P9-ARB-532

MILITARY HISTORY

THE DEFINITIVE VISUAL GUIDE TO THE OBJECTS OF WARFARE

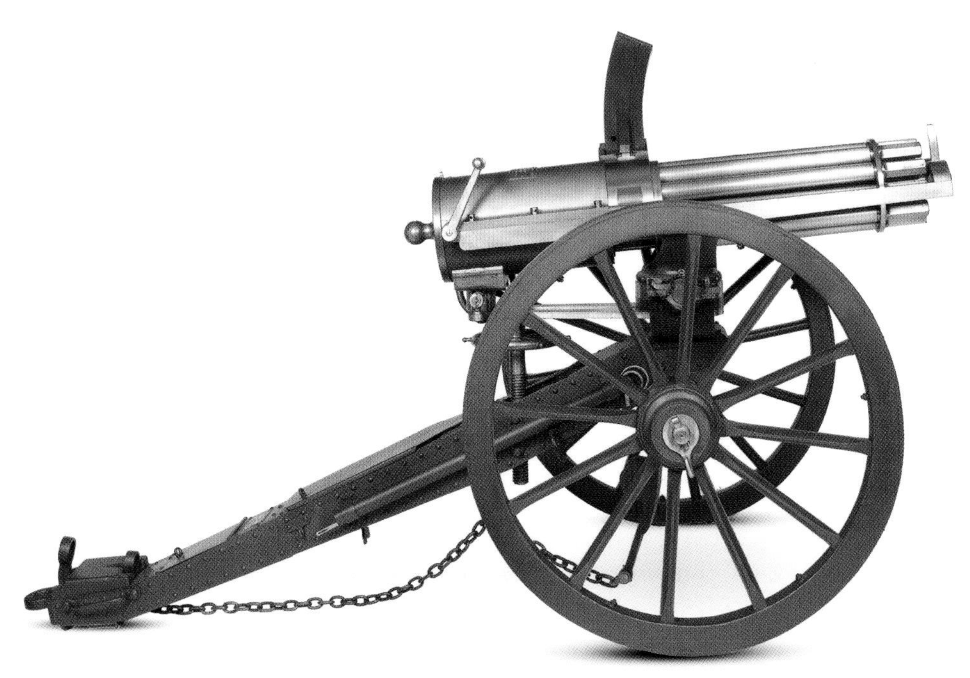

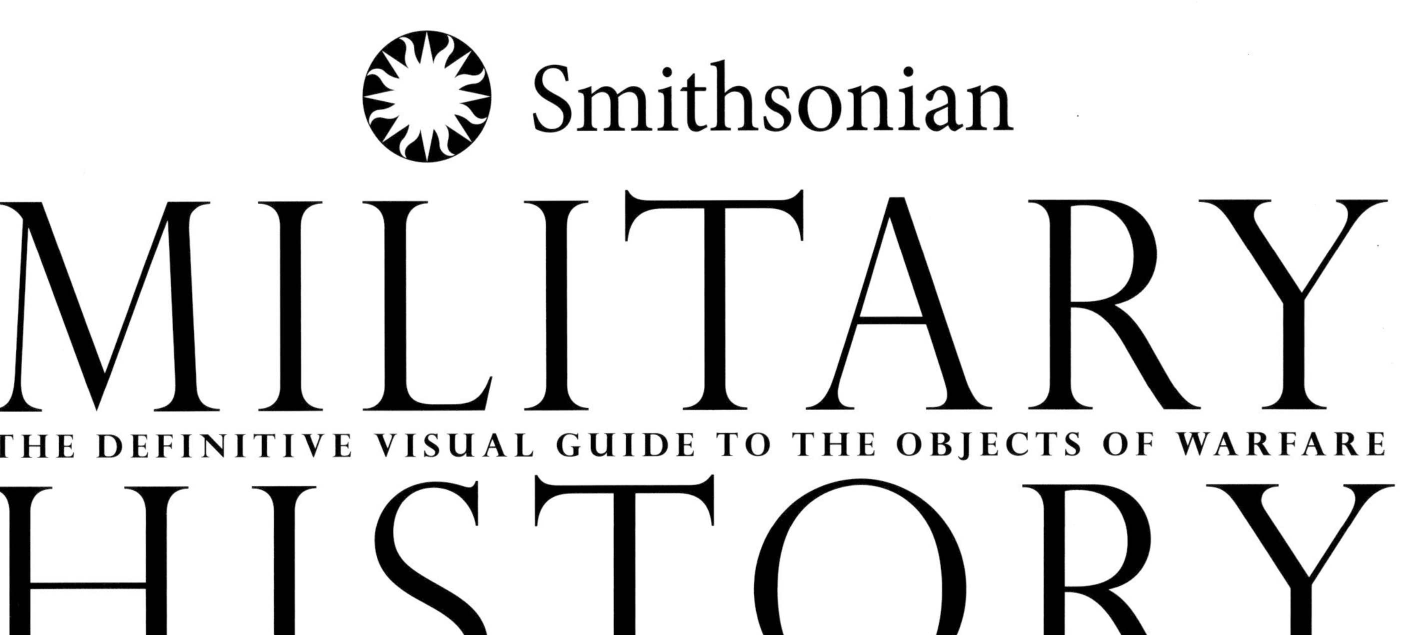
Smithsonian
MILITARY
THE DEFINITIVE VISUAL GUIDE TO THE OBJECTS OF WARFARE
HISTORY

DK

LONDON • NEW YORK
MUNICH • MELBOURNE • DELHI

Senior Editor Gareth Jones
Editorial Team Hannah Bowen, Hugo Wilkinson, Alison Sturgeon, Steve Setford, Andy Szudek, Satu Fox
Senior Art Editors Michael Duffy, Sharon Spencer
Design Team Keith Davies, Steve Woosnam-Savage
Photographer Gary Ombler
Production Editors Ben Marcus, Tony Phipps
Production Controller Linda Dare
Picture Research Sarah Smithies, Roland Smithies
Cover Designer Mark Cavanagh
Managing Editor Stephanie Farrow
Managing Art Editor Lee Griffiths
US Senior Editor Rebecca Warren
US Editor Jill Hamilton

Cobalt ID
The Stables, Wood Farm
Deopham Road, Attleborough
Norfolk NR17 1AJ
Managing Editor Marek Walisiewicz
Managing Art Editor Paul Reid
Editors Richard Gilbert, Louise Abbott
Art Editors Darren Bland, Lloyd Tilbury

DK India
Managing Editor Saloni Talwar
Senior Editors Neha Gupta, Priyanka Naib
Editorial Team Surbhi Nayyar, Suneha Dutta
Managing Art Editor Romi Chakraborty
Senior Designer Govind Mittal, Anis Sayyed
Design Team Pankaj Bhatia, Amit Varma, Honlung Zach
Senior DTP Designer Harish Aggarwal
DTP Designers Vishal Bhatia, Jagtar Singh, Dheeraj Arora
CTS Manager Balwant Singh
Production Editor Pankaj Sharma
Managing Director Aparna Sharma

First American Edition, 2012

Published in the United States by
DK Publishing
375 Hudson Street
New York, New York 10014

12 13 14 15 10 9 8 7 6 5 4 3 2 1
001—182907—Oct/2012

A catalog record for this book is available from the Library of Congress

ISBN 978-0-7566-9838-6

DK books are available at special discounts when purchased in bulk for sales promotions, premiums, fund-raising, or educational use. For details contact: DK Publishing Special Markets, 375 Hudson Street, New York, 10014 or SpecialSales@dk.com.

Printed and bound in China by Leo Paper Products Ltd

Discover more at
www.dk.com

CONSULTANTS

This trademark is owned by the Smithsonian and is registered in the US Patent and Trademark Office

Established in 1846, the Smithsonian—the world's largest museum and research complex—includes 19 museums and galleries and the National Zoological Park. The total number of artifacts, works of art, and specimens in the Smithsonian's collections is estimated at 137 million, much of which is contained in the National Museum of Natural History, which holds more than 126 million specimens and objects. The Smithsonian is a renowned research center, dedicated to public education, national service, and scholarship in the arts, sciences, and history.

SMITHSONIAN ENTERPRISES
Carol LeBlanc, Vice President
Brigid Ferraro, Director of Licensing
Ellen Nanney, Licensing Manager
Kealy Wilson, Product Development Coordinator

SMITHSONIAN
Staff of the Division of Armed Forces History, National Museum of American History, Smithsonian

THE ROYAL ARMOURIES, UK
Thom Richardson
Keeper of Armor and Oriental Collections

Robert C. Woosnam-Savage
Curator of European Edged Weapons

Jonathan Ferguson
Curator of Firearms

Mark Murray-Flutter
Senior Curator of Firearms

Trevor Weston
Manager of Modern Military Firearms

Karen Watts
Senior Curator of Armor and Art

Nicholas Hall
Keeper of Artillery

Philip Magrath
Curator of Artillery

ADDITIONAL CONSULTANTS
Brian Lavery
Curator of Naval History, National Maritime Museum, Greenwich, UK

Stephen Woolford MBE
Head of Interpretation and Collections, Imperial War Museum, Duxford, UK

CONTRIBUTORS

R. G. Grant
Philip Parker
Ian Bottomley
Charles Phillips
Roger Ford
Adrian Gilbert
Malcolm Claridge

Weights and measurements given in this book are expressed in their metric and imperial equivalents, wherever the information is available. However, there are various different conventions for the measurements of caliber and displacement. Please refer to p.446 for further details.

INTRODUCTION

The development of arms and armaments is central to the story of military history. While the aims and intentions of humans at war have remained essentially the same since the very dawn of civilization, the history of weaponry and tactics has been a process of near-constant adaptation, reinvention, and progression, with the result that battlefield technology has grown increasingly effective, and ever more deadly.

The earliest weapons took the form of stone axes and clubs, but, with the adoption of bronze, and then iron, these were improved, developed, and then superseded. Swords, spears, and bows dominated the field of battle from the era of Ancient Egypt and Assyria to the high Middle Ages, until the introduction of gunpowder weapons in Europe in the 14th century. This invention heralded a sea-change in warfare, as human strength was aided and then all but replaced by chemical and mechanical power, a process that accelerated during the Industrial Revolution, with an exponential growth in the range and accuracy of weapon systems, both on land and at sea. War then reached the skies in the early 1900s, expanding the reach of military might across the globe, and, while the advent of the nuclear bomb in 1945 made the prospect of full-scale conflict almost too terrible to contemplate, it did not stop the pace of technological change in conventional arms during the rest of the century. In the modern age, the increasing sophistication of "smart" weapons has heralded a revolution in warfare, and we have reached an era in which human combatants are slowly being replaced by computer-controlled machines.

The following pages offer a beautifully illustrated account of this process, showcasing significant armaments and other military pieces across 5,000 years and a vast geographical range. However, this majestic book—a fruitful collaboration between leading military history writers and expert consultants from the Royal Armouries, the Smithsonian, and other specialist institutions—is much more than simply a catalog of weaponry. It offers gripping accounts of the key battles, landmark events, and historical figures whose legacies have changed the reality of warfare; it explores the role technologies and tactics played in determining the outcome of conflicts; and it charts the impact of these events on the balance of power and boundary, the rise and fall of nation and empire, and on the course of human history.

CONTENTS

1500–1680

PIKES AND GUNPOWDER

1680–1815

FLINTLOCK AND BAYONET

1815–1914

INDUSTRY AND IMPERIALISM

1914–1945

THE WORLD WARS

1945–PRESENT

THE NUCLEAR AGE

TO 500CE

CHARIOTS AND SWORDS

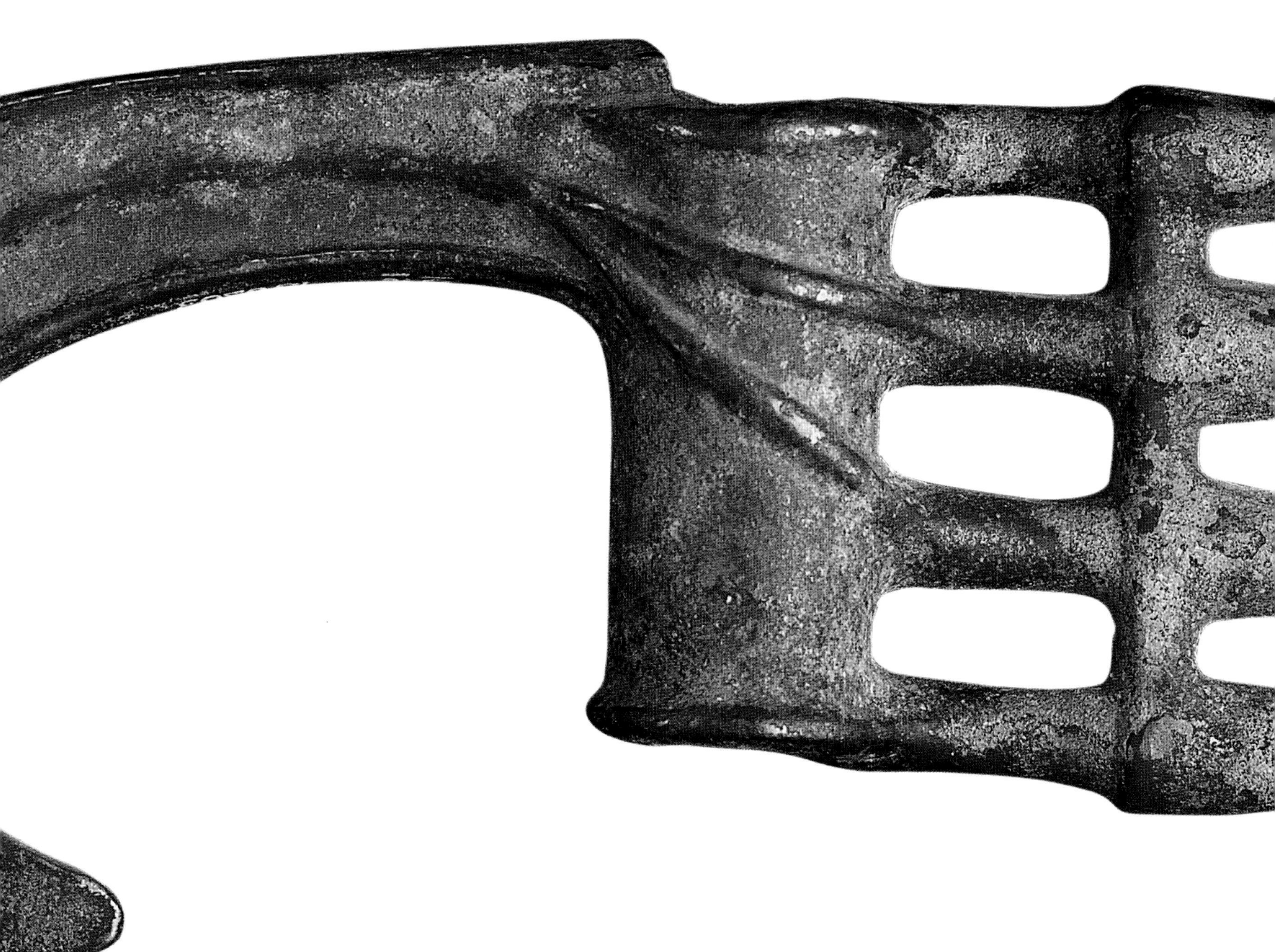

INTRODUCTION

Early humans developed weapons of wood and stone, such as clubs, axes, spears, and simple bows, for hunting and fighting; the growth of civilizations from around 3000BCE onward led to advances in both technology and organization.

The first military developments were slow, emerging over centuries, or even millennia. Stone weapons were gradually replaced by those of more effective materials—first copper and bronze, then iron and steel; meanwhile, missile weapons increased in range and penetrative power with the advent of the composite bow, and later, the crossbow. The invention of wheeled vehicles and the domestication of horses gave rise to the war chariot, which dominated battlefields from Egypt to China until, imitating the mounted warriors of central Asia, settled civilizations learned to fight on horseback. The building of fortifications led to the new art of siege warfare, and conflict also took to the sea, with oared war galleys operating in the Mediterranean by the 8th century BCE.

In ancient warfare, fighting methods and organization were generally more important to success than technological superiority. The Assyrians conquered an empire with the world's first permanent professional army, in the 1st millennium BCE, and the Romans ruled the most famous of ancient empires with an army of professional legionaries who also excelled as military engineers, building roads, bridges, forts, and frontier fortifications. The Greeks, meanwhile, won renown for their tactical skills—whether as infantry in their tightknit phalanx formations, or at sea, maneuvering their lightweight galleys, the triremes.

None of the settled civilizations, however, were safe against the nomadic peoples—or "barbarians" as they were known—outside their borders. The "civilized" technological advantages of torsion catapults and crossbows counted for little against bands of mounted warriors, who were highly skilled in raid and ambush. East and West Asia, India, and Europe all faced severe problems from incursions by central Asian nomadic horsemen.

KEY DATES

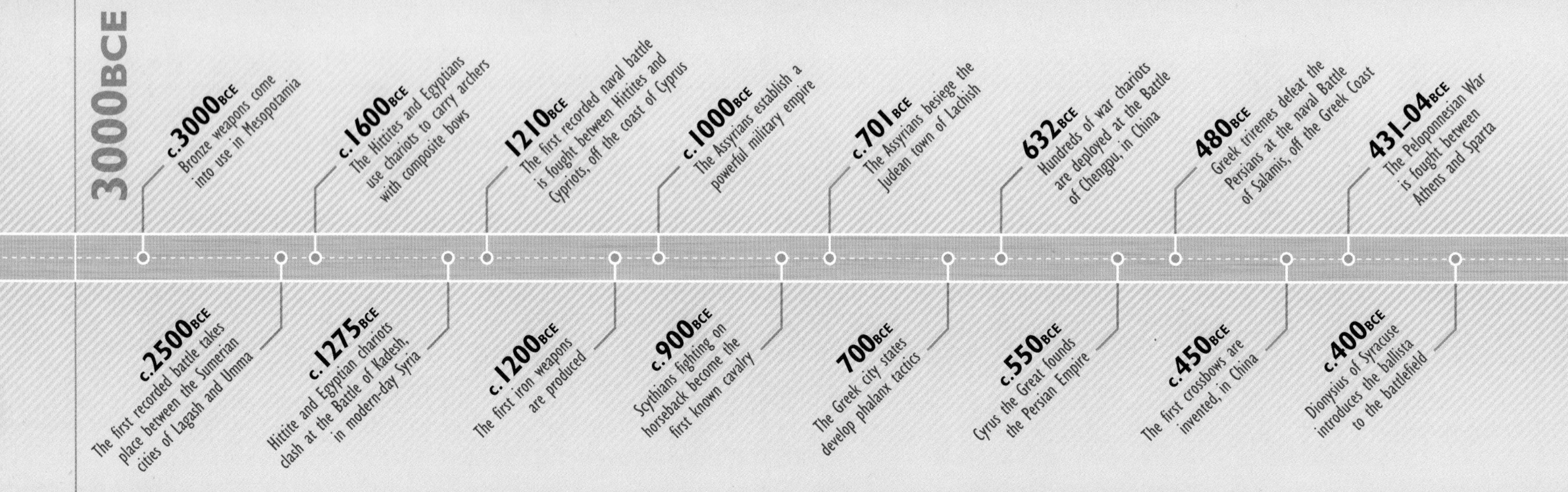

KING TUTANKHAMEN—c.1300BCE

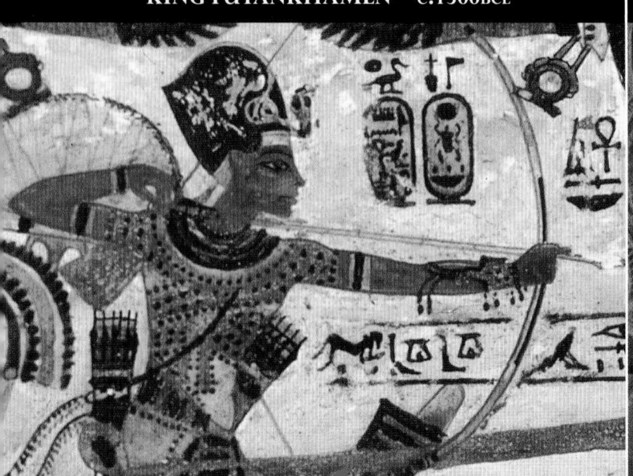

THE MAHABHARATAS WAR—c.1300BCE

THE SIEGE OF LACHISH—701BCE

333–31BCE Alexander the Great of Macedonia defeats the Persian empire in battles at Granicus, near Troy, Issus, in Anatolia, and Gaugamela, in Persia

c.310BCE Chandragupta Maurya creates an empire in northern India with an army using war elephants

264–41BCE Rome defeats Carthage in the First Punic war

c.220BCE The construction of the first Great Wall of China

218BCE Carthaginian commander Hannibal leads an army across the Alps to attack Rome

c.210BCE The Terracotta Army is made for the Chinese Emperor Qin Shi Huang

202BCE The defeat of Carthage by Rome, at the Battle of Zama, ends the Second Punic War

107BCE The Marian reforms create professional Roman legions, armed with sword, javelin, and shield

52BCE Roman general Julius Caesar defeats the Gauls under Vercingetorix, at the Siege of Alesia

31BCE Octavian, the future Roman Emperor Augustus, defeats Mark Antony and Cleopatra, at the Battle of Actium, off the Greek coast

122CE The Romans begin the construction of Hadrian's Wall, in Britain

208CE In China, the Battle of Red Cliffs, on the Yangtze River, ends the Han dynasty

260CE Persian Sassanid Emperor Shapur I defeats and captures Roman Emperor Valerian at Edessa, Mesopotamia

378CE Roman Emperor Valens is defeated by the Goths at the Battle of Adrianople, in Thrace

451–52CE The Huns, horsemen from central Asia, invade western Europe

476CE The fall of the western Roman Empire

500CE

HOPLITES—c.500BCE

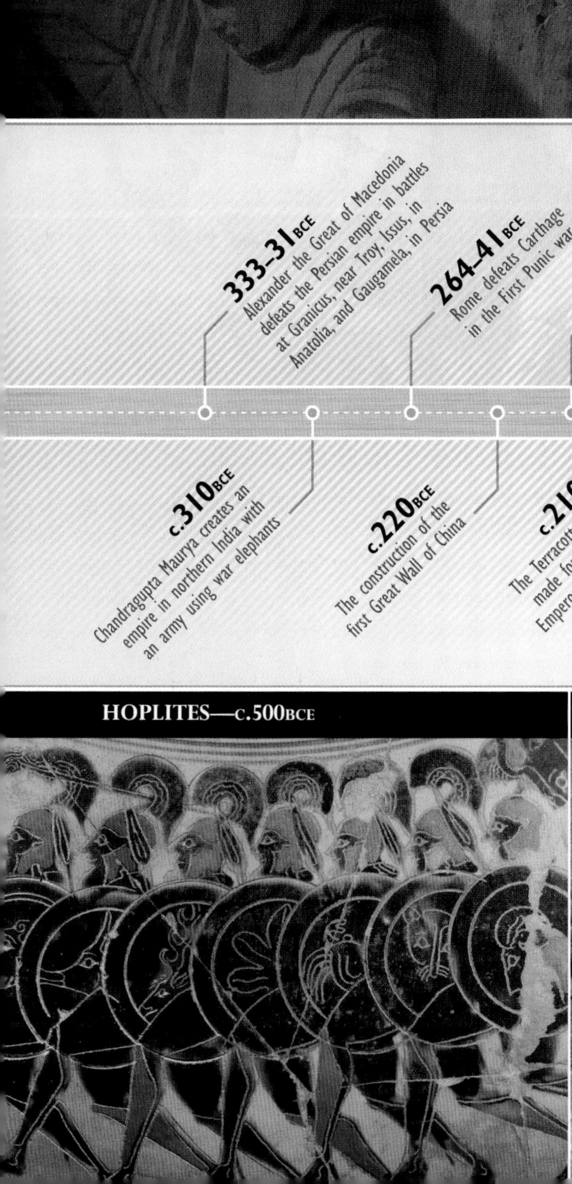

THE TERRACOTTA ARMY—c.200BCE

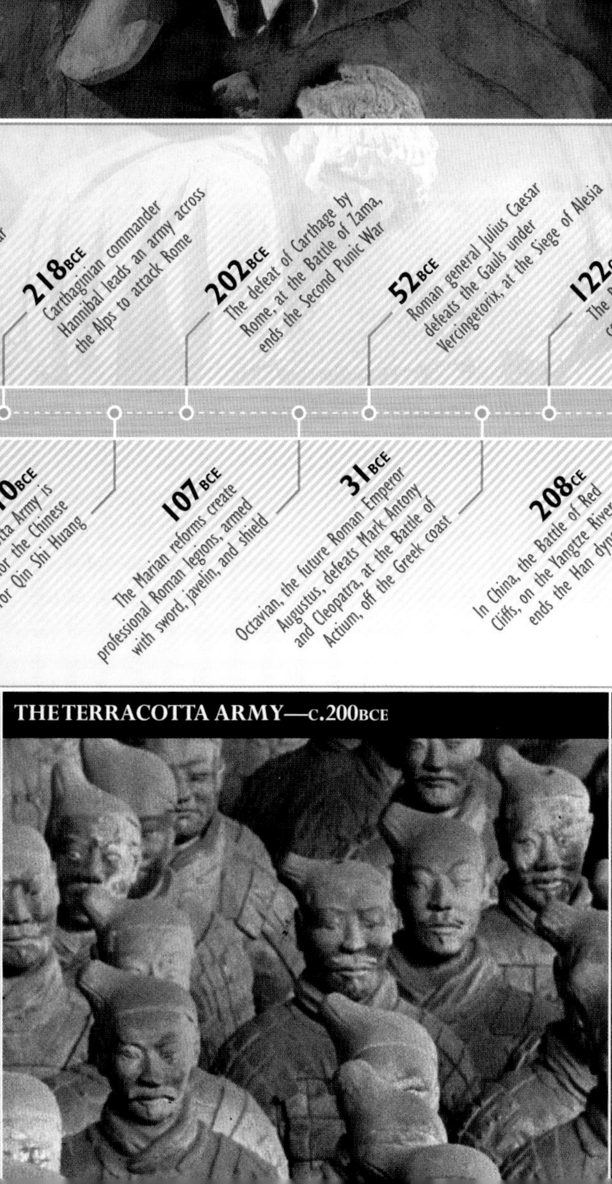

THE SIEGE OF MASADA—73CE

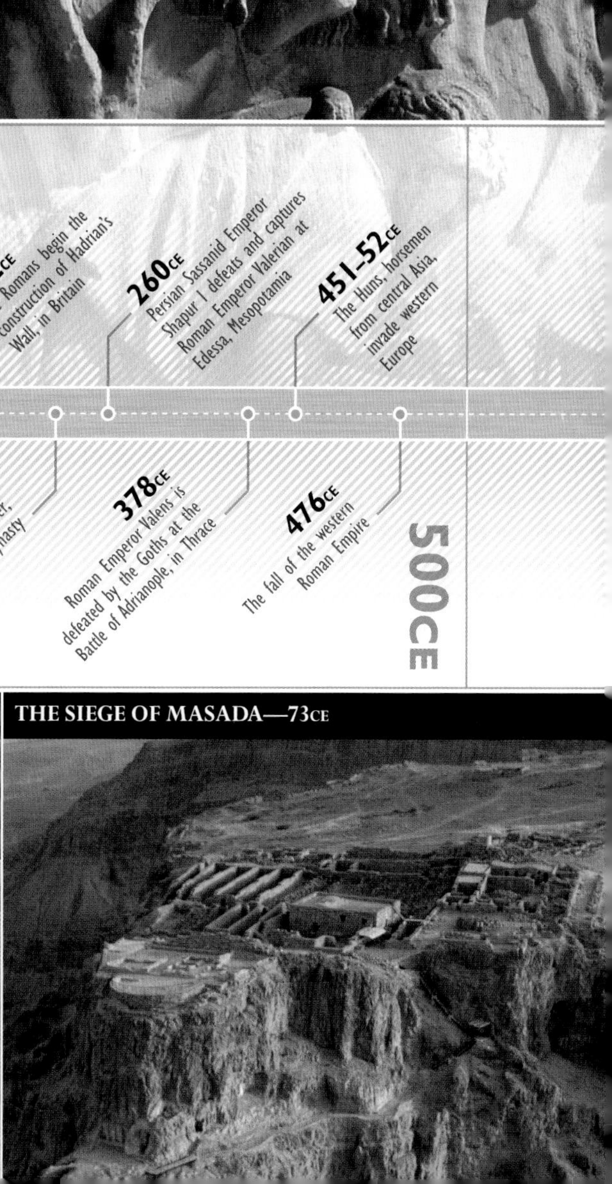

KEY **FIGURE**

RAMESSES II
1279–1213BCE

One of the longest-reigning Egyptian pharaohs, Ramesses II led numerous military campaigns, taking armies into Syria to the east, Libya to the west, and Nubia in the far south. His main rival was the Hittite emperor, Mutawallis. The climax of his second Syrian campaign was the Battle of Kadesh in 1275BCE, a clash with the Hittites that involved large chariot forces on both sides. Ramesses survived a devastating charge by the Hittite chariots to emerge victorious.

▲ The head from a colossal statue of Ramesses II at the Temple of Abu Simbel, in southern Egypt.

► TUTANKHAMEN
The Egyptian pharaoh Tutankhamen (reigned 1332–1322 BCE) is depicted shooting volleys of arrows at his fleeing enemies. In reality, the king was a boy who would not have led his troops in battle.

KEY DEVELOPMENT

THE FIRST WARRIORS

The birth of advanced civilizations in the Near East, around 3000BCE, heralded the emergence of organized military forces. Over the next 3,000 years, a series of technical developments led to advances in weaponry, which in turn shaped the development of military tactics.

While it is likely that there was conflict of some sort between groups of hunters before agriculture began, a permanent warrior class only arose with the first farming communities, which needed to protect their surpluses. The earliest agricultural societies built defenses (such as the walls of Jericho, in around 8000BCE) and adapted stone hunting weapons for use in battle, leading to the invention of weapons such as the mace. It was not until the rise of the city-states of Sumeria, however, in the late 4th millennium BCE, that true organized armies began to appear.

THE RACE FOR COPPER

The discovery of copper-refining methods around 4500BCE led to the manufacture of the first metallic weapons, and may also have set off competition between city-states for access to the copper mines of Anatolia. These two factors contributed to the endemic state of war between Sumerian city-states, such as Uruk, Ur, and Kish, during the 4th and 3rd millennia BCE. Sumerian soldiers fought largely on foot, armed with long spears and arranged in

▼ AN EGYPTIAN SPEAR
The thrusting spear was the main weapon of Egyptian infantrymen, particularly under the Old Kingdom (2686–2181BCE). Like many ancient armies, the Egyptians fought in phalanxes, which opponents found difficult to penetrate.

▲ **AN ASSYRIAN VICTORY**
This relief of the Battle of Til Tuba (655BCE) shows the Assyrian archers and spearmen who drove their Elamite foes into the Ulai River, where thousands drowned. The Elamite ruler, Teumanni, was captured and executed.

phalanxes—units comprising densely packed rows of troops. They were supported by cumbersome, four-wheeled battle-wagons drawn by onagers (a species related to the horse family).

The Akkadians overcame the Sumerians in around 2350BCE. Under a leader named Sargon, they established the first empire in the Near East, uniting the lands of many city states. Sargon was the first military leader to make use of archers on a large scale, giving the Akkadians a crucial advantage against their less versatile foes.

THE RISE OF BRONZE

In the second millenium BCE, two technical innovations occurred that would shape warfare in the ancient Near East for another thousand years. The first of these was the introduction of bronze. Emerging around 2800BCE, this alloy of copper and tin gave a more durable, sharper edge to weapons than copper alone. Until the technique of bronze-making became widely known, it was prohibitively expensive, but by around 1800BCE, bronze had replaced copper as the predominant metal used for armaments. At about the same time, horse-drawn chariots with two wheels also appeared, adding a new, highly mobile dimension to warfare.

From around 1300BCE, the Egyptian army—previously an almost entirely infantry force—was radically reorganized under the influence of the Hyksos, a group of foreign invaders who introduced chariots, bronze swords, and metal scale armor. This coincided with an era of Egyptian imperialism, when the armies of pharaohs such as Ramesses II expanded into the Levant and engaged in bitter struggles with rival kingdoms such as the Hittites.

THE AGE OF IRON

By around 1000BCE, iron, being stronger than bronze, was becoming the metal of choice for weapons. It was exploited to lethal effect by the Assyrians (see pp.20–21). During the reign of Tiglath-Pileser III (745–27BCE), Assyria established the world's first standing army, which, when boosted by drafting, numbered over 100,000 men. They wielded the longer swords that iron made possible, and were protected by knee-length metal tunics. Assyrian tactics combined the well-orchestrated push of a heavy phalanx of infantry, with supporting fire from archers and slingers, and assaults by auxiliary units of heavy cavalry and charioteers. With a clear chain of command and a reputation for ferocity and cruelty against their enemies, the Assyrian army was the most formidable fighting force the ancient world had yet produced.

KEY **EVENTS**

2600–750BCE

- **2600BCE** A Sumerian artifact known as the Standard of Ur provides the first depiction of an organized army, with mosaic scenes showing rows of infantry carrying spears and battle-axes, accompanied by onager-drawn battle-wagons. The infantry have no shields or armor.
- **2000BCE** The first metal swords appear in Mesopotamia as bronze-making spreads and the metal becomes cheaper to produce.
- **c.1300–1250BCE** New Kingdom Egypt undergoes its period of greatest expansion, while chariot warfare reaches its peak. The Hittite empire disintegrates, after which a period of disorder reigns in the Near East.
- **c.1000–750BCE** The introduction of iron weaponry aids the expansion of the Assyrian empire. Assyria is the dominant military power in the Near East by 750BCE.

> "**I tore down… their towns** and **set fire to them**, and turned them into **forgotten mounds**"
>
> **ASSYRIAN RULER SENNACHERIB**, ON A REVOLT BY THE CHALDAEANS, 703BCE

STONE AND BONE WEAPONS

The first human tools were made of stone, bone, or wood. The earliest were simple pebble choppers and scrapers, but by around 1.75 million years ago, these had developed into the first hand axes—shaped blades—that could be gripped firmly in the hand to strike an enemy. Gradually, the blades became narrower and sharper, most often made of flint, a stone that was hard but could be easily shaped. Wooden shafts were bound to sharp blades to form axes and spears, and eventually—with the invention of the bow—to act as arrowheads, vastly extending the range at which the warrior could attack. Most early stone weapons were made with multiple uses in mind, from domestic tasks to hunting, as well as warfare.

▼ ATLATL

Date c.10,500BCE
Origin France
Length Unknown

Atlatls, or spear throwers, were developed around 20,000 years ago. They increased a spear's velocity and range, which allowed the bearer to kill prey from a greater distance. This reindeer-ivory example is carved as a mammoth.

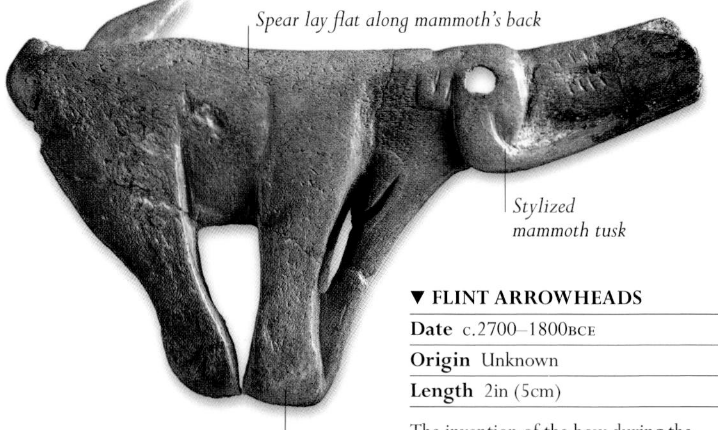

▼ STONE AXEHEAD

Date 4000–2000BCE
Origin UK
Length 8in (20cm)

Adding wooden handles gave axes greater reach and power, enabling the bearer to attack from a safer distance. This stone axehead was dredged from the Thames River in London.

▼ FLINT ARROWHEADS

Date c.2700–1800BCE
Origin Unknown
Length 2in (5cm)

The invention of the bow during the Paleolithic period made it possible to shoot projectiles at great range and with accuracy. Because these flint arrowheads were barbed, they embedded themselves deep in the victim's flesh.

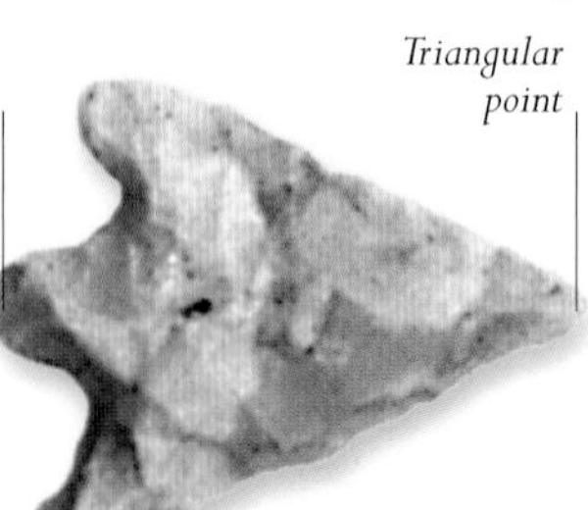

▼ OLDUVAI CHOPPER

Date Up to 2.5 million years ago
Origin Africa
Length Unknown

Olduvai tools are among the oldest known deliberately shaped objects, first appearing around 2.5 million years ago. Choppers such as this were versatile tools, used as cutting edges and scrapers, and for bludgeoning prey.

▼ SERRATED FLINT KNIFE

Date 1,500,000–10,000BCE
Origin Unknown
Length 8in (20cm)

Serrated edges were developed for sawing through bone or other tough materials. However, the jagged flint edges on this knife could also inflict savage cuts.

▶ FLINT HAND DAGGER

Date c.2000BCE
Origin Unknown
Length 12in (30cm)

The addition of wooden shafts to flint blades, bound with sinew or leather strips, created stabbing spears, and allowed the bearer to use the full force of his arm to strike blows.

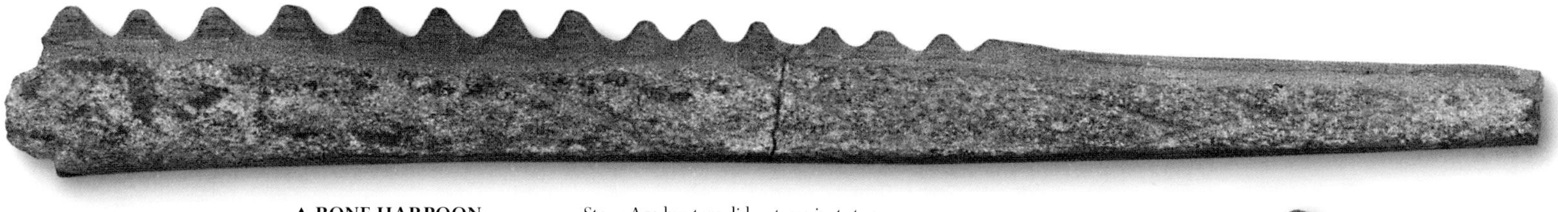

▲ BONE HARPOON

Date	c.28,000–13,000BCE
Origin	Unknown
Length	Unknown

Stone Age hunters did not use just stone for their weapons. From toward the end of the last Ice Age, 30,000–15,000 years ago, many weapons of bone survive, such as this harpoon, which might have been used for spearfishing.

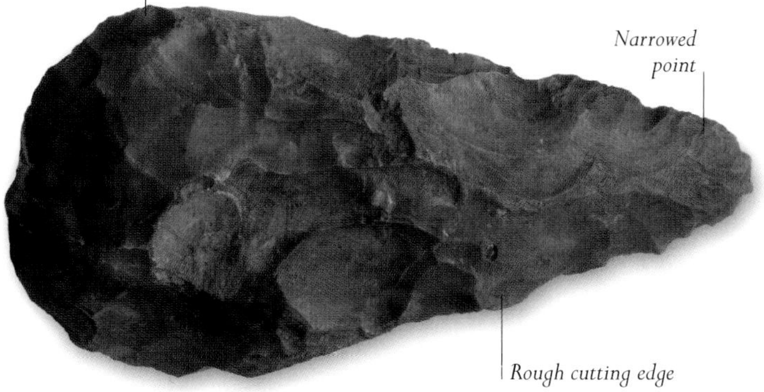
Broad end for handgrip
Narrowed point
Rough cutting edge

◀ HAND AX

Date	250,000–70,000BCE
Origin	Unknown
Length	6in (15cm)

The first hand-held weapons, hand axes were essentially small rocks shaped to form a handgrip and blade. They were useful both as domestic tools and for attacking enemies.

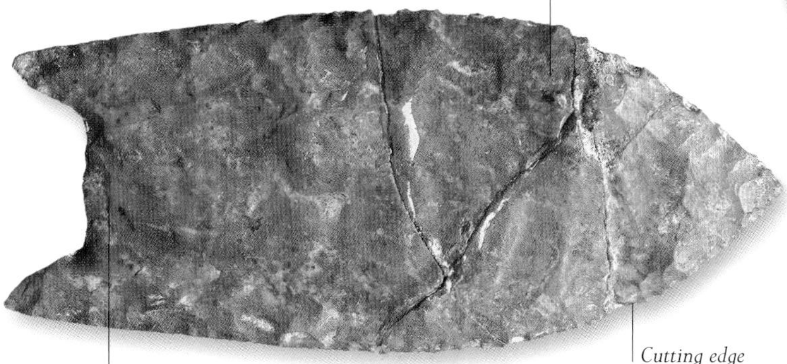
Fluted groove caused by striking off flakes
Cutting edge
Originally attached to shaft

▶ SMALL CLOVIS POINT

Date	c.10,000BCE
Origin	North America
Length	4in (10cm)

Clovis points were made by alternately flaking off pieces from both sides of the core, creating fluted edges. They were a characteristic feature of the weapons used by settlers in North America from around 15,000 years ago. Clovis points were replaced by shorter and thinner Folsom points 8,000 years ago.

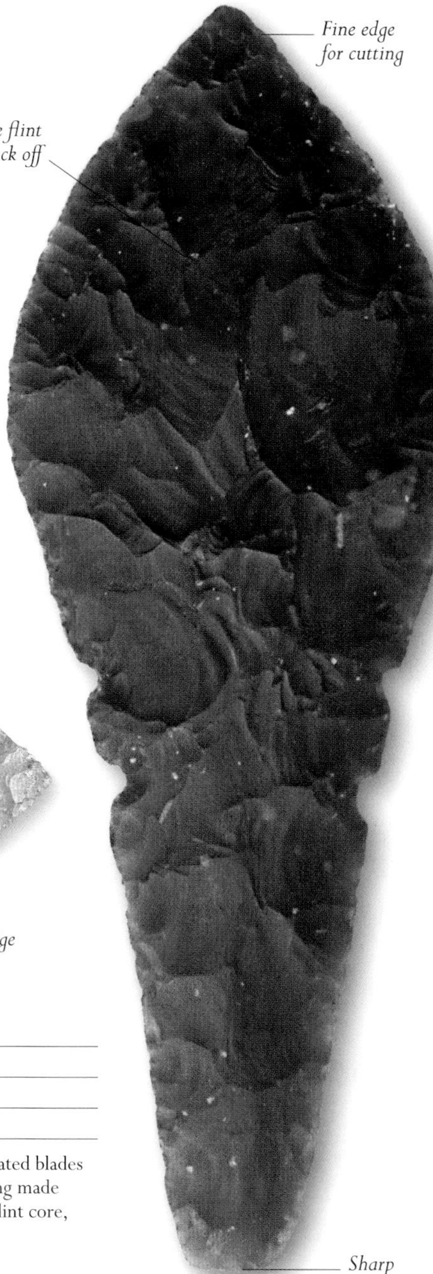
Fine edge for cutting
Indentations where flint flakes were struck off
Sharp broad point

▶ FLINT DAGGER HEAD

Date	c.2000BCE
Origin	Unknown
Length	6in (15cm)

By the Neolithic period, sophisticated blades such as this dagger head were being made by striking off flakes from a hard flint core, producing a sharp, flat blade.

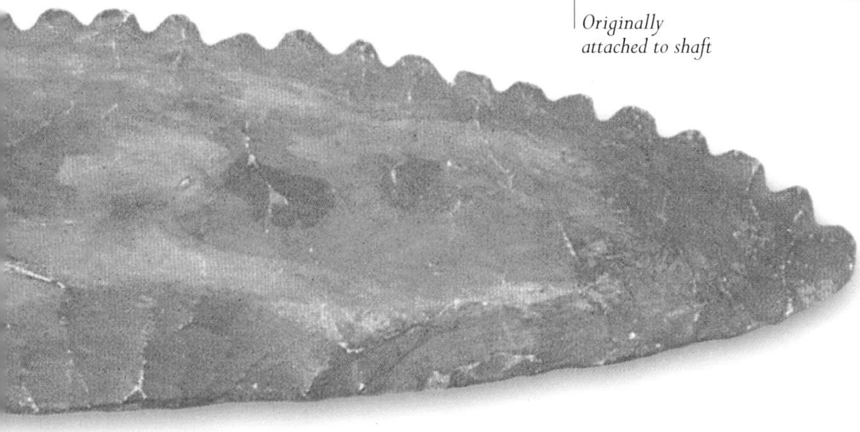

Leather or sinew binding
Pointed flint blade

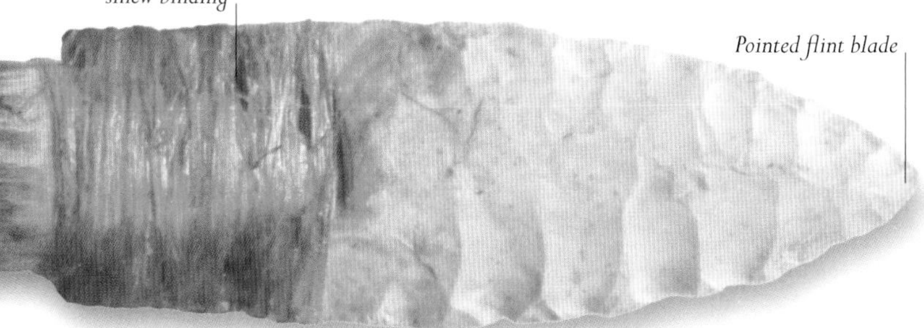

▶ LEVALLOIS FLAKE POINT

Date	Post-300,000BCE
Origin	Unknown
Length	Unknown

The Levallois point was made by flaking off points from a central flint core to create the pattern of the desired shape, which was then struck off to create the final object. It had a characteristic scarring pattern on its surface.

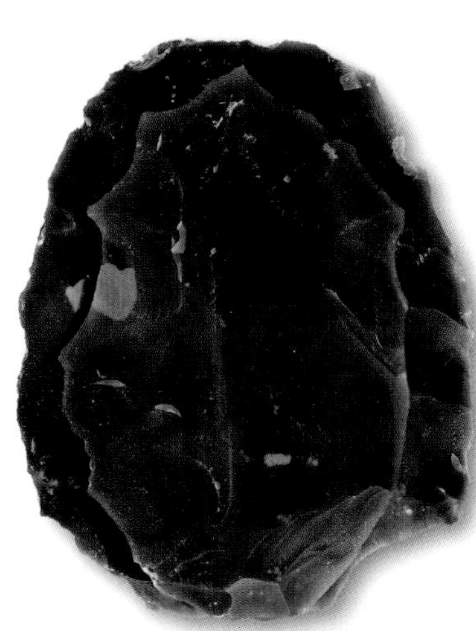

EARLY METAL WEAPONS

The first organized armies, those of the Sumerians, are recorded in around 3000BCE. While heavy war wagons were used, the Sumerians fought largely on foot and carried spears and shields. The development of the spoked wheel enabled much lighter, faster vehicles to be built—open chariots, from which archers could shower enemies with arrows. Thus, chariot warfare came to dominate conflict in the Near East in the second millennium BCE. But as advances in horse breeding produced more robust animals, mounted archers—even faster and more maneuverable than chariots—became more valuable to armies in the region, together with infantry foot soldiers equipped with spears, swords, and daggers.

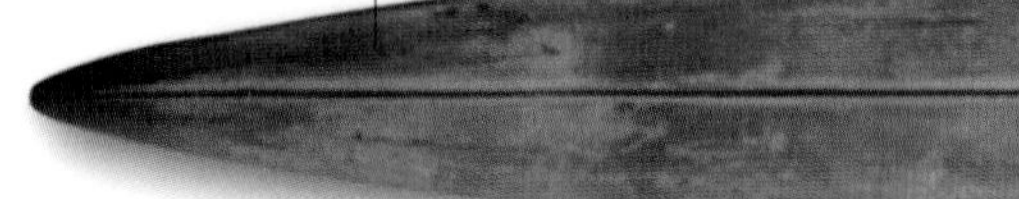

▲ SUMERIAN DAGGER

Date	c.2500BCE
Origin	Sumeria
Length	8–12in (20–30cm)

This ornate ceremonial dagger was excavated from the tomb of Queen Pu-Abi at Ur. Its blade and scabbard are crafted in gold, while the hilt is made from lapis lazuli trimmed in gold.

▲ HELMET OF MESKALAMDUG

Date	c.2500BCE
Origin	Sumeria
Length	8½in (22cm)
Material	Gold, silver

This ceremonial, gold-and-silver alloy helmet was found in the tomb of Meskalamdug at Ur in Sumeria. It is known as a wig helmet because of the intricately carved imitation of hair on the crown.

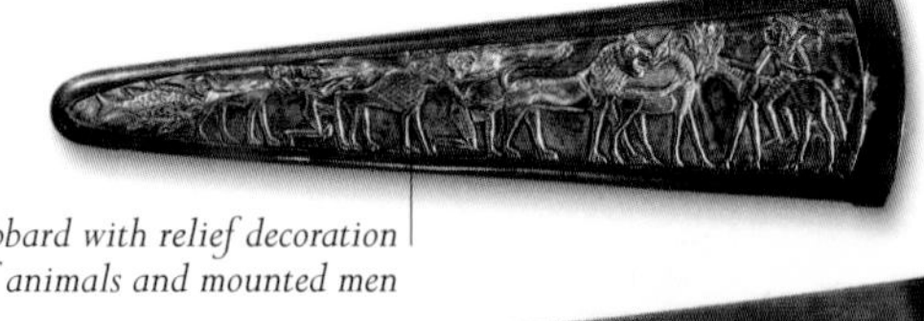

▲ PHOENICIAN DAGGER

Date	18th century BCE
Origin	Phoenicia
Length	15¾in (39.3cm)

The Phoenicians occupied trading cities of the Levantine coast and were known more as merchants than as warriors. This magnificent gold and ivory dagger and scabbard signified the bearer's wealth and were not intended for military use.

▲ ASSYRIAN SCALE ARMOR

Date	1800–620BCE
Origin	Assyria
Length	2in (5cm)

Assyrian soldiers wore a *sariam*, a long coat made of lamellar armor. Bronze scales, such as these, were laced together through holes punched in the side. A complete set of armor consisted of up to 1,000 scales, weighing 33–55lb (15–25kg).

◄ PERSIAN BRONZE AXEHEAD

Date	10th–7th century BCE
Origin	Persia
Length	8in (20.5cm)

The blade on this spike-butted ax is set at an angle, which would have been impractical in combat, suggesting that the ax was for ceremonial use.

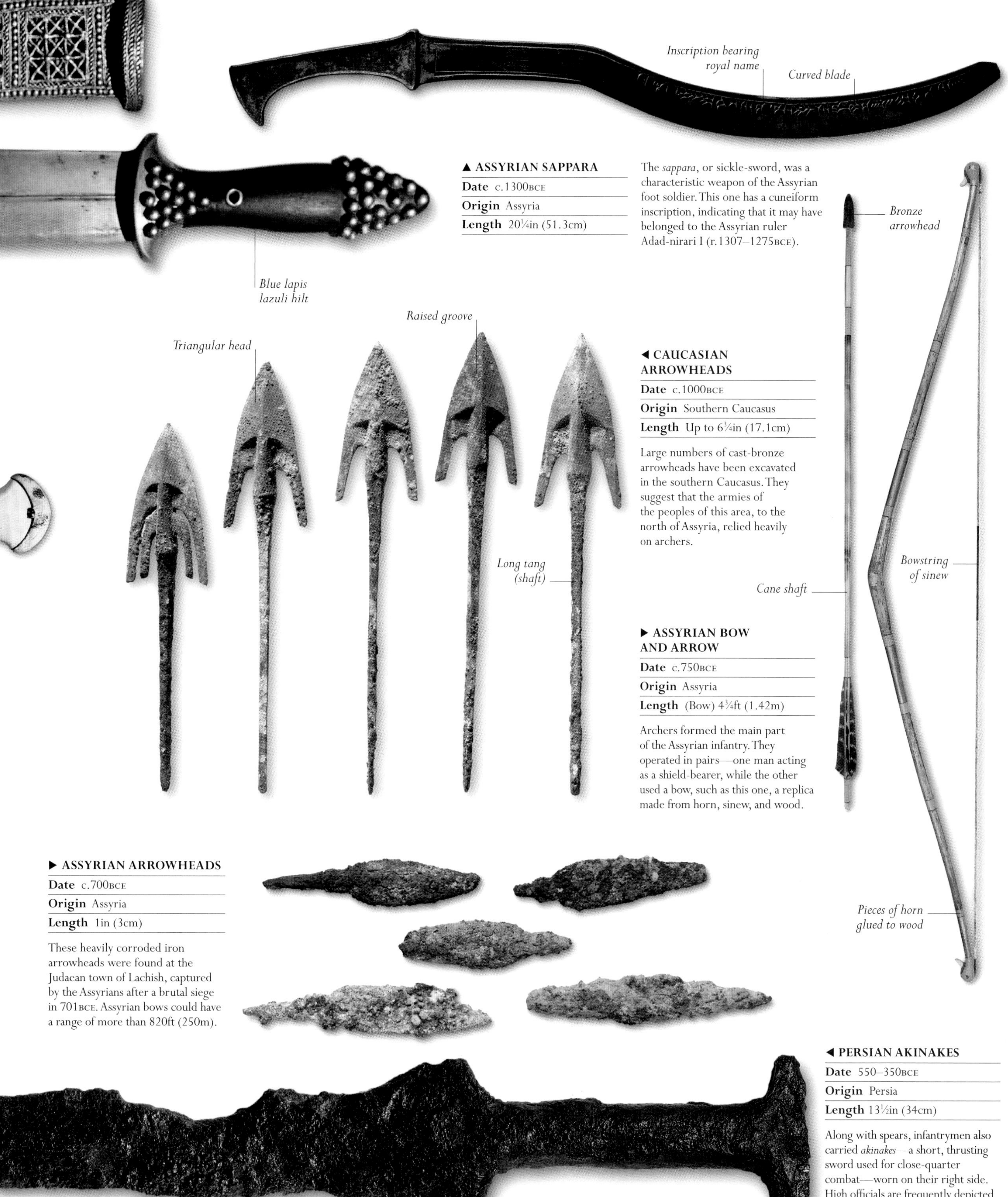

▲ ASSYRIAN SAPPARA

Date c.1300BCE

Origin Assyria

Length 20¼in (51.3cm)

The *sappara*, or sickle-sword, was a characteristic weapon of the Assyrian foot soldier. This one has a cuneiform inscription, indicating that it may have belonged to the Assyrian ruler Adad-nirari I (r.1307–1275BCE).

◀ CAUCASIAN ARROWHEADS

Date c.1000BCE

Origin Southern Caucasus

Length Up to 6¾in (17.1cm)

Large numbers of cast-bronze arrowheads have been excavated in the southern Caucasus. They suggest that the armies of the peoples of this area, to the north of Assyria, relied heavily on archers.

▶ ASSYRIAN BOW AND ARROW

Date c.750BCE

Origin Assyria

Length (Bow) 4¾ft (1.42m)

Archers formed the main part of the Assyrian infantry. They operated in pairs—one man acting as a shield-bearer, while the other used a bow, such as this one, a replica made from horn, sinew, and wood.

▶ ASSYRIAN ARROWHEADS

Date c.700BCE

Origin Assyria

Length 1in (3cm)

These heavily corroded iron arrowheads were found at the Judaean town of Lachish, captured by the Assyrians after a brutal siege in 701BCE. Assyrian bows could have a range of more than 820ft (250m).

◀ PERSIAN AKINAKES

Date 550–350BCE

Origin Persia

Length 13½in (34cm)

Along with spears, infantrymen also carried *akinakes*—a short, thrusting sword used for close-quarter combat—worn on their right side. High officials are frequently depicted wearing them in Persian art.

THE SIEGE OF LACHISH

By the 8th century BCE, the Assyrian empire had an army of unprecedented size and efficiency. Its assault on the fortified town of Lachish, recorded in reliefs in the Assyrian palace in Nineveh, demonstrated sophisticated, if well-established, siege techniques and the calculated use of terror.

The army that King Sennacherib led to Judah in 701 BCE comprised a mixture of foot soldiers and mounted troops on chariots or on horseback. There was also a dedicated body of engineers, skilled in building earthworks and siege machines. The army's mission was to crush a revolt by the Judean King Hezekiah, and to impose exemplary punishment to deter any further resistance to Assyrian imperial rule.

The Assyrians' principal missile weapon was the composite bow. Capable of shooting an iron-tipped arrow to an effective range of over 820ft (250m), it was used by charioteers and horsemen, as well as by troops on foot. Assyrian foot soldiers also employed slingshots, flinging shaped stones a distance of 330ft (100m). Both of these were deadly anti-personnel weapons, and during a siege arrows could be turned into incendiary devices by dousing their tips in flammable pitch. Neither arrows nor small stones posed any threat to the high mud walls of Lachish, however, which presented a formidable challenge, even to an armed force that must have far outnumbered the defenders.

To force entry into a walled town, the Assyrian troops had to advance to the walls and find ways either to breach them or go over them. Assyrian engineers had developed a range of techniques for assailing fortifications. They could attack the foundations, digging at the base of the walls to undermine them; they could build a ramp against a wall or tower, allowing troops a route to the summit of the battlements; they could attack the walls with siege towers and metal-tipped battering rams. Or, more simply, troops armed with spears and swords could be sent forward with ladders to scale the walls or fortifications.

SIEGE TOWER AND INFANTRY

At Lachish, engineers built a ramp of rocks and earth reaching to a point halfway up the fortifications. At the same time they assembled a large siege tower, with a ram in its lower story. Mounted on four wheels, the wooden tower was covered in hides and canvas. When the Assyrians were ready to attack, they manhandled the tower and ram up the ramp. While archers in the tower's upper story shot at the defenders, soldiers battered the ram against the exposed wall. The defenders fought back against the assault, throwing rocks and flaming torches onto the tower, but the Assyrian soldiers kept water-filled buckets in the tower for extinguishing the resulting fires. Meanwhile, tightknit groups of soldiers on foot launched a secondary assault on the walls, armed with spears and protected by shields and armor. Assyrian bowmen supported this advance with a barrage of arrows directed at the defenders on the walls, each bowman sheltered by a curved reed screen held by his shield-bearer.

The exact sequence of events leading to the fall of the town is not known, only that the Assyrians overcame the town's defenses. The aftermath of this victory, depicted in reliefs for the king's enjoyment, involved the cruel execution of a large number of Judeans and the exile of the survivors.

LACHISH UNDER SIEGE
Made to decorate the walls of King Sennacherib's palace in Nineveh (in modern-day Iraq), this relief shows the Assyrian siege tower rolling up a ramp to batter the defensive wall with its ram, while archers shoot at the defenders.

ANCIENT EGYPTIAN WEAPONRY

Egyptian soldiers were mainly peasant conscripts who fought almost exclusively on foot until around 1500BCE. The archers were the most important component of the army, and they carried light bows with a range of about 165ft (50m). The other infantry, known as the *nakhtu-aa* ("strong-armed"), fought in close formation using battle-axes and spears. Both types of warrior also carried a dagger in a leather scabbard, which was often strapped to the lower arm. For protection, the archers relied on a leather kilt, while the infantry carried a large, wooden-framed shield covered with cowhide. After the beginning of the New Kingdom in around 1550BCE, the Egyptian army began to use chariots, which were utilized by archers as a mobile platform from which to fire.

▼ BRONZE SPEARHEAD

Date c.2000BCE
Origin Egypt
Length 10in (25cm)

Egyptian infantrymen were usually equipped with a spear, which was generally used for thrusting rather than throwing. Before around 1500BCE, the blade was lashed to the haft rather than inserted into a socket.

Fine linen cloth covering blade

Triangular end for cutting into flesh

Hole for threading rawhide lashing

Wide half-moon shaped head

▲ FLINT ARROWHEAD

Date 5500–3100BCE
Origin Egypt
Weight ¼oz (2–2.5g)
Length 2¼in (6.1cm)

Archers formed a crucial component of Egyptian armies. They carried a simple bow, around 5ft (1.5m) long, made of acacia wood. The arrowheads were made of bone, flint, ebony, or copper, with triangular or barbed ends.

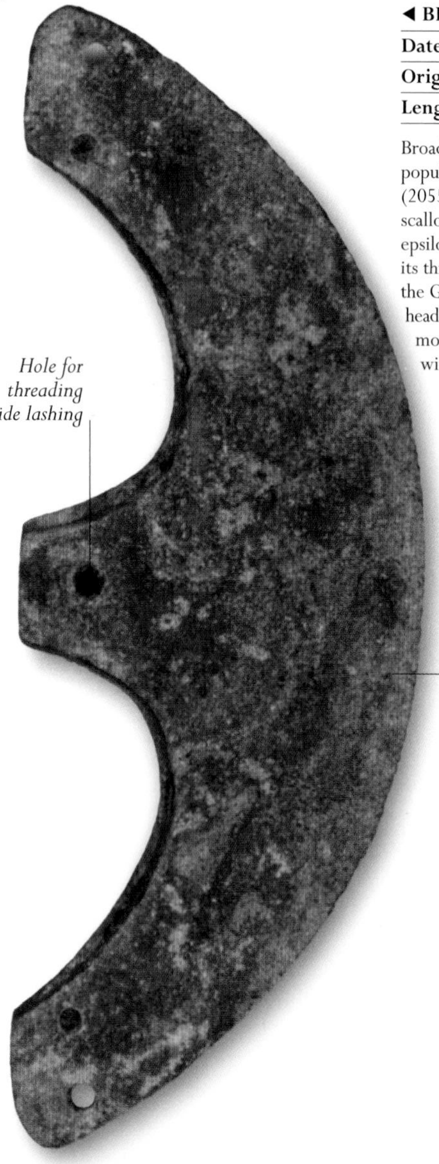

◄ BRONZE AXEHEAD

Date 2055–1650BCE
Origin Egypt
Length 6¾in (17.1cm)

Broad, round-headed axes were popular in the Middle Kingdom (2055–1650BCE). This broad, scalloped axehead was called an epsilon, due to the shape made by its three tangs, that was similar to the Greek letter. The shape of the head allowed a wide slashing action, most effective against opponents with minimal armor.

Bronze axehead

Rawhide binding

▲ BATTLE-AX

Date 1630–1520BCE
Origin Egypt
Length 16¼in (41.1cm)

Egyptian axes typically had a heavy, bronze, D-shaped head. This axehead was attached to the haft with wet rawhide thongs to ensure a stronger fit. The hafts were generally wider at the base, which was wrapped in linen to provide a stronger grip.

Falcon on the underside of the pommel

▼ LONG SWORD

Date 1539–1075BCE
Origin Egypt
Length 16in (40.6cm)

This double-edged copper sword, worn on a belt around the soldier's waist, dates from the New Kingdom. Its straight blade made it more suitable for thrusting than slashing. The gold hilt suggests it was crafted for an elite warrior.

Gilded hilt

Corroded blade

Leaf-shaped blade

▲ SHORT SWORD

Date	1539–1075BCE
Origin	Egypt
Length	12¾in (32.3cm)

Swords were probably introduced in the New Kingdom by invaders from the eastern Mediterranean, known as the "Sea Peoples." This broad-bladed short sword is a display weapon that probably belonged to a member of the royal family.

Cutting edge

▲ SICKLE SWORD

Date	1200–1000BCE
Origin	Egypt
Length	23½in (60cm)

The *khepesh*, or sickle-sword, came into use at the start of the New Kingdom. The curved blade had its cutting edge around the outside. The weapon was wielded more like an ax than a sword, and heavier specimens could be used to rip an opponent's armor open, leaving him vulnerable to blade thrusts.

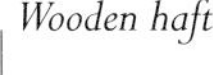

Wooden haft

► LION SHIELD

Date	c.1325BCE
Origin	Egypt
Width	21¼in (54cm)

The soldier's shield had a slightly convex shape. This protected the sides of his body and helped him push against a densely packed line of opponents. This ornate display shield from the tomb of Tutankhamen shows the Pharaoh in the shape of a sphinx trampling his enemies.

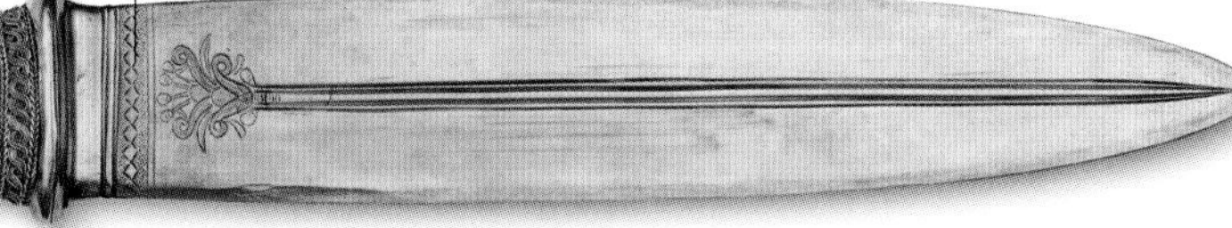

▲ PHARAOH'S DAGGER

Date	c.1325BCE
Origin	Egypt
Length	12½in (31.9cm)

This dagger was found with the mummy of Tutankhamen and, with its golden blade and ornate golden sheath, was intended strictly for ceremonial use. The falcon on the hilt symbolized protection for the Pharaoh in the afterlife.

KEY **BATTLE**

SALAMIS

480BCE

During the second Persian invasion of Greece, Athenian admiral Themistocles tricked Xerxes's Persian flotilla—three times the size of Themistocles' force of 378 triremes—into entering the Straits of Salamis. In the narrow waterway, the Persian force could not exercise its numerical advantage, and was badly mauled by the Greek ships.

▲ The Greek navy triumphed at Salamis through ingenious use of the terrain and waterways.

KEY DEVELOPMENT

HOPLITES AND PHALANXES

Around 700BCE, a new type of foot soldier emerged in Greece. The hoplite, equipped with a long spear, a sword, an elaborate bronze corselet and helmet, and a large wooden shield (*aspis*, or *hoplon*), would form the backbone of Greek armies for the next 500 years.

The earliest examples of hoplite equipment date back to about 710BCE, and within half a century of this date, depictions on vases show hoplites fighting in their signature tactical formation—the phalanx. Composed of rows of spear-wielding hoplites, the phalanx was normally eight men deep. With spears of around 95–105in (240–70cm) in length, only the first three ranks could reach the enemy line, but the phalanx's structure presented a fearsome barrier.

THE AGE OF THE HOPLITE

In the 7th and 6th centuries BCE, the main hoplite tactic involved colliding with the opposing phalanx, followed by concerted pushing and stabbing. There was little tactical sophistication, and the encounters continued until one side broke and fled. Only the hoplite's left side was fully protected, thanks to the *hoplon* (shield) of the man next to him: as a result, the phalanx tended to drift to the right, as each man tried to edge behind the *hoplon* of his neighbor.

By the early 5th century, bronze corselets had been superseded by linen or scale leather armor, allowing the wearer more freedom of movement. When Darius of Persia invaded Greece in 490BCE, the lightly armed Greek phalanx charged the Persian archers at Marathon, neutralizing one of their opponents' key advantages, and aiding an unlikely Greek victory against significant odds. Eleven years later, at Plataea, a renewed Persian invasion was defeated by the hoplites of Sparta, a militarized Greek city-state that trained its warriors from childhood. Sparta's rival, Athens, also participated in the land campaign against the Persians, but its most valuable contribution was a fleet of triremes—fast ships powered by triple banks of oarsmen—that outmaneuvered the Persians to victory at Salamis, in 480BCE.

▶ ALEXANDER THE GREAT
Alexander's tactical brilliance enabled him to defeat superior forces, which in turn allowed him to conquer the Persian empire within three years.

With the Persians defeated, Sparta and Athens clashed for almost the next 80 years, resulting in the Peloponnesian War (431–04BCE), which, although bloody, showed only a few innovations in equipment and tactics. The armies began to make more use of archers, and employed flexible light infantry, called peltasts, as skirmishers, armed with

javelins and swords. However, almost as soon as Sparta emerged victorious in 404BCE, its power was challenged by the Thebans, led by Epaminondas.

THE EVOLUTION OF THE PHALANX

The Thebans deepened their phalanxes to 12 ranks or more, made greater use of cavalry, and trained an elite force known as the Sacred Band. This helped them win a stunning victory at Leuctra, in 371BCE, which broke Spartan supremacy. However, Theban dominance was short-lived and Greece fell into civil wars, ending with the rise of Macedon, first under Philip II and then Alexander the Great.

The Macedonians further deepened the phalanx to 16 ranks, and their soldiers carried the *sarissa*, a longer spear of up to 20 feet (6m), which allowed the first five rows to strike at the enemy. These armored "phalangites" kept enemy infantry pinned down, while heavy cavalry, slingers, and peltasts launched their attack.

"Like some **ferocious beast** as it turns at bay and **stiffens its bristles**"

PLUTARCH, DESCRIBING THE APPEARANCE OF A PHALANX, c.100CE

KEY **EVENTS**

725–300BCE

- **c.725–700BCE** The earliest known war between Greek city-states (the Lelantine War between Chalcis and Eretria) is thought to have been fought in this period. Hoplite armor is also thought to originate in this era.
- **c.650BCE** The earliest depiction of hoplites in art shows them without swords, but carrying two spears: one for thrusting and one for throwing.
- **492–90BCE** The first Greco-Persian War takes place. Darius I of Persia invades Greece, attracting some allies in the north, but is defeated by the Athenians and their Plataean allies at the Battle of Marathon (490BCE), in which the Plataean hoplites surprise the Persians by charging into their ranks.
- **431–04BCE** Spartan and Athenian forces clash in the Peloponnesian War.
- **480BCE** Xerxes launches the second Persian invasion of Greece. The Persians are delayed by Spartan resistance at Thermopylae (480BCE). They are then defeated at Salamis (480BCE) by the Athenian navy, and at Plataea (479BCE), where Spartan hoplites break through the Persian line, causing the Persian army to flee.
- **378BCE** The Thebans, under Epaminondas, destroy the Spartan army at the Battle of Leuctra, marking the beginning of the eclipse of traditional hoplite forces.
- **338BCE** At Chaeronea, Philip II of Macedon defeats the Thebans by feigning a withdrawal, stretching one wing of the Theban army in pursuit. Philip's son, Alexander, then charges the enemy's left wing with cavalry, routing it. The Theban Sacred Band is destroyed.
- **331BCE** The Battle of Gaugamela takes place. A Macedonian attack on the left wing of the Persian army, opens up a gap in their ranks, into which Alexander advances. This flexible approach is far in advance of traditional hoplite tactics.

◀ **A HOPLITE CHARGE**
This vase shows Greek hoplites running into battle, their Corinthian helmets, horsehair crests, bronze greaves, and spears clearly visible. The artist has not depicted the other ranks in the phalanx, which made it even more intimidating to behold.

HOPLITE ARMOR AND WEAPONS

For four centuries from 700BCE, heavily armed citizen-soldiers called hoplites ("armed men") formed the armies of the Greek city-states. Each soldier typically provided all of his weaponry and armor at his own expense: a bronze corselet (made up of a bell-shaped breastplate and backplate), a helmet, greaves, a sword, a spear, and a large round shield. Fighting in tightly packed phalanxes, the soldiers were very well protected, although still vulnerable to spear-thrusts around the groin and throat, or to wounds inflicted by missiles before they closed in on the opposing army's line.

Cheek guard

◄ CORINTHIAN HELMET

Date Late 7th century BCE
Origin Greece
Material Bronze

The Corinthian was the most common form of hoplite helmet, made from a single piece of bronze. It protected the whole head, with only a T-shaped opening for the eyes, nose, and mouth. An inner lining helped cushion the wearer's head.

Molding to represent warrior's muscles

► LATE CORINTHIAN HELMET

Date 6th century BCE
Origin Greece
Material Bronze

More developed Corinthian helmets, such as this example, had sharply angled side pieces and thinner, more delicate nose protectors with a more pronounced neck guard. It is the type of helmet most commonly depicted on Corinthian vases.

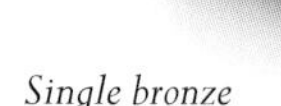

Single bronze piece forms helmet

▲ BRONZE CUIRASS

Date 8th century BCE
Origin Greece
Material Bronze

The backplate of the hoplite cuirass was secured to the front with hinges and rings for leather straps. The front was molded to the contours of the wearer's torso, suggesting that these cuirasses were probably crafted for individuals. Full plate cuirasses fell out of fashion around 500BCE.

Shaped to fit contours of leg

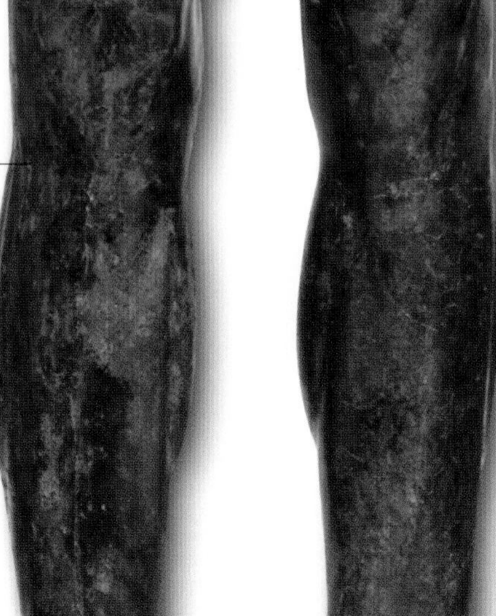

Hinged cheekflap

◄ ATTIC HELMET

Date 5th century BCE
Origin Greece
Material Bronze

The Attic helmet was a further development of the Chalcidian—a type that had more rounded cheekpieces than the Corinthian. However, the Attic gave lighter protection, with more space around the ears and hinged cheekflaps. It was often decorated on the front above the forehead.

◄ BRONZE GREAVES

Date 6th century BCE
Origin Greece
Material Bronze

While the hoplite's thighs were covered by his shield, the greaves protected the knees and shins. The greaves were thin and shaped to the wearer's legs, allowing them to be snapped into place without the need for straps or ties.

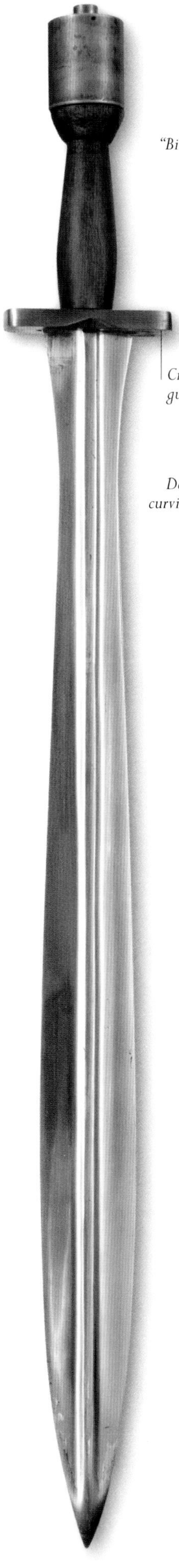

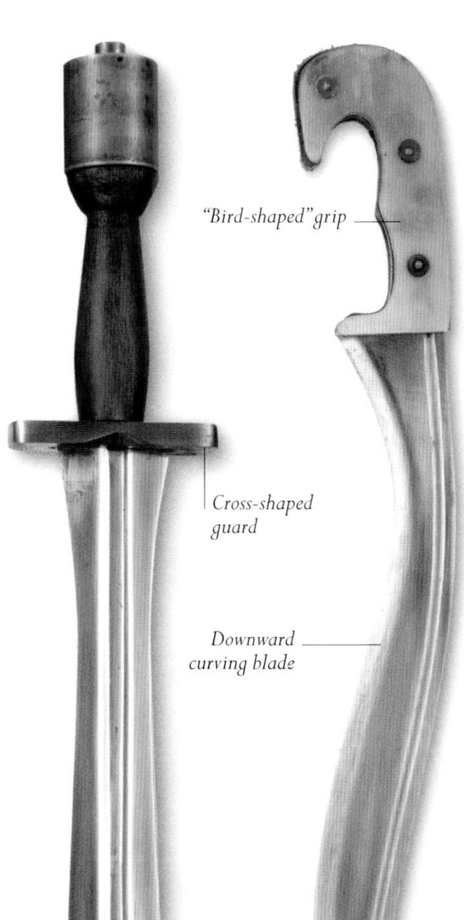

▲ GREEK SPEARHEAD

Date 6th–5th centuries BCE

Origin Greece

Weight 13oz (370g)

Length 12¼in (31cm)

The spear was the hoplite's main weapon; the *kopis* (short sword) was used only if the spear broke during fighting. Originally hoplites carried two spears that could be thrown, but these were later replaced by one long, thrusting spear.

Indentation for bronze securing ring

Socket for spear shaft

◀ KOPIS

Date 5th century BCE

Origin Greece

Material Iron

The *kopis* appeared in the late 6th century BCE, replacing earlier, broader, slashing blades. As can be seen in this modern replica, its curved shape was designed to inflict wounds with a downward slash, while its convex blade and back (noncutting edge) were designed to add weight to the weapon toward its tip.

▲ HOPLITE SPEAR BUTT

Date 4th century BCE

Origin Macedonia

Length 15in (38cm)

As hoplite spears grew longer, particularly from the 4th century BCE in the phalanxes of Philip of Macedon and Alexander the Great, they needed a counterweight to balance the spear point at the other end. The spear butt provided this support and could also be used as a weapon if the spearhead broke.

Scorpion was Spartan symbol of the city of Geronthrae

Bronze rim of shield

◀ XIPHOS

Date Early 6th century BCE

Origin Greece

Material Iron

The *xiphos* was the sword most commonly carried by hoplites in the 6th century BCE. Its thick hilt had a cross-shaped guard and the blade swelled to a wide point near the tip, making it a very strong weapon. Used for thrusting in close combat, it was carried in a sheath worn under the left arm. The version pictured here is a modern replica.

▶ ASPIS

Date c.500BCE

Origin Greece

Material Wood, bronze

This modern replica of an *aspis* (or *hoplon*) shield is made from wood, although they were also often covered with bronze, with further bronze reinforcement around the rim. Up to 3ft (1m) in diameter, they gently curved inward to provide some protection to the soldier's sides, and had an *antilabe* (handle) and a bronze *porpax* (loop) on the back. This allowed the soldier to carry a weapon and a shield in the same hand.

THE ALEXANDER SARCOPHAGUS
This representation of the Battle of Issus appears on a sarcophagus made in the 4th century BCE. After his victory at Issus, Alexander continued his invasion of the Persian Empire, finally defeating Darius at Gaugamela in 331BCE.

PHALANX AND CAVALRY

THE BATTLE OF ISSUS

The Macedonian army of Alexander the Great achieved remarkable conquests in the 4th century BCE, invading and destroying the mighty Persian Empire. Alexander's defeat of the Persians at Issus in 333BCE exemplified the Macedonian use of infantry phalanxes flanked by heavy cavalry.

As Alexander advanced along the eastern Mediterranean coast, the Persian ruler Darius III led an army through Syria to intercept him, reaching the sea behind Alexander's line of march. The Macedonians turned back and confronted Darius at Issus on a plain between the sea and the foothills of the Amanus Mountains. Alexander's army was outnumbered—possibly 40,000 men to the Persians' 100,000—but the restricted battlefield made it difficult for Darius to use his larger force to outflank the Macedonian line.

The Persians took up a position behind a river, fortifying its banks with wooden palisades. On the other side of the river, Alexander arranged his forces in a traditional fashion. His elite Companion cavalry took up position on the right, by the foothills, and the subsidiary Thessalian cavalry on the left, beside the sea. In the center were the infantry—most of them organized into tightknit phalanxes armed with long, two-handed sarissa pikes. The Macedonian phalanxes were usually 16 ranks deep, but at Issus the ranks were thinned to eight to spread the troops more widely. The Macedonians also deployed more flexible hypaspists—elite infantry equipped with shorter spears, swords, and pikes—and swarms of light skirmishing troops armed with bows, javelins, and slings.

Darius opened the battle, sending soldiers to infiltrate through the hills, but the Macedonian skirmishers countered this outflanking maneuver, halting the Persians with arrows and stones. The main body of heavily armored Persian cavalry, supported by slingers running alongside the horses, charged along the beach on the Macedonian left, but was contained and then repulsed by the Thessalian horsemen. In the center, Alexander ordered his infantry to advance against the Persian line, where Greek mercenary hoplites employed by Darius were drawn up in phalanxes with their traditional bronze armor, shields, and spears. As the Macedonian foot soldiers began to ford the river and scale the palisades on the far side, their own phalanxes lost formation, opening gaps in the ranks of pikes into which the enemy could penetrate.

TACTICAL PROWESS

The struggle in the center, however, was not Alexander's main tactical gambit—he intended to triumph through a cavalry charge on the right. With Alexander himself at their head, the Companion cavalry rode forward. The horsemen wore bronze cuirasses and helmets, but did not carry shields. Each was armed with a lance and a sword, mostly the curvaceous *kopis*. Having neither saddle nor stirrups, the men gripped their mounts firmly with their knees as they smashed into a mix of Persian light infantry, archers, and cavalry. The point of attack was well chosen, and the Persian left wing collapsed in the face of the onslaught. Already engaged with the Macedonian infantry to their front, Darius's Greek mercenaries were now exposed to cavalry attack from the flank and rear. Darius himself, on a command chariot behind his army, was also under threat. The Persian emperor fled the field, leaving his soldiers to be massacred or to scatter in search of safety.

GREEK TRIREME

OLYMPIAS

The Greeks were famed for their naval prowess, using light, fast galleys called triremes. No trireme has survived from antiquity, but the *Olympias* is a reconstruction based on historical evidence.

A Greek trireme was a shallow-draft vessel some 115ft (35m) long and less than 20ft (6m) wide. It cruised under sail, but in battle it was propelled by 170 oarsmen – all free citizens – in three tiers: 62 thranites on top, 54 zygians in the middle, and 54 thalamians at the bottom. With around 30 other men completing the crew, including marine hoplites and archers, it was a crowded vessel. There was room to carry only a few basic supplies and insufficient space for the whole crew to sleep on board.

The *Olympias* was built at Piraeus, Athens, between 1985 and 1987. It proved highly maneuverable in sea trials, reaching speeds of almost 8 knots under oar and turning around in twice its own length. In action, a trireme with a skilled helmsman and a disciplined crew could ram an enemy vessel or ride over its oars, then reverse and leave it crippled in the water. If its own hull was holed, a trireme would not sink because it was made from buoyant wood such as pine, poplar, or fir.

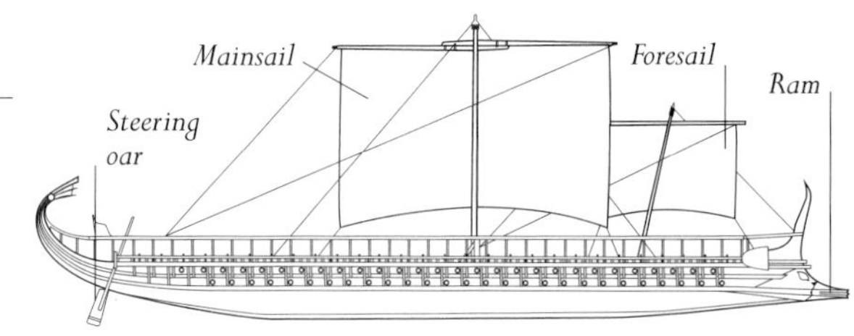

SIDE VIEW

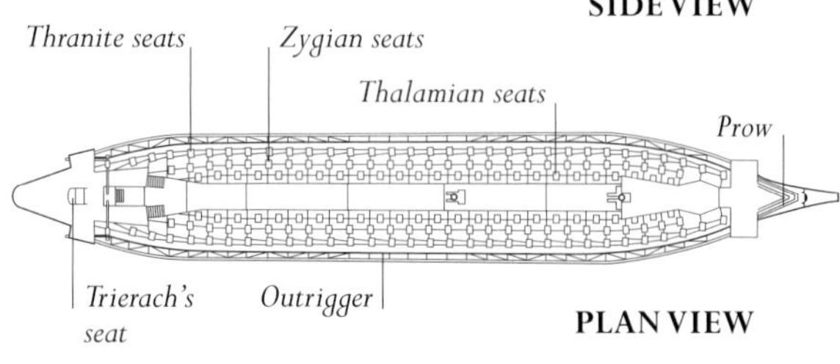

PLAN VIEW

THE *OLYMPIAS*
The side view shows the arrangement of the two sails and the three tiers of oar ports. The plan view shows the position of each individual oarsman's seat.

PROW AND HULL

◄ BRONZE RAM
A trireme's prow terminated in a bronze-clad ram for holing the hulls of enemy galleys in battle. The ram on the *Olympias* weighs 440lb (200kg).

▲ EAR AND ANCHOR
Sailors dropped and weighed anchor from platforms called *epotides* (ears) near the prow. The ears also protected the thranite oarsmen behind.

► OUTRIGGER
Built out from of the hull, the outriggers allowed the thranites on the upper tier to row from a position outboard of the two lower tiers.

► SAILING AT SPEED
Under sail, and with a favorable wind, the *Olympias* achieved a speed of almost 11 knots.

OARS AND OARSMEN

▲ **THRANITES' BENCHES**
The rowers on the topmost tier, the thranites, had the toughest job, because of the angle at which their oars entered the water. Consequently, they commanded higher wages than the other rowers.

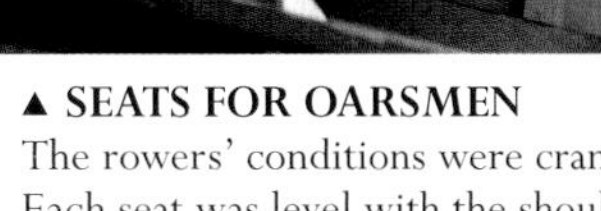

▲ **SEATS FOR OARSMEN**
The rowers' conditions were cramped. Each seat was level with the shoulders of the oarsman on the tier below.

▲ **FOOT STRETCHER**
The crew of the *Olympias* experimented with various rowing techniques, including securing one foot to the stretcher.

▲ **TIERS OF OARS**
The tiers were staggered to prevent oars from clashing. The lowest oars had leather sheaths to keep water out of the hull.

STEERING THE BOAT

▲ **VIEW FROM THE STERN**
The helmsman, who steered using a pair of tillers, overlooked the central slot between the decks, where the mast was stowed when not in use.

▲ **TILLER**
A single helmsman normally controlled both tillers, but if more force was required a man was assigned to each one.

▲ **STEERING OAR**
Operated by the tillers, the pair of steering oars (rudders) could also be used as brakes to slow the ship's forward movement.

KEY DEVELOPMENT

THE ROMAN WAR MACHINE

Until the collapse of the western Roman empire in the 5th century CE, the Roman legions formed the most formidable army of the Ancient World. Primarily an infantry force, it underwent a number of changes during its time of dominance.

The early Roman army was a citizen militia, drawn mainly from the wealthier classes. It owed its early successes to Rome's ability to conscript large numbers of recruits in times of war, and to its formidable tactical organization and training, which were far superior to those of its Italian enemies. The early legions had three categories of heavy infantry—the *hastati*, who were the least experienced, the *principes*, the best-quality troops, and the *triarii*, the veterans. The *hastati* and *principes* were armed with heavy javelins (*pila*), whereas the *triarii* had thrusting spears (*hastae*). The legionaries were protected by bronze helmets and semi-cylindrical body shields and, from the mid-3rd century BCE, they were armed with a short sword—the *gladius hispaniensis*—that became known as their signature weapon.

Drawn up in these three lines—each divided into 10 maniples (units) of around 150 men—the legion fought in much the same way as many ancient armies. Supporting cavalry (*equites*) and light infantry (*velites*) would attempt to turn the enemy flank, while the heavy infantry tried to breach their opponents' line. Few armies could match the Romans in number or skill, but the legion suffered major setbacks when faced with the tactical genius of the Carthaginian general Hannibal, during the Second Punic War.

THE MARIAN REFORMS

Although the Roman army ultimately won the Second Punic War, its performance during the 2nd century BCE was lackluster and it struggled in

KEY **FIGURE**

JULIUS CAESAR

100–44BCE

Roman general Julius Caesar secured his reputation in a series of campaigns in Gaul, from 58 to 50BCE, securing large new provinces for Rome. Dogged and tactically adept, Caesar ruthlessly suppressed tribes who opposed him, such as the Belgae and Nervii, and was made dictator for life. Soon after, however, he was assassinated.

◀ At the time of his assassination, Julius Caesar was planning further military conquests, of the Dacians and the Parthians.

▼ **THE BATTLE OF THE TREBIA**
In 218BCE, Hannibal turned the Roman flanks by defeating their cavalry, then attacking from the rear.

"The **Romans** instil into their **soldiers fortitude** not only of **body** but also **soul**"

JOSEPHUS, *THE JEWISH WAR*, c.75CE

wars against the Numantines, in Spain, and against Jugurtha, King of Numidia, in North Africa. From 107BCE, the Roman general Marius instituted a number of reforms. The army became a permanent force, not recruited fresh each campaigning season, and it became open to all, rather than only the propertied classes. There was now just one form of heavy infantry, issued with standardized equipment—the *pilum*, the *gladius*, mail armor, and the *scutum*, a long rectangular shield. A more flexible tactical sub-unit—the cohort—also came into use. This consisted of 480 men, divided into six centuries (a unit of 80 men).

THE LEGIONS UNDER THE EMPIRE

The new army was supremely well drilled and disciplined. It could advance to within 50ft (15m) of the enemy and would then let off a volley of javelins and charge. Once at close quarters, the legionaries used their shields to strike enemies, then stabbed them in the stomach with their short swords. Highly trained, they were able to withstand a cavalry charge by using their javelins to form a type of phalanx (see pp.24–25). They rarely lost field battles against infantry forces, and their skill in siege warfare meant that only mobile opponents with strategic depth, such as the horse archers of the Parthian Empire, were able to fend them off. With backup provided by professional auxiliaries—slingers, archers, and even specialized camel troops—armed with a wider range of weapons, the legions conquered much of Europe, North Africa, and the Middle East.

THE LATE ROMAN ARMY

Under the later empire, the Roman army became more diverse and was composed of smaller units. Smaller, oval or round shields were used instead of the *scutum* and lighter spears (*lancea*) replaced *pila*. Cataphracts (heavily armored cavalry) came into service, and the army became more adapted to defending the Empire's frontiers, rather than engaging in aggressive field battles. An increasing reliance on foreign mercenaries—mostly Germanic—meant that, by the fifth century, the Roman Empire's western provinces had few military resources of its own able to hold back waves of barbarian invaders—a factor that contributed to the empire's fall in 476CE.

▼ ROMAN ARTILLERY
Roman legions carried field artillery with them. The bulk of these were ballistas—giant torsion operated machines that shot lead-tipped bolts.

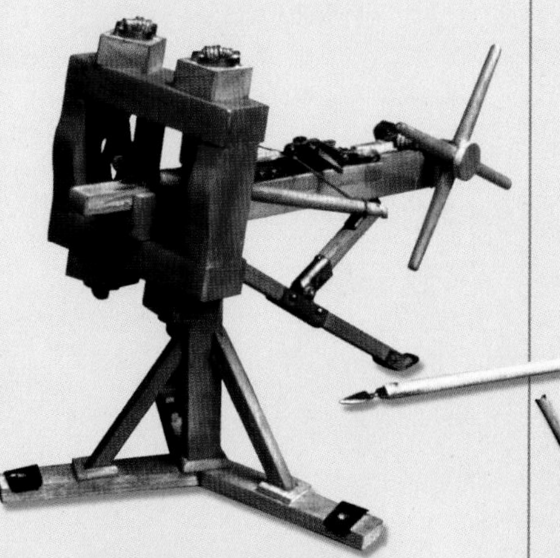

KEY **EVENTS**

2600–750BCE

- **264–241BCE, 218–201BCE, 149–146BCE** The Punic Wars between Rome and Carthage, in North Africa, end in a Roman victory. During the Second War, the Carthaginian general Hannibal crosses the Alps into Italy, defeating the Romans at Trebia and Cannae, but failing to capture Rome.
- **102BCE** At the Battle of Aquae Sextiae, Roman general Marius defeats the invading Teutones, who threaten to overwhelm Italy. This is the reformed Roman army's first success.
- **58–50BCE** Julius Caesar conquers Gaul, defeating numerous tribes and finally overcoming the resistance of the Gallic leader Vercingetorix at the decisive Siege of Alesia.
- **27BCE** Augustus becomes the first Roman emperor. After a long period of civil war, he reduces the number of legions from around 60 to 28, all of which now pledge their loyalty to the emperor rather than to a variety of generals.
- **101–02, 105–06CE** Emperor Trajan defeats the Dacian king Decebalus during the Dacian Wars. Dacia province becomes an outpost of the Roman Empire.
- **378CE** Gothic barbarians defeat the main field army of the eastern Empire at the Battle of Adrianople. Emperor Valens perishes during the battle—Rome's worst military disaster for nearly 400 years.

◀ TRAJAN'S CAMPAIGN
A scene from Emperor Trajan's campaign against the Dacians, in 105–06CE, shows the Romans fending off an attack from a field fortification.

ROMAN LEGIONARY'S ARMOR AND WEAPONS

The Roman legionary, the mainstay of the Roman army, fought in legions roughly 5,000 strong. Their equipment was well adapted for fighting in close formation, each soldier being equipped with two *pila* (javelins) that could be hurled, and a *gladius* (a short stabbing sword), which was used in hand-to-hand fighting. The dimensions of the equipment changed over time—a longer slashing sword, the *spatha*, came to be preferred over the *gladius*.

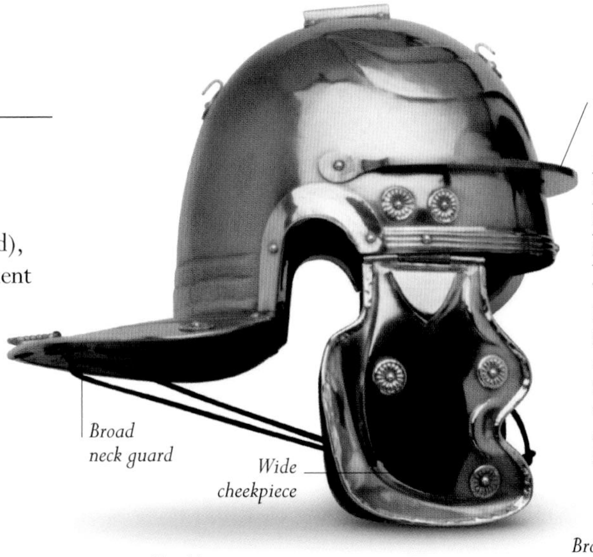

Brow guard

Broad neck guard

Wide cheekpiece

◄ **GALLIC HELMET**

Date Late 1st century CE

Origin Roman Empire

Material Iron

This modern replica depicts an Imperial-Gallic helmet that was influenced by Celtic models and had a deeper neck guard than earlier Roman helmets, which made it harder to crouch and dictated a more upright fighting style for its wearers.

▲ **LORICA SQUAMATA**

Date 1st century CE

Origin Roman Empire

Material Iron

Legionaries often wore armor of overlapping metal scales an inch long, made of copper or iron, bound together with iron and sewn onto a cloth underpiece. By the late 1st century CE, it was increasingly superseded by *lorica segmentata*.

▲ **LORICA SEGMENTATA**

Date Late 1st century CE

Origin Roman Empire

Material Iron, bronze, leather

This modern replica Roman armor is made up of overlapping iron plates with leather straps running underneath. It probably had its origins in gladiatorial equipment and, although providing good protection, the complicated fittings made it hard to maintain.

◄ **SCUTUM**

Date 1st century CE

Origin Roman Empire

Weight 15–20lb (6.8–9kg)

Width 29in (73cm)

The *scutum* (legionary shield) was a long rectangle that curved inward to form a part cylinder, giving greater protection to its wearer. As depicted on this modern replica, it was adorned with legionary insignia. When not in use, it was protected by a leather cover.

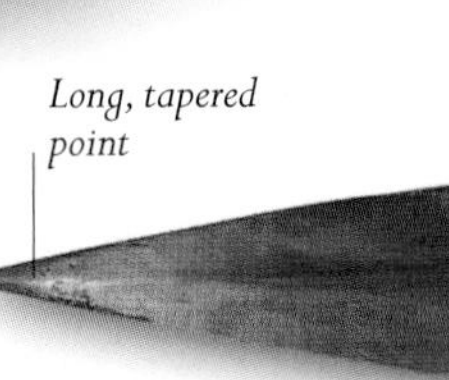

◀ GLADIUS AND SCABBARD

Date c.15CE

Origin Rome

Length 22½in (57.5cm)

This *gladius* (legionary sword) and ornate scabbard was probably presented by the Emperor Tiberius to a favored officer. Its decoration shows the Emperor dedicating a victory to his stepfather Augustus.

Legionary eagle standard in shrine

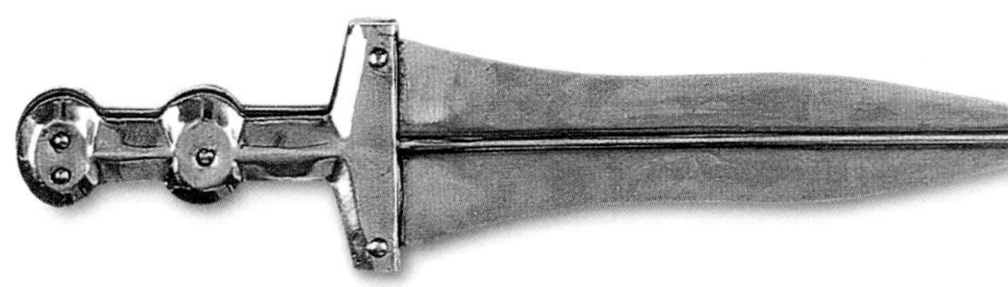

▲ PUGIO

Date 1st century CE

Origin Roman Empire

Material Steel

The legionary's *pugio* (dagger) was a backup weapon if his sword could not be deployed. It was worn on the left for ordinary soldiers and frequently had an ornate scabbard inlaid with metal or enamel. The object shown here is a modern replica.

▲ MASK FOR CAVALRY SPORTS

Date 1st century BCE–1st century CE

Origin Nola, Italy

Material Bronze

At military displays, cavalrymen wore ornate helmets with face masks, often when they took part in mock battles. The mask was attached to the main part of the helmet with leather straps, and a crest and streamers added to the impressive appearance.

HASTA

PILUM

▶ PILUM AND HASTA

Date Late 1st century CE

Origin Roman Empire

Length 6½ft (2m)

The Roman military *pilum* (javelin) was a throwing weapon, designed so that its pointed head would break off on hitting a target, making it impossible to hurl back. The *hasta* (thrusting spear) was a more substantial spear, used to thrust in close-quarter combat. The versions shown here are modern replicas.

▶ SLING BULLETS

Date 3rd–1st centuries BCE

Origin Roman Empire

Weight 1¼–2¼oz (37.5–64.5g)

Length 1¼–1¾in (3.2–4.4cm)

Roman armies included lighter-armed troops, whose weaponry included slings with lead pellets such as these. The legions also had some heavier artillery that shot larger, pointed bolts.

MAINZ-STYLE BLADE

Waisted blade

POMPEII-STYLE BLADE

Parallel cutting edges

◀ GLADII

Date 1st–3rd centuries CE

Origin Roman Empire

Weight 25–32oz (700–900g)

Length 26–28in (65–70cm)

Based on a short Spanish sword, the *gladius* had a narrow blade with a long point, making it effective for stabbing and thrusting. As can be seen in the modern replicas pictured here, the blade shape evolved from the waisted "Mainz" style to the straight-edged "Pompeii" type, which then evolved into the longer, straight-bladed *spatha* (slashing sword).

KEY **EVENTS**

146BCE–124CE

■ **c.146BCE** Work begins on the Via Egnatia, a road that will enable Roman armies to access most of the Balkans from Italy.

■ **134–133BCE** Roman forces, led by Scipio Africanus, besiege the Celtiberian stronghold of Numantia, surrounding it with fortifications (known as circumvallations) and attacking it with siege towers. The settlement falls after 16 months.

■ **52BCE** Julius Caesar traps Vercingetorix, leader of the Gallic Revolt, at Alesia. Roman engineers build complex siege-works, preventing relief forces from coming to the defenders' aid.

■ **73CE** Flavius Silva uses his engineers of the Tenth Legion to subdue the mountain fort of Masada.

■ **122–24CE** Hadrian's Wall becomes the Romans' most complex border system. It is 73 miles (117km) long and punctuated by forts.

KEY DEVELOPMENT

THE ENGINEERING OF ROMAN CONQUEST

The Roman legionaries were not only excellent in combat—they were also highly skilled military engineers, who were called upon to build forts, roads, and siege-works throughout the empire.

A Roman legionary's entrenching tools, it was said, were as dear to him as his sword. When on campaign, legionaries built a marching camp every evening, using a formulaic design that allowed them to organize encampments for up to 5,000 soldiers. Sited on level ground, the camps were usually rectangular, surrounded by a V-shaped ditch and an earth rampart bristling with wooden spikes that the legionaries carried with them.

Once an area was conquered, more permanent forts were built (see p.38), also based on this "playing-card design"—so-called because they had rounded corners. Each fort had four main gates, one of which (the *porta praetoria*) faced enemy territory; a network of roads; and a central block of buildings that contained the *praetorium* (commander's house), the *principia* (headquarters), and a shrine for the legionary standards.

Forts were built in various sizes, to accommodate either whole legions or smaller auxiliary cohorts (around 500 men). They sometimes formed part of complex linear defenses, or even walls (such as Hadrian's Wall in Britain). Over time, the earth and turf of many of the original forts were replaced with stone, and, during the later empire, the walls were stronger and had projecting corner towers allowing missile cross-fire. These developments reflected the fact that the forts had become places the army needed to defend, rather than bases from which to dominate the surrounding territory.

ROMAN SIEGES

The legionaries put their skill at constructing fortifications and ramparts to good offensive effect in siege warfare, as they encountered enemy bastions as diverse as the hill-forts of Gaul and Britain, and the elaborate walled towns of Judaea.

If an enemy fort could not be taken by stealth, it had to be surrounded and starved out or, as a last resort, stormed. To isolate an enemy position, the Romans built complex siege-works of ramparts, often with towers from which to fire heavy catapults. At the Siege of Alesia, Julius Caesar oversaw the building of 35km (55 miles) of ramparts that hemmed in Gaulish chieftain Vercingetorix, and cut off supplies. Vast earthworks called assault ramps intimidated

▼ LEGION INSIGNIA
Imperial legions were proud of their identity. This plaque shows the emblem of the Twentieth Legion, which took part in suppressing the Iceni revolt in Britain (60–61CE).

"There was also **a tower** made of the height of **sixty cubits**, and all over **plated with iron**, out of which **the Romans threw darts and stones** from the engines"

JOSEPHUS, *THE JEWISH WAR*, c.75CE

the besieged troops, provided the attackers with access to the walls for artillery points, and formed a platform for a final assault.

More than the surviving remains of their forts, the finest testament to the Romans' skills in military engineering is arguably the vast network of roads—some 120,000km (75,000 miles) long—they built to consolidate their rule. The first was the Via Appia, begun in 331BCE, which initially ran from Rome to Capua. Main roads linked the towns, making it possible to move troops quickly and to operate an efficient postal network. Military roads ran behind important frontiers, as in Britain and Germany. Roman roads were normally straight, regardless of local topography, and were carried over rivers and marshes by bridges or viaducts. Their durability owed much to their excellent construction, which involved a foundation of coarse gravel laid beneath layers of finer gravel, with large blocks of basalt added on top to form the pavement.

◄ **THE SIEGE OF MASADA**
To take possession of the inaccessible mountain fort of Masada, the last stronghold of the Jewish Revolt, in 73CE, the Romans had to build a counterwall with towers and a gigantic assault ramp on which to mount a battering ram. The ramp was 738ft (225m) long and up to 656ft (200m) wide.

◄ **A DACIAN CONQUEST**
Roman legionaries are depicted on Trajan's Column (in Rome, dated 113CE) leaving a fortress to cross the Danube on a bridge of boats at the start of Trajan's Dacian War, in 101–02CE.

KEY **FIGURE**

HADRIAN

76–138CE

The emperor Hadrian ordered a retreat from advanced Roman positions in Scotland and had a wall built to mark the Roman frontier in northern Britain. It was defended by a complex series of forts, milecastles, and turrets.

▲ Hadrian consolidated the Roman Empire rather than expanding it. He even withdrew from some territories.

ROMAN FORTIFICATION

ARBEIA FORT

The Roman army built the ancient world's greatest fortifications. Legionaries were more like combat engineers than ordinary soldiers, being trained in construction as well as the art of battle.

On campaign, a legion made a wooden camp, surrounded by an earth rampart, at every stop. Permanent forts were initially also made of wood and earth, but later ones, like the reconstructed Arbeia, in northeast England, were stone-built. Used as barracks, administrative centers, and supply depots, they maintained a military presence in potentially hostile territory.

Outposts of Roman civilization, the forts made no concessions to local climates or cultures, displaying similar features across the empire. Living conditions were basic and cramped—units of eight soldiers called *contubernia*, or "tent groups," shared small, two-roomed suites in the barracks. However, with heated bathhouses and latrines cleaned by running water, hygiene standards were relatively high.

Arbeia was a small fort, housing about 600 auxiliary troops, both infantry and cavalry. Built in the 2nd century CE, it was a major supply center for the troops on Hadrian's Wall to the north.

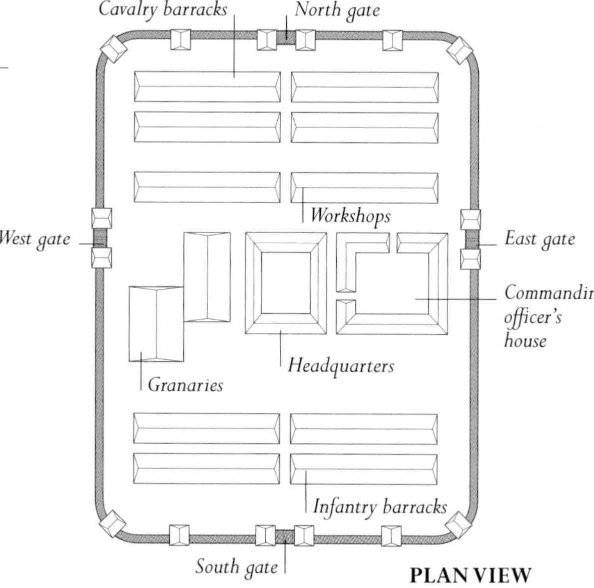

LAYOUT OF A ROMAN FORT
Large or small, most Roman forts were built to a similar plan, with barracks for cavalry and infantry, workshops, granaries, and a separate headquarters.

FORT ENTRANCE

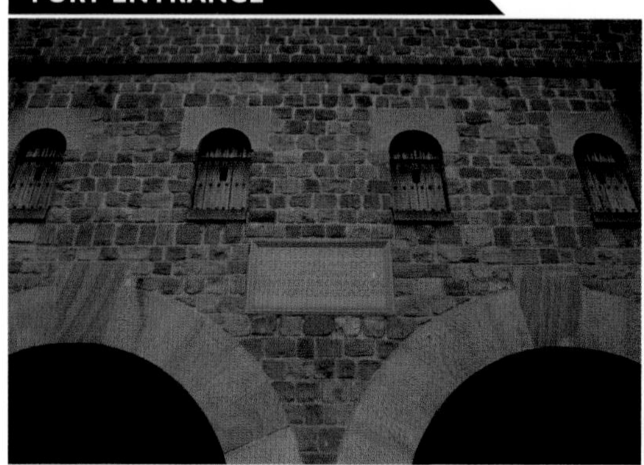

▲ GATEHOUSE PLAQUE
The plaque states that the fort was built by Legio VI Victrix under Sextus Calpurnius Agricola, governor of Britain (c.163–66CE).

▲ DOORS AND WALLS
Solid stone walls and thick wooden doors would have kept out the bands of tribal fighters who occasionally carried out raids in Roman Britain.

▶ GATEHOUSE
Although the twin towers of Arbeia's gatehouse are imposing, they are smaller than those at some other Roman forts and city walls.

CONTUBERNIA SUITE

▲ **BARRACK BLOCKS**
Each plastered-stone block housed five *contubernia*. There were a few small windows, and ventilators were set into the roof.

◀ **DORMITORY**
The eight soldiers of a *contubernium* slept in the larger room of their suite, either under woolen blankets on simple beds or on straw-filled mattresses on the floor.

◀ **SMALL ROOM**
The smaller room of a *contubernium*'s suite was used as either a living area or a storage space for the soldiers' military equipment.

▲ **INTERIOR BARRACK WALLS**
The internal walls were made of wattle-and-daub—a woven wooden lattice (wattle) daubed with a mixture of straw, mud, and animal dung.

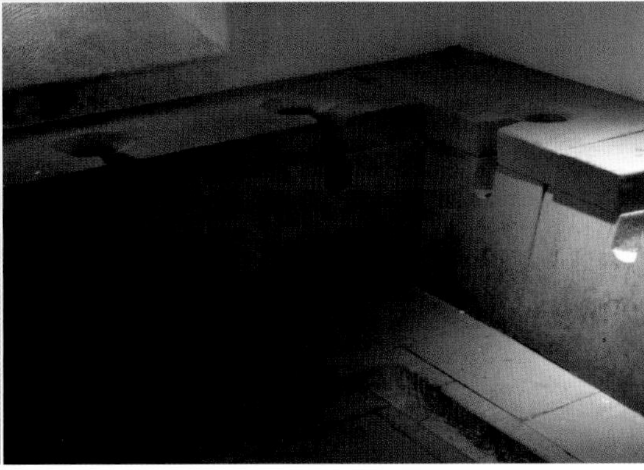

▲ **BATHHOUSE LATRINES**
There was also probably a bathhouse for the troops outside the fort. Its communal latrines lacked privacy, but they had high-quality plumbing.

OFFICER'S HOUSE

▲ **COURTYARD**
The commanding officer lived in a comfortable house within the fort. It had an open courtyard and rooms leading off a colonnaded walkway.

▲ **HEATED BEDROOM**
The commander's bedrooms were large, decorated, and warmed by the hypocaust (underfloor heating). Beds were often richly carved or painted.

ENEMIES OF ROME

The expansion of Rome's influence from a small settlement in central Italy to an imperial power that ruled a huge empire brought its armies face to face with a wide range of foes. Although the individual equipment of most enemy warriors may have been superb, their training and organization was almost always inferior to that of the Roman army. However, the Roman infantry did struggle against the mounted warriors of Persia and the Hunnish archers, and by the time the Franks, the Ostrogoths, and other Germanic groups poured into the empire from the 4th century CE onward, the Roman army was too weakened to resist them.

Bronze wings

▼ BRONZE SAMNITE BREASTPLATE

Date	4th century BCE
Origin	Central Italy
Material	Bronze

Made of three convex bronze disks, this breastplate would have been matched by a similar piece to protect the back. Such armor was worn by Rome's opponents, the Samnite tribes, in three wars in central Italy from 343–290BCE.

Red glass enamel studs

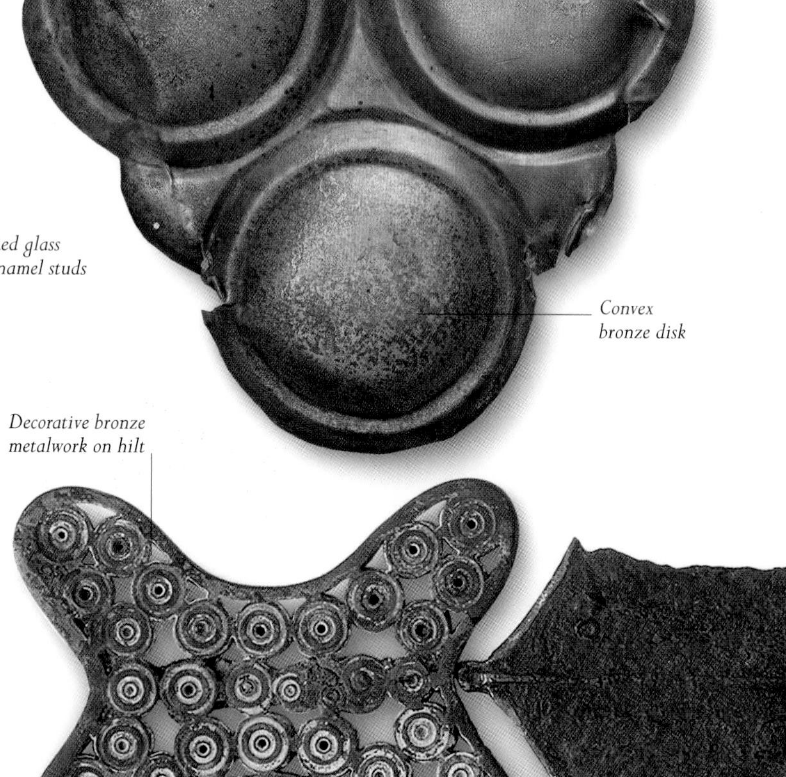

Rivet holes for fastening armor

Convex bronze disk

Decorative bronze metalwork on hilt

◄ BATTERSEA SHIELD

Date	350–50BCE
Origin	England
Weight	7½lb (3.4kg)
Diameter	14in (35.7cm)

This ornate decorative bronze cover to a wooden shield, found in the Thames River at Battersea, London, was probably for parade use. It is made of four sheets of bronze riveted together.

▲ CELTIC DAGGER

Date	250–50BCE
Origin	England
Length	11in (27.8cm)

The intricate spiral-pattern decoration on this Celtic dagger indicates that it was probably intended for funerary or display purposes, rather than combat. Its sharply tapering blade was typical of everyday weapons.

Silver-covered scabbard

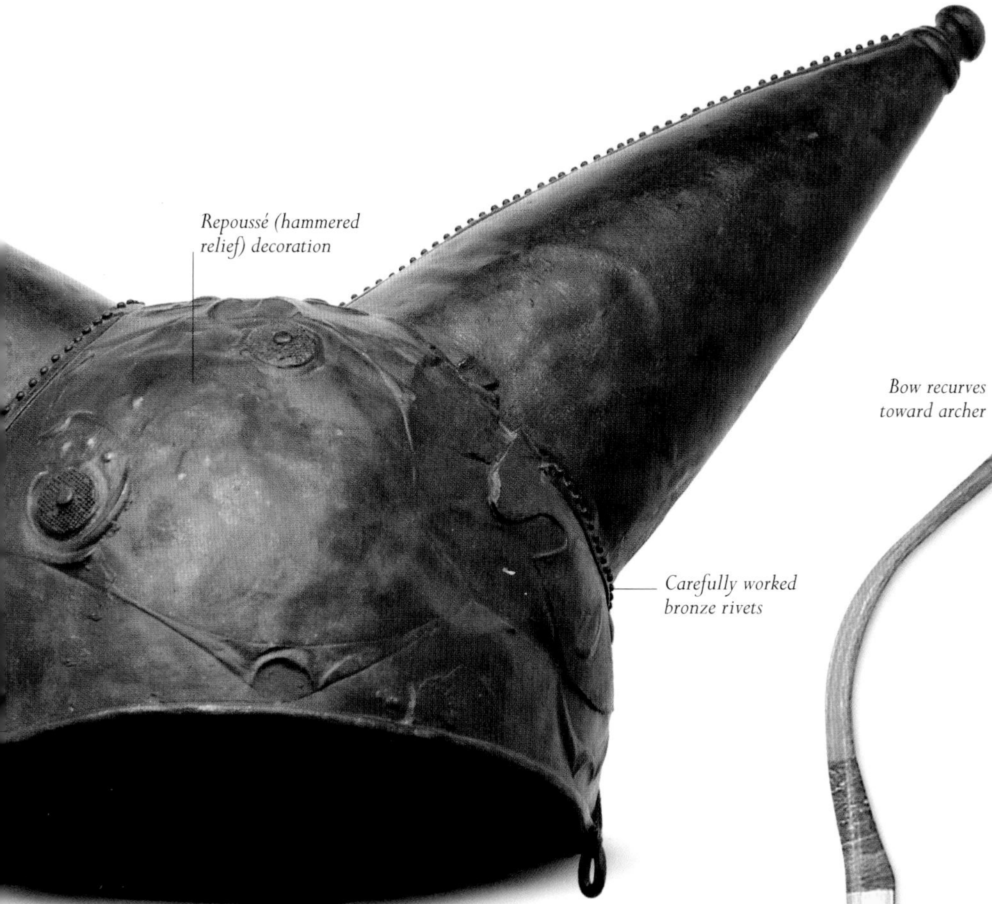

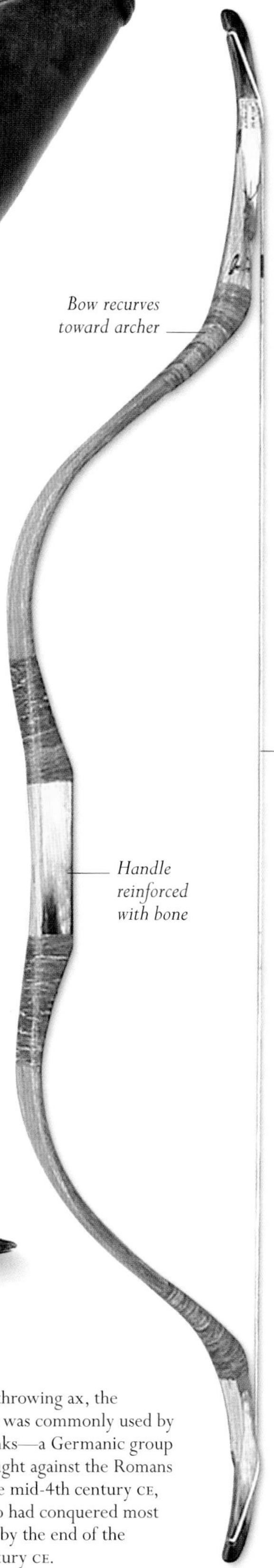

▲ BRONZE HELMET

Date 250–50BCE
Origin England
Material Bronze

This horned helmet is the only one of its type ever found in Europe, and was probably for ceremonial rather than combat purposes. It is made of bronze sheets riveted together.

▶ HUNNISH BOW

Date 5th century CE
Origin Central Europe
Length 4–5½ft (1.25–1.65m)

The Huns employed compound bows made of horn and wood, which had a greater range than simple bows. The Huns depended on a rapid rate of fire from horseback for their military successes against the Romans in the 5th century CE. The version pictured here is a modern replica.

▶ SICKLE SWORD

Date Early 1st century CE
Origin Germany
Length 10in (25.7cm)

This *falx*, or sickle-shaped sword, was found in the Teutoburg Forest in Germany, the site of one of Rome's greatest military defeats, at the hands of Germanic tribes in 9CE. This type of sword was also used by Rome's enemies in Dacia (modern-day Romania) in the 1st and 2nd century CE.

▶ EAGLE CLASP

Date c.500CE
Origin Italy
Material Gold, cloisonné

This eagle clasp was probably used to fasten the cloak of a high-status warrior. It comes from the Ostrogoths, a people who occupied Italy from the late 5th century CE.

▼ SASSANIAN PERSIAN SWORD

Date 6th–7th century CE
Origin Persia
Length 3½ft (1.05m)

Late Sassanian Persian swords were long with narrow blades. They were hung from the belt by two straps, which prevented the scabbard from trailing on the ground and allowed the rapid drawing of the sword.

▼ FRANCISCA THROWING AX

Date 500–600CE
Origin Europe
Weight 15¼oz (430g)
Length 6½in (16.5cm)

A light throwing ax, the *francisca* was commonly used by the Franks—a Germanic group who fought against the Romans from the mid-4th century CE, and who had conquered most of Gaul by the end of the 5th century CE.

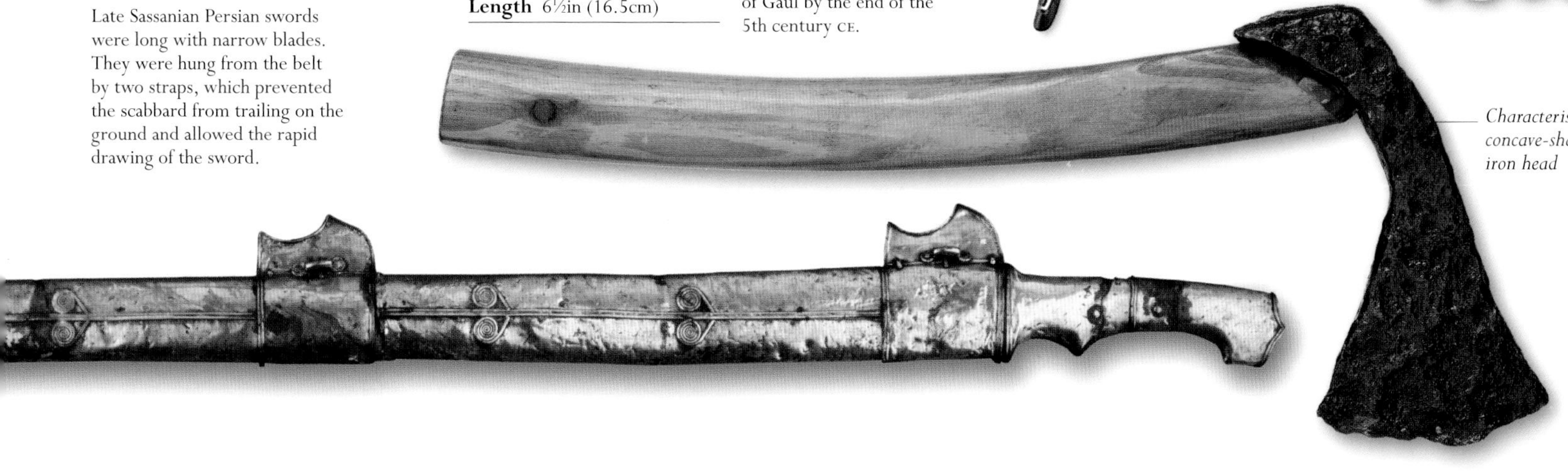

KEY **BATTLE**

THE BATTLE OF THE RED CLIFFS

208CE

The Battle of the Red Cliffs marked the culmination of the struggle between the northern Chinese warlord Cao Cao and his southern rival Sun Quan. Although Cao Cao lost, his fleet destroyed by fire, he escaped and continued to rule the northern kingdom of Wei.

▲ The warlord Cao Cao arrives by barge on the eve of the Battle of the Red Cliffs.

KEY DEVELOPMENT

ASIAN TRADITIONS

Asian societies, in particular India and China, had their own distinctive military traditions. From the 6th century BCE onward, large states began to appear in these areas that were able to deploy massive armies. In both China and India, however, these armies struggled to subdue nomads from Central Asia.

From the earliest times, China was the backdrop for fierce disputes between warring factions. The royal workshops of the Shang, the first historic Chinese Dynasty (1766–1122BCE), produced bronze dagger-axes, arrowheads, helmets, and shields, and early chronicles record battles against an enemy from the north called the "Tufang," with forces that numbered up to 5,000. Army sizes increased under the succeeding Western Zhou dynasty, but it was not until a period of political fragmentation known as the Spring and Autumn period (776–403BCE) that more organized military activity began.

Spring and Autumn armies combined chariots, ridden by noble warriors armed with bows, with infantry who fought with lances. This era gave way to the Warring States period (403–221BCE), a time of incessant warfare between rival powers such as Zhao, Qi, and Qin. As armies of up to 100,000 men fought in the battles between rulers, a shift occurred in favor of infantry-based armies, while traditional weapons such as the lance (*mao*) and dagger-ax (*ge*) became longer, making them more effective when used by large numbers of troops. The crossbow appeared, adding range to the armies' destructive power, while military organization also became more sophisticated, with the publication of the first work on military strategy, by Sunzi, in around 500BCE. After China became united under the Qin in 221BCE, its successor dynasty, the Han, was able to call on even greater military resources, with a war tax and a pool of recruits of up to a million enabling campaigns deep into Central Asia and as far afield as Vietnam (in 111BCE).

▲ ELEPHANTS AT WAR
War elephants are first mentioned in the Mahabharata around 1000BCE, and their use was subsequently adopted by Alexander the Great. Many other armies, such as Hannibal's Carthaginians, also employed them.

STRUGGLES IN INDIA

The earliest archaeological indications of warfare in India come from the Indus Valley civilization, where arrowheads and flat axes have been found in the ruined city of Mohenjo-Daro, dating toward the end of the 3rd millennium BCE. The India depicted in the Vedic poems (around 1500–1000BCE) had a similar aristocratic tradition to that of China, in which chariot-mounted nobles armed with bows were the most important military force. By the time of the era described in the epic poems, such as the Mahabharata (around 900BCE), warfare had become more varied, with larger numbers of infantry and the first appearance of swords. As early states coalesced after 600BCE, more realistic historical records begin to emerge, recounting, for example, the wars of Bimbisara and Ajatashastru of Maghada: in their struggle against the Vriji confederacy they are said to

have used large catapults to hurl rocks, as well as the *rathamusala*, a chariot fitted with a mace that scythed through the enemy's ranks. From the early 5th century BCE, the empire-building Nanda dynasty could deploy armies consisting of 20,000 cavalry and 200,000 chariots, as well as 3,000 war elephants, which the Greeks encountered for the first time when Alexander the Great's army invaded India in 327BCE.

HORSEBACK RAIDERS

From the 2nd century BCE, Indian dynasties lost territory in the north of the country to Central Asian nomadic groups such as the Yuezhi, and later the Sakas and Hunas. Horse-mounted bowmen, these warriors could travel rapidly, enabling them to carry out successful campaigns of harassment against Indian forces of greater number. The established Asian powers, with their more conventional military tactics, found these offensives difficult to repel. In China, the Han engaged in a long-running struggle against the nomadic Xiongnu people to the northwest, who several times during the 2nd century BCE seized control of the strategic Tarim Basin. They and many other tribes continued to plague the Chinese along the whole frontier of their empire well into the 5th century CE.

▲ TERRACOTTA ARCHER
Often aristocratic warriors, archers formed the elite of Chinese armies, until the rise of elite infantry and weapons such as the crossbow, which occurred during the Warring States period (403–221BCE).

> "Let your rapidity be that of **the wind**, your compactness that of **the forest**. In raiding and plundering, **be like fire**"
>
> **SUNZI**, *THE ART OF WAR*, 500CE

◄ EPIC BATTLE
A scene from the Mahabharata, an ancient Indian epic recounting a struggle between two armies over the Delhi area that ended in an 18-day battle.

KEY **EVENTS**

2600–100BCE

■ **c.1000BCE** The legendary Mahabharata War between the Kauravas and Pandavas is the first conflict described in Indian history.

■ **221BCE** After a long series of wars, the Qin kingdom under Qin Shih Huangdi conquers the last of the other Warring States, making China a unified country ruled by an emperor for the first time.

■ **261BCE** Mauryan forces kill around 100,000 Kalingan soldiers in a bloody battle during the conquest of Kalinga (in modern Orissa, India). The victorious Mauryan ruler, Ashoka, renounces war and turns to the non-violent creed of Buddhism.

■ **202BCE** At the Battle of Gaixia, the Chinese Han army under Liu Bang traps the rival Chu force under Xiang Yu in a canyon, killing most of them. Soon after, Chu surrenders, and Liu Bang becomes the first Han emperor.

■ **127BCE** General Wei Qing invades the Xiongnu lands north of the Chinese frontier, beginning a Han–Xiongnu war that carries on intermittently until 89CE.

TERRACOTTA WARRIORS
The life-size figures in the Terracotta Army were assembled from arms, legs, heads, and torsos that had been mass-produced separately. Each figure was then given individual facial features to create a realistic impression of a living army.

AN ANCIENT CHINESE ARMY

TERRACOTTA WARRIORS

Discovered near Mount Li in Shaanxi Province in 1974, the buried collection of sculptures known as the Terracotta Army opens a unique window on China's military past, providing a realistic representation of an army in the reign of self-styled "First Emperor" Qin Shi Huang over 2,000 years ago.

A towering figure in Chinese history, Qin Shi Huang unified all of China under his rule in 221 BCE, crushing his rivals by the relentless application of military power. As emperor he centralized power, suppressed dissent, and launched large-scale construction projects, including the first attempt to build a Great Wall to block the incursions of steppe nomads. The Terracotta Army was created as part of the emperor's burial complex: it comprises over 8,000 soldiers, 150 cavalry horses, and 130 chariots, each pulled by four horses.

The great majority of the army represented in these sculptures consists of peasant foot soldiers. They are depicted with armor of laced plates (the originals would have been made of bronze or hardened leather), and though helmets are not shown on the figures, archaeological finds of armor include them. The figures were also equipped with real weapons, fragments of which remain. Other sources reveal that infantrymen were equipped with a variety of axes and swords made of bronze, and with staff weapons, most typically the "dagger-axe." This was a long spear with a sharp blade attached to the haft, which could be used to stab in a prodding motion or wielded like a scythe. Many of the men also carried crossbows, a fundamental weapon in Chinese warfare: crossbows with sophisticated bronze trigger mechanisms were found during the excavation of the Terracotta Army.

Cavalry was a recent innovation that had helped Qin Shi Huang achieve his military ascendancy. With no native tradition of horsemanship, the Chinese had learned the importance of mounted troops from their wars with steppe nomads; some of the horsemen would have been armed with varieties of bows. The chariots represented a Western influence on Chinese armies; by this period, rather than being used as a shock force, on the battlefield they chiefly functioned as mobile command platforms for aristocrats and senior officers, kept to the rear of the fighting troops. Indeed, officers in the Terracotta Army are portrayed as taller than ordinary soldiers, and are also identifiable by their long double tunics and more elaborate armor.

SERRIED RANKS

The arrangement of the Terracotta Army in ordered ranks suggests a body of disciplined soldiers drilled to march in step. According to ancient texts, armies numbering hundreds of thousands of men were fielded in the largest Chinese battles. Even allowing for exaggeration, the massed peasant forces must have been large and difficult to command. Banners were used to signal messages across the battlefield, drums marked an advance, and bells were sounded to order a retreat. Crossbows were probably deployed in mass formations, with soldiers shooting volleys in sequence, one group loosing their bolts while another reloaded. An exchange of missiles at distance was probably more to the taste of poorly motivated peasant conscripts than close-quarters combat. The emphasis in ancient military writings on deception, rather than pitched battles, may well reflect the difficulty of executing decisive battlefield maneuvers with unwieldy forces.

500–1500

KNIGHTS AND BOWMEN

INTRODUCTION

During the era known in Europe as the Middle Ages, warfare was dominated by the mounted warrior—from the armored European knight to the steppe horseman. Military technology evolved slowly, and for a long time the bow was more influential than new gunpowder weapons.

Centers of settled civilization were often vulnerable to raids or conquest by marauding warrior tribes: despite being relatively advanced in terms of both technology and its government, China was conquered in the 1200s by the Mongols—steppe nomads using the composite bow. Religious zeal also proved as important as technological advantages: the foundation of Islam in around 600CE inspired an Arab expansionist drive, while from around 1090, militant Christianity inspired crusades to Palestine and the retaking of Spain from Muslim rule. These insecure times saw the building of castles and other fortifications, which then became the object of attack by siege engines.

During this period, developments in metallurgy improved the quality of the steel used for swords and armor. In western Europe, the mounted knight, clad in increasingly complex armor, became a central figure in the culture of chivalry, as well as a highly effective fighting man.

European warfare also repeatedly demonstrated the effectiveness of disciplined foot soldiers—from the Genoese crossbowmen, to the longbowmen of the English kings, to the Swiss with their pikes. The use of gunpowder also crept into warfare during this era—initially as a peripheral novelty, valued more for its surprise effect of flashes and bangs than for its practical impact. In 15th-century Europe, however, improvements in the construction of metal cannon, and in the quality of gunpowder, created the potential for a transformation in siege warfare and fortifications. Large guns had made the tall, stone walls of the medieval castle obsolete by 1500, but it would take considerably longer for the armored knight to disappear from the battlefield.

KEY DATES

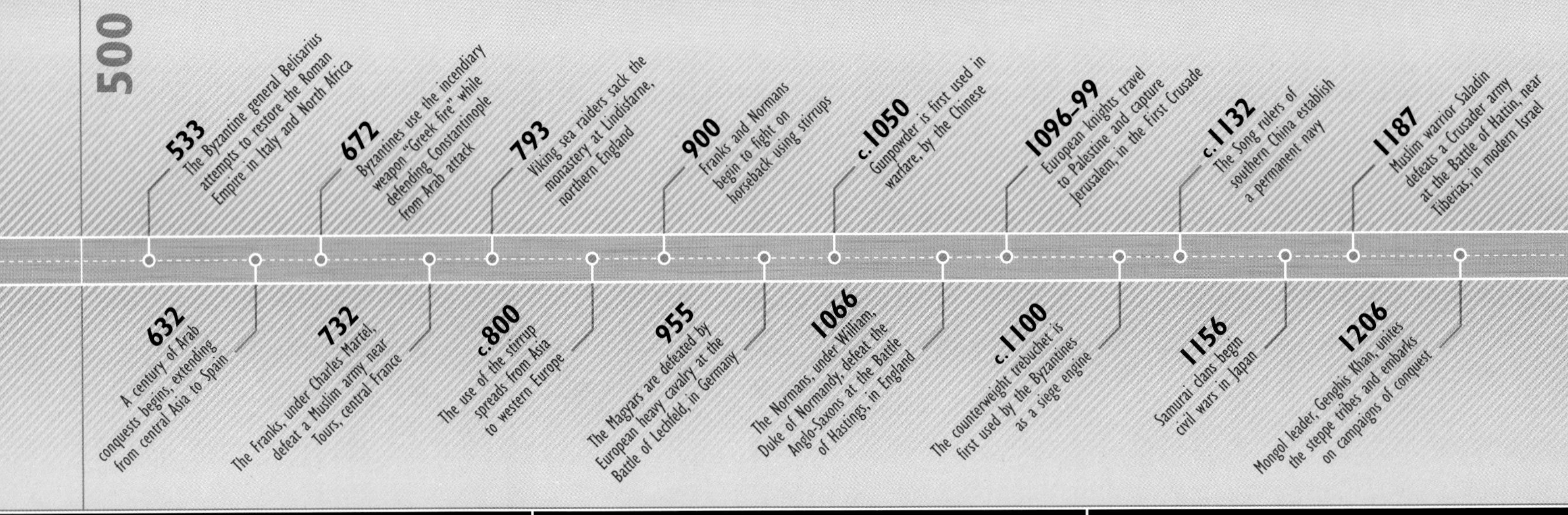

THE BATTLE OF POITIERS (TOURS)—732

THE BATTLE OF HASTINGS—1066

MONGOLS AT WAR—c.13TH CENTURY

1279 Mongol leader Kublai Khan completes the conquest of China

1281 The Japanese repulse a full-scale Mongol invasion

1291 The fall of Acre marks the end of the crusader kingdom

1302 French knights are defeated by Flemish infantry at the Battle of Courtrai, in western Flanders, Belgium

1324 The first recorded military use of cannon in Western Europe occurs at the Siege of Metz, in modern-day France

1346 Using massed longbows, English King Edward III defeats the French at the Battle of Crécy, in France

c.1380–1405 Timur, a central Asian leader, mounts campaigns of conquest from northern India to Turkey

c.1400 Most European knights wear plate armor as standard

c.1420 The use of corned powder improves the efficiency of gunpowder weapons

1421 The Hussites use gunpowder weapons on war wagons, at the Battle of Kutna Hora, Bohemia

1428 The Aztec Empire is founded in Mexico

1453 The Ottoman Turks capture Constantinople using heavy cannon

1453 The French are victorious in the Hundred Years War

1474 In China, the Ming dynasty begins rebuilding the Great Wall

1476 A Swiss victory over the Burgundians at Murten proves the effectiveness of massed pikemen

1494 King Charles VIII of France marches into Italy with an artillery train of cannon

1500

SAMURAI WARRIORS—c.13TH CENTURY

THE BATTLE OF ALJUBARROTA—1385

HUSSITE WAGENBURGEN—c.15TH CENTURY

KEY **BATTLE**

BATTLE OF POITIERS (TOURS)

732CE

An army of Arab and Berber horsemen from Spain—an area recently conquered by the Muslims—invaded Frankish territory in 732CE. Charles Martel, leader of the Franks, confronted them between Tours and Poitiers. The Frankish warriors fought dismounted in a tightly-packed square, and held off the Muslims with sword, spear, and shield to win a famous defensive victory.

▲ Charles Martel rides a white horse in this fanciful 19th-century painting of a battle said to have saved Christendom from Muslim domination.

▼ VIKING SWORD
The seafaring Scandinavians known as Norsemen, or Vikings, were well-armed with swords, axes, shields, spears, javelins, and bows; some also wore mail armor. Some of their swords were pattern-welded for extra strength.

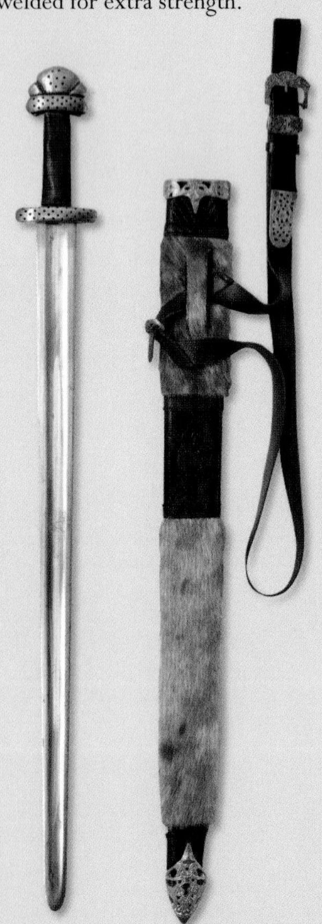

KEY DEVELOPMENT

THE WEAPONS OF EARLY MEDIEVAL EUROPE

From 500CE to 1000, the relatively weak states of western Europe were prey for raiders. By the 11th century, however, improved use of armored cavalry in mounted combat was becoming a significant factor on the battlefield.

The fall of the Roman Empire in western Europe, in the 5th century CE, was followed by a general decline in political organization and technology. This was not true, however, of the Byzantine Empire, the successor to the Roman Empire in the east. Despite many setbacks, the Byzantine imperial system retained its resources and organization to field an impressive army, centered around heavily armored cavalry, known as cataphracts. The empire also maintained a formidable navy, and even devised an advanced secret weapon: the flammable liquid known as Greek fire—a predecessor of napalm. Byzantine ships used pump-operated tubes in their prows to spray streams of flames at enemy vessels.

A CITIZEN MILITIA

Post-Roman western Europe, meanwhile, fell short of Byzantine sophistication. Even the kingdom of the Franks, the most prosperous successor state to the empire, at first had only a tribal warband for an army. By 800CE, under Charlemagne, the Franks ruled a large area of western Europe and were bold enough to proclaim a Holy Roman Empire. However, they still lacked the resources to sustain permanent armed forces, instead depending on a system of obligation that required local lords, their followers, and levies (peasants and freemen) to turn up, fully equipped, for service. In Anglo-Saxon England, local lords or "thegns" assembled armed men from their districts as the "fyrd"—a part-time militia. Armed with swords, spears, and simple bows, and protected at best by mail armor, iron helmets, and shields, they were often unable to defend coasts or ill-defined land borders against a substantial hostile force.

THE RISE OF THE VIKINGS

The Scandinavian Vikings first appear in European chronicles as seaborne raiders in late 700CE, using their longships to carry out hit-and-run attacks on coastal targets, and penetrating far inland along rivers. Later they became settlers and conquerors, ruling over much of the British Isles and part of northern France. Countermeasures against Viking raids were limited: the Franks built fortified bridges to block rivers; the Irish built tall towers as lookout posts; and the Anglo-Saxons created a network of fortified settlements—the "burhs". In battle, however, Viking axes and swords were a match for any technology available to the settled kingdoms.

Throughout the 10th and 11th centuries, a fresh dynamism emerged in western European warfare. Hardened, quenched steel was increasingly used for swords, crossbows began to appear, and motte-and-bailey castles were built—still made

"Shields, helmets and coats of mail were shivered by the **furious and impatient thrusts of his sword**; some he dashed to earth with his shield"

ORDERIC VITALIS, ON WILLIAM THE CONQUEROR AT HASTINGS, c.1130CE

▲ THE BATTLE OF LECHFELD
In 955CE, at Lechfeld, European armored horsemen led by Otto I defeated the previously invincible Magyars. The victory was achieved through a decisive cavalry charge, assisted by the use of stirrups.

◄ THE BATTLE OF HASTINGS
Following William, Duke of Normandy's invasion of England, Anglo-Saxon and Norman infantry and cavalry clashed at Hastings, in 1066.

of wood, but now featuring a keep on top of an earth mound as a central strongpoint. Until the 10th century, horsemen had mostly dismounted to fight, but the adoption in Europe of stirrups and of a saddle with a raised pommel and cantle (backrest) made the horse an effective fighting platform. The efficacy of mounted combat was demonstrated in 955CE, when Otto I of Germany defeated the Magyars by armored cavalry charge. At first, mounted troops wielded spears overarm, as the Normans did against an Anglo-Saxon infantry shield wall at Hastings in 1066. However, fifteen years later, at the battle of Dyrrachium in southern Italy, Norman horseman could be seen charging with lances held underarm—a tactic that became the trademark of later medieval European warfare.

KEY **EVENTS**

500–1100

- **From 533CE** Emperor Justinian tries and fails to restore the Roman Empire in North Africa and Italy; the eastern half of the empire becomes the Byzantine Empire.
- **c.677CE** The Byzantines use the incendiary weapon known as "Greek fire" against Arab forces besieging Constantinople.
- **752CE** Pepin the Short becomes the first Carolingian king of the Franks.
- **793CE** Vikings use longships to cross the North Sea and plunder the monastery of Lindisfarne, in northern England, signaling the beginning of the period of Viking raids around the coasts of Europe.
- **c.800CE** The Franks develop high-quality swords of hardened and tempered steel.
- **800CE** Charlemagne, the Frankish king, is crowned Emperor of the Romans by Pope Leo III in Rome.
- **900CE** Franks and Normans begin to fight on horseback, using stirrups and improved saddles.
- **911CE** Viking invaders form the Duchy of Normandy in northern France.
- **1015–1026** Danish warrior, Canute, creates a North Sea empire, ruling England and Scandinavia.

VIKING WEAPONRY AND ARMOR

The Vikings were warriors from Scandinavia who carried out raids across northwest Europe from about 800 to 1050CE, also reaching Russia, Iceland, and Greenland. Renowned as individual fighters, they defended from behind a wall of shields before emerging to strike their opponents. Their main weapon was an ax, although many also carried long, straight double-edged swords, while some brandished a single-edged, shorter version, the seax. Most were lightly armored with leather or, occasionally, mail coats, and carried heavy shields.

▲ **PATTERN-WELDED SWORD**

Date	700–800CE
Origin	Denmark
Weight	3¼lb (1.5kg)
Length	35in (90cm)

Many Viking swords, such as this one, were pattern-welded. This process involves adding carbon to red-hot iron and a number of rods, which are twisted together and hammered flat repeatedly to give a patterned appearance.

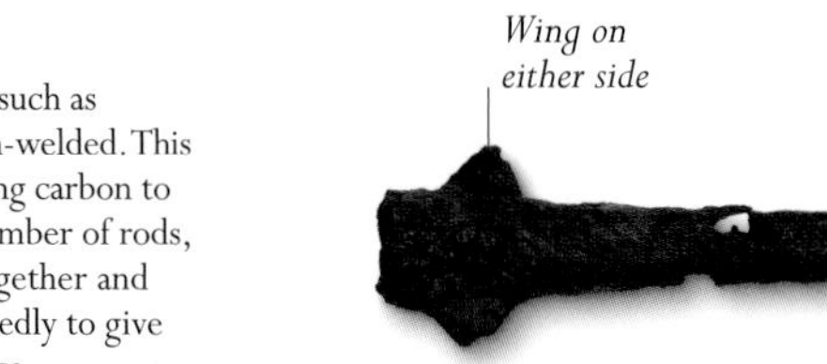

▲ **DOUBLE-EDGED SWORD**

Date	800–1100CE
Origin	Denmark
Weight	3¼lb (1.5kg)
Length	35in (90cm)

This blade, like most Viking swords, is quite blunt at the tip because it was used for slashing and cutting rather than stabbing. The fuller—a groove that runs the length of the sword—makes it lighter and easier to use.

◀ **MAIL COAT**

Date	c.1000CE
Origin	Northern Europe
Material	Iron

Mail coats had iron links—as visible on this modern replica—that were formed by winding iron wire tightly around a metal pole, then clipping individual coils from the spiral. Coats of mail could weigh up to 30lb (14kg) and were usually only worn by richer Vikings.

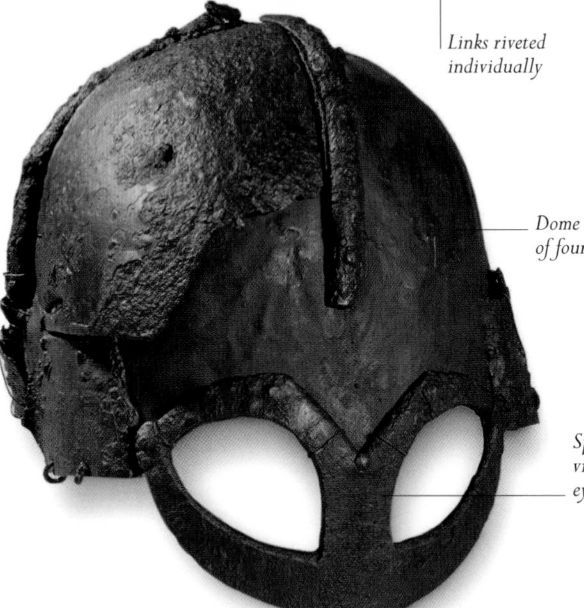

▲ **GJERMUNDBU HELMET**

Date	c.875CE
Origin	Norway
Material	Iron

Made from four iron plates, this helmet was found near Gjermundbu in Norway, in 1943. It is thought to have been used by Norsemen in the Viking Period.

▶ **SWEDISH HELMET**

Date	700–800CE
Origin	Sweden
Material	Iron

This helmet with a spectacled visor was found in a grave at Vendel in Sweden. Very few Viking helmets have been found, compared with axes and swords.

▼ WINGED SPEARHEAD

Date	700–800CE
Origin	Northern Europe
Length	18½in (47cm)

This lugged or "winged" iron spearhead has a leaf-shaped blade and a tapered iron socket. The wings could prevent the spear blade from getting stuck in an opponent's body or hook a shield out of the way.

Decoration also helps provide grip

▲ VIKING SWORD HILT

Date	950–1050CE
Origin	Northern Europe
Length	10in (25cm)

Crafted from copper and inlaid with geometric designs in silver, this ornate hilt was too fine to be used in battle, and probably belonged to a chieftain.

▼ LATE VIKING SWORD

Date	900–1000CE
Origin	Northern Europe
Weight	3¼lb (1.5kg)
Length	32–39in (80–100cm)

As with most swords found on archaeological sites, this later Viking sword blade is badly corroded, making the interpretation of runic inscriptions on the blade very difficult. Its wooden scabbard and hilt have also rotted away.

Blade tapers more towards the point

Two-edged pattern-welded blade

▲ STRAIGHT-SIDED SWORD

Date	900–1000CE
Origin	Scandinavia
Weight	3¼lb (1.5kg)
Length	35in (90cm)

The sword shown here is typical of Viking weapons, which were mostly straight-sided and of about the same size, with a simple cross-guard and pommel. Its blade is inlaid with a figure-eight mark.

▼ TAPERED SWORD

Date	900–1100CE
Origin	Scandinavia
Weight	3¼lb (1.5kg)
Length	35in (90cm)

This broad, straight, two-edged blade retains traces of an inlaid inscription—now indecipherable—and a scroll-design pommel, but its grip is missing. The sword is more tapered than earlier versions.

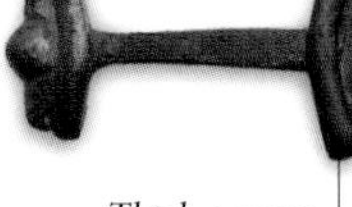

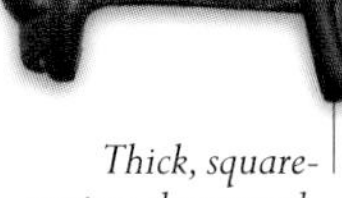

Fuller to lighten blade

Thick, square-section, downward-pointing quillons

Broad, crescent-shaped blade

Cutting edge made of hardened steel

Long handle to allow two-handed blow

◀ IRON AX

Date	c.900CE
Origin	Europe

The example shown here is one of the three forms of Viking ax, the "bearded" ax. Its elongated lower edge and slanting blade were suited for downward blows.

Brightly painted pattern

Edge bound with leather or iron

▶ PAINTED WOODEN SHIELD

Date	900–1000CE
Origin	Northern Europe
Weight	11lb (5kg)
Diameter	28–39in (70–100cm)

Viking shields were made from wood and covered with leather. They had an iron boss in the center, which could be used for striking opponents. This example is a modern replica.

VIKING LONGSHIP

HAVHINGSTEN FRA GLENDALOUGH

The Viking longship was a swift, sturdy, and versatile naval craft. Propelled either by a sail or by oars, it was one of the fastest vessels of its era, and able to travel great distances on the open sea.

A longship's shallow draft enabled it to penetrate far upriver or beach itself at speed in an early form of amphibious assault. It could also be hauled over narrow necks of land between waterways. The warriors it carried mostly took part in land raids, but occasionally crude sea battles took place involving exchanges of missiles and boarding with hand weapons.

The longship shown here, *Havhingsten fra Glendalough* (Sea Stallion from Glendalough), is a reconstruction of a vessel excavated from Roskilde Fjord, Denmark, that was built around 1042. As far as possible, the reconstruction used the techniques, tools, and materials of the Viking age, including timber from 300 oak trees. Steered by a side rudder, the longship has a strong keel and a high, curving prow and stern. It is clinker-built, meaning that its hull is made of overlapping planks, or "strakes," held together with iron nails. About 60 oarsmen—who doubled as warriors on raids—would have rowed such a ship. Their muscle power could have delivered a steady speed of 5–6 knots, but with its sail raised and a favorable wind, a longship could probably have made up to 17 knots.

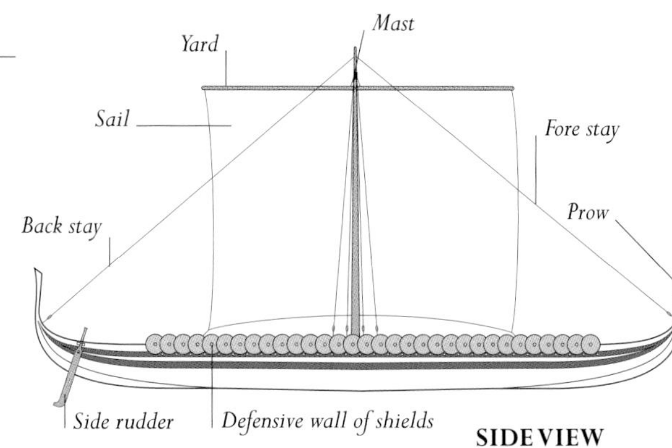

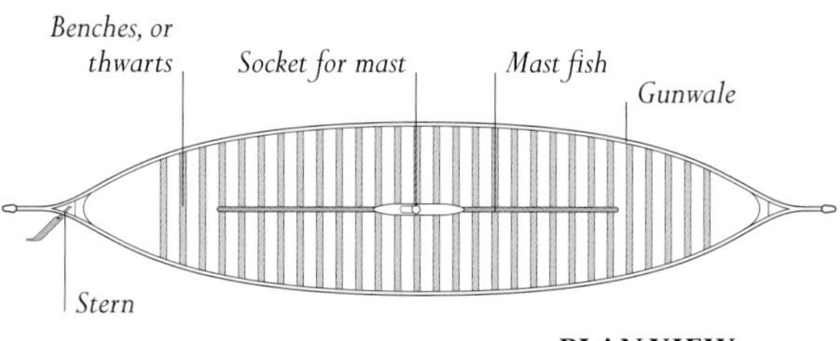

LONGSHIP PROFILE
The *Havhingsten* is about 98ft (30m) long but only 12½ft (3.8m) wide. This long, narrow shape makes it fast and enables it to sail in water less than 3¼ft (1m) deep.

LONGSHIP STRUCTURE

▲ PARREL
Attached by ropes, a horseshoe-shaped piece of wood known as a parrel held the yard onto the mast. Viking ship ropes were typically made of plant or animal fibers.

◄ CLEAT
The ropes that controlled the sail and the yard (the mast's horizontal wooden spar) were fastened to fixtures called cleats along the hull.

► STRENGTHENING TIMBER
Vertical timbers called top-ribs reinforced the hull's upper structure. They were butted into the gunwale and extended down over the first three strakes, to which they were secured with iron nails.

► MAST AND MAST FISH
The mast fitted into a socket in a block of wood called the kelson at the bottom of the boat. It was then secured in place by a horizontal piece of timber on the deck known as a mast fish.

OARS AND OARSMEN

◄ **PILE OF OARS**
The *Havhingsten*'s oars measure 15ft (4.5m) long and their blades are 6in (15cm) wide. Research has shown that this is the most effective blade width for rowing long distances at sea.

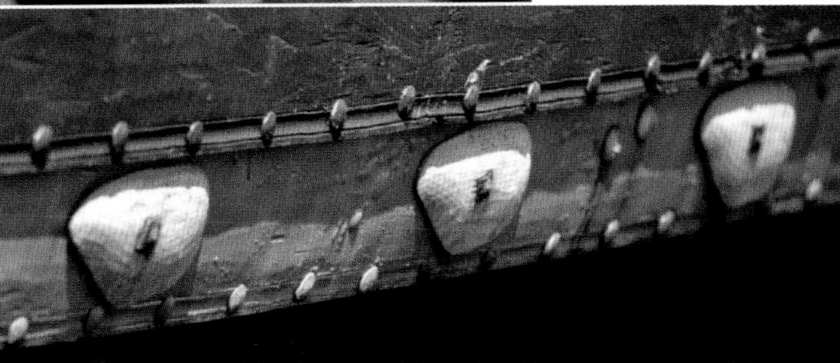

▲ **OAR PORTS**
The ports were large enough for the oar blades to pass through. When the ship was under sail and the oars were not in use, the ports were sealed with special locks.

▲ **SEATING FOR OARSMEN**
Although the benches were narrow, they allowed the oarsmen to shift position regularly on long journeys. Sometimes the rowers simply sat on sea chests instead of benches.

▲ **ROWING FOR THE SHORE**
As they neared a hostile shore, Viking warriors fixed their shields to the gunwale to create an impressive display and to deflect spears and arrows.

◄ **SHIP UNDER SAIL**
On the open ocean, Viking sailors relied on a large, rectangular sail. When maneuvering in coastal waters and up rivers, they dropped sail and rowed.

ANGLO-SAXONS AND NORMANS

The term Anglo-Saxon is used to refer to the various Germanic tribes who invaded and occupied the British Isles from the mid-5th century CE. They were mainly infantry fighters, armed with spears and short fighting knives (*seaxes*), although their elite troops had elaborate armor and fine pattern-welded swords. The Normans, originally a Viking group from Scandinavia, were established in northern France from 911CE. They conquered Sicily and parts of southern Italy by the early 11th century, and invaded England in 1066. Their army contained a larger number of mounted warriors than the Anglo-Saxons, and also made effective use of archers.

▲ LONG SAXON SPEAR

Date 400–500CE
Origin Northern Europe
Length 19in (48cm)

The spear was the Anglo-Saxon warrior's primary weapon. Many had long, leaf-shaped blades and wooden shafts traditionally made from ash. The warriors used the spears mainly with one hand, while holding a shield with the other.

Typical, slightly tapering double-edged blade

▲ ANGLO-SAXON SWORD

Date 500–600CE
Origin England
Length 3½ft (1.05m)

Anglo-Saxon swords were designed to inflict cutting blows, most often to the neck—which was usually fatal—or to the leg or sword arm, thus disabling the opponent. Their scabbards were attached to the wearer's belt by a loop.

Gilded dragon's head running over cap

Cheekpiece

► SUTTON HOO HELMET

Date c.625CE
Origin England
Material Tin, bronze, silver

Found in the royal ship burial at Sutton Hoo in England, this is one of the most elaborate Germanic helmets to have survived. Its cheekpiece, facemask, and neck guard are decorated with tinned bronze foil pieces.

Iron rings interlinked to form mail

► ANGLO-SAXON MAIL

Date 10th century CE
Origin England
Weight 50¾lb (23kg)
Length 35½in (90cm)

Full suits of Anglo-Saxon mail do not survive, but they could comprise up to 20,000 interlinked 0.3in (8mm) iron rings. They were extremely effective in protecting against cutting blows from swords or axes, but less so against sword thrusts. The item pictured here is a modern replica.

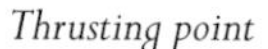

Thrusting point

Iron tang to attach grip

▲ LONG SAXON KNIFE

Date 600–1000CE
Origin Northern Europe
Weight 2oz (60g)
Length 9¾in (24.76cm)

The Saxon *seax*, a single-bladed knife, was as much a domestic implement as a weapon of war. A piece of wood or bone would have been attached to the tang to form a grip, but does not survive in this example.

▲ SHORT SAXON KNIFE

Date 600–1000CE
Origin Northern Europe
Weight 2oz (60g)
Length 7½in (19cm)

Most Saxon fighting knives, or *seaxes,* were made by twisting and hammer-welding hot bars of iron and steel—a process called pattern-welding—to produce a sharp, durable blade.

◀ LATE ANGLO-SAXON SWORD

Date 900–1050 CE

Origin England

Length (Surviving) 19¾in (50cm)

The blade of this pattern-welded sword is mostly broken off, and its upper and lower guards curve in opposite directions. Anglo-Saxon swords were balanced halfway down the blade, making them better adapted for cutting strokes.

▲ DECORATED ANGLO-SAXON SWORD HILT

Date Mid-8th century CE

Origin England

Material Silver, gold filigree

This ornate early Anglo-Saxon sword has an intricate gold-filigree pommel with interlaced snakes and grapes against a vine pattern. It would have belonged to a high-status warrior or noble.

◀ NORMAN SPUR

Date 11th century

Origin England

Material Iron

Knights riding on horseback played a key role in Norman armies. The riding boots of these warriors were equipped with spurs with spiked ends to help direct the horses.

▶ NORMAN HELMET

Date 11th century CE

Origin England or northern France

Material Iron

Norman warriors wore conical metal helmets, much like earlier medieval *Spangenhelms*. Norman helmets, however, also featured a long, thin nose guard for better facial protection.

▼ NORMAN ARROWS

Date 11th–12th century CE

Origin England

The narrow, pointed heads of Norman arrows were designed to penetrate mail. Despite their effectiveness on the battlefield, however, arrows were little used by the Normans before the Battle of Hastings against the English in 1066.

◀ NORMAN SWORD

Date c.1100

Origin England

Weight 2¾lb (1.28kg)

Length 38in (96.5cm)

Norman swords generally had brazil-nut-shaped pommels, long, flat cross-guards, and a broad, flat blade that was adapted for use both from horseback and on foot.

DARK AGES INVASION FORCE

THE BATTLE OF HASTINGS

The victory of William of Normandy over the Anglo-Saxon King Harold II at the Battle of Hastings on October 14, 1066 was a turning point in English history. It was a close-fought battle in which the Anglo-Saxons narrowly failed to hold their ground against Norman cavalry and bowmen.

The death of Anglo-Saxon King Edward the Confessor in January 1066 triggered a succession struggle. Harold Godwinson, Earl of Wessex, was crowned king, but his right to the throne was contested by his brother Tostig and by William, Duke of Normandy. William immediately began assembling an invasion fleet at Dives-sur-Mer on the Normandy coast. By August he was ready to sail, but was prevented by the winds, which fortunately worked in his favor. Having stood ready to face an invasion all summer, Harold's peasant army, the fyrd, had to be released to gather the harvest. Meanwhile Tostig had sought the aid of King Harald Hardrada of Norway, and in September Harald led his own invasion force across the North Sea. With his personal troops, the housecarls, and hastily raised levies, Harold marched north to defeat Harald at the Battle of Stamford Bridge. This left England's southern coast undefended.

NORMAN INVASION

William sailed across the Channel, his soldiers and horses packed into 700 vessels, and landed unopposed at Pevensey in Sussex. He advanced along the coast to Hastings, while Harold hurried his army southward. On October 13, William learned that the Anglo-Saxons were nearby, and the following morning he led his army out to meet them.

The strength of both forces is uncertain—estimates vary from a few thousand to tens of thousands on each side. Harold had taken up a strong defensive position on top of Senlac Ridge. His men were exhausted after the long journey from the north, but resolute. They would fight on foot, clustered together in close formation, wielding two-handed axes or spears and depending on the protection of their shields and armor. William had a mixed force of infantry and cavalry at his disposal: they would have to attack uphill, but hoped to break up the tightknit Anglo-Saxon formation with the impact of their arrows and cavalry charges.

THE LUCK OF THE DAY

The Norman bowmen opened the battle, attempting to weaken the enemy with their mix of simple bows and a few crossbows. Then the armored infantry advanced uphill, the horsemen following behind. But the Anglo-Saxons stood firm as the Normans assailed their shield wall, bringing the attack to a halt. William was in the heart of the action. When some of his men began to fall back in disarray, the Norman leader reportedly pulled off his helmet to show his face and called out for them to renew their efforts. Eventually, in the turmoil of combat, some Anglo-Saxons were tempted to rush forward in pursuit where they saw Normans apparently retreating. They were cut down in a Norman counterattack. As the Anglo-Saxon forces weakened and lost formation, Norman horsemen were able to penetrate their ranks, wreaking havoc. The Anglo-Saxon housecarls pulled back in a tightening circle around their king. Norman arrows continued to rain down on them and, tradition has it, Harold was among their victims. He was certainly killed (whether by an arrow in the eye, or not, is disputed), and by the day's end the Normans held the field.

CAVALRY CHARGE
The Battle of Hastings was commemorated shortly after the event in the Bayeux Tapestry. In this scene from the tapestry, Norman horsemen with kite-shaped shields charge Anglo-Saxon housecarls wielding double-handed axes.

KEY **FORCE**

KNIGHTS TEMPLAR

1119–1312

Founded in Jerusalem during the Crusades, the Knights Templar were a military organization dedicated to the defense of Christianity. While following religious rules of conduct, the Templars were also elite fighters in the Crusader wars against Muslim forces. They took part in the failed defense of the last of the Crusader kingdoms in 1291, after which they were suppressed by the papacy and their wealth was plundered by King Philip IV of France.

▲ A knight charges with his lance ready for combat. The cross on his shield identifies him as a crusader.

KEY DEVELOPMENT

ARMORED CAVALRY IN MEDIEVAL EUROPE

The armored knight appeared as the key figure in western European warfare around the 11th–12th centuries. The armor and weaponry of this elite warrior evolved constantly in search of better protection and more effective attack.

Heavily armored cavalry first developed in Asia, and reached Europe through the Roman Empire's contacts with Sassanid Persia from the 3rd century CE. As a result, the Byzantine Empire fielded cataphracts (early heavy cavalry) as its shock battlefield force. Both the cataphract and his horse were fully covered by scale armor, which was made of overlapping metal plates. His main weapon was a long lance. Sustaining such a warrior required a supply of specially bred large horses, skilled metalworkers, and the resources to pay for these.

DEVELOPMENTS IN ARMOR

Cavalry in western Europe evolved independently, but was influenced by the Byzantine example. Mounted forces had adopted the lance by the 12th century, but their armor was still relatively primitive. A coat of mail, the hauberk, covered the body, while the head was protected by a mail hood and conical iron helm, the face exposed except for a "nasal," a central metal guard covering the nose. The cylindrical great helm completely enclosed the heads of the knights who fought for Richard the Lionheart on the Third Crusade in 1191–92, improving protection but sacrificing all-round vision and ease of breathing. Over the years, plate armor was added, first on the legs, arms, and shoulders. The great helm was superseded by the pointed basinet with a hinged visor.

By the 15th century, suits of full plate armor had come into general use. A well-made suit of armor, its weight well distributed, never prevented a knight from mounting his horse unaided or fighting on foot: its main disadvantage was that it caused overheating. Both armor and helmets continued to evolve in terms of the skill of manufacture and complexity of design and decoration, reaching a pinnacle of elaboration in the 16th century, by which time display was as important a function as practical defense.

KNIGHTS IN COMBAT

The evolution of armor also led to changes in weaponry. The ideal knightly combat—rarely encountered outside jousting tournaments—started with a charge with couched lance (held in the attacking position), followed by a close-quarters mêlée. In the era of mail, knights hacked

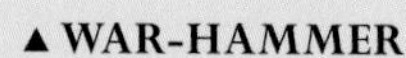

▲ **WAR-HAMMER**
The short-handled war-hammer was a weapon used by late medieval knights. The hammer could deliver a stunning blow to a helmet, while the spike might penetrate weak points in armor.

at one another with broad swords, while fending off blows with their shields. The adoption of full plate armor, which was itself as hard as a sword blade and curved to deflect blows, made shields redundant. The only way a sword could harm a knight was with a thrust of the point through one of the joints in the armor. More effective were the mace and the formidable war-hammer. A blow on the helmet with one of these percussive weapons could stun the knight inside, disabling him without needing to penetrate his armor. To their humiliation, mounted knights often proved vulnerable to foot soldiers. They rarely succeeded in adequately protecting their horses, especially against arrows, and being unhorsed in the middle of a battle was often a fatal experience. In practice, especially in western Europe, knights increasingly dismounted for combat, fighting as armored infantry.

◄ **HERALDIC SIGNS**
This 15th-century illumination shows a knight riding a horse, which is wearing a red caparison (cloth). The shields display a heraldic device: such devices were both a mark of status and a practical means of identification.

> "When **battle is joined** let all **noble knights** think nothing of the **breaking of heads and arms,** for it is **better to die** than be vanquished and live"
>
> **BERTRAN DE BORN**, FRENCH TROUBADOUR, c.1140–1215

KEY **EVENTS**

1000–1500

- **1081** Norman horsemen use the charge with couched lance against Byzantine forces at the Battle of Dyrrhachium.
- **From 1096** European knights fight Crusades to secure Christian states in Palestine and Syria.
- **1000–1500** Spanish knights fight the wars of the Reconquista, wresting Iberia from Muslim rule.
- **1350** The visored basinet becomes standard for knights.
- **c.1350** Full plate armor comes into general use for European knights; meanwhile, war-hammers are introduced as a means of attacking it.
- **1337–1453** The kings of England and France fight a series of conflicts known as the Hundred Years' War.

◄ **A SWORD BATTLE**
This 14th-century illustration shows sword-armed knights wearing basinet helmets and mail, with plate armor covering their vulnerable arms, torso, and legs. Cloth surcoats helped keep their armor cooler in the sun.

KNIGHTS' ARMOR AND WEAPONS

During the early Middle Ages, the most common form of armor was a mail coat of riveted iron rings, which by the 13th century had turned into elaborate mail protection from head to toe. In the 14th century, solid metal was introduced into armor, beginning with small plates worn over vulnerable parts of the body, followed by more complete sets of plate during the 15th century: mail was retained only behind exposed joints in the armor. The most elaborate sets of armor were produced in the 16th century. By then, however, firearms were rendering extensive armor redundant.

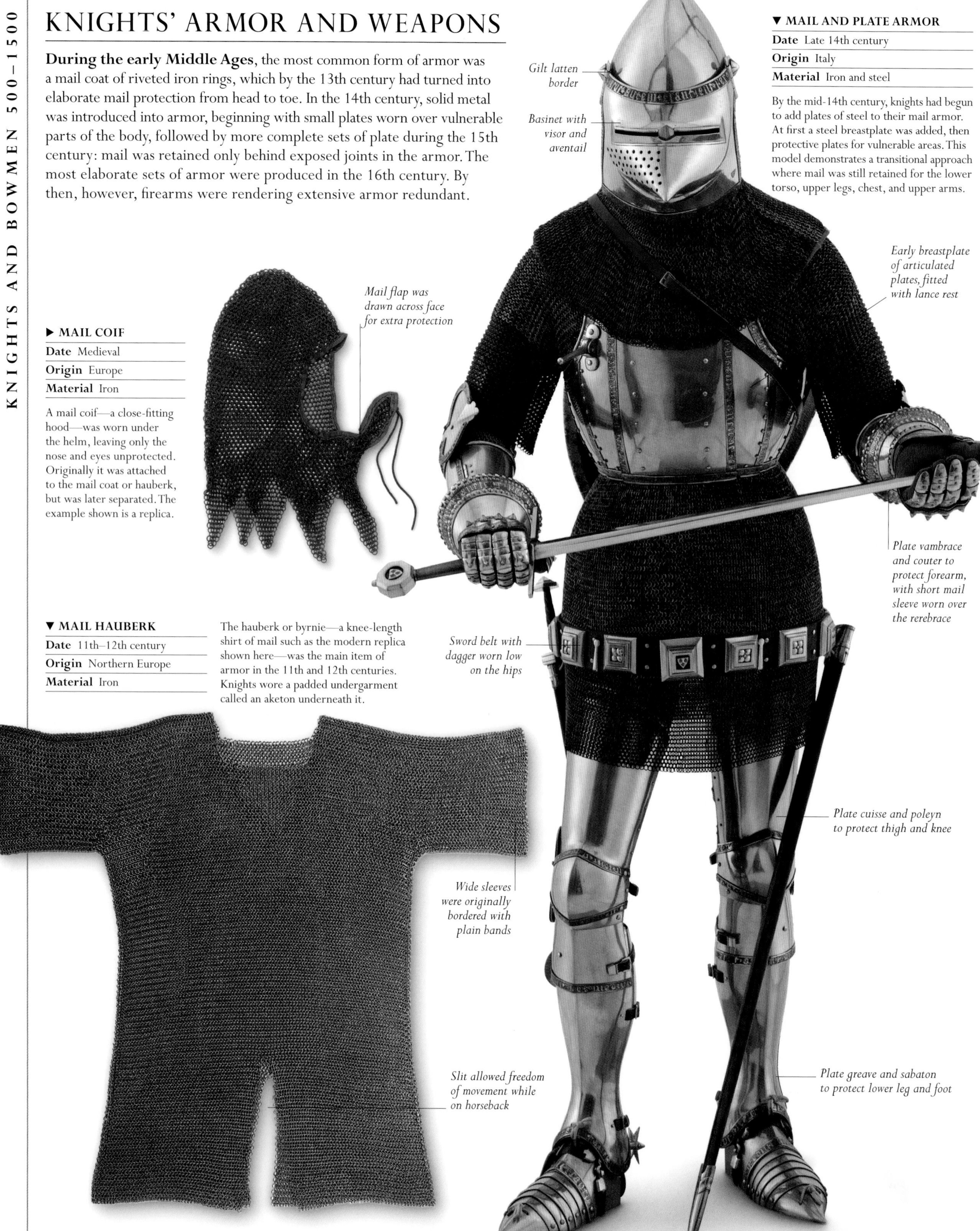

▶ MAIL COIF

Date Medieval

Origin Europe

Material Iron

A mail coif—a close-fitting hood—was worn under the helm, leaving only the nose and eyes unprotected. Originally it was attached to the mail coat or hauberk, but was later separated. The example shown is a replica.

▼ MAIL HAUBERK

Date 11th–12th century

Origin Northern Europe

Material Iron

The hauberk or byrnie—a knee-length shirt of mail such as the modern replica shown here—was the main item of armor in the 11th and 12th centuries. Knights wore a padded undergarment called an aketon underneath it.

▼ MAIL AND PLATE ARMOR

Date Late 14th century

Origin Italy

Material Iron and steel

By the mid-14th century, knights had begun to add plates of steel to their mail armor. At first a steel breastplate was added, then protective plates for vulnerable areas. This model demonstrates a transitional approach where mail was still retained for the lower torso, upper legs, chest, and upper arms.

▲ LANCE HEAD

Date	12th–13th century
Origin	Europe
Weight	3oz (90g)
Length	7½in (19.4cm)

Long lances were used as shock weapons after a charge in combat or in a tournament. Metal combat lance heads, such as this one, could pierce gaps in plate armor, leaving terrible wounds.

► CUISSE AND POLEYN

Date	16th century
Origin	Europe
Material	Steel

The cuisse was a plate that protected the lower thigh, fastened in place with buckles. It first became common in the 14th century and was sometimes made of two separate plates, which allowed for greater flexibility. The poleyn protected the knee.

▲ PRICK SPUR

Date	11th century
Origin	Europe
Material	Iron

The prick spur had a single iron spike to guide the horse by prodding its flank. It was the most common form of spur until the introduction of the rowel spur in the late 13th century, which featured multiple points.

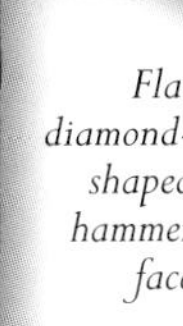

► WAR-HAMMER

Date	c.1490
Origin	Europe
Weight	3¼lb (1.51kg)
Length	27¼in (69.5cm)

War-hammers appeared around 1250, and were especially popular during the Hundred Years' War (1337–1453). They typically comprised a blunt hammer head or set of claws at the front with a sharp pick at the back.

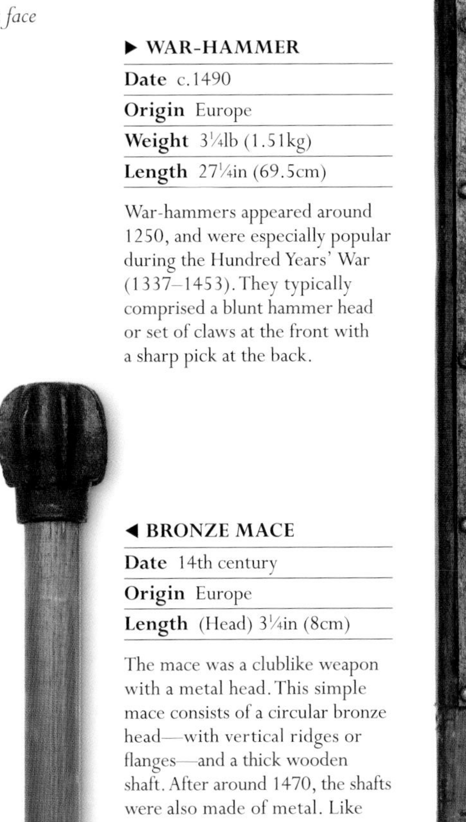

◄ BARDING

Date	c.1480
Origin	Northern Europe
Material	Steel

Barding, or horse armor, was little used before the 13th century. Initially, it consisted of a simple shaffron of mail to protect the horse's face. Later, plates of "cuir-bouilli" (hardened leather) or metal appeared as peytrals for the chest, and flanchards for the flanks. This is an elaborately decorated Gothic-style barding.

◄ BRONZE MACE

Date	14th century
Origin	Europe
Length	(Head) 3¼in (8cm)

The mace was a clublike weapon with a metal head. This simple mace consists of a circular bronze head—with vertical ridges or flanges—and a thick wooden shaft. After around 1470, the shafts were also made of metal. Like the war-hammer, maces were popular with cavalrymen.

FULL STEEL PLATE PROTECTION

MEDIEVAL ARMOR

The full steel plate armor worn by knights in the late 15th century offered excellent protection. The helmet was curved in order to deflect the impact of blows from blunt weapons, such as maces, while slashing strokes from swords glanced off almost any part of the surface. The armor was so effective that it offered its wearer protection from everything but crossbow bolts. This Gothic-style armor, with its elaborate decorative details, was made in Germany.

▶ ARMOR
Full plate armor was designed to offer a good degree of mobility to its wearer—certainly enough to participate in close-quarters combat on foot or horseback. At around 40lbs (18kg), it was also surprisingly light, and offered such good protection against blows from swords and other edged weapons that the use of more effective blunt weapons such as war-hammers grew increasingly widespread.

Poleyn (knee defense)

Greave (plate armor for lower leg)

Leather overshoes

FULL VIEW

◀ PLATE ARMOR

Date 15th century
Origin Germany
Material Steel

◀ BESAGEW
These small, round shields were attached to the buckle at the shoulder to defend the armpit. Although uncommon in the 14th century, they reappeared in later armor.

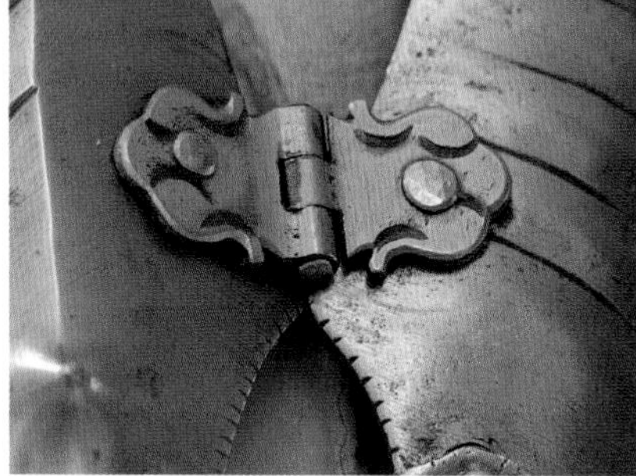

◀▲ GAUNTLET
This hand-protecting armor had a series of intricately articulated plates to allow movement.

▸ **VISOR ROSE**
Although mainly utilitarian, some plate armor also bore decorative motifs, such as this rose, located on the hinge of the sallet helmet's visor.

◂ **BUCKLE**
This buckle on the breastplate secured it to the back plate.

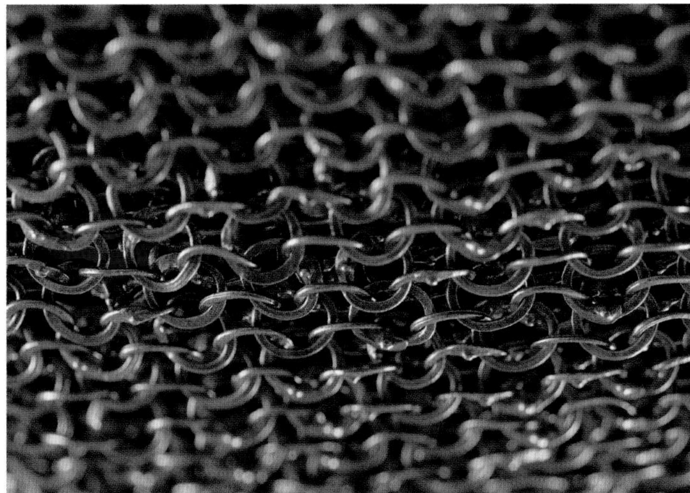

◂ **MAIL**
This protected exposed areas, such as the inner arms. Occasionally full mail hauberks were worn like undershirts beneath the plate armor.

▾ **CUISSE**
Named after the French word for "thigh," this armor for the upper leg was designed to protect against blows both from forward-facing opponents, and upward strikes that might be dealt to the wearer when he was on horseback.

IN ACTION

ARMOR IN BATTLE

Knights sometimes wore a combination of mail and plate armor, along with with a visored basinet, an aventail (mail collar), and a mail hauberk under a pair of plates covered with fabric. Despite the relatively high level of protection that plate armor offered its wearer, casualties were a regular occurrence, and mounted knights were particularly at risk from footsoldiers armed with staff weapons.

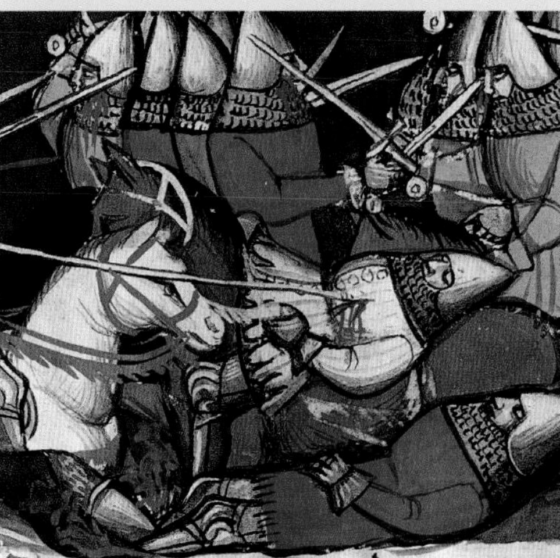

▴ The protection of full plate armor could count for little if a knight was unhorsed.

KNIGHTS' HELMETS

The helmets worn by the Normans in the 11th and 12th centuries were little different from the *Spangenhelms* of the Dark Ages—high, conical metal caps with nose guards. From the 12th century, however, rounder helmets evolved, which eventually covered the whole face. These great helms proved cumbersome and, in the 14th century, were superseded by basinets, which allowed the wearer extra mobility and visibility at the cost of some protection. Helmets appeared in ever greater varieties in the 15th century, including barbutes and the lighter sallets, as well as armets, which had hinged cheekpieces that fastened under the chin.

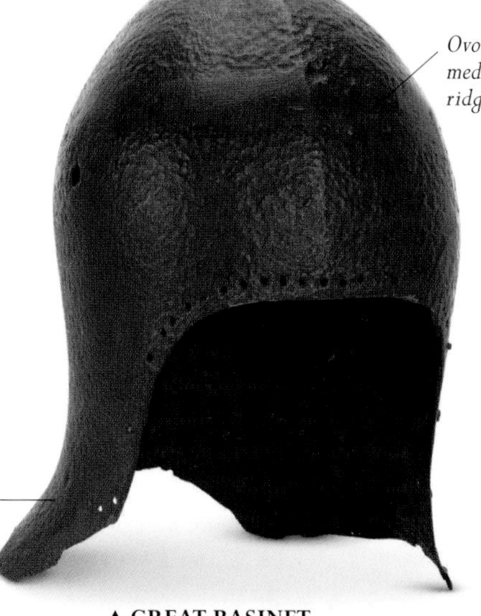

▲ GREAT BASINET

Date Late 14th century

Origin England

Material Steel

The origins of the great basinet helmet go back to the metal skullcap worn inside a mail coif and under a great helm. The holes for the vervelles—rivet-like metal staples—that secured this basinet to the mail aventail are visible.

Triangular plates, riveted together

Copper rivets with silver-bound heads

◄ SEGMENTED HELM

Date 11th century

Origin Poland

Material Iron, copper

Segmented helms are typical of early medieval designs. This helm was constructed from four triangular iron plates, originally covered in gilt copper sheet, and joined by copper rivets.

▲ PAINTED SALLET

Date 1490

Origin Northern Europe

Material Steel

Sallets were light helmets that developed from the basinet. They usually had a long tail to protect the neck. This one has a painted design, while others were covered with cloth.

▲ SHORT-TAILED SALLET

Date c.1440

Origin Northern Italy

Material Steel

Originally from Italy, sallets were worn by both knights and foot soldiers. This one has a much shorter tail than many other types, and does not have a visor.

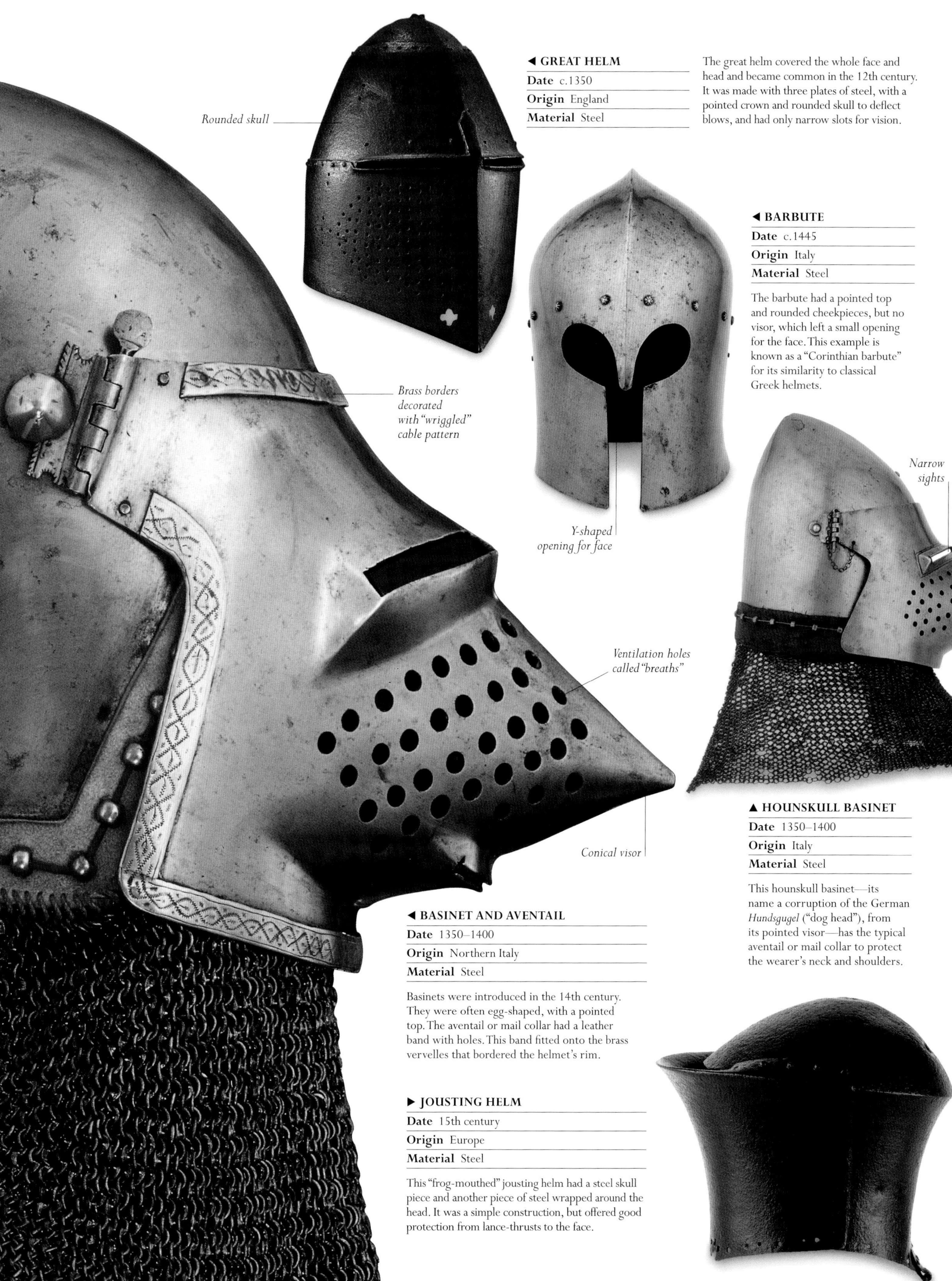

◀ **GREAT HELM**

Date c.1350

Origin England

Material Steel

The great helm covered the whole face and head and became common in the 12th century. It was made with three plates of steel, with a pointed crown and rounded skull to deflect blows, and had only narrow slots for vision.

◀ **BARBUTE**

Date c.1445

Origin Italy

Material Steel

The barbute had a pointed top and rounded cheekpieces, but no visor, which left a small opening for the face. This example is known as a "Corinthian barbute" for its similarity to classical Greek helmets.

▲ **HOUNSKULL BASINET**

Date 1350–1400

Origin Italy

Material Steel

This hounskull basinet—its name a corruption of the German *Hundsgugel* ("dog head"), from its pointed visor—has the typical aventail or mail collar to protect the wearer's neck and shoulders.

◀ **BASINET AND AVENTAIL**

Date 1350–1400

Origin Northern Italy

Material Steel

Basinets were introduced in the 14th century. They were often egg-shaped, with a pointed top. The aventail or mail collar had a leather band with holes. This band fitted onto the brass vervelles that bordered the helmet's rim.

▶ **JOUSTING HELM**

Date 15th century

Origin Europe

Material Steel

This "frog-mouthed" jousting helm had a steel skull piece and another piece of steel wrapped around the head. It was a simple construction, but offered good protection from lance-thrusts to the face.

A CLASH OF KNIGHTS

THE BATTLE OF BOUVINES

Although medieval rulers often launched military campaigns, they were wary of pitched battles. The meeting of European armies at Bouvines in 1214 was a rare clash between large bodies of knights, a set-piece battle that epitomized the fighting style of the era's armored horsemen.

In the summer of 1214, King Philip II of France faced an army led by the Holy Roman Emperor Otto IV and Ferdinand, Count of Flanders. The two armies encountered one another near Bouvines in Flanders on July 27, and engaged in battle. The French king was accompanied by his feudal lords and their armed followers, and by citizen militia from the towns. The Imperial army—Germans, Flemings, and English—was similarly structured, ranging from noblemen to the armed artisans of the Flemish towns. Both sides also employed mercenaries, fighting for pay or plunder.

It was symmetrical warfare, the two sides fighting with the same weapons (mainly edged or percussion mêlée weapons), tactics, and military codes. Both armies were drawn up with armored horsemen—nobles, knights, and unknighted sergeants—on the flanks, and foot soldiers in the center. The king and the emperor each placed himself behind the infantry in the midst of his household knights, who formed a cavalry reserve. The field was dotted with banners—a practical visual identification for the different feudal contingents. The Imperial army was larger, with around 25,000 men against 15,000 French, but the numbers of mounted men on each side were similar, probably about 4,000. Philip's army spread out thinly, matching the length of the enemy line to avoid being outflanked.

CLOSE COMBAT

The battle began without clear plan or central command. Amid a cacophony of trumpets, shouted insults, and prayers, some of the armies' troops attacked, while others hesitated or stood on the defensive. Bodies of knights lowered their lances and charged the facing cavalry, their lances shattering on impact, while some nobles sought out particular enemies against whom they held a grudge. Although knights would not shy away from clashes with infantry, they preferred to engage their peers; it was sometimes seen as degrading to fight against opponents of lower social status. However, soon such distinctions were lost as a vast mêlée broke out across the battlefield. Knights hacked at one another with swords, daggers, axes, and maces. Their mail armor and plate helmets were resistant to most blows, but horses were more vulnerable: many savagely wounded mounts fell, bringing their riders to the ground. Foot soldiers also proved adept at unhorsing knights, snagging their armor with hooks and spears. Philip himself was unhorsed by Flemish infantry, and was lucky to escape with his life.

Eventually the French gained the upper hand, their horsemen emerging victorious. In the center, the emperor was overrun and his banner captured, although Otto himself escaped the field. The last of the Imperial forces to hold out was Renaud of Boulogne, a doughty fighter who organized 700 pikemen in a circle, keeping the French knights at bay using the reach of their weapons. When they fell, the battle ended. Three counts, 25 barons, and about 100 knights were led off as privileged prisoners: it was not considered dishonorable to surrender and, because of the financial value of ransom, surrender was usually accepted. Thus, few nobles or knights fought to the death.

KNIGHTS IN BATTLE
A 14th-century illustration shows the knights in combat at Bouvines, with King Philip Augustus in the foreground. Despite the close hand-to-hand fighting that largely characterized the Battle of Bouvines, casualties were low among the knights and nobles.

EUROPEAN SWORDS

The sword was the medieval European warrior's most valued weapon. Magnificent blades were often handed down through the generations. Swords were also a symbol of the status and prestige of a knight—a man was made a knight by being dubbed on the shoulders with a sword. Early medieval swords were designed as hacking and slashing weapons to break the mail armor prevalent up to the mid-13th century. But between 1275 and 1350, a transition occurred, with the development of sharply pointed thrusting swords with longer blades that were better adapted to dealing with plate armor.

▲ GERMAN ULFBERHT SWORD

Date	c.900CE
Origin	Northern Europe
Length	30in (76cm)

Around 900CE, a new type of sword emerged, as long as its Celtic predecessors but tapering more sharply, with a balance point closer to the hilt. Some weapons of this type are known as Ulfberht swords, from the name of the swordsmith inscribed on many of the blades.

Rounded pommel

Finger ring below guard

Single-edged blade

▲ EAST EUROPEAN SABER

Date	9th–10th century CE
Origin	Eastern Europe
Length	37½in (95cm)

Early Eastern European cavalry swords typically had a single-edged blade and a double-edged point, making them suitable for both slashing and thrusting. This example has a sunburst motif on the blade, and the quillons are short with rectangular arms.

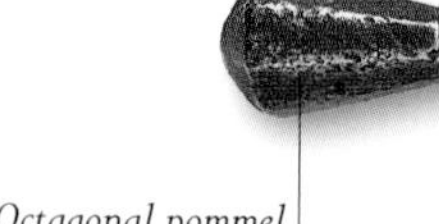

Octagonal pommel

Cross-guard with winged dragon figures

Gold pommel with diamond net pattern

▶ FRENCH CORONATION SWORD AND SHEATH

Date	12th century CE
Origin	France
Length	3½ft (1.05m)

This composite sword is traditionally said to have been "Joyeuse," the sword of Charlemagne, although it was first recorded as the coronation sword of Philip the Bold in 1271.

Gemstone mounted on filigree bezel

Sheath with fleur-de-lys pattern

Fish-tail pommel

Bronze gilded guard

Long grip

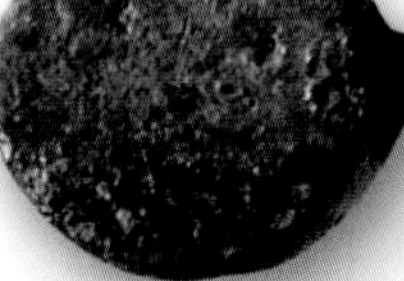

Outward-curving quillons

▲ GERMAN KNIGHT'S SWORD

Date	c.1300CE
Origin	Northern Europe
Length	3½ft (1.09m)

Belonging to one of the last generations of blades before the tips of swords became more pointed, this broad-bladed sword has a forward-curving cross-guard and flat, disk-shaped pommel. It came from Passau (in modern-day Germany), a town noted for its sword-makers.

Short tang

▼ ENGLISH SWORD

Date	14th century CE
Origin	England
Weight	27¼oz (760g)
Length	3½ft (1.04m)

The long, double-edged, tapering blade of this sword incorporated a shallow fuller for two-thirds of its length. It has a notably short tang, a small wheel-shaped pommel, and slightly down-curved quillons.

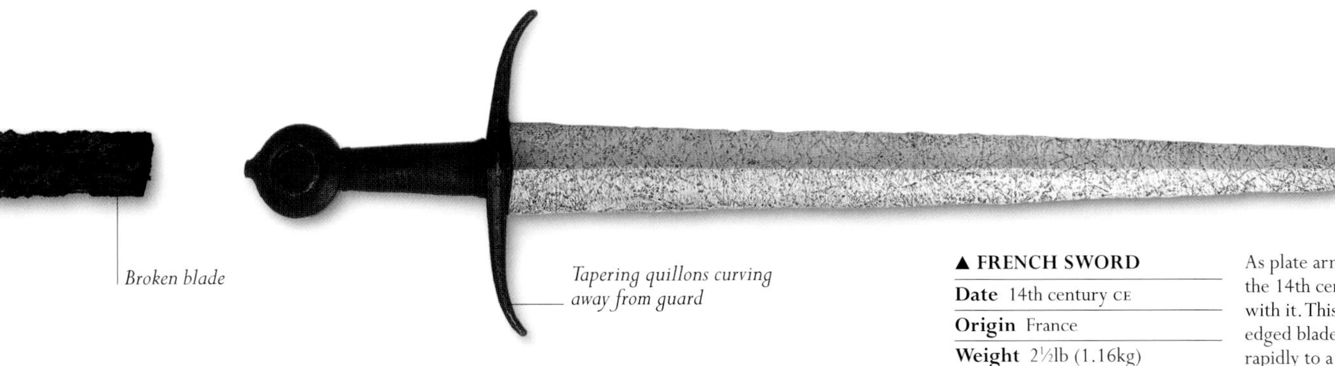

Broken blade

Tapering quillons curving away from guard

▲ FRENCH SWORD

Date	14th century CE
Origin	France
Weight	2½lb (1.16kg)
Length	33¾in (85.7cm)

As plate armor became more common in the 14th century, swords had to adapt to deal with it. This powerful sword has a double-edged blade that is wide at the hilt and tapers rapidly to a sharp point that could penetrate gaps in an opponent's armor.

Sharply tapered point

▲ ITALIAN SWORD

Date	c.1400CE
Origin	Italy
Weight	27¼oz (760g)
Length	3½ft (1.04m)

This sword was deposited in the Arsenal of Alexandria by the Egyptian Mamluk Sultan in 1432. It has a broad, flat blade and a short, sharp point—a style that became more common in the mid-16th century.

▼ ENGLISH HAND-AND-A-HALF SWORD

Date	Early 15th century CE
Origin	England
Weight	3½lb (1.54kg)
Length	4ft (1.19m)

Also known as a "bastard sword," this type of weapon had a long, slender blade, primarily for thrusting at an opponent. It had a long ricasso—an unsharpened length of blade—below the cross, allowing the bearer to grip this area with his left hand to deliver a powerful two-handed thrust.

Long, thin fuller

Ricasso

Blade heavily nicked and corroded

"Scent-stopper" pommel

▲ ENGLISH CASTILLON SWORD

Date	Mid-15th century CE
Origin	England
Weight	2¼lb (1kg)
Length	3½ft (1.09m)

This is one of around 80 swords found near the battlefield of Castillon, in France, where the French defeated the English in 1453. These swords mostly had sharply tapering points. Although the blade of this sword is heavily corroded, traces of the original wooden grip and gilding survive.

Sharp point for penetrating plate

◄ FLEMISH SWORD

Date	1460CE
Origin	Southern Europe
Weight	3lb (1.34kg)
Length	34¾in (88.3cm)

Both the hilt and the pommel of this extremely ornate sword were gilded. The grip carved from black horn was made to flow into the fish-shaped pommel. The double-edged blade has four sides that taper to a very sharp point.

Broad blade with central fuller

Curved tip

▼ ENGLISH SHORT SWORD

Date	1480–1520CE
Origin	England
Weight	20½oz (570g)
Length	27in (69cm)

Single-edged short swords were ideal for use against lightly armored opponents and were often used by ordinary soldiers across northwest Europe in the 14th and 15th centuries. The backward-extending rear quillon provided additional protection for the gripping hand.

Rear quillon bent toward blade

Single-edged blade

KEY **EVENTS**

11TH–15TH CENTURY

■ **11th century** The crossbow is used in European warfare, notably by the Genoese.

■ **1139** Pope Innocent II bans the crossbow (along with other bows) because of the number of Christian knights it kills. The ban is ineffectual.

■ **1176** The Battle of Legnano demonstrates the effectiveness of spear-armed infantry in tight formation, as Milanese foot soldiers defeat Emperor Frederick Barbarossa's knights.

■ **1333** Flemish infantry defeat French knights at Courtrai.

■ **1333** At Halidon Hill, King Edward III of England first deploys massed longbowmen, flanking dismounted knights.

■ **1476** Swiss Confederacy foot soldiers defeat Charles the Bold at Murten, attacking in columns with long pikes and halberds.

KEY DEVELOPMENT

MEDIEVAL INFANTRY

In the medieval European concept of war, foot soldiers were seen as a low-status, supporting body to mounted knights. In practice, however, when they employed tactics that made the best use of their weaponry, infantry often proved decisive on the battlefield.

Most foot soldiers were either citizen militia of prosperous cities, or peasant levies forced into service by their local lords. Correspondingly, the quality of their equipment depended directly upon the money available to finance it. The well-funded infantry from the cities of Flanders—who inflicted a notable defeat upon French knights, at Courtrai in 1302—were well protected, with mail hauberks (long mail shirts), steel helmets, shields, and gauntlets. Their weapons included bows, crossbows, pikes, and a distinctive staff weapon known as a "goedendag"—a long thick wooden staff tipped with a deadly steel spike—that functioned as both a spear and a club. Such resources were not commonly available to medieval peasant levies, however, who often entered combat without metal body armor and carrying only the simplest of spears. The success of infantry against mounted troops depended upon them fighting in a disciplined, tight formation on well-chosen ground, with natural obstacles augmented by the digging of ditches or the planting of sharp stakes.

THE CROSSBOW

Bowmen were unquestionably the elite among medieval foot soldiers, and of the weapons used by these infantry, the crossbow was the most sophisticated and powerful. The bolts shot even by earlier models had been able to penetrate mail armor—among their victims was King Richard the

"So great was the **undisciplined** violence… the **living fell on top of the dead**, and others falling on top of the living were killed"

GESTA HENRICI, DESCRIBING THE BATTLE OF AGINCOURT, c.1417

▶ **GENOESE CROSSBOWMEN**
Crossbowmen from Genoa, Italy, became the most sought-after mercenary soldiers in Europe, employed in particular by the kings of France. They fought in the First Crusade and other land battles as well as naval battles, continuing into the 16th century.

Lionheart of England in 1199. Initially, these early European models were drawn by the bowman bending forward, placing his foot in the stirrup at the end of the stock, and attaching the string to a hook on his belt; when he straightened his back, the string was drawn upward, "spanning" the bow. From the 14th century onward, however, mechanisms were introduced—first a windlass and pulley, and later a ratchet known as a cranequin. These systems allowed the use of composite and steel bows of even greater strength: the effect of these weapons on the battlefield was awesome.

ARCHERS AND PIKEMEN

The main drawback of the crossbow, however, was its slow rate of fire. One or two shots a minute was the best an experienced bowman could manage, and the crossbow was often a more effective weapon when used in sieges than on an open battlefield. The longbow, on the other hand, made a huge impact on European battlefields when deployed *en masse* by English armies in the 14th and 15th centuries. Preferably made of yew, the "self" bow (made from a single piece of wood) required constant practice, as well as great physical strength, on the part of the archer. Its effectiveness depended upon an experienced archer who could loose around 17 arrows a minute. English kings discovered that by packing thousands of longbows onto the battlefield, they could produce a great density of fire—from a modern perspective, almost a similar effect to that of the machine-gun. The longbow saw spectacular successes in battle against the French, at Crécy in 1346, Poitiers in 1356, and Agincourt in 1415.

A demonstration of the importance of combining tactics with existing military technology was provided by the Swiss pikemen in the late 15th century. The long pike was a supremely simple weapon, but the Swiss developed a new method of using it offensively, grouping their infantry together and fighting as massed columns of pikemen advancing rapidly upon the enemy. Even more so than the introduction of gunpowder weapons, their victories in the 1470s set the scene for a new era in infantry warfare.

▲ **SALLET**
The sallet, a form of helmet introduced in the 15th century and widely used by infantry, gave excellent protection to the neck.

◄ **BOWMEN IN PITCHED BATTLE**
A representation of the Battle of Aljubarotta, in 1385, shows bowmen shooting at unrealistically close range. The armor pictured is more typical of the late 15th century.

KEY **BATTLE**

THE BATTLE OF BANNOCKBURN

JUNE 24, 1314

Fought in June 1314, Bannockburn was a famous victory for Scottish foot soldiers, led by Robert Bruce, over King Edward II's mounted English knights. The Scots took up positions on a slope above a stream. Their unarmored soldiers formed a schiltron—a tight unit bristling with spears. The schiltron held off repeated charges by the English knights, before eventually driving them from the field in disarray.

▲ A modern illustration gives an impression of the chaos of fallen horses and knights at Bannockburn.

INFANTRY ARMOR AND WEAPONS

At the start of the Middle Ages, foot soldiers, armed with spears and axes, played an important role on the battlefield. They were gradually marginalized as mounted knights became the dominant military force, but enjoyed a resurgence after the 13th century with the development of staff weapons such as pollaxes and bills (billhooks), which gave them a longer reach and enabled them to keep horsemen at bay. At Courtrai in 1302, a Flemish army of townspeople and peasants, armed with *godendags* (long-hafted staff weapons with a spike), defeated a French army of feudal cavalry, marking the beginning of a new golden age of infantry.

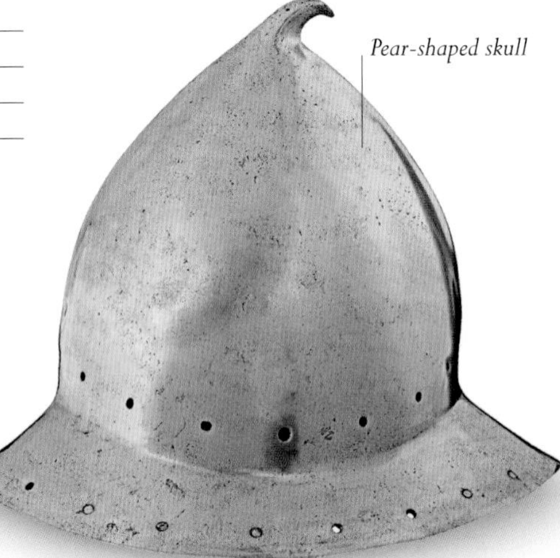

▶ CAPACETE

Date c.1470

Origin Spain

Material Steel

The capacete (or cabasset)—its name deriving from the Spanish *cabeza*, or "head"—was a form of "kettle" hat worn by Spanish and Portuguese infantry and men-at-arms. It had a conical headpiece and a narrow brim, and evolved into the "Spanish" morion, the popular infantry helmet of the 16th century.

▲ BRIGANDINE

Date Early 16th century

Origin Europe

Material Canvas, velvet, steel

The brigandine became very popular among foot soldiers in bands of condottieri (mercenaries) in the 15th and 16th centuries. It was a light armor of canvas and steel plates, often covered with rich material (in this case, crimson velvet, which has largely perished).

Blade narrow at base

Long wooden shaft

Wide curved cutting edge

▲ BEARDED AX

Date 900–1100

Origin Denmark

Weight (Blade) 27½oz (785g)

Axes of this period had broad blades—as long as 12in (30cm)—that could inflict terrible injuries. In Scandinavia, where this example was found, a hero's weapon might earn a bloodthirsty name, such as "Wound's Wolf."

Honed cutting edge

Tapered shaft for a tight fit

Fluke or spur

Triangular spike

◀ BILL

Date Late 15th century

Origin England

Weight (Head) 5lb (2.3kg)

Length (Head) 19¼in (49cm)

Developed from the rural laborer's billhook, the bill was used from the 10th to the 16th centuries. The spikes and flukes made it an effective parrying weapon. This example has two triangular spikes and a short triangular fluke.

▼ POLLAX

Date 1470

Origin France

Length (Head) 12½in (32cm)

The pollax had multiple blades: the spike for thrusting, the ax blade for cutting through armor, and the hammer head for crushing tissue and bones. It was used both by pure infantry and, from around 1350, by knights fighting on foot.

▲ GLAIVE

Date	c.1250–1500
Origin	Scotland
Weight	6lb (2.7kg)
Length	(Head) 31in (79cm)

The glaive had a blade that resembled a modern kitchen knife, with a sharp point at the end, as well as a wider, curved cutting edge.

Sharp hook

Long scythelike blade

▲ LOCHABER AX

Date	1400
Origin	Scotland
Weight	5lb (2.3kg)
Length	(Head) 17¾in (45cm)

A variant of the halberd, the Lochaber ax had a sharp hook on the back that could be used in close combat or to pull cavalry off their horses.

Straight quillon

Long grip

Tapering double-edged blade

▲ TWO-HANDED SWORD

Date	c.1500
Origin	Germany
Weight	6lb (2.7kg)
Length	4½ft (1.35m)

Too heavy to use in open combat, two-handed swords were generally reserved for single combat or to defend town walls. They had grips that were long in proportion to the blade, and sharply tapering points.

Long wooden shaft was gripped in both hands

Spearhead

▲ PIKE

Date	c.1500
Origin	Germany
Weight	(Head) 2oz (57g)
Length	13–16½ft (4–5m)

Evolving from a long infantryman's spear, the pike kept getting longer until the 15th century, when the Swiss began using them in formations. As with the hoplite phalanxes of Ancient Greece (see pp.24–25), these units were almost impenetrable to cavalry.

▲ BARDICHE

Date	c.1580
Origin	Russia
Weight	5½lb (2.5kg)
Length	(Head) 30¼in (77cm)

The bardiche was popular in Scandinavia, Eastern Europe, and Russia. It had a long narrow blade with no lugs or hooks (unlike halberds). The lower end of the axehead was attached to the wooden shaft.

Langet steel strip to protect shaft from other edged weapons

Rondel to protect hands

Long thin spike

Hammer head

MEDIEVAL ARCHERS

Armies up to the Middle Ages made good use of archers, although the simple bows they used made firepower relatively limited. Crossbows became common for a time in the 12th and 13th centuries, but by the mid-14th century the English, in particular, were deploying a powerful new weapon—the longbow—whose greater range enabled them to nullify the advantage the armored knights possessed. As with most medieval men-at-arms, the archers used a range of daggers to defend themselves at close quarters, should their volleys be insufficient to drive off attackers.

Pommel curling backward around rivet

Scrolling quillons

▲ QUILLON DAGGER

Date 14th century

Origin England

Weight 4oz (110g)

Length 12in (30.8cm)

This dagger has prominent quillons that curve down toward its blade. Its atypical pommel exhibits a similar curved effect, mirroring the quillons. Such daggers were especially popular with men of high rank, particularly when wearing civilian dress.

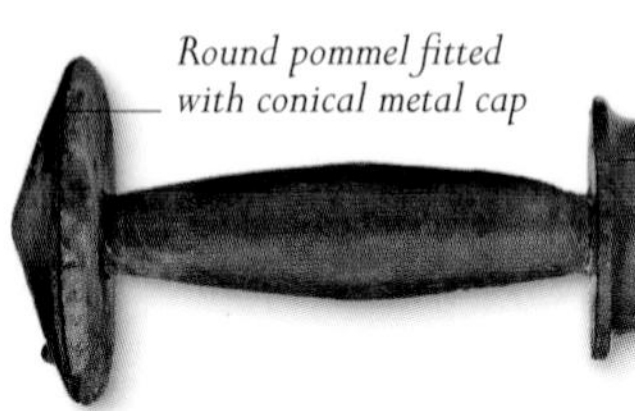

Round pommel fitted with conical metal cap

Lower rondel with wooden hilt and metal plate

▲ RONDEL DAGGER

Date 15th century

Origin England

Weight 8oz (230g)

Length 13¾in (35cm)

The rondel was the main military dagger during the early 15th century, distinguished by the round disks that formed the guard and the pommel. It was also known as the *dague à rouelles*, and was a popular dagger among those of high social status.

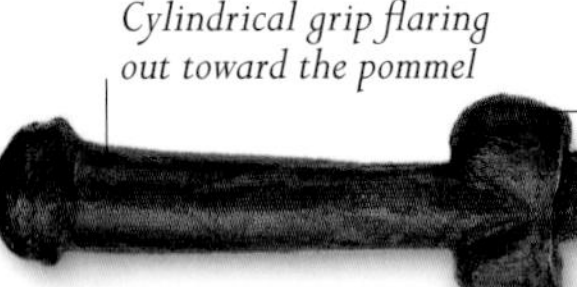

Cylindrical grip flaring out toward the pommel

Distinctive rounded haunches

▲ BALLOCK DAGGER

Date c.1500

Origin England

Weight 6oz (170g)

Length 13¾in (34.9cm)

Also known as a "kidney dagger," this weapon was named after the distinctive shape of its guard with two rounded lobes. It was popular in England and the Low Countries, and was most commonly worn with civilian dress rather than armor.

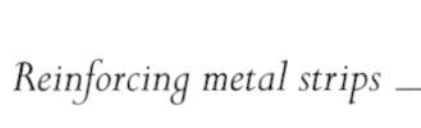

Raised central boss

Reinforcing metal strips

► BUCKLER

Date c.1500

Origin Europe

Diameter 6–18in (15–45cm)

The buckler, a small round shield, formed part of an archer's equipment for hand-to-hand combat. It was capable of deflecting light blows from maces or swords, while the raised central boss—as seen on this modern replica—could itself be used as a weapon to strike against an opponent.

Projecting gutter rising to a peak offered extra protection

▲ PAVISE

Date Mid-15th century

Origin Bohemia

Weight 21¼lb (9.7kg)

Length 3¾ft (1.13m)

Pavises (named after the Italian city of Pavia) were long convex wooden shields often used to protect archers, and crossbowmen in particular, whose slow rate of fire made them particularly vulnerable. This one formed part of a set of 40 ordered by the Swiss city of Zwickau, in 1441.

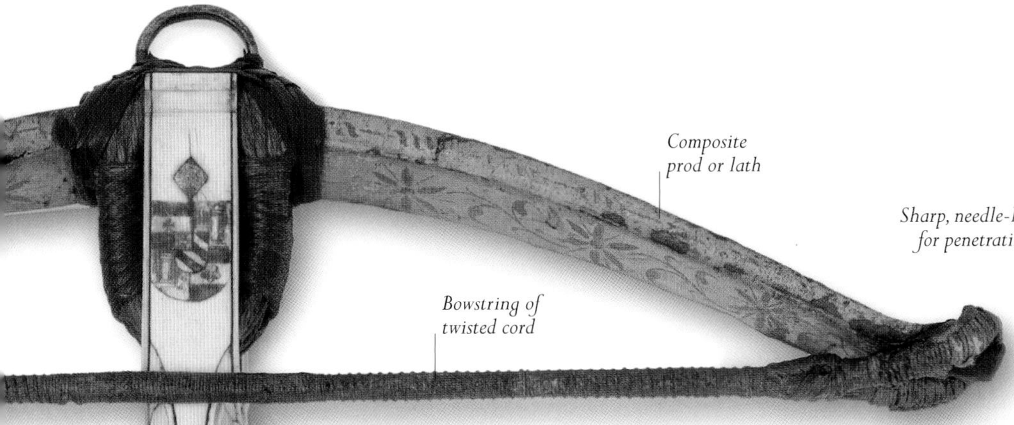

Composite prod or lath

Bowstring of twisted cord

Sharp, needle-like point for penetrating armor

▲ CROSSBOW

Date c.1460
Origin Europe
Weight 9¾lb (4.4kg)
Length 28¼in (72cm)

Widely used in Europe from the 12th century, the crossbow, when fired from the shoulder, was very effective against armored knights (see pp.78–79). Although the bolt was released with great power, crossbows were slow to reload, so their rate of fire was far lower than longbows.

Groove for bolt

Revolving nut released by trigger below

Steel pin to engage mechanism for spanning bow

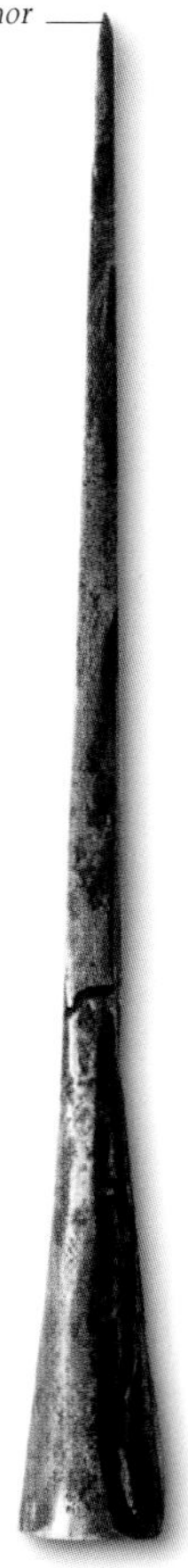

► LONGBOW

Date c.1540
Origin England
Weight 25¾oz (730g)
Length 6½ft (2m)

Originating in northern Europe during the "Migration Period" (c.400–800CE), the longbow came into general use only by the late 13th century. Drawn to the ear (rather than to the cheek), the superior tension of the bowstring gave increased range. A modern archer using a replica of this bow (recovered from the wreck of Henry VIII's *Mary Rose*, which sank in 1545), shot an arrow to a distance of 328m (360 yards).

Broadhead bolt

◄ CROSSBOW BOLTS

Date c.1500
Origin Germany
Weight 1¼oz (35g)
Length 14½in (37cm)

Shorter and heavier than longbow arrows, bolts (or quarrels) had different tips depending on the effect required. Barbed broadhead bolts were used primarily for hunting, whereas chisel-headed arrowheads were used against armored soldiers. The tip of the bolt served as a sight when aiming.

◄ BODKIN ARROWHEAD

Date 15th century
Origin Europe
Weight ¼oz (7g)
Length 4¾in (12cm)

With their sharp pointed ends, bodkin arrowheads could breach mail and were capable of penetrating weak points in plate armor. In battle an archer might stick such arrows in the ground in front of him for easy access.

Sharp point and edges

► LONGBOW ARROWS

Date c.1520
Origin England
Weight 1½oz (42g)
Length 29½in (75cm)

Longbow arrows, also called "clothyard" arrows (named after the standard early 14th-century length of cloth), were mass-produced in medieval England to supply the king's longbowmen. The fletching (feathers) stabilized the arrow in flight.

Barb

◄ BROADHEAD ARROWHEAD

Date c.1500
Origin Europe
Weight 1oz (28g)
Length 1¾in (4.5cm)

Broad iron arrowheads with barbs were able to inflict a deep, wide wound, and the barbs would cause terrible (often fatal) damage to the victim as they sliced through body tissue.

LONG RANGE POWER

CROSSBOW

This typical late medieval European crossbow could shoot a bolt roughly 330 yards (300m). Its composite bow (also known as a lath, or prod), made of layers of wood, sinew, and horn, had far too high a draw weight to be spanned by unaided muscle power—up to around 1,200lb (550kg). Crossbowmen used a rack-and-pinion device known as a cranequin (also called a cric or rack) to pull the bowstring back to the nut, where it was hooked, then released it by pressing the long trigger under the crossbow tiller. The crossbowman rested the butt against his shoulder, looking along the tiller and using the tip of the bolt as his sight.

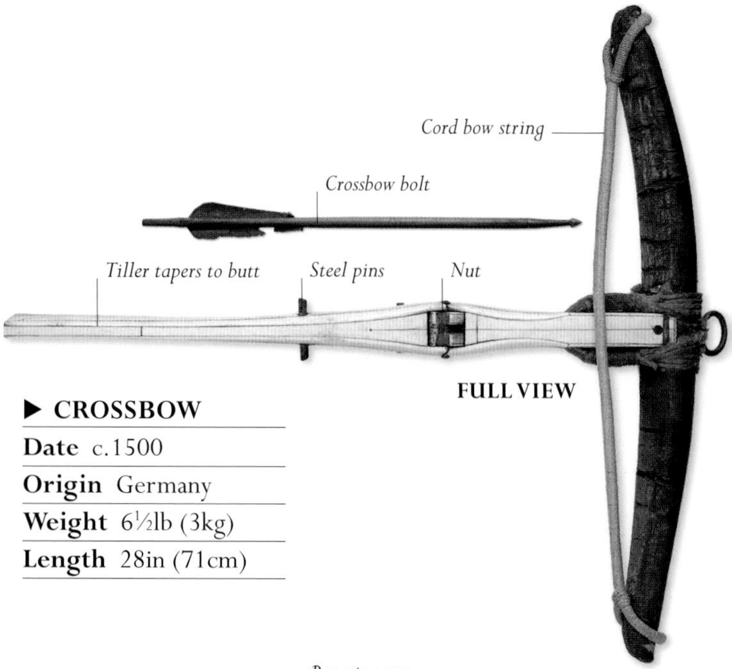

Cord bow string

Crossbow bolt

Tiller tapers to butt

Steel pins

Nut

FULL VIEW

▶ CROSSBOW

Date	c.1500
Origin	Germany
Weight	6½lb (3kg)
Length	28in (71cm)

▼ CROSSBOW
This German crossbow, with its handsome bone veneer, would have belonged to a wealthy individual who enjoyed hunting as a leisure pursuit. It was spanned by a small cranequin (below).

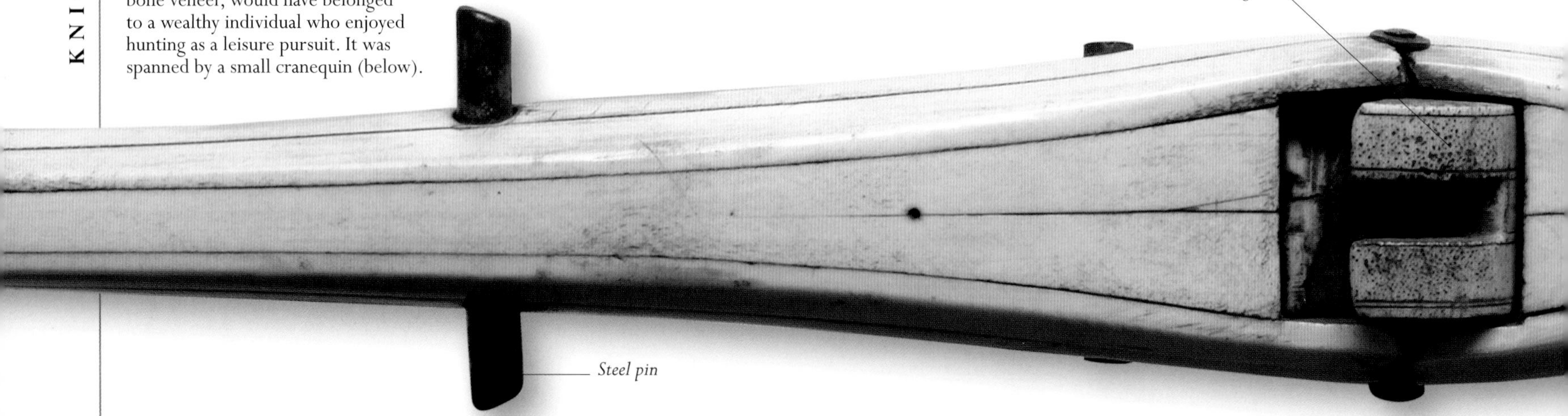

Rotating nut

Steel pin

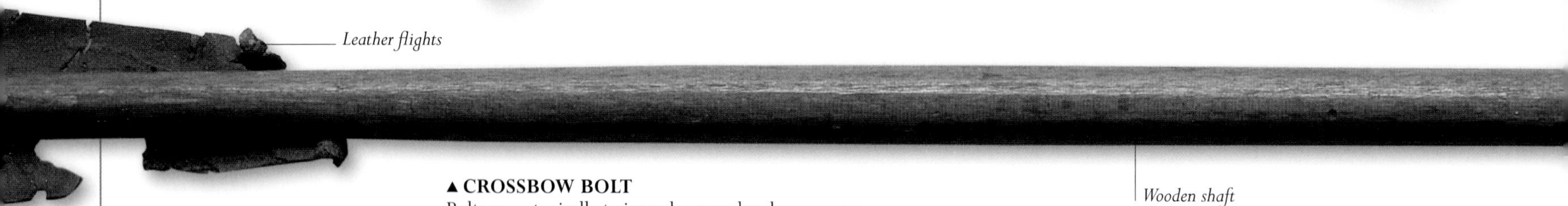

Leather flights

Wooden shaft

▲ CROSSBOW BOLT
Bolts were typically twice as heavy as longbow arrows. The flights were made of wood, paper, or leather, and only two were used, because a third would snag on the nut.

▲ CRANEQUIN
The cranequin was introduced in Europe in the late 14th century. One of its advantages was that it could be used on horseback. However, it was an expensive device and was slow to operate, two considerations that made it less suitable for warfare than hunting.

IN ACTION

LOADING THE CROSSBOW

To prepare the crossbow, the archer first anchored the cranequin to it by looping the cord over the steel pins on the tiller, and laid the claws at the front end of the toothed rack over the bowstring. Turning the lever, he then rotated the geared cogwheels against the teeth of the rack, drawing back the bowstring and bending the bow. When the string was hooked over the nut, he removed the cranequin, laid a bolt in the groove, and was ready to shoot.

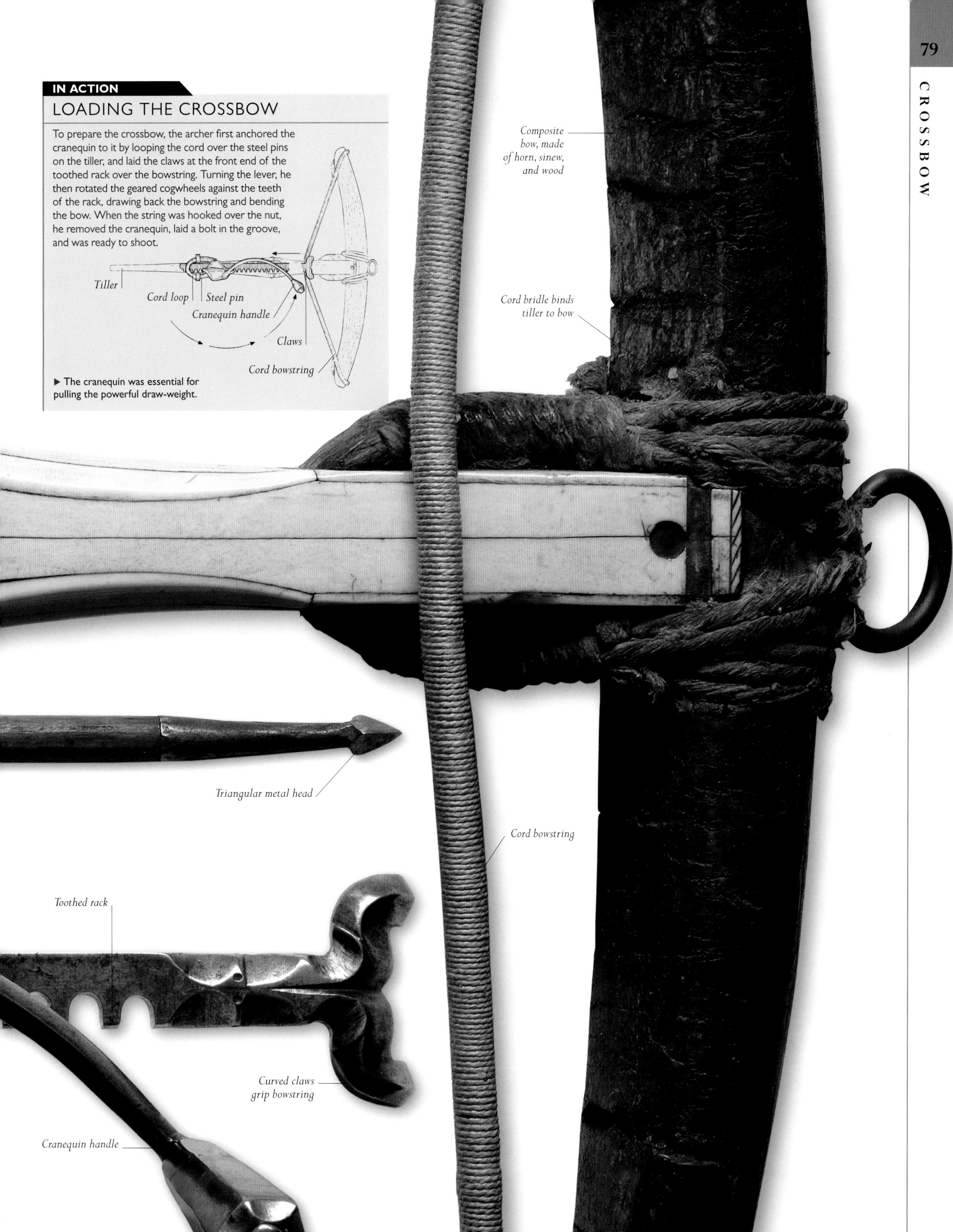

▶ The cranequin was essential for pulling the powerful draw-weight.

RIVAL BOWMEN
The key to the victory of the English at Crécy was the success of their longbows and the relative ineffectiveness of the Genoese crossbows. In this late 15th-century image, longbows and crossbows engage in an improbable close-quarters duel.

MEDIEVAL KNIGHTS AND BOWMEN

THE BATTLE OF CRÉCY

During the Hundred Years' War—the series of conflicts fought between the kings of France and England from 1337 to 1453—the medieval knight's dominance of the European battlefield began to wane. At Crécy in 1346, mounted armored warriors were shot down by common bowmen.

In medieval Europe, knights and men-at-arms were a social and military elite, traditionally accorded pride of place on the battlefield. Battles were supposed to be won by thundering charges in which nobles showed their prowess at fighting on horseback. In the course of wars with the Scots in the early 14th century, however, the English had learned the effectiveness of a different set of tactics. With knights and men-at-arms deployed on foot in a primarily defensive role, they used massed archers equipped with fast-shooting longbows to wreak havoc.

LONGBOW IN THE ASCENDANT

In 1346, King Edward III of England landed in France with some 7,000 longbowmen, about 4,000 mounted knights and men-at-arms, and several thousand assorted foot soldiers. Edward also brought with him a few small cannon, some of the earliest gunpowder weapons to be used in Europe. The king of France, Philip VI, was able to field a much larger army—his knights and men-at-arms alone probably numbered 12,000. He intercepted Edward south of Calais, forcing him to give battle. The English king drew up his forces in a defensive position on a ridge between Crécy and Wadicourt, dividing his dismounted knights and men-at-arms into three divisions, or "battles."

The encounter opened with a duel between Philip's archers (Genoese mercenaries armed with crossbows) and Edward's longbowmen. The Genoese advanced and shot their crossbow bolts to little effect. As they stopped to reload—a lengthy process—the longbows responded. According to chronicler Jean Froissart: "The English archers advanced one step forward, and shot their arrows with such force and quickness, that it seemed as if it snowed."

Overwhelmed by the mass of arrows, the Genoese fell back. But discipline on the French side was poor. Their high-spirited noblemen considered themselves the finest knights in Europe, and they were more concerned with seeking personal glory than obeying their king's commands. Not waiting for orders, they began a piecemeal charge through the ranks of the fleeing Genoese. As the knights lumbered uphill, the longbow arrows brought down horses and men, reducing the charge to floundering chaos. The firing of the handful of cannon was barely noticed amid the devastation wrought by thousands of bowmen, each shooting at least five arrows a minute. Edward's infantry, armed with spears and knives, rushed forward to finish off the unhorsed Frenchmen.

The English did not enjoy an easy victory. The fighting continued beyond nightfall, the rival knights wielding their swords, maces, and war hammers in close combat. Froissart describes the French noblemen gathering their surviving followers around their individual banners to stage a gallant defense against the advancing enemy. Eventually King Philip fled the field, where more than a thousand of his knights lay dead. The superiority of massed longbows over armored knights was to be witnessed again at Poitiers in 1356 and Agincourt in 1415—without, however, lessening the prestige or status of the mounted elite.

KEY DEVELOPMENT

SIEGES AND THE ART OF FORTIFICATION

Castles and siege warfare flourished in the medieval period, mainly as a result of widespread insecurity and the fragmentation of political power. As the technology of siege weapons and tactics evolved, it drove developments in the design of castles and city walls.

In the 11th century, most castles in western Europe were still made of wood and earth. When the first crusader armies from the west made their way to the Holy Land in 1096–99, they were awed by the defensive structures they found—massive stone fortifications ringed the great cities around the eastern Mediterranean, such as Constantinople and Jerusalem. During the following century, stone castles were to become the norm across western Europe, as well as in the crusader states in the east. At first these were mostly quite simple, with a tall curtain wall surrounding an elevated stone keep. This posed sufficient problems for besieging forces equipped with mangonels—stone-throwing torsion catapults inherited from the Romans. Unable to create a breach in the walls, armies mostly settled down to a long blockade.

INCREASED DEFENSES

The introduction of the counterweight trebuchet in the 12th century changed the balance between besiegers and besieged. These huge machines were capable of hurling rocks weighing over 220lbs (100kg), and made curtain walls vulnerable. Castle designers responded by creating concentric structures, with the outer wall merely as a first line of defense, behind which the even taller, thicker fortifications of an inner castle loomed. Towers in the battlements were made rounded, instead of square, to deflect the force of a hurled rock. A castle was surrounded by moats—either dry or filled with water—and fortified outworks to make it difficult for the besiegers to bring up rams or siege towers. Potential weak points, especially the main gate, were reinforced with extra fortifications. Arrow slits in the walls and towers were positioned to shoot directly onto troops advancing toward, or successfully breaching, the castle.

SIEGE LOGISTICS

A medieval siege was a major undertaking, and even maintaining a blockade could stretch an army's resources. Spread out around the fortified position, besiegers were vulnerable to sudden sorties by the defenders' garrison, as well as to sniping from crossbowmen on the battlements. If mangonels and trebuchets failed to make a breach in the walls, these could be attacked with rams, or by tunnelling to undermine the foundations. A portable roof—the cat—was deployed to protect troops against missiles from above as they advanced to bring forward a ram, or hack at the wall with picks. Occasionally an assault on unbreached walls succeeded, either by scaling ladders or by rolling a tall wooden siege tower forward. More often, a weak point such as an unlocked door was discovered—or the defenders were betrayed by treachery on the part of one of their own side.

The introduction of cannon became a transforming influence on sieges during the 15th century. French superiority in gunpowder artillery enabled them to overcome a series of English stone strongholds rapidly, in the 1440s and 1450s. The stone castle was soon rendered obsolete, but another revolution in the design of fortifications would soon make sieges as long and arduous as before—the era of the angle bastion (see pp.176–77).

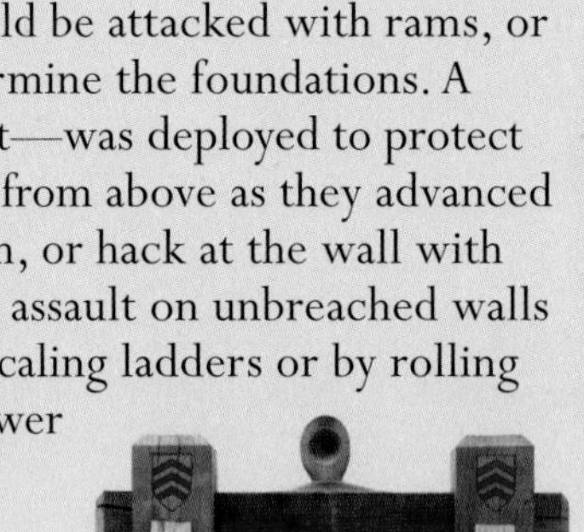

◂ MANGONEL
The catapult used the pulling power of a skein of twisted ropes. When released, the arm flew upward and hurled the projectile at its target—often a castle's fortified walls.

KEY **BATTLE**

THE SIEGE OF ROUEN
1418–19

In July 1418, the city of Rouen, in France, was beseiged by an English army under King Henry V. French crossbowmen held the attackers at bay, while primitive English cannon failed to batter a breach in the well-built masonry. After six months of tight blockade, the defenders were starved into submission.

▴ Painted in around 1480, this French image of the siege shows the attackers attempting to breach the city walls with their guns.

▾ CRUSADER CASTLE
The castle of Krak des Chevaliers, of the long-standing religious and military order the Knights Hospitaller (1099–present), was considered one of the world's strongest fortresses. In 1271, it fell to Muslim leader Baybars, who used it as a base for attacks on crusader strongholds on the coast.

◄ **AN ASSAULT ON FORTIFICATIONS**
A 14th century European artist's representation of a siege in progress shows men-at-arms in mail armor and surcoats attempting to scale walls, while archers with longbows provide covering fire. Both sides are suffering heavy casualties in this perilous assault.

KEY **EVENTS**

11TH–15TH CENTURY

- **c.1078–90** William the Conqueror builds stone keep castles in London and Rochester, England.
- **1096–99** The First Crusade introduces western European soldiers to the advanced fortifications of the eastern Mediterranean.
- **1120s–1130s** The counterweight trebuchet comes into use in battles between Muslims and Christians, in Palestine and Syria.
- **1143** The order of the Knights Hospitaller begin turning the Krak des Chevaliers, in Syria, into the most impressive crusader castle.
- **1196** Construction of Chateau Gaillard in Normandy begins—an early example of a series of high walls surrounding a central keep.
- **c.1450** Used in sieges by the French and the Ottoman Turks, cannon render medieval stone fortifications obsolete.

"The armed men… delivered a **terrific assault, firing stones and missiles**… from their **ballistas and engines**"

ITINERARIUM REGIS RICARDI, DESCRIBING THE 1191 SIEGE OF ACRE, c.1220

MEDIEVAL FORTIFICATION

BODIAM CASTLE

Europe's larger medieval castles were military strongholds and centers of administration. Smaller castles, such as Bodiam in southern England, were the homes of wealthy knights, built in martial styles.

Early European castles were built of wood and earth. With the adoption of stone as a construction material in the 11th century, castles became more expensive to build, but also longer lasting and more immune to fire and rot. The first stone castles had a central tower, or "keep," encircled by a defensive wall. By the time Sir Edward Dallingridge built Bodiam in 1385, towers had been integrated into the walls and the gatehouse had become the most strongly defended part of the castle.

A castle was a statement of the owner's wealth, power, and prestige, but it was also skillfully designed to give its occupants the best chance of fending off an enemy. Its walls and towers thus had to be resistant to stone-throwing siege engines and difficult for tunnel-digging engineers to undermine. However, the increasing use of gunpowder and cannon in the 15th century eventually made the stone walls of the medieval castle obsolete, for they could not withstand battering by powerful artillery.

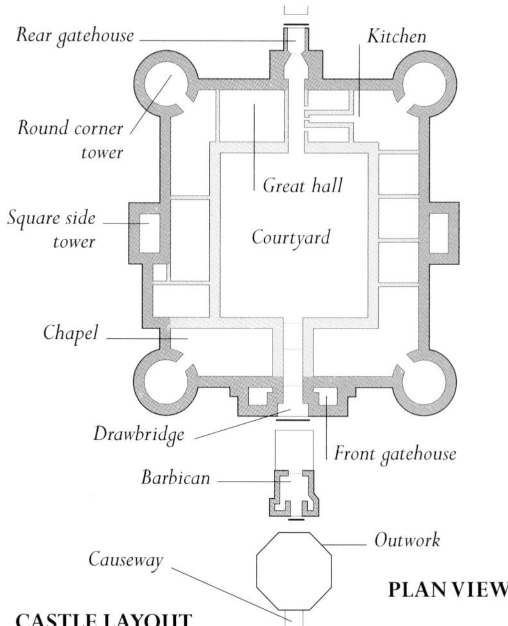

CASTLE LAYOUT
Built around a courtyard, Bodiam Castle had circular towers at each corner, square towers on each side, and fortified gatehouses at the front and the back.

MAIN ENTRANCE

▲ MAIN GATE
A potential weak point, vulnerable to a battering ram, the gate could be protected by lowering the iron portcullis.

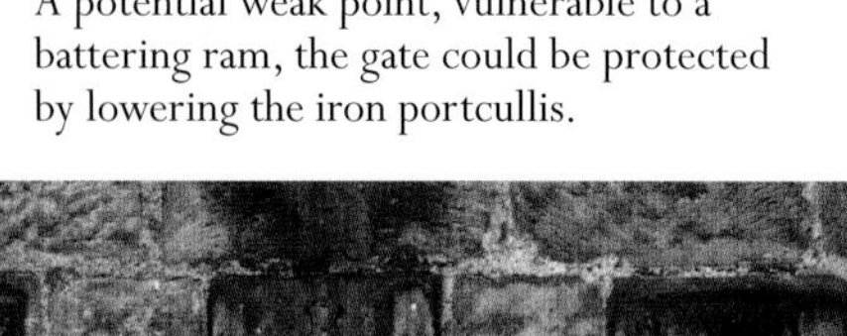

▲ SHIELDS OVER MAIN GATE
Heraldic shields were meant to impress visitors. The family coat of arms identified the owner and his status in the feudal order.

▶ SURROUNDED BY WATER
The moat forced attackers to approach the castle by the causeway at the front or a wooden bridge at the rear. It is also an impressive ornamental work that makes the castle appear larger than it really is.

CASTLE DEFENSES

▲ **BATTLEMENTS**
Supported by projections called corbels, the castle's battlements have crenels (gaps) through which archers could take aim at attackers below.

▶ **CORNER TOWER**
The round towers were excellent vantage points from which to keep watch over the surrounding land. Their curved surfaces deflected missiles hurled by siege engines.

▼ **GATEHOUSE MACHICOLATIONS**
Defenders could rain missiles onto the enemy through openings called machicolations between the battlement's corbels.

▼ **LOOPHOLE**
The walls are dotted with loopholes and arrow-slits that enabled the defenders to shoot outward.

CASTLE INTERIOR

▲ **GREAT HALL WINDOWS**
The hall, the castle's main room, was designed in a contemporary Gothic fashion, with arched windows.

▲ **VAULTED CEILING**
The castle's inner chambers had elaborate ceilings, emphasizing the owner's wealth and taste.

▲ **STURDY WALLS**
Deep window embrasures (recesses) reveal the impressive thickness of the castle's outer walls.

KEY **EVENTS**

11TH–15TH CENTURY

■ **1044** A document written for the Chinese emperor describes the use of gunpowder for smoke bombs and incendiary devices in sieges.

■ **1231** "Fire lances"—primitive flamethrowers—and "thunder-crash bombs" are employed in the defense of Kaifeng (Beijing) against the Mongols' forces.

■ **1326** The government of Florence, Italy, orders a supply of metal cannon and ammunition to be used in the defense of the city.

■ **1346** King Edward III of England uses small field cannon against the French, at the Battle of Crécy.

■ **c.1350** Chinese armies are regularly deploying hundreds of cannon and primitive handguns in field battles and sieges.

■ **1380s** Large siege guns (bombards) come into use in Europe; some are capable of firing stone shot weighing up to 500lb (230kg).

■ **1421** Using hand guns and cannon mounted on wagons, Hussites led by Jan Zizka defeat Sigismund, King of Hungary and Bohemia, at the Battle of Kutna Hora.

■ **1439–53** Brothers Jean and Gaspard Bureau create a powerful artillery train for King Charles VII of France, aiding him in the defeat of the English in the Hundred Years' War.

■ **1453** Sultan Mehmed II of the Ottomans uses large cannon to decisive effect during the successful siege of Constantinople.

KEY DEVELOPMENT

GUNPOWDER MAKES ITS MARK

The arrival of gunpowder is often dated to 1453, when the massive cannon of Sultan Mehmed II breeched the walls of Constantinople, a city that had resisted sieges for a thousand years. However, by this time, gunpowder had already been in military use in China for four centuries.

The explosive properties of a mix of charcoal, sulfur, and saltpeter were probably discovered by Chinese alchemists during the Tang dynasty (618–907CE). Documents from the Song dynasty, in the 11th century, make reference to the use of gunpowder-tipped arrows as incendiary devices, and of gunpowder fire-bombs that were hurled into besieged cities by catapult.

Over the following centuries, a whole family of gunpowder weapons was developed, from flame-throwing "fire-lances" to grenades, rockets, hand-held guns, and primitive cannon. These devices did not transform the Chinese practice of war, but took their place as a significant but subsidiary adjunct to traditional weaponry, often employed primarily for psychological effect.

THE NEW TECHNOLOGY

As the new gunpowder-based technology filtered through to the Muslim armies of West Asia and to Christian Europe, in the 12th and 13th centuries, its impact at first remained marginal. The few small cannon deployed at Crécy in 1346 were puny in their effect compared with the decisive firepower of the archers' longbows. However, European military artisans and their employers saw the potential of large guns for sieges. And so, by the 15th century, bombards (large siege guns) were being made, usually with barrels of wrought iron rods bound together with iron hoops. Exploiting the propulsive power of improved "corned" gunpowder, these mighty but cumbersome cannon were capable of hurling stone shot with crushing force against the walls of large structures, such as castles and towns, facilitating early siege warfare. The artillery used at the 1453 Siege of Constantinople, made for Ottoman Sultan Mehmed by a renegade Christian Hungarian artillery expert, included a bombard so large that it traveled on a cart drawn by 50 yoke of oxen and could fire a ball weighing up to half a ton.

For a brief period of time, heavy cannon were decisive weapons. At the same time that Mehmed was taking Constantinople, the French royal artillery, created by brothers Jean and Gaspard Bureau, was making a decisive contribution to the defeat of the English at the end of the Hundred

▶ **SIMPLE FIREPOWER**
Most early gunpowder weapons were crude by later standards, and did not make a great physical impact; their effect on the enemy was mainly psychological.

"We can compose artificially **a fire** that can be **launched over long distances**... It is possible with it to **destroy a town or an army**"

ROGER BACON, *OPUS MAIOR*, 1248

Years' War. A revolution in fortifications, however, soon tamed the siege guns. By the 16th century, medieval castles with their tall curtain walls were being replaced by lower-lying thick-walled fortifications, with angled bastions (see pp. 176–77) that provided the defenders with gun platforms to repel attack, enabling them to rake an enemy attempting an assault. Even after an additional use was found for gunpowder—packing it into a tunnel dug beneath wall, then exploding it to make a breach—besieging forces often found they could not regain the upper hand.

THE USE OF THE ARQUEBUS

A range of smaller, more mobile cannon was developed for use in field battles, along with a number of hand-held gunpowder weapons for infantry and cavalry. During the 16th century, one such weapon—the arquebus, a firearm with a matchlock mechanism—equipped numbers of infantrymen in armies from western Europe to India and Japan. Slow-firing, inaccurate, and unreliable, arquebuses and the matchlock muskets that eventually succeeded them by no means dominated the battlefield, and instead coexisted with pikes, edged weapons, and crossbows. Nor did the increased use of hand-held guns and cannon make the medieval armored knight instantly redundant. Charges by lance-wielding knights were still being executed well into the late 16th century. Instead, the adoption of firearms was a gradual process. It was only from the 1540s onward that wheellock pistols started to become the standard equipment of the cavalryman. And it would not be until the late 17th century that all infantrymen were equipped with firearms.

◄ THE HUSSITE WAGENBURGEN
Forerunners of modern armored vehicles, these heavy carts were used to provide protection and mobility for the Hussite soldiers, who rode in them to battle armed with simple gunpowder weapons.

KEY **FIGURE**

ODA NOBUNAGA

1534–82

Against the backdrop of 16th-century feudal Japan, hard-headed *daimyo* (warlord) Oda Nobunaga broke from the prevailing samurai tradition, which favored the sword and the bow. Using volleys of arquebus fire at the Battle of Nagashino, in 1575, he defeated the rival Takeda clan, demonstrating that gunpowder could be a significant force in battle.

▲ Oda Nobunaga introduced rotating volleys of fire together with the wooden stockade for defense.

◄ THE FALL OF CONSTANTINOPLE
The Ottomans' powerful cannon played a large role in the capture of Constantinople and the subsequent fall of the Byzantine Empire.

SIEGE ENGINES AND EARLY CANNON

During the Middle Ages, sieges were a far more common way of conducting warfare than open battle. Powerful siege engines that could batter fortification walls were used, allowing besieging armies to breach enemy defenses. The development of gunpowder weapons from the early 14th century onward increased the psychological aspect of siege warfare—the threat of devastation from this new form of firepower could drastically shorten a siege.

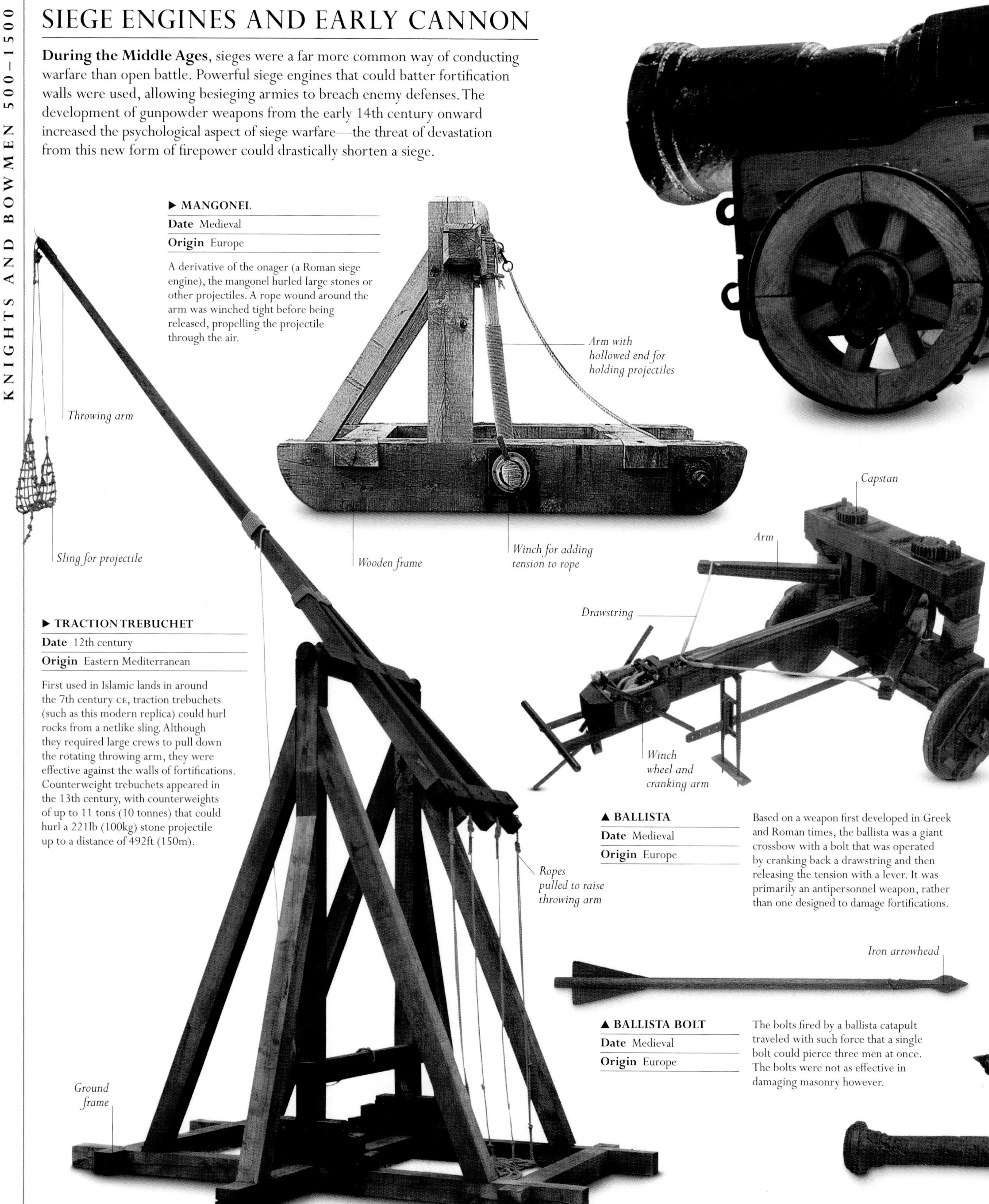

▶ MANGONEL

Date Medieval

Origin Europe

A derivative of the onager (a Roman siege engine), the mangonel hurled large stones or other projectiles. A rope wound around the arm was winched tight before being released, propelling the projectile through the air.

▶ TRACTION TREBUCHET

Date 12th century

Origin Eastern Mediterranean

First used in Islamic lands in around the 7th century CE, traction trebuchets (such as this modern replica) could hurl rocks from a netlike sling. Although they required large crews to pull down the rotating throwing arm, they were effective against the walls of fortifications. Counterweight trebuchets appeared in the 13th century, with counterweights of up to 11 tons (10 tonnes) that could hurl a 221lb (100kg) stone projectile up to a distance of 492ft (150m).

▲ BALLISTA

Date Medieval

Origin Europe

Based on a weapon first developed in Greek and Roman times, the ballista was a giant crossbow with a bolt that was operated by cranking back a drawstring and then releasing the tension with a lever. It was primarily an antipersonnel weapon, rather than one designed to damage fortifications.

▲ BALLISTA BOLT

Date Medieval

Origin Europe

The bolts fired by a ballista catapult traveled with such force that a single bolt could pierce three men at once. The bolts were not as effective in damaging masonry however.

◀ MONS MEG

Date	1449
Origin	Flanders
Weight	5.5 tons (5.08 tonnes)
Length	13¼ft (4.04m)
Caliber	49.6cm
Range	1½ miles (2.61km)

This massive bombard was presented to James II of Scotland in 1457. It fired stone balls that weighed almost 440lb (200kg), but was too cumbersome for regular service because it could be moved only 3 miles (5km) a day.

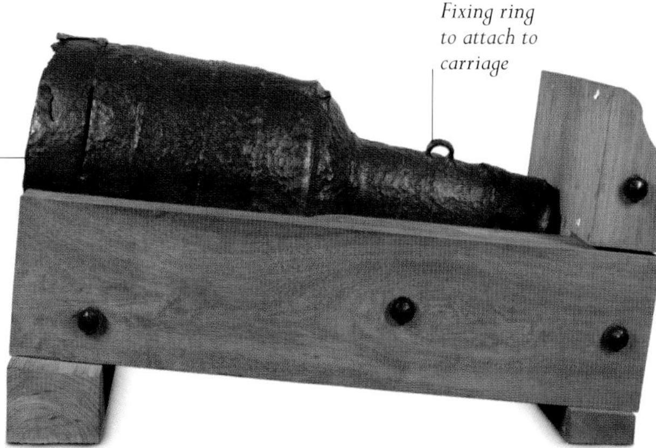

▼ FLEMISH BOMBARD

Date	Early 15th century
Origin	Flanders
Material	Forged hoop-and-stave iron
Shot	Stone balls

Large medieval siege guns, known as bombards, were muzzle-loaders. The stone balls they hurled were loaded through the muzzle after the powder charge. Flanders, where this bombard was made, had a strong tradition of gun-casting, particularly under Charles the Bold (1433–77).

▲ MORTAR

Date	15th–16th century
Origin	England
Length	4ft (1.25m)
Caliber	36cm

This mortar was found in the moat of Bodiam Castle, England (see pp.84–85). It was lit by a touch fuse at the end of the barrel, and was used to fire projectiles such as stones or perhaps incendiaries at a steep upward angle.

▼ ENGLISH SWIVEL GUN

Date	Late 15th century
Origin	England
Length	4½ft (1.36m)
Caliber	2in

Swivel-loading guns were frequently employed for naval use. This model was mounted on the gunwales of a ship, where the superior arc of fire could be used to rake enemy vessels. Like most swivel guns, it is a breech-loader.

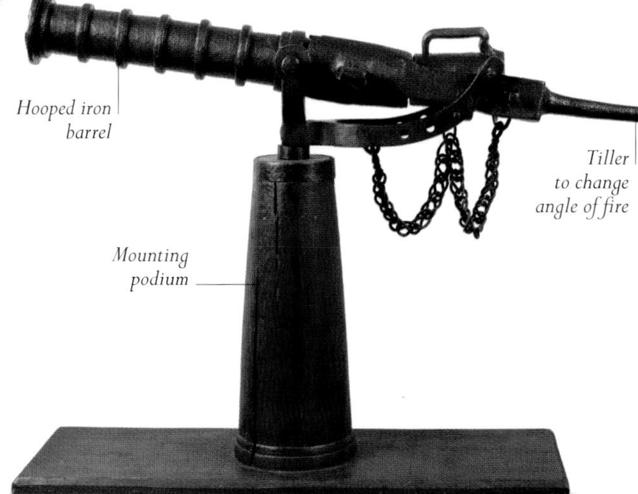

▶ CANNONBALLS

Date	14th–16th century
Origin	Italy
Material	Stone

In the early days of artillery, the most common form of projectile was stone balls. Cannonballs for the largest bombards could weigh up to 440lb (200kg) and inflict devastating damage on city walls.

◀ SWEDISH SWIVEL GUNS

Date	c.1500
Origin	Sweden
Material	Iron
Shot	Round or grapeshot

Swivel guns first appeared in the late 14th century, providing a greater arc of fire. They were mainly breech-loading, with the preloaded charge placed in a chamber at the back of the bore for firing. These Swedish models would have been mounted on a boat or a building.

KEY **EVENTS**

7TH–15TH CENTURY

- **634–36CE** The Arab armies launch their campaigns of conquest, with decisive defeats of the armies of the Persian Sassanid and Christian Byzantine Empires.
- **648CE** In possession of Egypt, the Arabs begin construction of a fleet of war galleys, making them a Mediterranean naval power.
- **9th century CE** The Arab Abbasid caliphs, ruling from Baghdad, make Turkish slave soldiers the hub of their military forces.
- **1071** Seljuk Turkish horsemen outmaneuver and destroy a Byzantine army at Manzikert.
- **1095–1291** The Crusades ignite prolonged combat between Muslim and Christian forces in the eastern Mediterranean.
- **1396** The Ottoman Turkish army of Sultan Bayezid shows its superiority to heavily armored European knights at the battle of Nicopolis.
- **1453** The Ottomans take Constantinople, using heavy cannon to batter the previously impregnable city walls.

KEY DEVELOPMENT

ARAB AND TURKISH CONFLICT

From the 7th century CE onward, Arab and Turkish armies dominated large areas of Asia, Africa, and Europe. These Muslim forces' military achievements were a combination of tactical subtlety, fighting spirit, and the skilled use of available weapons technology.

The founding of Islam by the prophet Muhammad, in Arabia in the early 7th century CE, had dramatic military consequences as well as religious significance. In the century from 634CE onward, Muslim Arab armies embarked on a series of campaigns of conquest that swept east as far as Afghanistan and west to the Iberian peninsula.

At first, the Arab military forces depended on camels to carry foot soldiers and supplies. But they quickly proved adept at absorbing new technology and tactics from the states they defeated. Soon, cavalry was the outstanding feature of Arab armies—including both light mounted bowmen and heavier armored cavalry with spears and lances. The craftsmen of the cities they captured, meanwhile, manufactured high-quality swords; "damascene" steel, from Damascus in Syria, for example, was renowned for its resilience and cutting edge. Not previously a seafaring people, after conquering the ports of Egypt and Palestine, the Arabs developed a navy using the expertise of shipbuilders and sailors. They also adopted siege machines and tactics from the conquered Sassanid Persian Empire, and the Byzantine Empire, which they did not conquer. Muslim states later efficiently adopted such advanced siege engines as the counterweight trebuchet from their Christian enemies.

TURKISH FORCES

The migratory Turkish peoples, who inhabited large areas of central Asia, became a source of military manpower for Arab states from the 9th century CE, employed as "Mamluks" ("slave soldiers")—in effect an elite, professional standing army. By tradition, the Turks were central Asian horsemen, armed with composite bows and fighting as fast-moving light cavalry. But like the Arabs, they proved adept at absorbing useful technology and tactics from settled civilizations. During the 10th century, they began to convert to Islam and some groups, such as the Ghaznavids and the Seljuks, carved out empires for themselves, as Arab power fragmented and declined. In 1071, combined Seljuk forces led by Alp Arslan inflicted a crushing defeat on a Byzantine army at Manzikert (in modern-day Turkey)—a heavy setback, from which the Byzantine Empire never fully recovered.

The Christian invasions of the eastern Mediterranean, known as the Crusades, brought various Muslim armies into combat with forces

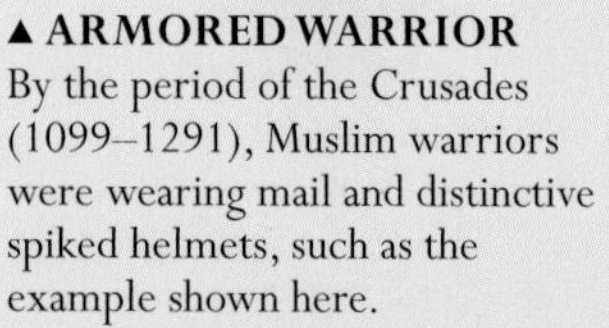

▲ **ARMORED WARRIOR**
By the period of the Crusades (1099–1291), Muslim warriors were wearing mail and distinctive spiked helmets, such as the example shown here.

"The Turks at a **given signal** rode about them like swarms of wasps, **showering arrows upon them** from all sides"

BYZANTINE HISTORIAN ANNA COMNENA, *THE ALEXIAD*, c.1140

from western Europe between the late 11th and late 13th centuries. Although more lightly armored than the Christian knights, forces led by Saladin, Kurdish ruler of Egypt and Syria, and Baybars, Mamluk sultan of Egypt, inflicted a number of defeats on crusaders' heavily armored bodies of knights. The Muslim forces' flexible tactics were based on rapid maneuvers, such as hit-and-run attacks by light horsemen, and they closed in for hand-to-hand combat only once they had gained the upper hand.

THE RISE OF THE OTTOMANS

During the course of the 14th century, a band of Turkish warriors established themselves in Anatolia, at the heart of the old Byzantine Empire. Initially led by Sultan Osman, they became known as the Ottoman Turks. Their military successes soon carried them deep into southeastern Europe. Originally mounted bowmen, the Ottomans also proved to be exceptionally quick to learn to use newer military technologies, adding gunpowder weapons to their armory during the 15th century. Unlike other Muslim armies of the time, they also made successful use of foot soldiers as well as mounted troops. In 1453, the Ottoman sultan, Mehmed II, captured the Byzantine capital of Constantinople using cannon—a groundbreaking use of gunpowder weapons. The city went on to become the capital of the Ottoman Empire all the way until the early 20th century.

▲ ARAB CAVALRY
An 11th-century Byzantine illustration shows Arab mounted troops armed with spears. Their armor was usually mail, with distinctive pointed helmets and aventails, which protected the neck.

◄ THE BATTLE OF HATTIN
In 1187, Muslim forces led by Saladin encircled, and subsequently defeated, an army of crusader knights at Hattin in Palestine, as depicted in this 15th-century illustration.

KEY **FIGURE**

BAYEZID I
1360–1403

Bayezid I was sultan (leader) of the Ottoman Turks from 1389 to 1403. Through a series of aggressive campaigns, he extended Ottoman rule across the Balkans and threatened Hungary. European knights organized an army to counterattack on the Danube, but Bayezid's army slaughtered this multinational force at Nicopolis in 1396. However, he met his match in 1402, when his army faced the Tatar warlord Timur at the Battle of Ankara. The Ottomans were defeated and Bayezid was taken prisoner, later dying in captivity.

▲ Sultan Bayezid was known as "Yilderim"—"the Thunderbolt"—because of his ruthless, decisive manner of waging war.

THE MIDDLE EAST

Between the 11th and 16th centuries, the weapons and armor of the Muslim world displayed greater variation than that of their western counterparts, although the most common type of armor was a mail coat (a *dir* or *zirh*), which was similar to the mail hauberk of European knights. Muslim helmets were most often conical, egg- or turban-shaped, and of metal or organic material. Swords were generally straight and double-edged until the 11th century, when cavalry sabers appeared under Turkish influence. Muslim armies employed a large number of horse archers, as well as cavalry bearing lances and swords, while the infantry carried maces and a variety of pole-arm weapons.

▲ ÇIÇAK HELMET

Date c.1525–1550

Origin Anatolia

Material Steel, silver, gilt

Made in the turban shape characteristic of many Muslim helmets, this parade helmet belonged to a grand vizier of the Ottoman Sultan, Suleyman the Magnificent (see p.130). It is decorated in gold with Koranic inscriptions and arabesques.

◀ MUSLIM SWORD

Date 12th–13th century

Origin Spain or Sicily

Length 35in (89.5cm)

Most early Muslim blades were straight, rather than curved. This wide, double-edged blade with a disk-shaped pommel lacks quillons. The grip, which was probably made of leather, has also perished. The blade bears inscriptions in Persian on both sides.

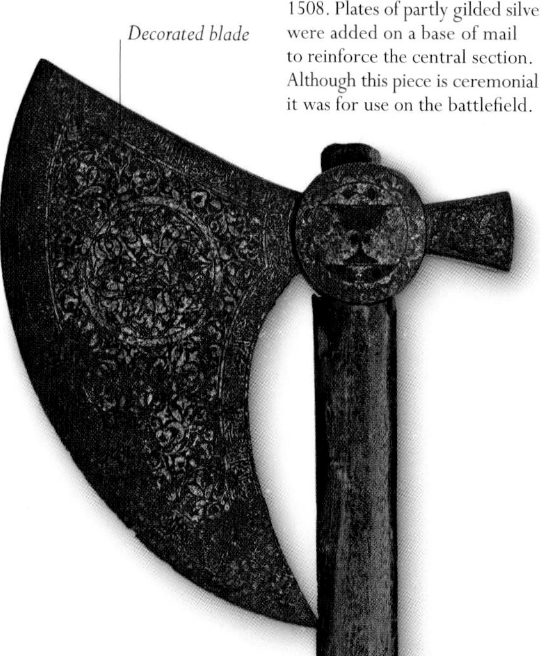

▶ MAMLUK AX

Date c.1400

Origin Syria

Length 27in (69cm)

This ceremonial ax, with its asymmetrical, crescent-shaped blade, probably belonged to Mamluk Emir Nawruz al-Hafizi. He was executed for staging a revolt against the sultan in 1413–14.

▶ MAIL AND PLATE ARMOR

Date Late 15th century

Origin Anatolia

Material Steel, silver, gilt

This mail and plate armor is characteristic of the Ak Koyunlu Turkomans, who ruled eastern Anatolia and parts of the Caucasus from 1378 to 1508. Plates of partly gilded silver were added on a base of mail to reinforce the central section. Although this piece is ceremonial, it was for use on the battlefield.

◀ **KILIÇ**

Date c.1500
Origin Anatolia
Weight 2½lb (1.15kg)
Length 37½in (95cm)

Long, single-edged cavalry sabers that curved slightly from the hilt were characteristic of Central Asian Turkic groups. Known as *kiliç*, they came into common use in the Muslim world from the 11th century.

▲ **MAMLUK HELMET**

Date 15th century
Origin Anatolia
Material Iron

This turban-style iron helmet is typical of Mamluk protective headgear. Despite bearing a rich silver damascened inscription, it was for battlefield use, and would have been lined and fitted with a metal aventail.

▶ **MAIL SHIRT**

Date Late 15th century
Origin Anatolia
Material Iron

Known as the *zirh*, this type of mail coat was particularly common in Anatolia and the Levant for several centuries before the 15th century. The iron rings were riveted together.

▶ **MUSLIM SHIELD**

Date Late 15th century
Origin Anatolia
Weight 3½lb (1.67kg)
Diameter 18in (45.8cm)

This type of shield was characteristic of the cavalry of the Ak Koyunlu. It had a high steel boss and, in battle, was generally strapped to the wearer's left arm. It was embossed with a geometric pattern.

THE CRUSADES

Throughout the crusading era (from 1095 to the fall of Acre in 1291), the weapons of the knights who formed the crusading elite remained relatively unchanged. The lance played a crucial part in the shock tactic of the mass charge, but at close quarters the sword was the crusader knight's most valuable weapon. Generally straight and double-edged, it was well adapted for use against mail. Later it was complemented in the Levant by daggers—considered unchivalrous in western Europe—and in the 13th century by axes, flails, and maces.

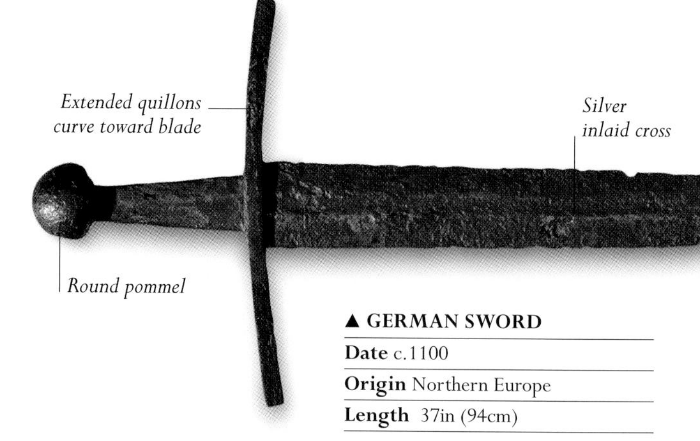

▲ GERMAN SWORD

Date	c.1100
Origin	Northern Europe
Length	37in (94cm)

This heavy blade was typical of the swords used in the First and Second Crusades (1096–99 and 1147–49 respectively). It had a narrow edge, with wide quillons that curved toward the blade.

Straight, slightly tapering quillons

Oval, conical pommel

Fuller almost reaches point

▼ FIRST CRUSADE SWORD

Date	c.1100
Origin	Northern Europe
Length	39in (99.5cm)

The massive double-edged blade of this early 12th-century sword is typical of the weapons that would have been carried by knights on the First Crusade (1096–99).

Double-edged cutting blade

▶ DOUBLE-EDGED SWORD

Date	1150–1200
Origin	Northern Europe
Weight	4¼lb (1.95kg)
Length	32¼in (82.2cm)

The blade of this heavy cutting sword was long and had two cutting edges. Its simple cross-guard, short hilt, and brazil-nut-shaped pommel are characteristic of 12th-century swords.

Wide, narrow cross

Fuller tapers off near point

▲ EUROPEAN SWORD

Date	Early 13th century
Origin	Europe
Weight	2½lb (1.2kg)
Length	3¼ft (1m)

Common between the 10th and 14th centuries, swords known as "Type X" generally had wide blades with a brazil-nut-shaped pommel. They also had a narrower and longer cross-guard than preceding Viking types.

▶ NORTH EUROPEAN SWORD

Date	1280–1320
Origin	Northern Europe
Weight	2½lb (1.2kg)
Length	36in (91.4cm)

Plate armor became increasingly common during the 13th century. As a consequence, swords with stiffer, pointed blades, better adapted to thrusting and exposing gaps in plate armor, were developed.

Pommel with horn-like projections

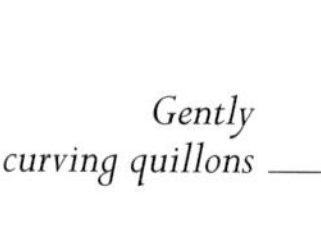

Gently curving quillons

▲ LATE "CRUSADER" SWORD

Date	c.1270–c.1350
Origin	France
Weight	3lb (1.45kg)
Length	29¼in (74.5cm)

Swords of the late crusading period typically had a flattened cone-shaped pommel with slightly curved quillons and a double-edged blade that tapered to a point. This example bears its maker's mark some 8in (20cm) up the hilt.

Sharply tapered blade

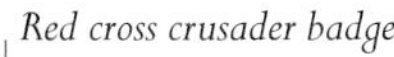

▶ GREAT HELM

Date 1250–1300

Origin Northern Europe

Material Iron

In use from the time of the Third Crusade (1189–92) for about a century, the cylindrical *heaume* or great helm completely enclosed the wearer's face, so became stifling in battle. Narrow visor slits allowed limited vision.

Cross-shaped plate on front

Red cross crusader badge

The Dreux family arms

▲ SWORD POMMEL

Date 1250

Origin France or England

Material Iron, enamel

Enamelled with the Dreux family arms, this pommel probably came from the sword of Peter de Dreux, Duke of Brittany. He fought alongside Louis IX of France at the disastrous Battle of Mansourah in 1250, during the Seventh Crusade.

Flattened diamond-shaped blade in cross section

▲ "CRUSADER" SWORD

Date 12th century

Origin Western Europe

Weight 2¾lb (1.27kg)

Length 38in (96.5cm)

Swords with broad blades and simple cross-guards and pommels became popular during the Crusades, and were used widely throughout Europe.

Flattened diamond-section blade

Mail aventail

▶ MAIL ARMOR

Date 1339–65

Origin Austria

Material Iron

This suit of mail, composed of hundreds of linked iron rings, has a short hem, and was probably worn with extra plate protection. The head was protected by a basinet and a mail aventail.

KEY **FIGURE**

GHENGHIS KHAN
1162–1227

Originally named Temujin, the founder of the Mongol Empire took the title Genghis Khan after uniting the steppe tribes in 1206. By the time of his death, his horsemen had campaigned as far west as the Black Sea coast and begun the conquest of China.

▲ Genghis Khan inspired the steppe horsemen with his ambition to create a universal empire.

KEY DEVELOPMENT

EAST ASIAN WARFARE

Three distinct approaches to weapons and warfare evolved in medieval East Asia. While steppe tribesmen depended upon horses and the compound bow, and China combined advanced technology with mass peasant armies, the Japanese, developed the idiosyncratic, highly ritualized fighting style of the samurai warrior.

Under the dynasties of the Tang (618–907CE) and the Song (960–1279), China was the world leader in technological innovation. However, defending its long frontier from bow-armed nomadic horsemen often overwhelmed the country's military resources.

The Song fielded large armies of conscripted foot soldiers. Although most were equipped with basic staff weapons, such as the halberd, they also used an impressive array of crossbows, ranging from simple, hand-held bows to large, lever-operated repeating crossbows capable of emptying a 10-bolt magazine in under 20 seconds. By the 13th century, the Song armies also had primitive gunpowder weapons, although these had only a marginal impact.

INVADING FORCES

Despite its technological and numerical advantages, China was often invaded by steppe peoples. In the 12th century, the Song lost control of northern China to federations of steppe tribes —first the Jurchen, and then the Mongols. The vulnerability of China was partly due to its military failings—primarily the lack of cavalry—but it also reflected the remarkable effectiveness of the steppe warriors. When a leader united them in sufficiently large numbers, the steppe tribes' ability to campaign over long distances and their deadly efficiency in battle enabled them to achieve wide-ranging conquests; they campaigned as far west as Hungary and Poland. Between the 1380s and 1405, Timur—who claimed descent from Genghis Khan—campaigned victoriously from Delhi, in India, to Ankara, in Turkey. The Song dynasty retained control of southern China by exploiting its naval strength on the Yangtze River, which formed a barrier against the north. The permanent Song navy, founded in 1132, deployed a remarkable variety of vessels, including multi-deck "tower ships" that were armed with various kinds of catapult. Some warships were propelled by human-powered paddlewheels; others were fast-moving, oared galleys. The Song could not hold out against the Mongol forces of Kublai Khan, however, who created his own fleet to conquer southern China in 1279, and later sailed to Japan and Java, a tradition continued by the next native Chinese dynasty, the Ming (1368–1644). From 1405 to 1433, the eunuch admiral Zheng He led the Ming fleet to East Africa. But he soon turned his attention to defending the steppe frontier, diverting resources to build the Great Wall.

Meanwhile, a distinctive military culture had developed in Japan. Samurai warriors emerged in the 10th century as soldiers in the service of the Japanese emperors, and over time they formed

▼ TIMUR
A Turco-Mongol warrior from Uzbekistan, Timur defeated the Mongol Golden Horde, the Egyptian Mamluks, and the Ottoman Turks. Before he died in 1405, he was planning an invasion of China.

warrior-clans with regional power bases. In the 12th-century Gempei Wars, the Minamoto and Taira clans fought, the Minamoto emerging as military rulers of Japan—the shoguns.

In this period, the samurai were primarily mounted bowmen; the art of Japanese sword-making only evolved in the late middle ages. Samurai warfare was highly stylized: battles opened with archery duels between notable warriors, and defeat led to ritual suicide (*hara-kiri*). Nevertheless, when Kublai Khan tried to invade Japan by sea, in 1274 and 1281, he found them to be formidable foes: the Mongols were repulsed, albeit with help from the bad weather that wrecked the invasion fleets.

◄ **A SAMURAI RITUAL BEHEADING**
It was the custom in medieval Japan for a samurai killed in combat to be beheaded by his enemies. The severed head was then returned to his relatives, mounted on a spiked board.

"They come with the **swiftness of lightning**, ravaging and slaughtering, **striking everyone with terror** and with incomparable horror"

ENGLISH MONK MATTHEW PARIS, DESCRIBING THE MONGOLS, c.1250

◄ **THE BATTLE OF AIN JALUT**
One of the very few defeats suffered by the Mongols came at Ain Jalut, in Palestine, in 1260. The steppe horsemen were beaten by the army of Mamluk Egypt, which fought in a not dissimilar style.

KEY **EVENTS**

10TH–15TH CENTURY

- **10th century** The samurai are first mentioned, as the Japanese emperor's guards.
- **11th century** In China, gunpowder is first used in warfare.
- **1132** The Song rulers of southern China establish a permanent navy.
- **1180–85** The Gempei Wars between samurai clans lead to the establishment of the Minamoto shogunate in Japan.
- **1241** At the battles of Liegnitz, in Poland, and Mohi, in Hungary, Mongol horsemen prove their military superiority to forces of European knights.
- **1385–1405** Timur carries out campaigns of conquest across much of Asia.
- **1474** Ming China begins the reconstruction of the Great Wall as a barrier against steppe horsemen.

MONGOL ARMOR AND WEAPONS

The Mongol warriors who swept through Central Asia, Eastern Europe, and China in the 13th century came from a nomadic tradition that valued mobility and the ability to strike from a distance. Mongol discipline was fierce—the army punished unlicensed plundering with death. They were organized into *tümens* (units of 10,000 men) centered around an imperial guard. Fighting from horseback, the Mongols were armed with composite bows that had a range of up to 655ft (200m), and a mixture of light arrows for greater range and heavier ones for penetrative power. Once an enemy had been softened up by multiple volleys of arrows, heavier cavalry armed with sabers moved in to finish off the survivors.

▶ MONGOL HELMET

Date 13th century
Origin Mongolia
Material Iron, leather, fur

The warrior's helmet had a traditional conical shape, trimmed with a padded roll of fur for a snug fit and protection against extreme cold.

▶ MONGOL ARMOR

Date 13th century
Origin Mongolia
Material Leather, iron

Lamellar, or scale armor, was made from overlapping leather or metal strips. Arrows that penetrated the armor would get caught in the silk layer beneath, making it easier to extract them.

▲ MONGOL BOOTS

Date 18th century
Origin Mongolia
Material Leather, felt

A Mongol warrior generally wore felt boots in both summer and winter. The boots provided protection from the bitter cold of the steppes and prevented their legs from rubbing against the horse's back and chafing.

Elaborately decorated head

Wooden shaft covered with polished rayskin

Small iron grip

Leather wrist loop

▲ IRON MACE

Date 14th century
Origin China or Mongolia
Weight 2½lb (1.17kg)
Length 15¾in (40cm)

This iron mace dates from the period when the Mongols, under Kublai Khan, overthrew the native ruling dynasty of China and took power. The intricate decoration suggests that it belonged to a warrior of high status.

Ivory-inlaid handle

Silver blade with deep fuller

▲ MONGOL DAGGERS

Date 14th century
Origin Mongolia

Various types of short swords and daggers were used by Mongol warriors for close-quarter combat. These are modern replicas in the style of the 14th century.

▲ BOW CASE

Date 15th century
Origin Mongolia
Material Leather

Mongol warriors protected their precious composite bows by carrying them in leather cases, which were slung on their left side while riding. They were designed to give the warrior easy access to his bow while on horseback.

Quiver carried about 60 arrows

Silver inlaid crest

Animal hide string

Steel neck protector

Tip recurves away from archer

◀ BOW IN MONGOL STYLE

Date 18th century
Origin China
Weight 2½lb (1.07kg)
Length 31¼in (79.4cm)

The composite bows used by the Mongols were made up of laminated layers of wood, horn, and sinew, which gave them greater elasticity and thus a longer range than a simple wooden bow. These bows had maximum strength for minimum length, a valuable attribute on horseback.

▲ QUIVER

Date 15th century
Origin Mongolia
Material Leather

A Mongol quiver was divided into a number of sections, allowing the warrior to quickly select different arrows for different purposes: heavy ones for piercing armor, or light ones for long-range firing. Arrows with scissor-shaped heads were designed to make deep flesh wounds in the bow arms of their enemies.

▲ NOGAI HELMET

Date Late 16th century
Origin Russia
Material Steel, iron, silver

This late Mongol helmet of the Nogai people (descendants of Genghis Khan) retains the conical shape of earlier types, but the neck guard is made of mail rather than leather.

THE MONGOLS AT WAR

Under the leadership of Genghis Khan from the early 13th century, the Mongols created the largest empire in history. Their secret was the ability to blend the traditional fighting tactics of nomadic horsemen with technology adopted from the settled civilizations that they subjugated.

Born Temüjin, the son of a tribal chief, the future Genghis Khan spent two decades uniting the various Mongol and Turkic peoples of eastern Central Asia. Although they had similar lifestyles—living in tents and in close proximity to their horses—the Mongols, Merkits, Naimans, Keraits, Tatars, and Uighurs were traditionally hostile to one another. However, using a combination of savage warfare and cunning diplomacy, Temüjin united them into a vast steppe confederation. In 1206, the tribes formally acknowledged his authority and he assumed the title Genghis Khan, or "lord of all." With a huge army at his disposal, Genghis embarked on campaigns that reached from Beijing (Zhongdu) in China, to the wealthy Central Asian cities of Samarkand and Bukhara (in modern-day Uzbekistan), before his death in 1227.

The Mongols' style of warfare originated from hunting. With their powerful composite bows and sturdy, nimble horses, large groups of riders would pursue herds across the steppe, then encircle and kill the animals with arrows; this is also how they attacked their enemy in battle. The Mongols had none of the obsession with personal bravery and honor that governed medieval European knights at the time. A traditional steppe horseman would use his bow to kill from a distance whenever possible, instead of risking his life in a close-quarters encounter. Similarly, Mongol commanders directed battles from a position of safety, using flags, smoke signals, and trumpets to convey orders; they considered it foolish to risk personally leading their men into combat. However, they also learned to augment their traditional mounted bowmen with armored cavalry equipped with swords and lances, and protected by metal armor, instead of their usual felt or silk tunics. Rather than avoiding close combat, this heavy cavalry would charge an enemy already weakened by the bowmen, and deliver the final, crushing blow.

Overall, their approach to warfare was ruthlessly practical: they would lure the enemy into a position of weakness, then destroy them. Speed of maneuver was therefore of the essence. Traveling light and living off the land, they could overcome the more cumbersome armies of settled civilizations.

THE OLD AND THE NEW

However, if traditional steppe warfare was the foundation for Genghis Khan's empire, then its expansion was strongly based on new technology adopted from conquered territories in China and the Muslim world. From Beijing in 1214–15 to Baghdad in 1258, the Mongols demonstrated their skill at siege warfare, battering city walls with projectiles hurled by mangonels and trebuchets. They were also pioneers in the use of gunpowder as a military explosive and incendiary material, using primitive bombs hurled by catapult, and handheld devices that were ancestors of the flamethrower and the handgun.

At their peak the Mongols were a near-unstoppable military force, but their high-casualty tactics prevented the long-term consolidation of their far-flung realms. By the end of the 14th century, the mighty empire that Genghis had so skillfully founded was reduced to fragments.

WARFARE ON THE STEPPE
After the death of Genghis Khan, the Mongols often fought one another in a series of bloody power struggles. Here sword-wielding Mongol cavalry pursue defeated rivals, who are shooting their composite bows from the saddle.

EAST ASIAN WEAPONS AND ARMOR

Lamellar (scaled) armor—made from small rectangular iron, leather, or bronze plates laced together—originated in the classical world, but was perfected by the Japanese: from the 11th century onward, nobility wore the *o-yoroi* (armor), specifically designed for mounted archers. By the 14th century, the design of Japanese swords reached its peak; a superior *tachi* or curved blade, worthy of an expensive mount (hilt and scabbard), was a symbol of high status, and samurai wore their swords not only on the battlefield but also when in civilian dress. In China, lamellar armor was replaced by armor made from plates riveted to a fabric backing, similar to the European brigandine. Following the Mongol invasion of China in the 13th century, curved swords influenced by the steppe saber became more widely used alongside the classic straight-edged *jian*, and by the middle of the Ming dynasty (1368–1644), many swords had also been imported from Japan into China. It was during this period that Chinese gunpowder weapons were first used in battle.

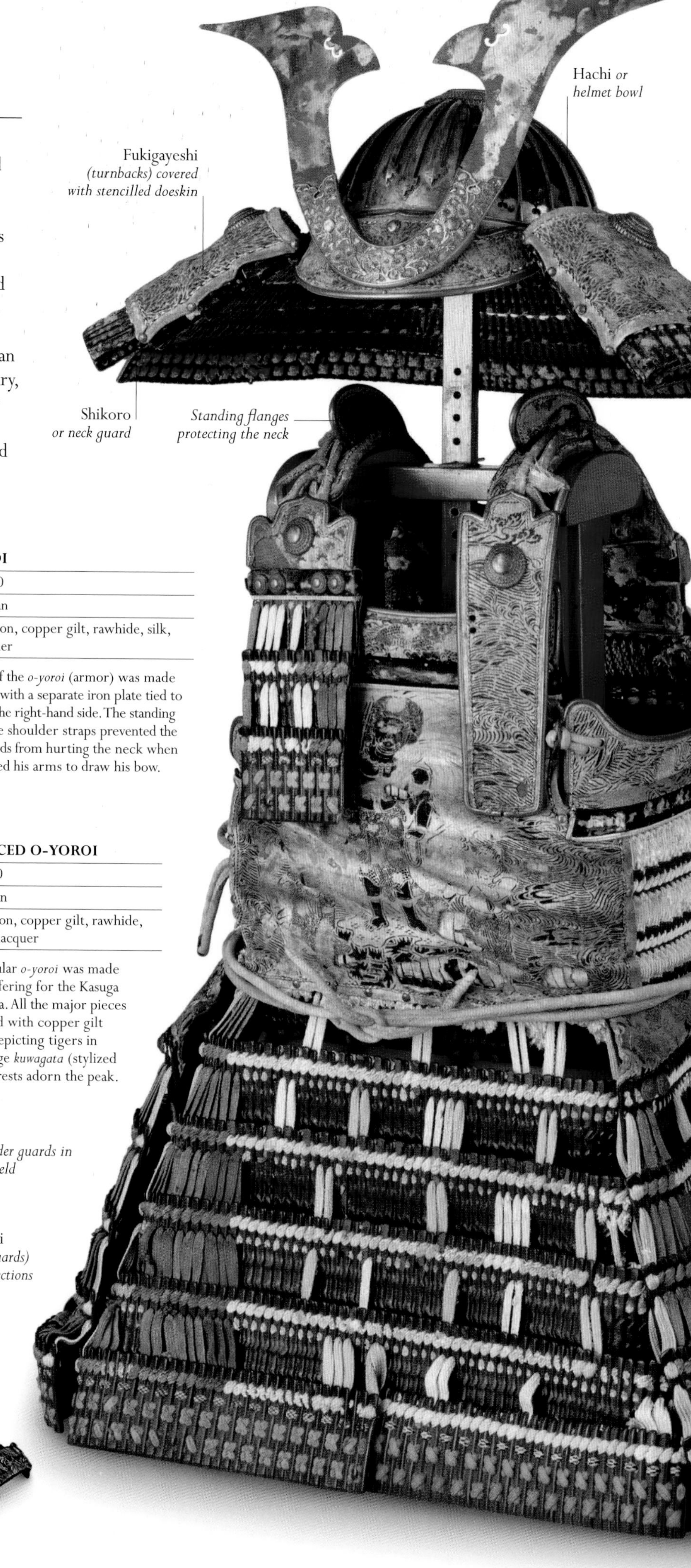

▶ **O-YOROI**

Date c.1340

Origin Japan

Material Iron, copper gilt, rawhide, silk, leather, lacquer

The cuirass of the *o-yoroi* (armor) was made of two parts, with a separate iron plate tied to the body on the right-hand side. The standing flanges on the shoulder straps prevented the shoulder guards from hurting the neck when a soldier raised his arms to draw his bow.

Kuwagata *crest*

Large shoulder guards in lieu of a shield

Kuzasuri *(thigh guards) in four sections*

◀ **RED-LACED O-YOROI**

Date c.1360

Origin Japan

Material Iron, copper gilt, rawhide, silk, leather, lacquer

This spectacular *o-yoroi* was made as a votive offering for the Kasuga Shrine in Nara. All the major pieces are decorated with copper gilt ornaments depicting tigers in bamboo. Large *kuwagata* (stylized deer horn) crests adorn the peak.

▶ KOBOSHI KABUTO

Date 15th–16th century
Origin Japan
Material Iron, copper gilt, leather, silk, lacquer

High-sided, multi-studded helmets in the style known as *koboshi kabuto* could contain as many as 2,000 rivets. It was quite common for a good helmet bowl to be recycled: this one was refurbished with a new neck guard, visor, and crest ornaments, for a member of the Honda family.

▶ YUMI

Date 19th century
Origin Japan
Weight 7¾oz (220g)
Length 4½ft (1.36m)

The design of the *yumi* (Japanese bow) has been unchanged since at least 1000CE. It was built with bamboo glued to the back and front. The grip was positioned near the lower end to allow the bow to be used on horseback.

Rattan binding to prevent joints weakening from damp

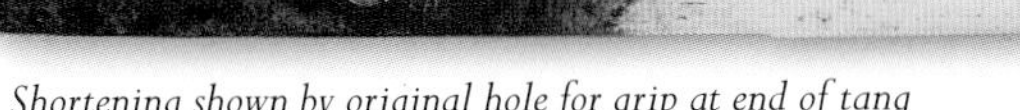

▲ TANTO BLADE

Date 1400
Origin Japan
Weight 5oz (145g)
Length 8½in (21.8cm)

Daggers were thrust through a sash on the left-hand side when wearing armor. The *tanto* (dagger) blade was acutely pointed and sturdy, designed to pierce armor when opponents were engaged in hand-to-hand combat.

▶ IRON CANNON

Date c.1400
Origin China
Length 18½in (47cm)
Bore 10cm

This small cannon was fired from a trestle-like stand. It was cast with a bulbous breech region to resist pressure. Rather than firing a single projectile, it was loaded with a number of smaller missiles.

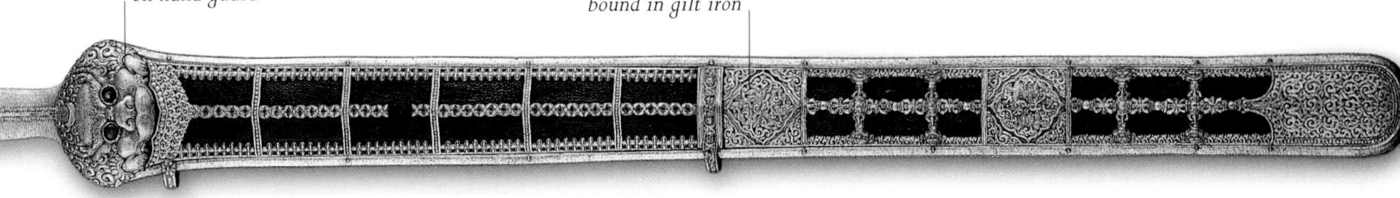

▲ JIAN

Date Early 15th century
Origin China
Weight 2¾lb (1.3kg)
Length 35½in (90.3cm)

The *jian* (Chinese straight sword) was the favored weapon of figures in both Taoist and Buddhist mythology. This sword, with a richly decorated hilt and scabbard, was made for presentation to a Tibetan monastery.

Cutting edge

Tang to fit bamboo arrow shaft

▲ YA NO NE

Date 18th century
Origin Japan
Weight ¾–1½oz (20–40g)
Length 7–9½in (18–24cm)

Japanese archers used many shapes of *ya no ne* (arrowheads). These examples are forked heads called *karimata* because of their resemblance to a skein of geese. They have a long tang to fit into the bamboo shaft.

▼ TACHI

Date 18th century
Origin Japan
Weight 4½oz (130g)
Length 29¼in (74.5cm)

The *tachi* was a long sword worn slung from the belt, attached by the *sageo* (cord) on its scabbard. The *tachi* was superseded by the *katana* for civilian wear by samurai, but remained the proper weapon to be worn with armor.

Wooden hilt covered with rayskin and bound with silk

Sageo (cord) of gilded Dutch leather

Wooden scabbard covered with lacquered cloth

Bronze kojiri (tip guard) decorated with a butterfly

EPIC FORTIFICATION

THE GREAT WALL OF CHINA

The longest defensive fortification ever built, the Great Wall of China protected northern China from incursions by mounted warriors from the steppe. First constructed more than 2,000 years ago and rebuilt in the 15th century, it was a piece of military infrastructure on an unprecedented scale.

China's settled civilization was always vulnerable to the nomadic, bow-wielding horsemen living in the vast spaces of inner Asia to the north and west. The wealth of Chinese cities and agricultural lands had long attracted these highly mobile steppe raiders, from the Xiongnu and the Jurchen to the Mongols and the Manchu. Qin Shi Huang, known as the first emperor because of his unification of China in 221 BCE, created the original Great Wall by joining up a number of existing fortifications, some already 500 years old. Built mostly of packed earth, with some wood and stone, over successive centuries, the Qin Wall was only partially and sporadically maintained, leaving northern China exposed to pillage.

THE NEED FOR DEFENSES

The Ming dynasty came to power in the 14th century, and represented a reassertion of Chinese national pride after a period of rule by Mongol conquerors. At first, the Ming were expansionist in outlook, seeking to extend Chinese territory by sea into the Indian Ocean, and by land into Central Asia. But ambitions to subdue the steppe tribes came to a halt in 1449, when Emperor Zhengtong was defeated and captured by Oirat Mongols on the frontier at the Battle of Tumu. As well as this military disaster, the need for protection against the steppe horsemen had become more acute since 1421, when the northern city of Beijing was made the official Ming capital, instead of the more southerly city of Nanjing. Beijing was virtually a frontier town, and was critically exposed to attack. and blades, although deadly when used in a pitched battle, would be unsuited to assailing fortifications.

In 1474, work began on a new Great Wall made from brick and stone, strong enough to withstand attack by the horsemen. Built mostly along the line of the old Qin Wall, in many places the remains of the original earth structure were used as foundations. Vast resources of human labor were devoted to building 3,510 miles (5,650km) of fortification, much of it across difficult terrain. The function of this wall was partly symbolic—to mark the territory in which Chinese civilization held sway. But it was mainly a practical, utilitarian military structure. As a physical barrier, it was sufficiently solid to repel the parties of horsemen armed with composite bows and bladed weapons. Sturdy fortresses were sited along its length, protecting key towns, mountain passes, or river crossings. More than 7,000 lookout towers enabled small garrisons of soldiers armed with pikes, swords, and crossbows to keep watch for intruders, and signal for reinforcements in case of attack. The walkway along the top of the wall allowed for the rapid movement of infantry from barracks or forts to any point that was under threat.

The wall outlasted the Ming dynasty, which disintegrated in the 17th century. The invading Manchu horsemen were only able to conquer China because Chinese General Wu Sangui, guarding the Great Wall at the Shanhai Pass, deliberately opened its gates to allow them through to Beijing. The wall itself remained an effective

MOUNTAIN DEFENSES
The builders of the Great Wall made extensive use of natural features, such as mountains and rivers, to enhance defensive effectiveness. Its walkway provided a means of moving troops through otherwise almost impassible terrain.

KEY DEVELOPMENT

WARRIORS OF PRE-COLUMBIAN AMERICA

The first substantial records of war in Mesoamerica relate to the Maya, who ruled parts of Mexico, Guatemala, and Honduras from around 250CE until the 16th century, when the Spanish conquistadors arrived, ushering in the end of an era.

From 250–900CE, the Mayan lowlands were divided between city-states such as Tikal, Copan, and Yaxchilan, which were in a state of constant war with each other. Mayan warriors fought with spears and sometimes with wooden clubs that were inset with stone or obsidian blades. Records indicate that armor and shields were rarely used by Mayan warriors: their equipment appears to have been more suitable for sporadic raids than large-scale battles. Mayan armies were small and aristocratic, and Tikal's army, the largest, would have numbered no more than 1,000 warriors.

AZTEC TRADITIONS

The Aztecs (Mexica) originated from the Valley of Mexico and eventually settled at their future capital, Tenochtitlán, in 1325, but emerged as an imperial power only in the mid-15th century. They built up a system based on tribute, which ennobled successful warriors and created a society that valued military training, encouraging commoners to join the Aztec army. With a core of trained veterans and a ready supply of fresh warriors, the Aztecs were able to field armies of over 8,000 men and could overwhelm their opponents by sheer force of numbers. In battle, they relied on a barrage of arrows and slingstones, followed by an advance of close-order fighters armed with axes, maces, and clubs. Warriors wore body armor of cotton or leather, and elite soldiers covered these with the skins of fierce animals, such as jaguars.

THE INCA EMPIRE

From 1438, under Pachacutí, the Inca, who had controlled a small state in the Cuzco area of Peru, took over the whole of the central Andes, absorbing other civilizations, such as the Chimú of northern Peru. As well as looting the capital, Chanchan, of its gold and precious stones, the Inca borrowed aspects of Chimú organization to consolidate their rule, handing control of the growing empire's provinces to a hereditary nobility. A series of well-built roads linked all parts of the empire, and a network of relay stations made it possible to send messages, enabling efficient central control of the provinces. To help rule a vast area that stretched from Ecuador to northern Chile, the Inca built hilltop fortresses and fortified outposts in the border regions of the empire, such as southern Bolivia.

Inca armies' success on the battlefield was not reliant on superior weaponry, but instead on numerical advantage and better use of tactics. Their equipment was equal to, or even less advanced than, that of their rivals; unlike the neighboring Amazon tribes, they did not even use bows and arrows. Their warriors fought mainly with clubs (initially of stone, then of bronze fitted with stone spikes), slings, and short wooden lances, and they were protected by padded armor. To swell their ranks, they instituted compulsory military service for all men between the ages of 25 and 50, producing a vast pool of recruits; in combat, warriors would employ their long-range weapons (principally the slings) before closing in for hand-to-hand combat. If they suffered a setback in one area, they were able to call on substantial military resources from elsewhere in the empire. Just as the Aztecs fought "flower wars" (see box, right), the Inca seem to

▲ PLACE OF SACRIFICE
The Aztec ruler Axayacatl (1468–81) is seen presiding over a human sacrifice of captives at the Pyramid of Huitzilopochtli, in the Aztec capital Tenochtitlán. The skulls of the victims were placed in racks at the foot of the temple steps.

> "And the curs **fought back furiously,** dealing us **wounds and death** with their **lances** and their **two-handed swords**"
>
> **BERNAL DÍAZ DEL CASTILLO**, *THE TRUE HISTORY OF THE CONQUEST OF MEXICO*, c.1568

◄ OBSIDIAN SPEAR
Inca warriors usually carried one or two throwing spears made of wood, featuring blades edged with sharp flakes of stone capable of inflicting deep cuts.

have engaged in a form of ritual warfare known as "tinkuy." The spilling of blood on the ground was believed to ensure the earth's fertility, so the purpose of this type of conflict was not outright conquest. As in their major battles, the Inca forces' superiority in numbers would also have helped them in this ritualized form of combat.

THE COMING OF THE EUROPEANS

The arrival of Europeans, in Mexico in 1519, and in Peru in 1532, heralded the rapid collapse of the principal pre-Columbian civilizations. Although Spanish military technology was superior—they possessed firearms, horses, and metal armor—their numbers were vastly inferior. They achieved a series of victories through their advanced weapons, but also through military aggression, by disregarding Aztec and Inca ritual proprieties (such as the Inca reluctance to fight at the new moon), and by exploiting the resentment that existed among the subject peoples of the two empires. Once the vulnerability of the Inca and Aztec emperors had been established, the Spanish, who then arrived in greater numbers, never allowed their opponents to regain their strength. The Aztec empire lasted only until 1521, when it was overthrown by the Spanish; by 1572, the last Inca stronghold had also fallen.

◀ **WARRIOR GOD**
Mixcoatl was the Aztec god of hunting and warfare, and is normally pictured with warpaint, a bow, and his kills.

KEY **EVENTS**

800–1550

■ **c.800–830** The Classic Mayan civilization collapses. The main cities of the Maya—Calakmul, Tikal, and Yaxchilan—are abandoned one by one, for reasons that are not clear, but may have included the effects of overpopulation on poor land.

■ **1428** The Aztecs of Tenochtitlán form a triple alliance with the neighboring city-states of Texcoco and Tlacopan, marking the start of the Aztec rise to power in the Valley of Mexico.

■ **c.1470** After a series of campaigns, the Pachacuti Inca conquer the Chimor capital at Chanchan, giving them dominance in the Andes.

■ **1519–21** The Spanish, under the command of Hernan Cortes, overthrow the Aztec empire.

■ **1529–33** Led by Francisco Pizarro, the Spanish overthrow the Inca, capturing and killing the Inca emperor Atahuallpa.

KEY **TRADITION**

AZTEC FLOWER WARS

The Aztecs and neighboring tribes indulged in a type of ritual fighting known as "flower wars." At an agreed time and place, restricted numbers of warriors armed with non-lethal weapons would fight; captives on either side were taken off and used for human sacrifice.

▲ Aztec warriors as depicted in the *Codex Mendoza*, an Aztec pictorial record dated around 1541.

PRE-COLUMBIAN WEAPONRY

Weapons technology did not advance significantly in the Americas in the thousand years before European contact in the late 15th century. The most common weapons were thrusting spears, slings, and wooden clubs, with padded cotton armor forming the principal protection. Warfare, although common (especially between the Mayan cities of Mesoamerica), occurred on a small scale until the 14th and 15th centuries. This period saw the emergence of the more organized Inca and Aztec states, which were able to construct large empires dominating most of Peru and Mexico, respectively. It was their ability to deploy resources effectively, rather than superior military technology, that ensured their supremacy.

▶ AZTEC CHIMALLI

Date 1400–1500
Origin Mexico
Diameter 30in (75cm)

An Aztec warrior's *chimalli* (shield) was usually made of fire-hardened bamboo, tied together with fibers from the maguey plant. They were backed with cotton or leather and covered with feathers, which often hung down in tassels. The object pictured here is a replica.

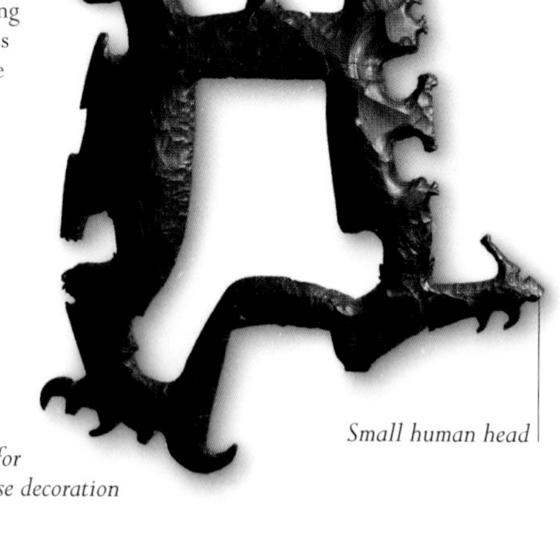

▶ MAYAN AXEHEAD

Date 9th century CE
Origin Mexico
Length 12½in (32cm)
Material Obsidian

Axes were not commonly employed by Mayan warriors in battle—this axehead bearing the form of human silhouettes was probably ceremonial. The Mayans instead used mainly spears and long clubs.

▼ MIXTEC GOLD BREASTPLATE

Date 1300–1450CE
Origin Mexico
Material Gold

This gold breastplate in the form of a deity came from the Mixtec people of Monte Alban, near modern-day Oaxaca. Mixtec nobles fought with thrusting spears, while commoners probably used slings and *atlatls*.

▲ CEREMONIAL TUMI

Date 9–11th century CE
Origin Peru
Length Approx. 13¾in (35cm)
Material Gold, bronze

Tumis were ceremonial knives with semicircular blades, characteristic of the Sicán and the Moche, pre-Inca peoples of Peru. They depicted the mythical founder of the Sicán people, the Sicán Lord, and were used in sacrifices to slit the victim's throat.

▲ AZTEC MAQUAHUITL

Date	1400–1500
Origin	Mexico
Length	Approx. 23½in (60cm)
Material	Wood, obsidian

The *maquahuitl* (broadsword) was a long war club that was used as one of an Aztec warrior's primary shock weapons. Although made of wood, it was often studded with razor-sharp flakes of obsidian or flint.

▲ AZTEC FLINT KNIFE

Date	1400–1530
Origin	Mexico
Length	Approx. 8in (20cm)
Material	Flint

This flint knife is of an earlier type than the wood and flint *maquahuitl*. The sharp stone blade could inflict serious gashes, but was more difficult to repair than a wooden broadsword.

▲ AZTEC ATLATL

Date	1400–1500
Origin	Mexico
Length	23½in (60cm)
Material	Wood

The *atlatl*—a device into which a javelin or long dart was placed—was retained in the hand when the projectile was thrown, giving it around 60 percent more force than a normal spear-throw. The darts or javelins were held in the hand and not in a quiver.

◀ AZTEC SLING

Date	1400–1530
Origin	Mexico
Length	Approx. 19½in (50cm)
Material	Maguey-plant fibers

Slings complemented bows as the main long-range Aztec missile weapons. Made of maguey-plant fibers, they were used to fire specially shaped spherical stones for maximum effect and had a range of up to 656ft (200m).

▶ MOCTEZUMA'S HELMET

Date	1500–1520
Origin	Mexico
Material	Gold, feathers

This is a reproduction of a helmet said to have belonged to Moctezuma, the last ruler of the Aztecs. It was made of gold, with 400 feathers of the sacred quetzal bird bound together with beadwork.

MOCTEZUMA'S PALACE
The Spanish, holding Moctezuma hostage in his palace, are besieged by hostile Aztec warriors. The Aztec had difficulty adjusting to the European intruders and their fighting methods, which had no equivalent in the Aztecs' previous experience.

AZTECS AND CONQUISTADORS

From 1519, the Aztec Empire faced an invasion by Spanish conquistadors—men from an alien military tradition with superior technology. The struggle for control of the capital, Tenochtitlán, revealed the Aztec army's dependence on stone weaponry and their ritualistic attitude to warfare.

The Aztec Emperor Moctezuma II at first welcomed the Spanish and their Indian allies, the Tlaxcaltec, into his palace in Tenochtitlán, but relations soon soured. The Spanish took Moctezuma hostage, and the Aztec population became increasingly hostile. In June 1520, fighting broke out. Moctezuma was killed—whether by the Spanish, or his own people, is not known—and the Spanish were besieged in the royal palace. On the night of June 30, they attempted to escape along the causeways that linked the city, built on an island in Lake Texcoco, to the shore. Aztec warriors in war canoes attacked the Spanish, shooting arrows and climbing onto the causeways to strike them with clubs. Of about a thousand conquistadors, probably two-thirds were killed, taken prisoner, or wounded.

THE SHOCK OF THE NEW

Under a new emperor, Cuitláhuac, the Aztecs sought to complete their victory by pursuing the remnants of the Spanish force. An Aztec army set out, splendidly arrayed, the officers wearing elaborate feathered displays on bamboo frames and marching under colorful standards. They caught up with the Spanish at the plain of Otumba. The Aztecs greatly outnumbered their enemy, probably by at least twenty to one. Their noble warriors, hardened to warfare from an early age, were physically fearless fighters. They had no metal weapons, but their wooden clubs and spears were edged with razor-sharp black obsidian blades. As well as bows and arrows, they had javelins that could be launched to considerable distance The primary objective of a warrior was not to kill his opponents but to maim them and capture them alive. Nonetheless, after battle was joined the Spanish suffered steady attrition. The tide was turned not by the conquistadors' few gunpowder weapons or their steel swords, but by their horses—animals unknown to the Aztecs before the Europeans' arrival. The Spanish commander Hernán Cortés led a small cavalry charge into the Aztec ranks and ran down their commanders. The psychological impact of this bold and unexpected action routed the Aztecs, who soon abandoned the field in disarray.

THE TAKING OF TENOCHTITLÁN

The following year, reinforced with large numbers of Tlaxcaltec and other native allies, Cortés placed Tenochtitlán under siege. In the defense of the city the Aztecs proved far more resolute than in open field. They fought fiercely to hold the causeways giving access to the city across the lake, until these were made untenable by the fire of small cannon mounted in Spanish boats. Then they defended their city street by street. Confronting crossbows, arquebuses, and steel swords with their weapons of wood and stone, they repeatedly repelled incursions by the Spanish and their allies, throwing missiles from the rooftops and ambushing isolated groups of soldiers. The Aztecs remained undefeated through 10 weeks of siege, but eventually the Spanish blockade of the city led to a shortage of food, forcing them to surrender. In August 1521, the Aztec civilization

1500–1680

PIKES AND GUNPOWDER

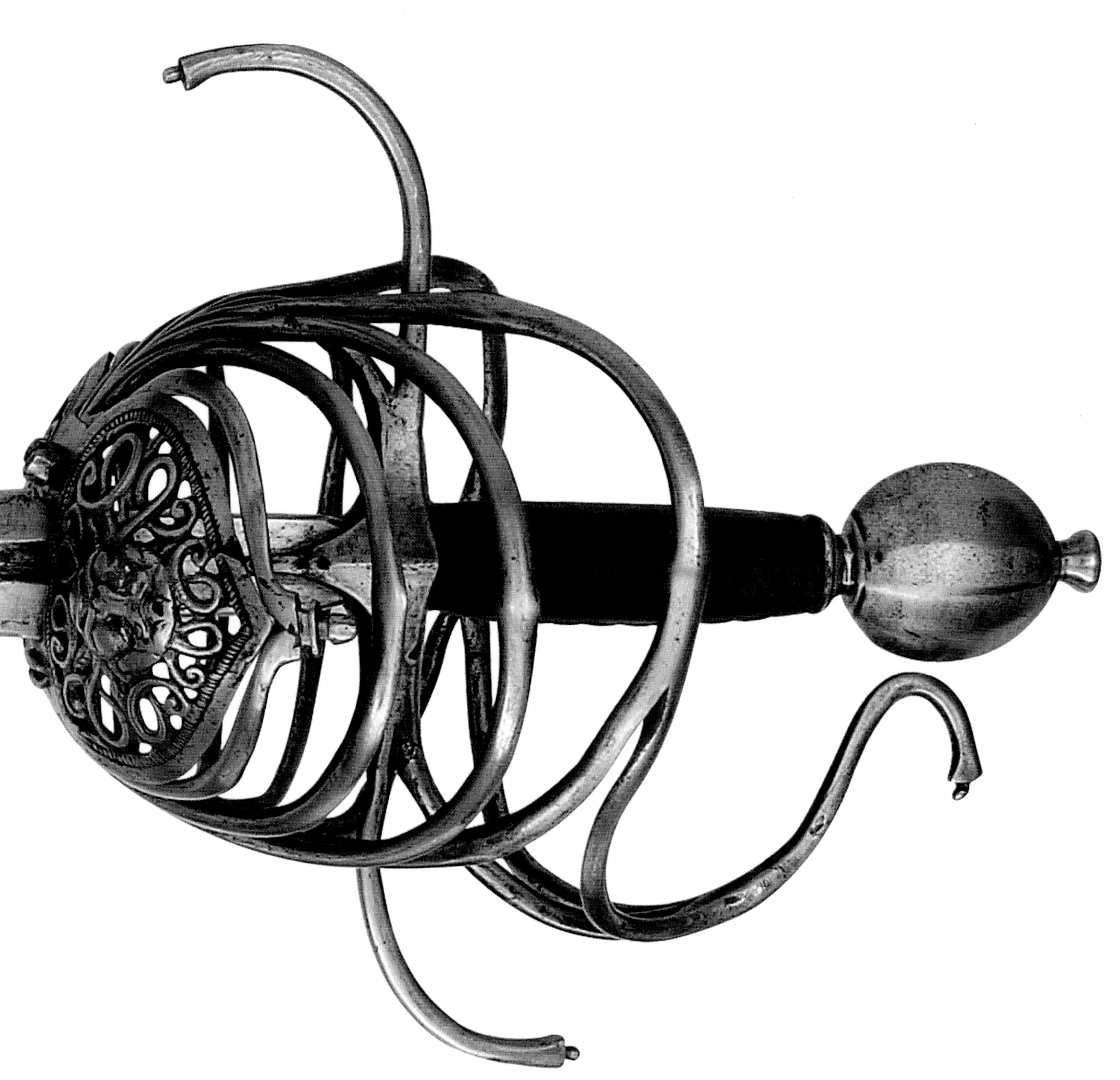

INTRODUCTION

Around 1500, warfare entered a phase of intensive innovation. The growing impact of gunpowder weapons led to a re-evaluation of siege warfare, battlefield tactics, and the training of soldiers. At sea, sailing ships armed with cannon gave Europeans unprecedented control of the seas.

Although military developments varied worldwide, there were certain trends. In 16th-century Japan, for example, commanders realized that peasant footsoldiers, if equipped with firearms and properly disciplined, could be a match for the elite mounted samurai. A similar idea underpinned the strict drills of European musket-armed infantry, who learned to fire in volleys and maneuver together on the battlefield. In Europe, the use of massed pikemen became standard: the issue of how to combine muskets and pikes in battle preoccupied European military theorists for a century and a half, before the advent of the bayonet, in the late 17th century, made the issue redundant.

The conquest of the Aztec and Inca empires by small Spanish forces, in the 1520s and 1530s, was atypical of European military achievement—the most effective army in the 16th century was arguably that of the Turkish Ottoman Empire. The largest wars of the 17th century were fought by the Manchu in China, while Europe's incessant religious and dynastic conflicts were stimuli for technological development.

The armored knight evolved into the cavalryman, armed with pistol and sword. Adapting successfully to the challenge of cannon, fortifications became ever more elaborate, as did the techniques used to besiege them. In the Mediterranean, war fleets still consisted of oared galleys but, in the Atlantic, sailing ships evolved into remarkable weapons platforms, with a single ship mounting as many cannon as an entire land army. Permanent regular armies—drilled, disciplined, and uniformed—eventually replaced the former European military traditions of mercenaries, feudal retainers, levies, and militias. The wealth of increasingly centralized European states sustained these expanding military establishments.

KEY DATES

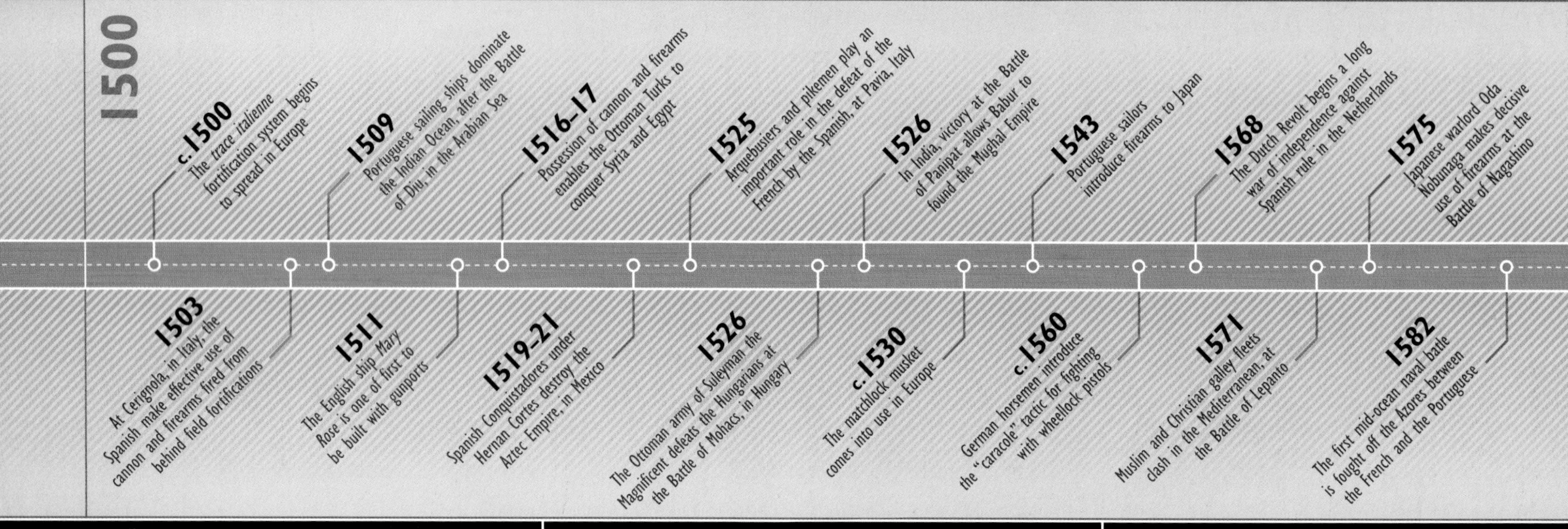

SÜLEYMAN I—1494-1566

THE BATTLE OF MOHACS —1526

THE BATTLE OF NAGASHINO—1575

THE SPANISH ARMADA—1588

THE BATTLE OF WHITE MOUNTAIN—1620

THE BATTLE OF BREITENFELD—1631

KEY DEVELOPMENT

PIKES AND MUSKETS

In the 16th and 17th centuries, Europe was a continent almost constantly at war. Over the course of these decades of conflict, European armies experimented with fighting methods that bestowed new importance on infantry armed with pikes and firearms.

Medieval European foot soldiers were often effective but were generally seen as being of low repute. In the early 16th century, however, the Renaissance rediscovery of the military techniques of Ancient Greece and Rome—the Greek phalanx and the Roman legion—suddenly made infantry fashionable. The most admired fighting men of 16th-century Europe, such as the German Landesknechte and the Spanish *tercios*, fought on foot, utilizing massed bodies of pikemen. This technique had been pioneered by the Swiss, but now firearms were added to the formations: although some foot soldiers continued to use the bow, the matchlock arquebus overtook it as the key infantry missile weapon during the Italian Wars (1494–1559). The arquebus was neither accurate nor powerful, but it could weaken an enemy pike square or help hold off a cavalry charge. Mobile field cannon—of bronze and firing iron shot—also began to make their mark on the battlefield.

INFANTRY DISCIPLINE

When they could afford it, 16th-century infantry wore extensive plate armor for protection against arquebus fire, as well as against pikes, swords, and halberds. But during the second half of the 16th century, the matchlock musket came into use. A heavier weapon that required a forked rest to aim, the musket could penetrate most plate armor at moderate range, and the proportion of foot soldiers carrying them gradually increased. The importance of discipline in the effectiveness of

▲ **MUSKETEER'S KIT**
Musket soldiers in the English Civil Wars (1642–51) rarely wore armor. The red coat was the uniform of men of Parliament's New Model Army.

"Advanced within **musket shot** of the enemy, the **foot on both sides** began to give fire"

FUTURE KING OF ENGLAND, JAMES II, DESCRIBING THE BATTLE OF EDGEHILL, 1642

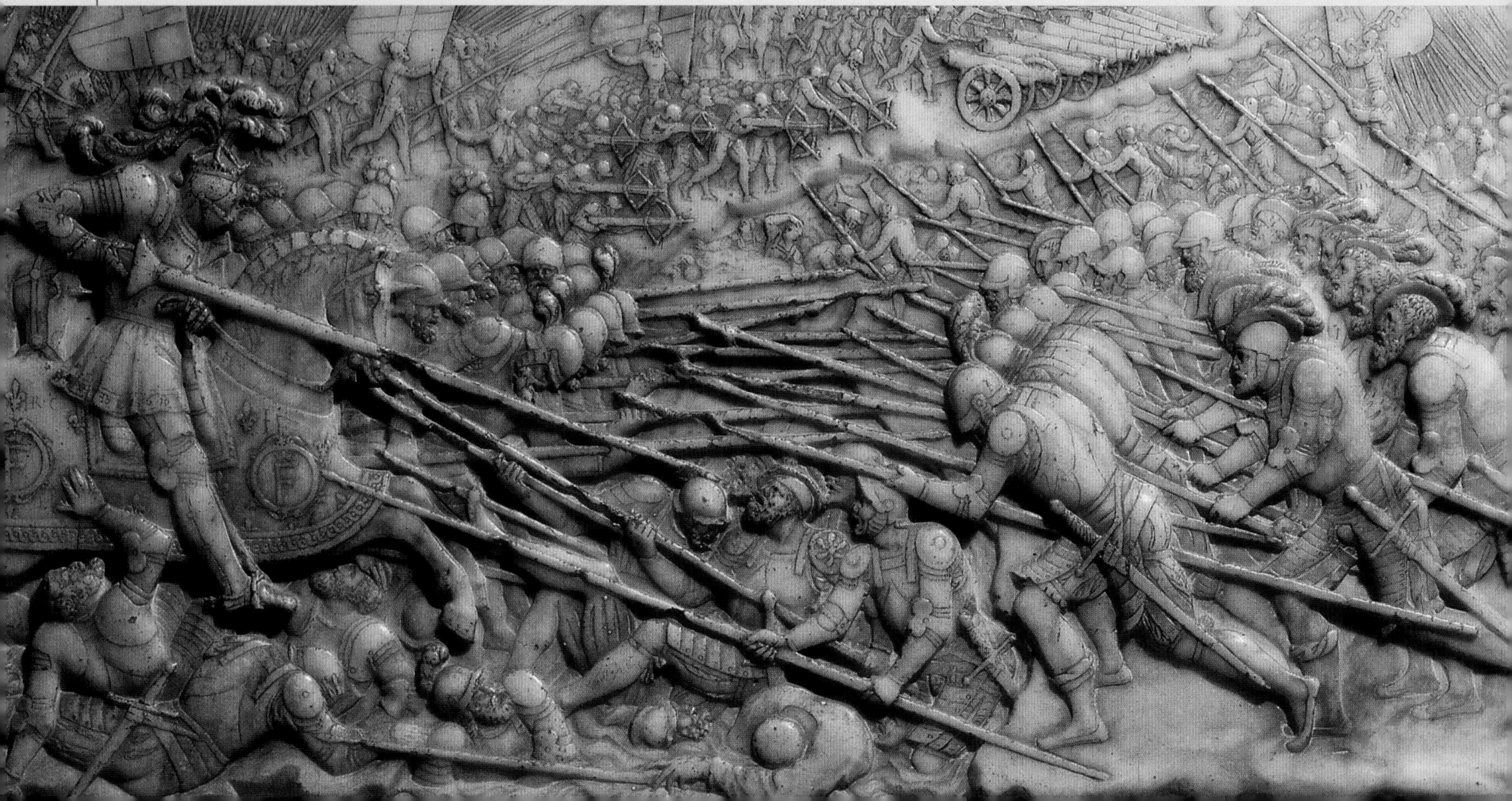

▼ **BATTLE OF MARIGNANO**
The tomb of King François I of France is decorated with this image of his victory at Marignano in 1515. In it, François leads his knights in a charge with couched lance against Swiss pikemen backed by field artillery.

◄ SPANISH TERCIOS
Spanish royal troops fight in a deep pike formation during the Eighty Years' War (1568–1648) against the Dutch. The Spanish *tercios* were considered the best infantry in Europe.

KEY **EVENTS**

16TH–17TH CENTURY

- **1503** At Cerignola, the Spanish demonstrate the effectiveness of firearms and cannon deployed defensively behind field fortifications.
- **1513** Swiss pikemen attacking in dense columns beat the French at Novara.
- **1525** French armored cavalry suffer heavy losses to Spanish arquebusiers in the defeat of François I by Habsburg forces at Pavia.
- **1580s** The matchlock musket comes into use.
- **c.1600** Dutch commander Maurice of Nassau trains and organizes his pike-and-musket infantry to carry out flexible battlefield maneuvers.
- **1619–48** During the Thirty Years' War, the proportion of musket-armed infantry increases, sometimes outnumbering pikemen.
- **c.1660** The flintlock musket begins to replace the matchlock musket as the key European infantry weapon.

infantry was already apparent from the pike square—a man with an 18ft (5.5m) pike was formidable as part of a tight formation, but useless on his own. However, as the use of firearms increased, so did the need for further precision in drills: loading and firing the gun was a complex operation, particularly *en masse*, and its success in battlefield formation depended on tight discipline. The 17th century saw musket-armed troops maneuvering in formation alongside pike squares, firing in volleys—either together for shock effect, or in sequence to maintain a continuous fire. The impact of gunpowder weapons on European siege warfare, however, was far more rapid than that on field battles. Tall stone castle walls were obsolete by 1500, but during the Italian wars they were gradually replaced by star forts that were designed not only to resist bombardment by cannon, but also to enable the defenders to make optimal use of cannon and firearms themselves. As a result, sieges became even longer and more elaborate than before, with besieging infantry forced to spend long months in trenches that protected them from the defenders' firepower.

KEY **STRUCTURE**

STAR FORT

Originally called the "trace italienne," the star fort's projecting triangular bastions enabled its defenders to cover all approaches to the walls with converging musket fire. The walls themselves were thick and low, surrounded by a wide ditch and an earth slope—the *glacis*.

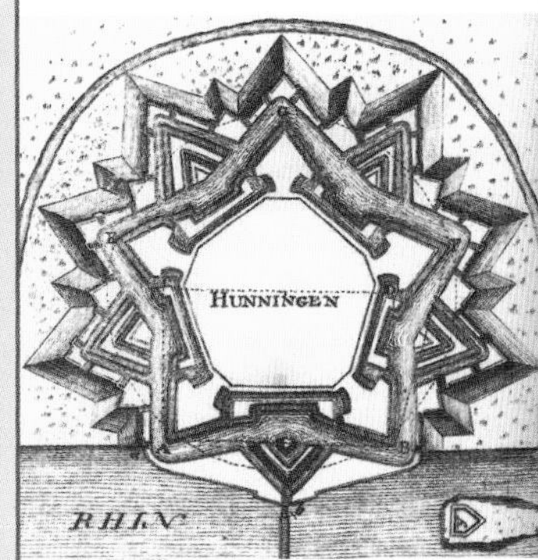

▲ Plans for fortifications at Hunningen were drawn up in the 1670s. Star forts often had additional outworks, as here across the Rhine.

FIELD ARTILLERY AND NAVAL CANNON

Artillery was established as an effective battlefield weapon by the early 16th century, leading to the appearance of a wide range of ordnance, including practical field artillery and lighter pieces for naval use. Improvements in gun-casting technology led to the replacement of wrought-iron guns with stronger bronze cannon, while the introduction of superior corned gunpowder in the late 16th century allowed the construction of longer-range guns with short barrels. By the time of the Thirty Years' War (1618–48) and English Civil War (1642–51), artillery was firmly established, with gun units integrated into infantry regiments.

▲ BRONZE FALCON WITH TEN-SIDED BARREL

Date c.1520

Origin England or Flanders

Length 9ft (2.78m)

Caliber 6.6cm

Range 262½ yards (240m)

This falcon was cast by a Flemish master gun-founder for Henry VIII as part of a consignment of 28 guns. It fired balls weighing 2¼lb (1kg).

▲ BRONZE FALCON

Date c.1520

Origin Flanders or France

Length 8¼ft (2.54m)

Caliber 6.3cm

Shot c. 2¾lb (1.3kg)

The falcon was a light cannon typical of the early 16th century. This model was ordered by Henry VIII, possibly from Flanders, because England did not have an established gun-manufacturing industry at the time.

▲ BRONZE SAKER

Date 1529

Origin England

Length 7¼ft (2.23m)

Caliber 9.5cm

Range 1½ miles (2km)

Like many early guns, the saker was named after a bird of prey—in this case, the saker falcon. This one was acquired from an Italian master craftsman as part of Henry VIII's campaign to enlarge his army's artillery force.

▲ BRONZE ROBINET

Date 1535

Origin France

Length 7¾ft (2.39m)

Caliber 4.3cm

Shot 1lb (0.45kg)

Weighing 425½lb (193kg), this is an extremely ornate example of the robinet, a light cannon. This model was made in Metz, France. It was seized in Paris by Allied troops in 1815.

Small-bore barrel

▲ BRONZE MINION

Date c.1550

Origin Italy

Length 8¼ft (2.5m)

Caliber 7.6cm

Shot 3¼lb (1.5kg)

Minions, light cannon that were particularly well adapted for use at sea, saw service on many English ships during their engagement with the Spanish Armada (see pp.148–49).

▼ IRON BREECH-LOADING SWIVEL GUN

Date 16th century

Origin Europe

Length 5¼ft (1.63m)

Caliber 7.6cm

Shot 3½lb (1.5kg) or grape shot

Pivots that allowed a gun to fire across a wide arc turned a fixed barrel into a swivel gun, especially useful aboard a ship when firing on other moving vessels. This model was used in an antipersonnel role, shooting stone ammunition.

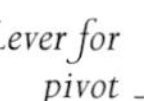

Bronze barrel

▼ BRONZE DEMI-CULVERIN

Date	1636
Origin	France
Length	9½ft (2.92m)
Caliber	11cm
Shot	8¾lb (4kg)

This naval version of a demi-culverin, a medium cannon, was cast for Cardinal Richelieu, who reorganized the French fleet and established a foundry at Le Havre.

Lifting handles in the shape of dolphins

Reinforcing bronze strips

▼ BRONZE DEMI-CANNON

Date	1643
Origin	Flanders
Length	10¼ft (3.12m)
Caliber	15.2cm
Shot	26lb (12kg)

This demi-cannon, a heavy piece designed for naval use, was cast in the famous Flemish gun-foundry at Malines. It was capable of firing heavy shots, which could cause devastating damage at short range.

Widely flared muzzle

Ornamental figure of pouncing lion

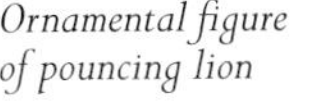

▶ MALAYSIAN BRONZE SAKER

Date	c.1650
Origin	Malaysia
Length	7½ft (2.29m)
Caliber	8.9cm
Shot	4½lb (2kg)

These light cannon were designed for long-range attack. This ornate model was cast in Malacca, Malaysia, by local craftsmen who probably followed a Dutch model.

Decoration depicting arms of Prince Maurice of the Netherlands

Slots for wedge to secure breech chamber

◀ BRONZE BREECH-LOADING SWIVEL GUN

Date	c.1670
Origin	Netherlands
Length	4ft (1.22m)
Caliber	7.4cm
Shot	2½lb (1.16kg) or grape shot

This swivel gun was owned by the Dutch East India Company, and was most probably used as an antipersonnel weapon.

EUROPEAN INFANTRY ARMOR AND WEAPONS

Peacetime armies hardly existed prior to the 16th century: professional troops were either bodyguards or employed for garrison duties. However, during wartime troops were recruited and mercenaries hired. Permanent infantry units, such as the Spanish *tercio* (see p.117), were established in the early 16th century. They were drilled in battlefield tactics and trained in the effective use of their weapons. Such forces, together with the increased availability of handguns, challenged the supremacy of the fully armored knights. Manufacturers in Italy, Germany, and the Low Countries increased their production of swords, staff weapons, handguns, and armor, transporting them all over Europe to equip these new military units.

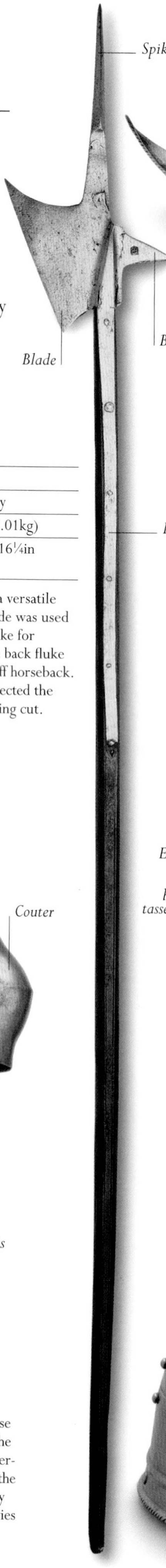

Spike

Blade

Back fluke

Langet

▶ HALBERD

Date c.1500

Origin Germany

Weight 4½lb (2.01kg)

Length (Head) 16¼in (41.2cm)

The halberd was a versatile weapon—the blade was used for cutting, its spike for thrusting, and the back fluke for pulling men off horseback. The langets protected the shaft from being cut.

MORION

▼ SPANISH TERCIO ARMOR

Date c.1570

Origin Italy

Material Iron, leather

Italy, and especially Milan, made munition armor of this type in large quantities. This cuirass was worn with full arms and an open helmet such as the morion shown. The *tercios* were armed with a pike or gun and a sword.

Gorget

Movable gussets at armholes

Embossing on breast plate and tassets (thigh guards)

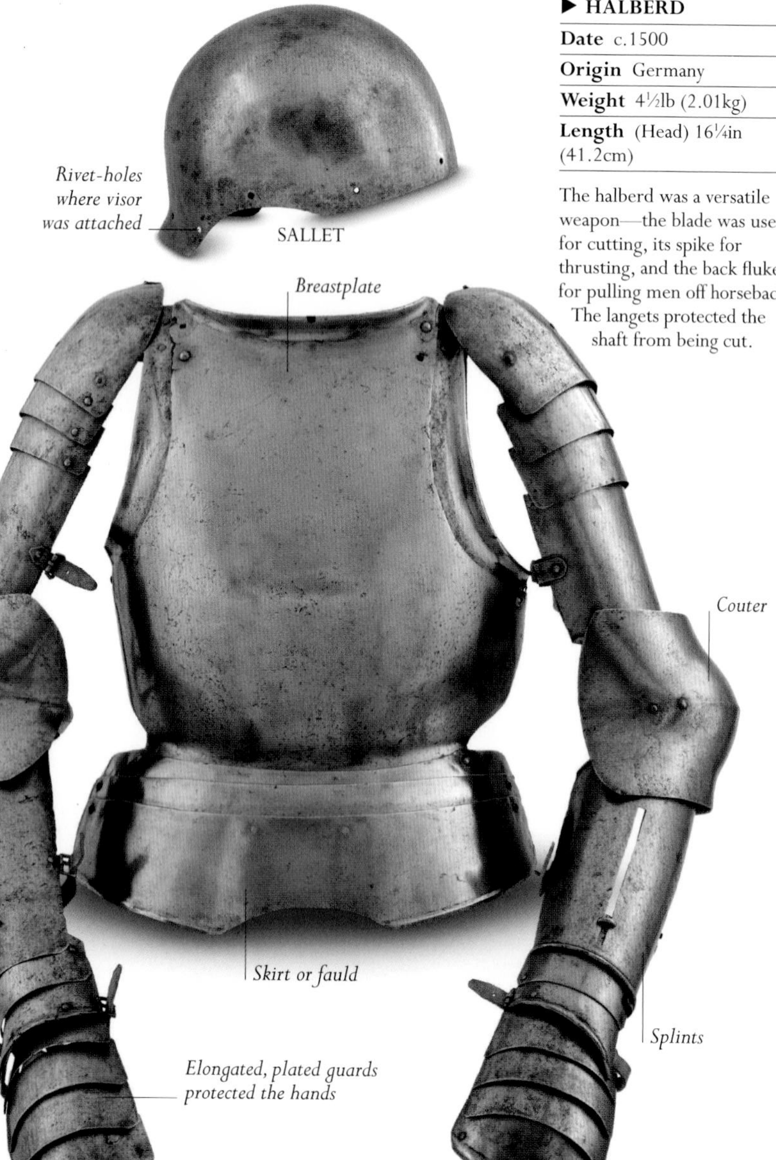

▲ ALMAIN RIVET (MUNITION ARMOR)

Date c.1520

Origin Italy

Material Iron, leather

In 1512, King Henry VIII ordered 2,000 of these simple armors from a merchant in Florence. The arm defenses, called "splints," consisted of gutter-shaped plates attached to a dished couter over the elbow. The plates and the couter were joined by leather on the inside. Instead of gauntlets, a series of laminations covered the hands.

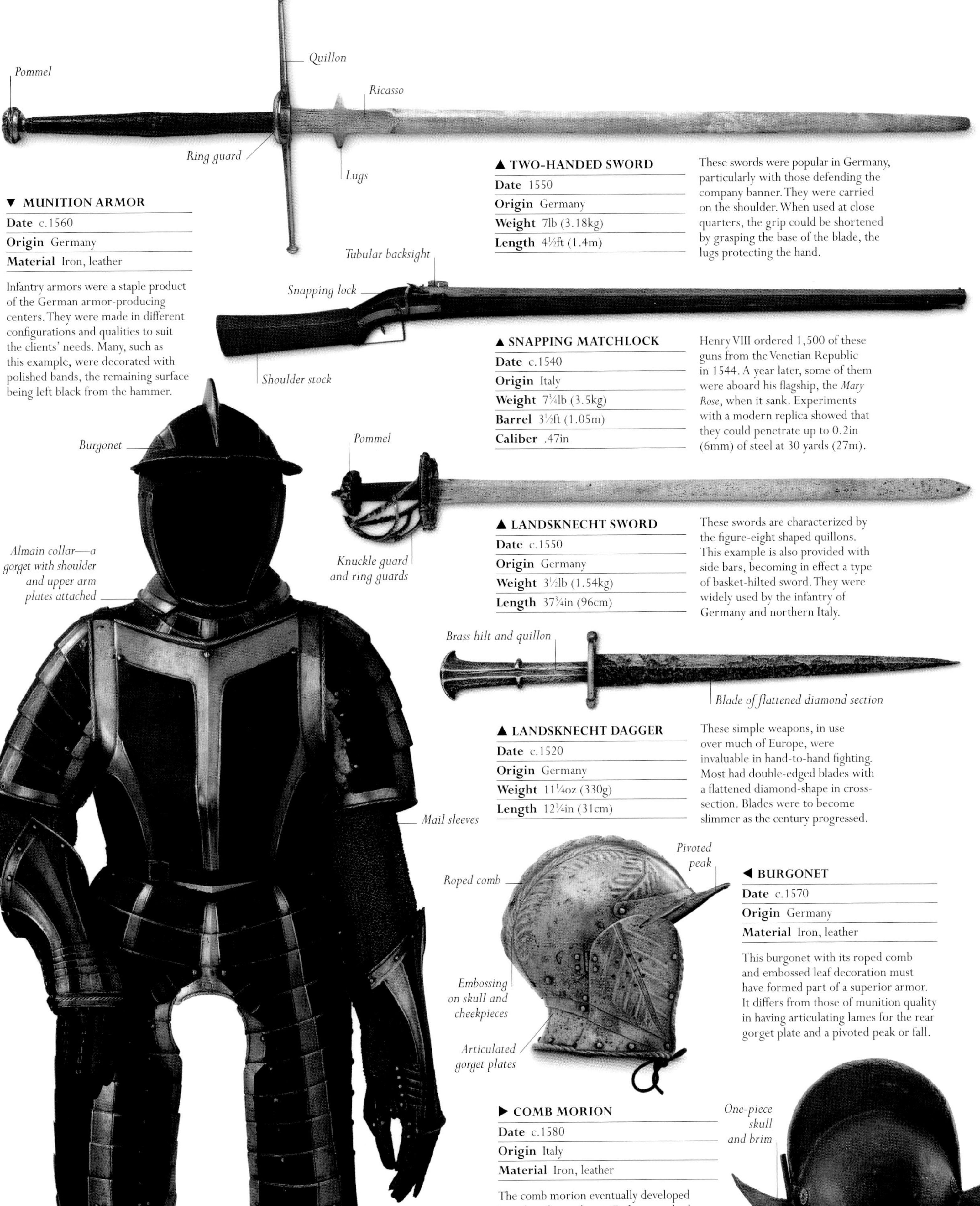

▲ **TWO-HANDED SWORD**

Date 1550
Origin Germany
Weight 7lb (3.18kg)
Length 4½ft (1.4m)

These swords were popular in Germany, particularly with those defending the company banner. They were carried on the shoulder. When used at close quarters, the grip could be shortened by grasping the base of the blade, the lugs protecting the hand.

▼ **MUNITION ARMOR**

Date c.1560
Origin Germany
Material Iron, leather

Infantry armors were a staple product of the German armor-producing centers. They were made in different configurations and qualities to suit the clients' needs. Many, such as this example, were decorated with polished bands, the remaining surface being left black from the hammer.

▲ **SNAPPING MATCHLOCK**

Date c.1540
Origin Italy
Weight 7¾lb (3.5kg)
Barrel 3½ft (1.05m)
Caliber .47in

Henry VIII ordered 1,500 of these guns from the Venetian Republic in 1544. A year later, some of them were aboard his flagship, the *Mary Rose*, when it sank. Experiments with a modern replica showed that they could penetrate up to 0.2in (6mm) of steel at 30 yards (27m).

▲ **LANDSKNECHT SWORD**

Date c.1550
Origin Germany
Weight 3½lb (1.54kg)
Length 37¾in (96cm)

These swords are characterized by the figure-eight shaped quillons. This example is also provided with side bars, becoming in effect a type of basket-hilted sword. They were widely used by the infantry of Germany and northern Italy.

▲ **LANDSKNECHT DAGGER**

Date c.1520
Origin Germany
Weight 11¼oz (330g)
Length 12¼in (31cm)

These simple weapons, in use over much of Europe, were invaluable in hand-to-hand fighting. Most had double-edged blades with a flattened diamond-shape in cross-section. Blades were to become slimmer as the century progressed.

◀ **BURGONET**

Date c.1570
Origin Germany
Material Iron, leather

This burgonet with its roped comb and embossed leaf decoration must have formed part of a superior armor. It differs from those of munition quality in having articulating lames for the rear gorget plate and a pivoted peak or fall.

▶ **COMB MORION**

Date c.1580
Origin Italy
Material Iron, leather

The comb morion eventually developed into the pikeman's pot. Early examples have the comb, skull, and brim forged in one piece, while later examples were made in two halves. The earpieces on this example are missing.

SIMPLE BUT EFFECTIVE FIREARM

MATCHLOCK MUSKET

The invention of the matchlock *hackenbüsche*, or arquebus, cannot be dated precisely, but evidence points to it being around 1475, of German origin. Its source of ignition was a length of smouldering "match"—cord soaked in saltpeter. On pulling the trigger, the match, held in a pivoting holder, swung down and touched off a small quantity of priming powder held in a pan, which lit the main gunpowder charge via a narrow touch-hole. Matchlocks were superseded by flintlocks in the early 1600s, but were still used until the end of that century, due to their simplicity and low cost.

▶ MATCHLOCK MUSKET

Date	Mid-17th century
Origin	Britain
Weight	13¼lb (6.05kg)
Barrel	49½in (126cm)
Caliber	.75in

▲ MATCHLOCK MUSKET
While the matchlock was a significant improvement over the hand-cannon, it was still a very clumsy weapon. Early examples were unwieldy and not very accurate. Even in dry weather, the match could be extinguished all too easily, and its glowing end was a giveaway at night.

▸ BANDOLIER
This "collar of charges," worn diagonally over the shoulder, carried around 12 wooden flasks, each of which held a measure of powder for one shot.

IN ACTION

MATCHLOCK DRILL

In the first of these pictures from a Dutch drill manual, the match in the musketeer's left hand is already lit. In the second, he pours gunpowder from a flask on his bandolier. He then rams down a musket ball, before preparing to pour priming powder into the pan from a priming flask, keeping the smoldering match at a safe distance in his left hand.

▶ Good dexterity was required to load matchlocks in the field.

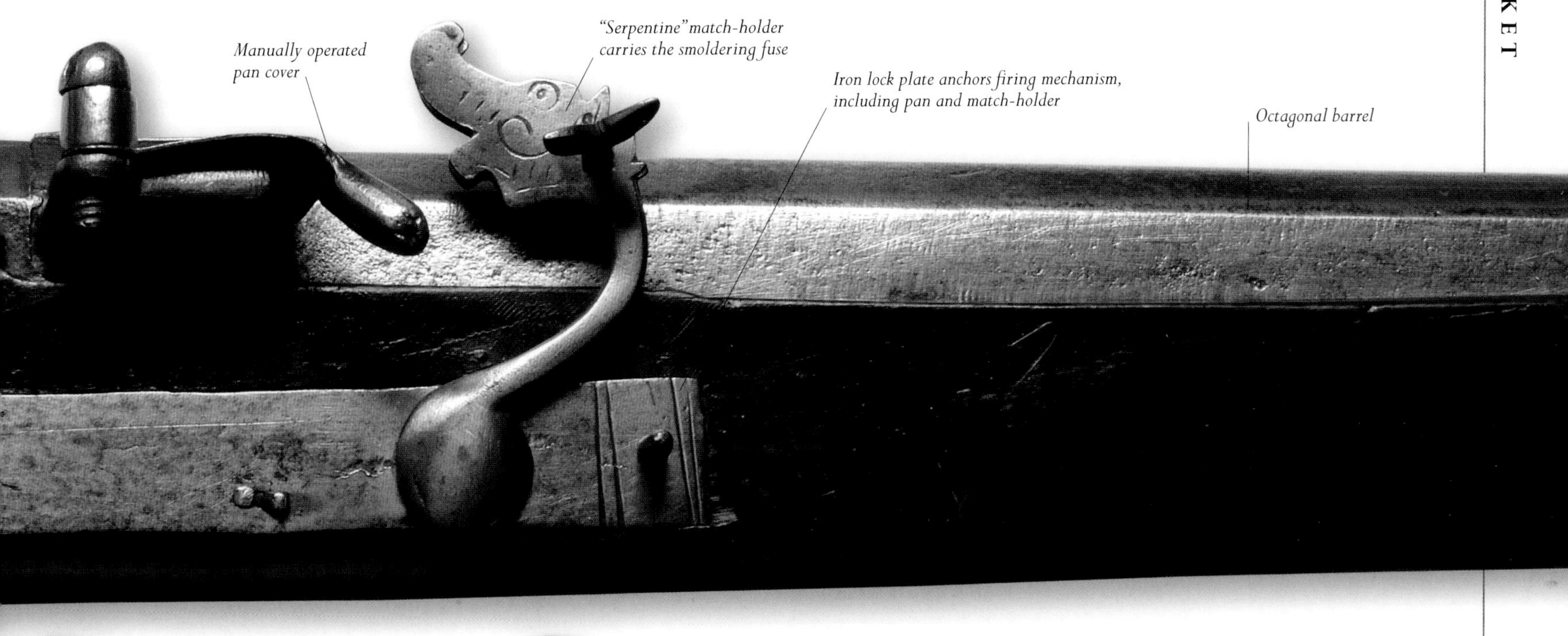

▼ MUSKET REST
The earliest military matchlocks were massive, and required the use of a rest, which had to be of sturdy design and increased the gunner's load. By about 1650, guns had become light enough for rests to be dispensed with.

▶ POWDER FLASK
This example is made of wood covered with velvet and reinforced with iron. It is designed to hold fine-grained priming powder—the narrow spout makes it easier to pour into the pan.

▼ LEAD BALL
Matchlock muskets fired a ball made from lead that was cast slightly smaller in diameter than the bore of the gun. This was because residues from the burning powder quickly fouled the barrel, making loading difficult.

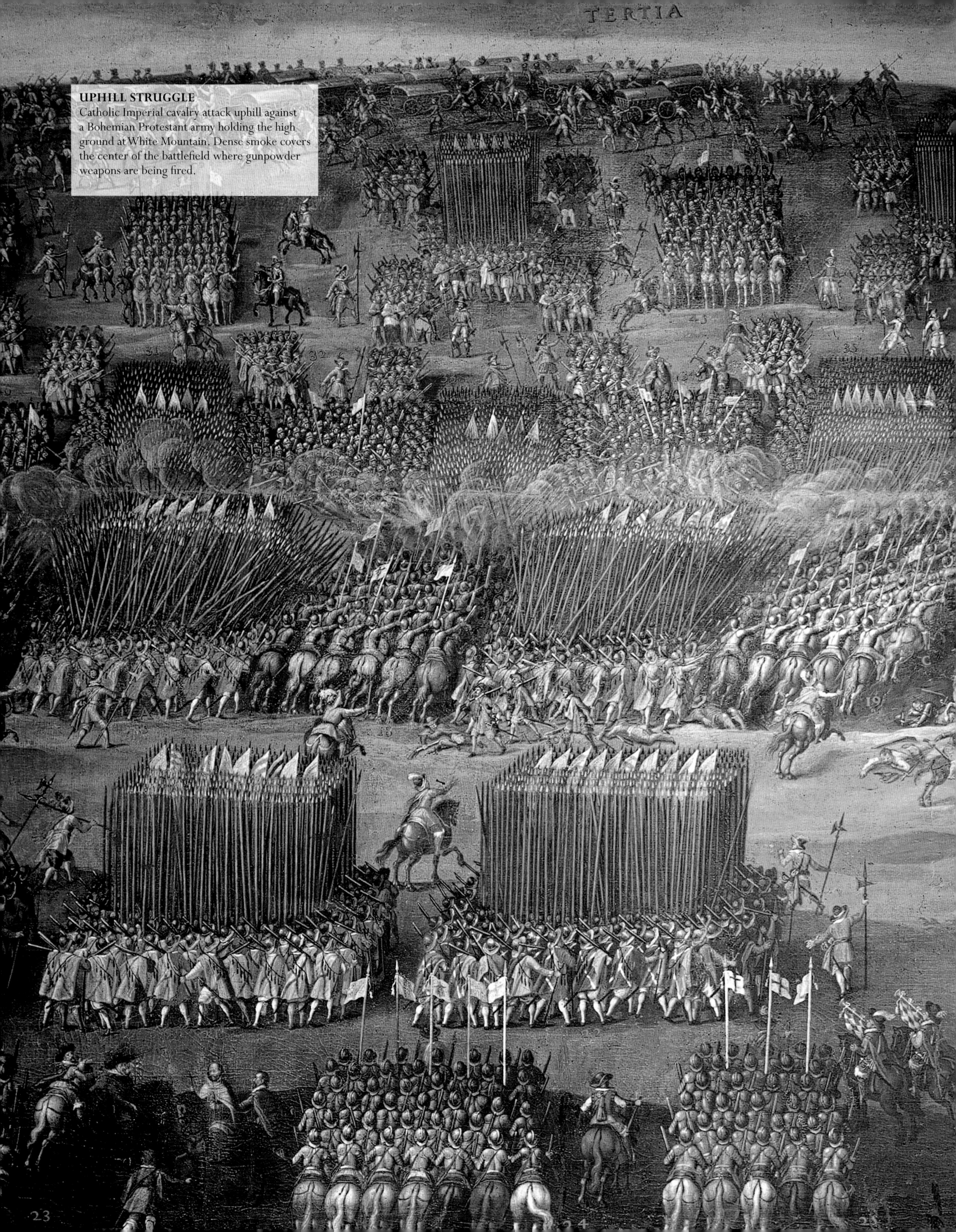

UPHILL STRUGGLE
Catholic Imperial cavalry attack uphill against a Bohemian Protestant army holding the high ground at White Mountain. Dense smoke covers the center of the battlefield where gunpowder weapons are being fired.

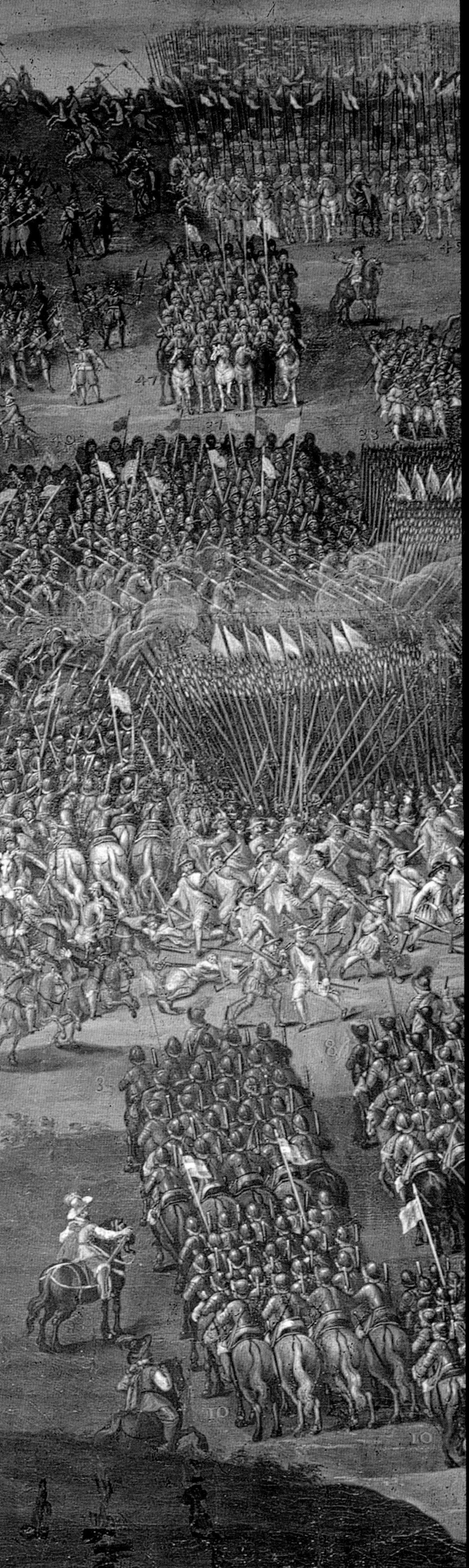

PIKE AND MATCHLOCK MUSKET

THE BATTLE OF WHITE MOUNTAIN

In the Thirty Years' War, fought in central Europe between 1618 and 1648, all armies used infantry armed with pikes and matchlock muskets. This distinctive form of warfare is exemplified by the Battle of White Mountain, an important encounter in the opening phase of the conflict.

The Battle of White Mountain was fought outside Prague on November 8, 1620, when Bohemian Protestants, rebelling against the authority of the Holy Roman Emperor, were confronted by a mix of Catholic Imperial forces. Both armies numbered between 20,000 and 30,000 men—quite substantial amounts by the standard of the time. Commanded by Christian of Anhalt, the Bohemian Protestants had taken an advantageous defensive position on high ground, but the Catholics, led by Johann Tserclaes, Count von Tilly, were more experienced and enjoyed superior morale.

PIKE SQUARES

On both sides the pikemen formed up in tightly packed squares, a practice that had been commonplace in European warfare for over a century. The smaller number of infantry equipped with firearms—predominantly matchlock muskets—were either positioned in a "sleeve" around the outside of the pike square, or formed into squads known as "horns" at the four corners of each square. Influenced by recent tactical developments initiated by the Dutch, the Protestants deployed their pikemen in shallower squares than the Catholics, with fewer lines from front to back. Like the infantry, the cavalry were deployed in tight formations. Each rider carried several wheellock pistols, preloaded in preparation for the battle. Their armor was less extensive and elaborate than that of a medieval knight, but the steel plate provided some protection, even against musket balls.

A SHORT ENGAGEMENT

The Protestants were first to take the offensive. The squares of pikemen advanced down the hill, directed by sergeants marching at the flanks with their halberds. Lowering their long, unwieldy weapons, the pikemen intended to engage the enemy infantry at close quarters with a "push of pike." The cavalry also came forward, riding knee-to-knee at a steady jog rather than a gallop. Following the established tactics of the time, each body of horsemen advanced toward an enemy pike square and discharged their pistols in a volley at as close a range as possible before turning away.

Count von Tilly, however, was confident in the quality of his troops and not inclined to stand on the defensive. He ordered his own cavalry and infantry aggressively up the slope. The Protestant musket troops were trained to fire in rolling volleys—the front row fired, then moved to the back to reload while the second row fired, and so on—to compensate for the slowness of reloading the matchlock, theoretically allowing a continuous fire to be maintained. But the Catholic squares advanced relentlessly forward through the thickening fog of gunpowder smoke, and their cavalry drove the Protestant horsemen into flight.

Unable to sustain an unsupported encounter with determined Catholic pikemen and pistol-armed cavalry at close range, the Protestants' pike squares began to break up and the pikemen were swiftly routed, fleeing for their lives. Almost 5,000 men were killed in the battle—a victory for the Catholics that was completed in less than two hours.

KEY **FIGURE**

GUSTAVUS ADOLPHUS
1594–1632

King Gustav II Adolf of Sweden, known as Gustavus Adolphus, was an innovative tactician who emphasized the central battlefield role of the cavalry charge. From 1630, he intervened in the Thirty Years' War in Germany. Initially victorious, he later died in battle at Lützen, in 1632.

▲ Proud and aggressive, Gustavus Adolphus was dubbed "The Lion of the North."

▶ **CAVALRY AND ARTILLERY**
The Battle of First Breitenfeld, in 1631, was a triumph for King Gustavus Adolphus of Sweden. It showed how effective cavalry could be when used alongside pike-and-musket infantry and artillery.

KEY DEVELOPMENT

FROM LANCE TO PISTOL

In the gunpowder age, cavalry lost their dominance on the battlefields of Europe. Fresh tactics had to be invented to restore a vital role to cavalry, working in combination with infantry and artillery.

At the start of the 16th century, European armies were still led by bodies of chivalrous knights, clad in elaborate armor, and employing the charge with couched lance (in the attacking position). Traditions such as jousting were also at the height of their popularity—as late as 1559, King Henri II of France died after a lance splintered against his visor in a joust. On the battlefield, however, infantry often prevailed, and horsemen with lances were rarely able to break up formations of pikemen.

Full plate armor was supposed to protect against firearms—breastplates were tested by the manufacturers by firing a ball at them—but this did not always work in practice. Its limitations were shown by the death of the renowned Chevalier de Bayard, in 1524, whose armor could not save him when he was struck by an arquebus ball. The following year, the French aristocratic cavalry suffered at the hands of arquebusiers at the Battle of Pavia, in the Italian War. From the 1550s, however, heavier, bulletproof armor began to appear.

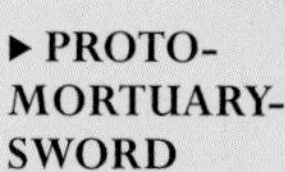

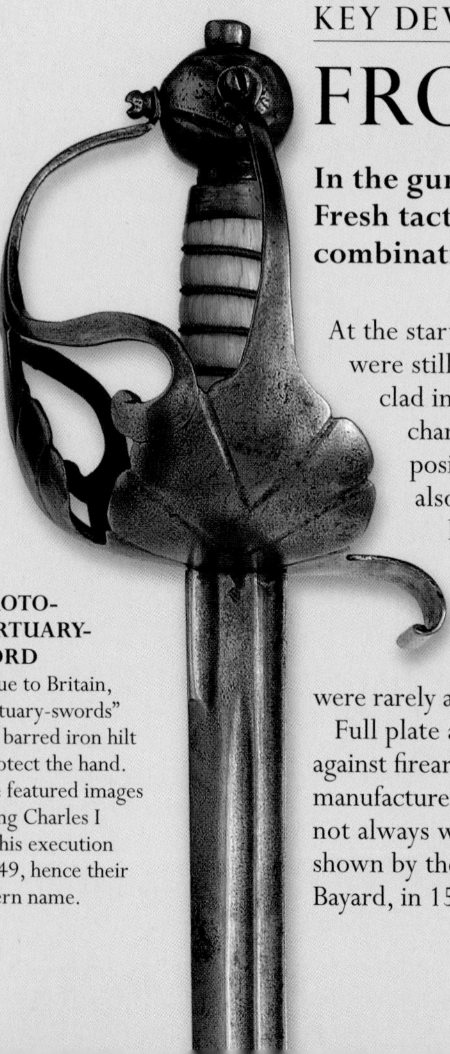

▶ **PROTO-MORTUARY-SWORD**
Unique to Britain, "mortuary-swords" had a barred iron hilt to protect the hand. Some featured images of King Charles I after his execution in 1649, hence their modern name.

A NEW ERA

With infantry rising in status and the lance approaching obsolescence, new technology and tactics began to emerge. Mounted troops were unable to use matchlocks because these required two hands to operate, and they needed one hand to control their horses. However, the invention of the self-igniting wheellock allowed cavalry to use pistols. In the 1540s, the Reiters, German mounted mercenaries, adopted firearms and reduced their armor to a helmet, cuirass, and arm defense. For use against pike squares, they invented the "caracole"—a

KEY **EVENTS**

1500–1650

- **1515** King François I of France wins the Battle of Marignano, with a charge by fully armored horsemen with couched lance.
- **c.1540** German cavalry, the Reiters, adopt the wheel-lock pistol as their main armament.
- **1562** Cavalry use the "caracole" tactic at the Battle of Dreux, during the French Wars of Religion.
- **1590** At the Battle of Ivry, Henry of Navarre triumphs using a cavalry charge with pistol and sword.
- **c.1600** European armies introduce dragoons—horsemen who fought dismounted with carbines (shorter muskets).
- **1610** Polish hussars defeat the Russians and Swedes at the battle of Klushino.
- **1630** In the Thirty Years' War, the Swedish combine cavalry with other arms.
- **1640s** In the English Civil Wars, Oliver Cromwell's Ironside cavalry fights in a disciplined close formation.

maneuver in which the horseman turned his horse to one side and then the other, enabling him to discharge a pistol to the left and right. The pistoleers rode at the pikemen in a column and fired at close range, each rank firing a volley and then retreating to reload as another line took its turn.

By the start of the 17th century, European cavalry had largely abandoned the lance, and also the percussive weapons that had been essential against full armor, such as the war-hammer. A cavalryman's armament consisted of a sword and a firearm, or sometimes several preloaded pistols. Companies of dragoons rode to the battlefield, but fought unmounted with firearms, like musketeers. Commanders were, however, unwilling to abandon the cavalry charge: it was seen as glamorous, and could still be decisive in battle.

In the hands of leaders such as King Gustavus Adolphus of Sweden, cavalry recovered its shock effect. Deployed on the flanks of infantry, horsemen would first charge the opposing cavalry. Then, after discharging their firearms, they would attack with swords drawn; breaking through the lines would allow them to overrun enemy cannon. Bodies of musketeers augmented the mounted firepower, combining to drive the opponent's cavalry from the field, exposing enemy infantry to attack.

> "God made them as **stubble to our swords**. We charged their regiments of foot with our horse, and **routed all** we charged"
>
> **OLIVER CROMWELL**, WRITTEN AFTER THE BATTLE OF MARSTON MOOR, 1644

◄ **CAVALRY CHARGE**
The English Civil War battle at Marston Moor, in July 1644, was won by the Parliamentarians through the success of Oliver Cromwell's cavalry, the Ironsides. Their charge scattered the Royalist horses, leaving their infantry open to attack.

CAVALRY ARMOR AND WEAPONS

As firearms became more common, armor was made thicker and its less important features were abandoned to reduce its weight. At the beginning of the 17th century, cavalry—armed with wheellock pistols and swords—still wore knee-length armor. New tactics such as the caracole, which involved successive ranks of riders discharging their pistols before riding to the rear to reload, were developed in order to defeat pikemen. By the middle of the century, most cavalry, now called harquebusiers due to the weapons they carried, wore only a heavy cuirass and an open helmet over a buff coat.

▲ FLEMISH CUIRASSIER'S HELMET

Date c.1600
Origin Holland
Material Iron, leather

Most helmets of this period were made in two halves that were joined along the comb. The bevor covering the chin and the peak pivoted at the same point. Attached to the peak was an almost flat plate covering the face; the plate was pierced for vision and breathing.

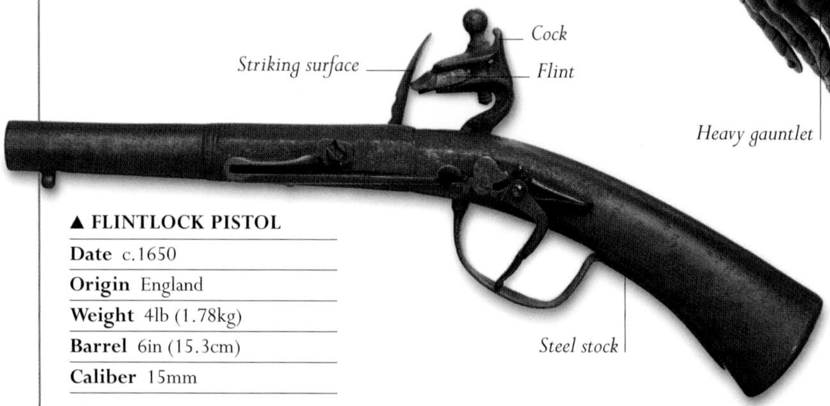

Cock
Striking surface
Flint
Steel stock

▲ FLINTLOCK PISTOL

Date c.1650
Origin England
Weight 4lb (1.78kg)
Barrel 6in (15.3cm)
Caliber 15mm

This all-steel pistol is interesting because its mechanism is exposed on the outside of the stock. A spring-loaded tumbler that runs through the stock governs the striking action of the cock when the trigger is pulled.

► FIELD ARMOR

Date c.1630
Origin Germany
Material Iron, leather

At the beginning of the 17th century, heavy cavalry cuirassiers wore three-quarter-length armors such as this, with the lower legs protected by boots. The lance was mostly abandoned in favor of a sword and a pair of pistols carried in holsters at the saddle.

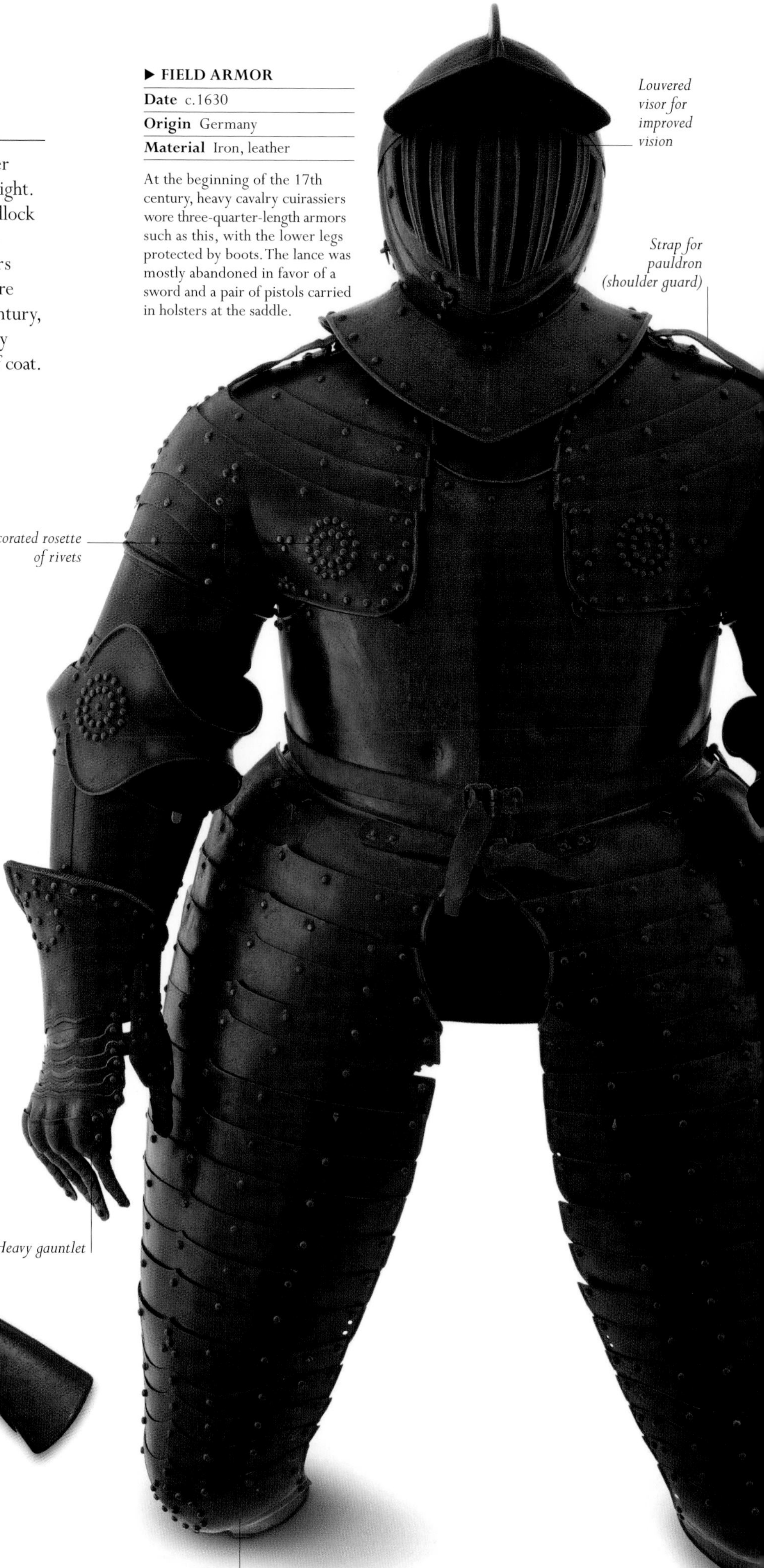

Louvered visor for improved vision
Strap for pauldron (shoulder guard)
Decorated rosette of rivets
Heavy gauntlet
Long tassets (thigh guards) to the knees

▶ BUFF COAT

Date c.1640

Origin England

Material Leather

These coats were made from cowhide about $\frac{1}{4}$in (3–4mm) thick. They provided fair protection from swords and long-range pistols. The lacing on this coat has been added for display: the original fastenings were hooks and eyes.

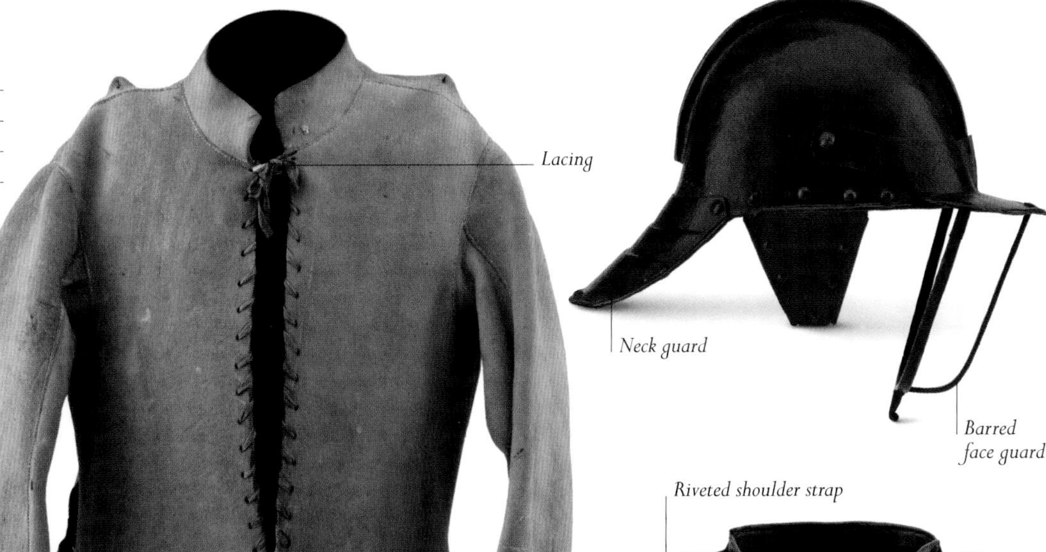

◀ TRIPLE-BARRED POT

Date c.1640

Origin England

Material Iron, leather

Troopers on both sides wore these simple helmets during the English Civil War. The two-piece skull is fitted with a neck guard—embossed to simulate lames—a pivoting peak with a barred face guard, cheekpieces, and a neck guard.

◀ HARQUEBUSIER'S CUIRASS

Date c.1640

Origin England

Material Iron, leather

This simple cuirass was worn over a buff coat. The breastplate was thick—sometimes double-layered—and bulletproof. The backplate was thinner, but robust enough to resist blade thrusts in close-combat skirmishes.

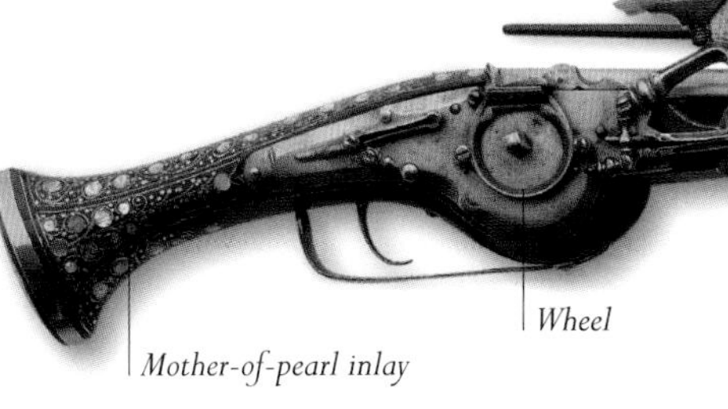

▲ WHEELLOCK PISTOL

Date 17th century

Origin Italy

Military wheellock pistols were expensive and used only by cavalry. Pairs of these pistols were carried in holsters in front of the saddle. This example is more decorative than most, having mother-of-pearl inlay in the stock.

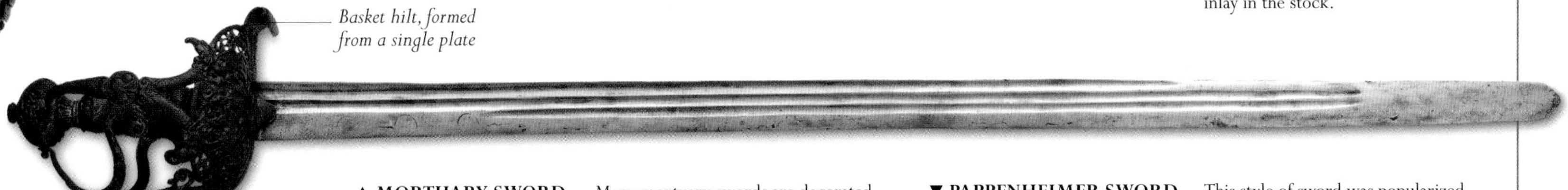

Basket hilt, formed from a single plate

▲ MORTUARY SWORD

Date 1640

Origin England

Weight 2lb (0.89kg)

Length $36\frac{1}{4}$in (92.1cm)

Many mortuary swords are decorated with a chiseled portrait head amid foliage—the head supposedly of the executed King Charles I—giving the swords their name. They were used by both sides in the English Civil War.

▼ PAPPENHEIMER SWORD

Date 1625–50

Origin Northern Europe

Weight $2\frac{1}{2}$lb (1.17kg)

Length $4\frac{1}{4}$ft (1.28m)

This style of sword was popularized by Count Pappenheim, a Bavarian field marshal in the Thirty Years' War. It is characterized by the pommel, the complex side bars, and the pierced plate or shell guard on either side of the blade.

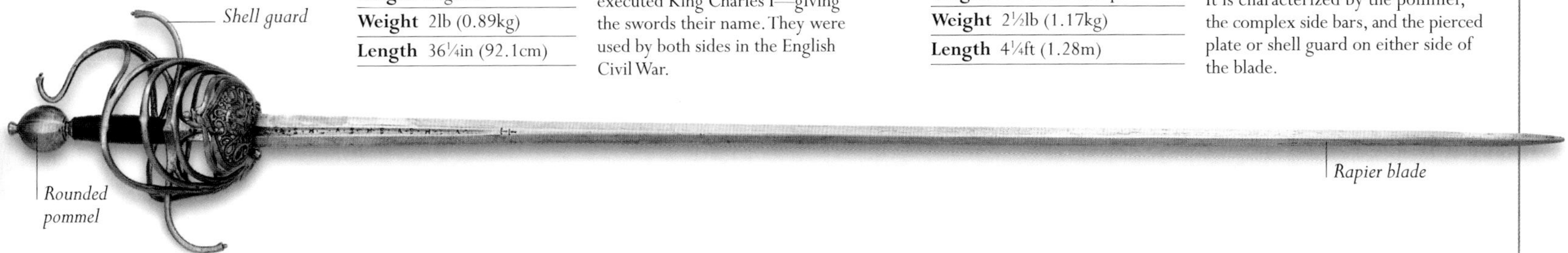

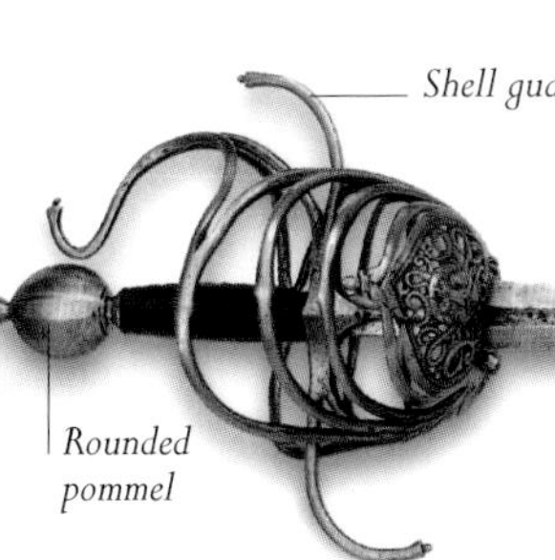

KEY DEVELOPMENT

THE ISLAMIC EMPIRES AT WAR

The Muslim empires of the Ottomans, Mughals, and Safavids ruled a large swathe of Eurasia in the 16th and 17th centuries. Their armies combined Asian tribal heritage, reflected in the importance of horsemen, with gunpowder weapons.

The Mughals originated from Central Asia. Led by Zahir-ud-Din Babur, they conquered Afghanistan and northern India in the early 16th century, founding the Mughal Empire. Under Babur's successors, Mughal rule extended over the Indian subcontinent through near-constant campaigning.

The Mughal emperors recruited nomadic tribesmen from Central Asia, who fought as light horsemen with powerful composite bows. The army also absorbed the forces of conquered Indian states such as the Rajputs—aristocratic Hindu warriors armed with swords and daggers. Other Indian nobles supplied peasant infantry from their lands.

Mughal foot soldiers carried matchlock muskets, made by imitating foreign models; they also used brass and bronze cannon. In battle, musket- or spear-armed infantry lined up alongside field guns to form a block in front of the commanders, who sat on elephants that served as mobile command posts. Light horsemen on the flanks rode forward to shower the enemy with arrows, before the armored cavalry in the center charged with mace, sword, and lance. Their engineers built roads and mined under walls during sieges. Their main weakness was their infantry, a low-status, undisciplined rabble.

THE OTTOMANS

The Ottoman Turks were originally from Central Asia but, by 1500, they had ruled most of Turkey and the Balkans for over 100 years. In the 16th century, they extended their empire into Hungary, west Asia to the Persian border, Egypt, and North Africa.

The Ottoman army comprised infantry, cavalry, and artillery. Their elite infantry were Janissaries, seized as children from Christian families in the Balkans and raised as Muslim slaves. They carried firearms, and formed a disciplined corps of musket troops as part of the sultan's household guard. The household troops also featured a core of cavalry, the *sipahis*, who served in return for the right to raise rent from land. With mail-and-plate armor, lances, javelins, and swords, they were supported by lighter horsemen with composite bows, known as *akinji*, who acted as scouts, raiders, and skirmishers. The power of Ottoman cannon was famous, and their artillery boasted almost 3,000 gunners by the late 16th century. Their navy, meanwhile, dominated the eastern Mediterranean.

THE SAFAFIDS

The Safavids came to power in Persia in 1501. At first, their army consisted of tribal horsemen, the Kizilbash. Lacking firearms, they were defeated by the Ottomans along the border of their two empires. But the Safavid monarch Shah Abbas (ruled 1587–1629), created a standing army that combined cavalry with musket-armed infantry and gunpowder artillery, drawing on European expertise. This more balanced force kept the Safavids in power until 1732.

▲ **MUGHAL WAR ELEPHANT**
Elephants were widely used in Mughal armies. Commanders rode them into combat, and used them both as heavy cavalry and as vantage points from which to survey and direct the battle.

◄ **OTTOMAN JANISSARIES**
Elite Janissaries head for war on horseback to the beat of drums. Ottoman soldiers were noted for their good discipline and morale.

KEY **FIGURE**

SULEYMAN I
1494–1566

Suleyman the Magnificent ruled the Ottoman Empire from 1520. He alternated campaigns in Europe with attacks on Safavid Persia, and his triumphs included the conquest of Hungary in 1526, and the capture of Baghdad in 1534. He failed, however, in a bid to take the island of Malta in 1565.

▲ In his younger years, Suleyman was an imposing figure, known for his chivalry as well as his valour. He later suffered from poor health.

> "I am the **sultan of sultans**, the sovereign of sovereigns, the **shadow of god** on earth"

SULEYMAN I, IN A LETTER TO THE KING OF FRANCE, 1536

◄ **MUGHAL CHARGE**
The armored cavalry of Mughal ruler Akbar the Great charges its enemies in the 1560s, using swords and lances. Akbar was fond of war elephants, with 5,000 in his army, although they are reputed to have been panicked by gunpowder weapons.

KEY **EVENTS**

1500s–1700s

■ **1514–17** Ottoman Turks defeat the Persian Safavids at Chaldiran, and the Egyptian Mamluks at Raydaniya, exploiting the use of gunpowder weapons against opponents who lack them.

■ **1526** Led by Babur, the Mughals defeat the Sultan of Delhi at the battle of Panipat, their cannon terrifying the Sultan's force of war elephants.

■ **1571** Ottoman war galleys, short of gunpowder weapons, are defeated by a Christian fleet at Lepanto (see pp.154–55).

■ **1587** In Persia, Shah Abbas I begins a successful modernization of the Safavid armed forces, employing European military experts.

■ **1658–1707** The Mughal Empire reaches its greatest extent under the rule of Aurangzeb, gradually declining after his death.

■ **1683** The Ottoman defeat at the Siege of Vienna marks the beginning of a sharp and irreversible decline in the success of the Ottoman army.

OTTOMAN ARMOR AND WEAPONS

At its height, during the 16th century, the Ottoman Empire extended from modern-day Algeria in the west to the Caspian Sea in the east, pushing north into Central Europe. The Janissaries, a well-paid and well-equipped infantry corps, were credited with the empire's success. They were primarily archers, who later fought with guns and their characteristic swords (*yatagans*). The cavalry was divided into two groups: the *akinji*, the lightly armored archers whose primary roles were reconnaissance and harrying of the enemy; and the *sipahis*, the heavy cavalry, who wore mail and plate and rode armored horses, fighting with bows, lances, maces, and axes.

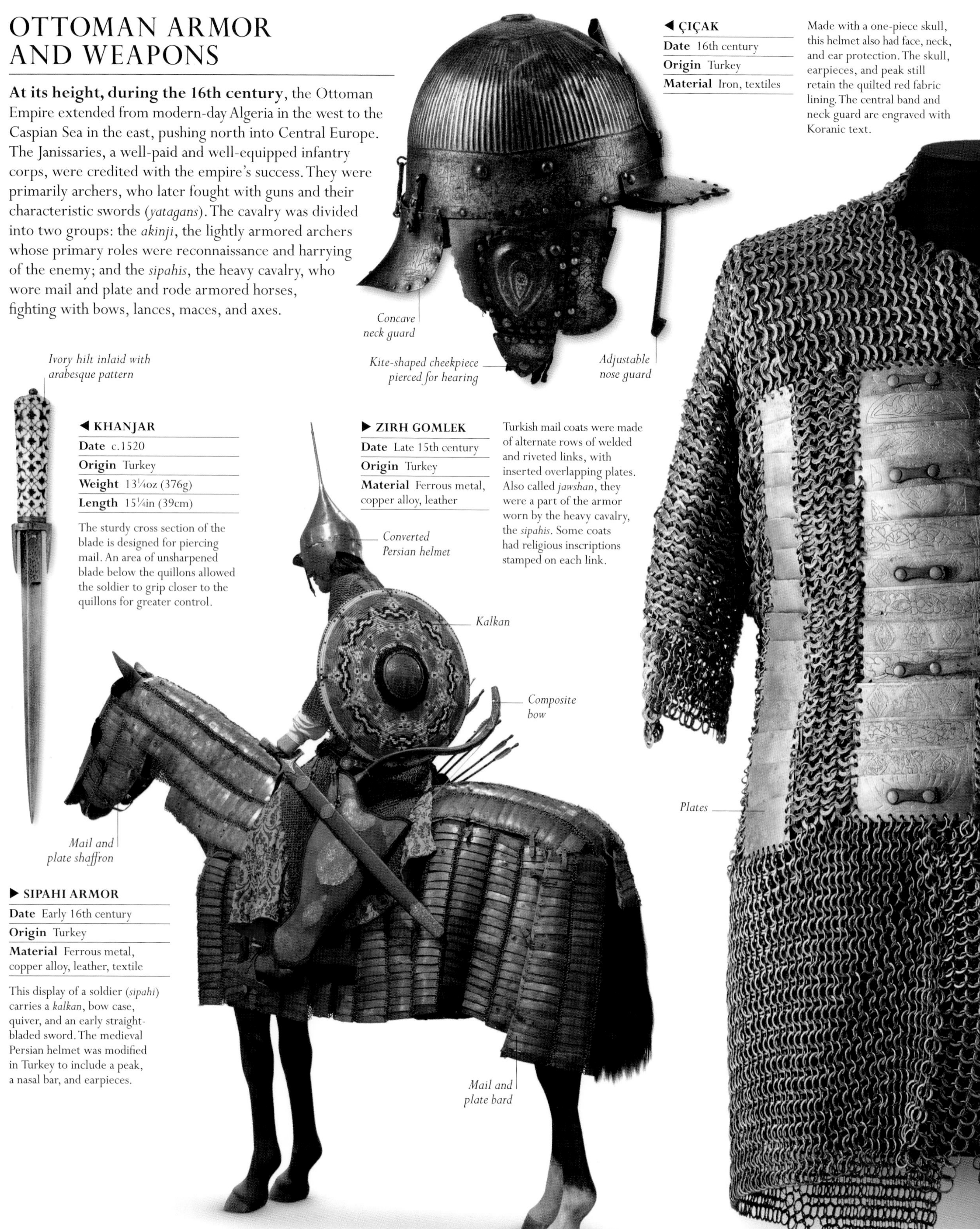

◀ **ÇIÇAK**

Date 16th century
Origin Turkey
Material Iron, textiles

Made with a one-piece skull, this helmet also had face, neck, and ear protection. The skull, earpieces, and peak still retain the quilted red fabric lining. The central band and neck guard are engraved with Koranic text.

◀ **KHANJAR**

Date c.1520
Origin Turkey
Weight 13¼oz (376g)
Length 15¼in (39cm)

The sturdy cross section of the blade is designed for piercing mail. An area of unsharpened blade below the quillons allowed the soldier to grip closer to the quillons for greater control.

▶ **ZIRH GOMLEK**

Date Late 15th century
Origin Turkey
Material Ferrous metal, copper alloy, leather

Turkish mail coats were made of alternate rows of welded and riveted links, with inserted overlapping plates. Also called *jawshan*, they were a part of the armor worn by the heavy cavalry, the *sipahis*. Some coats had religious inscriptions stamped on each link.

▶ **SIPAHI ARMOR**

Date Early 16th century
Origin Turkey
Material Ferrous metal, copper alloy, leather, textile

This display of a soldier (*sipahi*) carries a *kalkan*, bow case, quiver, and an early straight-bladed sword. The medieval Persian helmet was modified in Turkey to include a peak, a nasal bar, and earpieces.

▶ **KILIC**

Date 1625
Origin Turkey
Weight 26½oz (750g)
Length 28in (71cm)

The characteristic sword of the Ottomans, the *kilic*, with its enlarged point section, was designed for slicing. The hilt is made of horn, while the quillon assembly is of gilded copper. The blade is chiseled and inlaid at the forte (the strong part of the blade).

"Pistol grip" pommel

Forte

Chiseled inlaid decoration

Curved steel blade

Mail

Side plate with holes for straps

◀ **KORAZIN**

Date c.1656
Origin Turkey

This mail and plate cuirass, worn over a mail coat, had plates around the neck and back. The front and back were fastened together with straps and buckles. It was worn with a helmet, tubular plate arm guards, and thigh guards.

Cane wrapped in colored silks

▶ **KALKAN**

Date 17th century
Origin Turkey
Weight 4lb (1.9kg)
Diameter 20½in (52.5cm)

This shield is made from a spiral of cane with a central iron boss. The four inner rivets were for the handgrips; the six outer rivets were for straps that held the shield to the body.

Handgrip rivets

▼ **MIQUELET RIFLE**

Date 18th century
Origin Turkey
Weight 5¼lb (2.39kg)
Barrel 31in (78.5cm)
Caliber 16mm

By the 17th century, the Ottoman army had adopted a version of the Mediterranean miquelet lock for its firearms. Most of these guns were of high quality, with rifled barrels and elaborately inlaid stocks. The lock and mounts of this example are lavishly decorated with gold inlay, while the barrel bands are silver.

Ball trigger

▼ **GURZ**

Date 18th century
Origin Turkey
Weight 2½lb (1.16kg)
Length 27½in (70cm)

Made of iron, this mace has a spirally fluted hollow shaft and a ribbed head, surmounted by a gilt finial. It was primarily a horseman's weapon.

Hollow shaft

Ribbed head

SULEYMAN AT MOHACS
Sultan Suleyman the Magnificent, seated on a white horse, observes his gunners firing their cannon and his Janissaries in action with their arquebuses. The Ottomans showed far greater tactical subtlety than their Christian opponents.

THE BATTLE OF MOHACS

In 1526, Sultan Suleyman the Magnificent of the Turkish Ottoman Empire led a powerful army into the territory of King Louis II of Hungary and Bohemia. Meeting Louis' army at Mohacs, Süleyman's forces resisted with skillfully deployed weaponry and traditional fighting skills.

When Suleyman's army marched out of Constantinople on April 16, 1526, its goal was no secret. Expanding his empire in southeastern Europe, Süleyman had already taken the Serbian capital, Belgrade, in 1521. Hungary was the next stepping stone toward his ultimate goal, the Habsburg city of Vienna. King Louis had time to prepare his defenses during the Turks' slow progress north. Appeals to other Christian leaders for military aid fell on deaf ears, however, and even the Hungarian nobles who owed Louis allegiance were reluctant to accept his authority.

Through a wet summer that made progress arduous, Suleyman's army advanced along the bank of the Danube, accompanied by a fleet of supply boats. On August 14 they reached the Drava River, a tributary of the Danube that formed Hungary's natural border. Louis' best policy might have been to defend the river crossing here, but the Ottoman forces crossed the rain-swollen flood unmolested. It took them five days to move 300 cannon and an estimated 50,000 to 100,000 men across a skillfully constructed bridge of boats. Louis, meanwhile, awaited the invaders near Mohacs, blocking their road to his capital, Buda.

KNIGHTS AND CANNON

The battle took place on August 29. Most of Louis' army consisted of armored knights, although he also had a significant number of cannon. In the tradition of Christian Europe, he intended to gamble on the shock impact of his charging knights to win the day. Suleyman arranged his variegated forces in anticipation of this. His impressive array of cannon were tied together to form a barrier across the battlefield, reinforced by the Ottomans' elite Janissary infantry armed with arquebuses (small-bore matchlock weapons). In front of this line of gunpowder weapons he placed his own heavy cavalry, the *sipahi*. They were less well armored than their Christian counterparts, and many were still armed with the composite bow of their Central Asian ancestors. On the flanks, the light irregular horsemen, the *akinji*, awaited the chance to harass, pursue, and plunder. The sultan himself took up position in the rear, surrounded by his household cavalry.

The Hungarians opened the battle by firing their cannon. Then the armored knights, with King Louis in their midst, thundered forward toward the Ottoman army. Most likely following a prearranged tactical plan, the *sipahi* melted away in front of the knights' onslaught, revealing the line of cannon behind them. As the knights bore down upon the muzzles of the guns, the Ottomans opened fire. Amid a carnage of slaughtered horses and fallen riders the charge was brought to a halt. The Ottoman cavalry then launched a counterattack, and a savage mêlée ensued. Meanwhile the *akinji* had stolen around to the Christian rear, and were plundering the camp and massacring the camp followers.

Louis' army disintegrated. The individual survivors sought to escape through woods and swamps, and the king himself died while fleeing—his body was not found for months. Buda was occupied and Hungary became an Ottoman territory.

MUGHAL ARMOR AND WEAPONS

The Mughal Empire had its beginnings in 1526, when steppe nomads from Central Asia swept into India from the northwest, occupying much of the subcontinent by the late 17th century. They were heavily influenced by Persia, and brought with them similar weapons, including guns. The Mughal army was divided into cavalry, infantry, and artillery. In similar style to the Mamluks, the heavy cavalry wore mail and plate armor and rode armored horses, fighting with bow, lance, and sword. Armored elephants saw limited use because they were unreliable and difficult to control. The infantry fought chiefly with guns and swords, but lacked a coordinated command structure, which limited their effectiveness.

Scalloped plates protect the skull

Heaviest links over chest

▼ ELEPHANT ARMOR

Date c.1600

Origin India

Material Ferrous metal, copper alloy, leather

Panels of mail and plate were used for elephant armor. These were inset with plaques that were decorated with flowers, fish, and running elephants. A pair of swords could be sheathed above the tusks.

▲ TOP

Date 17th century

Origin India

Material Ferrous metal, textile (lining fragment)

Made of horizontal bands of vertically arranged plates joined by mail, this helmet originally had a heavily padded lining. The triangular section of mail hung in front of the face.

▶ ZEREH BAGTAR

Date Early 17th century

Origin India

Material Ferrous metal, copper alloy, leather, red silk, gold threads

A Mughal horse-warrior wore a plated cuirass combined with a coat of mail that reached his knees. It was often zinc-plated to prevent rusting and damage to the padded garment worn underneath. Although it did not offer the level of protection of an all-over plate armor, it was relatively light and flexible.

▼ TALWAR

Date	Early 17th century
Origin	India
Weight	2¼lb (1.04kg)
Length	37¾in (95.7cm)

The carved ivory grip is different from the usual iron Indo-Muslim hilts fitted to *talwars*, but is typical of the luxurious tastes of the Mughal court. The early blades, such as this, were slightly less curved than later models.

Brocade facings

Iron quillon block decorated with gold koftgari *(inlay work)*

Ivory grip carved as a lotus bud

Wootz steel blade

▶ DHAL

Date	18th century
Origin	India
Weight	5½lb (2.5kg)
Diameter	23½in (60cm)

This domed shield was made of thick rawhide dried in a mold and coated with lacquer to keep the moisture out. The four iron bosses, which secure the handgrips on the inside of the shield, are decorated with gold *koftgari* (inlay work).

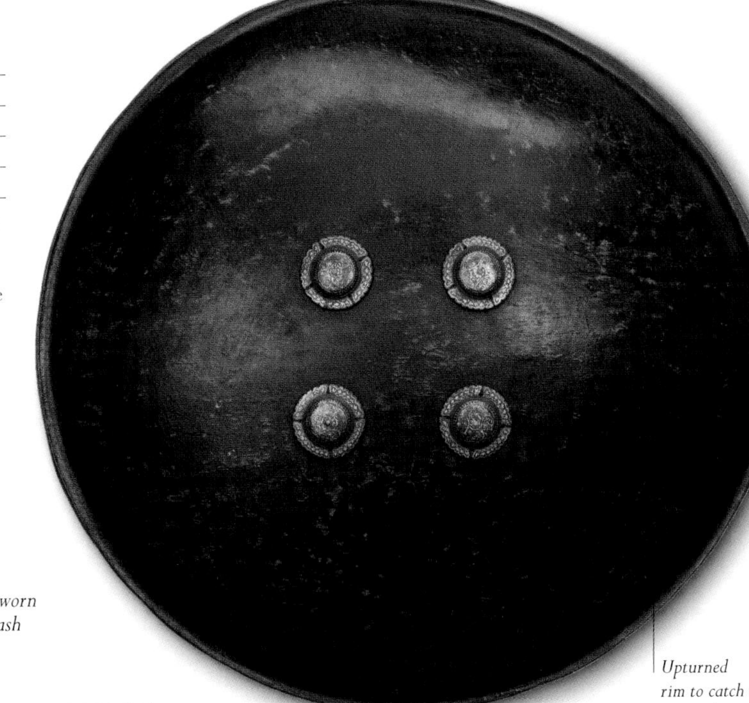

Upturned rim to catch a weapon's point

Side-bar

Cross-handles

Scabbard worn through sash

Religious inscription in gold

Thickened mail-piercing blade tip

◀ KATAR

Date	1760
Origin	India
Weight	18½oz (525g)
Length	17½in (44.6cm)

The tip of the curved blade of this dagger is thickened to pierce mail, while the sunken panels have been etched to show the structure of the wootz steel. The *katar* was held by gripping the cross-handles, with the side-bars extending on either side of the wrist.

Solid ends, called siyahs *in Persian*

Grip

Limb

◀ KAMAN

Date	18th century
Origin	North India
Weight	19½oz (550g)
Length	(Strung) 37½in (95cm)

Mughal bows were made from horn and sinew glued onto a wooden core. Unstrung, they bent the opposite way to when strung. The ends of the limbs were solid, acting as levers to assist in drawing.

Ivory nock

Fletching

▶ TARKASH AND TIR

Date	18th century
Origin	India
Weight	25oz (710g); (Arrow) ¾oz (18g)
Length	(Arrow) 28¾in (73cm)

This embroidered velvet quiver (*tarkash*) was worn on the right hip, balanced by a matching bowcase on the left. The painted bamboo arrows (*tir*) were fitted with ivory nocks, three low-cut fletchings, and armor-piercing heads.

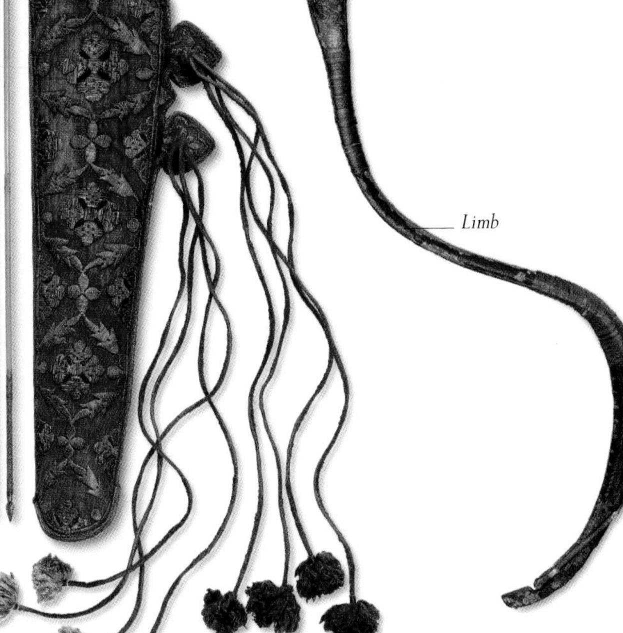

Velvet hilt pad

Gilded basket hilt

Reinforcement decorated with floral pattern

▶ KHANDA

Date	Early 19th century
Origin	India
Weight	2¾lb (1.3kg)
Length	36¾in (93.3cm)

The blade of this sword is made of wootz steel, which could only be produced in limited quantities. When hammered out into a sword, it was of necessity rather thin and had to be reinforced to stiffen it. This sword was made for the Great Exhibition of 1851.

KEY **EVENTS**

16TH–17TH CENTURY

■ **1543** Portuguese voyagers land in southern Japan and introduce the matchlock arquebus, which is quickly copied by Japanese craftsmen.

■ **1592** Korean admiral Yi Sun-sin inflicts a crushing defeat on Japanese naval forces at the Battle of Hansando, leading Japan to abandon its first invasion of Korea.

■ **1598** A second Japanese invasion of Korea fails, after fierce fighting on land, and naval defeats at Myongyang and Noryang.

■ **1600** Victory in the Battle of Sekigahara enables Tokugawa Ieyasu to take supreme power in Japan. He founds the Tokugawa shogunate.

■ **c.1615** Jurchen warrior Nurhaci creates the Manchu Banner system, a military organization that proves highly effective against the Chinese.

■ **1644** Allowed passage through the Great Wall by a renegade Chinese general, the Manchu occupy Beijing and establish the Qing dynasty.

■ **1673–83** Emperor Kangxi of China defeats rebel warlords in the War of the Three Feudatories, and against Ming loyalists on Taiwan.

KEY DEVELOPMENT

CONFLICT IN EAST ASIA

In the 16th and 17th centuries, a number of large-scale wars were fought throughout Japan, Korea, China, and southeast Asia. Many of these conflicts used innovative technology, including early gunpowder weapons and heavily armored ironclad ships.

In Japan, the era from 1467 to 1615 is known as the Sengoku Period, "the age of the country at war," during which powerful regional warlords, the *daimyo*, clashed regularly. The most ambitious of them—such as Oda Nobunaga and Toyotomi Hideyoshi—aspired to unite Japan under single rule, a goal eventually achieved by Tokugawa Ieyasu, founder of the long-lived Tokugawa shogunate.

THE SAMURAI AND THE ASHIGARU

The samurai warriors of the warlords' armies were shifting away from their origins as mounted archers, in favor of fighting on foot, using spears and swords. Their main sword was the two-handed *katana*, worn blade-upward so that a samurai could draw it and deliver a cut in a single, sweeping movement. Although individual samurai became legendary for their fighting prowess, the peasant foot soldiers, the *ashigaru*, were also a notable force. After earlier experiments with Chinese firearms, from the 1540s onward, the *ashigaru* adopted the European matchlock arquebus, which could be used to great effect by trained, disciplined squads. Castle-building was another important feature of the period, and many elaborate stone-and-wood structures were constructed at this time, often with additional outworks.

GUNPOWDER AND WARSHIPS

During the 1590s, Japan attempted to invade Korea twice, led by Toyotomi Hideyoshi. Chinese forces helped defend Korea, and successfully repulsed the invaders. Korean and Chinese land forces had superior gunpowder weapons, typified by the Korean *hwacha*, a multiple rocket launcher capable of firing batches of a hundred incendiary rockets. The main reason for Korean victory, however, was their naval prowess, which was at its peak in 1592–98, during which time Korean admiral Yi Sun-sin won a series of battles with a fleet of cannon-armed, oar-powered ships—the *panokseon* and the iron-armored *kobukson* (turtle ships).

After 1615, the Tokugawa shogunate ended Japan's era of civil war; in China, however, the 17th century was still a period of major conflict. The Manchu, a federation of Jurchen tribes north

▼ A KOREAN TURTLE SHIP
Used against the Japanese in the 1590s, Korea's turtle ships had their upper decks enclosed with iron plates and spikes, while cannon fired through portholes.

"As one man can **defeat ten men**, so can a thousand men **defeat ten thousand**"

MIYAMOTO MUSASHI, *THE BOOK OF FIVE RINGS*, c.1645

of the Great Wall, created a military organization known as the Eight Banners. In 1644, the decline of the Chinese Ming dynasty led to political chaos that the Manchu exploited, seizing Beijing and establishing the Qing dynasty. It took 40 years of warfare, however, to extend Manchu rule over the whole of China. Originally steppe cavalry fighting with bows, swords, and spears, the Manchu had to adapt to the use of mass peasant armies, naval warfare on river and sea, and an array of Chinese gunpowder weaponry. However, the capture of Taiwan in 1683 by means of a seaborne invasion marked the final triumph of Emperor Kangxi of the Manchu over the Ming loyalists.

In southeast Asia, meanwhile, the warring kingdoms of Burma and Siam were maintaining a very different tradition of warfare, in which armies were based around units of massed war elephants used as a shock force.

▲ EMPEROR KANGXI'S NAVY
The Manchu Emperor Kangxi completed the defeat of resistance to his rule on the island of Taiwan with a victory for the Chinese navy at the Battle of Penghu in 1683.

◄ THE BATTLE OF NAGASHINO
Fought in Japan in 1575, the Battle of Nagashino is famous for warlord Oda Nobunaga's use of firearms. Protected by a wooden palisade, a mass of Oda's foot soldiers firing arquebuses in rotating volleys shattered the charging cavalry of Takeda Katsuyori.

KEY **FIGURE**

TOYOTOMI HIDEYOSHI

1536–98

Japanese warlord Toyotomi Hideyoshi rose from peasant stock to prominence in the service of Oda Nobunaga. After Oda—by then the most powerful man in Japan—died in 1582, Hideyoshi won succession. Despite two failed invasions of Korea, he remained in power up to his death.

▲ During his reign, Hideyoshi tried to pacify Japan by banning peasants from bearing arms.

EAST ASIAN SWORDS

The earliest Chinese swords were straight and double-edged, but single-edged swords date at least as far back as the late Han dynasty (206BCE–220CE), their blade shape evolving into a variety of forms. At first, the Japanese imported swords from China, but by 1000CE, they had perfected their own style of the single-edged, curved blade that did not materially change for the next 1,000 years. Japanese blades were designed to be removable from the rest of the sword, enabling the same blade to be worn for generations, becoming an heirloom within a family. The blades were reset in new mounts, consisting of the *tsuka* (hilt or grip), *tsuba* (hand guard), and *saya* (scabbard). Some swords, particularly short swords and daggers, had pockets in the scabbard for a *kozuka* (a small knife) and a *kogai*, a skewerlike implement for dressing the hair.

Tang

▲ KATANA BLADE

Date	15th century
Origin	Japan
Weight	22¼oz (630g)
Length	34¼in (87cm)

This *katana* blade has been removed from its mountings. It was secured into the wooden hilt by the taper of the tang, and by a bamboo peg, which passed through the hole in the tang and corresponding holes in the hilt.

▶ DAO

Date	17th century
Origin	China
Weight	18¼oz (520g)
Length	25in (64cm)

This short, single-edged sword or *dao* has a near-straight *yanmaodao* (goose quill) blade. Primarily a cavalry weapon, its single edge was used for cutting and its point for thrusting.

Disk-shaped hand guard

Rayskin-covered grip

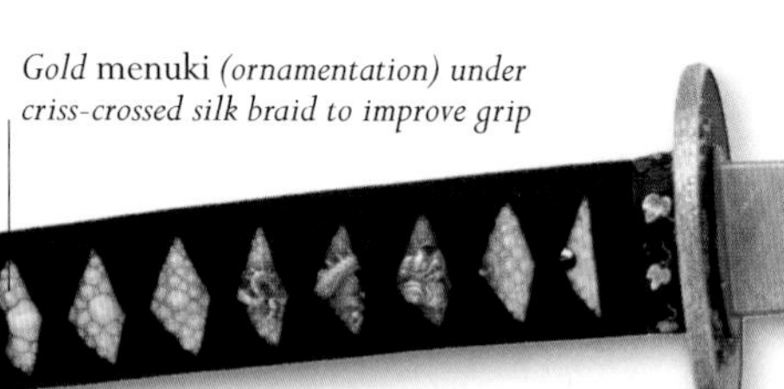

Shinogi-ji *or the area above ridge*

WAKIZASHI

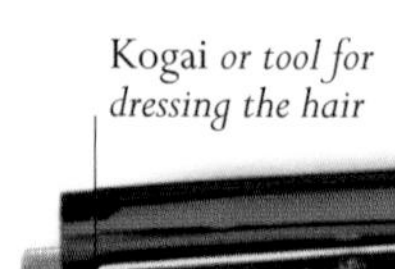

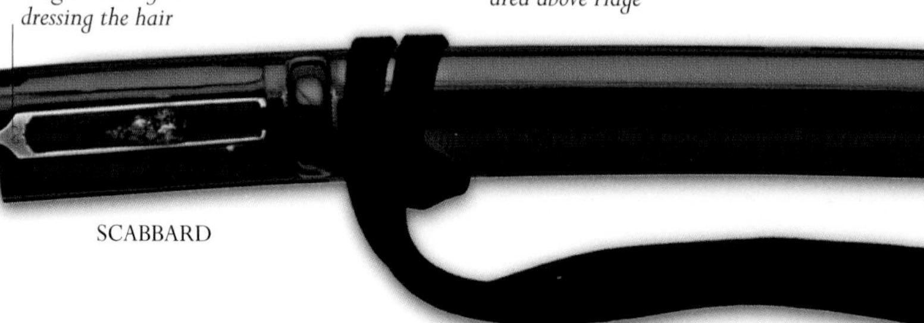

SCABBARD

▲ WAKIZASHI

Date	c.1640
Origin	Japan
Weight	17oz (480g)
Length	21in (53.4cm)

The samurai wore the *wakizashi* (short sword) as an accompaniment to the *katana*. It was also the only sword permitted to be worn by other social groups.

Hole for a peg that held the blade in the hilt

Nakago *or tang*

KATANA BLADE

Sageo *(heavy silk braid) tied the sword into the belt*

Tsuba *(hand guard) of iron or soft metal*

Tsuka *(wooden hilt) wrapped in rayskin under silk braid*

Koi guchi *or the mouth of the scabbard*

BLADE IN MOUNT

▲ EDO PERIOD KATANA BLADE AND MOUNT

Date	17th century
Origin	Japan
Weight	2¾lb (1.3kg)
Length	3½ft (1.06m)

During the 16th century, samurai began to wear an *uchiganata* (striking sword) thrust edge upwards through their belt; it was easier to draw than the earlier slung *tachi* (long sword). This style of sword came to be known as *katana*, and could be worn only by the samurai class.

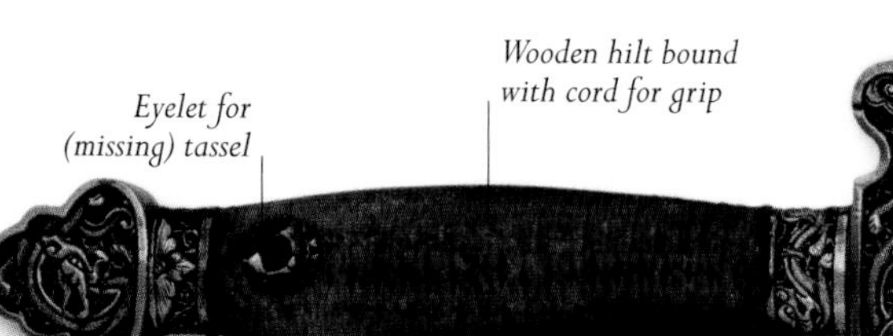

Shinogi *(ridge)*

Menuki *(ornamentation) in the form of Shimazu heraldry*

▶ TANTO

Date	1792
Origin	Japan
Length	11¼in (28.5cm)

A *tanto* was a sword or dagger with a blade less than 12in (31cm) in length. It was often worn as an alternative to a *wakizashi*. This example is black-lacquered, with the scabbard housing a *kogai* on the outer face and a *kozuka* at the rear.

TANTO

SCABBARD

Blade is a composite of iron and steel

KOGAI

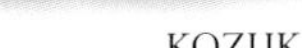

KOZUKA

Kissaki *or point section*

Black lacquered wooden saya *(scabbard)*

▶ TSUBA

Date	19th century
Origin	Japan
Material	Iron, gold
Diameter	2¾– 3in (6.5–7cm)

Originally, *tsuba* (hand guards) were relatively plain, becoming more decorative later. The example with a silhouetted goose flying in front of the moon and clouds (left) is enhanced with gold overlay, while the *tsuba* with a floral motif (right) is chiselled out of an iron plate.

Decoration probably by Owari school

Signed by master swordsmith Masayoshi

Blade more than 23½in (60.6cm) long

Kissaki *or point section*

Lacquered wooden saya *(scabbard)*

▼ JIAN

Date	19th century
Origin	China
Weight	33½oz (950g)
Length	34½in (88cm)

Straight, double-edged swords were used in China for over 2,500 years, and were regarded as one of the four traditional weapons. The blades were made of hard steel, with a softer steel welded to each side. Many had a medial ridge.

Medial ridge

EAST ASIAN WEAPONS

Staff weapons, the bow and the gun—rather than the sword—were often the primary weapons of Japanese and Chinese military forces. Despite their technological advances, east Asian armies' firepower was initially limited: although the Chinese had invented gunpowder, it was reintroduced in a more effective form in the Middle East and Europe in the 16th century. Around the same time, in 1543, the matchlock gun arrived in Japan, and was used in large numbers; however, during the peaceful Edo period (1603–1868), gun-making in Japan all but ceased.

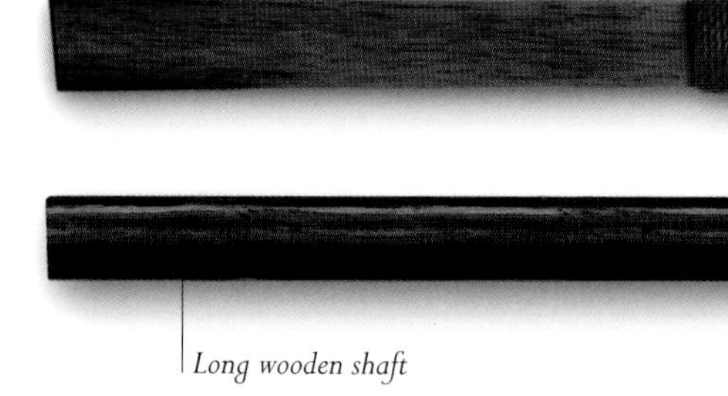

Long wooden shaft

► **YARI**

Date	16th century
Origin	Japan
Length	3¼–19½ft (1–6m)

The *yari* was a straight-headed spear. Its length ranged from 3ft (1m) to 20ft (6m). The longer versions were called *omi no yari*, while the shorter ones were known as *mochi* or *tae yari*. The longest versions were carried by foot troops, and the shorter versions by samurai.

Brass-bound shaft

Hand guard of brass

Hook on rear edge of blade

▲ **GUANDAO**

Date	19th century
Origin	China
Weight	11½lb (5.2kg)
Length	8¼ft (2.52m)

Staff weapons of this type, resembling European glaives, had been in use for centuries in China. Made in the style of a 16th-century weapon, this example has a thin, flexible blade issuing from a cast-brass guard that resembles a dragon's head.

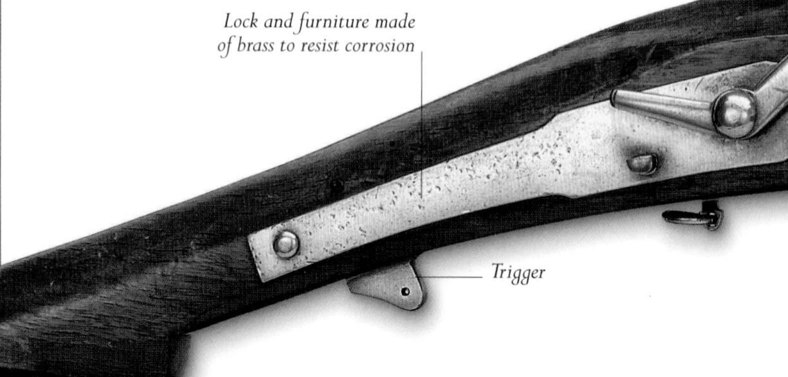

Match-holder

Elaborate sight block holds blades of varying heights for different ranges

Lock and furniture made of brass to resist corrosion

Trigger

▲ **KAKAE ZUTSU**

Date	17th–19th century
Origin	Japan
Weight	14¾lb (6.7kg)
Barrel	26½in (67.5cm)
Caliber	18.7mm

Kakae zutsu (hand cannon), some with bores of up to ¾in (2cm) in diameter, were used to batter down doors and to launch incendiary missiles. Their weight meant that they had to be shot from the waist, or from a support. The lock in this example has an internal spiral spring to operate the match-holder.

Serpentine match-holder is forward-facing

Owner's heraldry

Bore standardized to simplify ammunition supply

Brass lock cover plate

Decorative brass inlay

▲ **HI NAWA JU**

Date	17th–19th century
Origin	Japan
Weight	2¾lb (1.29kg)
Barrel	36¾in (93.7cm)
Caliber	15mm

The *hi nawa ju* (matchlock gun) was introduced to Japan by the Portuguese from their base at Goa, India, in 1543. Within 25 years, manufacturing centers were producing thousands of these guns for arming foot soldiers, and the matchlock had become a decisive weapon in battle. The decoration in black and gold lacquer was added later.

Match-holder

Steeply bent butt

Long bar-trigger

Leather-covered grip

Disk-shaped guard

▲ **CHANGDAO**

Date	16th century
Origin	China
Weight	6lb (2.72kg)
Length	5¼ft (1.57m)

Chinese long swords of this kind are similar to the Japanese swords known as *ōdachi*. However, unlike the *ōdachi*, the *changdao* has a long tang riveted through the brass pommel cap.

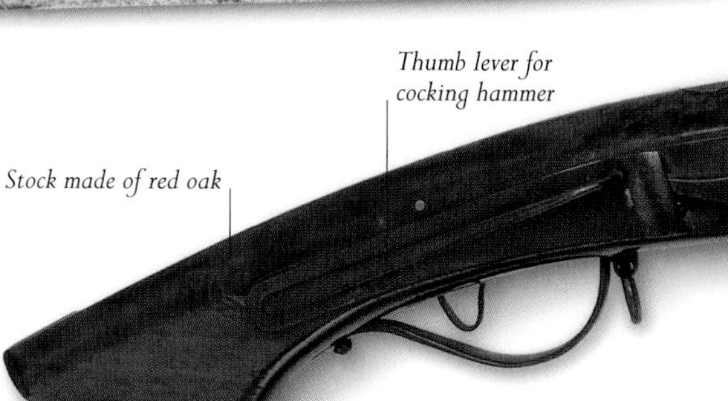

Thumb lever for cocking hammer

Stock made of red oak

▲ NAGINATA

Date	19th century
Origin	Japan
Weight	$4\frac{1}{4}$lb (1.95kg)
Length	9ft (2.75m)

Naginata blades, mounted on oval wooden shafts about $6\frac{1}{2}$ft (2m) long, were the standard weapon of foot soldiers in medieval Japan. Used as a spear or a fighting staff, they were especially associated with warrior monks, the *sōhei*.

◀ CHINESE SILK GUN

Date	c.1825
Origin	China
Weight	3lb (1.42kg)
Length	$37\frac{3}{4}$in (83.2cm)
Caliber	63.5mm

This cannon, designed for portability, was made from a copper tube wrapped with iron wire and silk cord. It derived from earlier guns, which were made from bamboo wound with cord. Chinese paintings show soldiers lying on the battlefield firing similar guns.

▶ TSUKUBO

Date	19th century
Origin	Japan
Weight	3lb (1.36kg)
Length	$27\frac{1}{4}$in (69cm)

Although not principally a weapon of war, implements such as this *tsukubo* (pushing pole) were used to overcome and detain criminals in Japan. In towns and cities, racks of these devices were positioned at strategic sites for use by law enforcement officers.

▲ CHINESE MATCHLOCK

Date	c.1830
Origin	China
Weight	19lb (8.6kg)
Barrel	$5\frac{1}{4}$ft (6m)
Caliber	15mm

Unlike the matchlocks used in Japan, on most Chinese guns the match-holder and trigger are one piece, so that when the trigger is pulled up, the match-holder dips down to apply the flame to the touch-hole. This is a simple, functional example, undecorated save for the stock, which is painted red.

▼ JAPANESE PILL-LOCK CARBINE

Date	c.1850
Origin	Japan
Weight	8lb (3.64kg)
Barrel	$26\frac{1}{4}$in (67cm)
Caliber	12.5mm

In 1853, American warships forced Japan to open its ports for trade, introducing new technology. Within a few years, the Japanese had adopted percussion ignition for their guns. This example has an automatic dispenser for detonating pills (its ignition primers).

JAPANESE ARMOR

Prior to the 16th century, Japanese armor was lamellar in construction—made from scales of rawhide or lacquered iron, laced together with leather or silk braid. During the Japanese civil wars of the 16th and 17th centuries, armor made of plate, which was lighter and more effective, was devised. This development proved fortuitous when guns were introduced from Europe in 1543. Although the samurai owned their own distinctive armor, commanders issued simple munitions, armor, and weapons to low-ranking troops. During the peaceful Edo period (1603–1868), samurai were still required to own armor, primarily as a symbol of status and rank.

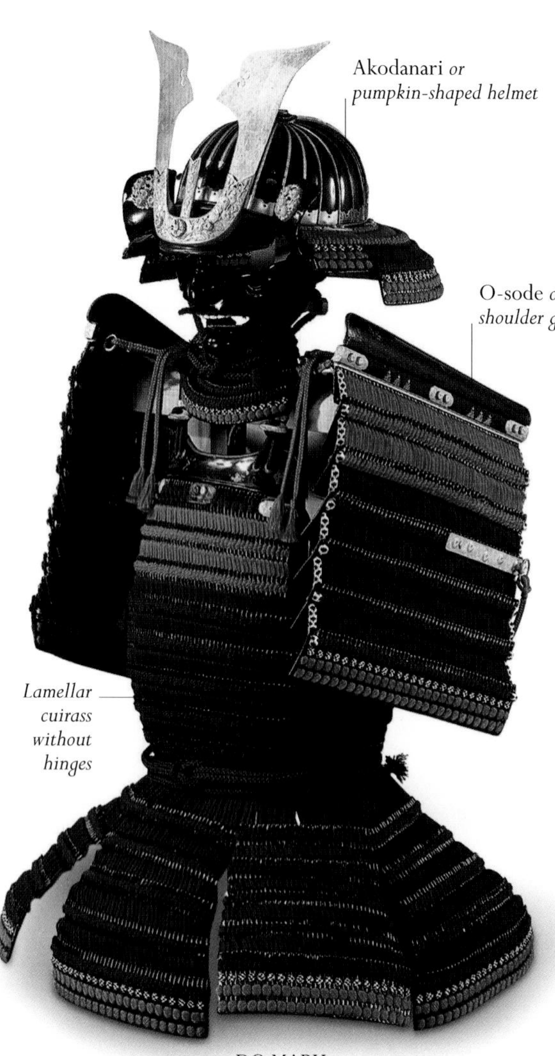

DO MARU

SUNEATE

▲ DO MARU

Date	c.1610
Origin	Japan
Material	Iron, lacquer, rawhide, silk braid

This formal armor, decorated with the heraldry of Takeda Katsuyori (1546–82), was given to King James I of England as a diplomatic gift. It is signed by the armorer Iwai Yosaemon of Nara.

KUSAZURI

▲ MOGAMI HARAMAKI

Date	c.1570
Origin	Japan
Material	Steel, lacquer, silk braid, textiles

This armor was given to King Philip II of Spain, in 1585. It opened down the back, with each plate in the body divided into five sections and joined by individual small hinges and *sugake* lacing.

▲ HINENO ZUNARI KABUTO

Date	c.1600
Origin	Japan
Material	Iron, lacquer, silk braid

This *hineno zunari kabuto*, or head-shaped helmet, was made for a retainer of the Ii family. The neck guard was made up of three sections so that a spear would exit through a gap rather than be deflected onto the neck.

▲ HISHINUI GUSOKU

Date c.1750

Origin Japan

Material Iron, rawhide, lacquer, silk braid, textiles

Made in the Edo period, this armor was more decorative than practical. The gold finish was achieved by dusting wet lacquer with gold dust. Some elements of the armor were made of rawhide to reduce the weight.

▲ KABUTO AND MEMPO

Date c.1750

Origin Japan

Material Iron, rawhide, lacquer, silk

The multi-plate helmet bowl (*kabuto*) is smoothly lacquered, and fitted with a brow plate and crests of lacquered wood and yak hair. The helmet cord was tied to hooks on the cheeks of the iron face mask (*mempo*).

THE SIEGE OF OSAKA CASTLE

The Sengoku period in Japan was a 150-year era of civil conflict when rival *daimyo* (feudal lords) and their samurai vied for power. The Siege of Osaka castle in 1614–15 was the climax and conclusion of this turbulent era.

The *daimyo* Tokugawa Ieyasu, effective ruler of Japan from 1600, took the title of shogun (military dictator) for the Tokugawa family. The impressive castle at Osaka was the power base of the rival Toyotomi clan, whose leader, Toyotomi Hideyori, had a better hereditary claim to the shogunate than the Tokugawa. In 1614, Ieyasu invented a pretext to attack the Toyotomi, assembling an army possibly 190,000-strong. *Daimyo* and samurai discontented with Tokugawa rule flocked to join Hideyori in Osaka. They included many masterless samurai, the *ronin*. An experienced warrior, Sanada Yukimura, oversaw the strengthening of the castle's defenses, ordering the digging of moats and the building of an earthwork barbican outside the tall stone walls.

The siege began in November 1614. First the Tokugawa captured various strongpoints in the country around Osaka. They then confronted Sanada's earthworks, but their siege weapons—a handful of imported European culverins and several hundred Japanese or Chinese artillery pieces—were powerless against thick earth walls. The Tokugawa decided to attack. They surged forward in their thousands, the *ashigaru* (peasant foot soldiers) armed with long pikes or arquebuses, the samurai, dismounting, wielding spears and swords. It was an impressive sight, the samurai arrayed in elaborate armor, the foot soldiers displaying a mass of fluttering flags attached to their backs by poles. But when they mounted ladders to scale the walls, the attackers were cut down by arquebuses fired through loopholes at the top of the fortifications. Where they breached the outer wall they found themselves trapped in front of inner defenses and fired down upon from all sides. The Tokugawa, suffering heavy losses, abandoned their assault and retreated to siege lines, where they camped in the bitter winter cold. The defenders nestled inside the castle, living off plentiful food stores.

A TREACHEROUS TREATY

Toyotomi Hideyori then made the fatal error of negotiating a peace deal with the Tokugawa. He was tricked. As soon as the armies dispersed, the Tokugawa ordered the Osaka moats filled in and the earthworks leveled. By the time fighting resumed in the spring of 1615—after Ieyasu pressed another spurious cause for war—Osaka castle was no longer defensible. The reassembled Toyotomi forces instead sought to preempt a siege by winning victory in the open field. The climactic encounter, known as the Battle of Tennoji, came in early June. The Toyotomi adopted a plan in which part of their forces would use a flanking movement to take the enemy from the rear, and then a reserve would enter the battle at the crucial moment. But this strategy was too complex for their loosely coordinated army. Many of the *ronin* attacked at will, and arquebusiers assigned to the reserve opened fire without waiting for orders. In the midst of a chaotic struggle Sanada was killed and his severed head displayed to the demoralized troops. A belated sortie by the garrison from the castle, led by Hideyori himself, was driven back through the gates. As Tokugawa cannon battered the stone walls and parts of the castle caught fire, Hideyori committed *seppuku* (ritual suicide). The Tokugawa shogunate was destined to last another 250 years.

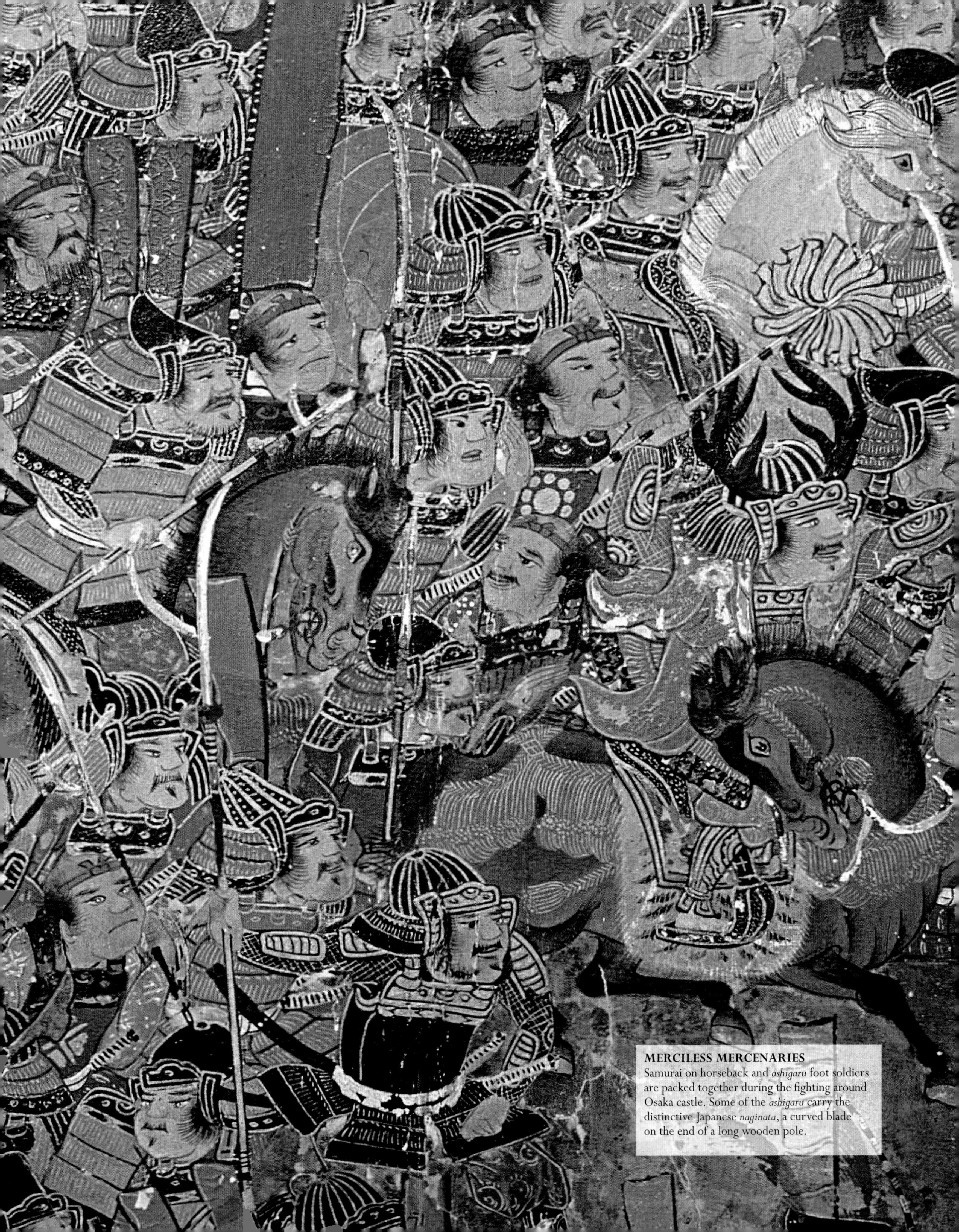

MERCILESS MERCENARIES
Samurai on horseback and *ashigaru* foot soldiers are packed together during the fighting around Osaka castle. Some of the *ashigaru* carry the distinctive Japanese *naginata*, a curved blade on the end of a long wooden pole.

KEY **FIGURE**

SIR FRANCIS DRAKE
1540–96

The English privateer Francis Drake ravaged Spanish colonies and shipping in the Caribbean and Pacific in the 1570s. His daring raid on Cadiz, in 1587, was said to have "singed the king of Spain's beard." Drake was made vice-admiral of the English fleet that would resist the Armada.

▲ Drake was knighted in 1580, as the first Englishman to sail around the world.

▶ **THE SPANISH ARMADA**
Phillip II of Spain's "Invincible Armada," which was sent to facilitate a cross-Channel invasion of England, is engaged by English galleons firing cannon at the Battle of Gravelines, in August 1588.

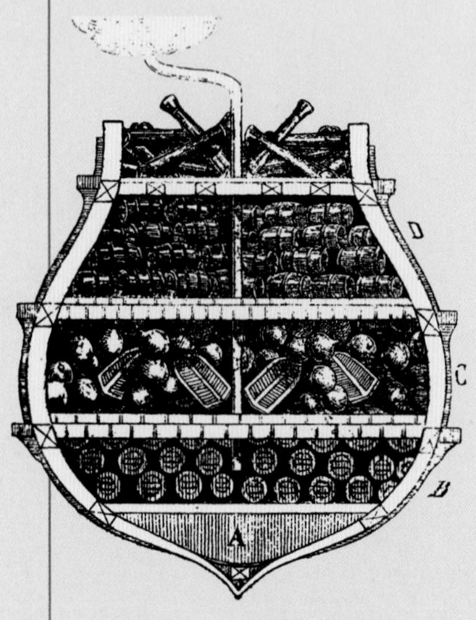

▲ **FRENCH FIRESHIP**
A ship was packed with combustible material, then set alight and steered toward enemy vessels.

KEY DEVELOPMENT

EUROPEAN NAVAL WARFARE

European sailors established oceanic sea routes linking Europe to Asia and the Americas from the late 15th century. The rise of ocean-going sailing ships ushered in a new era of naval warfare, while oared galleys fought for dominance of the Mediterranean.

Galley warfare peaked in the 16th century, as the Turkish Ottoman Empire, aided by privateers, sought control of the Mediterranean. Muslim galleys raided the coast of Italy and landed armies on Christian-held islands, such as Rhodes, Malta, and Cyprus. Christian states responded by deploying large galleys rowed by prisoners using the clumsy but powerful "*scalaccio*" (echelon) system, with five to seven men on each massive oar. Cannon were mounted on the galleys, and the soldiers on board also carried firearms. This firepower was no guarantor of success, however: although a Christian alliance won a major naval victory at Lepanto, in 1571, the Muslims largely had the upper hand at sea.

Galleys tended to dominate the Mediterranean at the end of the 17th century, while sailing ships were traditionally considered of little use in combat: dependence on the wind left them outflanked by nimbler, oared vessels. However,

▲ AT CLOSE QUARTERS
The last naval encounter of the Anglo-Dutch Wars was the Battle of Texel, fought off the coast of the Netherlands, in August 1673. While inconclusive, the battle was contested with savage cannon broadsides and hand-to-hand fighting with cutlasses, daggers, and axes.

galleys struggled to survive in heavy oceanic seas. By the 16th century, states around Europe's Atlantic coast had developed carracks—vessels with high castles (multi-deck structures) fore and aft, and a combination of square and lateen (triangular) sails. They were effective warships, and large carracks, known as "great ships," became prestigious status symbols for early 16th-century monarchs.

EVOLVING SHIPS

From the mid-16th century, the galleon, a slimmed-down, faster version of the carrack, was the pivotal warship. The invention of the gunport allowed large numbers of heavy cannon to be mounted on ships' lower decks, and firing broadsides (from the ship's sides) became the norm. In the 17th century, the galleon evolved into the ship of the line, built to fight in lines together, firing broadsides, and supported by smaller frigates and fireships.

Warships were essential to the states of western and northern Europe as they competed for trade routes and colonies, but permanent navies were expensive to maintain. All countries conscripted armed merchantmen into their navies, and also depended on privateers—licensed pirates who preyed upon foreign states' shipping and colonies.

In the 16th century, Spain had been the dominant naval power, using galleys in the Mediterranean, and galleons in the Atlantic. By the 17th century, the Dutch and English were vying for naval supremacy in a series of large-scale naval battles in the Anglo-Dutch Wars from the 1650s to the 1670s. France, on the other hand, devoted serious resources to naval development only in the reign of Louis XIV, in the 1660s.

The tactics of battles between sailing ships evolved in an ad hoc fashion. When the Spanish sent their Armada against England, in 1588, the smaller English galleons sought to duel with cannon, while the Spanish, their ships packed with soldiers, would have preferred to board: since it was hard to sink a wooden sailing ship with cannon fire, boarding remained a prime tactic. In the 17th century, however, navies formalized a system for exchanging broadsides, but despite this, naval battles remained brutal due to their sheer quantity of firepower.

"Every squadron **shall endeavor to keep in line** with the chief, **unless the chief be maimed** or otherwise disabled (which God forbid!)"

FIGHTING INSTRUCTIONS ISSUED TO THE ENGLISH FLEET, MARCH 1653

KEY **EVENTS**

1500–1700

■ **1509** The defeat of an Ottoman, Egyptian, and Gujarati (western Indian) fleet by the Portuguese at the Battle of Diu establishes the superiority of European sailing ships in the Indian Ocean.

■ **1511** The English carrack *Mary Rose* is one of the first ships to be built with gunports.

■ **1571** The Battle of Lepanto takes place. Fought between Christian and Muslim fleets in the Mediterranean, more than 400 oared galleys and over 100,000 men are involved (see pp.154–55).

■ **1582** The first naval battle in mid-ocean occurs off the Azores—an archipelago in the North Atlantic ocean—with Spanish galleons beating the French and Portuguese.

■ **1588** Spain assembles 130 ships for its Armada to sail to the English Channel; less than half return, with most losses due to storms.

■ **1639** Dutch admiral Maarten Tromp destroys a Spanish fleet at the Battle of the Downs by making effective use of fireships; this marks the end of the era of Spanish naval dominance.

■ **1653** Fighting Instructions drawn up for the British Royal Navy by Admiral Robert Blake (known as the "Father of the Royal Navy") order captains to enter combat in a disciplined line of battle.

MEDITERRANEAN GALLEY

GALERA REAL

The *Galera Real* was no ordinary war galley but a luxury vessel made for Don John of Austria, commander of the Holy League fleet that defeated the Ottoman Turks at the Battle of Lepanto in 1571.

The ship carried up to 400 men, of whom 236 rowed the galley, with four men per oar. In addition, there were a number of skilled sailors to steer and manage the two lateen sails, as well as a large detachment of soldiers, many of them armed with arquebuses. On the covered forecastle, beneath a raised fighting platform, the galley had a large central cannon and four medium-sized guns. Four small guns were sited among the oarsmen's stations, two on either side of the ship. In preparation for Lepanto (see pp.154–55), the end of the prow, with its classical figurehead, was cut off so that the central cannon could be angled to shoot down on the Ottoman ships.

During the battle, the *Galera Real* was rammed by the Ottoman flagship *Sultana*, the enemy prow penetrating as far inboard as the innermost oarsman. Turkish soldiers boarded the galley but were driven back.

This replica of the *Galera Real* was made for Barcelona's Maritime Museum to mark the battle's 400th anniversary.

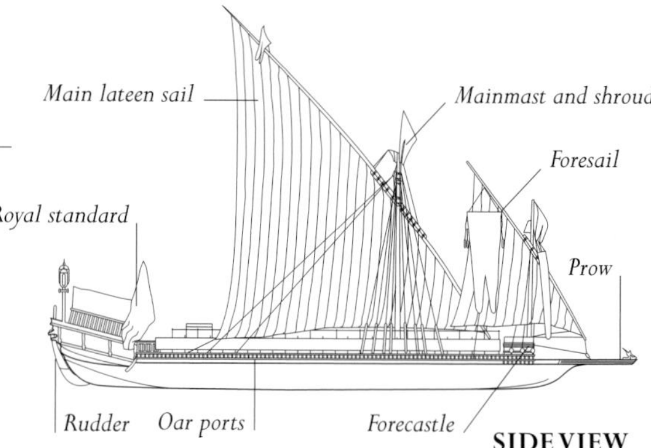

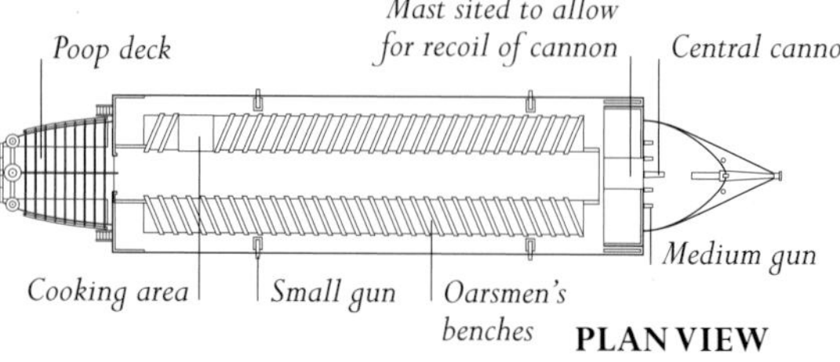

GALERA REAL
The palatial royal flagship was 197ft (60m) long and 20¼ft (6.2m) wide. Sails were used on the open sea, but in battle the galley relied on its oarsmen.

AROUND THE SHIP

▲ AUXILIARY GUN
The small, breech-loading guns on either side of the galley could be swiveled on their mountings. They were loaded with small shot and used as anti-personnel weapons against the deck crew of an enemy galley.

▲ ORNATE SCUPPER
Small ports called scuppers were opened to let water run off the deck.

▲ DECK RANGE
One of the luxuries on Don John's galley was a range toward the stern. The cooking pots were suspended over the fire.

▲ REAR VIEW
The leading sculptors of Renaissance Spain created the statues and reliefs. Projecting from the deck beyond the stern is an outrigger, which supported the long oars.

THE OARS AND OARSMEN

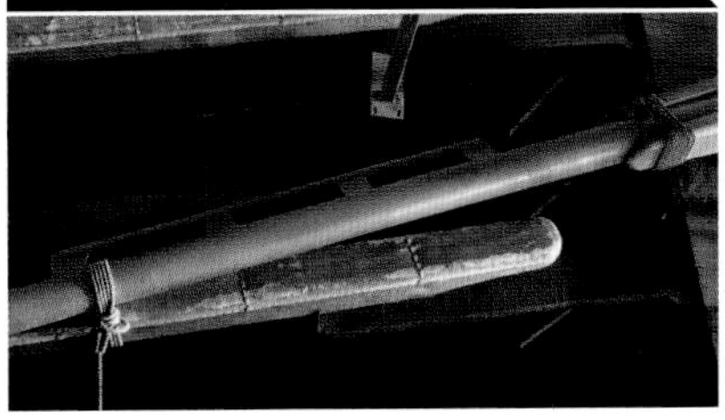

▲ ROWING BENCH AND OAR
The most experienced oarsman took the inner seat and dictated the timing of the strokes to the other three oarsmen, who pulled on the battens.

▲ THE BINDING OF THE OARS
The beechwood oars were 37ft (11.4m) long. Oars made from a single piece of wood were more likely to break, so they were usually made from two lengths bound together.

◄ FRONT VIEW
The forecastle housing the main cannons lay behind the long prow.

▼ THOLE PIN
Each oar pivoted around a peg called a thole pin as the oarsman drove its blade into the water. The oar was simply tied to the pin with a loop of rope.

► COAT OF ARMS
The *Galera Real* was a gift to Don John from King Philip II of Spain, his half-brother. The prow is decorated with the king's coat of arms, supported by two mermen.

► CLASSICAL FIGUREHEAD
The prow ends in a magnificent figurehead of a gilded Neptune, the Roman god of the sea, who is shown riding on a dolphin and brandishing a trident. The prow of the original ship was removed before Lepanto.

STERN, POOP, AND HOLD

The ship's most striking feature is its ornate stern. This was painstakingly recreated from a contemporary description. Although elaborately decorated, the poop deck became the center of resistance if the galley was boarded in battle, with fighting men clustering there to defend their flag and commander. The *Galera Real* had a larger hold than ordinary war galleys, with plenty of space for stores.

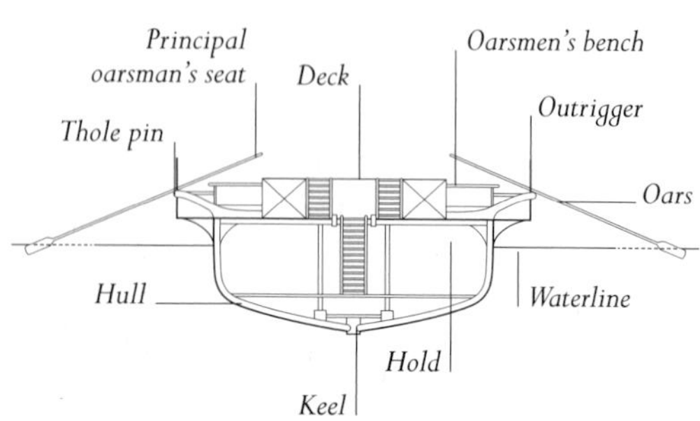

CROSS SECTION

GALLEY HOLD

▲ SPACIOUS HOLD
The hold stored food, drink, weapons, armor, sailcloth, spars, clothing, ropes, and a number of lockable chests in which the ship's gentlemen kept their possessions. There was also a gunpowder room and a surgery.

▲ BASIC STORES
Grain, wine, and water were always in store. Fresh vegetables and bread were taken aboard whenever possible.

GALLEY STERN

► GILDED BALUSTER
Every tiny detail around the stern, where the admiral resided in the poop, is richly carved and gilded or painted.

► EAGLE
The gilded eagles on the stern are a reference to the Roman Empire and Christian Europe's desire to win back Rome's former lands from Ottoman control.

◄ FACE OF MEDUSA
The snake-headed gorgon Medusa stares out from the stern of the *Galera Real*, deflecting evil and bringing destruction on the ships of Don John's enemies.

▲ DECORATED STERN
The *Galera Real* was built in Barcelona in 1568 and decorated in Seville. The frieze at the top of the stern shows Hercules in the Garden of the Hesperides. Below, the two lions hold the coats of arms of Austria and the Order of the Golden Fleece, while the four female figures represent Christian virtues.

POOP DECK

▲ **BOARDING STEPS**
A pair of curved ladders, one on either side of the poop deck, were used for embarking and disembarking.

▼ **NIGHT LIGHT**
Above the helmsman's position on the poop deck are three large, ornate lanterns. They were used as beacons for keeping the fleet together at night.

▼ **LATIN MOTTO**
The rudder's inscription extols prudence and strength—virtues needed to rule the waves.

▲ **RUDDER**
Galley rudders were smaller than those on sailing ships, and curved rather than straight.

▲ **POOP DECOR AND CANOPY**
The backrests of the benches depict episodes from Greek myths, most of which have a nautical theme and a moral message. An awning was draped over the canopy to keep out the sun, wind, and rain, and to give protection in battle.

THE BATTLE OF LEPANTO

Fought off the coast of Greece on October 7, 1571, the Battle of Lepanto was the climax of the era of galley warfare in the Mediterranean. More than 400 oared warships engaged in a close-fought battle that resulted in one of Christian Europe's greatest victories over the Ottoman Turks.

In the 16th century, Muslim naval forces—the well-funded fleet of the Ottoman Empire, and the piratical Barbary corsairs from the ports of North Africa—were bidding for control of the Mediterranean. The states of Christian Europe were rarely capable of uniting to face this threat; however, in 1571, they forged a Holy League to resist an Ottoman attack on Cyprus. The combined fleets of Habsburg Spain, Venice, Genoa, the Papacy, Savoy, and the Knights of St. John were led by Don John of Austria, illegitimate half-brother of Philip II of Spain. Heading into the eastern Mediterranean, they met the Ottoman fleet and its corsair allies in the Gulf of Patras.

The galleys carried large contingents of soldiers, but their use of equipment showed a clear division of technology and approach. The Christian forces were mostly armored and carrying arquebuses, while the Muslims were more lightly clad and equipped with composite bows. Galley battles had traditionally involved engaging enemy ships so that soldiers could board and attack at close quarters. But now the Christian fleet also depended heavily on the firepower of naval guns: their galleys had cannon in the bows, and smaller swivel guns to sweep an enemy's deck. They had also rebuilt six large Venetian cargo ships as "galleasses"—unwieldy gun platforms heavily armed with cannon, which had to be assisted into action in front of their fleet. The Muslim galleys, meanwhile, were smaller and lighter, and depended on speed of maneuver to gain advantage; on the Christian side, only the Venetian galleys, oared by free men, could move as nimbly. The rest of Don John's galleys, heavy with cannon and clumsily rowed by prisoners and slaves, kept in line abreast, to protect their flanks and maximize the power of their forward-firing guns.

JOINING THE FRAY

Commanded by Ali Pasha from the flagship *Sultana*, the Ottomans and corsairs took the initiative. They advanced in crescent formation, attempting to outflank the Venetians on their left, and the Genoese on their right. The Ottoman center came under bombardment from the galleasses, causing damage to the ships. Ali Pasha, undeterred, pressed forward toward Don John's flagship *Real* at the heart of the Christian fleet. Soon galleys were locked together in deadly combat, soldiers fighting hand-to-hand on the decks. The Genoese were outflanked by corsair captain Uluj Ali, who threatened to break through on the Christian right. On the left, the Venetian commander Agostino Barbarigo was killed by an arrow in the eye, while in the center Ottoman Janissaries boarded *Real*.

The Christians were saved by the experienced Habsburg admiral Álvaro de Bazán. Leading a reserve force of galleys, he directed ships into the battle at crucial moments, shoring up the flanks and rescuing Don John's flagship. The turning point came when Ali Pasha's flagship *Sultana* was boarded and taken, and his severed head displayed on a pike. The Muslim fleet disintegrated, with only Uluj Ali succeeding in rescuing his ships from the rout.

COMBAT AT SEA
Battle is joined between galleys of the Christian and Muslim fleets at Lepanto. The oarsmen are crowded together at their benches below decks while soldiers fight above their heads.

1680–1815

FLINTLOCK AND BAYONET

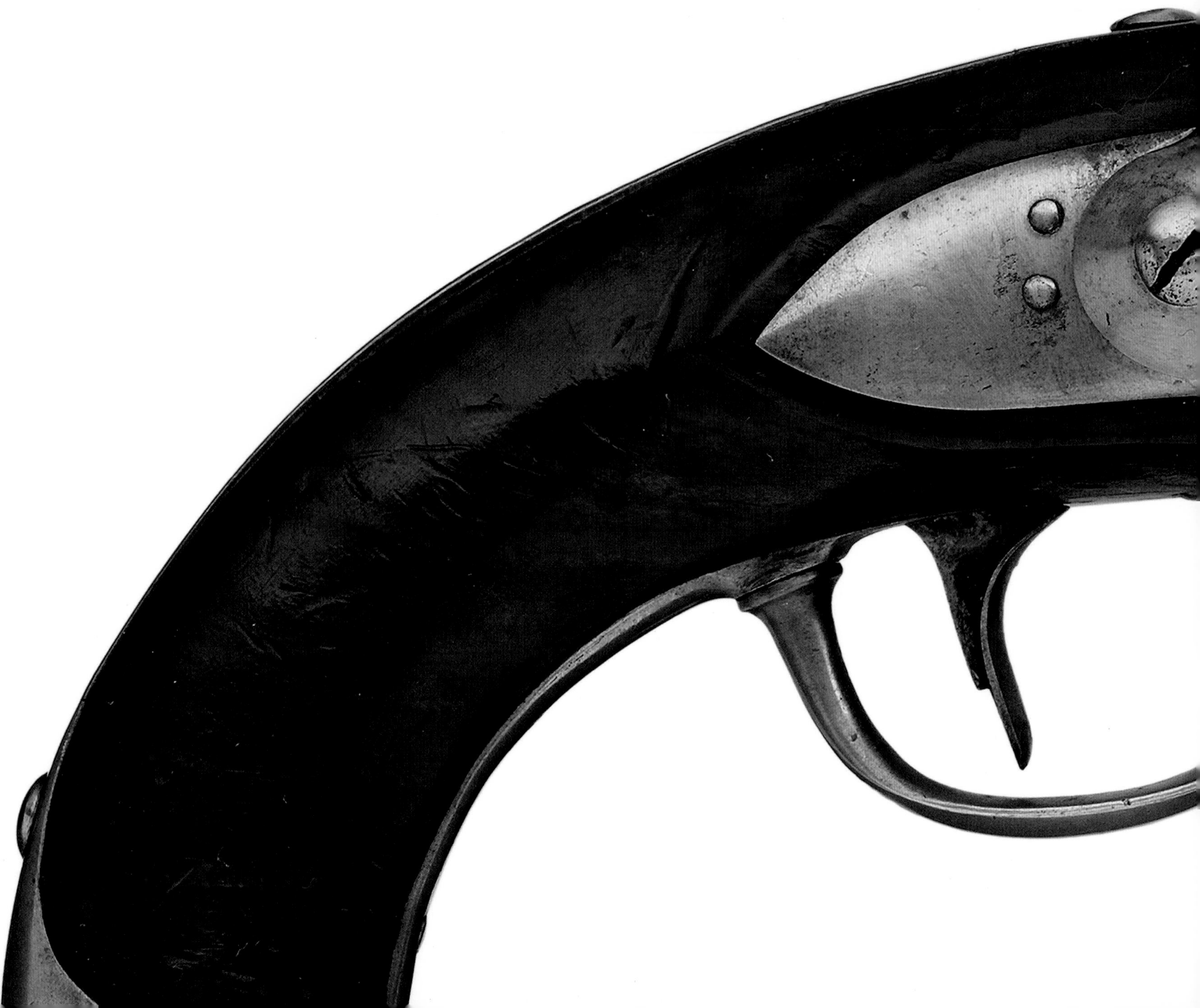

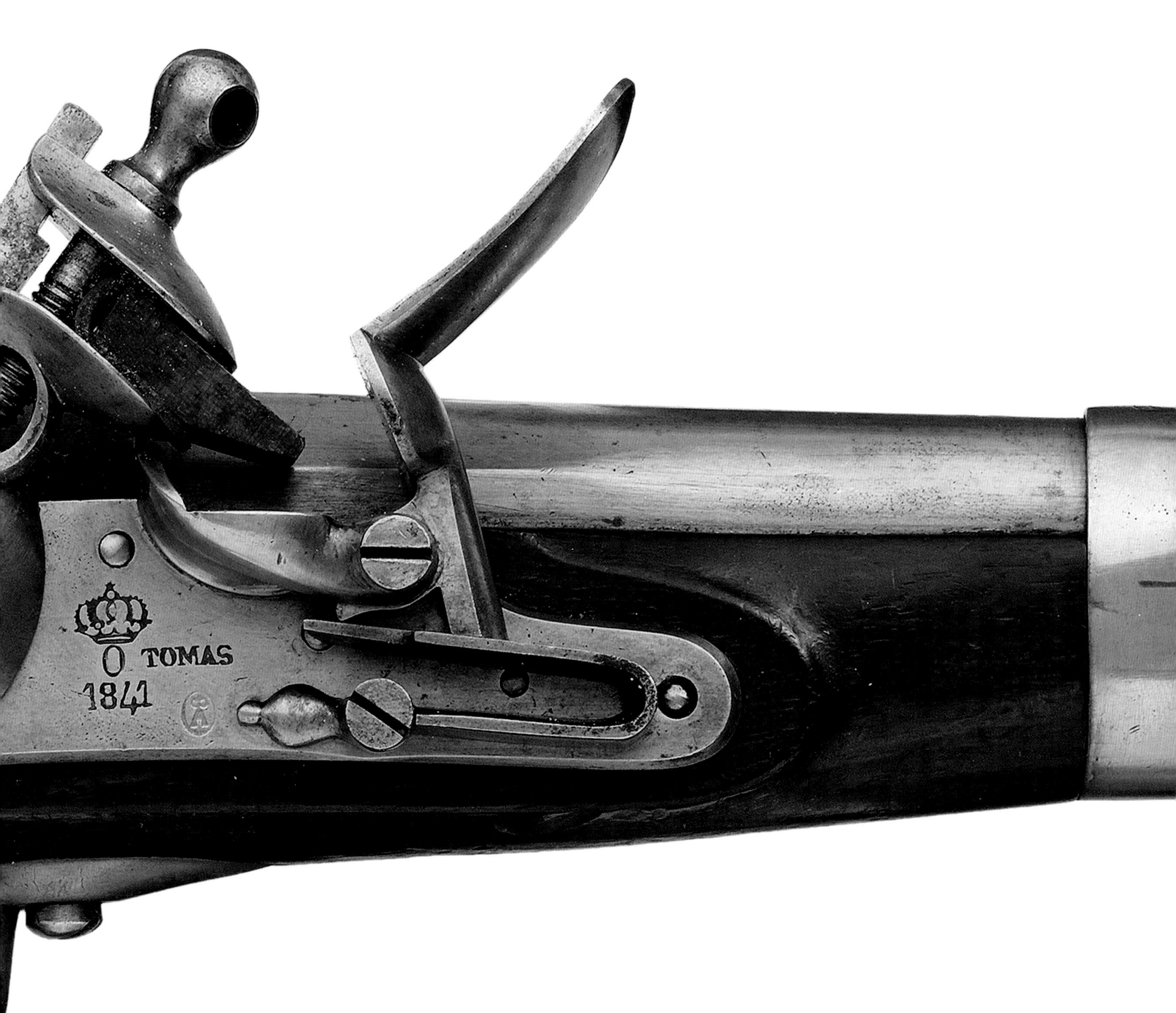

O TOMAS
1841

INTRODUCTION

From the late 17th to the early 19th centuries, there were few dramatic changes in military technology. The basic infantry weapon was the flintlock musket with bayonet attached; artillery consisted of smoothbore muzzle-loading cannon. However, the nature of warfare developed in organization, ideology, strategy, and tactics.

Eighteenth-century European states maintained permanent armies commanded by officers, with regiments and formal hierarchies of rank. Infantry were uniformed and issued with standard equipment, harshly disciplined, and drilled to march and fight in formation with automatic obedience. Cavalry performed a variety of roles, from reconnaissance to charges or pursuit of the enemy, while field artillery was also now a key part of armies. At sea, a ship of the line might mount 70–130 cannon in broadside. Thus, non-European states, such as Ottoman Turkey or Indian princedoms, found themselves at a military disadvantage.

From the second half of the 18th century, a new spirit infused European warfare, related to the currents of revolution that swept America in the 1770s, and France from 1789. Although the American Revolution, waged by America against Britain, was fought mostly by conventional armies, irregular troops with rifles showed their effectiveness. This encouraged European armies to make better use of skirmishers as an adjunct to their line infantry, and to arm some of their forces with rifles. In 1793, the French revolutionary government created a mass national army, based on the idea that men should fight due to patriotic enthusiasm, rather than fear of punishment. After rising to power in 1799, Napoleon Bonaparte reorganized the French army into a unified force of four corps, each capable of independent operations. Like the British Royal Navy's Admiral Nelson, at sea Napoleon favored an offensive strategy and aggressive tactics. By 1815, European armies had grown to unprecedented size and states had shown an ability to mobilize vast resources for victory in war.

KEY DATES

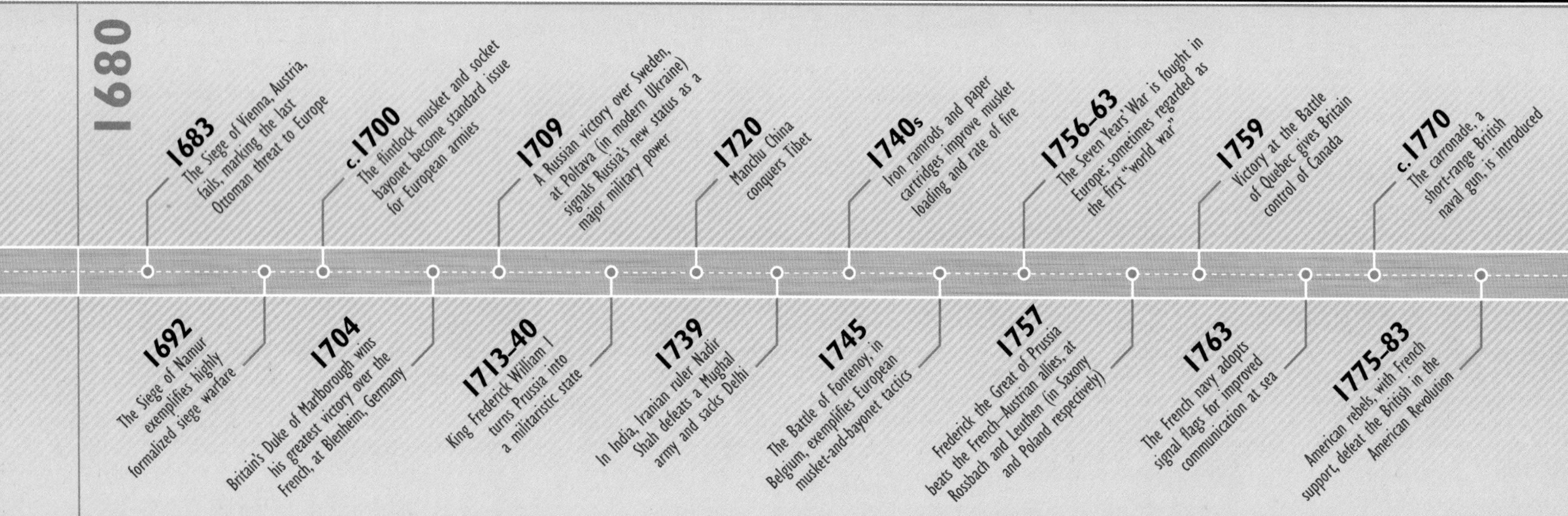

THE SACK OF MAGDEBURG—1631

THE SIEGE OF NAMUR—1692

THE BATTLE OF YORKTOWN—1781

THE BATTLE OF THE NILE—1798

THE BATTLE OF AUSTERLITZ—1805

THE BATTLE OF WATERLOO—1815

KEY DEVELOPMENT

18TH-CENTURY UNIFORMED ARMIES

The armies that fought such conflicts as the wars of the Spanish Succession (1701–14) and Austrian Succession (1740–48), the Seven Years' War (1756–63), and the American Revolutionary War (1775–83), followed the tradition of uniformed regular forces, with a formal hierarchy of ranks.

Permanent regiments, identified by banners, uniforms, and other symbols, provided a focus for loyalty. Cavalry retained high status and were given important tasks: light horsemen carried out reconnaissance and raids, while heavy cavalry were used in field battles to charge with sabres drawn. Although field artillery was growing in use, muzzle-loaded smoothbore cannon as yet played only a supporting role. Consequently, the success or failure of an army depended mainly upon its infantry.

MUSKETS AND RIFLES

Around the start of the 18th century, European infantry adopted the flintlock musket and socket bayonet. The bayonet replaced the pike, in effect making every foot soldier a musketeer. Usually recruited from the lowest levels of society, infantry were subject to brutal discipline and relentlessly drilled to execute orders without question. They were trained to maneuver with mechanical precision, marching in columns and deploying in lines for combat, to bring maximum firepower to bear. Since armor was no longer used, soldiers walked unprotected into enemy muskets and cannon, while maintaining close formation. They shot their muskets in controlled volleys, relying on volume of fire rather than individual marksmanship.

Alongside the line infantry, European armies deployed light infantry, who were supposed to take on a freer role. Some of these light troops, notably the Austrian and Prussian Jäger, were armed with rifles. Line infantry were not trained in aimed fire, which was hardly possible with the inherently inaccurate smoothbore musket. The Jäger were accomplished sharpshooters, however, capable of accurate sniping and skilled in the use of cover. Elsewhere, rifle-armed American frontiersmen gained a legendary reputation for success against the British Army in the American Revolutionary War, although the reality was not as clearly defined.

HEAVY LOSSES

The level of combat casualties during this period was often astonishingly high. At the Battle of Zorndorf in 1758, during the Seven Years' War, the Prussians suffered 11,000 casualties out of an army of 36,000, while the Russians lost 22,000 men out of 43,000. Commanders such as Frederick the Great aspired to battles of sweeping maneuver, making coordinated use of infantry, cavalry, and artillery to achieve victories. Some battles, however, simply degenerated into incoherent mêlées, obscured by great clouds of gunpowder smoke. Although many European armies had developed into highly efficient killing machines, commanders typically found it difficult to translate successes on the battlefield into permanent strategic gains.

KEY **FIGURE**

FREDERICK THE GREAT
1740–86

Frederick the Great (Frederick II, King of Prussia) was the most admired commander of his time. His greatest battles were at Rossbach and Leuthen, in November and December, 1757, during the Seven Years' War. He won each victory against far larger forces, through aggressive battlefield maneuvers.

▲ Frederick commanded his army in person, priding himself upon his tactical handling of artillery, cavalry, and the disciplined Prussian infantry.

▶ **CUIRASSIER'S UNIFORM**
Cuirassiers were French heavy cavalry who wore plumed helmets. Their tunics were less spectacular than those of the light cavalry, but they were usually covered by armor—a cuirass and back plate.

▶ **THE BATTLE OF BLENHEIM**
A British army led by the Duke of Marlborough, and Austrian forces under Eugene of Savoy, defeated Franco-Bavarian forces at Blenheim, in 1704, during the War of Spanish Succession. More than 30,000 soldiers were killed or wounded in the day's fighting.

◀ **THE BATTLE OF YORKTOWN**
The final battle of the American Revolutionary War, in 1781, set American troops and their French allies against British redcoats. Although the Americans made fun of the formality of the British, they created their own disciplined, uniformed army to fight the war.

"If my soldiers were **to begin to think**, not one would **remain in the army**"

FREDERICK THE GREAT (FREDERICK II, KING OF PRUSSIA), c.18TH CENTURY

KEY **EVENTS**

1700–1800

- **c.1700** European armies abandon the pike and adopt the socket bayonet, which fits over the barrel of a flintlock musket.
- **1713–40** By employing draconian punishments, King Frederick William I of Prussia transforms the Prussian army into Europe's most rigorously disciplined military force.
- **1740s** Ramrods made of iron, rather than wood, and cartridges (paper containers that combine both ball and powder) are introduced. These innovations improve the speed of musket loading—and also rates of fire.
- **1744** Frederick the Great of Prussia, the son of Frederick William I, recruits Jäger (huntsmen) as light rifle-armed troops in the Prussian army.
- **1775** American commander-in-chief George Washington creates the Continental Army, a European-style uniformed force armed with muskets, to fight against the British during the American Revolutionary War.
- **1776** General Jean Baptiste de Gribeauval initiates a major reform of French artillery, introducing standardized sizes and lighter gun carriages to improve mobility.

UNIFORMS OF EUROPEAN ARMIES

European military uniforms of the 18th century generally took the form of a tricorn hat, a waistcoat, breeches, canvas gaiters, and a coat with a long skirt. Infantrymen wore coats in national colors—blue for the Prussians, green for the Russians, and red for the British. One notable component of uniform was the elongated, brimless grenadier's cap. The grenadiers were established in the mid- to late 1600s as an elite infantry unit of the tallest and strongest men, who attacked with heavy grenades from the front rank of the infantry. They chose a brimless cap to enable them to sling their musket over their shoulders and throw grenades more easily.

Monogram of Peter III

◀ RUSSIAN GRENADIER'S CAP

Date 1762

Origin Russia

Material Silvered brass

The silvered-brass front plate on this grenadier cap bears the monogram of the Russian Emperor Peter III. After a reign of just six months in that year, he was succeeded by his wife, Catherine II ("Catherine the Great").

▲ RUSSIAN OFFICER'S UNIFORM

Date 1687

Origin Russia

Material Broadcloth, silk

This uniform and tricorn hat of an officer in the elite Preobrazhensky Regiment of the Russian army was worn by Peter I ("Peter the Great"), who established the regiment in 1687. The regiment had significant success against Swedish forces in the Great Northern War of 1700–21, and later formed the bodyguard of Empress Catherine the Great.

Decorated pocket

Green was the traditional color of Russian infantry

▶ RUSSIAN GENERAL'S UNIFORM

Date 1760

Origin Russia

Material Wool, silk

This ornate uniform belonged to the Russian general Alexander Suvorov, who never lost a battle in his entire career. Shortly before his death in 1800 he was made Generalissimo of the Russian Empire, taking command of all Russian troops, following his masterminding of a tactical retreat across the Alps in 1799.

Imperial crown

◀ **PRUSSIAN GRENADIER'S CAP**

Date 1713

Origin Prussia

Material Wool

This cap was worn by grenadiers in the infantry regiment of Frederick Henry, Margrave of Brandenburg-Schwedt, in 1713. At the time, Henry was just four years old and under the guardianship of his uncle, Frederick I.

▶ **GRENADIER'S POUCH**

Date 1750

Origin England

Material Leather, brass

Grenadiers carried leather pouches containing essential equipment for use on the battlefield. The brass facing depicts a grenadier wearing a tall cap, which made him look even more imposing to enemy forces.

Canvas belt

▶ **PRUSSIAN OFFICER'S GORGET**

Date 1750

Origin Prussia

Material Brass

In the 18th and 19th centuries, army officers wore gorgets—a metal collar originally designed to protect the throat—as a symbol of their rank.

Prussian coat of arms

▲ **BRITISH GRENADIER'S CAP**

Date 1746

Origin England

Material Wool

This cap for an officer in the Norwich Company of Artillery bears the personal coat of arms of Sir John Hobart. He raised the company in 1746 to defend the city in the event of attack during the Jacobite Rebellion.

▼ **PRUSSIAN INFANTRY UNIFORM**

Date 1740

Origin Prussia

Material Wool

The infantrymen in the Prussian army under Frederick II ("Frederick the Great") wore long, dark blue coats with red facings and lining. They fought with flintlock muskets and were fiercely disciplined and highly trained.

Shirt and waistcoat worn beneath coat

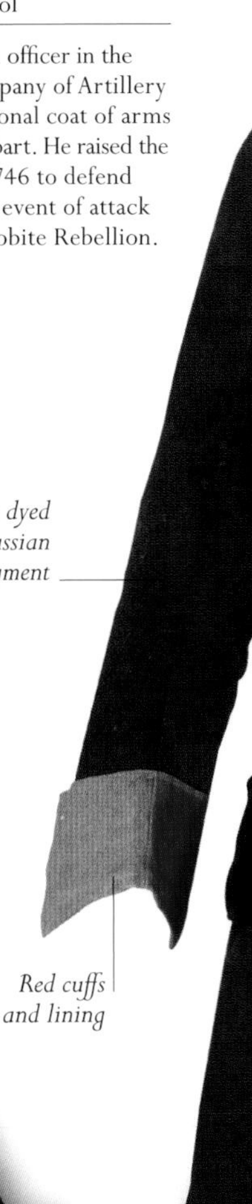
Uniform dyed with "Prussian blue" pigment

Red cuffs and lining

▲ **MILITARY GREATCOAT OF FREDERICK THE GREAT**

Date 1760

Origin Prussia

Material Wool

Frederick the Great (see p.160) often led the Prussian army in person and frequently dressed in a simple blue military uniform and greatcoat. Frederick was widely praised for his battlefield tactics—in fact, Napoleon Bonaparte regarded Frederick as the greatest military tactician in history.

PLUG, SOCKET, AND SWORD BAYONETS

Infantrymen fighting with muskets were vulnerable to enemy attack while loading their weapons after firing, so they originally fought alongside pikemen for protection. At the end of the 17th century, bayonets were developed to enable musketeers to defend themselves. The first type, plug bayonets, were daggers thrust into the musket's muzzle. They had to be removed to fire the weapon, and were superseded by socket bayonets, which were attached by a metal tube that engaged with a stud on the gun's barrel. In the early 19th century, many armies issued the longer sword bayonet, which could be removed from the gun and used in hand-to-hand combat.

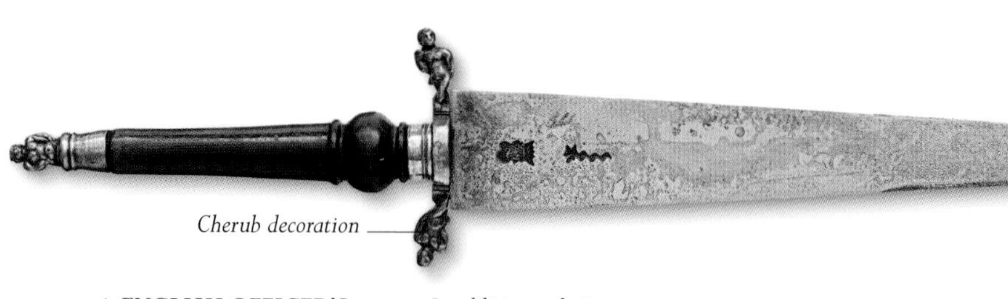

▲ ENGLISH OFFICER'S PLUG BAYONET

Date	c.1680
Origin	England
Weight	21oz (600g)
Length	17¼in (44cm)

In addition to being weapons, bayonets could be removed from the gun and used for practical tasks. Officers' bayonets might also have ornate features, such as the cherubs on the handle of this blade.

▲ SPRING-LOADED PLUG BAYONET

Date	c.1685
Origin	Europe
Weight	13oz (370g)
Length	19in (48.2cm)

A musketeer equipped with a bayonet could hold enemy cavalry at bay. The bayonet handle was tapered to fit in the muzzle of the gun. A catch on the spring-loaded blades secured them in position.

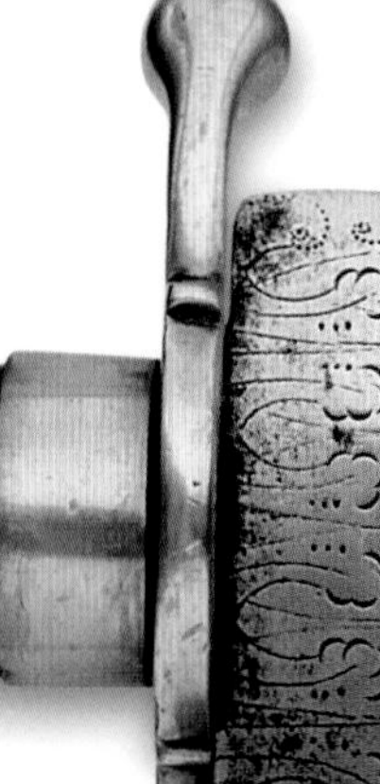

▲ PLUG BAYONET

Date	1686
Origin	England
Weight	11½oz (328g)
Length	18in (46.2cm)

The blade of this plug bayonet is inscribed "God save King James the 2 1686," a reference to the monarch who lost the English and Scottish thrones to William III and Mary II in 1688.

▲ OFFICERS' PLUG BAYONET

Date	1695
Origin	England
Weight	24¾oz (700g)
Length	25in (64cm)

This type of bayonet had to be fitted into a gun barrel before use. English Royalist troops were defeated by charging Highlanders at the Battle of Killiecrankie, Scotland, in 1689, because they were too slow to mount their plug bayonets in the heat of battle.

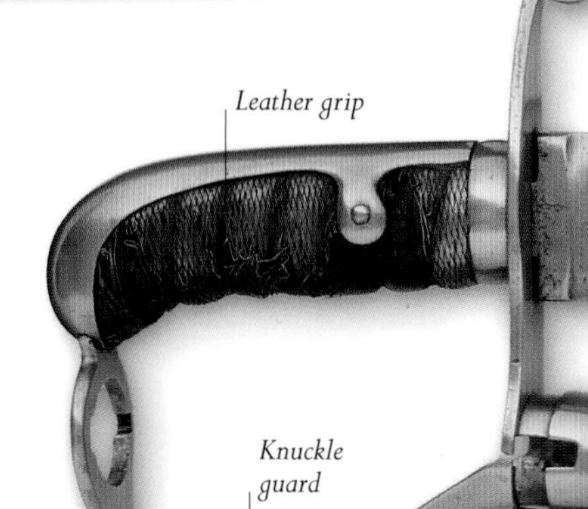

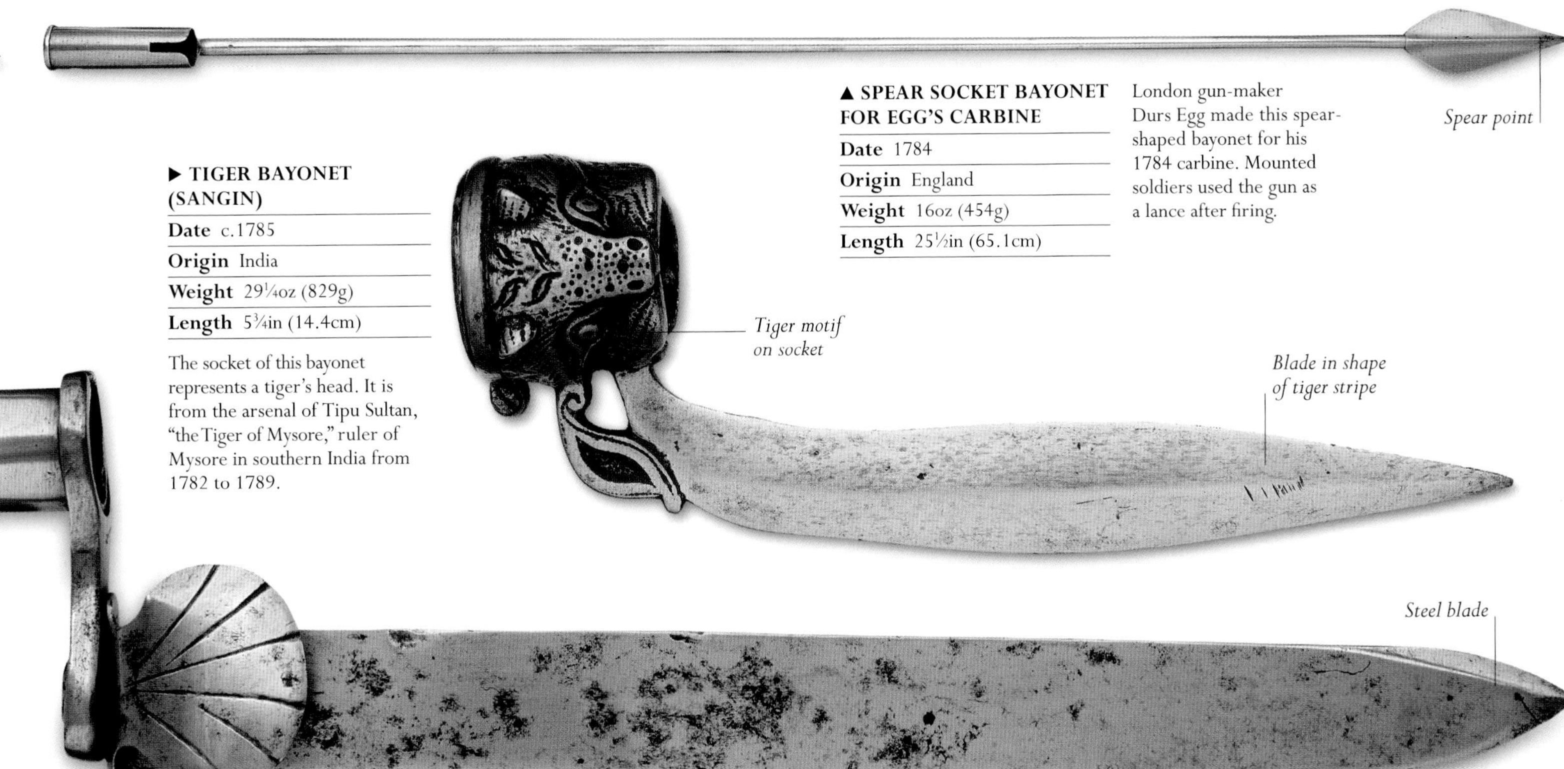

▲ SPEAR SOCKET BAYONET FOR EGG'S CARBINE

Date 1784
Origin England
Weight 16oz (454g)
Length 25½in (65.1cm)

London gun-maker Durs Egg made this spear-shaped bayonet for his 1784 carbine. Mounted soldiers used the gun as a lance after firing.

▶ TIGER BAYONET (SANGIN)

Date c.1785
Origin India
Weight 29¼oz (829g)
Length 5¾in (14.4cm)

The socket of this bayonet represents a tiger's head. It is from the arsenal of Tipu Sultan, "the Tiger of Mysore," ruler of Mysore in southern India from 1782 to 1789.

▲ SOCKET BAYONET

Date c.1790
Origin England
Weight 16oz (454g)
Length 13in (33cm)

The socket bayonet, which was first used by the French army in the 1670s, was fitted by means of a slot that connected to a stud on the barrel.

Knuckle bow

▲ BRITISH BAKER RIFLE SWORD BAYONET

Date c.1810
Origin UK
Weight 32oz (907g)
Length 24in (61cm)

The Baker rifle was the first British army firearm to come with a sword bayonet (see pp.192–93). Regular army troops were equipped with a Baker and its sword bayonet during the Napoleonic Wars.

▼ VOLUNTEER INFANTRY SWORD BAYONET

Date 1810
Origin UK
Weight 17½oz (500g)
Length 30½in (77.5cm)

This sword bayonet, made by London gun-maker Staudenmayer, equipped volunteer infantrymen in the Napoleonic Wars. The bayonet used a knuckle grip to lock the rifle to the bayonet.

Straight steel blade

18TH-CENTURY SWORDS

Through the 1700s, the sword was becoming less important as an infantry weapon, although it was still valued by the heavy and light cavalry, and also often fulfilled a ceremonial role. In China, it accounted for two out of the four main weapons—the staff, the spear, the singled-edged *dao* sword, and the double-edged *jian* sword. Tibetans, too, had a tradition of sword manufacture, with designs that were similar to Chinese models. Swordsmiths of the Ottoman Empire, established by Turks who migrated from central Asia to Anatolia, favored a curved blade derived from the Turko-Mongolian saber of the 13th century.

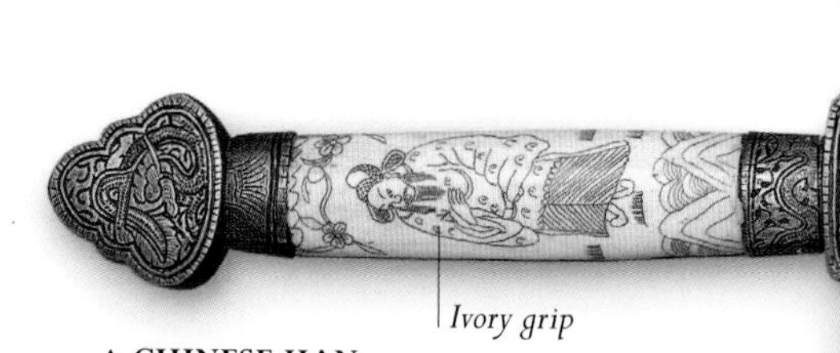

▲ CHINESE JIAN

Date	1735–1796
Origin	China
Weight	2¾lb (1.25kg)
Length	3½ft (1.07m)

Chinese swordsmen chose the straight, double-edged *jian* sword to show off their skills. This sword dates from the reign of Emperor Qianlong (ruled 1735–96), of the Manchu Qing dynasty.

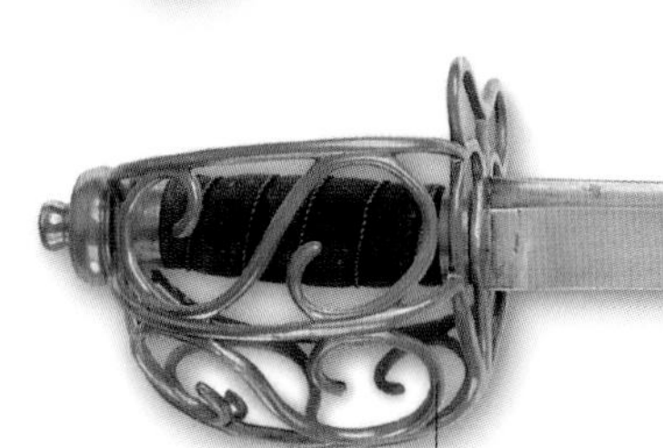

▲ DRAGOON SWORD

Date	c.1750
Origin	UK
Weight	2½lb (1.15kg)
Length	3¾ft (1.13m)

In the mid-18th century, British heavy cavalry regiments were redesignated as either Dragoon Guards or Heavy Dragoons, and the light cavalry as Light Dragoons. Long, single-edged swords were used by both divisions of heavy cavalry through the 18th century and into the Napoleonic era.

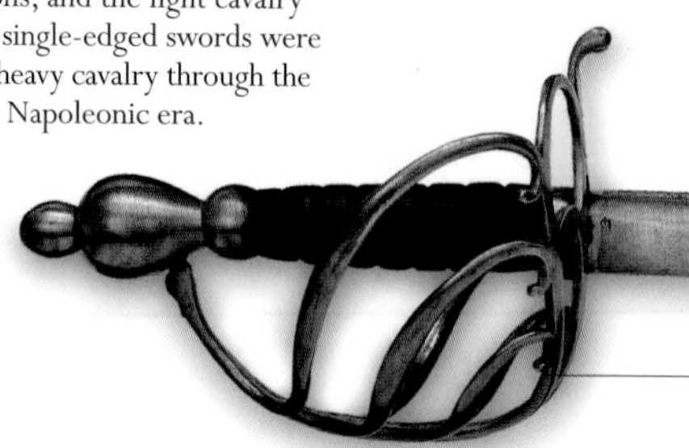

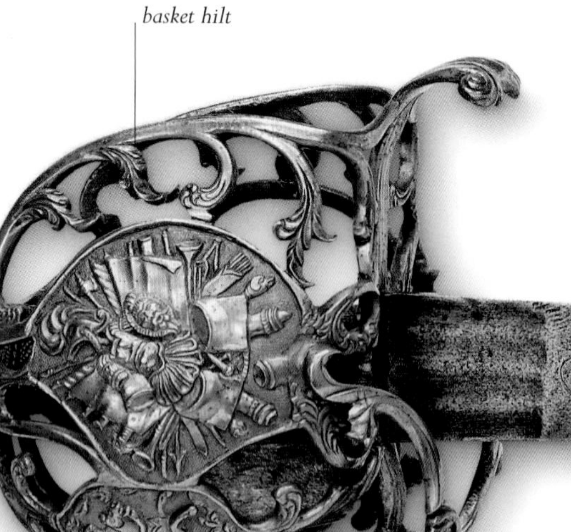

▲ CAVALRY OFFICERS' SWORD

Date	1730
Origin	UK
Weight	3½lb (1.6kg)
Length	33¾in (86cm)

This English cavalry officers' sword has a highly ornate, decorated, gilt-brass basket hilt. The blade is inscribed with the royal monogram "GR"—King George II—beneath a crown.

▼ SHAMSHIR

Date	18th century
Origin	Persia
Weight	31oz (890g)
Length	36½in (93cm)

The Persian *shamshir* sword, with its curved, single-edged blade, is better known to Europeans as the "scimitar." It was an excellent slashing weapon, but less effective for thrusting.

Back guard with three horizontal bars

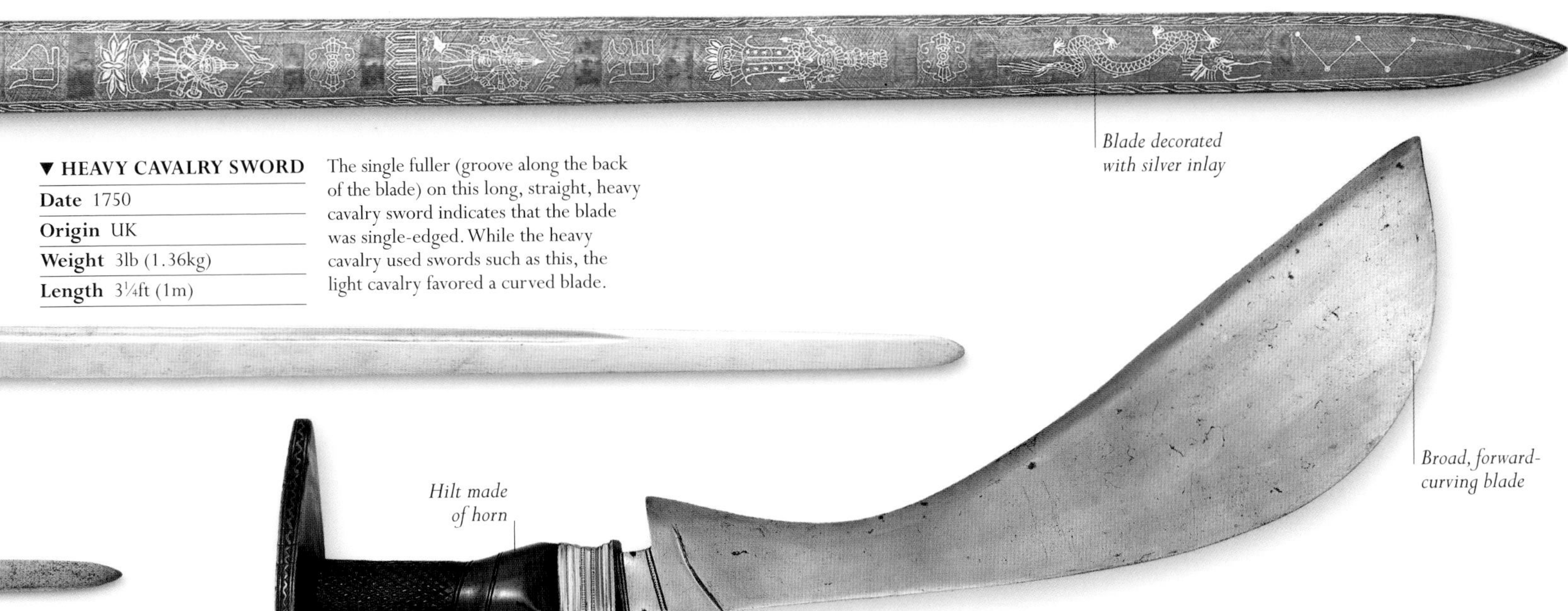

▼ HEAVY CAVALRY SWORD

Date	1750
Origin	UK
Weight	3lb (1.36kg)
Length	3¼ft (1m)

The single fuller (groove along the back of the blade) on this long, straight, heavy cavalry sword indicates that the blade was single-edged. While the heavy cavalry used swords such as this, the light cavalry favored a curved blade.

▲ AYUDHA KATTI

Date	18th century
Origin	India
Weight	2½lb (1.15kg)
Length	23½in (59.5cm)

The *ayudha katti*, or the Indian *moplah* sword, was used by the Muslims in the Malabar Coast of southwestern India. It was developed from an implement used to cut through dense undergrowth.

Blade flattened toward tip

▲ CAVALRY TROOPER'S SWORD

Date	1770–1790
Origin	UK
Weight	2¼lb (1kg)
Length	32¼in (82cm)

This cavalry trooper's sword was probably manufactured for the East India Company, an English enterprise formed in 1600 for trade with Asian countries. The sword's overall length, including the hilt, is 40in (102cm).

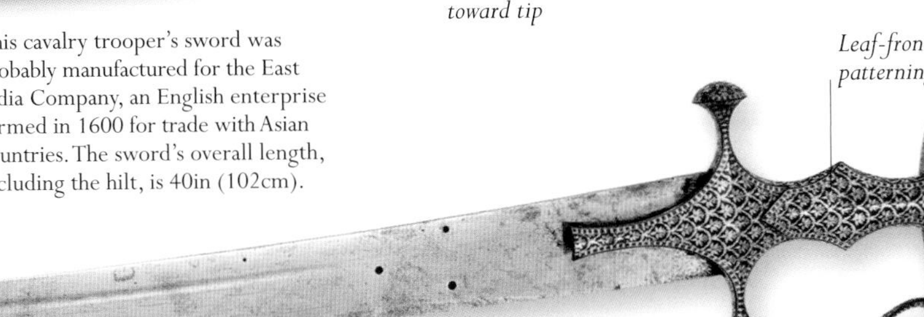

◀ NIZAMS' TALWAR

Date	18th century
Origin	India
Weight	2½lb (1.1kg)
Length	37¼in (94.9cm)

The blade inscription on this Indian *talwar*, or curved sword, suggests that it was made for the Nizams of Hyderabad, Muslim princes who ruled part of southern India from 1724.

Narrow fuller on back of blade

▲ NORTH AFRICAN SAIF

Date	Late 18th century
Origin	North Africa
Weight	24¾oz (700g)
Length	33in (83.5cm)

This *nimcha* or *saif* (Arabic words for sword) is of a type made in North Africa—a part of the Ottoman Empire from the 16th century—and in parts of Arabia associated with Yemen and the Hadramaut.

▼ HALF-BASKET CAVALRY SWORD

Date	c.1780
Origin	UK
Weight	2½lb (1.1kg)
Length	36¼in (92cm)

This half-basket cavalry sword is single-edged and marked "Gills Warranted": the manufacturer Gills of Birmingham was a major supplier of cavalry swords in the late 1700s.

18TH-CENTURY GUNS

In 18th-century Europe, the flintlock musket was developed to a very high standard, one such example being the "Brown Bess" Land-Pattern musket—the weapon of choice for British infantry from 1722 to 1838. In Japan and India, however, the matchlock gun remained the dominant form of firearm. Japanese traders had come into contact with Portuguese matchlock guns in 1543, and within a few years their craftsmen had begun making weapons of this type. Because of Japan's subsequent isolationist policies, the matchlock remained the dominant gun design until well into the 1800s. Indian matchlocks were often superbly built and featured exquisite decorations using inlaid ivory, gold, silver, or bone.

Serpentine match holder

Octagonal barrel

Shishi *(guardian lion) made of inlaid brass*

▲ JAPANESE HI NAWA JU

Date	Early 18th century
Origin	Japan
Weight	9lb (4.14kg)
Barrel	3½ft (1.03m)
Caliber	13.3mm

Japanese *hi nawa ju* (matchlocks) could fire three bullets a minute and pierce typical samurai armour at 165ft (50m). This matchlock was made by Kunitomo Tobei Shigeyasu of Omi, western Japan. The influence of the Sakai school is evident in its red-oak stock, although it has limited decoration.

Stock decorated with kara kusa *(foliage) scrolls in gold lacquer, with inlays of brass and silver*

▲ JAPANESE HI NAWA JU

Date	c.1700
Origin	Japan
Weight	6lb (2.77kg)
Barrel	39¼in (100cm)
Caliber	11.4mm

This early 18th-century matchlock musket is the work of the Enami family of Sakai, widely held to be among the finest Japanese gunmakers of the preindustrial era. The stock is made of red oak, while the decoration may have been added at a later date.

Pentagonal-section shoulder stock

Cock

Rear sight

Barrel-retaining pin

Ramrod pipe

Stock has high comb

Small of stock gripped in hand

▲ LIGHT DRAGOON FLINTLOCK CARBINE

Date	1756
Origin	England
Weight	7¼lb (3.3kg)
Barrel	36in (91.4cm)
Caliber	15-bore

British dragoons carried this carbine during the Seven Years' War (1756–63). It was a scaled-down version of the Long Land-Pattern musket, with a shorter barrel and in a smaller caliber.

Comb of stock to put shoulder in line of recoil

▲ PRUSSIAN RIFLED FLINTLOCK CARBINE

Date	1722
Origin	Prussia
Weight	7½lb (3.37kg)
Barrel	37in (94cm)
Caliber	15-bore

This carbine was manufactured until 1774 at the Prussian state arsenal at Potsdam (in modern-day Germany). The small of the stock is sized to fit in the hand, while the name of the armory is stamped on the lock plate.

Steel spring

Trigger guard

▲ SEA SERVICE MUSKET

Date	Mid-18th century
Origin	England
Weight	8¾lb (4kg)
Barrel	37in (94cm)
Caliber	.75in

This English Sea Service musket is fitted with a discharger cup on the muzzle. The discharger fired cast-iron hand grenades, making this an ideal weapon for use prior to boarding.

Ramrod

Rest terminates in forked antelope horn

▲ TIBETAN MEDA

Date c.1780
Origin Tibet
Weight 9lb (4.15kg)
Barrel 3¾ft (1.11m)
Caliber 17mm

Tibet was largely isolated from the rest of the world but carried out trade with India and China. This *meda* (matchlock) shows Chinese influence in form and decoration. Attached to the fore stock is an unusual rest, while the ramrod is a modern replacement.

Folding spike bayonet

▲ DOUBLE-BARRELED FLINTLOCK WITH BAYONET

Date c.1800
Origin England

The blunderbuss-type muzzle of this double-barreled weapon features a folding spike bayonet. Naval crews appreciated guns that combined short-range firepower with a stabbing weapon.

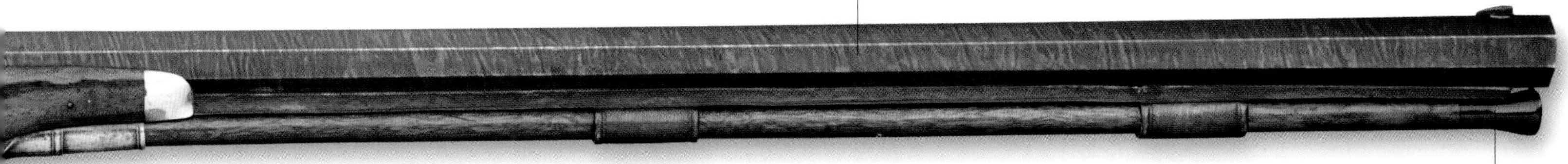

▲ TURKISH SNAPHAUNCE

Date Late 18th century
Origin Turkey
Weight 6lb (2.69kg)
Barrel 28½in (72.4cm)

The smoothbore Turkish *tüfek*, or musket, combines a pentagonal-section butt with an octagonal barrel. Its lock is a snaphaunce, a predecessor of the flintlock, which had become obsolete in northern Europe by the early 1600s.

Grooved barrel

Ramrod

▲ ENGLISH FLINTLOCK RIFLE

Date 1791
Origin England
Weight 7¾lb (3.5kg)
Barrel 32in (81cm)
Caliber .680in

Innovative London gunsmith Henry Nock made several volley guns for the Royal Navy and numbered Ezekiel Baker among his apprentices. Nock designed this flintlock weapon—possibly an officer's private purchase—with nine-groove rifling.

Fore sight

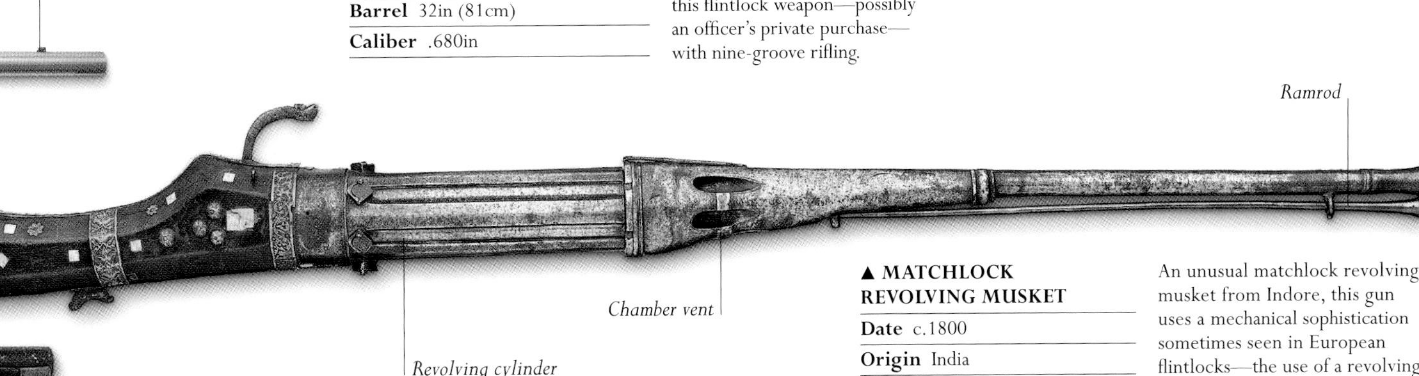

▲ MATCHLOCK REVOLVING MUSKET

Date c.1800
Origin India
Weight 13lb (5.9kg)
Barrel 24½in (62cm)
Caliber .6in

An unusual matchlock revolving musket from Indore, this gun uses a mechanical sophistication sometimes seen in European flintlocks—the use of a revolving cylinder to create a multi-shot weapon. The cylinder is indexed manually.

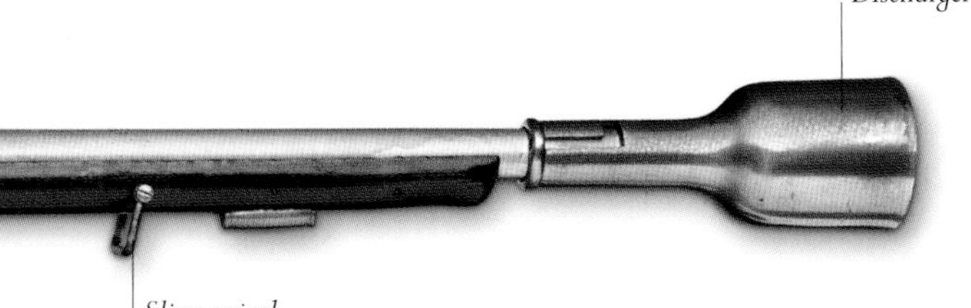

▼ INDORE TORADAR

Date c.1800
Origin India
Weight 7½lb (3.4kg)
Barrel 3¾ft (1.12m)
Caliber .55in

This simple matchlock from Indore, central India, has a pronounced recurve. Four leather thongs serve as barrel bands, although the one closest to the breech is made of wire.

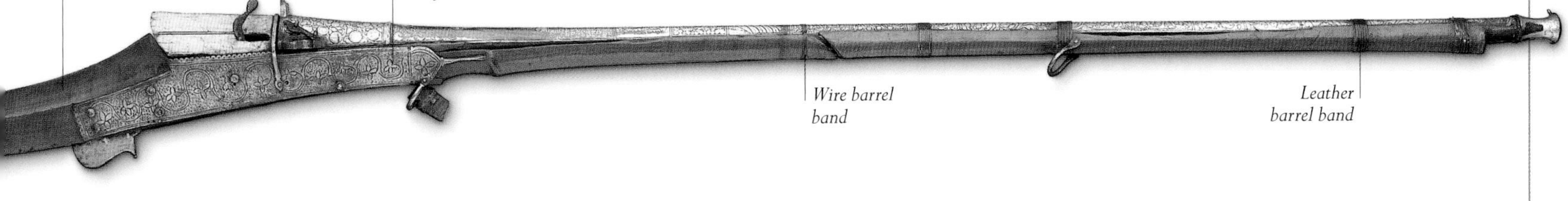

Pentagonal-section butt

Decorated iron lock plate

Wire barrel band

Leather barrel band

THE BATTLE OF FONTENOY

The European wars of the mid-18th century were contested with a mixture of formality and savagery. The battle at Fontenoy is a classic example of an era dominated by the musket-volleys of disciplined infantry, maneuvering with parade-ground precision in spite of heavy casualties.

In 1745, during the War of the Austrian Succession, a French army, commanded by Maurice de Saxe, was campaigning in Flanders. Its opponent, the Pragmatic Army, consisted of Dutch, British, Austrian, and Hanoverian forces under the command of the Duke of Cumberland, son of King George II. Saxe seized the strategic initiative by laying siege to the fortress town of Tournai. The Pragmatic Army had to aid the town, thus allowing Saxe to meet them on a ground of his choosing. He took up a defensive position along a ridge in front of Tournai, anchored by the Scheldt River on his right flank and woods on his left. He fortified two villages, Antoing and Fontenoy, and had five redoubts—earthwork strongpoints—constructed in front of the line. The Pragmatic Army approached Fontenoy on May 9 after an exhausting march. Without having fully appreciated the strength of Saxe's position, the Allied commanders decided to attack on May 11.

HOLDING THE FIELD

The rival armies were each around 50,000 strong. Aristocratic officers led bodies of mostly professional soldiers, the infantry armed with flintlock musket and bayonet. The French had over 100 cannon, probably more than their opponents, and were also superior in cavalry. The Pragmatic Army deployed with the Dutch and Austrians on its left, the Hanoverians and British on the right. The attack began badly. After an ineffectual preliminary bombardment by heavy cannon, frontal infantry assaults against the French right crumbled in the face of withering firepower. On the French left, the Redoubt of Eu remained intact because the British officer ordered to take it refused to move, apparently unnerved by French skirmishers in the nearby woods.

With the attack having failed to his left and right, Cumberland decided to advance. Urged on, the British infantry marched smartly up the hill between Fontenoy and the intact redoubt. Cannonballs fired from the flanking strongpoints carved gaps in the British ranks, but, undeterred, they progressed to the top of the ridge, bringing them face to face with the opposing infantry. According to the French writer Voltaire, the commanders of the British and French guards each politely called on the other to fire first. There was an end to civilities once the point-blank exchange began, for soldiers fell in heaps, hundreds cut down by a single volley. The British pushed their field guns forward to batter the French with grapeshot, at which point the French line collapsed.

Saxe mustered reserves of infantry and cavalry to launch desperate counterattacks. Having advanced deep into the French position, the British faced assaults from the flanks as well as the front. The Irish Brigade, the "Wild Geese," fighting as mercenaries in the French army, delivered an especially destructive charge. Forced to give way, the British infantry managed an orderly retreat, screened by their cavalry. The French held the field and claimed the victory. The day's fighting had cost some 5,000 lives, with more than twice that number wounded, and many of them maimed for life.

BATTLEFIELD PANORAMA
French King Louis XV came to Flanders to witness the battle. He was close to fleeing at the moment of crisis, before Saxe organized the counterattack.

RIFLEMEN OF THE AMERICAN REVOLUTION

At the start of the American Revolutionary War in 1775, skilled riflemen were among the first companies of soldiers raised by the rebellious North American colonies to fight the British Army and its Loyalist supporters. These riflemen had their origins in the American frontier world of hunters and farmers, and relied on their skill with a long-barreled rifle to carve out a life in the wild. Some riflemen were incorporated into units of General George Washington's army, but others retained their independent spirit along with their own equipment and clothing. They proved themselves effective snipers and skirmishers.

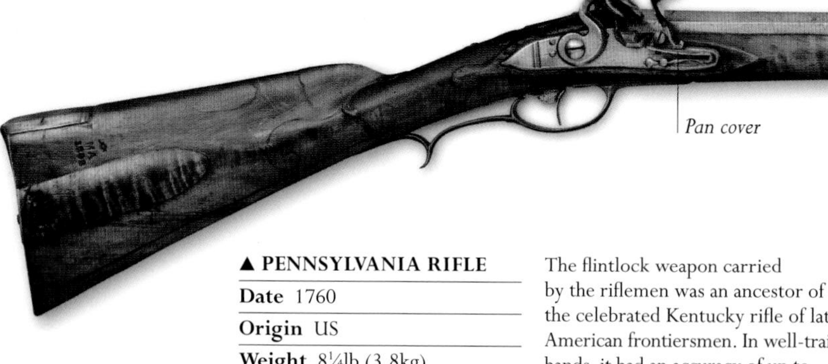

▲ PENNSYLVANIA RIFLE

Date 1760
Origin US
Weight 8¼lb (3.8kg)
Barrel 3¾ft (1.14m)
Calibre .45

The flintlock weapon carried by the riflemen was an ancestor of the celebrated Kentucky rifle of later American frontiersmen. In well-trained hands, it had an accuracy of up to 1,200ft (365m). The long, rifled barrel made it far more accurate than the muskets used by European armies.

◄ HATCHET

Date c.1775
Origin US
Weight 24oz (680g)
Length 14in (35.5cm)

A skilled hunter and woodsman, the rifleman usually carried a hatchet—tucked into his belt—for constructing shelters and making fires.

► GUN POUCH

Date c.1775
Origin US
Material Leather

Riflemen carried a leather gun pouch slung over the shoulder. The pouch contained only the essentials for their rifle, while a linen knapsack held personal items.

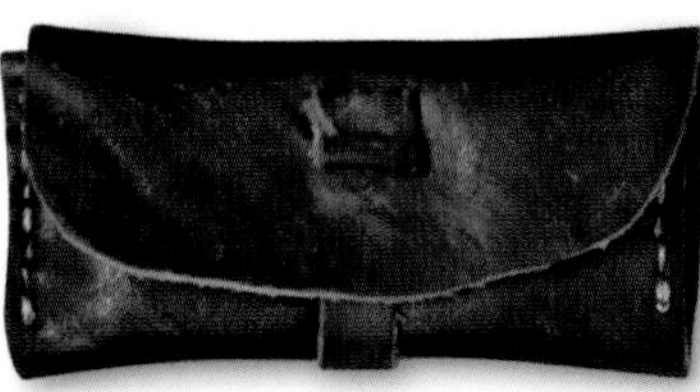

▲ FLINT POUCH

Date c.1775
Origin US
Material Leather

Using tow (hemp or flax fibers) to catch sparks struck from his flint and steel, a rifleman could light a fire. He often also carried a pouch of dry kindling.

Undershirt

▲ HUNTING SHIRT

Date c.1775
Origin US
Material Linen

Many riflemen favoured a fringed linen shirt worn with a belt fastened around the waist. The shirts were often dyed in natural shades of brown or green for camouflage.

◀ **FELT HAT**

Date c.1775

Origin US

Material Felt

The flamboyant headgear of the riflemen reflected their prewar life spent in tracking and hunting animals. Many riflemen decorated their hats with animal tails instead of feathers.

▶ **POWDER HORN**

Date c.1775

Origin US

Material Horn

Riflemen carried their gunpowder in a horn. They measured out the main charge, which was poured down the muzzle, as well as the primer, which was tipped into the pan.

▶ **CANTEEN**

Date c.1775

Origin US

Material Wood

A rifleman's wooden canteen was constructed like a barrel with side staves. It had to be refilled whenever possible or the wood would shrink, resulting in leakage.

◀ **BREECHES**

Date c.1775

Origin US

Material Wool

Riflemen wore woolen breeches with leggings made of hide or a simple blanket material. They were fastened with pewter buttons at the waist, pockets, front flap, and knee.

◀ **MOCCASINS**

Date c.1775

Origin US

Material Deerhide

Frontiersmen followed the example of Native Americans in making lightweight moccasins out of deerhide, although the styles they favored showed elements of European taste.

WEAPONS, UNIFORMS, AND KIT OF THE AMERICAN REVOLUTION

At the Continental Congress, in June 1775, the 13 American colonies in revolt against British rule decided to form an army under the command of General George Washington. Initially made up of New England militiamen and rifleman volunteers, this Continental Army was later recruited on a quota basis from the 13 states. On the opposite page, the Continental Army uniform is that of the 4th Maryland Independent Company, formed in January 1776. A significant number of Americans joined up to fight alongside the British. Some Loyalists formed British regiments, while others fought in irregular militias. The uniform shown here is that of the Queen's Rangers, a Loyalist regiment established in 1776, in New York.

▲ **QUEEN'S RANGERS PLUMED CAP**

Date 1776
Origin US
Material Leather, feather

The Queen's Rangers were named in honor of George III's wife, Queen Caroline. Their leather cap bore the black cockade of the royal house of Hanover.

▶ **QUEEN'S RANGERS JACKET AND TROUSERS**

Date 1776
Origin US
Material Linen, canvas

This Loyalist regiment was the first in the British Army to wear green uniforms for the purpose of camouflage. The short green jacket was known as a "round jacket."

▲ **QUEEN'S RANGERS KNAPSACK AND CARTRIDGE BOX**

Date 1776
Origin US
Material Canvas, leather

Both the knapsack and the cartridge box bear an image of George III's crown. The brass badge on the cartridge box has the initials GR (*George Rex*).

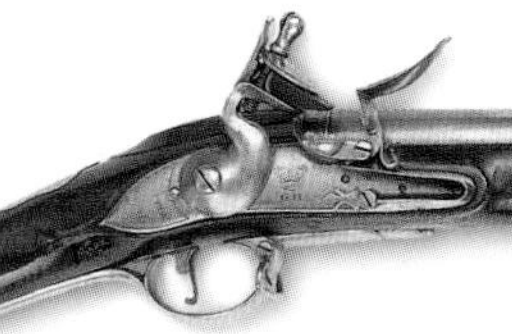

Fore stock sized to fit in hand

Ramrod pipe

▲ LONG LAND-PATTERN FLINTLOCK MUSKET

Date	1742
Origin	England
Weight	10¼lb (4.7kg)
Barrel	4ft (1.17m)
Caliber	10-bore

Most British infantrymen in the American War used the "Brown Bess" Land-Pattern musket. This long version of the gun was first issued in 1722, while shorter versions followed in 1768 and 1797.

▼ FERGUSON RIFLE

Date	1776
Origin	England
Weight	7½lb (3.5kg)
Length	4–5ft (1.21–1.52m)
Caliber	.65in

The breech-loading Ferguson rifle was used in limited numbers on the British side in the American Revolutionary War. It was designed by a Scottish army officer, Major Patrick Ferguson.

Trigger guard—one turn lowered the breech plug

Linen dyed purple with red collar and cuffs

▶ MARYLAND INDEPENDENT COMPANY SHIRT AND WAISTCOAT

Date	1776
Origin	US
Material	Linen

The men of the 4th Maryland Independent Company wore a purple hunting shirt with a white waistcoat. The unit was one of seven companies of 100 men authorized by Maryland in January 1776.

▲ MARYLAND INDEPENDENT COMPANY TRICORNE HAT

Date	1776
Origin	US
Material	Wool, linen

The soldiers wore a tricorne (three-cornered) hat similar in style to British regulars. By spring 1776, nine companies together formed the 1st Maryland Regiment under Colonel William Smallwood.

HUNTING SHIRT

WAISTCOAT

BAYONET ON BELT

▶ MARYLAND INDEPENDENT COMPANY KNAPSACK AND BELT

Date	1776
Origin	US
Material	Canvas, leather

The Maryland troops were highly regarded by General George Washington after they distinguished themselves at the Battle of Long Island in August 1776. Their knapsacks bore the company insignia.

Shoulder straps

KNAPSACK

Trigger guard

▲ RAPPAHANNOCK PISTOL

Date	c.1776
Origin	US
Barrel	9in (23cm)
Caliber	.69in

At the Rappahannock Forge near Falmouth, Virginia, Scottish émigré James Hunter produced the first American-manufactured military pistol. It was a copy of the British Light Dragoon pistol, and was used by the Light Dragoons in the Continental Army.

KEY **FIGURE**

MARQUIS DE VAUBAN
1633–1707

France's greatest military engineer, Vauban, directed his first siege in 1657, aged 24. Having won the confidence of King Louis XIV, he oversaw the construction of 37 French fortresses and improved more than 300. But he was, above all, valued for his innovative and aggressive conduct of sieges, employing the system of saps and parallels.

▲ After directing 48 sieges during the course of his career, Vauban retired in 1703 with the rank of marshal.

KEY DEVELOPMENT

THE DEVELOPMENT OF SIEGE WARFARE

By the late 17th century, the construction of fortifications and the conduct of sieges in Europe had become elaborate and formalized, and were the subject of learned treatises by renowned engineers, as well as the focus of military campaigns.

The introduction of cannon into European siege warfare from the 15th century triggered the rapid evolution in defensive fortifications. The challenge was to make a fortress that was less vulnerable to cannon fire than the old stone castles, while being capable of using cannon as a defensive armament. In place of high castle walls, military engineers developed a squat structure known as a "star fort" (see p.117). This was a polygonal fortification, half buried behind a deep, wide ditch, with bastions protruding at each angle. The bastions were wedge-shaped artillery platforms that provided an all-round field of fire, so that soldiers assaulting the walls, or another bastion, would come under fire from the flank or rear. A slope, or "glacis," of earth in front of the ditch further protected the walls against cannon shot. This basic model was soon developed further, with outworks—fortifications built outside the fortress to delay or prevent besieging forces advancing their guns and soldiers to the main walls.

NEW STRUCTURES

During the 17th century, the complexity of major fortifications left the simple "star fort" model behind. Triangular fortifications, or outworks, called "ravelins" (or "demi-lunes") thrust forward between angle bastions. Vulnerable points were defended by "hornworks"—defensive structures comprising two bastions joined by a short wall. Citadels were built as backup forts within fortress towns, where garrisons could continue resistance after the town had fallen. These complex fortifications were expensive to build and man. Many fortifications were built by the Dutch Republic, which was threatened first by Spain in the Eighty Years' War (1568–1648) and then by France in the wars of Louis XIV (reigned 1643–1715). Louis XIV, meanwhile, authorized his chief engineer, the Marquis de Vauban, to build a string of fortresses along the frontiers of France.

By the time of Louis XIV's reign, sieges were the focal points of conflicts. In the Nine Years' War (1688–97), pitting France against a Grand Alliance that included the Dutch, there were 21 major sieges. Field battles resulted chiefly from efforts to relieve ongoing sieges.

▲ **MORTAR SHELL**
Mortars fired explosive shells consisting of a spherical iron casing packed with gunpowder and ignited by a burning fuse. They saw much use during sieges.

WEAPONS OF WAR

Special weaponry evolved for siege warfare, including mortars that launched explosive shells over walls or into siege trenches, and grenades, which were hurled by a new type of elite soldier, the grenadier. Engineers, such as Vauban and his Dutch counterpart, Menno van Coehoorn, formalized and set out the conduct of sieges in treatises. Despite this formality, the siege tactics

of Louis XIV's wars were aggressive and designed to produce a rapid result. These tactics involved digging trenches toward enemy fortifications in a zigzag, so that fire could not rake the trench from end to end. At intervals, engineers dug transverse "parallels," lines to which the siege cannon then advanced. Under Vauban's system, the third parallel was the last. From there, soldiers might emerge from their trenches, with grenadiers at the fore, to mount an assault on the "covered way"—the defensive position held by the enemy infantry, on the outer edge of the fortress's ditch. Once this position was taken, siege cannon could advance close to the walls, and the defenders would be expected to surrender—a gesture rewarded by honorable treatment. Of course, actual sieges only approximated this pattern: for example, tunneling sappers might blow up walls using mines, or moats might be drained or crossed by soldiers on rafts.

Ironically, despite the money lavished upon them, by the 18th century fortifications rarely resisted a siege for long. The golden age of siege warfare and fortifications was over by 1720.

"The **more powder we burn**, the **less blood we lose**"

ATTRIBUTED TO MARQUIS DE VAUBAN, AT THE SIEGE OF CHARLEROI, 1693

◄ **THE SACK OF MAGDEBURG**
If defenders refused to surrender, they faced massacre when fortifications were taken by assault. At Magdeburg, in 1631, more than 20,000 people were killed when the city fell after a six-month siege.

◄ **THE SIEGE OF MAASTRICHT**
In June 1673, French King Louis XIV, invading the Netherlands, besieged the fortress city of Maastricht with an army of 45,000 men. Vauban directed the siege, overcoming the defenses within the month.

KEY **EVENTS**

1650–1700

- **1667** The French army details specific soldiers to specialize in throwing grenades—the first instance of grenadiers.
- **1674** Dutch military engineer Menno van Coehoorn introduces a man-portable mortar gun for use in sieges.
- **1678** French King Louis XIV appoints Vauban his commissioner-general of fortifications, embarking on a large-scale program of fortress-building around the frontiers of France.
- **1685** Van Coehoorn publishes his influential treatise entitled *New Fortress Construction.*
- **1692** Vauban conducts the Siege of Namur (see pp.180–81), in which van Coehoorn directs the defense; the fortress falls to the French in five weeks.
- **1695** After a two-month siege conducted by van Coehoorn, the Grand Alliance retakes Namur from the French.

FIELD AND SIEGE ARTILLERY

Through the 17th and 18th centuries, artillerymen continued to use smoothbore cast-bronze and cast-iron firing stone or cast-iron shot. The next breakthrough in artillery design came in the mid-19th century with the development of rifled cannon, improved gunpowder, elongated projectiles, and special instruments. While guns fired in a level trajectory, the lighter, short-barreled mortar was used to fire in an elevated trajectory—generally more than 45 degrees. Smaller hand mortars were also developed for firing fuzed grenades. These are often named after the Dutch military engineer Menno, baron van Coehoorn, who developed a design for this weapon.

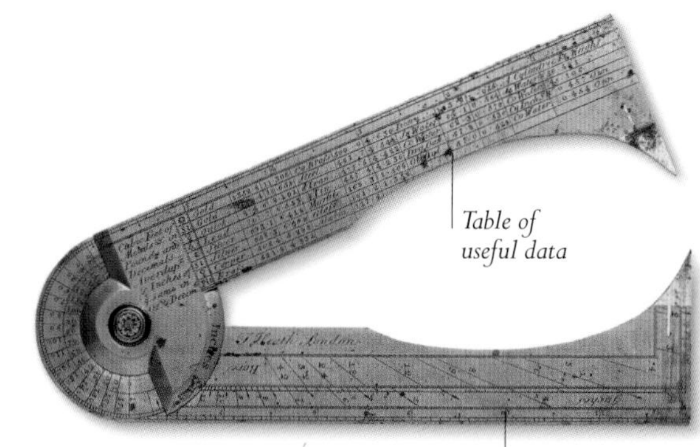

► GUNNER'S CALLIPERS

Date	18th century
Origin	England

Callipers were used to measure the diameter of the cannonball. When the two arms were crossed over, they could also make internal measurements, such as that of the cannon's bore.

▲ GUNNER'S STILETTO

Date	18th century
Origin	Italy
Weight	5½oz (150g)
Length	13½in (34cm)

Artillerymen used this specialized dagger for measuring the bore of the gun and the size of the shot. It could also be used for self-defence in close-quarters combat.

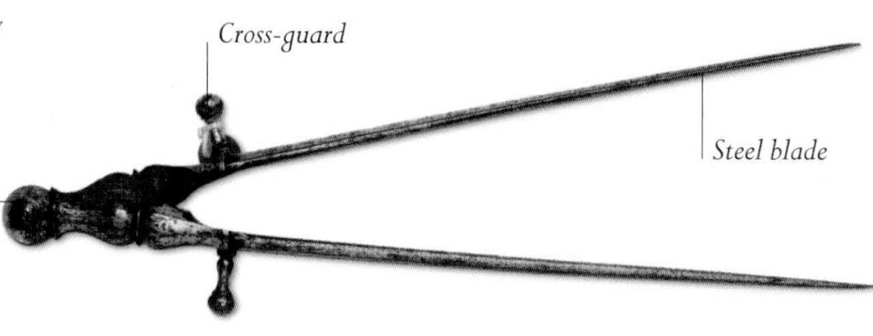

▲ GUNNER'S DIVIDERS

Date	18th century
Origin	England
Length	17¼in (44cm)

Dividers were used with a rule to perform calculations on the proportions of fortifications. This steel pair has a cross-guard, indicating they could also be used as a dagger if the artillery position came under attack.

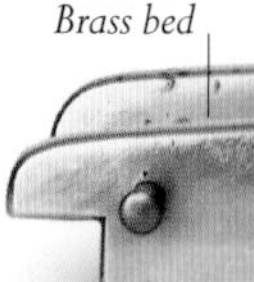

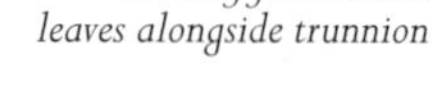

▲ INDIAN 6-POUNDER

Date	1693–1743
Origin	India
Weight	3.7 tons (3.4 tonnes)
Length	12½ft (3.86m)
Caliber	9.5cm

The bore of this gun is sleeved with an iron tube made from parallel strips welded together. This made the gun and the bore more durable, especially when the gun was used to fire stone shot.

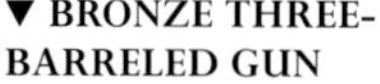

▼ BRONZE THREE-BARRELED GUN

Date	1704
Origin	France
Weight	1,996lb (905kg)
Length	5¼ft (1.62m)
Caliber	11.5cm

Three barrels, two side by side with the third above, were cast in one piece and could be fired one at a time or simultaneously. The intriguing design did not prove successful in practice, because the gun was difficult to reload and very heavy to maneuver.

◄ COEHOORN MORTAR

Date	c.1720
Origin	England
Weight	86lb (39kg)
Length	12½in (32cm)
Caliber	4.5in

The Coehoorn mortar was a small, portable mortar used to despatch grenades. Swiss-born Andrew Schalch, first Master Founder of the Royal Brass Foundry at Woolwich in England, cast this one. It is mounted on its original wooden bed, which is just 12in (30cm) wide and 20in (51cm) long.

Winch used to lift heavy bomb and lower it into muzzle

13in mortar bomb

◀ BRITISH MORTAR

Date	1760
Origin	England
Weight	1.4 tons (1.27 tonnes)
Length	27½in (70cm)
Caliber	33cm

The mortar was a muzzle-loading artillery weapon in use since the 15th century, especially in sieges. This gun, in use for about 100 years, was the largest in British service.

Gun has range of 601½ yards (550m)

▲ FRENCH 6-POUNDER FIELD GUN

Date	1813
Origin	France
Weight	844¼lb (383kg)
Length	5½ft (1.68m)
Caliber	9.6cm

A crew of eight could fire two rounds a minute with this 6-pounder field gun. The gun's carriage is marked "taken at Waterloo."

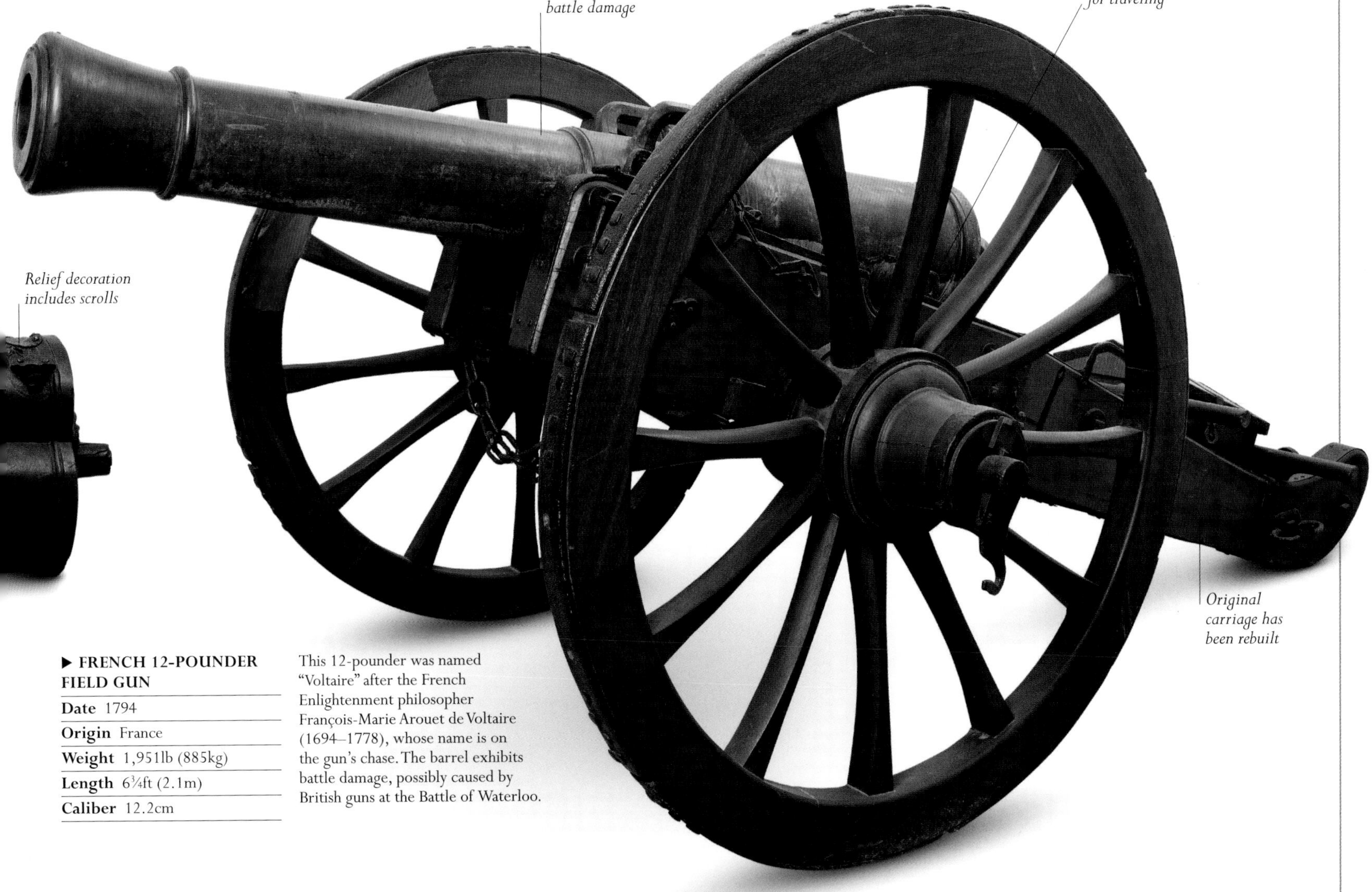

Barrel shows battle damage

Second set of trunnion holes to position gun for traveling

Relief decoration includes scrolls

Original carriage has been rebuilt

▶ FRENCH 12-POUNDER FIELD GUN

Date	1794
Origin	France
Weight	1,951lb (885kg)
Length	6¾ft (2.1m)
Caliber	12.2cm

This 12-pounder was named "Voltaire" after the French Enlightenment philosopher François-Marie Arouet de Voltaire (1694–1778), whose name is on the gun's chase. The barrel exhibits battle damage, possibly caused by British guns at the Battle of Waterloo.

THE KING AT THE SIEGE
French King Louis XIV (in blue) and his entourage observe the Siege of Namur. The detail of the fortifications is clearly shown, with bastions projecting forward from the town walls and the citadel on the rocky outcrop behind.

THE SIEGE OF NAMUR

During French King Louis XIV's reign (1643–1715), sieges were the most characteristic operations in European warfare. The Siege of Namur in 1692 is a famous example of this formalized combat, which was led by military engineers who designed the fortifications and also conducted the sieges.

Namur in Flanders was a strongpoint of the Grand Alliance (comprising the British, Dutch, Austrians, and Spanish), opponents of the French during the Nine Years' War. The fortified town stood on a plain on the north bank of the Sambre River; the citadel—an elaborate complex of fortifications—was set on rocky heights behind the town, on the south bank of the river.

In May 1692, King Louis came to witness his army's siege of Namur, led by his master engineer, the Marquis de Vauban. The fortress's defense was organized by Vauban's rival, Dutch engineer Menno van Coehoorn.

Vauban followed his standard procedures: beginning on May 25, two lines of earthworks were dug encircling Namur. These were both to blockade the town and protect the French, who were encamped between the lines, against attack from an Alliance relief army. Then, within this encirclement, men dug lines of zigzag trenches, or saps, toward the weakest point of the fortification. At intervals a transverse trench, or parallel, was dug and positions created for gun batteries. The cannon were then moved forward to the parallel, thus steadily advancing toward the fortress. The initial aim of the French batteries was to clear the fortifications of artillery. Vauban used ricochet fire, sending cannon balls bouncing into the defenses, to force defenders to abandon their positions.

The town's low-lying fortifications, fronted by a ditch and a glacis (a slope at the fortification's base), offered a minimal target while giving defenders a clear field of fire: the French troops in their trenches were bombarded by explosive shells lobbed by high-trajectory mortars and howitzers.

Despite heavy fire, the French trenches were able to be dug close enough for troops to batter a breach in the walls with their siege guns. Once the breach was opened, the defenders negotiated the surrender of the town.

THE FIGHT FOR THE CITADEL

The siege was not over, however, for the garrison withdrew to the citadel, where the fighting resumed in earnest. Under the surrender terms the French agreed not to attack the citadel from the side nearest the town, where the defenses were weakest. Instead they had to overcome an elaborate series of outworks fronting the main citadel.

Coehoorn directed the defense of the strongest of these, Fort William, in person. While Vauban dug his saps and parallels, French mortars bombarded the defenders with explosive shells launched over the walls. On June 22, after a French infantry assault, Coehoorn surrendered the fort and was taken prisoner. The main citadel, however, remained unbreached.

The French, meanwhile, had run into supply difficulties: without sufficient fodder, their many thousands of horses began to starve. Persistent wet weather had also turned the ground to a quagmire and carts trying to bring heavy ammunition up to the batteries foundered. It was a profound relief to Vauban and his king when the citadel's defenses were breached with sudden ease—possibly through an act of betrayal from within the garrison, which somehow left a section of the fortifications undefended. The garrison formally capitulated on June 30 and was granted the honors of war, marching out with drums beating and banners flying.

KEY **FIGURE**

NAPOLEON BONAPARTE
1769–1821

Born in Corsica, Napoleon was an artillery officer who became the most charismatic general in the French Revolutionary armies. In 1799, he seized power in a military coup, declaring himself Emperor in 1804. Defeated at Waterloo in 1815, he died a prisoner of the British.

▲ An aggressive risk-taker, Napoleon used cavalry and artillery as shock forces on the battlefield. He fought 50 battles, winning most of them.

KEY DEVELOPMENT

ARMIES OF THE REVOLUTIONARY ERA

The French Revolution of 1789 ushered in a new era of mass citizen armies, with battles fought on an unprecedented scale. The military genius of French emperor Napoleon Bonaparte, meanwhile, whose empire grew out of the revolution, gave European warfare a fresh dynamism.

From 1792 to 1815, the French Revolutionary Wars and the Napoleonic Wars kept Europe in an almost continuous state of warfare. There were a number of technological innovations during this period, some of which had an impact on the battlefield. The Chappe telegraph system, introduced by the French, in 1792 allowed messages to be sent rapidly over long distances via a chain of visual semaphore signaling stations—an invention of great value for military commanders. Meanwhile in 1794, at the Battle of Fleurus, the French also experimented with the use of a manned balloon for reconnaissance—the first ever instance of aerial warfare. Elsewhere, the British adopted shrapnel shells as anti-personnel munitions, and Congreve rockets as auxiliary artillery. However, the impact of these innovations was overshadowed by the changes that took place in military organization and tactics.

THE LEVÉE EN MASSE

In 1793, threatened with invasion by a coalition of hostile powers, the revolutionary French Republic issued a call for a *levée en masse*—the conscription

▶ **THE BATTLE OF AUSTERLITZ**
The mounted Russian Imperial Guard, flourishing their sabers, clash with Napoleon's infantry, armed with musket and bayonet, at Austerlitz in 1805.

KEY **EVENTS**

1792–1815

■ **1792** The French Revolutionary Wars begin, with a declaration of war against Austria.

■ **1793–94** Lazare Carnot, war minister of the French Republic, orders mass conscription, raising an army of around one and a half million soldiers.

■ **1805–06** Victories over the Austrian and Russian armies at Austerlitz, and the Prussians at Jena-Auerstadt, establish the dominance of Napoleon's Grande Armée.

■ **1807** Prussia reforms its armed forces by mass conscription, ending corporal punishment, and adopting combined arms tactics.

■ **1812** Napoleon invades Russia with an army of half a million men; about one in five of these survive the army's retreat from Moscow.

■ **1815** Napoleon is defeated at Waterloo by a British army under the Duke of Wellington, and the Prussian army of Field Marshal Gebhard Leberecht von Blücher.

"They came upon us **crying and shouting**, to the very **point of our bayonets**"

BRITISH OFFICER CAPTAIN THOMAS POCOCKE, DESCRIBING THE FRENCH AT VIMIERO, 1808

of all able-bodied men under 25. It was an appeal for what would later be called "total war": the rest of the population was to devote itself to supporting the war effort. The citizen-soldiers were expected to fight out of devotion to the nation and the revolution—rather than through fear of the lash and the gallows—and the officer ranks, previously monopolized by the aristocracy, were opened up to competent soldiers of all social backgrounds.

THE GRANDE ARMÉE

The new political climate brought about by the French Revolution transformed France into an expansionist power. Napoleon Bonaparte established himself as the country's most popular general and then became, in effect, a military dictator. By 1805, he had built the "Grande Armée," an army divided into six all-arms corps, each capable of independent maneuver. Freed from reliance on a supply train by living off the land, Napoleon moved his army at speed to bring the enemy to battle and destroy them. On the battlefield he emphasized the attack: musket-armed infantry advanced in dense columns preceded by swarms of skirmishers, and the cuirassiers (armored heavy cavalry) mounted massed charges. Gunners deployed cannon aggressively—Napoleon regarded the artillery as potential battle-winners, rather than a mere support to infantry and cavalry.

France's enemies took time to adjust to this new scale and dynamism, but over time they mobilized resources in their own version of total war. In Spain from 1808, and later, in Russia in 1812, France was defeated by relentless resistance, in the form of guerrilla warfare and pitched battles. At Leipzig in 1813, in the largest battle Europe had ever seen, Napoleon commanded an army of 200,000 men, but was outnumbered by two-to-one. With mass conscription and ever-improving weapons, this was the era that saw European societies begin a path to militarization—one that would bear bitter fruit in the world wars of the 20th century.

▲ THE CONGREVE ROCKET
Inspired by the rocket artillery of the Indian kingdom of Mysore, the British Congreve rocket was propelled by black powder and had an explosive warhead.

▼ THE BATTLE OF VALMY
The first battle of the French Revolutionary Wars, fought in September 1792, was a victory for French artillery defending the heights of Valmy.

FRENCH REVOLUTIONARY AND NAPOLEONIC INFANTRY

Infantrymen in the French Revolutionary and Napoleonic Wars fought mainly with smoothbore flintlock muskets and bayonets, and most of them also carried a sword. Their white trousers and coat were complemented by a "shako," or hat, complete with regimental badge and pompom. The infantry comprised fusilier companies fighting alongside grenadiers—the senior infantry regiment, who were particularly well kitted out—and, after 1805, *voltigeurs* (shorter soldiers who specialized in skirmishing and scouting). The troops of Napoleon's "Grande Armée" were celebrated not only for their discipline, courage, and devotion, but also for their ornate uniforms.

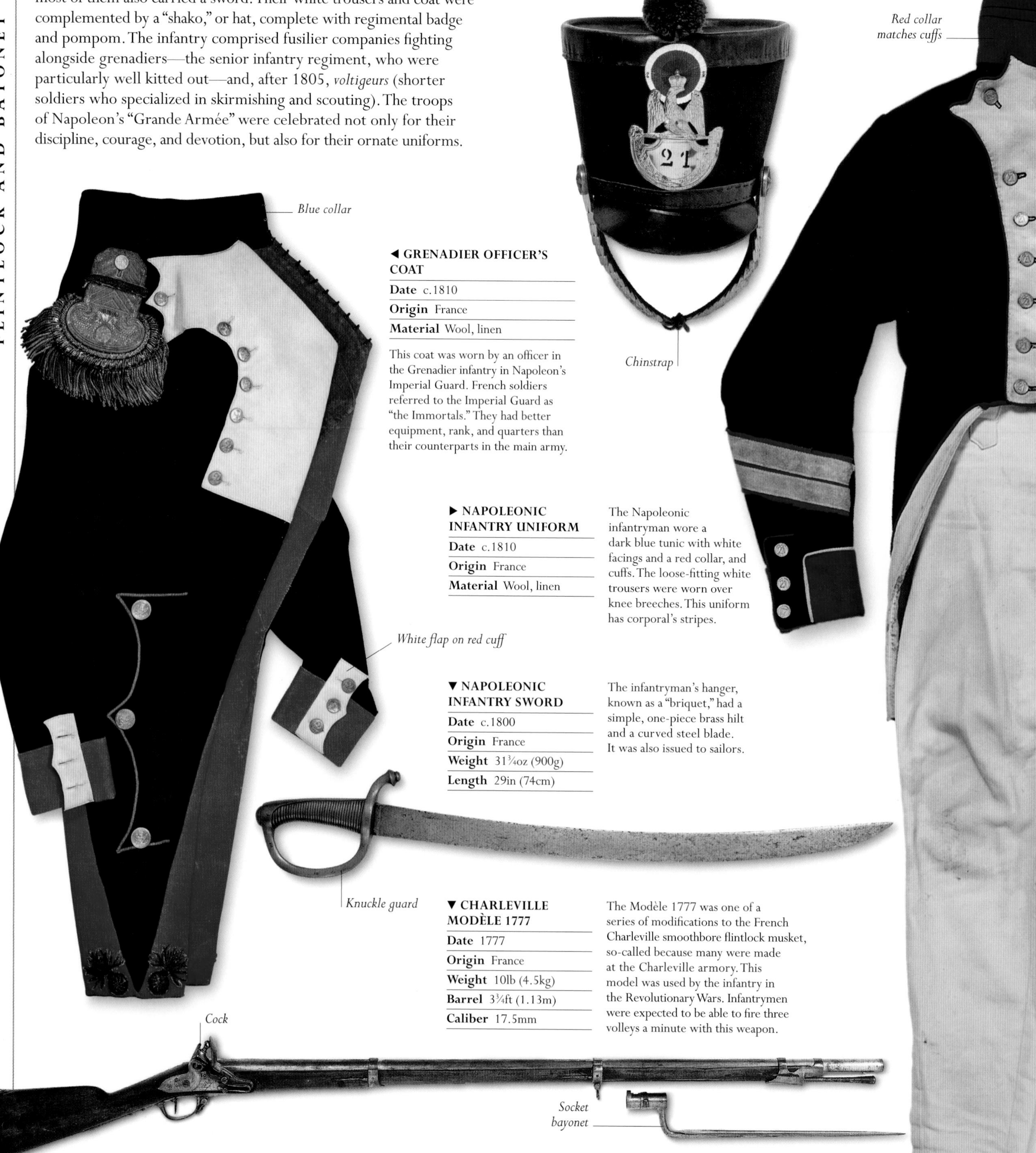

▼ INFANTRYMAN'S SHAKO

Date 1806
Origin France
Material Felt, leather

The shako replaced the earlier bicorn hat of the French infantry in 1806. On this shako, the front plate bears the imperial eagle and the regimental number, as well as a tricolor cockade.

◀ GRENADIER OFFICER'S COAT

Date c.1810
Origin France
Material Wool, linen

This coat was worn by an officer in the Grenadier infantry in Napoleon's Imperial Guard. French soldiers referred to the Imperial Guard as "the Immortals." They had better equipment, rank, and quarters than their counterparts in the main army.

▶ NAPOLEONIC INFANTRY UNIFORM

Date c.1810
Origin France
Material Wool, linen

The Napoleonic infantryman wore a dark blue tunic with white facings and a red collar, and cuffs. The loose-fitting white trousers were worn over knee breeches. This uniform has corporal's stripes.

▼ NAPOLEONIC INFANTRY SWORD

Date c.1800
Origin France
Weight 31¾oz (900g)
Length 29in (74cm)

The infantryman's hanger, known as a "briquet," had a simple, one-piece brass hilt and a curved steel blade. It was also issued to sailors.

▼ CHARLEVILLE MODÈLE 1777

Date 1777
Origin France
Weight 10lb (4.5kg)
Barrel 3¾ft (1.13m)
Caliber 17.5mm

The Modèle 1777 was one of a series of modifications to the French Charleville smoothbore flintlock musket, so-called because many were made at the Charleville armory. This model was used by the infantry in the Revolutionary Wars. Infantrymen were expected to be able to fire three volleys a minute with this weapon.

▼ PARADE SHAKO

Date 1806
Origin France
Material Felt, leather

Made of felt or sometimes board with a leather peak, the top of the shako was treated to make it waterproof. When on parade, troops attached cords to them—white for fusiliers, red for grenadiers, and yellow for *voltigeurs*.

White cords for fusilier companies

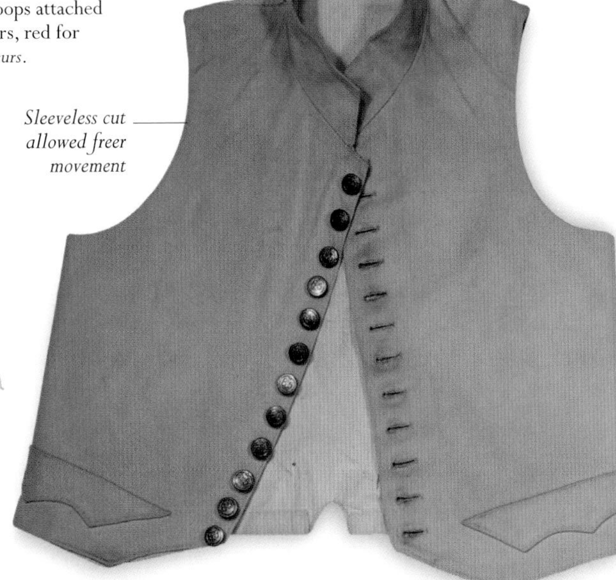

Sleeveless cut allowed freer movement

◀ FUSILIER'S WAISTCOAT

Date c.1810
Origin France
Material Leather

Waistcoats—also known as undercoats—came in a range of colors and materials. Fusiliers often wore white. On hot days, soldiers sometimes took off their coats and fought in waistcoats.

Corporal's stripes

White lapels often treated with pipe clay

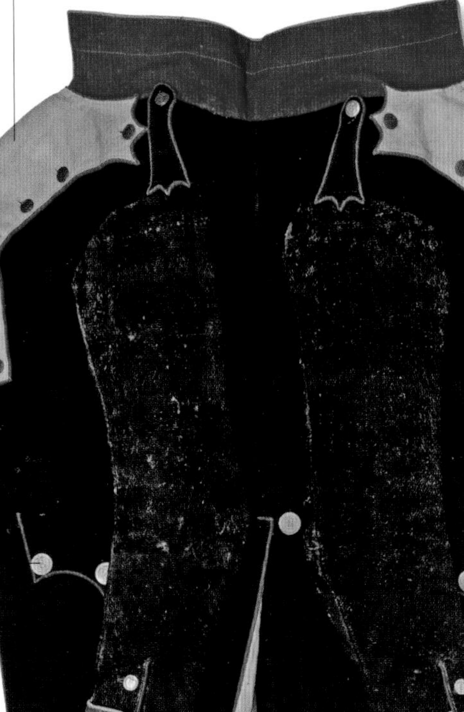

Regulation red cuff with dark blue flap

Buttons on pockets

Three buttons at the cuff

Cream trim

▶ FUSILIER'S COAT

Date c.1810
Origin France
Material Wool, linen

A fusilier in Napoleon's army wore a coat (*habit à la française*) that was dark blue with red collar and cuffs, together with cream trim and lining. The fusilier would normally also wear a white cross belt and white trousers. Dust, mud, rain, or blood often changed the color of a uniform when it was worn on campaign.

Leather straps were whitened with clay

Rolled-up greatcoat

▲ SOLDIER'S PACK

Date c.1810
Origin France
Material Leather

The soldier's compact knapsack was used for storing extra clothing and bread rations. Held securely in position by its shoulder straps, the top of the pack also featured stowage points for carrying the soldier's greatcoat.

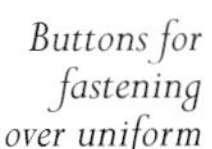

Buttons for fastening over uniform

Leather covering kept lower legs dry

▶ FUSILIER'S GAITERS

Date c.1810
Origin France
Material Leather

Gaiters kept dirt and stones out of the soldier's shoes, which often did not fit very well. French military gaiters were often made long, to be worn over the knee, but soldiers cut them down to wear them below the knee.

UNIFORMS OF CHASSEUR AND CUIRASSIER

Napoleon Bonaparte (see p.182) relied on his light cavalry (chasseurs) and heavy cavalry (cuirassiers) to mount charges and press home a decisive advantage in pursuing routed opponents. These are examples of the uniforms of the chasseurs and the cuirassiers. The chasseur uniform is that of the *1er Chasseurs à Cheval de la Ligne, 2e Compagnie*, from around 1806. The cuirassier was the descendant of the mounted and armored medieval knight, and took his name from the *cuirasse* (armor breastplate) he wore. Napoleon found an important role for cuirassiers in his army at a time when the use of armored heavy cavalry was declining.

▲ **SHAKO**

Date c.1806

Origin France

Material Felt, leather

The shako was adopted by many European cavalry and infantry regiments in the late 1700s. This chasseur shako had a waterproof top and was secured under the chin by brass chinscales.

▲ **FULL DRESS SHAKO**

Date c.1806

Origin France

Material Felt, leather

When on parade, the chasseur wore a plume on his shako instead of the pompom he wore when in battle. This is the full dress shako of the First Regiment of Chasseurs.

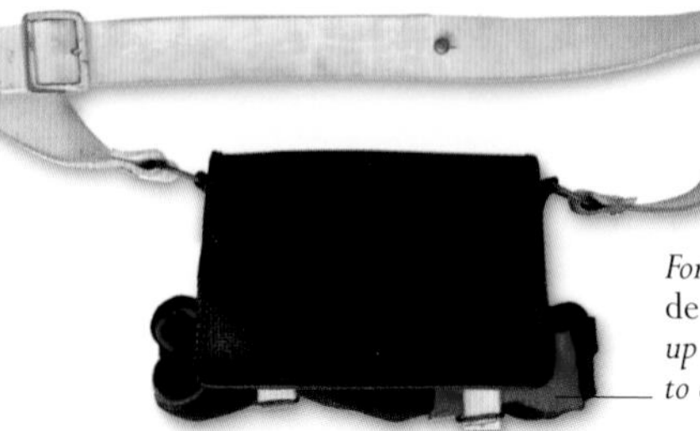

▲ **CARTRIDGE BOX**

Date c.1806

Origin France

Material Leather

The chasseur carried a box of prepared cartridges for his carbine and pistols. He hung the box from a crossbelt worn over the left shoulder.

► **BREAD BAG**

Date c.1806

Origin France

Material Linen

A lightweight cloth bag was used by the chasseurs to carry rations. They were not issued with water bottles and often had their own leather wineskin.

► **CHASSEUR UNIFORM**

Date c.1806

Origin France

Material Wool

Under the tight-fitting braided jacket, known as a dolman (originally from a Turkish word for a looser garment), the chasseur wore a splendid red waistcoat. A long white cotton shirt was tucked into the breeches and tied between his legs. The collar was fastened with an unobtrusive black stock.

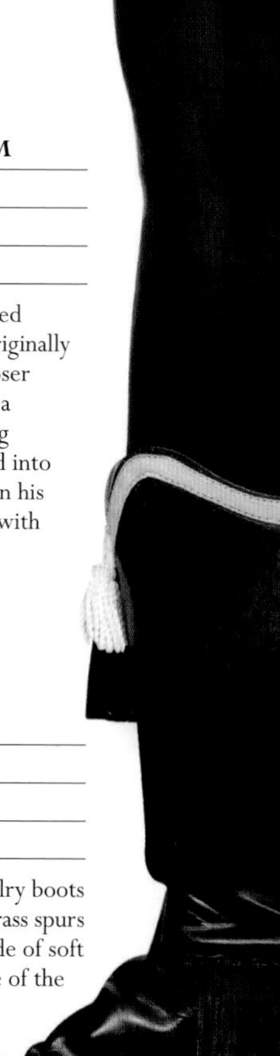

► **RIDING BOOTS**

Date c.1806

Origin France

Material Leather

The well-made, tasselled cavalry boots of the chasseurs had iron or brass spurs on them. The boots were made of soft leather in the traditional style of the Hungarian hussar.

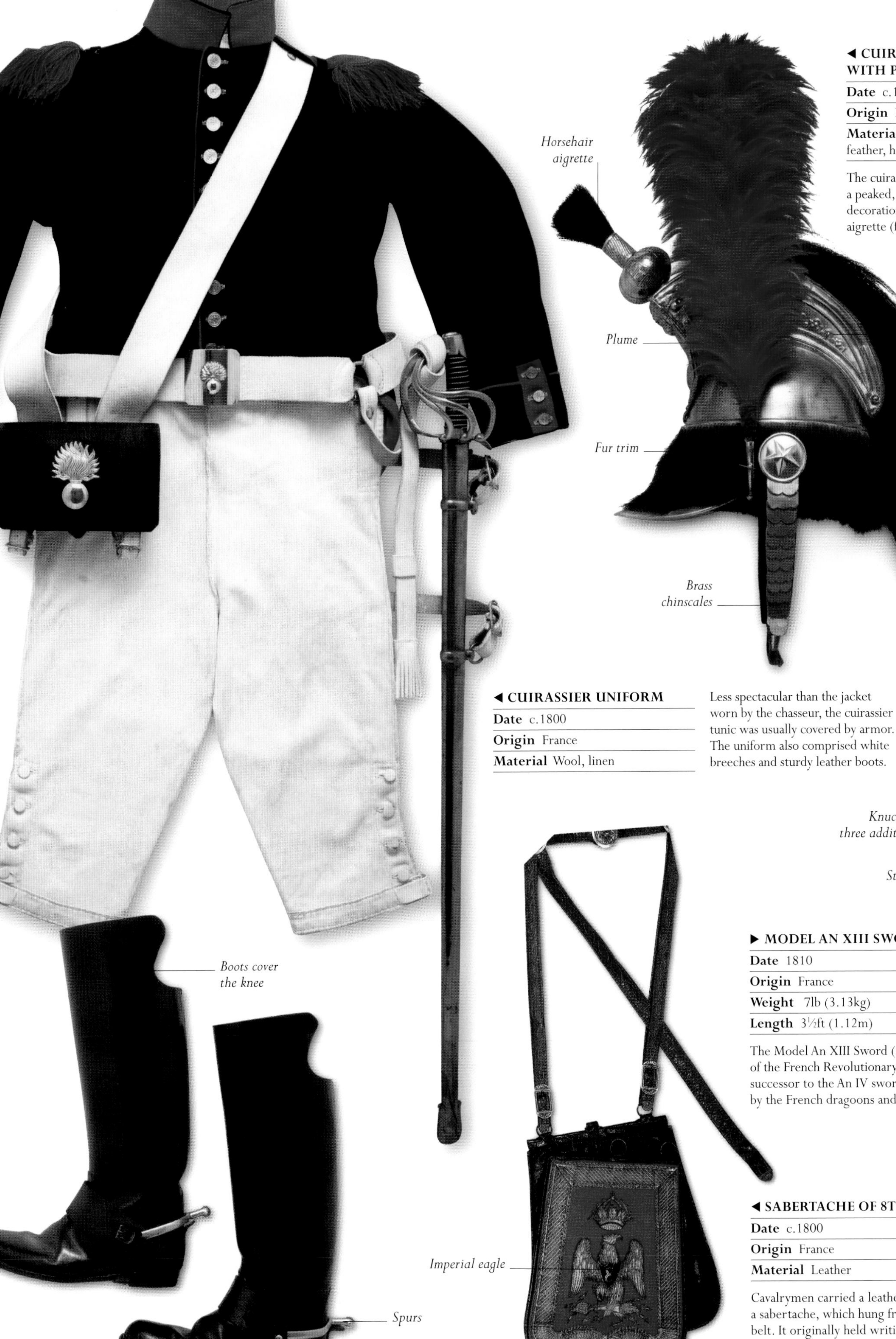

◀ **CUIRASSIER HELMET WITH PLUME**

Date c.1810

Origin France

Material Brass, copper, fur, feather, horsehair

The cuirassier's plumed helmet combined a peaked, copper-crested iron cap with fur decoration, feather plume, and horsehair aigrette (front) and tail (rear).

◀ **CUIRASSIER UNIFORM**

Date c.1800

Origin France

Material Wool, linen

Less spectacular than the jacket worn by the chasseur, the cuirassier tunic was usually covered by armor. The uniform also comprised white breeches and sturdy leather boots.

▶ **MODEL AN XIII SWORD**

Date 1810

Origin France

Weight 7lb (3.13kg)

Length 3½ft (1.12m)

The Model An XIII Sword (from the 13th year of the French Revolutionary Calendar) was the successor to the An IV sword, and was carried by the French dragoons and heavy cavalry.

◀ **SABERTACHE OF 8TH HUSSARS**

Date c.1800

Origin France

Material Leather

Cavalrymen carried a leather satchel called a sabertache, which hung from the saber belt. It originally held writing and sketching materials, but by Napoleonic times had become largely decorative.

BRITISH UNIFORM AND KIT OF THE NAPOLEONIC WARS

The British line and light infantry in the Napoleonic Wars wore bright red jackets. The eye-catching color was a sensible choice in an era when visibility during battles was often severely reduced by clouds of gunpowder smoke, making it difficult to distinguish friend from foe. Infantrymen wore the "stovepipe" shako as standard from 1801 to 1812. A soldier's most important piece of equipment was the flintlock Land-Pattern musket known as "Brown Bess," but he also had to carry a knapsack, food bag, kettle, overcoat, blanket, and water canteens, as well as ammunition. This represented a heavy burden on marches of up to 15 miles (25km) a day.

▶ GREEN-PLUMED LIGHT INFANTRY SHAKO

Date 1801
Origin UK
Material Felt, leather

The cylindrical British light-infantry shako was made of felt with a leather peak. The bugle-horn badge and green plume were symbols of light infantry.

▶ TUNIC

Date c.1810
Origin UK
Material Wool, linen lining

Private soldiers wore a single-breasted brick-red tunic. The green facings on the collar and cuffs and the shape, color, and spacing of the lace were all light infantry features.

▶ TROUSERS

Date c.1810
Origin UK
Material Wool

During the Peninsular War, the light infantryman's white breeches and black gaiters gave way to the gray trousers shown here. Made of thick wool, they were stiflingly hot in summer.

▲ CARTRIDGE POUCH

Date c.1800
Origin UK
Material Leather

The bag could hold 60 cartridges, each of which contained powder and a musket ball. The powder was used as both primer and charge, while the paper served as wadding to keep the musket ball in the barrel.

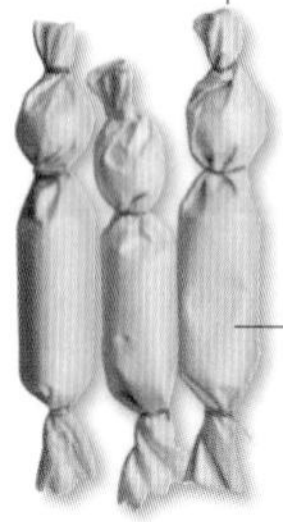

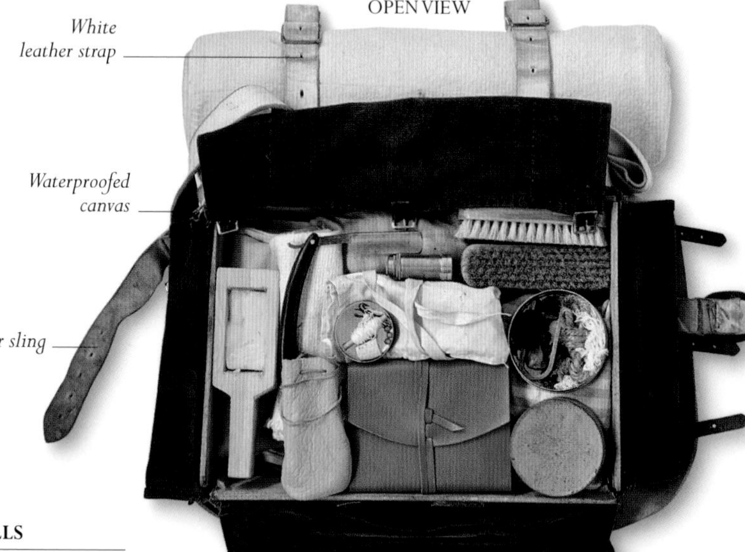

▲ BRITISH LIGHT INFANTRY "TROTTER" KNAPSACK

Date c.1805
Origin UK
Material Wood, canvas

The envelope (or "Trotter") knapsack, marked with the regimental number, was introduced in around 1805 for light infantry. By 1812, it was being used across the British Army.

◀ MUSKET BALLS

Date c.1800
Origin UK
Weight 1oz (32gm)
Diameter ¾in (1.7cm)

Musket balls were made of lead. Balls were classified by their "bore," the number of balls that could be cast from 1lb (0.45kg) of lead.

▲ SHOES

Date c.1800
Origin UK
Material Leather

Shoes were issued "straight-lasted" (with neither left nor right) and were often of extremely poor quality. A soldier was issued only two pairs each year.

◀ BRITISH OFFICER'S KIT

Date c.1815

Origin UK

Material Wool, leather

This is the uniform of an officer in the Royal Fusiliers from the time of the Battle of Waterloo in 1815. He carried his sword on a shoulder belt, and wore a gorget and silk sash.

▲ GORGET

Date c.1800

Origin UK

Material Brass

Gorgets were pieces of armor that protected the throat and symbolized the rank of officer in the British Army. They were tied around the neck using holes just visible at the top.

WEAPONS OF THE REVOLUTIONARY AND NAPOLEONIC WARS

Armies in the Revolutionary and Napoleonic Wars fought with a range of weapons including bayonets and cannon. The massed infantry used muskets, and only the specialist regiments of sharpshooters carried rifles. Swords were the preferred weapon in a cavalry charge, except for light cavalry regiments, who carried lances topped with pennons or flags. Many cavalrymen also had two loaded pistols, for emergency use, while dragoons often regarded the carbine as their principal weapon.

▲ BRITISH HEAVY DRAGOON PISTOL 1747

Date	18th century
Origin	UK
Weight	2½lb (1.2kg)
Barrel	12in (30.5cm)
Caliber	.65in

Officers in the French chasseurs, hussars, and dragoons generally carried flintlock pistols similar to this British example. One of a pair, it has a heavy brass butt plate, which could be used as a club in hand-to-hand fighting.

Striking steel

▲ INDIA-PATTERN MUSKET

Date	1797
Origin	UK
Weight	9lb (4.1kg)
Barrel	39in (99cm)
Caliber	.75in

The British Army introduced the India-Pattern musket, the final form of the "Brown Bess," in 1793. A simplified version, it was cheaper and quicker to produce.

Barrel band secures the barrel to the stock

▲ AUSTRIAN MUSKET

Date	1798
Origin	Austria
Weight	9¼lb (4.2kg)
Barrel	3¾ft (1.14m)
Caliber	.65in

In 1798, Austria introduced a new flintlock musket to match the latest French gun of this type, the Modèle 1777.

Striking steel and open pan cover

Jaws to hold flint

Trigger guard

Sling swivel

▲ CARBINE MODEL AN IX

Date	1801
Origin	France
Weight	7¼lb (3.3kg)
Barrel	3¾ft (1.15m)
Caliber	.69in

French cavalrymen carried a smoothbore flintlock carbine. This An IX model was manufactured at Charleville, the French government armament factory, in year nine of the Revolutionary calendar—that is, 1801.

Battle-scarred butt

▲ HEAVY DRAGOON CARBINE PATTERN 1770

Date	c.1805
Origin	UK
Weight	8½lb (3.9kg)
Barrel	26in (66cm)
Caliber	.75in

Napoleonic-era carbines had shorter barrels than earlier models. Each dragoon clipped the carbine to his belt, from which it hung next to the thigh.

Cock

Steel

Trigger

▲ PRUSSIAN 1809 PATTERN MUSKET

Date	1809
Origin	Germany
Weight	8¾lb (4kg)
Barrel	3½ft (1.04m)
Caliber	.75in

The 1809 Pattern musket was the Prussian equivalent of the British Brown Bess and the French Charleville. Unlike its competitors, it had a brass flash guard around the pan as standard. Most of these flintlocks were later converted to percussion.

Leather grip

Three-barred hilt

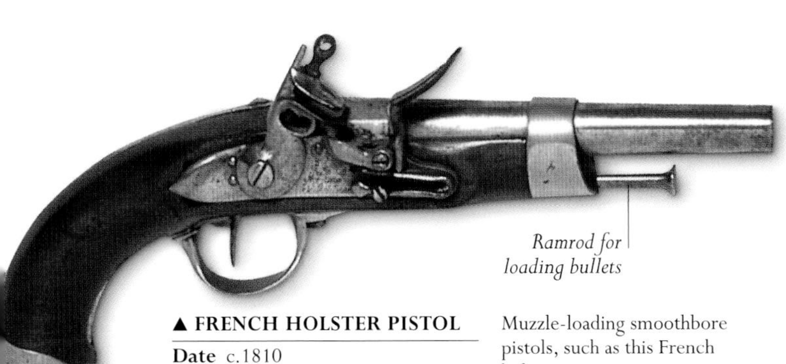

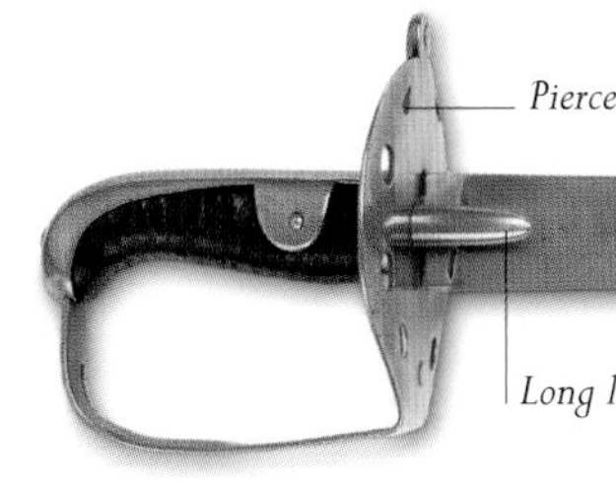

▲ FRENCH HOLSTER PISTOL

Date	c.1810
Origin	France

Muzzle-loading smoothbore pistols, such as this French holster weapon, were easy to carry but often inaccurate and unreliable.

▲ NEW LAND-PATTERN 1802

Date	1810
Origin	UK
Weight	17½oz (500g)
Barrel	9in (23cm)
Caliber	.65in

The British Army's New Land-Pattern pistol, first introduced in 1802, was a competent, sturdy design that remained in service until flintlocks gave way to percussion in the 1840s. A version with a flat butt and lanyard ring was produced for the cavalry.

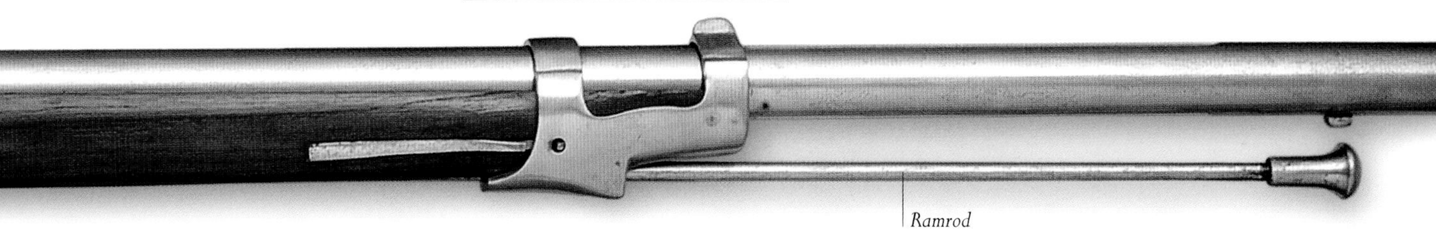

▲ HEAVY CAVALRY TROOPER'S SWORD PATTERN 1796

Date	1796
Origin	UK
Weight	2½lb (1.13kg)
Length	3¼ft (1.01m)

British heavy cavalry used the stirrup-hilt British Heavy Cavalry Sword of 1796 in the Napoleonic Wars. They criticized it for being unwieldy, but it was a forceful cutting sword.

Ramrod

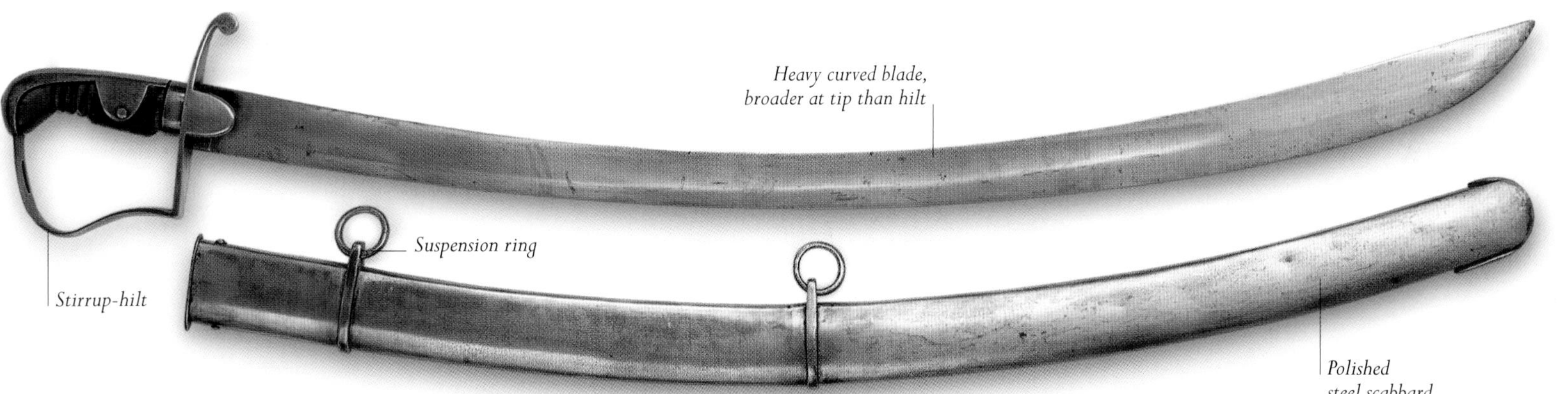

▲ LIGHT CAVALRY TROOPER'S SWORD PATTERN 1796

Date	c.1800
Origin	UK
Weight	2¼lb (1kg)
Length	38in (96.5cm)

This British light cavalry sword had a heavy blade that broadened toward the tip. This added power at the point of impact—a single blow could sever an arm or split a skull.

▼ FRENCH CAVALRY SABER

Date	1802
Origin	France
Weight	2¼lb (1kg)
Length	3¼ft (1m)

French cavalry sabers had narrower blades than their British counterparts. The iron scabbard was tougher than earlier brass and leather examples.

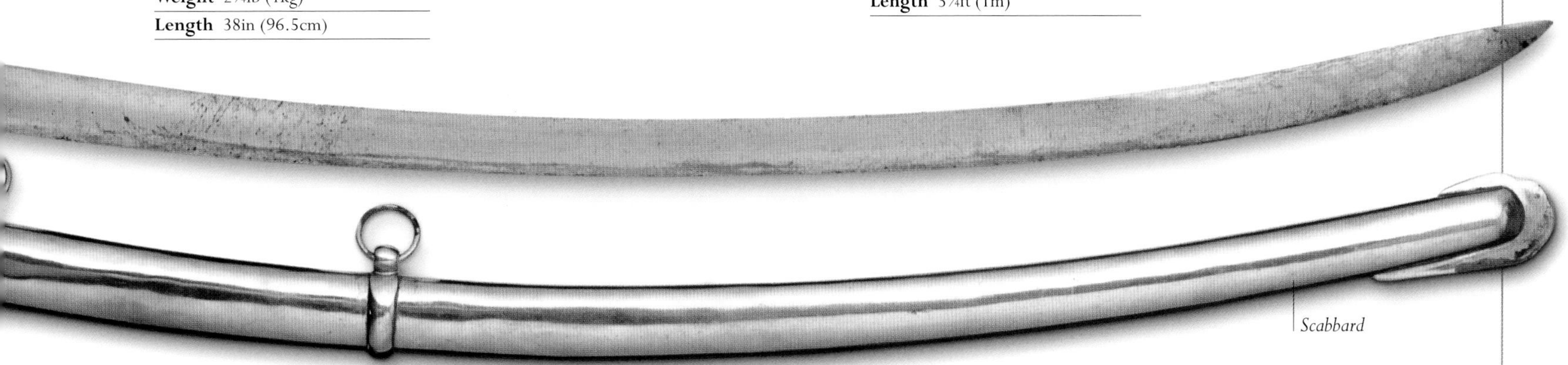

FOREFATHER OF THE MODERN RIFLE

BAKER RIFLE

In February 1800, the Baker rifle won a competition organized by the Army's Board of Ordnance and became the first rifle officially adopted by the British Army. It was similar to weapons in use in Germany, and its novel feature lay in its barrel. With shallow or "slow" rifling—just a quarter-turn in the length of the barrel—it stayed clean and thus usable for longer, a great practical advantage for the rifleman in the field. It was superseded from 1837 by the heavier, muzzle-loading Brunswick rifle.

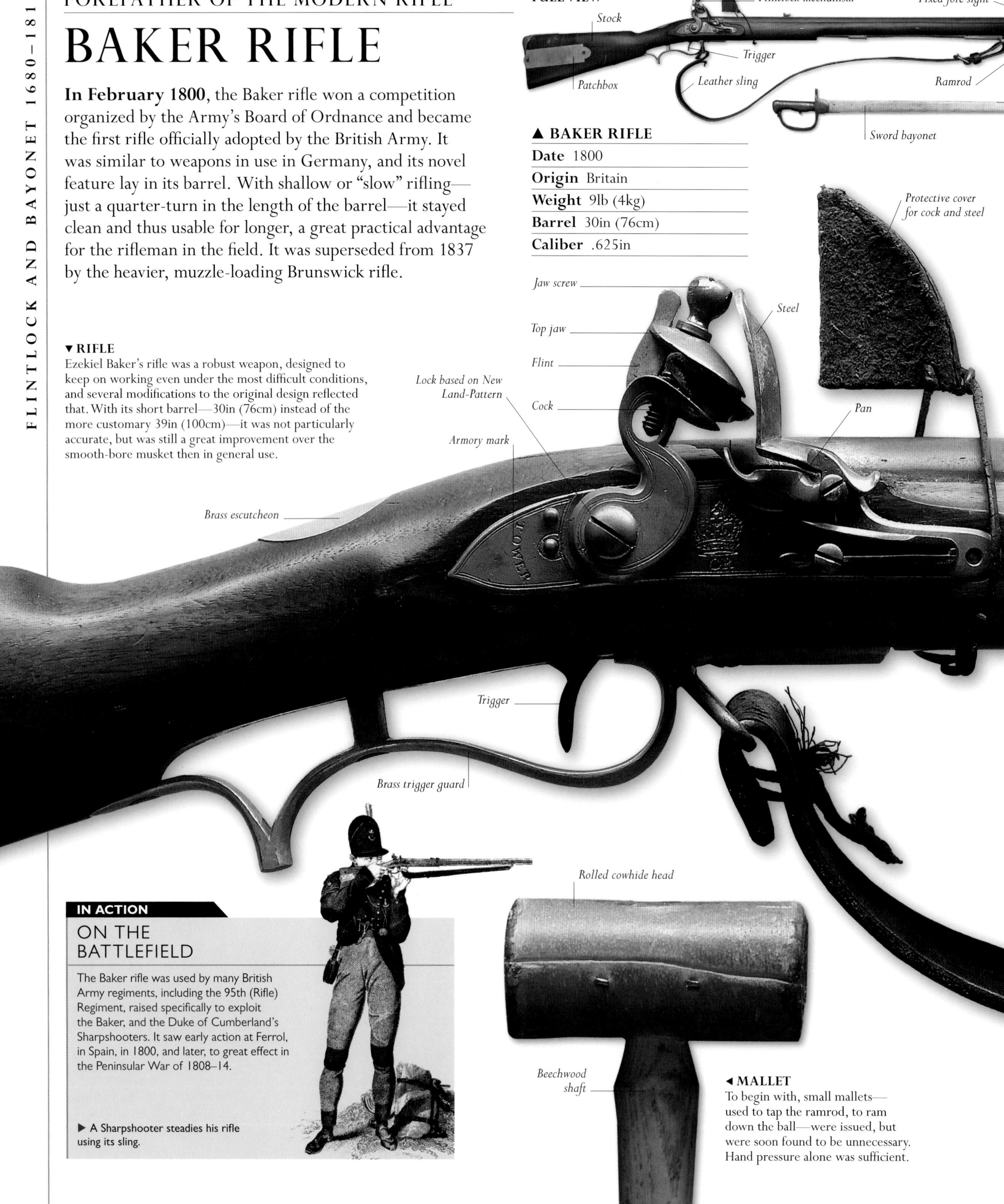

▲ BAKER RIFLE

Date	1800
Origin	Britain
Weight	9lb (4kg)
Barrel	30in (76cm)
Caliber	.625in

▼ RIFLE
Ezekiel Baker's rifle was a robust weapon, designed to keep on working even under the most difficult conditions, and several modifications to the original design reflected that. With its short barrel—30in (76cm) instead of the more customary 39in (100cm)—it was not particularly accurate, but was still a great improvement over the smooth-bore musket then in general use.

◄ MALLET
To begin with, small mallets—used to tap the ramrod, to ram down the ball—were issued, but were soon found to be unnecessary. Hand pressure alone was sufficient.

IN ACTION

ON THE BATTLEFIELD

The Baker rifle was used by many British Army regiments, including the 95th (Rifle) Regiment, raised specifically to exploit the Baker, and the Duke of Cumberland's Sharpshooters. It saw early action at Ferrol, in Spain, in 1800, and later, to great effect in the Peninsular War of 1808–14.

► A Sharpshooter steadies his rifle using its sling.

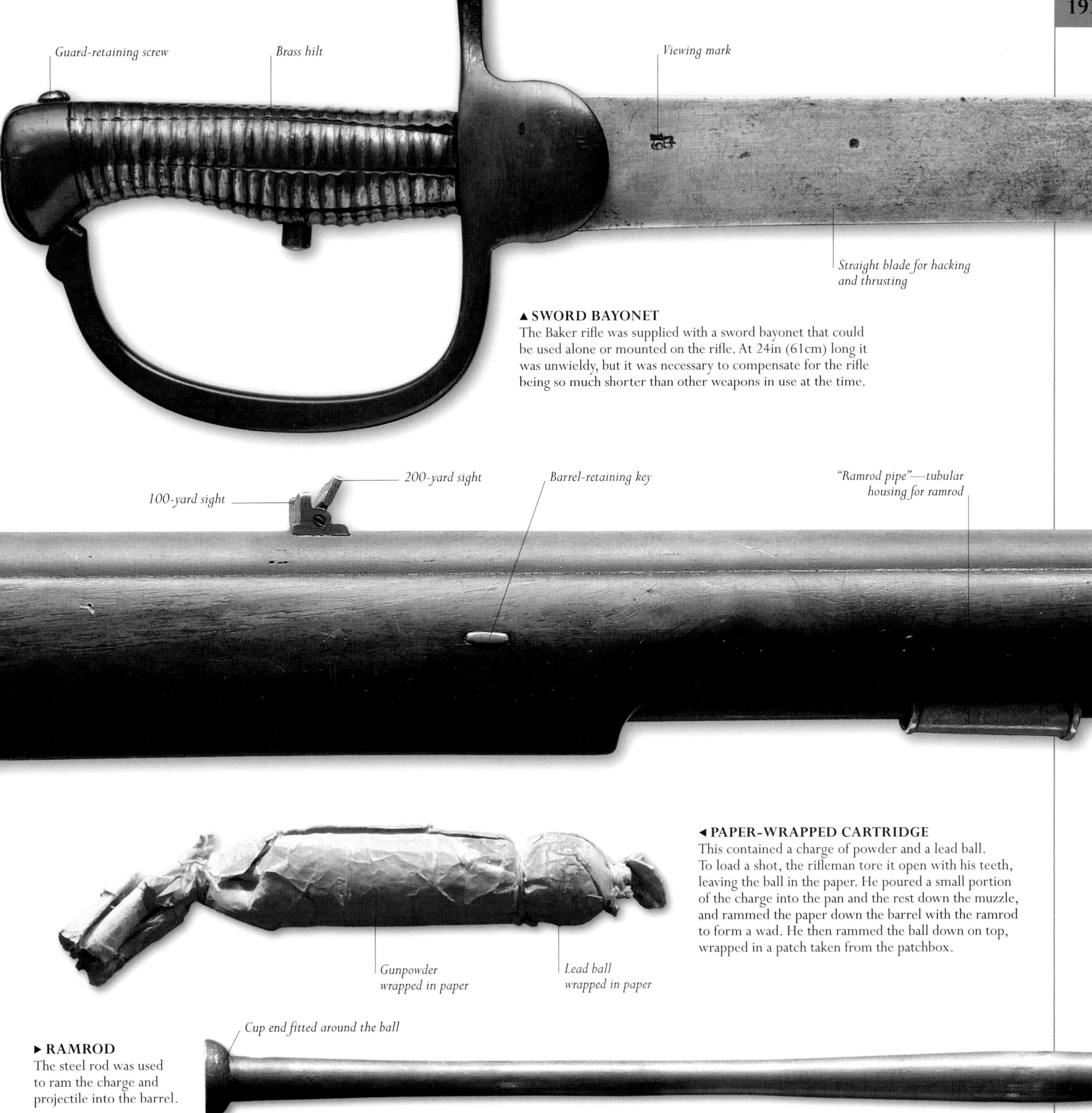

▲ SWORD BAYONET
The Baker rifle was supplied with a sword bayonet that could be used alone or mounted on the rifle. At 24in (61cm) long it was unwieldy, but it was necessary to compensate for the rifle being so much shorter than other weapons in use at the time.

◄ PAPER-WRAPPED CARTRIDGE
This contained a charge of powder and a lead ball. To load a shot, the rifleman tore it open with his teeth, leaving the ball in the paper. He poured a small portion of the charge into the pan and the rest down the muzzle, and rammed the paper down the barrel with the ramrod to form a wad. He then rammed the ball down on top, wrapped in a patch taken from the patchbox.

► RAMROD
The steel rod was used to ram the charge and projectile into the barrel.

INFANTRY SQUARE
Gallant British redcoats under attack from French cavalry form a defensive square around their regimental banners. A square that held firm could repel horsemen on the charge but was an inviting target for cannon fire.

CAVALRY AND THE INFANTRY SQUARE

THE BATTLE OF WATERLOO

Throughout the 18th and early 19th centuries, European warfare centered around the use of rigidly disciplined infantry armed with smoothbore flintlock muskets and bayonets. This style of fighting reached its climax at Waterloo on June 18, 1815, when superior French artillery and cavalry failed to crack the Duke of Wellington's steady foot soldiers.

Waterloo was the last battle of the Napoleonic Wars. On June 18, Wellington drew up his forces in a defensive position on a ridge, intending to hold off Napoleon's 70,000-strong army until Britain's allies, the Prussians, could reach the battlefield and tip the balance decisively against the French.

Wellington fortified a chateau and farmhouse in the front of his position as strongpoints to delay the French attack, but he knew his eventual success or failure would depend on the firmness of his infantry fighting in an open field. The infantry were strictly trained to march in columns, deploy in lines, and fire in volleys. The great majority were equipped with inaccurate but reliable flintlock muskets. Additionally, British riflemen, armed with the effective Baker rifle, could fight as skirmishers in loose formation or in line.

Napoleon opened the battle with a bombardment by the heavy cannon parked at the rear of his position. While fighting raged around the chateau and farm, the French launched a corps-strength infantry attack on the center of the British line. At first skirmishing troops, the *voltigeurs*, swarmed forward to snipe at Wellington's men, who were drawn up in formation two lines deep. The main body of French troops then advanced in large close-packed columns with bayonets fixed. Each British soldier could fire three rounds a minute, and with two lines firing alternate volleys, the infantry poured six volleys a minute into the dense French ranks. As field artillery joined in, sweeping the columns with canister, grapeshot, and shrapnel, the French were halted and driven back, sustaining heavy casualties.

HOLDING THE SQUARE

In the afternoon, around 4:00pm, Wellington's infantry were exposed to repeated attacks by French cavalry. Napoleon's horsemen ranged from heavily armored cuirassiers to lighter dragoons, chasseurs, and hussars, and a body of Polish lancers. The standard infantry response to a cavalry charge was to form squares. The square's "walls" consisted of soldiers three or four lines deep. The bayonets of the front line, bristling outward, held the enemy horses at bay on all four sides while the men farther inside the square fired at the cavalry. The lancers' weapons were long enough to reach into the square, but the real threat lay in artillery. In the late afternoon, after taking the fortified farm, the French moved their cannon forward to blast at the infantry squares. Once savaged by shot or shell, a square could be penetrated by cavalry, who cut down the foot soldiers with their swords.

Wellington later commented that he was "never as near being beat" as at Waterloo. But ultimately his line held both against the cavalry charges and a final attack by the infantry of Napoleon's elite Imperial Guard. As the Prussians, led by Count von Blücher, arrived on the French flank, Wellington ordered a general advance. The French were driven from the field and Napoleon's remarkable military career was finally brought to an end.

KEY **FIGURE**

HORATIO NELSON

1758–1805

Nelson was a fearless and often insubordinate British admiral who was brought to prominence by a bold maneuver at Cape St. Vincent, in 1797. His victories at the Nile (1798), Copenhagen (1801), and Trafalgar (1805) made him a national hero.

▲ Nelson lost an arm, and the sight in one eye, while leading from the front. He died on board HMS *Victory*.

KEY DEVELOPMENT

NAVAL BATTLES IN THE AGE OF SAIL

By the early 1800s, naval power had become a crucial concern for European powers ruling overseas empires. Substantial resources were devoted to sailing ship fleets, heavily armed with muzzle-loading, smoothbore cannon.

The basic tactics and technology for sailing-ship warfare were established in the 17th century, and did not fundamentally alter until the end of the age of sail in the mid-19th century. Cannon were mounted in broadside (along the ship's sides) and fleets fought in line, side-on to the enemy. Shots were aimed either at the hull, to cause maximum damage to the ship and crew, or at the masts and rigging to disable the vessel. However, wooden ships were almost impossible to sink with solid shot, and explosive shells were considered too dangerous for use at sea. As a result, engagements ended only when a ship was taken by boarding, or when a captain surrendered to avoid further carnage.

THE AGE OF THE WARSHIP

By this period, navies consisted entirely of purpose-built warships. The role of raiding an enemy's merchant ships, once filled by privateers, was now allotted to naval frigates. The French, who tended to lead in ship design, introduced the classic frigate in 1740, a fast-sailing vessel with a single gundeck mounting at least 28 cannon. Ships of the line were either 74- or 80-gun vessels, with two or three decks and 100 cannon or more. To put this in

▼ **NOCK VOLLEY GUN**
Volley guns were used in ship-to-ship fighting during the Napoleonic Wars. This model proved to be unwieldy due to the powerful recoil caused by seven barrels firing simultaneously.

▲ A GUN CREW AT BATTLE STATIONS
To fire a naval cannon, the crew rammed a gunpowder cartridge and cannonball down the barrel, "ran" the gun out so the barrel protruded from the gun port, and ignited the charge.

◄ THE BATTLE OF QUIBERON BAY
In November, 1759, British Admiral Edward Hawke pursued a French invasion fleet of 21 ships into Quiberon Bay, off the coast of France. The 24 British ships of the line shattered the French navy, effectively ending its role in the Seven Years' War.

perspective, in 1805 an entire corps of Napoleon's army had only 40 cannon. Over time there were significant but limited technological improvements. A flintlock mechanism was first applied to naval cannon in 1745, but the slow-burning linstock (a forked staff that held a match) was still used in the early 19th century to fire cannon aboard many warships. The carronade, a light but powerful short-range gun introduced in the 1770s, was a notable addition to the firepower of naval fleets.

TECHNOLOGY AND TACTICS

More influential were general improvements in sailing technology, from accurate navigation to progress in nutrition and medical care. The practice of sheathing underwater wooden hulls with copper, widely adopted from the 1770s, made ships faster and able to stay at sea for longer periods without docking for careening (cleaning and repair). The chief developments, however, were tactical rather than technological. Britain's Royal Navy—by the early 17th century the world's leading naval power—traditionally had a commitment to attack and, with superior gunnery, expected to defeat its enemies if it could bring them to battle. In the Seven Years' War (1756–63), the boldest British admirals practiced aggressive tactics known as the "general chase"—each ship racing to engage a fleeing enemy without waiting to take its allotted place in a formal line of battle. From the 1780s onward, the British developed the tactic of cutting through the enemy line, instead of sailing parallel to it, so that part of the opposing fleet could be surrounded and destroyed. This strategy was taken to its extreme by Admiral Horatio Nelson, who sought to force the enemy into a "pell-mell" battle—a savage and chaotic close-quarters mêlée in which British gunnery and fighting spirit would carry the day. Nelson won decisive victories with these risky tactics and helped secure British naval dominance for another century.

> "No captain **can do very wrong** if he places his ship alongside that of **an enemy**"
>
> **ADMIRAL NELSON**, BEFORE THE BATTLE OF TRAFALGAR, OCTOBER 1805

KEY **EVENTS**

1740–1805

- **1740** The French warship *Médée* is the first of a new type of frigate that will play a large part in naval warfare into the 19th century.
- **1761** On an experimental basis, the British Royal Navy coppers the hull of the 32-gun frigate HMS *Alarm*.
- **1763** The French navy adopts a system of signal flags that includes a number code. These greatly improve the visual communication of messages at sea.
- **1782** At Saintes, in the Caribbean, a British fleet under Admiral George Rodney breaks through the French battle line, initiating a new phase in British naval tactics.
- **1794** The US Navy is founded by an act of Congress, leading to the construction and manning of six powerful 44-gun or 38-gun frigates.
- **1805** Victory over a French and Spanish fleet at Trafalgar establishes a durable British command of the sea; Admiral Nelson of the British fleet is killed in the battle.

NAVAL GUNS AND KIT

Naval cannon first appeared in the mid-14th century in the form of wrought-iron breech-loaders. Cast-bronze muzzle-loaders were developed in the 16th century, and by the 18th century all European navies were widely using cast-iron muzzle-loaders, such as the British versions shown here. To charge muzzle-loaders of this type, a fabric powder cartridge was loaded down the muzzle and into the chamber, followed by a rope wad to hold it in place, the shot, and a second rope wad. The charge was pricked by inserting a wire pricker into the vent, then the gunpowder was poured in. Either a gunlock or a slow match held at the vent hole was used to fire the gun.

Slow match burned at a rate of 12in (30cm) every three hours

Wooden keg

◀ MATCH TUB AND SLOW MATCHES

Date	c.1800
Origin	UK
Material	Wood, hemp

A slow match was lit at the start of the battle and placed in the match tub. It kept burning and was used to ignite the charge if the gunlock failed. Made from hemp, the slow match was boiled in a solution of spirits of wine and saltpeter.

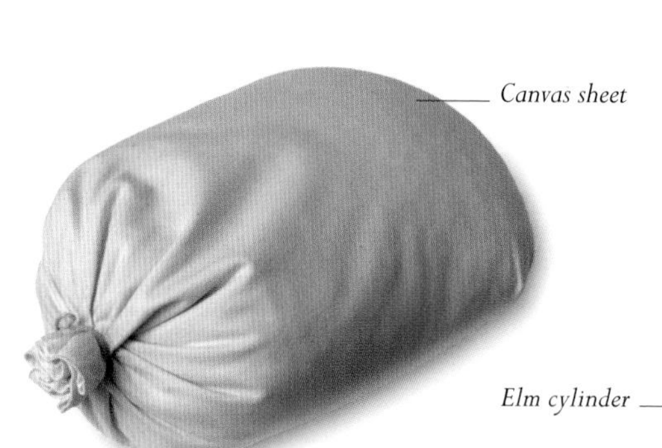

Canvas sheet

▲ CARTRIDGE

Date	c.1800
Origin	UK
Material	Canvas

Paper, canvas, or parchment were sewn into different size cylinders as gunpowder containers. A precise amount of gunpowder was used depending on the gun and the type of charge.

Poplar lid

Rope strap for carrying

Elm cylinder

▲ CARTRIDGE CASE

Date	c.1800
Origin	UK
Material	Wood

To prevent accidental explosions, cartridges had to be carried with great care from the magazines to the guns. A lightweight wooden cylinder was used to protect and carry each cartridge.

◀ ROPE WAD

Date	c.1800
Origin	UK
Material	Rope

Oddments of rope and rope fiber (oakum, or "junk") were used to make wads, which were rammed down the barrel of the gun to hold the charge and shot in place.

▶ CAST-IRON 24-POUNDER

Date	1785–1822
Origin	UK
Weight	3.2 tons (2.9 tonnes)
Length	9½ft (2.9m)
Caliber	5.8in
Shot	24lb (11kg)

Naval guns were mounted on wheeled wooden carriages, allowing them to run backward under recoil. This motion was controlled by restraining ropes around the breech or carriage.

Vent for igniting powder charge

Wooden trucks

Wooden gun carriage, usually made from elm

◀ **ROUND SHOT**

Date c.1800

Origin UK

Material Iron

Naval ammunition generally had three purposes—to punch holes in the side of an enemy ship, to bring down masts and sails, or to kill the enemy. An accurate and long-range type of munition, round shot was used for its penetrating effect against a ship's hull.

◀ **CHAIN SHOT**

Date c.1800

Origin UK

Material Iron

The chain shot—two or more cannonballs linked by a chain—could scythe down enemy crew on an exposed deck. As with other nonround shot, the range and accuracy of chain shot was poor.

Extendable sections

Solid iron

◀ **BAR SHOT**

Date c.1800

Origin UK

Material Iron

The bar shot was made by linking two or more shot pieces by a fixed bar or extendable bar sections. It was designed to hack away at lines and rigging as it flew over the top of the ship's deck.

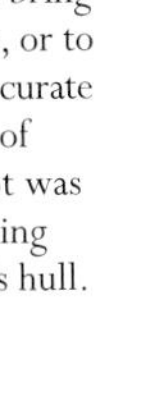

◀ **GRAPESHOT**

Date c.1800

Origin UK

Material Canvas, iron

Grapeshot consisted of balls of metal housed within a tin or a canvas bag. The container shattered when a gun was fired, producing a shotgunlike effect against an enemy crew.

▼ **RAMMER**

Date c.1800

Origin UK

Material Ash

The rammer was used to push the cartridge, wads, and shot down the full length of the bore and pack it into the firing chamber of the gun.

Concave ramming head

Wooden stave

Damp sheepskin sponge for swabbing the barrel

▲ **SPONGE**

Date c.1800

Origin UK

Material Ash, copper nails, sheepskin

A damp sheepskin sponge was pushed down the barrel after every shot had been fired to extinguish residual burning embers. Copper nails attached the sponge to the head of a wooden stave.

Barrel

Muzzle

Button to help in lifting and moving gun

Naval rear-chock carriage

▶ **CAST-IRON 3-POUNDER**

Date Late 17th century

Origin England

Length 6½ft (2m)

Caliber 3in

Shot 3lb (1.36kg)

Cast-iron guns were much cheaper to make than bronze guns and gradually replaced them during the 17th and 18th centuries. They were cast solid and bored out. The rear-chock carriage lessened recoil when the gun was fired.

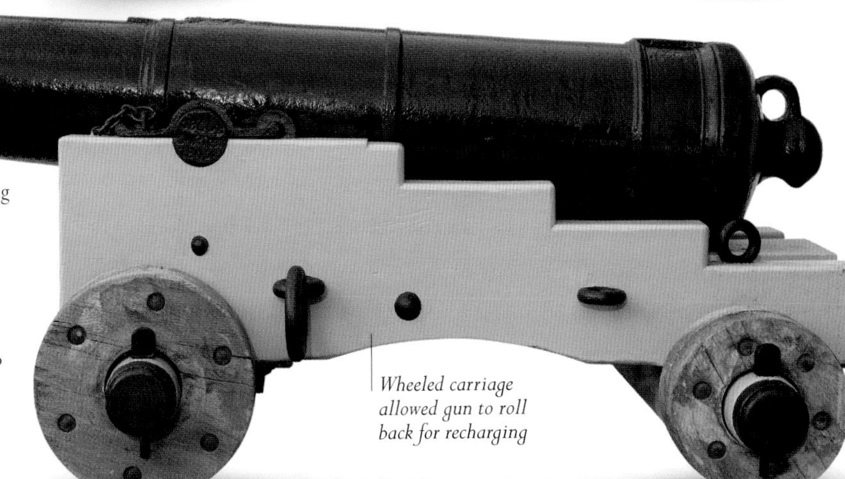

Wheeled carriage allowed gun to roll back for recharging

▶ **MUZZLE-LOADING 12-POUNDER**

Date 1805

Origin UK

Weight 1.2 tons (1.1 tonnes)

Length 9½ft (2.95m)

Caliber 4.5in

Shot 12lb (5.4kg)

This cast-iron muzzle-loading naval gun sits on a later sea-service carriage. In the Battle of Trafalgar, in 1805, HMS *Victory* had thirty-four 12-pounders, in addition to twenty-eight 24-pounders, thirty 32-pounders, and two 68-pounder carronades.

CARRONADES AND OTHER NAVAL GUNS

Carronades—a type of smoothbore cast-iron cannon—were an important addition to naval firepower in the late 18th and early 19th century, supplementing light weapons such as multi-shot guns, swivel guns, rockets, and mortars. Quickly adopted by the British, US, Russian, and French navies, carronades—so-called because they were manufactured by the Carron Ironworks in Falkirk, Scotland—were powerful, short-barreled guns that were relatively lightweight and could be operated by a small crew, but were devastating in close-range engagements. Moreover, while heavy guns such as 32-pounders had to be carried near the waterline so as not to destabilize a ship, carronades were light enough to be mounted on the upper deck.

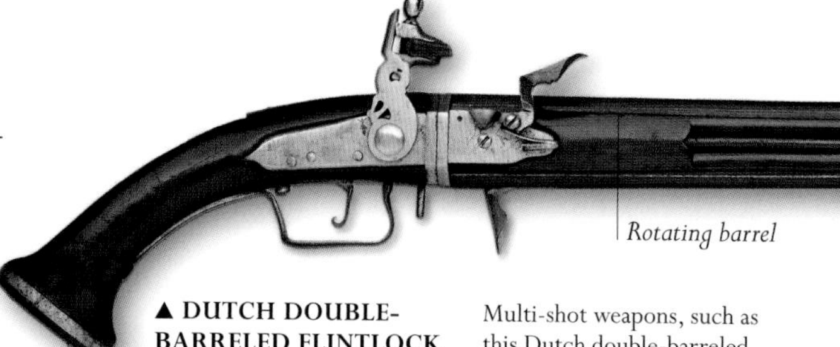

▲ DUTCH DOUBLE-BARRELED FLINTLOCK

Date	17th century
Origin	Netherlands
Weight	2½lb (1.2kg)
Barrel	19¾in (50.3cm)
Caliber	36-bore

Multi-shot weapons, such as this Dutch double-barreled flintlock, were used for boarding actions, due to the difficulty of reloading single-shot weapons at close quarters or on an often-pitching deck.

◀ SWEDISH 20-POUNDER MORTAR

Date	1735
Origin	Sweden
Weight	4.5 tons (4.1 tonnes)
Length	5ft (1.5m)
Caliber	13in
Shot	20lb (9kg)

The Swedish navy of the mid-18th century equipped smaller vessels (bomb ketches) with trunnioned mortars, which were adjustable to fire at an elevated angle for improved range. This bronze mortar was mounted toward the bow and generally used to bombard fortifications on land.

Reinforce ring

▶ BRITISH 4-POUNDER SWIVEL GUN

Date	1778
Origin	Scotland
Length	12½in (31.8cm)
Caliber	8.4cm
Shell	4lb (1.8kg)

This short, heavy swivel gun was one of the prototypes for the carronade made by the Carron Ironworks. Its trunnions are fitted with pivots and the cascabel connected to a long, curved handle for moving the gun.

Pivots at trunnion

Trunnion inscription reads "Carron 1778" with "180" above

Carrying handles

▶ BRITISH 13IN MORTAR

Date	1726
Origin	England
Weight	4.5 tons (4.1 tonnes)
Length	5½ft (1.6m)
Caliber	13in

The reinforce ring of this sea service mortar shows the royal arms of the British king, George II. The mortar may have been made for HMS *Thunder*, which saw action at the Siege of Gibraltar in 1727.

Replacement bed, 8½ft (2.64m) long

▲ FLINTLOCK SWIVEL GUN

Date c.1800
Origin UK
Weight 15lb (6.8kg)
Barrel 24in (61cm)
Caliber 28mm

Loaded and fired in the same way as a musket or pistol, this gun was fired at enemy ships prior to a boarding attempt. Because it could be swiveled, the gun—moving from side to side—had a wide arc of fire.

▲ NOCK VOLLEY GUN

Date 1795
Origin England
Weight 9lb (4.1kg)
Barrel 20½in (52cm)
Caliber .39in

A version of this seven-barreled volley gun was used by the British Royal Navy in close-range fighting when boarding a ship or attempting to repel enemy boarders. The central barrel fired normally, and the other six were set off by the detonation of its charge.

▼ CONGREVE ROCKETS

Date 1805
Origin UK
Weight 32lb (14.5kg)
Length 3¼ft (1.03m)

William Congreve's rockets were propelled by black powder and could be fitted with incendiary or shrapnel heads weighing 3–24lb (1.4–10.9kg). Their accuracy could be poor and they were prone to exploding prematurely.

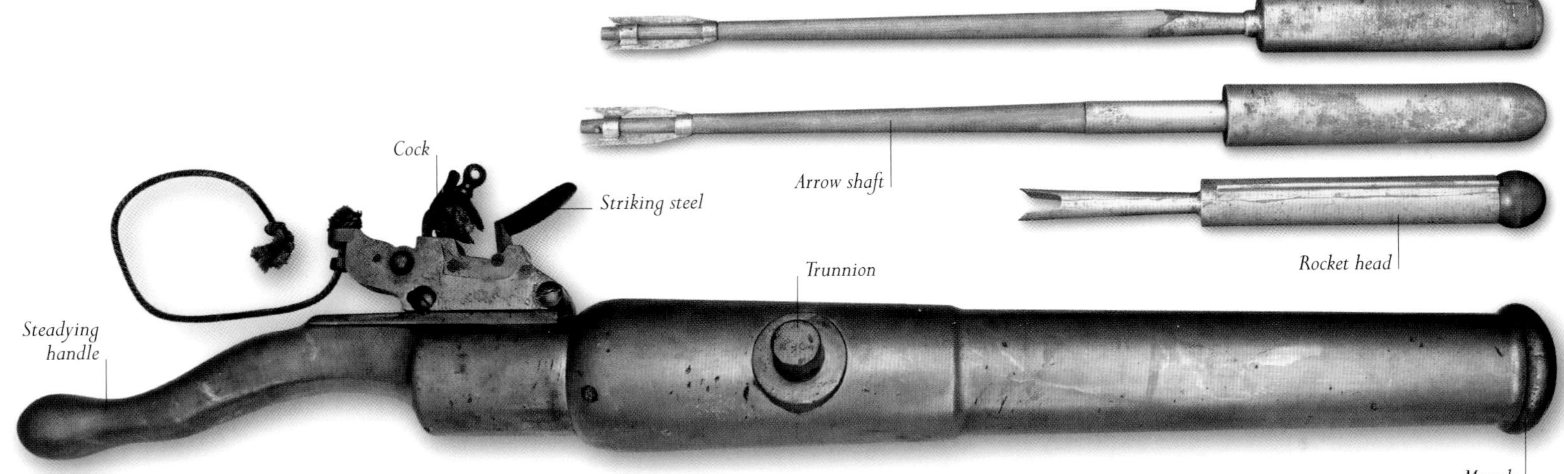

▲ FRENCH NAVAL SWIVEL GUN

Date 1812
Origin France
Barrel 33in (84cm)
Caliber 75-bore

Flintlock guns were unreliable weapons at sea because they were liable to misfire in bad weather. This bronze gun was marked with its place and date of manufacture: the armory of Toulon, France, 1812. The yoke or swivel post on which the gun rested would have been attached to the small trunnions on the barrel.

Muzzle

Raised sight

Fluted "cascabel" fixing point for ropes to secure the gun when firing

Curved handle

▶ CAST-IRON CARRONADE

Date 1808
Origin Scotland
Weight 1,481lb (671.7kg)
Length 3½ft (1.1m)
Caliber 14.5cm

This 24-pounder carronade was made with a raised sight in the reinforce ring and a recess in the muzzle ring for a removable sight. The muzzle was recessed for easy loading.

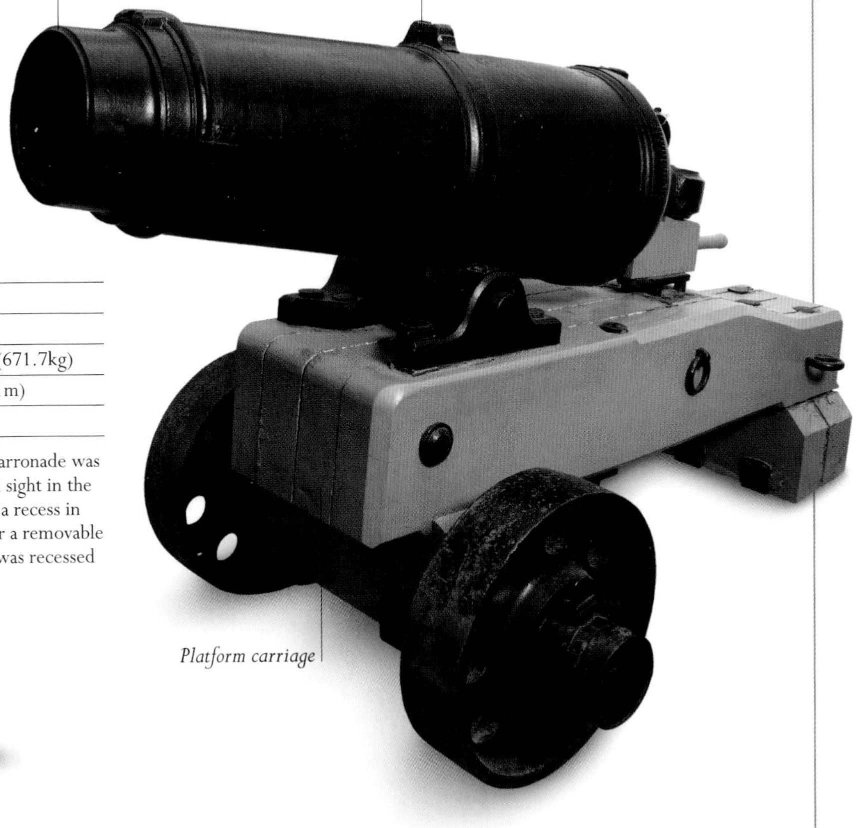

Platform carriage

NAVIGATION AND COMMUNICATION AT SEA

Specialized tools were used at sea to communicate signals, calculate position, and plot navigational routes. Aside from the magnetic compass, the navigator's principal tools were instruments such as the astrolabe and sextant, used for measuring the altitude of the Pole Star or the sun at noon. In conjunction with astronomical almanacs, these readings indicated the ship's latitude (how far north or south of the equator it was). Until the mid-18th century, longitude (a ship's east–west position) was calculated by "dead reckoning," using the ship's direction of travel and its speed. However, the invention of timepieces of unprecedented accuracy, such as John Harrison's marine chronometer of 1730–35, and his H4 timepiece of 1759, made precise calculations of longitude possible. The difference between the time on the clock—set to the time at Greenwich in London, England—and noon—as observed from the sun's position—indicated how many degrees the ship had sailed east or west of Greenwich.

Gnomon hinged for folding down when traveling

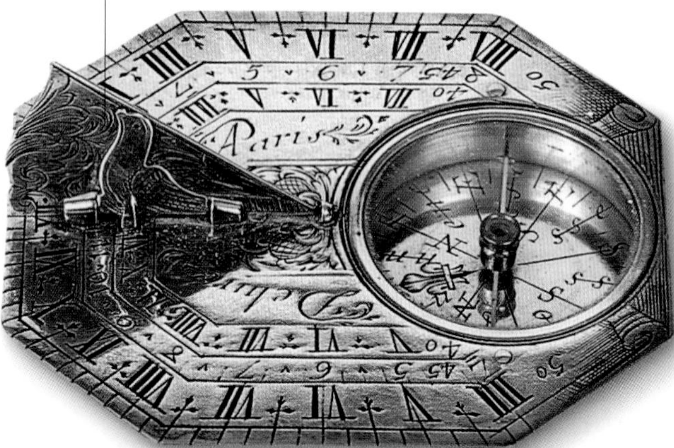

▲ BUTTERFIELD DIAL

Date Late 17th century

Origin France

Material Silver, glass

A Butterfield dial was a small portable sundial with an incorporated compass. The dials took their name from their inventor, Michael Butterfield (1635–1724), an English instrument-maker who worked in Paris. The gnomon (the raised blade that casts the shadow) was adjusted according to the latitude.

Suspension ring

Animals represent constellations or specific stars

Movable elements set to display date and time

▲ ASTROLABE

Date 1690

Origin Austria

Material Brass

The astrolabe was used by medieval astronomers to observe the stars. A simplified version was adopted by mariners from c.1450 onward.

Hand-colored card

North point marked with a fleur-de-lys

Wooden surround

Arrow labeled "S" for the south-easterly sirocco wind

▶ NAVIGATIONAL COMPASS

Date c.1719

Origin Italy

Material Wood, card

Developed in China, the navigational compass came to be used in Europe by the 12th century. On this mariner's compass, a quadrantal degree scale runs around the outer edge of the face. The cardinal and intercardinal points are identified by the initial letter of the Italian name for the wind that blows from that direction. North is the exception, being marked by a fleur-de-lys.

Retractable eyepiece

Pillar stand

Three folding legs

▶ GREGORIAN TELESCOPE

Date 1752

Origin England

Material Brass

The Gregorian telescope, named after its 17th-century Scottish inventor James Gregory, used two concave mirrors. This one, made by James Short of London, is 3¼in (8.5cm) in diameter and 20½in (52.5cm) long with its eyepiece extended. Its inclination could be adjusted and it could be moved easily from side to side.

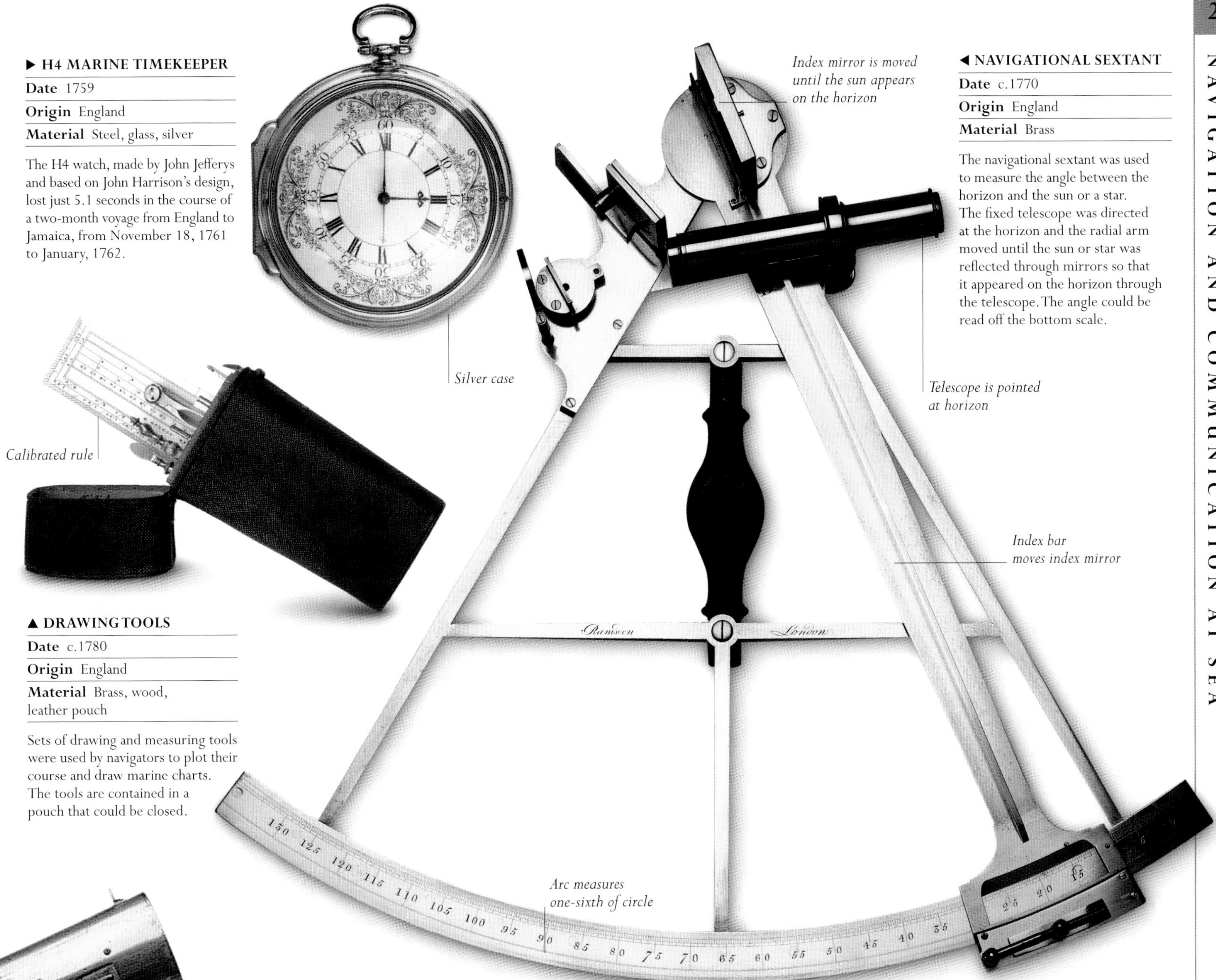

▶ H4 MARINE TIMEKEEPER

Date 1759

Origin England

Material Steel, glass, silver

The H4 watch, made by John Jefferys and based on John Harrison's design, lost just 5.1 seconds in the course of a two-month voyage from England to Jamaica, from November 18, 1761 to January, 1762.

Silver case

◀ NAVIGATIONAL SEXTANT

Date c.1770

Origin England

Material Brass

The navigational sextant was used to measure the angle between the horizon and the sun or a star. The fixed telescope was directed at the horizon and the radial arm moved until the sun or star was reflected through mirrors so that it appeared on the horizon through the telescope. The angle could be read off the bottom scale.

Index mirror is moved until the sun appears on the horizon

Telescope is pointed at horizon

Index bar moves index mirror

Arc measures one-sixth of circle

Calibrated rule

▲ DRAWING TOOLS

Date c.1780

Origin England

Material Brass, wood, leather pouch

Sets of drawing and measuring tools were used by navigators to plot their course and draw marine charts. The tools are contained in a pouch that could be closed.

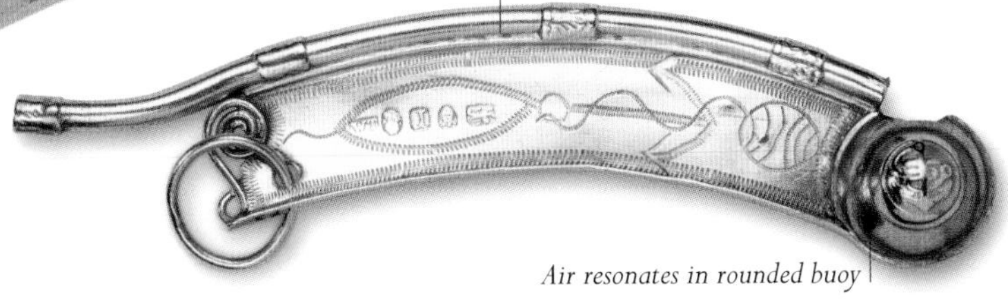

Air passes along an elongated tube called a "gun"

Air resonates in rounded buoy

▲ BOATSWAIN'S CALL

Date 1792

Origin England

Material Silver

The boatswain's call was a pipe used to convey orders aboard ship. Its shrill whistle could be heard above the sound of wind and waves. A finger was held over the hole to vary the tone—different combinations of tone and length of note signaled different orders.

▶ BRITISH NAVAL SIGNAL FLAGS

Date 1800

Origin England

Material Linen

Signal flags were used by most navies for communication at sea, but one of the first efficient, codified systems was developed by British Admiral Sir Home Popham in 1800. His system of numerary flags preceded the International Code of Signals, which was adopted worldwide in 1889.

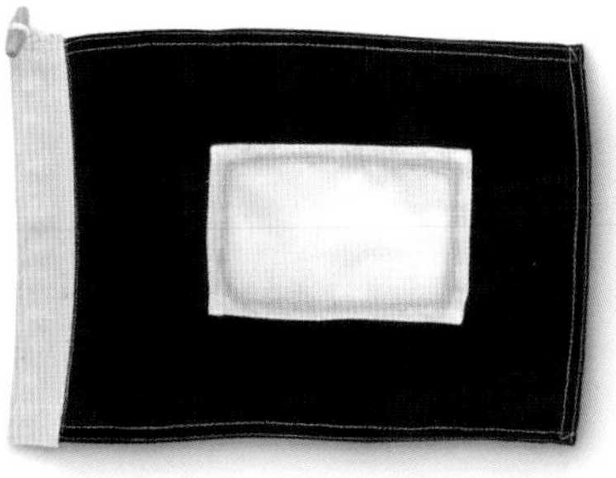

NUMERIC 1

NUMERIC 2

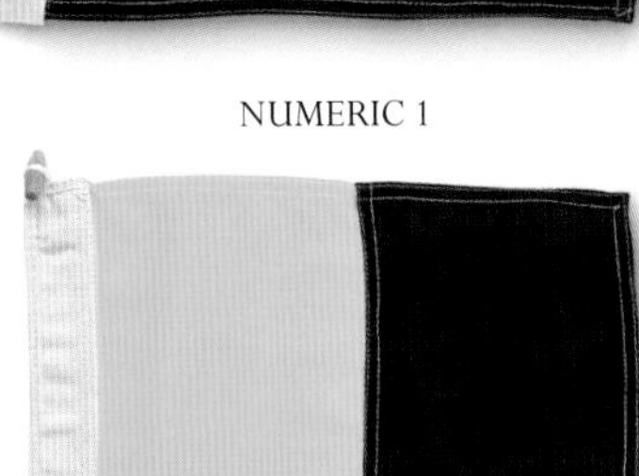

NUMERIC 4

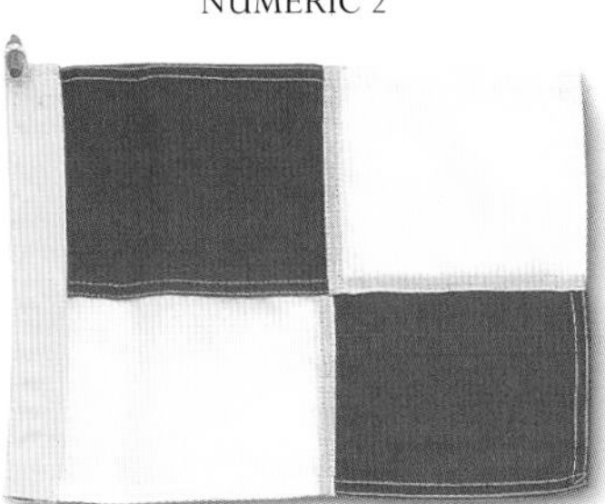

NUMERIC 9

NAVAL SWORDS

An ordinary sailor in the late 18th century made do with a simple cutlass, alongside a boarding pike, ax, and blunderbuss pistol. Naval officers, however, could choose from a wider range of swords. In addition to a short, curved sword with a plain hilt, officers' weapons included the ceremonial small sword, often worn when going ashore, and the spadroon—a light sword with a "five-ball hilt." The spadroon, with the decorative spheres on its hilt, was highly fashionable among officers in both armies and navies towards the close of the 18th century. Officers' swords also often had an anchor decoration on the hilt.

▲ SMALL SWORD

Date 1770

Origin UK

Length 32½in (82.5cm)

This ceremonial small sword, which probably belonged to British diplomat Sir William Hamilton (1731–1803), had a silver knuckle guard and grip bound with silver wire. The ornate pommel was embossed with a motif of a goat and dogs.

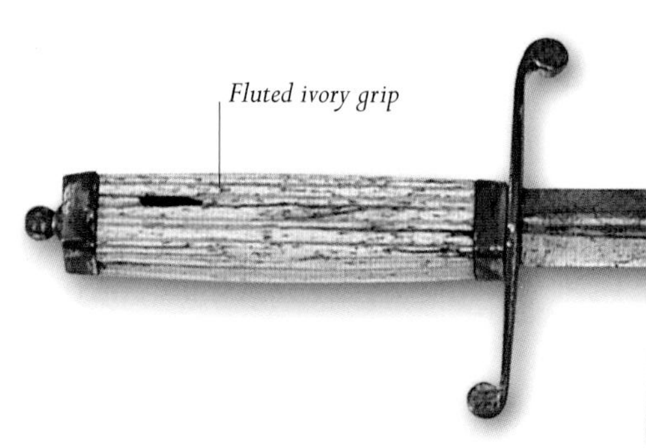

▲ OFFICER'S DIRK

Date 1790

Origin UK

Length 20½in (52cm)

The dirk was carried by officers and midshipmen from 1750 onwards. The daggerlike sword could be used as a stabbing weapon in boarding operations.

▶ DUTCH S-BAR HILTED SWORD

Date 1797

Origin Netherlands

Length 33in (84cm)

This Dutch sword with an S-bar hilt may have been given to Captain William Bligh by a Dutch admiral, perhaps Vice-Admiral Reijntjes, on board HMS *Director* in October 1797.

Reeded ivory grip

Lion's head pommel and back-piece

Gilt metal stirrup guard

Royal monogram

▲ ROYAL MARINES SWORD

Date c.1798

Origin UK

Length 34¼in (87cm)

The British Royal Navy's corps of the Royal Marines was established in 1664. It was initially called the Duke of York and Albany's Maritime Regiment of Foot. Half the length of this fine sword's blade featured blue and gilt decoration.

Ornate decoration

Blued blade

Leather scabbard

▶ NAVAL OFFICER'S SWORD

Date 1790

Origin UK

Weight 33oz (935g)

Length 33½in (85cm)

Many of the ceremonial swords worn by naval officers featured etched designs, gilding, and a "blued" blade. Gold and mercury were used in the gilding, and when the blade was fired, the mercury evaporated, leaving the gold design highlighted against a dark background. English swordsmiths were renowned around the globe for their skill in these techniques.

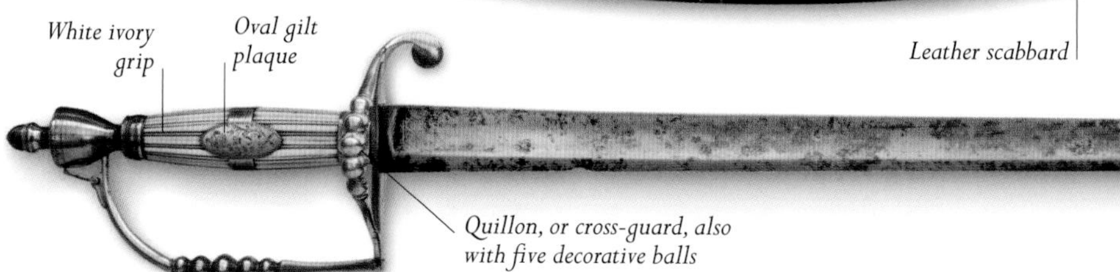

▶ FIVE-BALL SPADROON

Date c.1790

Origin UK

Length 31½in (80.5cm)

This five-ball spadroon, or light sword, was straight-bladed with a "five-ball hilt"—the "five-ball" referring to the decorative spheres on the hilt's knuckle guard and counter-guard.

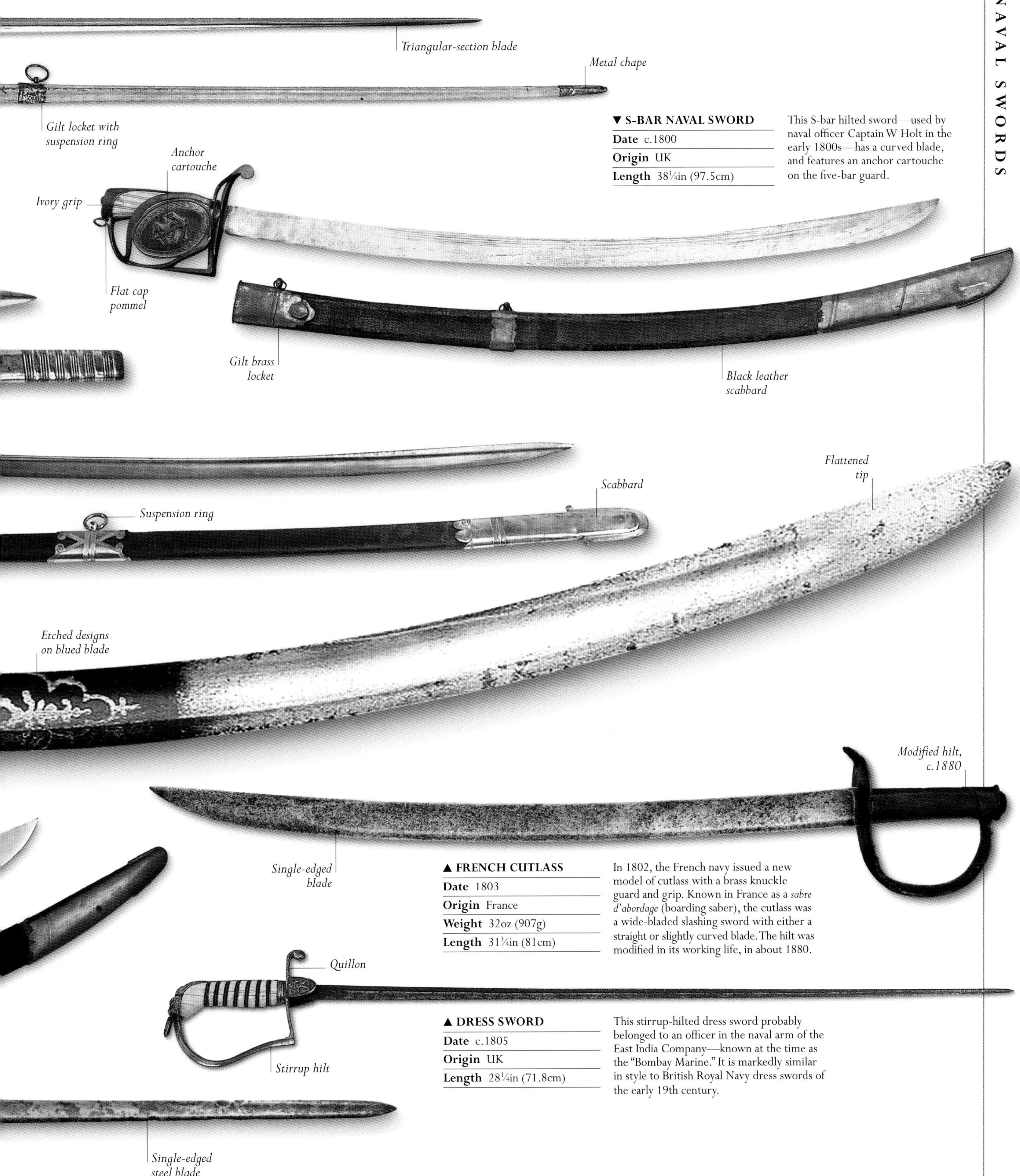

▼ S-BAR NAVAL SWORD

Date	c.1800
Origin	UK
Length	38¼in (97.5cm)

This S-bar hilted sword—used by naval officer Captain W Holt in the early 1800s—has a curved blade, and features an anchor cartouche on the five-bar guard.

▲ FRENCH CUTLASS

Date	1803
Origin	France
Weight	32oz (907g)
Length	31¾in (81cm)

In 1802, the French navy issued a new model of cutlass with a brass knuckle guard and grip. Known in France as a *sabre d'abordage* (boarding saber), the cutlass was a wide-bladed slashing sword with either a straight or slightly curved blade. The hilt was modified in its working life, in about 1880.

▲ DRESS SWORD

Date	c.1805
Origin	UK
Length	28¼in (71.8cm)

This stirrup-hilted dress sword probably belonged to an officer in the naval arm of the East India Company—known at the time as the "Bombay Marine." It is markedly similar in style to British Royal Navy dress swords of the early 19th century.

CARNAGE IN THE BAY
The climax of the battle came when the French flagship *L'Orient* caught fire and exploded. Of the ship's crew of over a thousand, probably less than a hundred survived, most of whom were rescued from the sea by British boats.

THE BATTLE OF THE NILE

The victories of British Rear-Admiral Horatio Nelson are among the most renowned examples of naval combat in the age of sailing ships. At Aboukir Bay in 1798, Nelson demolished a French fleet with a typically risky attack that rewrote the rules and tactics of fighting in line.

During the French Revolutionary War, the French fleet escorted General Napoleon Bonaparte's expeditionary force from France to Egypt. By August 1, 1798, 13 French ships of the line and four frigates were anchored at Aboukir Bay, on the Egyptian coast near Alexandria.

Britain's Admiral Lord Nelson had been seeking to intercept Bonaparte's troop convoy, chasing it with his 14 ships of the line. The ships, with one exception, were all 74-gun. On the afternoon of August 1 his lookouts sighted the French fleet, which had adopted an apparently impregnable defensive position: the ships were anchored in line of battle with their port side close to the shore, ready to fire broadsides to starboard. The French fleet was also mainly composed of 74-gun ships, but the fleet's commander, Admiral François-Paul Brueys, had a flagship, *L'Orient,* that was larger than any of the British ships—a massive 120-gun three-decker. Meanwhile, the shallow bay had numerous unmarked sandbanks and shoals that any attacker would need to negotiate with care.

Nelson decided to attack at once, although it was late in the day, focusing on the leading French ships (the van) and the center of the fleet. Due to wind direction, the ships of the French rear would be unable to join the fight, leaving the British with a local superiority in numbers.

When the British ships sailed into the bay it was nearly sunset. Many French sailors had been ashore and were still hurrying to rejoin their ships. Only one British vessel came to grief on a shoal, a tribute to the quality of Royal Navy seamanship. Five British ships sailed around the head of the French line and into the shallow water between the French ships and the shore. This maneuver took the French by surprise—the gunports on the landward side of their ships were closed. Nelson's ships also sailed into position on the seaward side of the French van, trapping each of the five French ships between a pair of British vessels. Shattered by point-blank broadsides from port and starboard, the French ships were soon in a desperate state.

The British attack on the French center, however, did not go as well at first. *L'Orient* dismasted *Bellerophon* by firing repeated broadsides, and the crippled ship drifted out of the battle. Nelson, standing in full view on the deck of his flagship *Vanguard*—as was customary—was cut across the forehead by a metal shard.

DESTRUCTION AND DEFEAT

The fighting continued after dark, and the valiant resistance of the French fleet began to fail. At around 10:00pm, *L'Orient* caught fire and when the flames reached the ship's powder magazine it exploded, scattering burning wreckage over a wide area. Admiral Brueys was already dead, cut almost in half by a cannon shot. During the night the fighting died down, and dawn broke over a scene of desolation: wreckage and dismembered bodies filled the bay. The ships in the rear of the French line had remained mere spectators of the carnage, while several French vessels had slipped away in the night. Nelson had destroyed two French ships of the line and captured nine

WEAPONS, UNIFORM, AND KIT OF AN ORDINARY BRITISH SAILOR

The phenomenal success of British sea power in the French Revolutionary and Napoleonic Wars depended not only on the tactical genius of commanders, but also on the bravery of the Royal Navy's well-drilled seamen, or "Jack Tars." Ordinary sailors' onboard duties chiefly involved the upkeep and running of the ship and the firing of its guns, although the men were issued with a pike, ax, cutlass, and pistols for boarding raids. A Jack Tar did not have a uniform, but he would have been identifiable from his outfit, which typically included a checked shirt, a short jacket, and a waistcoat.

Brim, usually of narrow width

▶ **ROUND HAT**

Date	c.1800
Origin	England
Material	Tarred straw

Sailors sported a variety of headgear. Straw hats, popular in sunny latitudes, were often tarred to make them waterproof. The "round hat" had a tall crown like that of a top hat.

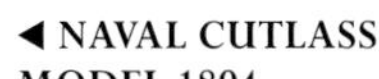

Black-painted iron grip

◀ **NAVAL CUTLASS MODEL 1804**

Date	1804
Origin	England
Weight	3lb (1.32kg)
Length	33½in (85.5cm)

The British Model 1804 cutlass was a utilitarian, straight-bladed, cut-and-thrust weapon with a double disk guard and a ribbed iron handle, painted black to protect against corrosion.

Straight, almost flat steel blade

Blade tapered to stabbing point

▶ **WAISTCOAT**

Date	c.1800
Origin	England
Material	Wool

A colorful waistcoat was a fairly standard piece of clothing for seamen. Being skilled at repairing sails, many sailors were accomplished needleworkers, making and mending most of their own clothes.

Red woolen cloth

Spike could be driven into hull of an enemy ship to make a step or handhold

Axehead riveted to handle

Tough hardwood handle

▶ **BOARDING AX**

Date	c.1800
Origin	England
Weight	4lb (1.8kg)
Length	3¼ft (1m)

The boarding ax was used by seamen to cut stays, cables, and rigging when boarding an enemy ship, and to hook away debris. The ax could also be used as a weapon in hand-to-hand fighting.

▶ **TROUSERS**

Date	c.1800
Origin	England
Material	Cotton

Seamen generally wore loose trousers for ease of movement. They favored "white duck," a hard-wearing cotton weave, and the trousers could be of any color or pattern—many were striped.

▼ JACKET

Date	c.1800
Origin	England
Material	Linen

A sailor's jacket was short with no tails, and usually blue. Sailors often bought material or clothes from the same outfitter or from the ship's purser, so there was considerable uniformity in their appearance.

▲ PAIR OF SEA SERVICE PISTOLS

Date	c.1790
Origin	England
Weight	2½lb (1.1kg)
Barrel	12in (30cm)
Calibre	.56in

First introduced in 1757, these pistols are of the Pattern 1757/1777 type. Pistols issued to sailors were normally fired only once—in the initial attack or as a last resort. The pistol's brass butt could also be used as a club.

◀ SHIRT AND NECK CLOTH

Date	c.1800
Origin	England
Material	Linen

A checked shirt and neck cloth were the hallmarks of a Royal Navy seaman. The neck cloth could double as a bandanna tied around the head to keep sweat out of the eyes.

▶ BOARDING PIKE

Date	c.1800
Origin	England
Weight	6½lb (3kg)
Length	8ft (2.4m)

Pikes were kept in a rack on the main deck. They were handy weapons in the mêlée of confused fighting that ensued when a ship was boarded.

▲ BELT

Date	c.1800
Origin	England
Material	Leather

To keep his cotton-weave trousers in place, a seaman usually wore a simple, wide, black leather belt with a brass buckle.

◀ BUCKLED SHOES

Date	c.1800
Origin	England
Material	Leather

Although sailors went barefoot much of the time on board, they would put on their best pair of shoes for the captain's inspection and church service on Sunday.

BRITISH NAVAL OFFICERS' UNIFORM

The British Royal Navy's officer class in the 18th and early 19th centuries was primarily made up of men as young as 12 to 14 years of age who came from respectable backgrounds. The Navy offered a tempting career during wartime, despite the hazards of life at sea. In addition to opportunities for promotion, there was the chance to become rich from the prize money paid by the Admiralty to those officers and crew who took possession of enemy ships. These young recruits initially learned how to navigate and operate a warship as midshipmen. They would hope for promotion to lieutenant after around six years, and for command of their own ship by the age of 21. Uniforms for officers, predominantly in white and navy blue, were first issued in 1748, and a new pattern was introduced in 1774.

▲ CAPTAIN'S HAT

Date c.1750

Origin England

Material "Half-beaver" felt

A captain would usually carry his hat under his arm so that his wig was not displaced. The material was "half-beaver"—a type of felt with beaver hair added to increase its firmness. The hat was then lined with silver lace.

▶ MIDSHIPMAN'S FROCK COAT

Date 1748

Origin England

Material Wool, velvet

The "mariner's cuff" in white with a three-point blue section was widely fashionable beyond the Royal Navy, appearing in suits and riding clothes as well. The wool collar is lined with white velvet.

Mariner's cuff

▲ OFFICER'S TELESCOPE

Date c.1800

Origin England

Material Glass, brass, rayskin, sharkskin

An officer used a hand-held telescope to identify approaching vessels, view flag signals, and help him gauge possible navigational hazards. This telescope had seven draw tubes, and the eyepiece cover, draw tubes, and fittings were made of brass. It could be retracted and fitted into a sharkskin case.

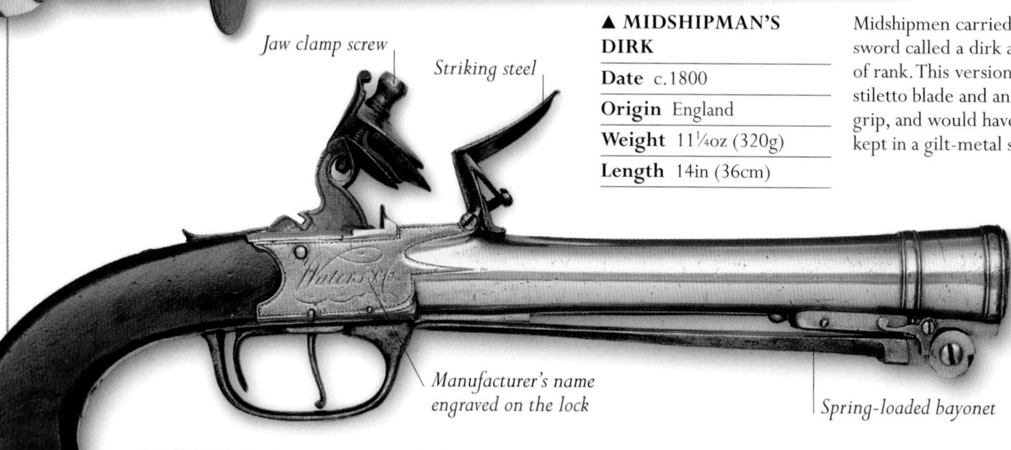

▲ MIDSHIPMAN'S DIRK

Date c.1800

Origin England

Weight 11¼oz (320g)

Length 14in (36cm)

Midshipmen carried a short sword called a dirk as a mark of rank. This version has a stiletto blade and an ivory grip, and would have been kept in a gilt-metal sheaf.

▲ JOHN WATERS BLUNDERBUSS PISTOL

Date 1785

Origin England

Weight 33½oz (950g)

Barrel 7½in (19cm)

Caliber 1in

The blunderbuss (from the Dutch *donderbus* or "thunder gun") was used in boarding operations—its bell-mouth ensured a wide spread of shot when fired at close quarters. This box-lock model was made by John Waters of Birmingham, who held the patent on the pistol bayonet. His name is legible on the rectangular box enclosing the lock mechanism.

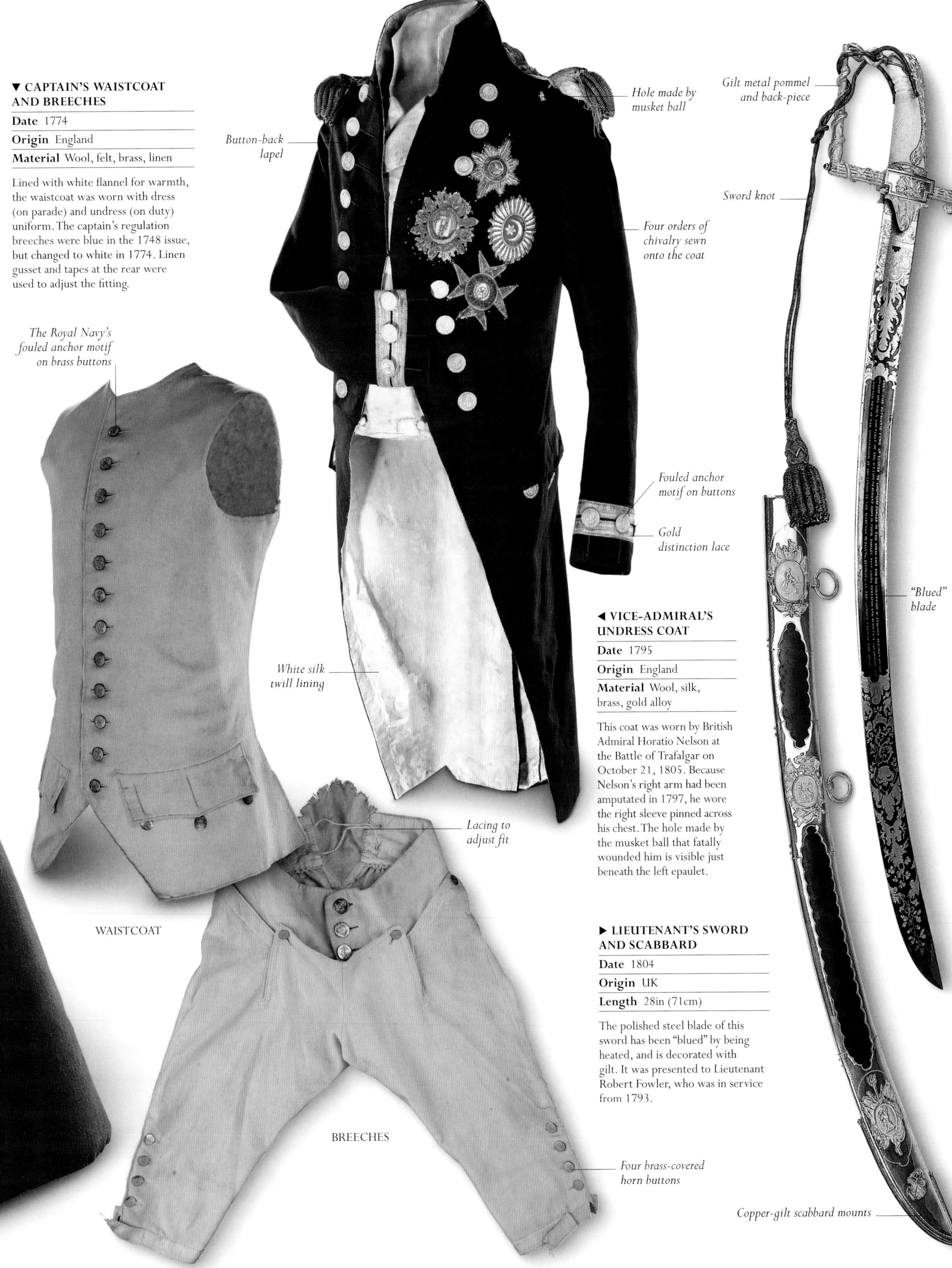

▼ **CAPTAIN'S WAISTCOAT AND BREECHES**

Date 1774

Origin England

Material Wool, felt, brass, linen

Lined with white flannel for warmth, the waistcoat was worn with dress (on parade) and undress (on duty) uniform. The captain's regulation breeches were blue in the 1748 issue, but changed to white in 1774. Linen gusset and tapes at the rear were used to adjust the fitting.

◀ **VICE-ADMIRAL'S UNDRESS COAT**

Date 1795

Origin England

Material Wool, silk, brass, gold alloy

This coat was worn by British Admiral Horatio Nelson at the Battle of Trafalgar on October 21, 1805. Because Nelson's right arm had been amputated in 1797, he wore the right sleeve pinned across his chest. The hole made by the musket ball that fatally wounded him is visible just beneath the left epaulet.

▶ **LIEUTENANT'S SWORD AND SCABBARD**

Date 1804

Origin UK

Length 28in (71cm)

The polished steel blade of this sword has been "blued" by being heated, and is decorated with gilt. It was presented to Lieutenant Robert Fowler, who was in service from 1793.

18TH-CENTURY SHIP OF THE LINE

HMS VICTORY

A first-rate ship of the line, the *Victory* won fame as Admiral Horatio Nelson's flagship when the British Royal Navy triumphed over the Spanish and French fleets at the Battle of Trafalgar, in 1805.

More than 6,000 trees, mostly oak, were felled for *Victory*'s construction. Launched in 1765, it was not commissioned until war with France broke out in 1778, and the ship saw its first action at the Battle of Ushant. It later became the Royal Navy's flagship in the Mediterranean and led the action that destroyed the Spanish fleet at the Battle of Cape St. Vincent, in 1797. By then the *Victory* was showing its age, so at the end of 1797 it was retired to serve as a hospital ship. This decision was soon reconsidered, and, after being repaired, the *Victory* was recommissioned as Nelson's flagship in 1803. Two years later it played a key role in the Battle of Trafalgar, with 57 men killed, including her admiral, and 102 injured. The ship remained in active service until 1812.

The *Victory* carried 820 men, including 146 marines. Its 104 smoothbore, muzzle-loading cannon gave it immense firepower: in comparison, the entire French army at the Battle of Austerlitz, in the same year as Trafalgar, fielded 139 cannon.

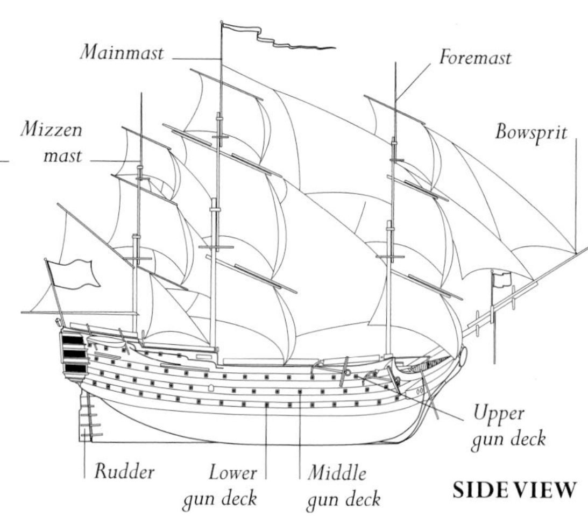

SIDE VIEW

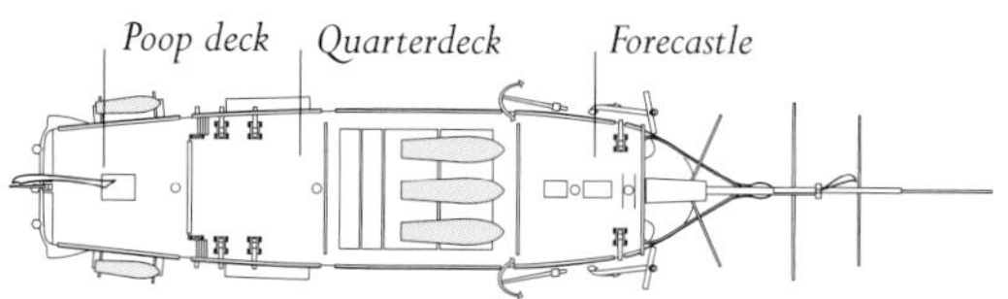

PLAN VIEW

HMS *VICTORY*
The ship was up to 52ft (16m) wide, and the gun-deck length was 107ft (57m). The 37 sails had a combined area of 6,510 sq yards (5,468 sq m).

TOWARD THE STERN

◄ **STERN**
Housed in the rear of the ship were the cabins of the admiral, captain, and other officers. There was less decoration on the *Victory*'s stern than on earlier ships of her kind.

▲ **WHEEL AND BINNACLE**
The double wheel, located aft on the quarterdeck and under the poop, was operated by four men in calm weather and up to eight in a storm. The binnacle, in front of the wheel, holds a lantern and two compasses.

▲ **GUN PORTS**
The ports were opened and closed using ropes located on the gun decks. The muzzles of the guns are blocked by tompions (plugs that are designed to keep out dust and moisture).

MASTS AND RIGGING

▲ **MAINMAST**
The three masts are supported by ropes called standing rigging. With men climbing along the yardarms to set or furl the sails, fatal falls were common.

▲ **ROPE LADDER**
"Shrouds" are standing rigging ropes fitted to the ship's sides; "ratlines" run across them, forming ladders up the masts.

TOWARD THE PROW

▲ **CARRONADE**
Two powerful short-barreled guns known as carronades were mounted on the forecastle. They were devastating at close range.

▲ **HEAVY ANCHOR**
The largest of the seven anchors weighed more than 4.6 tonnes (4½ tons) and required 144 men to raise it.

◄ **FIGUREHEAD**
Supported by two cupids, the royal coat of arms was topped by a crown and surrounded by the motto *Honi soit qui mal y pense* ("Shame on he who thinks evil of it").

▼ **AT REST**
Now restored to its pre-Trafalgar condition, the *Victory* sits in dry dock at Portsmouth, England. It is the oldest ship in the world that is still officially in naval service.

▲ **RIGGING BLOCK**
Ropes that raise, lower, and manipulate sails are known as running rigging. In total, the *Victory*'s rigging used 768 blocks, or pulleys.

▲ **PLATFORM**
The top—a platform halfway up each mast—was used by the crew to access the sails. In battle, seamen stood on the tops to fire down on the enemy.

▲ **JEER BLOCKS**
One of the most complex areas of rigging is just below the top, where the lower yard is held in place using large pieces of wood called jeer blocks.

BELOW DECK

To keep the *Victory* stable, the heaviest guns—the 32-pounders—were positioned on the lower gun deck. The middle gun deck held the 24-pounders, while the 12-pounders were located on the upper gun deck. The orlop deck and hold, which were beneath the water line and safe from enemy fire, contained the magazines. The hold was also used for storage and ballast.

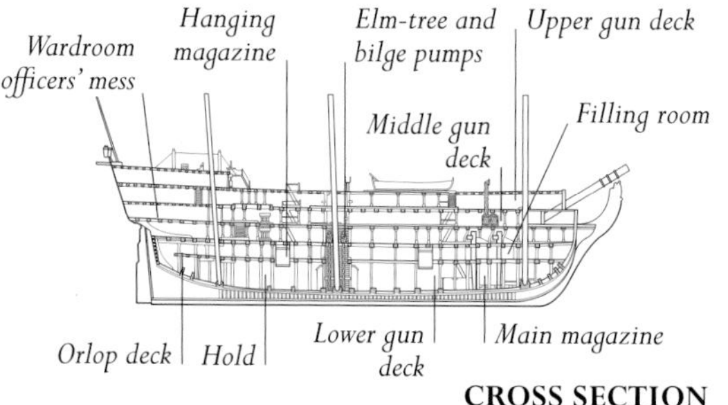

CROSS SECTION

▲ MESS TABLE
The gun decks not only housed the guns but also served as living areas for most of the ship's crew and its complement of marines. Meals were taken at tables suspended between the guns.

GUN DECKS

► 32-POUNDER GUNS
Each gun's recoil was controlled by a thick breeching rope. The rope allowed the gun to move back enough to be in-board of the gunport, so that the gunners could reload it via the muzzle.

► ELM-TREE PUMP
Two pumps made from elm trunks drew water up from the sea to fight fires and wash down the decks. They were operated from beside the mainmast on the lower gun deck. The *Victory* also had four chain pumps to remove bilge water or pump out water if the hull became holed (damaged).

▲ SICK BERTH
Sick or injured men were moved to a small area near the bow on the upper gun deck. In battle, they were taken below to the orlop deck, enabling the sick berth to become a functioning part of the gun deck.

▲ **FLINTLOCK**
The guns had flintlocks. Pulling the cord made a flint strike a spark to fire the gun.

▲ **HAMMOCKS**
Most of the ship's men slept in hammocks slung from the beams of the gun deck.

SENIOR OFFICERS' ROOMS

▲ **CAPTAIN'S DAY CABIN**
At the stern of the ship, the admiral and the captain both had light and spacious cabins that provided separate areas for sleeping, dining, and working.

▲ **ADMIRAL'S COT**
The admiral and other high-ranking officers slept in boxlike cots that hung from the deckhead. An officer's cot would also serve as a coffin in the event of his death.

ORLOP DECK AND HOLD

▲ **DISPENSARY**
The surgeon's dispensary was located on the orlop deck. The cockpit, an open area nearby, acted as an operating theater.

▲ **BOSUN'S STOREROOM**
The boatswain (bosun) was in charge of the deck crew. His store in the hold held supplies to repair the rigging.

▲ **CHARGE RACKS**
Gunpowder charges were made up in the filling room in the hold, and then stored on racks in magazines.

▲ **BALLAST**
On the floor of the hold lay 511 tons (464 tonnes) of ballast, which was needed to keep the ship level and upright. The ballast consisted of iron ingots and gravel.

▲ **SHOT LOCKERS**
Around 134 tons (122 tonnes) of cast-iron shot were kept in the hold. The largest shot weighed 32lb (14.5 kg). At Trafalgar, the *Victory* fired a total 31 tons of shot.

1815–1914

INDUSTRY AND IMPERIALISM

INTRODUCTION

Between 1815 and 1914, technological progress transformed conflict. High-explosive and rapid-fire mechanisms greatly increased the killing power of weaponry; railroads enabled greater mobility; the telegraph, telephone, and radio revolutionized communications; and warfare spread into the skies and beneath the oceans.

Developments were relatively slow at first, but, in the 1830s, a forty-year transition period began, in which many hybrid and experimental technologies flourished. The long reign of the flintlock musket came to an end, although at first mostly replaced by the rifle musket, which was still muzzle-loaded and slow-firing. Breech-loading rifles and pistols capable of repeated fire were invented, but armies were slow to accept them. At sea, ships used both steam engines and sails, and their wooden hulls were armored with iron cladding. Even in the American Civil War of 1861–65, more soldiers still died of disease than in combat—as in wars of old.

The pace of change increased from the 1870s. The Franco-Prussian War of 1870–71 was fought by infantry with breech-loading rifles; the French fielded machine-guns, while German rifled, breech-loading Krupp cannon bombarded Paris. In the 1880s, the use of smokeless propellants and high explosives in shells marked the end of the gunpowder era. New navies were built, with steel ships equipped with breech-loading rifled turret guns, as bolt-action repeater rifles became standard infantry equipment. Army organization was also changing, with the widespread adoption of the Prussian model of a professional general staff, and European powers committing to military service as a basic duty of their male citizens. More advanced nations amassed vast army and navy establishments, using them with success against tribal peoples and technologically inferior states, such as China or Turkey. The Russo-Japanese War of 1904–05 provided a glimpse of 20th-century conflict between industrialized states, with the presence of machine-guns and heavy artillery, barbed wire, and trenches.

KEY **DATES**

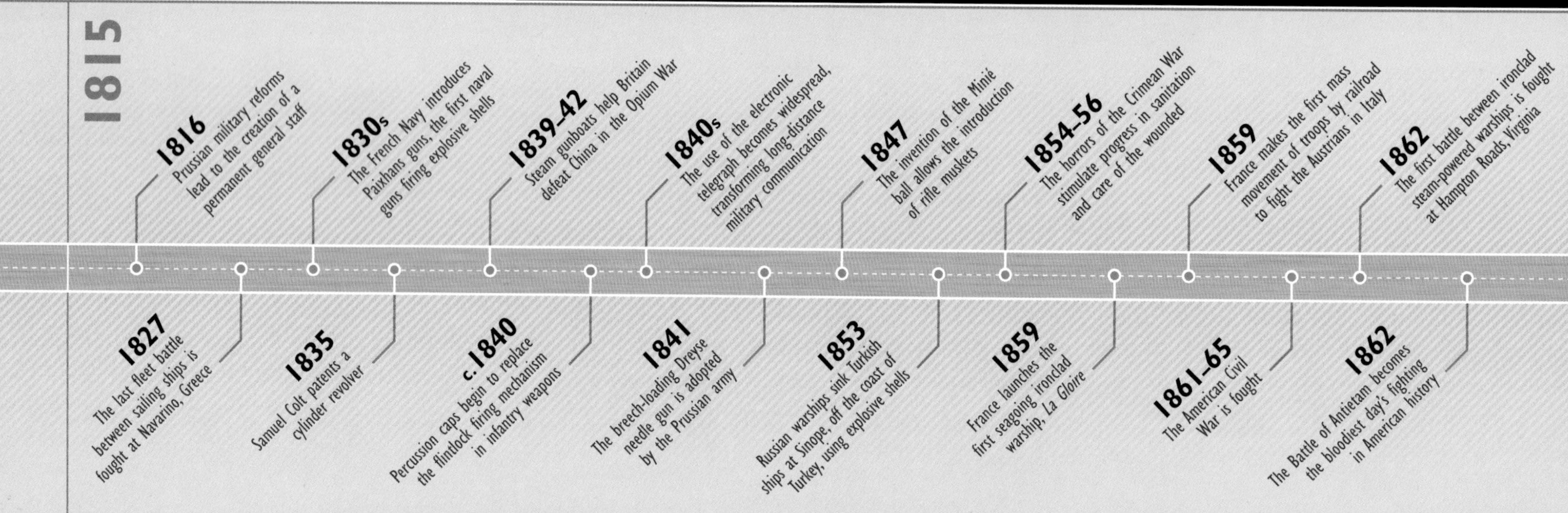

THE AMERICAN CIVIL WAR—1861–1865

THE FRANCO-PRUSSIAN WAR—1870–71

THE BATTLE OF MANILA—1898

1866 The Gatling gun, the forerunner of the machine-gun, is adopted by the US Army

1867 The Meiji Restoration begins in Japan, during which Japan modernizes its armed forces

1870–71 Prussia defeats France in the Franco-Prussian War

1871 The British Army adopts the single-shot, breech-loading Martini-Henry rifle

1879 British soldiers defeat Zulus at the Battle of Rorke's Drift, in South Africa, aided by the Martini-Henry rifle

1880s Armies adopt bolt-action repeater rifles as their standard infantry weapon

1883 Hiram Maxim makes the first recoil-operated machine-gun

1886 A smokeless propellant replaces gunpowder

1897 France introduces the 75mm field gun, which is capable of firing 15 rounds per minute

1898 An Anglo-Egyptian army defeats the Sudanese Mahdists at Omdurman using Maxim guns

1899–1902 The Second Boer War is fought in southern Africa

c.1900 Submarines begin to enter service with the world's navies

1904–05 The Russo-Japanese War demonstrates new technology, including field telephones and barbed wire

1905 The Imperial Japanese Navy defeats a Russian fleet at Tsushima, aided by the use of radio

1906 Britain launches the first Dreadnought-class battleship

1911 Italian aircraft drop bombs in a war against Turkey in Libya—the first use of aircraft in war

1914

THE BATTLE OF OMDURMAN—1898

THE BOER WAR—1880–1902

THE BATTLE OFTSUSHIMA—1905

KEY DEVELOPMENT

THE BEGINNINGS OF MODERN WARFARE

In the 19th century, weaponry was transformed by the cumulative effect of technological innovations. Armies clung to well-established tactics, such as the cavalry charge and frontal infantry assault, but improved firepower made these methods increasingly obsolete.

KEY **BATTLE**

CHARGE OF THE LIGHT BRIGADE
OCTOBER 25, 1854

During the Crimean War, Lord Cardigan led an attack by British hussars, lancers, and dragoons on a heavy Russian artillery battery. Charging along a valley covered by dense Russian fire, the light cavalry lost almost half their number.

▲ The British horsemen reached the Russian guns, but at the cost of an excessive number of lives.

The transformation of infantry weapons began in 1839, with the adoption of the percussion cap as an ignition system for muskets, over the long-established flintlock mechanism. However, in the 1840s, the Prussian army rearmed its infantry with the Dreyse needle gun, a bolt-action, breech-loading rifle firing a cartridge with integrated percussion cap, powder, and bullet. This had a higher rate of fire than muskets, and could be fired lying or kneeling behind cover.

In 1853, the British Army adopted the Enfield rifled musket, which fired the Minié ball: this ingenious bullet was small enough to be rammed down the barrel, but expanded when fired to engage the rifling. First used in the Crimean War (1854–56), fought between Russian and allied forces, the rifled musket had more than twice the range of a conventional musket, and it became the standard infantry weapon of the American Civil War (1861–65). It greatly increased the infantry casualties across open ground, even when they advanced in a loose skirmish line rather than traditional columns.

▲ THE COLT DRAGOON REVOLVER
Supplied to American mounted troops from 1848, the Colt Dragoon pistol had six revolving chambers. The soldier loaded each chamber with a ball, black powder, and a percussion cap.

TECHNOLOGICAL DEVELOPMENTS

In the Franco-Prussian War of 1870–71, infantry on both sides used breech-loading rifles firing the self-contained cartridge, an invention that led to repeater rifles, revolvers, and machine-guns: early rapid-fire weapons emerged in the 1860s, with the French Mitrailleuse and the American Gatling gun (see pp. 246–47), although the first true machine-gun, the Maxim gun, came into service in the 1880s. Cavalry in the American Civil War often carried Colt or Remington revolvers and Spencer repeating carbines, but only a few infantry had repeating rifles.

By the 1880s, advanced armies were adopting bolt-operated magazine rifles as standard, whereas innovations in artillery were slower. The American Civil War featured muzzle-loading, smoothbore cannon that were only a marginal improvement on

"The fire **was so destructive** my line wavered like a **man trying to walk against [the] wind**"

CONFEDERATE COLONEL WILLIAM OATES, WRITING ABOUT GETTYSBURG, 1905

cannon of the Napoleonic era. However, from the 1870s, breech-loading, rifled artillery, pioneered by the Prussians, transformed both range and rate of fire. Firing high-explosive steel shells, the French 75 field gun, introduced in 1898, could fire up to 30 rounds a minute up to 5 miles (8.5km).

LOGISTICS AND COMMUNICATION

Military commanders were mostly quick to adopt new technology. Two of the most important influences on 19th-century warfare—railroads and the electric telegraph—were civilian inventions. Large-scale military use of railroads came in 1859, when the French moved over 100,000 soldiers by train to fight the Austrians in northern Italy; soon after, both the railroad and the telegraph were to prove invaluable in the American Civil War.

▲ LONG-RANGE SIEGE GUNS During the Franco-Prussian War of 1870–71, Paris was bombarded with heavy Krupp siege guns. The superior performance of these breech-loading cannon was a major factor in Prussia's victory in the war.

◄ CIVIL WAR CAVALRY While cavalry still had an important role in the American Civil War, as in conflicts of old, the traditional charge with sabers drawn was increasingly rare, as the revolver and carbine proved their superiority.

KEY **EVENTS**

19TH CENTURY

- **1854–56** The rifled musket is employed in the Crimean War, which also sees use of the electric telegraph, and the beginnings of war photography.
- **1863** At the Battle of Gettysburg, an assault by Confederate infantry—known as Pickett's Charge—fails, with 50 percent casualties caused by the combined firepower of Union rifled muskets and cannon.
- **1866** Prussia defeats Austria in the Seven Weeks' War, helped by its efficiency in mobilizing its forces by rail, and its use of the breech-loading Dreyse needle gun.
- **1870–71** France is defeated in the Franco-Prussian War, chiefly because of the superiority of Prussian artillery.

FLINTLOCK MUSKETS AND BREECH-LOADING RIFLES

Muzzle-loading flintlock muskets, such as the French Charleville and the British "Brown Bess," proved reliable and robust. Thousands of these were made and remained in service until around 1840, by which time armed forces had recognized the ballistic advantages of rifled guns. The development of the unitary cartridge—which combined the bullet and ignition components in a single unit, and could be loaded by way of the breech—inspired new designs. Initially, many were conversions of muzzle-loading weapons, but these were followed by a range of specially built breech-loaders. The bolt action, pioneered by Johann von Dreyse and Antoine Alphonse Chassepot, was perfected by the Mauser brothers.

Barrel band

Rear sling swivel

▲ CHARLEVILLE MUSKET

Date	1776
Origin	France
Weight	9¼lb (4.2kg)
Barrel	3¾ft (1.13m)
Caliber	.65in

Charleville muskets were introduced in 1754, and modified a number of times. Large numbers of the 1776 model found their way to the US, where they were the main armament of the Continental Army.

Bolt handle

Trigger guard

▶ DREYSE NEEDLE GUN MODEL 1841

Date	1841
Origin	Prussia
Weight	10lb (4.5kg)
Barrel	28in (70cm)
Caliber	13.6mm

Dreyse's rifle had a simple straight-handed bolt, terminating in a needle that penetrated the length of a (linen) cartridge to detonate a percussion cap in the base of a Minié bullet.

Leather sling for steadiness while shooting

▲ BAKER RIFLE

Date	1800–37
Origin	UK
Weight	8¾lb (4kg)
Barrel	30in (76cm)
Caliber	.625in

The rifle designed by English gunsmith Ezekiel Baker was chosen for riflemen in the British Army (see pp.192–93). Accurate to around 460ft (140m), it was a great improvement over smoothbore muskets.

Tape primer compartment

Sliding breechblock

Rear sling swivel

▲ SHARPS PERCUSSION-CAP CARBINE

Date	1848
Origin	US
Weight	7¾lb (3.5kg)
Barrel	18in (45.5cm)
Caliber	.52in

This percussion-cap breech-loader used a sliding breechblock to load a combustible cartridge, which was ignited by a tape primer or, in other models, a percussion cap.

"Trapdoor" breech cover incorporates firing pin

Breech cover hinge

▲ CHASSEPOT PERCUSSION CARBINE

Date	1858
Origin	France
Weight	6¾lb (3.03kg)
Barrel	28¼in (72cm)
Caliber	13.5mm

In France, Chassepot produced a breech-loading carbine that used a rubber washer to seal the breech. The later, definitive Chassepot system replaced the hammer with a needle striker within a turn-bolt.

▲ WESTLEY RICHARDS "MONKEY TAIL" CARBINE

Date	1866
Origin	UK
Weight	6½lb (3kg)
Barrel	18in (45.5cm)
Caliber	.45in

Birmingham gunmakers Westley Richards produced two carbines for the British Army. This one had a front-hinged, tilting breech with a long, curved actuating lever, which gave the weapon its nickname.

◀ MARTINI-HENRY MK I

Date	1871
Origin	UK
Weight	10¼lb (4.7kg)
Barrel	33½in (85cm)
Caliber	.45 Martini

The British Army's first purpose-designed, breech-loading rifle, the Martini-Henry incorporated a tilting breech block. Lowering the under-lever opened the breech and cocked the action.

◀ SPRINGFIELD TRAPDOOR

Date	1874
Origin	US
Weight	10lb (4.5kg)
Barrel	32½in (82.5cm)
Caliber	.45in

In this converted muzzle-loader, the top of the barrel was milled out, creating a chamber for the cartridge, while the front-hinged breech cover incorporated a firing pin.

▲ MAUSER M/71

Date	1872
Origin	Germany
Weight	10lb (4.5kg)
Barrel	32½in (83cm)
Caliber	11mm × 60R

In Germany, Waffenfabrik Mauser began modifying Dreyse guns to accept brass cartridges. Subsequently, Peter Paul Mauser produced this new design, which was strong enough to handle much more powerful ammunition.

FLINTLOCK AND PERCUSSION PISTOLS AND EARLY REVOLVERS

American Samuel Colt patented the design of a new type of pistol in 1835—a six-shot cylinder revolver that fired percussion-cap ammunition. Colt was the first manufacturer to prove that it was commercially viable to mass-produce revolvers—no fewer than 215,348 of his .36 caliber Model 1851 revolver were sold from 1851 to 1876. British interest in pistols was sparked by Colt's display at the Great Exhibition of 1851 in London. By the end of the 1850s, revolvers made by London gunmakers such as Robert Adams had become more popular in Britain than American Colts. Adams's pistols had double-action ("self-cocking") locks—an element of British revolver design from the start.

Brass trigger guard

▲ HARPER'S FERRY PISTOL

Date	1805
Origin	US
Weight	31¾oz (900g)
Barrel	10in (25.4cm)
Caliber	.54in

The Model 1805 was the first pistol manufactured at the newly established United States Federal Arsenal at Harper's Ferry (in modern-day West Virginia). It was robust enough to be reversed and used as a club if required.

Plain unfluted cylinder has eight chambers

▲ COLT PATERSON REVOLVING RIFLE

Date	1837
Origin	US
Weight	8½lb (3.9kg)
Barrel	32in (81.3cm)
Caliber	.36in

Samuel Colt's first factory in Paterson, New Jersey, produced revolver rifles as well as pistols. However, it had limited facilities and went bankrupt. Paterson-built Colts, such as this first-pattern concealed-hammer eight-shot rifle, are extremely rare.

Hammer

Ramrod retainer

Lock plate

► PATTERN 1842 COAST GUARD PISTOL

Date	1842
Origin	UK
Weight	2¼lb (1.05kg)
Barrel	6in (15cm)
Caliber	24-bore

In the 1842 coast guard pistol, the ramrod retainer swivelled to allow the captive rod to be inserted in the barrel. These pistols were replaced by revolvers from the 1850s.

Brass trigger guard

Brass-bound butt

Octagonal barrel

▲ COLT POCKET PISTOL MODEL 1849

Date	1849
Origin	US
Weight	24½oz (690g)
Barrel	4in (10.2cm)
Caliber	.31in

A revised version of his 1848 revolver, the Baby Dragoon, Samuel Colt's 1849 Pocket Pistol had a standard compound rammer, the choice of three barrel lengths, and a five- or six-shot cylinder.

Cutaway to facilitate placing of cap

▲ COLT NAVY MODEL 1851

Date	1853
Origin	UK
Weight	2½lb (1.2kg)
Barrel	7½in (19cm)
Caliber	.36in

At the Great Exhibition of 1851 in London, Samuel Colt introduced the Navy Model, a lighter pistol in .36in rather than .44in caliber. After the display, he obtained an order from the British government. This is one of the pistols produced at the company's London factory.

▲ COLT SECOND MODEL DRAGOON PISTOL

Date	1849
Origin	US
Weight	4¼lb (1.93kg)
Barrel	7½in (19cm)
Caliber	.44in

Colt's mainstay during the first 15 years of the percussion era was the Dragoon Pistol, so called because it was intended as a sidearm for cavalrymen. A new factory was built at Hartford in Connecticut to produce the Dragoon Pistol to fulfill an army contract.

▲ COLT POCKET PISTOL MODEL 1855

Date 1855
Origin US
Weight 17½oz (500g)
Barrel 3½in (8.9cm)
Caliber .28in

Elisha Root, the Colt Works Superintendent, designed the 1855 Pocket Pistol. It had a top strap—the first in a Colt pistol—a side-mounted hammer, and a stud trigger. However, it was not very popular and was discontinued in 1870.

▲ ADAMS SELF-COCKING REVOLVER MODEL 1851

Date 1851
Origin UK
Weight 2¾lb (1.27kg)
Barrel 7½in (19cm)
Caliber 40-bore

In this revolver—British gunsmith Robert Adams's first—the entire frame, barrel, and butt were forged out of a single iron billet, making it extremely strong.

▼ SPANISH CAVALRY PISTOL

Date 1841
Origin Spain
Weight 2¾lb (1.3kg)
Barrel 7¾in (19.6cm)
Caliber .71in

The Spanish Army introduced a bridled flintlock closely modelled on those in French service. A small boss on the barrel's surface held the ramrod in place, rather than the swivel mount found on other martial pistols of this period.

▲ KERR DOUBLE-ACTION REVOLVER

Date 1856
Origin UK
Weight 2½lb (1.2kg)
Barrel 5¾in (14.7cm)
Caliber 54-bore

Adams's cousin James Kerr fitted his revolver with a simple box-lock and a side-mounted hammer. The lock was retained by two screws, and could be easily removed. If a component broke, any gunsmith would have been able to repair it.

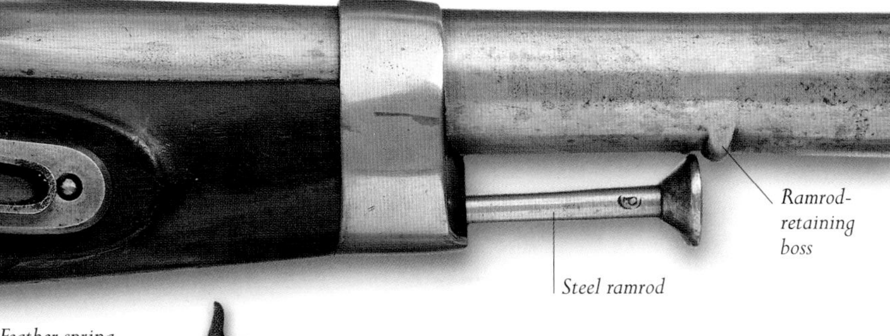

▲ DEANE-HARDING ARMY MODEL

Date 1858
Origin UK
Weight 2½lb (1.15kg)
Barrel 5¼in (13.5cm)
Caliber 40-bore

Deane and Harding's double-action lock was the forerunner of modern actions. In a double-action pistol, pulling the trigger cocks and then releases the action.

▲ SHARPS BREECH-LOADING PISTOL

Date c.1860
Origin US
Weight 33¾oz (960g)
Barrel 5in (12.7cm)
Caliber .34in

American inventor Christian Sharps was famous for his breech-loading rifles and carbines. He also made pistols based on the same principles of his early rifles.

▲ STARR SINGLE-ACTION ARMY MODEL

Date 1864
Origin US
Weight 3lb (1.35kg)
Barrel 7½in (19.2cm)
Caliber .44in

American gunmaker Nathan Starr was the pioneer of the break-open pistol, in which the barrel, top strap, and cylinder were hinged at the front of the frame before the trigger guard. The forked top strap passed over the hammer and was retained by a knurled screw.

Loading/ ejection gate

Extractor-rod housing

▲ COLT NAVY CONVERSION

Date 1861
Origin US
Weight 2¾lb (1.25kg)
Barrel 7½in (19cm)
Caliber .36in

Colt replaced its 1851 Navy revolver with a new, streamlined version ten years later. This revolver has been converted to accept brass cartridges. Many percussion revolvers were adapted in this way.

► LEMAT PISTOL

Date 1864
Origin France
Weight 3½lb (1.64kg)
Barrel Lower 5in (12.7cm)
Caliber .3in and 16-bore

In this revolver, designed by Frenchman Jean-Alexandre LeMat, the nine-chambered cylinder revolved not around a pin but a second, unrifled barrel, charged from the muzzle with pellets.

METALLIC-CARTRIDGE PISTOLS

After the Colt percussion-cap revolvers, the next major breakthrough in pistol design was the Smith & Wesson Model 1, produced in 1857. Horace Smith and Daniel Wesson had purchased a patent from gunsmith Rollin White for a revolver in which the chambers were bored through the full length of the cylinder, which made breech-loading possible. This design was combined with their .22in rim-fire brass cartridge to enable fast reloading, which transformed the use of handguns. Smith & Wesson won important international orders for their No. 3 Model in 1871, by which time more powerful center-fire cartridges were replacing the earlier rim-fire ones.

Trigger guard with steadying spur

▲ LEFAUCHEUX PIN-FIRE REVOLVER

Date	1853
Origin	France
Weight	33½oz (950g)
Barrel	5¼in (13.5cm)
Caliber	12mm Pin-fire

French gunsmith Casimir Lefaucheux invented the pin-fire cartridge in the mid-1830s, and his son Eugène later produced a six-shot, double-action revolver for it in 12mm caliber. This is a cavalry model.

◄ SMITH & WESSON NO. 3 RUSSIAN MODEL

Date	1871
Origin	US
Weight	2¾lb (1.25kg)
Barrel	8in (20.3cm)
Caliber	.44in S&W Russian

Smith & Wesson won a contract to supply the Russian Army with 20,000 of their No. 3 pistol, chambered for a special cartridge. These were the most accurate revolvers of the day.

Octagonal barrel

Fore sight

Grip screw

Lanyard ring

▲ DUTCH M1873 ARMY REVOLVER

Date	1873
Origin	Netherlands
Weight	2¼lb (1.04kg)
Barrel	6¼in (16cm)
Caliber	9.4 × 21mm Rim-fire

Two models of the M1873 were made for the Dutch Army. The earlier model had an octagonal barrel, while the later one had a round barrel.

Notched hammer acts as rear sight

Barrel screws into frame

◄ COLT SINGLE-ACTION ARMY MODEL 1873

Date	1873
Origin	US
Weight	2½lb (1.1kg)
Barrel	7½in (19cm)
Caliber	.45in

The Colt SAA ("Peacemaker") married the single-action lock of the old Dragoon model to a bored-through cylinder in a solid frame, into which the barrel was screwed.

Six-shot cylinder

▲ REMINGTON ARMY MODEL 1875

Date	1875
Origin	US
Weight	2½lb (1.1kg)
Barrel	7½in (19cm)
Caliber	.45in

The single-action Model 1875 was the same size and had the same removable cylinder as the Model 1858. The gun was also adapted for .40in and .44in cartridges.

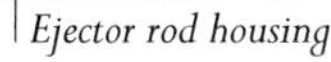

▶ COLT FRONTIER DOUBLE-ACTION

Date	1878
Origin	US
Weight	2¼lb (1kg)
Barrel	5½in (14cm)
Caliber	.44/.45in

Colt produced its first double-action pistol, the Lightning, in 1877, and the following year produced this double-action version equivalent of the SAA "Peacemaker" in .44 and .45 calibers.

▼ MAUSER M1878 "ZIG-ZAG"

Date	1878
Origin	Germany
Weight	2½lb (1.2kg)
Barrel	6½in (16.5cm)
Caliber	.43in

The "Zig-Zag" was a six-shot revolver with a top-hinged frame. Diagonal slots cut into the cylinder face were used with a corresponding arm link to rotate the cylinder.

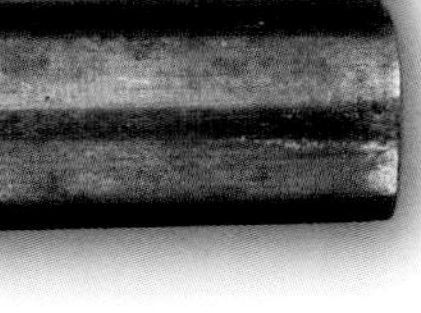

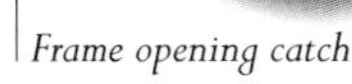

▶ REICHSREVOLVER M1879

Date	1879
Origin	Germany
Weight	2¼lb (1.04kg)
Barrel	7in (18cm)
Caliber	10.6 × 25mm Rim-fire

This solid and reliable single-action six-shot revolver was used by the German Army until 1908. Some guns even saw service in World War I.

▲ LEBEL MODÈLE 1892

Date	1892
Origin	France
Weight	28¼oz (800g)
Barrel	11¼in (28.6cm)
Caliber	8 × 27mm Rim-fire

The double-action solid-frame Lebel Modèle 1892 was loaded by means of a gate. It was used by the French Army in World War I.

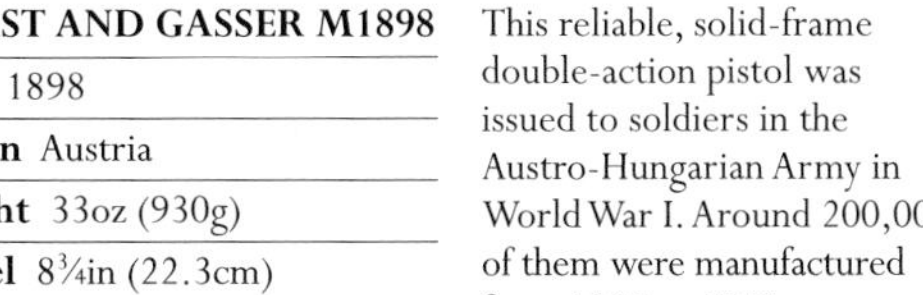

▼ RAST AND GASSER M1898

Date	1898
Origin	Austria
Weight	33oz (930g)
Barrel	8¾in (22.3cm)
Caliber	.32in

This reliable, solid-frame double-action pistol was issued to soldiers in the Austro-Hungarian Army in World War I. Around 200,000 of them were manufactured from 1898 to 1912.

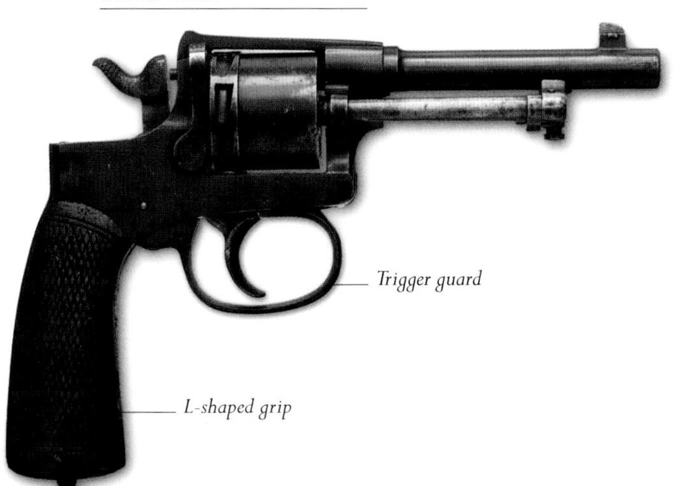

EARLY REPEATING RIFLES

The development of the unitary cartridge in the mid-19th century paved the way for the "repeater" rifle. This new weapon fed ammunition from a magazine to the breech as part of a single action that emptied the used cartridge case from the chamber, cocked the action, and readied the gun to fire. The first repeaters were mostly American, and used an under-lever design. Europeans, however, were familiar with the bolt action from single-shot Mauser and von Dreyse rifles of the 1870s, and came to prefer it in repeating guns. They considered the bolt action not only easier to use in a prone position, but also safer—because when the bolt was turned, the action was locked by lugs connecting with other parts in the receiver.

Hammer

Cylinder axis rod

▼ SPENCER RIFLE

Date	1863
Origin	US
Weight	10lb (4.55kg)
Barrel	28¼in (72cm)
Caliber	.52in

The Spencer, which had a tubular seven-round magazine in the butt stock, was the world's first practical military repeater. It was adopted by the Union Army in the American Civil War.

▲ COLT REVOLVING RIFLE MODEL 1855

Date	1855
Origin	US
Weight	7½lb (3.45kg)
Barrel	26¾in (68.2cm)
Caliber	.56in

The 1855 was the third model of the Colt Manufacturing Company's 1838 revolving rifle. It made a considerable impact, even though the loading procedure of the five-chambered cylinder was cumbersome.

Butt contains tubular magazine

Barrel band

Trigger guard and breech-operating lever

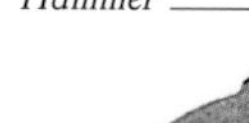

▶ SPENCER CARBINE MODEL 1865

Date	1865
Origin	US
Weight	8lb (3.7kg)
Barrel	20in (51cm)
Caliber	.50in

For this model, Christopher Spencer amended the design of his original repeater rifle and carbine to eliminate minor faults. The 1865 carbine had six-groove rifling. It was also made under contract by the Burnside Rifle Company.

Rear sight

Hammer

Trigger guard and cocking lever

Locking catch for cocking lever

▲ HENRY MODEL 1860

Date	1860
Origin	US
Weight	8¾lb (4kg)
Barrel	20in (51cm)
Caliber	.44in Rim-fire

In Tyler Henry's repeating rifle, an under-lever ejected a spent round, chambered a new one, and left the action cocked. A two-piece bolt joined by a toggle-joint locked the action.

▼ WINCHESTER CARBINE MODEL 1866

Date	1866
Origin	US
Weight	9¼lb (4.2kg)
Barrel	23in (58.5cm)
Caliber	.44 Rim-fire

A modified Henry Model 1860, the 1866 allowed the reloading—even part-full—of a magazine via a port on the receiver. This doubled the rate of fire to 30 rounds per minute.

Trigger guard and cocking lever

◄ LEMAT REVOLVER RIFLE

Date	1872
Origin	France/US
Weight	4¾lb (2.2kg)
Barrel	24¾in (62.8cm)
Caliber	.44in and 16-bore

Based on a similar pistol, the LeMat Revolver Rifle had two barrels. The lower, charged with shot, acted as the axis pin for the nine-chambered cylinder, which was charged with ball cartridges.

▲ MAUSER MODEL 71/84

Date	1884
Origin	Germany
Weight	10lb (4.6kg)
Barrel	33in (83cm)
Caliber	11 × 60mm Rim-fire

Peter Paul Mauser made many attempts to turn the single-shot bolt-action M1871 rifle into a repeater. The Model 71/84 suffered from weaknesses in the design of its magazine.

▼ LEE-METFORD MARK I

Date	1888
Origin	UK
Weight	9½lb (4.3kg)
Barrel	30in (76.7cm)
Caliber	.303in (black powder)

The Lee-Metford Mark I had an enclosed bolt action and a box magazine, designed by James Lee, and anti-fouling rifling, developed by William Metford. The Mark II followed in 1890.

▲ SCHMIDT-RUBIN M1889

Date	1889
Origin	Switzerland
Weight	9¾lb (4.45kg)
Barrel	31in (78cm)
Caliber	7.5 × 55mm

Colonel Rudolf Schmidt of the Swiss Army developed a straight-pull bolt-action rifle with a 12-round box magazine. It remained in service, though slightly modified, until 1931.

▼ LEBEL MLE 1886/93

Date	1893
Origin	France
Weight	9½lb (4.3kg)
Barrel	32in (80cm)
Caliber	8mm × 50R

The Lebel MLE 1886 was the first rifle to fire a small-caliber, jacketed bullet propelled by smokeless powder. This modified version followed in 1893.

UNIFORMS AND INSIGNIA OF 19TH-CENTURY ARMIES

The taste for elaborate, colorful, and imposing uniforms established by European armies in the Napoleonic era influenced the outfitting of soldiers throughout the 19th century. The French army under Napoleon Bonaparte is often celebrated as the high point of style and decoration in military uniforms, but—if anything—uniforms became even more intricately embellished and detailed in the decades following his defeat in 1815. Right through until the eve of World War I, in 1914, many armies were clad in distinctive uniforms in traditional colors, featuring outmoded elements of equipment, such as the sabertache.

Horsehair plume

▶ BRITISH BELL-TOP SHAKO

Date 1830

Origin UK

Material Felt, leather, brass

This cavalryman's bell-top shako—designed to make the wearer look taller and more imposing—was one of several rather impractical designs of the period that followed the highly ornamented "Regency" shako of 1822.

▼ BRITISH CAVALRY OFFICER'S SABERTACHE

Date 1830

Origin UK

Material Leather

British cavalry wore the sabertache—a leather bag suspended from a cavalryman's belt—from the late 1700s onward. In the 1800s, the sabertache was often restricted to ceremonial wear, but British cavalry wore it in the Crimean War (1853–56).

Embroidered cover

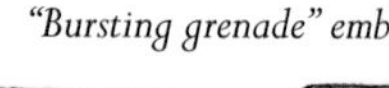

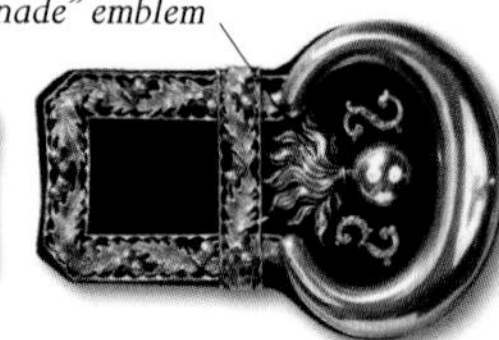

"Bursting grenade" emblem

▲ BRITISH CAVALRYMAN'S EPAULETS

Date 1830

Origin UK

Material Wool, metallic thread

These epaulets were probably worn by a cavalryman in the "Scots Grays" (officially the 2nd Dragoons), who were celebrated for their mounted charge at the Battle of Waterloo. The "bursting grenade" emblem, originally belonging to the Grenadiers, was associated with elite regiments.

▼ BRITISH INFANTRY CORPORAL'S DRESS COAT

Date c.1850

Origin India

Material Wool

This coat was worn by a corporal in the East India Company's 2nd European Light Regiment. The regiment served in the Anglo-Persian War of 1856–57, and became part of the British Army in 1862.

Corporal's stripes

Four buttons on cuff

▲ **FRENCH HUSSAR'S PARADE JACKET**

Date 1871

Origin France

Material Wool

This lieutenant's jacket is from the 9th Regiment of Hussars in the French army. Right through to 1914, hussar regiments kept a role in the French, British, Russian, and several other European armies. They functioned as light cavalry, and were celebrated for their highly elaborate parade uniforms.

◀ **PRUSSIAN PICKELHAUBE**

Date 1867

Origin Prussia

Material Leather

The *Pickelhaube* spiked military helmet was designed in 1842 by King Frederick William IV of Prussia. It was made of boiled leather with metal trim and spike. This 1867 version was worn in the Franco-Prussian War of 1870–71.

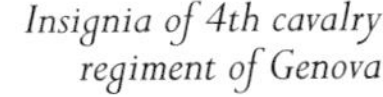

▶ **ITALIAN CAVALRY OFFICER'S CAP**

Date 1876

Origin Italy

Material Felt, leather

Italy was one of the first countries to move away from wearing brightly colored uniforms, introducing gray-green ones in 1909—around the same time that the Russians switched to khaki. This blue cap was worn by a cavalry officer in the late 19th century.

▶ **ITALIAN CAVALRY FLAG**

Date c.1880

Origin Italy

Material Wool

The guidon, or military standard, remained brightly colored as uniforms became more muted, functioning as a symbol of identity and tradition. This cavalry flag bears the coat of arms of the Italian House of Savoy, which ruled Italy for 85 years from 1861–1946.

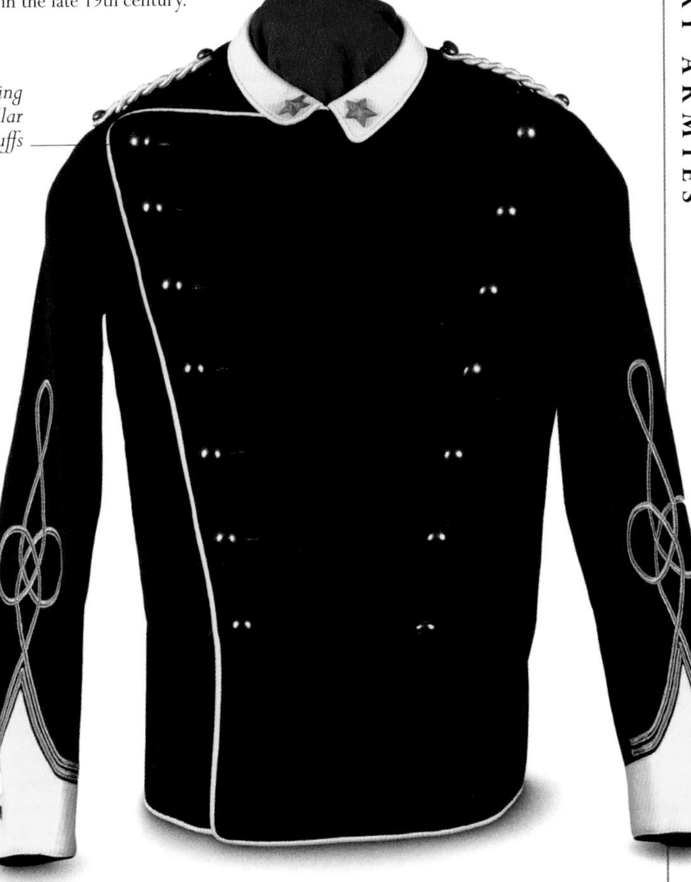

▲ **ITALIAN CAVALRY JACKET**

Date 1876

Origin Italy

Material Wool

Until the development of chemical dyes toward the end of the 19th century, many colorful uniforms, such as this elegant blue Italian cavalry jacket, would have been issued in slightly varying shades.

THE BATTLE OF ANTIETAM

Antietam displayed the weaponry and tactics of the American Civil War at their most deadly. Fought at Sharpsburg, Maryland, on September 17, 1862, it was the costliest day's fighting in American history, with 22,700 Union and Confederate soldiers killed or wounded.

At Sharpsburg a Union army about 75,000 strong, commanded by General George B. McClellan, faced a much weaker Confederate army led by General Robert E. Lee. The Confederates had taken up a defensive position behind Antietam Creek, where they did not dig earthworks but made optimal use of features such as woods, hills, and fences. Lee was still assembling scattered forces when the battle began, but eventually 38,000 Confederate troops would take part.

After a hard marching campaign in Maryland, the Confederates were in poor shape—a Union officer described the troops as "filthy, sick, hungry, and miserable." The Union troops, on the other hand, had been well equipped and supplied by Northern factories.

On the day before the battle began McClellan sent troops across Antietam Creek to General Lee's left. The Confederates observed the movement, and soldiers under General Thomas "Stonewall" Jackson got into position to face a flank attack at dawn on September 17.

The battle opened with an exchange of cannon fire from the batteries that each side had established on high ground. Union troops then marched onward to a cornfield where Jackson's infantry awaited them. After bringing forward their cannon, the Union divisions swept the cornfield with canister shot—anti-personnel munitions that decimated the Confederates. The Union troops pressed forward and hours of desperate infantry fighting ensued. Men exchanged fire in the open, inflicting and sustaining heavy losses. Groups of men were marshalled by their officers in attacks and counterattacks, especially around and through an area known as West Wood. Soldiers were armed with rifled muskets—muzzle-loaded weapons capable of three or four shots a minute—although in places men fought at close quarters with bayonets or wielded their muskets as clubs. Combat on the left flank eventually subsided due to shock and exhaustion on both sides.

FIRING FROM COVER

Meanwhile, elsewhere on the battlefield, the Confederates, using their muskets, were demonstrating the effectiveness of infantry when firing from cover against troops advancing in the open. In the center, some 2,500 men held a sunken road—later known as Bloody Lane—against repeated frontal assaults, inflicting thousands of casualties before being overrun.

Farther to the Confederate right, Union General Ambrose Burnside tried to move troops over the Creek across a bridge, under the fire of Confederate sharpshooters and cannon. Time and again the Union soldiers were cut down, and only established themselves on the other side of the Creek after bringing up their own artillery in support.

By late afternoon the Confederates had been outflanked on the right and looked about to be beaten, when Confederate reinforcements marching from Harpers Ferry arrived and counterattacked, causing Union troops to retreat. The cautious McClellan had held 20,000 infantry and cavalry in reserve throughout. He made no attempt to resume fighting the next day, and Lee withdrew his battered army to Virginia.

SURVIVORS OF BATTLE
A Union field artillery battery is photographed after the battle. Smoothbore cannon, like the one shown here, caused a large percentage of the casualties.

AMERICAN CIVIL WAR UNIFORMS

In the American Civil War of 1861–65, soldiers of the northern Union were well kitted out. From 1861, they were given standard issue uniforms and equipment mass-produced in factories in the north, on the orders of the War Department. By contrast, the soldiers of the southern Confederate states were often ill-equipped, and had to overcome a shortage of cartridges, uniform, tents, blankets, pay, and food. Sometimes they even had to march barefoot or rely on supplies of boots "liberated" from the Union forces.

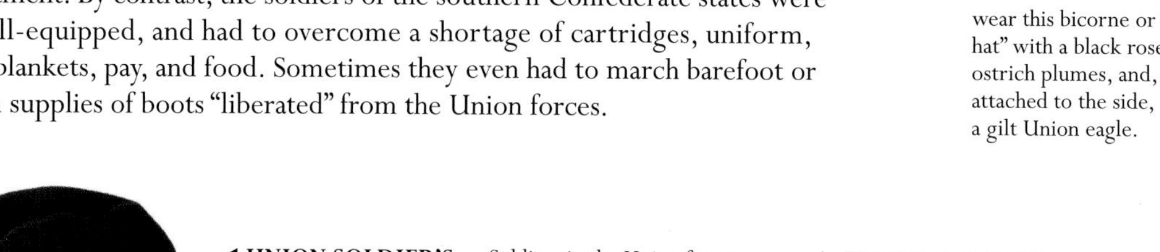

▶ UNION OFFICER'S COCKED HAT

Date 1861
Origin US
Material Wool

Officers were entitled to wear this bicorne or "cocked hat" with a black rosette, ostrich plumes, and, attached to the side, a gilt Union eagle.

◀ UNION SOLDIER'S FORAGE CAP

Date 1861
Origin US
Material Wool

Soldiers in the Union forces attached a regimental corps badge and brass numbers to the top of their forage cap. In this case, the "I" signifies "First Corps" and the "124" the New York 124th regiment.

▶ UNION OFFICER'S DRESS JACKET

Date 1861
Origin US
Material Wool

Rather than wearing standard issue, officers bought their own uniform. The influence of the French army is evident in this dress jacket with upright collar, sleeve braid, and brass buttons.

Four brass buttons on the front

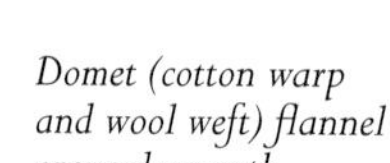

Domet (cotton warp and wool weft) flannel ensured warmth

◀ UNION SOLDIER'S UNIFORM

Date 1861
Origin US
Material Wool

Union soldiers wore a dark blue fatigue jacket and standard issue light blue trousers. Union forces kit was produced in a range of standard sizes to facilitate mass production.

▼ UNION SOLDIER'S BOOTS

Date 1861
Origin US
Material Leather

Union leather "bootees" were made with heavy leather soles. The heels were tacked together with wooden pegs or stitched with thick thread.

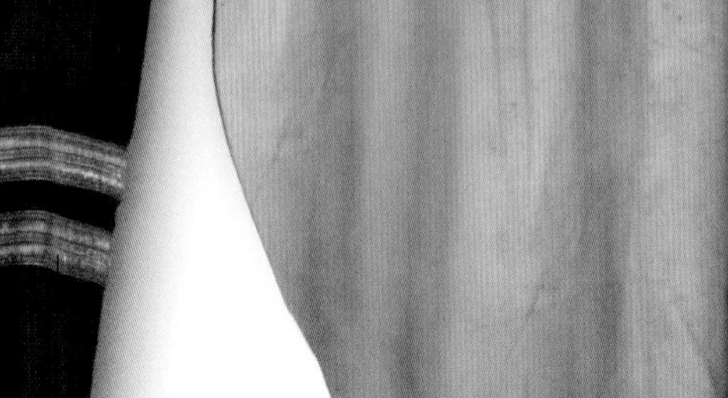

Sleeve braid indicated rank

Trousers were usually worn rolled up or tucked into socks when on campaign

▲ **CONFEDERATE OFFICER'S FROCK COAT**

Date 1861
Origin US
Material Wool

Frock coats were issued at the beginning of the war, but shortages of cloth later led to the introduction of waist-length jackets. The color gray was initially chosen because the dye could be made cheaply.

◀ **CONFEDERATE "BEEHIVE" SLOUCH HAT**

Date 1862
Origin US
Material Wool, felt

Many Confederate infantrymen wore low-crown "beehive" slouch hats, some with a star or another symbol to indicate their home state. Others wore an angled *képi* (peaked cap) or straw hats in summer.

▶ **CONFEDERATE INFANTRY UNIFORM**

Date 1862
Origin US
Material Wool, brass

Confederate uniforms were dyed in a range of colors, including gray, blue, and beige. The soldiers usually wore a white muslin or gray flannel shirt underneath their jacket. The trousers were made of wool, and could be very hot to march in.

◀ **UNION SOLDIER'S CARTRIDGE BOX**

Date 1861
Origin US
Material Leather

This box held 40 cartridges—each a paper tube filled with a Minié ball and black powder. The shoulder strap bears the brass Union eagle emblem.

▲ **CONFEDERATE SOLDIER'S BACKPACK**

Date 1862
Origin US
Material Canvas

Backpacks had a single pocket and sometimes a wooden frame. Soldiers carried a woolen blanket, extra food, and personal items in them, and usually had a cherrywood canteen for drinking water.

◀ **CONFEDERATE HOBNAILED BOOTS**

Date 1862
Origin US
Material Leather

Army boots were usually square-toed with hobnails, and had curved horseshoe protectors on the heels to protect against wear and tear during long marches.

INFANTRY AND CAVALRY SWORDS AND BAYONETS

By 1815, infantry swords were becoming little more than ceremonial weapons, although officers and senior NCOs continued to carry them as symbols of rank. The design of these swords was increasingly decorative. In the course of the 19th century, the sword bayonet replaced the infantryman's socket bayonet and hanger sword. The rise of long-range firearms meant that the bayonet was of little use in combat, but infantrymen were still equipped with it because armies believed the weapon fostered an aggressive spirit. In these years, light cavalry used a curved saber designed for slicing and cutting, while heavy cavalry carried a thrusting sword with a long, straight blade.

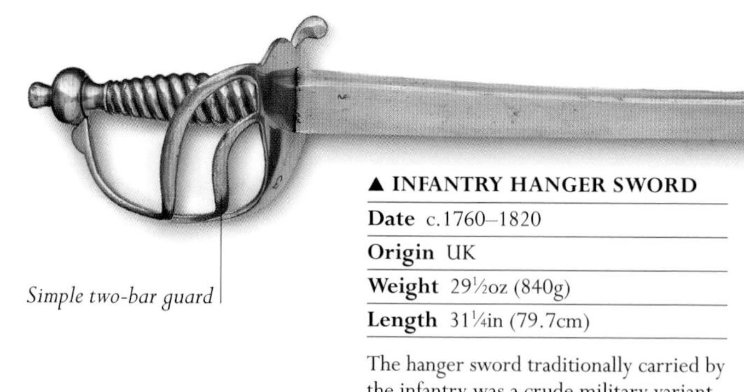

Simple two-bar guard

▲ INFANTRY HANGER SWORD

Date	c.1760–1820
Origin	UK
Weight	29½oz (840g)
Length	31¼in (79.7cm)

The hanger sword traditionally carried by the infantry was a crude military variant of a short hunting sword, almost always with a straight or slightly curved blade.

▶ "FOOT" OFFICER'S SWORD

Date	c.1820
Origin	US
Weight	2½lb (1.13kg)
Length	29in (73.6cm)

In the American Civil War (1861–65), the artillery had its own swords. This Confederate artillery saber was made by Boyle, Gamble & McFee, of Richmond, Virginia.

Guard with forward-facing quillon

Knuckle guard

Guard branches

Pommel cap

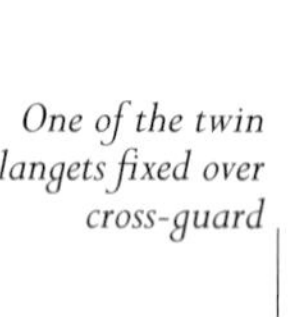

One of the twin langets fixed over cross-guard

D-shaped single knuckle guard

▲ MODEL 1827 CAVALRY TROOPER'S SWORD

Date	c.1827
Origin	Russia
Weight	2¾lb (1.22kg)
Length	3½ft (1.02m)

The Russian Model 1827 cavalry trooper's sword had a curved, single-edged blade with a single, wide fuller and a brass hilt. Twin langets could be used to trap an enemy's sword.

Tang stud

Muzzle ring with locking screw

Locking-bolt spring

Steel cross-guard with curved "blade-breaker" quillon

Single-edged steel blade with wide fuller

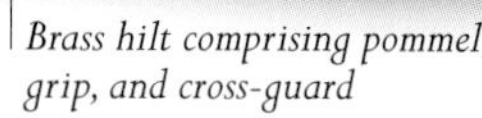

Brass hilt comprising pommel, grip, and cross-guard

Straight quillons with circular finials

▶ SWORD BAYONET

Date	Mid-19th century
Origin	France
Weight	27¾oz (790g)
Length	3¾ft (1.15m)

This French sword bayonet, with a long, narrow blade, is unusual in having a basket hilt—a feature usually associated with a cavalry sword.

▲ PIONEER SWORD MODEL 1847

Date	1847
Origin	Russia
Weight	2½lb (1.18kg)
Length	25in (63.5cm)

The hilt of this Russian sword is based on the French Model 1831 infantry sword. Both reflect the influence of the Roman gladius short sword.

Hilt with D-ring and two branches

▲ INFANTRY SWORD MODEL 1850

Date	c.1850
Origin	US
Weight	2½lb (1.13kg)
Length	30¼in (76.8cm)

In the American Civil War, edged weapons such as this Model 1850 equipped most infantry officers on the Union side. Its single-edged blade is slightly curved, and the leather grip is wrapped in twisted brass wire.

▲ CAVALRY TROOPER'S SWORD PATTERN 1853

Date	1853
Origin	UK
Weight	2½lb (1.13kg)
Length	3½ft (1m)

Of fairly conventional construction, the 1853 Pattern cavalry trooper's sword equipped British heavy cavalry in the Crimean War and during some of Britain's subsequent colonial campaigns.

▲ LIGHT CAVALRY SABER MODEL 1860

Date	c.1860
Origin	US
Weight	3lb (1.36kg)
Length	35in (90cm)

The Model 1860 Light cavalry saber was an effective thrusting and hacking weapon for the cavalry in the American Civil War. It was a lighter version of the 1840 saber.

◄ MLE 1866 CHASSEPOT BAYONET

Date	1866
Origin	France
Weight	27¾oz (760g)
Length	27½in (70cm)

This bayonet is from the Chassepot breech-loading rifle that armed the French during the Franco-Prussian War of 1870–71. The recurved *yataghan*-style blade influenced many European and American designs.

▲ PATTERN 1869 TRIALS BAYONET

Date	1869
Origin	UK
Weight	22½oz (640g)
Length	25in (64.2cm)

The Elcho bayonets, with their broad blade end, were considered too ungainly, and were not taken up as an official model. This earlier design with a narrower blade had also failed to impress the authorities.

▼ PATTERN 1871 ELCHO BAYONET

Date	1871
Origin	UK
Weight	23oz (650g)
Length	25in (64cm)

Lord Elcho designed this bayonet to go with the Martini-Henry rifle. Elcho extended the bayonet's range of tasks to include those of hacking down brush and sawing wood.

MUZZLE-LOADING ARTILLERY

In the 19th century, infantrymen firing rifled small arms were able to achieve greater range than smoothbore cannon, so attempts were made to apply rifling to field artillery. The first rifled cannon were developed in the 1840s by pioneers including Giovanni Cavalli of Italy, Martin von Wahrendorff of Sweden, and Joseph Whitworth and Charles Lancaster of Britain. Some of these early rifled field guns—such as the rifled Whitworth 12-pounder, which saw service in the American Civil War—were breech- rather than muzzle-loaders. Breech-loaders permitted a higher rate of fire and were generally safer to use, but muzzle-loaders were cheaper to manufacture and required less expensive ammunition. As a result, muzzle-loaders continued to be popular for military use.

Later replacement carriage

▶ CHINESE 18-POUNDER

Date	1830
Origin	China
Weight	2.75 tons (2.5 tonnes)
Length	10½ft (3.2m)
Caliber	5.25in

With inscriptions in Chinese on top of its breech, this 18-pounder is 19in (48cm) in diameter. It is mounted on a Russian wrought- and cast-iron carriage, which dates to 1853.

Muzzle diameter 16in (41cm)

Wrought- and cast-iron garrison carriage

▲ RUSSIAN LICORNE

Date	1793
Origin	Russia
Weight	3 tons (2.76 tonnes)
Length	9ft (2.8m)
Caliber	205mm

This gun, which saw action in the Crimean War (1853–56), could fire horizontally or at an elevated trajectory. The licorne was a development of the howitzer, with a powder chamber in the shape of a cone. It could shoot shells as well as cannonballs.

Plain bronze barrel

Limber (cart)

◀ ▶ INDIAN 6-POUNDER FIELD GUN WITH AMMUNITION CART

Date	1840
Origin	India
Weight	672½lb (305kg)
Length	11½ft (3.5m)
Caliber	3.66in

This smoothbore muzzle-loader gun has a plain bronze barrel and an ornate carriage and limber (cart) with decorative brass inlay. It was built on a British model for the army of Ranjit Singh, and was captured by the British at the Sutlej River in February 1846, during the First Sikh War.

Hardwood carriage could be linked to cart for transport

◀ CHINESE 32-POUNDER

Date	1841
Origin	China
Weight	5.3 tons (4.84 tonnes)
Length	8¾ft (2.74m)
Caliber	19cm

Engravings on the breech indicate that this imposing bronze 32-pounder was cast in August 1841, during the reign of Chinese Emperor Daoguang (1820–50), for coastal defense duties.

Steel barrel

Original wooden carriage

▲ BLAKELY RML MOUNTAIN GUN

Date	1865
Origin	UK
Weight	800¼lb (363kg)
Length	3¼ft (1m)
Caliber	2.75in

In mountainous terrain, armies needed lighter, more maneuverable field guns, and mountain guns were developed to meet this need. This gun, manufactured by the innovative Blakely Ordnance Company, has a steel barrel with six-groove rifling and reinforcement at the breech in the form of an additional steel tube ("jacket").

▼ BRITISH 9-POUNDER FIELD GUN

Date	1876
Origin	UK
Weight	1.14 tons (1.04 tonnes)
Length	5¾ft (1.79m)
Caliber	3in

Field guns like this muzzle-loading rifled British 9-pounder played an important role in both sieges and field battles in the British Army's overseas engagements of this period.

▼ ARMSTRONG RML 12-POUNDER

Date	1878
Origin	UK
Weight	915lb (415kg)
Length	7¼ft (2.23m)
Caliber	3in

The initials RML in the gun title stand for "rifled muzzle-loader." This steel 12-pounder was manufactured by Armstrong in Newcastle, northern England, for merchant marine use.

KEY **EVENTS**

19TH CENTURY

■ **1830–48** France invades Algeria, but Abd el-Kadir leads resistance to the French occupation of the territory until forced to surrender in 1848.

■ **1845–72** Maori opposition to the British colonization of New Zealand is overcome in a series of hard-fought wars.

■ **1857–58** A rebellion against British rule in India is put down by armed force.

■ **1860** A combined Anglo-French army invades China and occupies Beijing, looting and burning Chinese imperial palaces.

■ **1868** In Japan, the Tokugawa Shogunate ends and the period of the Meiji Restoration begins, during which time Japan modernizes its armed forces and society.

■ **1876–77** In the Black Hills War, Sioux warriors led by Crazy Horse mount the last serious resistance to the westward expansion of the United States.

■ **1879** At Rorke's Drift, 150 British soldiers armed chiefly with Martini-Henry rifles successfully resist repeated attacks by 4,000 Zulu warriors.

■ **1898** An Anglo-Egyptian army defeats the Sudanese Mahdists at Omdurman (see pp.250–51). The Sudanese are cut down by rapid-fire rifles and Maxim guns.

■ **1900** In the Boer War, Boer militia armed with the latest German weapons inflict a notable defeat on the British Army at Spion Kop.

▼ MAXIM GUN
Invented in 1884 by Sir Hiram Maxim, the recoil-operated Maxim gun was the first fully automatic weapon, firing for as long as the trigger was held down. Its maximum rate of fire was 500 rounds a minute.

KEY DEVELOPMENT

THE WARS OF EMPIRES

In the 19th century, a gulf opened up between the military technology of Europe and North America, and the rest of the world. Preindustrial societies, such as China, Japan, and Africa, could not withstand the firepower of imperial armies.

The armies of the world's great powers underwent a technological revolution between 1815 and 1914, progressing from flintlock muskets to repeater rifles firing metal cartridges, and from smoothbore muzzle-loading cannon to rifled guns firing high-explosive shells. Widely adopted in the1890s, the Maxim gun—the first self-powered machine gun —became a symbol of technological progress and the alleged superiority of European civilization. Steamships projected this increased firepower worldwide in campaigns waged on every continent.

Some wars of the imperialist era were between powers that had fallen behind in the race for military modernization. The defeat of China by European forces, in the Opium Wars of 1839–42 and 1856–60, demonstrated how a country long at the forefront of technological innovation and military organization could suddenly find itself defenseless at a time of rapid change. Both China and Japan attempted to adopt the technology of the West, but China's defeat by Japan in the war of 1894–95, and its invasion by European powers in response to the Boxer rebellion of 1900, showed that the Chinese had failed. Japan, in contrast, established itself as the sole Asian modern military power after its victory over Russia in 1904–05 (see pp.264–65), in which it deployed the latest military technology, from steel battleships and torpedo boats to machine guns, rifled artillery, and field telephones.

BATTLES WITH TRIBES

Other conflicts of the era led the armies of Europe and North America into combat with indigenous tribal societies. These tribal groups were formidable in their varied traditional styles of warfare, and often succeeded in integrating modern firearms into their fighting techniques. The Maori of New Zealand, for example, acquired muskets from the early 1800s, and used them in a series of wars—first against one another, and then against European settlers backed by the British Army. Firing rifled muskets from elaborate defensive earthworks and wooden palisades, the Maori inflicted notable reverses upon the British in the 1860s, although they were eventually defeated.

By contrast, however, the Zulu of southern Africa failed to make effective use of firearms. Turned into an impressive military machine under the leadership of Shaka (1816–28), they had achieved regional dominance by fighting aggressive wars against neighboring peoples with stabbing spears and cowhide shields. They mostly relied on the same equipment against an invading British Army in 1879, using rifles only for a scattered volley, before charging to engage at close quarters. Despite a victory at Isandlwana, the Zulu were soon forced to concede defeat due to casualties inflicted by British bullets and bayonets.

FRONTIER BATTLES

Expanding their territory westward, the US fought Plains Indian tribes such as the Sioux, Cheyenne, and Arapaho from the 1860s to the 1880s. The Plains Indians used modern technology—firearms, including repeater rifles, and steel knives—but they fought best with traditional bows and spears.

Although they inflicted a memorable defeat on General George Custer's 7th US Cavalry at the Battle of the Little Bighorn in June, 1876, the Plains Indians mostly fought a guerrilla-style war of small-scale raids and ambushes. The US used brutal but effective counterinsurgency tactics, attacking encampments and destroying food supplies.

The UK resorted to a similar strategy in the later stages of the Boer War of 1899–1902 (see pp. 256–57), when the mounted Boer commandos turned to guerrilla warfare. Armed with Mauser magazine rifles, Creusot artillery, and Maxim guns, the Boers shocked the British Army out of its complacency. By the early 20th century, it had become clear that any war fought between armies equally equipped with the latest weaponry was simply a bloodbath.

◄ **THE BATTLE OF ISANDLWANA**
In January, 1879, about 1,500 British soldiers were attacked by a Zulu force outnumbering them then to one. After losing their field guns early in the action, the British were overrun, and almost all were killed.

> "I rejoice to find that the sympathy of **well-nigh the whole world** is on our side in **this struggle for right and liberty**"
>
> **STATE PRESIDENT OF THE SOUTH AFRICAN REPUBLIC, PAUL KRUGER,**
> *THE MEMOIRS OF PAUL KRUGER*, 1902

KEY **BATTLE**

THE BATTLE OF ADOWA
1896

Ethiopia was the only African state to retain full independence in the imperialist era. In March 1896, an Italian army invaded Ethiopia from Eritrea, launching an ill-planned attack on King Menelik II's army at Adowa. Losing their cohesion on difficult terrain, the Italian forces were massacred.

Le Petit Journal
SUPPLÉMENT ILLUSTRÉ
Le Négus Ménélik à la bataille d'Adoua

▲ A contemporary French magazine featuring King Menelik II, victor of Adowa, on its cover.

◄ **A ZULU WARRIOR HUNTING DANCE**
The Zulu were a pastoral people in southern Africa. They became a dominant regional power in the early 19th century, through the adoption of a rigorous military organization and effective fighting tactics with the stabbing spear and shield.

MANUALLY LOADED REPEATER RIFLES

By the 1890s, refinements to the repeater rifle had made it reliable enough for use in many of the world's armies. In Britain, the .303 Lee-Metford was developed into the Lee-Enfield Mark I of 1895, the first in an enduring line of bolt-action rifles, while in Germany, the Mauser Gewehr 98 of 1898 was a near-faultless design. Thereafter, changes in design were made mostly to reduce the weapon's weight, or to cut manufacturing costs. After the turn of the century, the barrel length was often reduced to improve handling, although French Berthier and Japanese Arisaka weapons did not follow the general trend.

▲ MOSIN-NAGANT M91

Date	1891
Origin	Imperial Russia
Weight	9¾lb (4.43kg)
Barrel	31½in (80.2cm)
Caliber	7.62mm × 54R

The "3-line," as it was called, was Imperial Russia's first repeater rifle and its first in a modern caliber. The "line" was a measure approximating one-tenth of an inch and refers to its caliber.

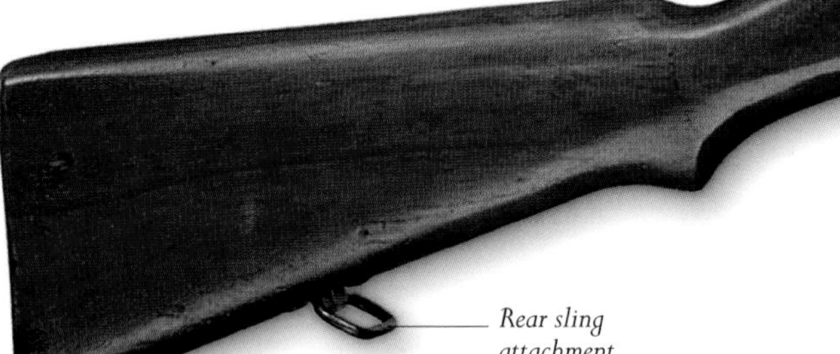

▲ MANNLICHER M1895

Date	1895
Origin	Austria
Weight	8¼lb (3.78kg)
Barrel	30in (76.5cm)
Caliber	8mm × 50R

The straight-pull, bolt-action M1895, designed by German engineer Ferdinand von Mannlicher, used a rotating locking lug turned in a camming (spiraled) groove. Ammunition was fed from a fixed box magazine.

▼ MAUSER INFANTERIEGEWEHR 98

Date	1898
Origin	Germany
Weight	9lb (4.15kg)
Barrel	29in (74cm)
Caliber	7.92mm × 57

In the Gewehr 98, Mauser brought the bolt action magazine rifle close to perfection by adding a third rear-locking lug, as well as improving gas sealing and refining the magazine. If the rifle had a fault, it lay in the design of its bolt handle.

▲ LEE-ENFIELD MARK I

Date	1895
Origin	UK
Weight	8¾lb (4kg)
Barrel	25in (63.5cm)
Caliber	.303in

A redesigned version of the .303 Lee-Metford of 1888, the ".303 caliber, Rifle, Magazine, Lee-Enfield"—or Mark I—had a detachable ten-round magazine, and, with the bolt handle near the trigger, was faster to operate than the rival Mauser rifle.

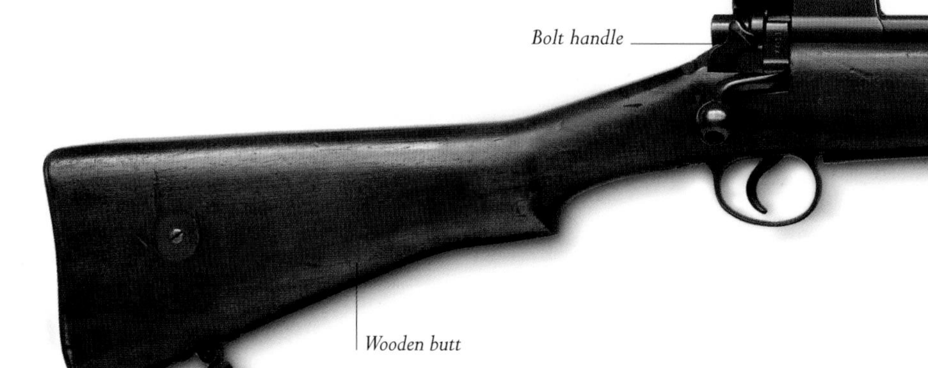

▲ ARISAKA MEIJI 30

Date	1897
Origin	Japan
Weight	9½lb (4.3kg)
Barrel	31½in (79.8cm)
Caliber	6.5mm × 50SR

Designed by Colonel Nariakira Arisaka, this gun was chambered for a 6.5mm semi-rimmed round and used a turning bolt of the Mauser pattern with forward-locking lugs.

▲ MAUSER M1896

Date	1896
Origin	Germany
Weight	8¾lb (3.97kg)
Barrel	29in (74cm)
Caliber	6.5mm × 55

Mauser began exporting to China in 1875, and made rifles for Serbia, Belgium, Turkey, Argentina, and Spain before manufacturing the M1896 for Sweden. Licensed Swedish production of the rifle continued until 1944.

◄ LEE-ENFIELD MARK III

Date	1907
Origin	UK
Weight	8¾lb (3.96kg)
Barrel	25in (64cm)
Caliber	.303in

A shorter version of the Lee-Enfield Mark I had been introduced in 1904 as the Short Magazine Lee-Enfield (SMLE, often nicknamed "Smellie"). The SMLE Mark III introduced improvements to the rear sight, magazine, and chamber.

▲ BERTHIER MLE 1916

Date	1916
Origin	France
Weight	9lb (4.15kg)
Barrel	31¼in (79.8cm)
Caliber	8mm × 50R

A modified version of the 1902 model Berthier rifle, this gun had a five-round magazine in place of the original's three-round magazine. The piling hook below the fore sight was used to stack the rifles "teepee-style" when troops were encamped.

▲ ENFIELD PATTERN 1913

Date	1913
Origin	UK
Weight	8½lb (3.9kg)
Barrel	26in (66cm)
Caliber	.276in

This experimental design was produced as a potential replacement for the Lee-Enfield SMLE, firing a more powerful 7mm round. After trials in 1913, the experiment was abandoned due to the onset of World War I.

MACHINE-GUNS

The first self-powered machine-gun was developed by American Hiram Maxim in Britain in 1884. In that design, the recoil energy—the backward force created by firing a cartridge—was used to eject the spent cartridge and then load and fire a new one from the ammunition belt. Earlier rapid-fire guns, such as the Nordenfelt and the Gardner, all relied on an operator turning a hand-cranked lever. The Maxim was adopted in Austria and Italy in 1887, and by the British Army in 1889. Versions of the gun were manufactured in the US, Germany, Russia, and Switzerland from 1904–11. In 1896, Maxim's company was taken over by the British firm Vickers, and their improved, lighter versions of the weapon—in particular the enduring Mk 1, launched in 1912—were to remain in service in the British Army through two world wars and beyond.

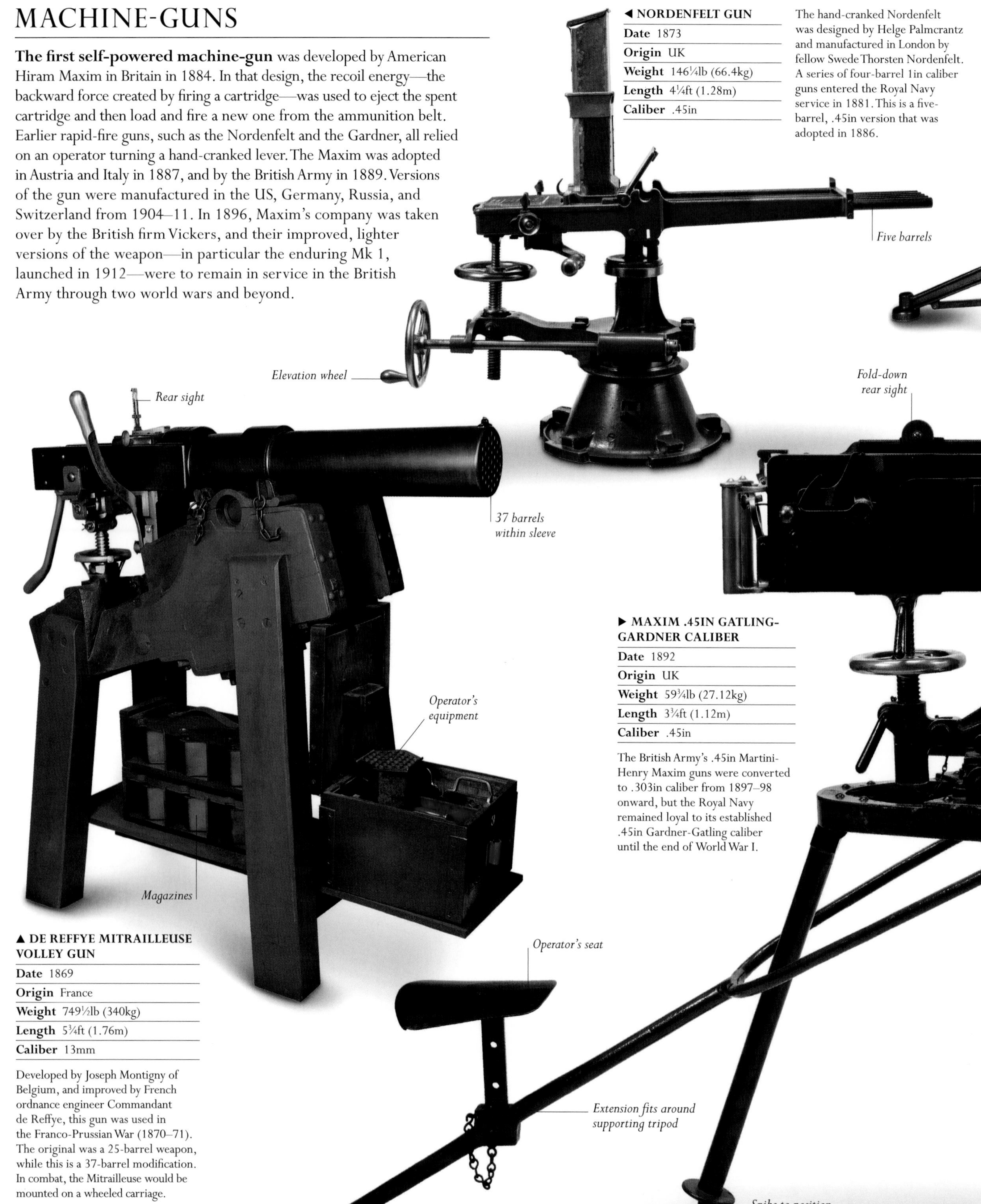

◀ NORDENFELT GUN

Date 1873
Origin UK
Weight 146¼lb (66.4kg)
Length 4¼ft (1.28m)
Caliber .45in

The hand-cranked Nordenfelt was designed by Helge Palmcrantz and manufactured in London by fellow Swede Thorsten Nordenfelt. A series of four-barrel 1in caliber guns entered the Royal Navy service in 1881. This is a five-barrel, .45in version that was adopted in 1886.

▶ MAXIM .45IN GATLING-GARDNER CALIBER

Date 1892
Origin UK
Weight 59¾lb (27.12kg)
Length 3¾ft (1.12m)
Caliber .45in

The British Army's .45in Martini-Henry Maxim guns were converted to .303in caliber from 1897–98 onward, but the Royal Navy remained loyal to its established .45in Gardner-Gatling caliber until the end of World War I.

▲ DE REFFYE MITRAILLEUSE VOLLEY GUN

Date 1869
Origin France
Weight 749½lb (340kg)
Length 5¾ft (1.76m)
Caliber 13mm

Developed by Joseph Montigny of Belgium, and improved by French ordnance engineer Commandant de Reffye, this gun was used in the Franco-Prussian War (1870–71). The original was a 25-barrel weapon, while this is a 37-barrel modification. In combat, the Mitrailleuse would be mounted on a wheeled carriage.

◀ GARDNER GUN

Date 1874
Origin US
Weight 56lb (25.4kg)
Length 30in (76.2cm)
Caliber .45in or .40in

In this gun—developed by William Gardner of Ohio—cartridges were fed by gravity from a vertical magazine. The Gardner found favor in Britain—it was used by the British Army in the Mahdist War (1881–99), and by the Royal Navy from 1880, where it was installed on fixed mountings on ships.

◀ MAXIM MACHINE-GUN

Date 1889
Origin UK
Weight 59½lb (27kg)
Length 3½ft (1.1m)
Caliber .45in

The Maxim was approved for the British Army in 1889 and issued in 1891. Chambered for the .45in Martini-Henry rifle ammunition, it was first used in combat near Shanghai, China, in 1893.

▼ MAXIM-NORDENFELT MODEL 1893

Date 1893
Origin UK
Weight 49½lb (22.5kg)
Length 3½ft (1.08m)
Caliber 11mm

Maxim and Nordenfelt entered into partnership in 1888. This 11mm Maxim-Nordenfelt, intended for French trials, featured a steam-operated trigger lock. In 1896, their joint venture was subsumed into Vickers, Sons & Maxim.

◀ COLT-BROWNING MODEL 1895

Date 1895
Origin US
Weight 37lb (16.8kg)
Length 28¼in (72cm)
Caliber 7.65mm

This air-cooled, gas-operated Colt-Browning 1895 had a swinging arm that descended vertically beneath the barrel when the gun was firing, earning it the nickname "the potato digger." This gun could fire 400–500 rounds per minute.

▶ MAXIM QF 1-POUNDER "POM-POM"

Date 1890
Origin UK
Weight 410lb (186kg)
Length 3½ft (1.09m)
Caliber 37mm

The "Pom-Pom"—so-called because of the noise it made when in use—was an enlarged version of Maxim's machine-gun. It was the world's first autocannon—unlike a machine-gun, it fired shells rather than bullets. The "Pom-Pom" served as an artillery weapon and an anti-aircraft gun.

A NEW KIND OF FIREPOWER

GATLING GUN

By the second half of the 19th century, improvements in engineering had made it possible to manufacture reliable multiple-fire weapons. This gun, patented by Richard Gatling in 1862, employed multiple barrels, as would all early machine-guns. It also took advantage of the new brass cartridge—earlier paper cartridges were dangerous, being liable to combust unpredictably. The Gatling gun was first developed in the American Civil War, and was deemed a success. It subsequently saw action with the British Army in various overseas campaigns.

▶ GATLING GUN

Date 1865	**Origin** US
Weight 2,200lb (1,000kg)	
Barrels 10	
Caliber .45, .65, or 1in	

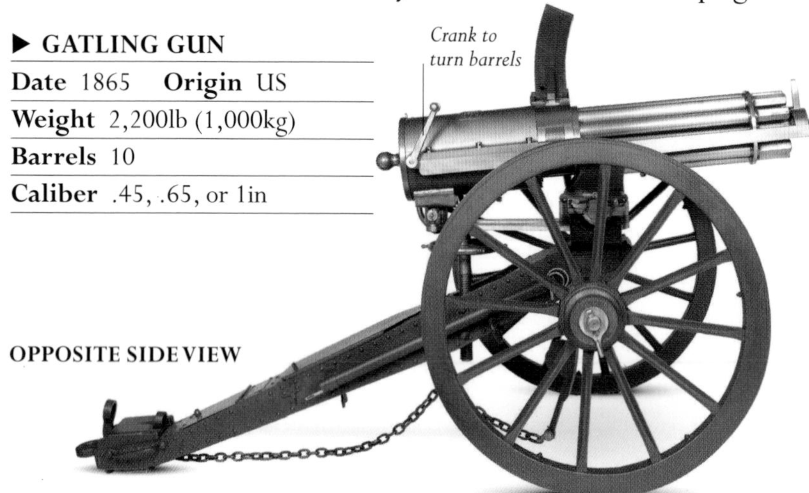

OPPOSITE SIDE VIEW

◀ FORE SIGHT AND BARRELS
The fore sight enabled the gunner to make adjustments to the gun's targeting. Having 10 barrels reduced the risk of overheating. In combat use the gun could average around 400 rounds per minute.

IN ACTION

ON THE BATTLEFIELD

The Gatling gun's method of operation enabled unskilled users to maintain a reasonably high rate of fire. This had its most notable effect in colonial wars against adversaries with less advanced arms, such as its use against the Plains Indians in North America by the US Army, and against the Zulus in southern Africa by the British Army. Some of the guns were also used as naval weapons, although with a slightly reduced rate of fire.

▶ The British Army used the Gatling to devastating effect in the Zulu Wars.

THE GATLING GUN
The gun's barrels—at first six, later ten—were arranged around a cylindrical shaft. A hand-operated crank made the barrels revolve, and cartridges dropped into place from above as each barrel came around. A firing pin then struck and fired the bullet; the barrel turned and the process was repeated. As each barrel descended, its spent case was ejected.

▸ **ANTI-ROTATION PAWL**
The breech plugs contain firing pins; each pin has a small cam head to catch hold of the gun body.

◂ **MAGAZINE SLOT**
The 40-round magazine was constructed with a groove to help prevent the gun from jamming.

▸ **LOWERING GEAR**
This wheel was used to raise and lower the barrels of the gun.

▸ **WHEEL HUB**
To make transportation easier, a towing ring was secured to the wheel hub by a cotter (a wedge-shaped fastener).

▸ **TRAVERSING HANDSPIKE STOWAGE**
Stored on the side of the gun, the handspike was used for additional grip when maneuvering the gun carriage.

BREECH-LOADING ARTILLERY

British engineer William Armstrong designed the first efficient breech-loading rifled field gun in 1855. The shell and gunpowder propellant were loaded at the breech, which was closed with a "vent-piece" secured in a slot with a hollow screw. Armstrong's 12-pounder gun, of 1859, was the first rifled breech-loading field gun to enter British Army service, and the Armstrong RBL 40-pounder was an adaptation of this gun as a medium artillery piece. The French Canon de 75mm Modèle 1897 added a key element to artillery design—a recoil-dampening mechanism that kept the trail and wheels perfectly still when firing, which freed gun crews from having to re-aim the gun after each shot.

Barrel

▲ ARMSTRONG RBL 40-POUND GUN

Date	1861
Origin	UK
Length	9¾ft (3m)
Caliber	12cm
Range	1.59 miles (2.56km)

The Armstrong rifled breech-loading 40-pounder was used by the British Royal Navy as a broadside gun, and by the army as a defensive gun in military forts. It saw action in the Royal Navy's bombardment of Kagoshima, Japan, in August 1863.

▶ ARMSTRONG RBL 12-POUNDER

Date	1859
Origin	UK
Length	7ft (2.13m)
Caliber	7.62cm
Range	1.92 miles (3.1km)

The Armstrong rifled 12-pounder gun required a crew of nine men to operate it. The gun that entered British Army service in 1859 had a 7ft (2.13m) barrel, while the British Royal Navy used a 6ft (1.83m) barrel version. In 1863, the shorter version became standard.

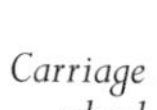

Rifling within barrel

Trail

Carriage wheel

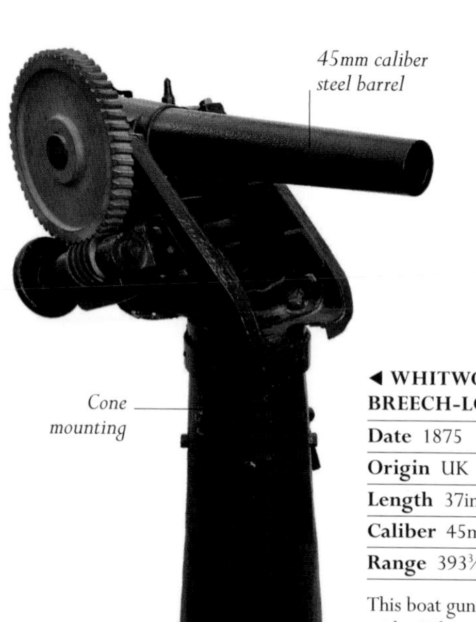

◀ WHITWORTH 45MM BREECH-LOADING BOAT GUN

Date	1875
Origin	UK
Length	37in (94cm)
Caliber	45mm
Range	393¾ yards (360m)

This boat gun had hexagonal rifling with a Whitworth sliding-lock breech-loading mechanism. It was set on a cone mounting mostly used for small naval guns. This example was mounted on an armed yacht.

▶ BL 15-POUNDER 7CWT

Date	1892
Origin	UK
Length	7ft (2.13m)
Caliber	76.2mm
Range	3.26 miles (5.26km)

This 15-pounder was fitted with an early recoil device—a spade that dug into the ground on firing, and was connected to a spring on the trail. The gun jumped backward on firing and then forward under the pressure of the spring. It could fire eight rounds per minute.

▶ HOTCHKISS QUICK-FIRING 3-POUNDER NAVAL GUN

Date	1885
Origin	France
Length	(Barrel) 6½ft (2m)
Caliber	47mm
Range	2.27 miles (3.66km)

The Hotchkiss QF (Quick-Firing) 3-pounder was used by the British Royal Navy from 1885, as well as the French, Russian, and US navies. These guns were made by a division of the Armstrong armaments business. Operated by two men, the gun could fire up to thirty 3¼lb (1.5kg) steel shells per minute.

◀ FRENCH CANON DE 75MM MODÈLE 1897

Date	1897
Origin	France
Weight	1.7 tons (1.54 tonnes)
Length	8¾ft (2.7m)
Caliber	75mm
Range	4.28 miles (6.9km)

The Canon de 75mm Modèle 1897 used a hydro-pneumatic recoil mechanism that kept the trail and wheels stationary when firing, making the model widely regarded as the first modern artillery gun. It could fire 15 rounds per minute.

◀ KRUPP 8.9CM FIELD GUN

Date	1895
Origin	Germany
Weight	1.25 tons (1.13 tonnes)
Length	8½ft (2.6m)
Caliber	8.9cm

This rifled breech-loading field gun was fitted with high brackets to make it sit in an elevated position in the carriage, and enable it to fire over the parapet of a fortified site. It is thought to have been captured by British forces from Boers at Pietersburg (modern-day Polokwanè), South Africa, in 1901.

▼ 7.7CM FK 96 NA

Date	1905
Origin	Germany
Length	(Barrel) 6¾ft (2.1m)
Caliber	77mm
Range	4.84 miles (7.8km)

The 7.7cm Feldkanone 96 neuer Art was an upgraded version of the FK 96, featuring improvements to the carriage and the breech, and the addition of a recoil system. It was the standard German field gun at the start of World War I, and although reliable, its elevation was limited. A crew of five could fire ten rounds per minute.

SURPRISE AMBUSH
After the first wave of the battle, the British 21st Lancers charged what they thought was a small troop of Mahdist forces—in fact it numbered several thousand, most of them hidden in a dip in the desert. Thanks to superior firepower, British casualties were few.

THE BATTLE OF OMDURMAN

The battle fought between General Herbert Kitchener's Anglo-Egyptian army and the Muslim Mahdists at Omdurman, in Sudan on September 2, 1898, was an overwhelming victory for European industrial technology over a determined African army of superior numbers but limited firepower.

As *Sirdar* (commander-in-chief) of the British-officered Egyptian army, Kitchener was entrusted with avenging the death of General Gordon at the hands of Sudanese Mahdists. The Mahdists were in revolt against British-supported Egyptian rule, and had killed Gordon in 1885 at Khartoum; tactically, Britain also wanted to deter the ambitions of the rival French in Sudan.

Kitchener's army of 8,000 British and 18,000 Egyptian troops advanced down the Nile, accompanied by river gunboats carrying supplies and heavy equipment and providing extra firepower. The land forces were equipped with field artillery as well as 40 Maxim guns, each capable of firing 600 rounds per minute. The infantry, meanwhile, carried the latest Lee Metford and Lee Enfield rifles, rapid-fire bolt-action weapons with box magazines. Some of the riverborne guns were also provided with shells containing Lyddite, a new high explosive that would later be used in World War I.

The Mahdist leader Khalifa Abdullah al-Taashi waited at Omdurman, near Khartoum. About one-third of his army of over 50,000 men had rifles, though often without adequate or appropriate ammunition. The rest relied on spears and swords, still perfectly serviceable weapons at a time when European infantry still practiced the bayonet charge.

On September 1, British cavalry scouts made contact with the Mahdist army. Kitchener took up a defensive position on the bank of the Nile, with his infantry in the center and cavalry on the flanks. At dawn the following day some 8,000 Mahdist warriors dressed in white and flourishing banners, made a frontal assault on the defensive perimeter. Their charge across the open plain was met by the fire of field artillery and gunboats and then, as they drew closer, of Maxim guns and rifles. As infantry were to find during the carnage of World War I, an advance into such density of fire from these new weapons was near-suicidal. Not a single warrior reached the defensive line.

RIFLES AND DISCIPLINE

The majority of the Mahdist forces, however, remained in concealed positions around the Anglo-Egyptian camp. When Kitchener's troops left their defensive perimeter and advanced over the body-strewn ground toward Omdurman, they entered a trap. The 21st Lancers, with young war correspondent Winston Churchill in their ranks, inadvertently rode into the midst of several thousand Mahdists hidden in a dry streambed, and suffered 61 casualties. Potentially more serious was the fate of General Hector Macdonald's infantry brigade, caught in the open by some 15,000 Mahdists emerging from hiding, but the 3,000-strong brigade held off the attackers with disciplined rifle fire until reinforcements arrived.

Kitchener's forces advanced relentlessly on Omdurman while it was bombarded with Lyddite shells. By the end of the day the remnants of the Mahdist army had withdrawn, and the town was in British hands. Around 10,000 Mahdists died, compared with only 48 Anglo-Egyptian troops—a striking display of the killing power of European military technology.

CLOTHING AND WEAPONS OF AFRICA AND OCEANIA

By the late 19th century, European invaders were firmly established in Africa and the Pacific Basin. Except in the settlements themselves, their presence actually impinged little on the day-to-day lives of the indigenous peoples, who continued to behave much as they had done for centuries. In particular, while firearms sometimes found their way to the indigenous population, the weapons and tactics they used when fighting among themselves remained largely unchanged. This often had horrific consequences when the native warriors tried to resist conquest. Occasionally, however, as at Isandlwana in 1879 when the Zulus defeated the British, superiority in numbers combined with complacency on the part of the imperialists allowed native warriors using traditional weapons to inflict a crushing defeat.

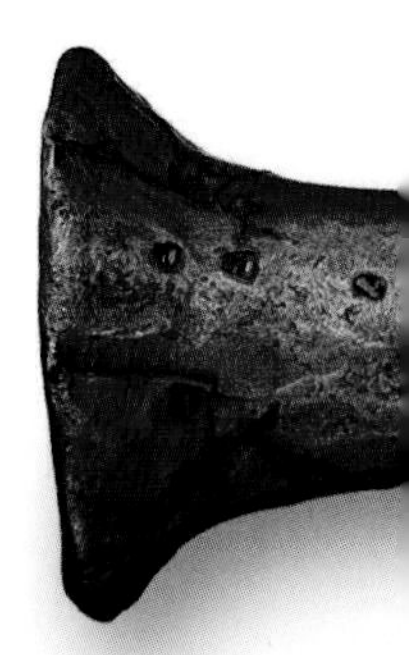

▼ ZULU KNOBKERRIE

Date	19th century
Origin	South Africa
Length	36in (91cm)

Knobkerries were simple hardwood rods with round finials, usually around 4in (10cm) in diameter. Clubs such as these were carried by Zulu warriors together with a short shaped stabbing spear and stiff cowhide shield.

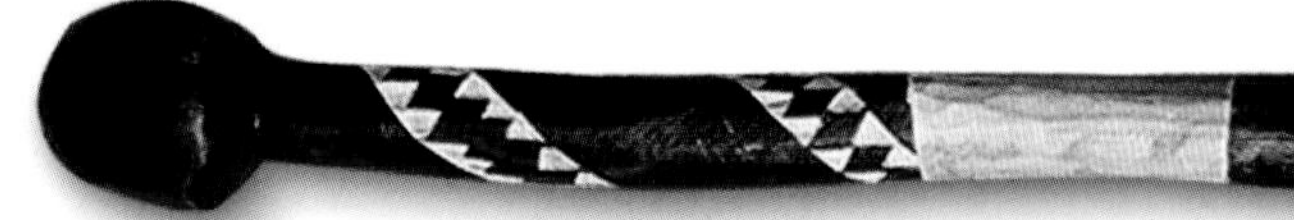

Hardwood shaft

▲ ZULU IKLWA (STABBING SPEAR)

Date	19th century
Origin	South Africa
Length	4ft (1.2m)

The celebrated Zulu king Shaka was responsible for introducing the short, broad-pointed stabbing spear known as the *iklwa*, which was used along with a shield.

Slits cut in shield with strip of hide threaded through

▲ ZULU HEADDRESS

Date	19th century
Origin	South Africa
Material	Monkey skin, feathers, fur

The warrior's headdress consisted of a decorative skin band that was set over a monkey-skin cap, with flaps for the neck and ears surmounted by further decoration, such as feathers or fur strips.

▲ ZULU UMUTSHA (APRON)

Date	19th century
Origin	South Africa
Material	Cowhide, goathair

The Zulu warrior's *umutsha* (apron or loincloth) covered his front and back. This example is decorated with goathair, and the pattern would have been unique to an *amabutho* (regiment).

Carved geometric design

◄ ZULU SHIELD

Date	19th century
Origin	South Africa

The Zulu warrior aimed to use the left side of his shield to hook the adversary's aside, exposing his body to a spear thrust. The pointed lower end of the shield-shaft was also employed as a weapon.

◀ **CONGOLESE AX**

Date	19th century
Origin	Congo Basin
Weight	3lb (1.35kg)
Length	17in (42.8cm)

This ornate ceremonial ax is of a type carried by chiefs of the Songye people, from the southeast Congo Basin. The hardwood haft is entirely sheathed in copper, a metal common in the region.

▲ **WEST AFRICAN FIGHTING PICK**

Date	19th century
Origin	Ghana
Weight	1½lb (0.65kg)
Length	20in (51cm)

The barbed head of this unusual fighting pick would have certainly caused a serious wound, but made the weapon potentially difficult to recover.

▲ **MAORI CEREMONIAL TOKI**

Date	19th century
Origin	New Zealand

Maori warriors used the *toki*, an adzelike weapon with a transverse blade, as well as clubs and *taiahas* (club-spears). This *poutangata* (ceremonial) version has a blade of carved *pounamu* (jade), a symbol of chieftainship.

Red bead

Cylindrical hardwood shaft

◀ **MELANESIAN CLUB**

Date	19th century
Origin	Vanuatu
Weight	1¼lb (0.6kg)
Length	32in (82cm)

This lightweight, ceremonial wooden club has a stylized human face carved on each side of the head. This kind of decoration is frequently found across Oceania.

Human figure carving

◀ **TONGAN CLUB**

Date	19th century
Origin	Tonga
Weight	3lb (1.3kg)
Length	32in (82cm)

This heavy, two-handed war club is carved along its length with geometric patterns, human figures, animals, and fish. The diamond-shaped head would have inflicted a crushing blow to the skull.

▲ **POLYNESIAN "CUTLASS"**

Date	19th century
Origin	Polynesia
Weight	3¼lb (1.5kg)
Length	30½in (77.5cm)

Based on the *ayudha katti* of South India, this cleaverlike club's triangular panels of geometric motifs are reminiscent of patterns found in ceremonial weavings.

SELF-LOADING PISTOLS

When Maxim's patents on the mechanism of the recoil-operated machine-gun expired, firearms designers began applying the same principle to pistols. The first successful attempt, by Borchardt, actually copied Maxim's breaking-toggle locking system, but his followers found new ways of locking breech and barrel together in such a way that the recoil generated when a round was fired separated the two, allowing the breech to open and the spent cartridge to be expelled. The breech then rebounded against a spring, chambering a fresh round, cocking the action, and leaving the pistol ready to be fired in the process. This cycle took just a fraction of a second.

▶ **WEBLEY-FOSBERY MODEL 1903**

Date	1896–1924
Origin	UK
Weight	2½lb (1.1kg)
Barrel	7½in (19cm)
Caliber	.455in

Designed by Fosbery, the cylinder of this unique semi-automatic revolver was made to turn when the pistol's upper frame was driven back by recoil and returned by a spring.

▶ **GABBETT-FAIRFAX "MARS"**

Date	1899–1902
Origin	UK
Weight	3½lb (1.55kg)
Barrel	10½in (26.5cm)
Caliber	8.5mm Mars/.45 Webley

The "Mars" pistol was too big, too expensive, too complex—and too unforgiving—to succeed in the already congested and competitive weapon market of 1900.

▶ **STEYR M1905**

Date	1905–15
Origin	Austria-Hungary
Weight	33¼oz (940g)
Barrel	6½in (16cm)
Caliber	7.63mm Mannlicher

The Mannlicher-designed M1905 was chambered for a round generally thought too powerful for a "blowback" action, but succeeded—although it was never especially popular—due to the high standard to which it was manufactured.

▲ BORCHARDT C93

Date	1894
Origin	Germany
Weight	3¼lb (1.66kg)
Barrel	6½in (16.5cm)
Caliber	7.65mm

The C93 was the first successful self-loading pistol. For its locking mechanism, it drew on the design of Maxim's machine-guns, which Borchardt's employer, Loewe, was producing under license in Berlin.

Fixed five-round magazine

▶ BERGMANN NO. 3

Date	1896
Origin	Germany
Weight	31oz (880g)
Barrel	4½in (11.2cm)
Caliber	6.5mm Bergmann

The Louis Schmeisser-designed "No. 3" was amongst the simplest of pistols, with a "blowback" breech and a small-capacity fixed magazine. The spent case was ejected by gas pressure alone.

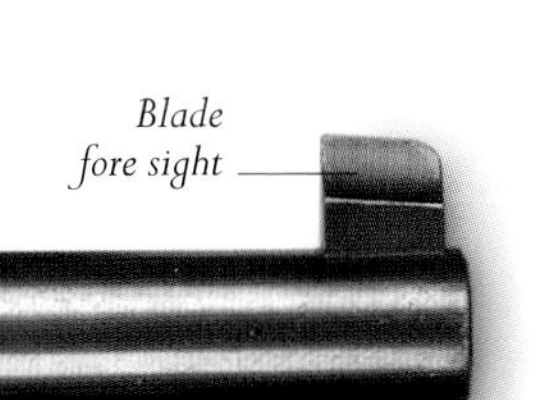

▲ MAUSER C96

Date	1896–1930s
Origin	Germany
Weight	2½lb (1.15kg)
Barrel	5½in (14cm)
Caliber	7.63mm Mauser

Despite shortcomings, chief among which was its complexity, the Mauser C96, chambered for a particularly effective and popular round, was one of the most successful designs of its day.

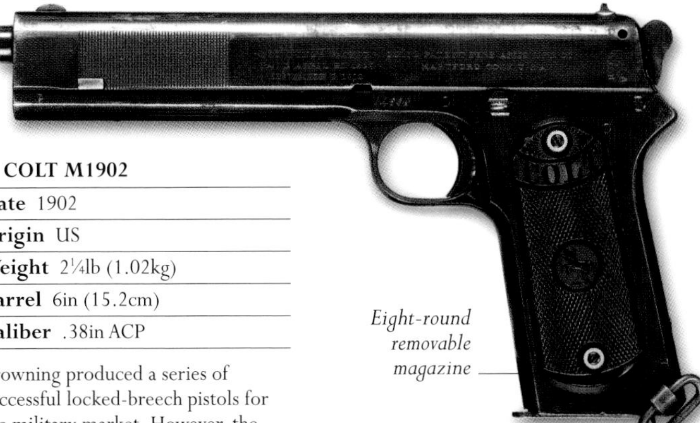

▶ COLT M1902

Date	1902
Origin	US
Weight	2¼lb (1.02kg)
Barrel	6in (15.2cm)
Caliber	.38in ACP

Browning produced a series of successful locked-breech pistols for the military market. However, the Model 1902—designed with a double-link mechanism and chambered for a lighter round—was not as popular.

Barrel locking-lug

Hammer (or "hahn")

▶ STEYR "HAHN" M1911

Date	1911
Origin	Austria
Weight	34½oz (980g)
Barrel	5in (12.7cm)
Caliber	7.63mm Mannlicher

This was the first successful locked-breech semi-automatic pistol Steyr produced. Its weakness was its non-removable magazine, which was charged from above using a clip. This version was used by the Chilean armed forces.

▶ WEBLEY MODEL 1910

Date	1910–30s
Origin	UK
Weight	33¾oz (960g)
Barrel	5in (12.7cm)
Caliber	.38in

Better known for revolvers, Webley also produced semi-automatic pistols. The unsophisticated Model 1910 was the most successful, and was adopted by the British Royal Navy and the Royal Flying Corps.

BOER FIGHTERS
In the Boer republics, all men aged from 16 to 60 had to present themselves to fight when called upon. Many of them fought using the German Mauser Model 1895, an excellent bolt-operated rifle with a box magazine.

SECOND BOER WAR

In October 1899 the independent Boer republics of the Transvaal and the Orange Free State launched a preemptive attack on British-ruled South Africa. The conflict later became a guerrilla war, in which lightly armed, mounted Boer commandos defied the military might of the British Empire.

The Boer forces were a citizen militia. Every adult male was issued with a rifle by the central government and was obliged to turn up for military service when called upon, bringing his weapon, ammunition, and a horse. The basic military unit was known as a "commando"—before the term took on its current meaning. The Boers' equipment was light but of high quality. They had the latest Mauser rifles and some state-of-the-art field artillery from the Krupp and Creusot factories in Europe. British infantry were equipped with Lee-Metford and Lee-Enfield rifles, and both sides made use of the machine-gun.

The advent of smokeless powder meant that rifles had become more accurate with better range, an advance which played to a Boer strength: they were excellent sharpshooters, skilled in exploiting cover, especially now that positions were no longer given away by gun smoke. They were also experienced in surviving on the South African veld. But the commandos had their weaknesses: officers were elected, which, though democratic, did not encourage strict discipline. Also most Boers were reluctant to fight far from their home areas, which limited offensive operations.

The Boer army had a series of initial successes, but then suffered repeated defeats as the British counterattacked in strength. In the summer of 1900 British troops occupied the Boer republics and declared the war won, but while some Boers accepted this outcome many did not. Battle-hardened Boer commanders such as Louis Botha, Koos de la Rey, and Christiaan de Wet decided to fight on. They launched a coordinated campaign of guerrilla warfare that caught the British occupying forces utterly unprepared. Able to move swiftly across the veld and resupply with the local Boer population, the mounted commandos struck at will against railroad lines and telegraph wires, supply convoys, and isolated garrisons. Although hugely outnumbered by the British troops, the commandos' hit-and-run attacks denied Britain the chance to bring its superior forces into play. When Boer horsemen did enter into combat against British troops they were usually the victors, exploiting their speed of maneuver and superior knowledge of the terrain.

A SCORCHED EARTH POLICY

The British commander-in-chief, Lord Kitchener, responded with a ruthless counterinsurgency campaign. He built a chain of fortified blockhouses linked by barbed wire to protect the railroads, before fencing in whole areas of the veld, which could then be swept to flush out the guerrillas. Large numbers of mounted troops were deployed in roaming columns to hunt the commandos. Most controversially, Boer farms, livestock, and crops were also destroyed to deny the guerrillas sustenance, and Boer women and children were herded into British "concentration camps," where thousands died of malnutrition and disease. Thus a pattern was established that was to recur through the 20th century—a major power drawn into deploying large-scale forces against an elusive enemy, and in the process politically discrediting its own cause.

In the end the commandos were not defeated, but their leaders recognized that the damage suffered by their own people was too great to be allowed to continue. The British were also eager to end the fighting and a compromise peace was agreed in May 1902.

MILITARY MEDALS BEFORE 1914

The 19th century saw the birth of the military medal as we know it today. Previously such recognition of notable valor was reserved largely for those of high rank. During the Napoleonic Wars, however, medals began to be awarded to both officers and other personnel. The most prestigious medals were for exceptional acts of bravery, but others were given simply for participation in an action. The medals varied from coinlike medallions to more elaborate designs incorporating national symbols and mottos. In many cases clasps were used to specify the action or battle.

◀ WATERLOO MEDAL

Date 1815

Origin UK

Conflict Napoleonic Wars

The first award to be issued to all ranks in a specific campaign, this was also the first to be awarded to the next-of-kin of fallen soldiers.

▶ INDIA GENERAL SERVICE MEDAL

Date 1854

Origin UK

Conflict Indian campaigns

This medal was awarded to British and Indian servicemen from 1854 to 1895. Different ribbon clasps denoted specific battles or actions.

▼ HANOVERIAN MEDAL FOR WATERLOO

Date 1815

Origin Hanover

Conflict Napoleonic Wars

Authorized by George, the British Prince Regent, in his position as Elector of Hanover, this medal was given to Hanoverian troops who survived the Battle of Waterloo (1815).

Head of the Prince Regent on the front

◀ VICTORIA CROSS

Date 1856

Origin UK

The Victoria Cross is the UK's premier award for gallantry. Originally struck from the gunmetal of captured Russian cannon, it was introduced to honor acts of exceptional valor in the Crimean War (1853–56).

Reverse (shown) depicts Britannia with a lion

▶ TURKISH CRIMEA MEDAL

Date 1855

Origin Turkey

Conflict Crimean War

The Turkish Crimea Medal, "Kinm Harbi Madalyasi," was awarded by Sultan Abdulmecid I of the Ottoman Empire to all allied military personnel, including British, French, and Sardinian troops, who fought in the Crimean War (1853–56).

Clasp denotes actions in which recipient was involved

▲ INDIAN MUTINY MEDAL

Date 1858

Origin UK

Conflict Indian Rebellion

Initially given to British and Indian troops who had fought the Indian rebels, this award was later extended to civilians who had played a role in the suppression of the revolt.

◀ PUNJAB MEDAL

Date 1849

Origin UK

Conflict Punjab campaign

This award was made to officers and men of the British Army and East India Company who served in the Punjab campaign of 1848–49.

▲ MEDAL OF HONOR

Date 1861

Origin US

The Medal of Honor is the highest medal for "valor in combat" that can be awarded to members of the US Armed Forces. First authorized in 1861 for issue to sailors and marines, the medal was extended to soldiers in 1862. Since then, more than 3,400 Medals of Honor have been awarded to personnel from all the armed services.

◀ QUEEN'S SOUTH AFRICA MEDAL

Date 1899

Origin UK

Conflict Anglo-Boer Wars

Awarded to personnel who served in the Second Anglo-Boer War in South Africa (1899–1902), with 178,000 medals issued and 26 authorized clasps, this is one of the most widespread of all military medals.

Laurel wreath symbolizes victory

A total of six silver clasps were authorized

Imperial crown joins cross and ribbon

▲ SOUTH AFRICA MEDAL

Date 1879

Origin UK

Conflict South Africa campaigns

This was issued by the British Government to members of the British Army and Naval Brigade who served in the South African tribal wars between 1877 and 1879. Most awards were made for actions during the Anglo-Zulu War (1879), especially the battles of Isandlwana and Rorke's Drift.

▶ ORDER OF THE RISING SUN

Date 1875

Origin Japan

Established in 1875 by Emperor Meiji of Japan, the Order of the Rising Sun was the country's first national decoration. The version shown here is a 7th class medal, showing Paulownia flowers and leaves.

▶ LÉGION D'HONNEUR

Date 1802

Origin France

Instituted by Napoleon Bonaparte in 1802 as an award for outstanding civil or military service to France, the Ordre Royal, Imperial, et National de la Légion d'Honneur is still one of France's highest awards. The pictured design was awarded between 1870 and 1951.

◀ AFGHANISTAN MEDAL

Date 1881

Origin UK

Conflict Anglo-Afghan Wars

This medal was awarded to British and Indian forces, who took part in the Second Anglo-Afghan War, which consisted of a series of battles between 1878 and 1880. The war ended with a British victory at Kandahar in 1880.

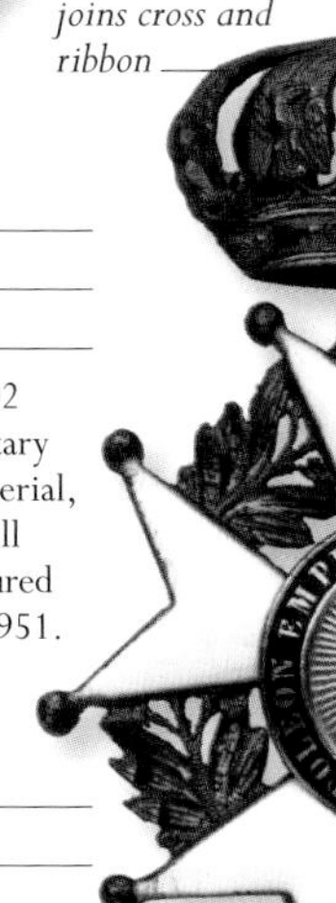

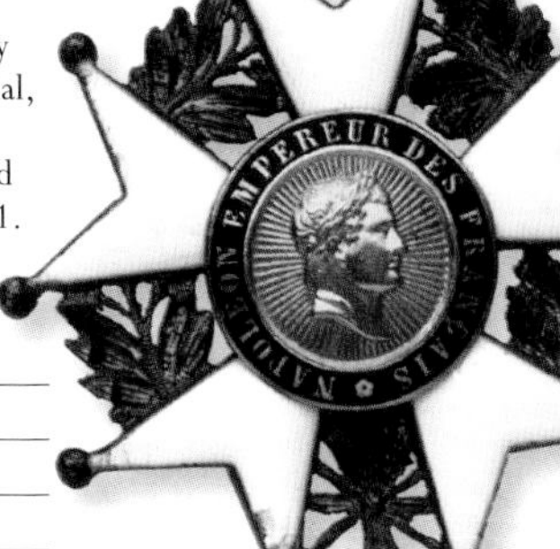

KEY DEVELOPMENT

STEAM, IRONCLADS, AND THE FIRST BATTLESHIPS

In the century between the Napoleonic Wars and the outbreak of World War I, new technology transformed naval warfare. Sail gave way to steam, wooden hulls were superseded by metal ones, and high-explosive shells replaced cannonballs.

The sailing ship navies of Nelson's era (see p.196) did not disappear overnight; at first, steamships were only viable in coastal and inland waters. Their large paddlewheels limited the space available for gunports and were vulnerable to enemy fire, but steamships had the clear advantage of being able to maneuver at will, even in a dead calm. The introduction, in the 1840s, of screw propellers as an alternative to paddlewheels led to the adoption of steam engines as a standard feature of warships, although initially as an auxiliary to the sails.

RISE OF THE IRONCLAD

The 1840s also saw the Paixhans gun revolutionize naval armament: it was the first naval gun designed to fire explosive shells instead of solid shot. In response, during the 1850s, some wooden-hulled ships were armored with thick iron plate above the waterline. These ironclad ships were deemed a success during the Crimean War (1853–56), fought between Russia and the allied forces of Britain, France, the Ottoman Empire, and Kingdom of Sardinia. In 1859, France built the first ironclad battleship, *La Gloire*, which was matched by the British HMS *Warrior* the following year.

The American Civil War began in 1861. The Confederates rebuilt an existing ship as the ironclad CSS *Virginia*, while their opponents sponsored a radical new design, the USS *Monitor*—a metal raft equipped with two Dahlgren guns in a rotating turret. At the Battle of Hampton Roads, in March 1862, CSS *Virginia* sank two conventional Union frigates with frightening ease, but then fought a stalemated duel with USS *Monitor* in what was to be the first battle between two ironclad steamships.

Experiments with ironclad ships continued throughout the Civil War: the Union forces built more monitors (named after the original), as well

KEY **EVENTS**

1800–1950

- **1841** An iron-hulled steam-powered gunboat, *Nemesis*, plays a key role in the British defeat of China in the First Opium War.
- **1853** Making the first use of explosive shells in a naval battle, a Russian squadron destroys 11 Turkish ships at the Battle of Sinope, during the Crimean War.
- **1897** The US Navy adopts the first successful powered submarine, designed by Irish-American John Holland.
- **1904** Japanese destroyers armed with Whitehead torpedoes make a surprise attack on the Russian fleet at Port Arthur.
- **1911** Britain's Royal Navy decides that its new *Queen Elizabeth*-class battleships will use oil as fuel, instead of coal.

▼ METAL AGAINST METAL
In 1864, during the American Civil War, Union admiral David Farragut penetrated Confederate-held Mobile Bay with a squadron of metal monitors and wooden ships. One monitor was sunk by a mine, but Farragut disabled the Confederate ironclad CSS *Tennessee*.

"The **storm of shot and shell** launched against the Spaniard was **destructive beyond all description**"

LIEUTENANT J L STICKNEY, EYEWITNESS TO THE BATTLE OF MANILA, 1898

as a fleet of iron-armored paddle steamers, to fight on the Mississippi. By the conclusion of the Civil War, in 1865, the superiority of ironclad steamships over wooden sailing ships was generally accepted. In 1871, the British built HMS *Devastation*, the first capital warship to have no sails at all. However, a new configuration of naval warfare still took time to emerge: the design of naval guns and their positioning on ships went through a stuttering development. For a time, naval designers became obsessed with rams, imagining that armor would make warships immune to gunfire; they pictured a return to the tactics of Ancient Greece in which steamships maneuvered like triremes in a bid to sink enemy vessels with their reinforced prows.

Eventually a system was devised for mounting large rifled guns in rotating armored turrets, with the magazine and ammunition stored in the hull below. These guns fired high-explosive shells at long range, requiring the invention of complex range-finding devices. Hulls were now made from metal and clad in steel armor, but the increasing power of explosives meant that ships remained vulnerable to this kind of gunfire. In addition, the adoption of steam power was not without its drawbacks. Sailing ships had not needed fuel, but coaling stations were now essential to naval operations, giving a new twist to geopolitics. When coal began to be replaced by oil, the possession of oilfields became a primary strategic concern for naval powers.

NAVAL RACE

By the end of the 19th century, navies had become supreme status symbols for competing imperial powers. The US, Japan, and Germany embarked on large-scale naval construction programs, to which the UK actively responded, determined to maintain its long-established naval supremacy. In the first decade of the 20th century, a frenzied naval race between the British and the Germans saw the UK repeatedly raise the bar with faster, more powerfully armed battleships, starting with the epoch-making HMS *Dreadnought* in 1906. Yet while naval commanders and a jingoistic public were obsessed with large warships—battleships, battlecruisers, and cruisers—other developments in naval warfare made these expensive vessels worryingly vulnerable. Sea mines, first used in the Crimean War, could sink any capital ship—and so could boats armed with torpedoes, whose worth was ably demonstrated by the Japanese during their war with Russia from 1904 to 1905. Destroyers were devised to defend the fleet against attack by torpedo boats, as well as launching torpedoes themselves, but navies had no technology for defense against torpedo-armed submarines, which became a practical element of navies in the first decade of the 20th century.

KEY **BATTLE**

THE BATTLE OF MANILA

MAY 1, 1898

The Spanish–American War of 1898 was the first test of the American "New Navy" of modern battleships and cruisers. The Asiatic Squadron under Commodore George Dewey sank seven Spanish warships in the Philippines without loss.

▲ American battleships steaming in line destroy Spanish warships in Manila Bay.

▼ WHITEHEAD TORPEDO
In the 1860s, British engineer Robert Whitehead invented the first effective self-propelled torpedo. Carried by small ships, the torpedo threatened to undermine the dominance of heavily gunned warships.

▼ DAHLGREN GUN
Invented by US naval officer John A Dahlgren, the Dahlgren gun was in frequent use during the American Civil War. Its distinctive soda-bottle shape gave more power than a conventional naval gun.

BATTLESHIPS

The second half of the 19th century was a time of considerable technological innovation at sea. Already the world's naval forces had begun to embrace steam propulsion, but now the very essence of the warship was to undergo a complete transformation, as wood and wind gave way to steel and steam. New types of weapons, as well as new ways of handling them, were developed and introduced. A dramatic transition occurred in a period of just 40 years, and in a world known for its innate conservatism and reluctance to accept change, this was no mean achievement.

▲ HMS WARRIOR

Commissioned 1861 **Origin** UK
Displacement 9,140 tons
Length 420ft (128m)
Top speed 14.1 knots

The *Warrior* and its sister-ship HMS *Black Prince* were the first ocean-going "ironclads," with 4½in (11.5cm) of armor on 18in (45.7cm) wooden hulls, screw propellers as well as a full sailing rig, and breech-loading guns.

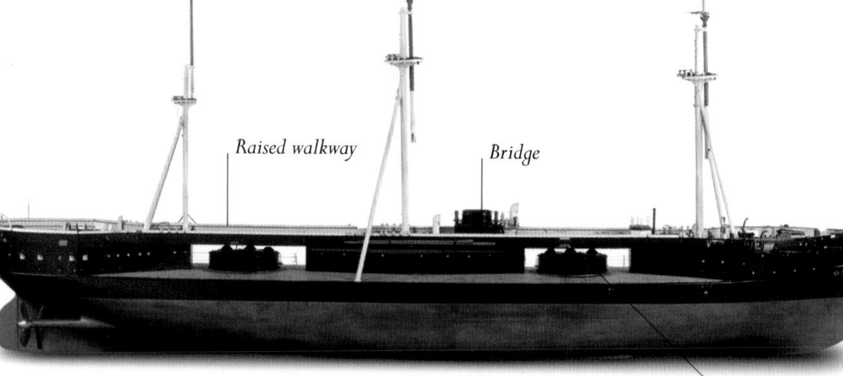

▲ HMS CAPTAIN

Commissioned 1870 **Origin** UK
Displacement 7,770 tons
Length 320ft (97.5m)
Top speed 15.25 knots

An experimental ship produced to the design of Captain Cowper Phipps Coles, a pioneer of the gun turret, HMS *Captain* proved to be a disastrous mistake. Its low freeboard contributed to its loss during a severe storm in September 1870.

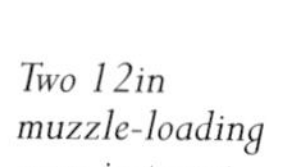

▲ HMS DEVASTATION

Commissioned 1873 **Origin** UK
Displacement 9,330 tons
Length 307ft (93.6m)
Top speed 13.5 knots

Devastation and its sister-ship *Thunderer* were the first mastless sea-going battleships, with their armament contained in turrets fore and aft of the superstructure. This feature set the pattern for future development.

▲ HMS RUPERT

Commissioned 1874 **Origin** UK
Displacement 5,440 tons
Length 264ft (80.5m)
Top speed 14 knots

Following the success of ramming tactics at the Battle of Lissa in 1866, many navies built ships specifically designed to sink others by ramming them. The British Royal Navy commissioned four, including *Rupert*, but none ever saw combat.

▶ HMS INFLEXIBLE

Commissioned 1881	**Origin** UK
Displacement 11,880 tons	
Length 344ft (104.9m)	
Top speed 15 knots	

Inflexible was a hybrid: a full-rigged "ironclad" with its main armament—the heaviest muzzle-loaders in the British Royal Navy—in turrets. It was specifically designed to match similar Italian ships in the Mediterranean, but never met them in conflict, although it participated in the bombardment of Alexandria in 1882.

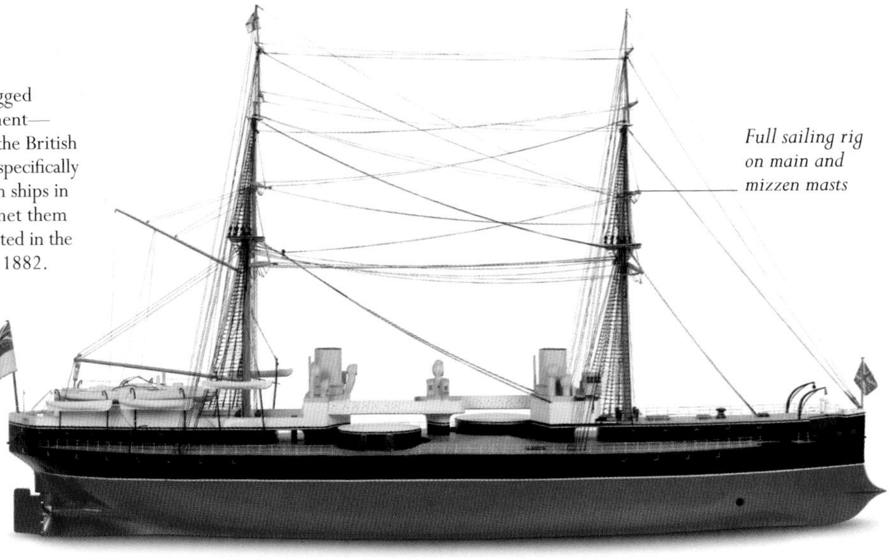

Full sailing rig on main and mizzen masts

Gardner machine-guns in fighting top
Two 13.5in guns in barbette

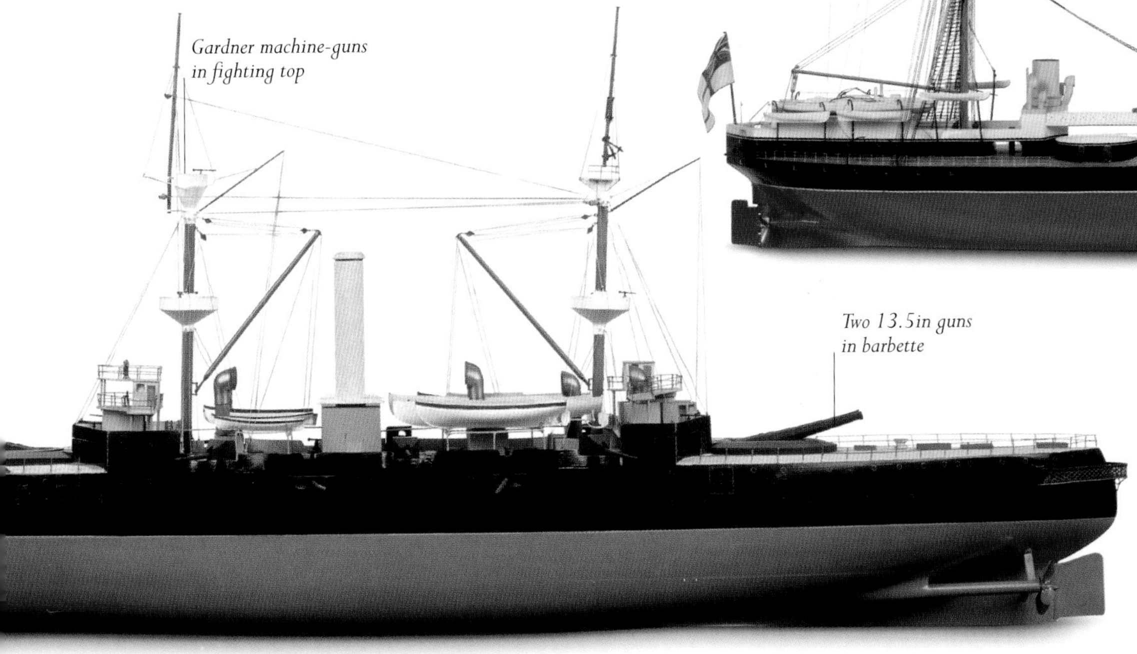

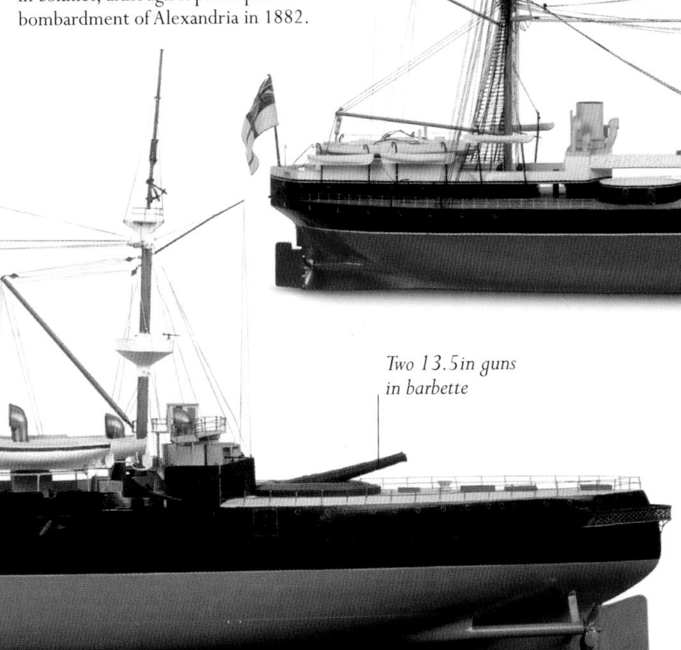

◀ HMS ROYAL SOVEREIGN

Commissioned 1892	**Origin** UK
Displacement 15,580 tons	
Length 410ft (124.9m)	
Top speed 15 knots	

The leader of a class of seven ships, the *Royal Sovereign* was the first of what became known as the pre-dreadnought battleships, mounting just four large-caliber guns and a sizeable battery of smaller, quick-firing weapons designed to fight off cruisers and destroyers.

▶ HMS HINDUSTAN

Commissioned 1905	**Origin** UK
Displacement 17,290 tons	
Length 454ft (138.3m)	
Top speed 18.5 knots	

One of the second generation of pre-dreadnoughts, with 9.2in guns to supplement their main armament, the *Hindustan* was one of the eight-strong *King Edward VII* class. It was considerably bigger than previous British battleships.

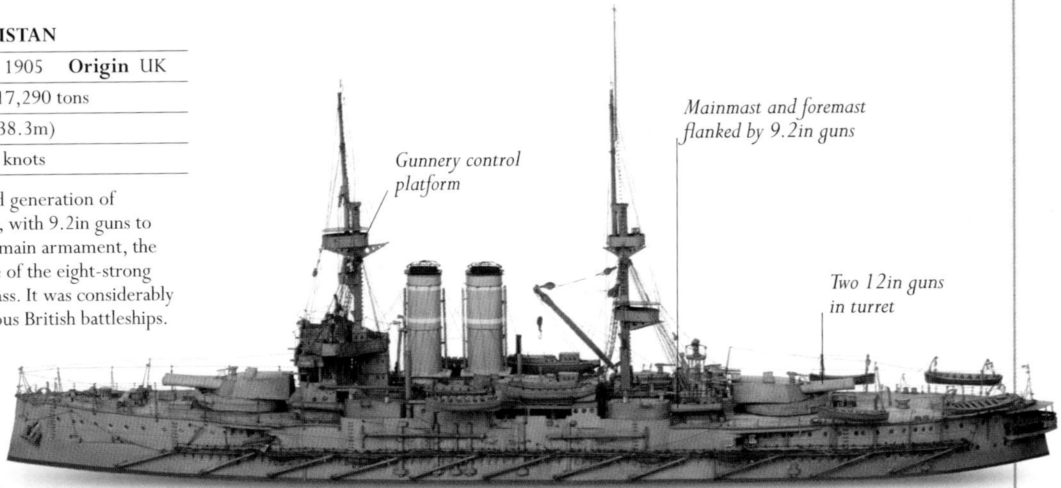

Gunnery control platform
Mainmast and foremast flanked by 9.2in guns
Two 12in guns in turret

6in gun in shielded mount
Ventilators for forecastle living spaces
18in thick armor belt at waterline

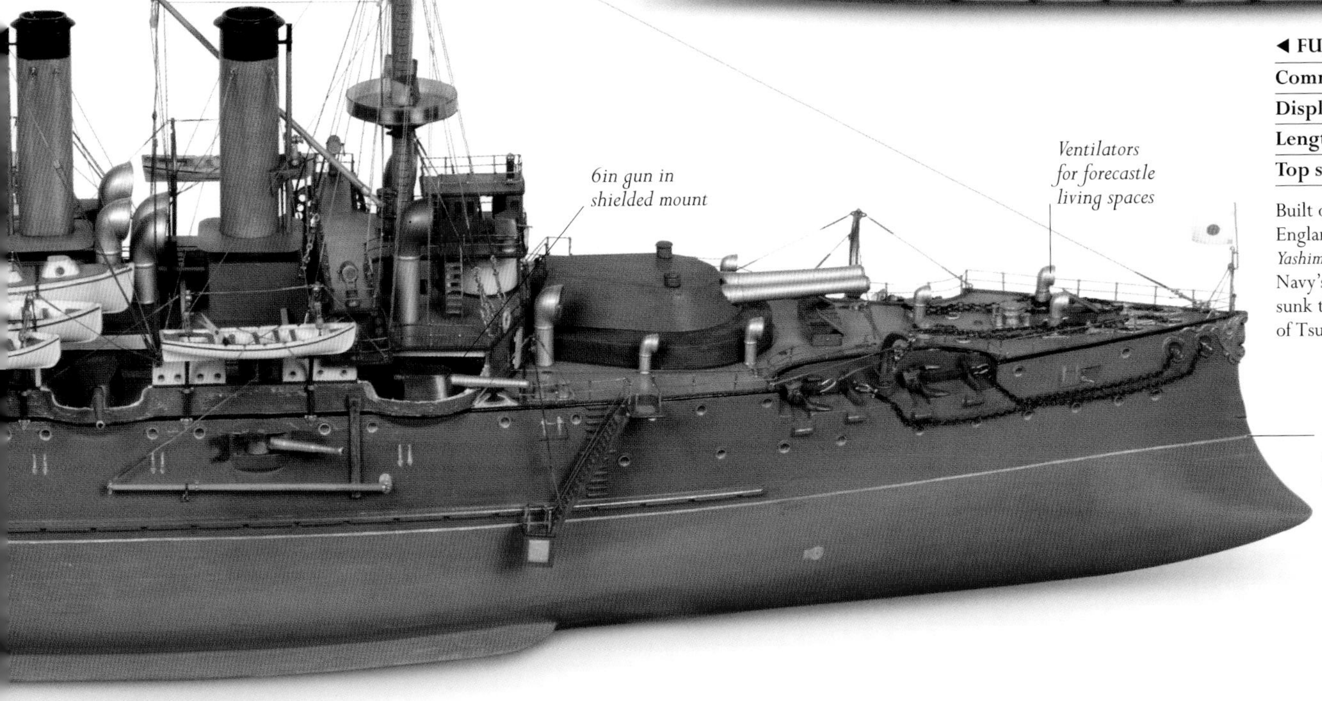

◀ FUJI

Commissioned 1897	**Origin** Japan
Displacement 12,535 tons	
Length 412ft (125.5m)	
Top speed 18 knots	

Built on the Thames in London, England, the *Fuji* and its sister-ship *Yashima* were the Imperial Japanese Navy's first modern battleships. The *Fuji* sunk the Russian *Borodino* at the Battle of Tsushima, Japan, on May 25, 1905.

THE AGE OF STEAM AND BIG GUN

THE BATTLE OF TSUSHIMA

In the second half of the 19th century, new technology transformed the world's navies. Wooden sailing ships were replaced by steel warships with coal-fired engines, armed with powerful rifled guns in rotating turrets. The Russians and Japanese fought the first fleet encounter between these formidable vessels in the Tsushima Strait in May 1905.

Russia and Japan went to war in 1904 over their rival ambitions to control Manchuria and Korea. From the outset the Japanese Imperial Navy outclassed the Russian Pacific Fleet based at Port Arthur and Vladivostok. In a bold bid to redress the balance, Russia decided to send a large part of its Baltic Fleet from European waters to East Asia, a grueling voyage that took seven months. By the time the Russian ships reached the Pacific, Port Arthur had fallen to the Japanese. The Russians had to head for Vladivostok, farther north, which meant steaming past Japan. Short of coal, Russian Admiral Zinovy Petrovich Rozhestvensky chose the shortest route, through the Tsushima Strait between Japan and Korea.

Japanese commander Admiral Togo Heihachiro was on the lookout for the Russian fleet, the progress of which around the world had been a public event. Rozhestvensky hoped to dash through the Strait under cover of darkness, and he might have succeeded but for a new invention: wireless telegraphy (radio). When a Japanese vessel patrolling the Strait spotted the Russian fleet, it was able to inform Admiral Togo instantly. Fast-moving Japanese cruisers kept in visual contact with the Russians, radioing their position to Togo so he could direct his main force in pursuit. The Japanese fleet had no difficulty intercepting the Russians because it enjoyed a substantial speed advantage, steaming at around 15 knots against the 6 knots of the Russian vessels. Battle was joined on the afternoon of May 27.

Both fleets steamed in "line astern" formation—one vessel following another—allowing their turret guns a maximum field of fire without the risk of hitting a friendly ship. Togo turned his fleet to sail parallel to the Russians, with his flagship *Mikasa* in the vanguard. The exchange of fire began at a range of around 6,000 yards (5,500 meters). Crucially, the Japanese had superior range-finding technology, vital if gunners were to hit a target at such distance. They also had shells more suitable for the conditions: whereas the Russians fired armor-piercing rounds, the Japanese shells were fused to explode on contact. Packed with high explosives, they devastated the superstructure of ships they hit, starting fires and raking the decks with deadly steel splinters. Moreover, the Japanese fleet's speed advantage enabled them to "cross the T," sailing their ships across the front of the Russian line. This maneuver brought all their guns to bear on the Russians, while the Russians could only reply with some of their forward guns.

ENDGAME

By nightfall the outclassed Russian fleet had suffered devastation; Admiral Rozhestvensky, wounded by a piece of steel embedded in his skull, was among thousands of casualties. When one of the Russian battleships, the *Borodino*, exploded, a shell striking one of its magazines, 784 of its 785 crew were killed. After dark, the Japanese unleashed their destroyers and torpedo boats upon the fleeing, disorganized enemy. Repeated torpedo runs completed the rout begun by the heavy guns. In total, 17 Russian warships out of the original fleet of 27 were destroyed, including seven battleships. Only three reached Vladivostok.

"CROSSING THE T"
The battle line of Japanese warships, with Admiral Togo's flagship *Mikasa* (see pp. 266–69) leading the fleet, wreaks destruction upon the Russians, triggering fires and explosions with its accurate gunnery.

PRE-DREADNOUGHT BATTLESHIP

MIKASA

The only remaining example of a pre-dreadnought battleship, the *Mikasa* was the Japanese flagship at the Battle of Tsushima, in 1905 (pp.264–65), which saw the Imperial Russian fleet virtually annihilated.

Based on the Royal Navy's Majestic class, the *Mikasa* was the last of four similar battleships built in British yards for the Imperial Japanese Navy. Constructed by Vickers at Barrow-in-Furness, the *Mikasa* entered service on March 1, 1902.

The ship's main armament consisted of four 12in guns, 40 calibers long, mounted in twin center-line turrets fore and aft. These could be fired at a rate of three shots every two minutes. The *Mikasa*'s secondary armament included fourteen 6in quick-firing guns, lighter guns for defense against destroyers and torpedo-boats, and four submerged torpedo tubes.

The *Mikasa* was one of the first ships to have "Krupp Cemented" steel armor. In addition to forming the main deck, this armor was fitted in belts around the waterline up to 9in (23cm) thick, and in 14in- (356mm-) thick "barbettes" around the 12in gun installations. The armor proved effective at Tsushima, when some 30 hits from Russian guns failed to put the *Mikasa* out of action. Ironically, the ship sank in the harbor four months later after an accidental explosion in a magazine. Although raised in 1906 and repaired, the *Mikasa* never saw combat again and was decommissioned in 1923. It is now a museum ship at Yokosuka.

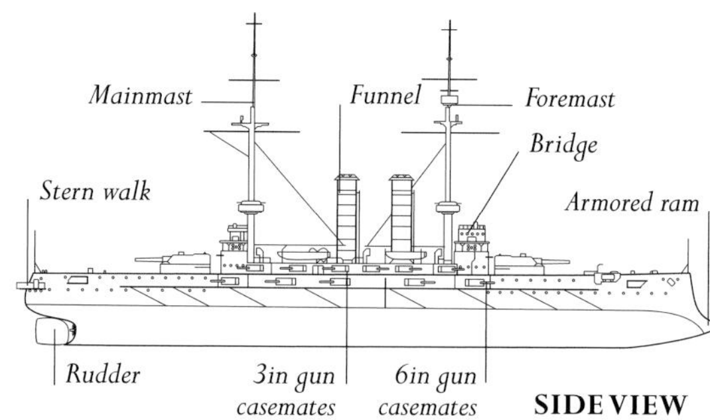

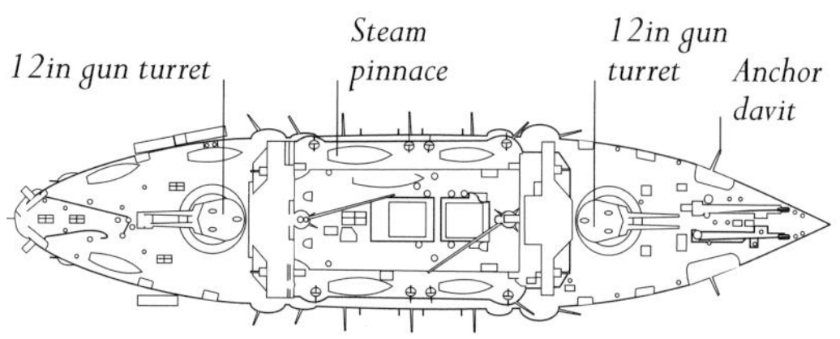

▲ ***MIKASA***
About 432ft (132m) long and displacing 15,180 tons, the *Mikasa* was powered by two triple-expanding steam engines that gave a top speed of 18 knots.

◄ BRIDGE
The pilot house (*left*) and chartroom (*right*) are topped by an open platform bearing a compass and rangefinder. It was from here that Admiral Togo Heihachiro commanded the Japanese fleet at Tsushima.

▼ 12IN GUN TURRET
The *Mikasa*'s original 12in guns could fire a 850lb (385kg) projectile 8½ miles (13.5km). They were replaced by 45-caliber pieces during the 1906 rebuild.

BRIDGE AND FORWARD

▲ FORE ANCHOR
Once raised, the anchor was returned to a platform just below upper-deck level, rather than to the hawsehole. It was brought there by a davit.

▲ COMMAND POST
Orders were given to the pilothouse via speaking tubes (*left*) beside the compass.

▲ SEARCHLIGHT
The wing searchlights were used to locate other vessels at night and for long-distance signaling.

▲ REAR VIEW OF BRIDGE
Situated in front of the foremast, the bridge gives an uninterrupted view forwards and to each side. The long "wings" of the bridge, on which two 35in (90cm) electric searchlights are mounted, extend the full width of the ship.

▲ PORTHOLE
Small glazed portholes, which could be sealed closed, were located only in unarmored parts of the hull.

AMIDSHIPS AND AFT

▲ **FUNNELS**
The flues from the *Mikasa*'s 25 coal-burning boilers connected to two tall, closely set vertical funnels.

▲ **STERN WALKWAY**
As always in such ships, the admiral's cabin was located in the very stern of the vessel, and was furnished with a private walkway. The gilded metal characters spell out the name "*Mi-ka-sa*" in hiragana script.

▲ **MAINMAST**
The two masts flew signals flags, supported radio antennae, and provided lookout positions.

▲ **AFT SKYLIGHT**
Shuttered skylights on the poop deck aft—and also the forecastle deck forward—allowed light and fresh air into the living quarters below.

ARMAMENTS AND QUARTERS

To supplement its main armament, the *Mikasa* mounted a variety of smaller-caliber guns, from 6in ones for use against cruisers and destroyers to 12-, 3-, and 1-pounders. There were also rifle-caliber machine-guns. Living conditions were almost unchanged from the days of sail, with the men sleeping in hammocks and eating at fold-up tables.

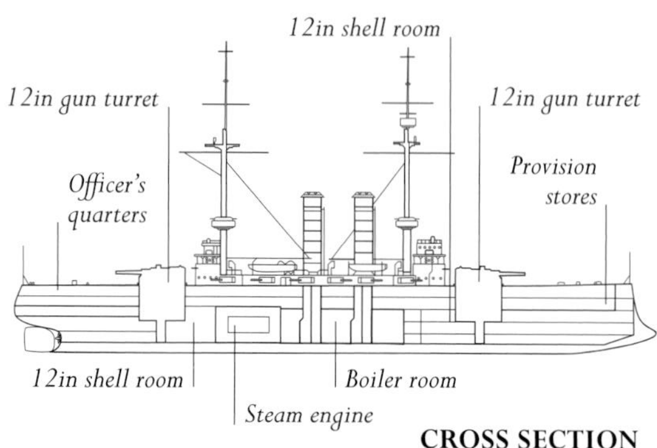

CROSS SECTION

SMALLER GUNS

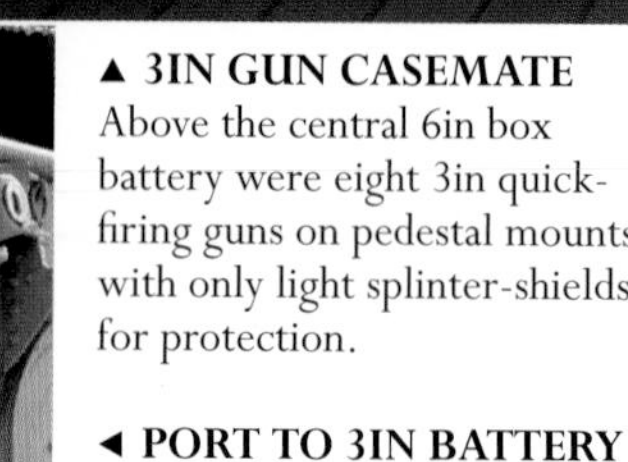

▲ 3IN GUN CASEMATE
Above the central 6in box battery were eight 3in quick-firing guns on pedestal mounts, with only light splinter-shields for protection.

◄ PORT TO 3IN BATTERY
It was through this port that the Russian second-in-command, Rear-Admiral Nikolai Nebogatov, boarded the *Mikasa* to surrender at Tsushima.

► 6IN GUNS
Protected by 2in (5cm) of armor, a central box battery on the main deck housed six 6in guns. A further eight 6in guns in casemates, fore and aft of this battery, and repeated on the deck above, gave a total of 14.

▲ HOTCHKISS 3-POUNDER GUN
These lightweight guns were mounted on simple pedestals, allowing the gunners to follow fast-moving targets such as torpedo-boats.

► RANGEFINDER
The *Mikasa*'s Barr & Stroud rangefinders were far superior to the types used by the Russian ships at Tsushima. They were decisive in the battle, giving the Japanese fleet long-range firepower superiority.

◄ 6IN GUN BREECH
The 6in guns were "quick-firers," their ammunition comprising both projectile and charge in a brass cartridge. They could fire up to six rounds per minute.

BELOW DECK

▲ **PILOT HOUSE**
The ship was "conned" (controlled) from here. The wheel, brass-mounted compass, and engine room telegraphs (used to indicate the speed required) were duplicated in an armored conning tower one deck below.

▲ **PANTRY**
Food prepared below in the galley was brought up to the pantry, where it was plated-up by stewards to be served to officers in the wardroom.

▲ **OFFICERS' WARDROOM**
As well as acting as the officers' dining room, the wardroom was used for meetings. The Imperial Japanese Navy had long adopted the European style of dining, even for ratings (non-officers).

▲ **ADMIRAL'S CABIN**
The admiral's quarters included a day cabin, where he worked, and a sparsely furnished night cabin with a high-sided bunk and limited storage space.

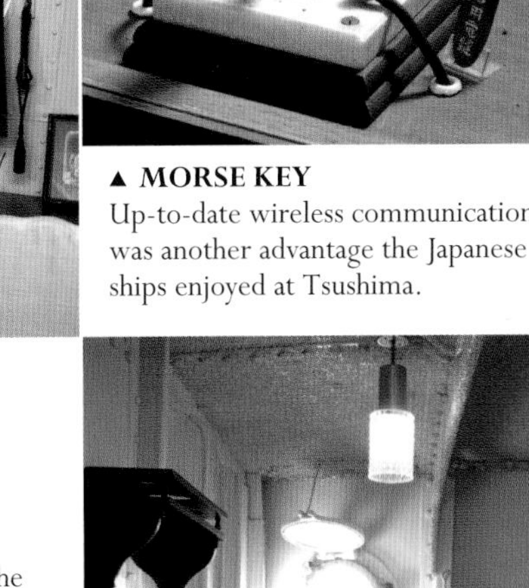

▲ **MORSE KEY**
Up-to-date wireless communication was another advantage the Japanese ships enjoyed at Tsushima.

▼ **ADMIRAL'S SALOON**
For formal meals and discussions with senior staff, the admiral used his saloon. The 3in gun on its pedestal mount was a reminder that this was a warship.

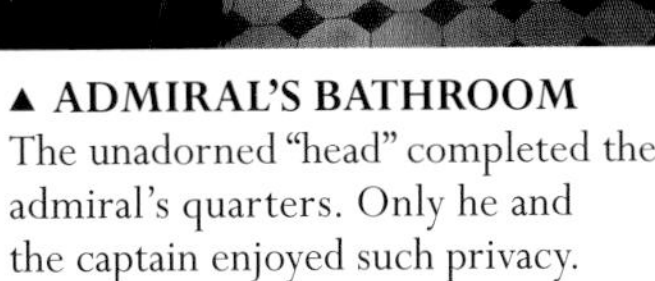

▲ **ADMIRAL'S BATHROOM**
The unadorned "head" completed the admiral's quarters. Only he and the captain enjoyed such privacy.

EARLY CRUISERS

Prior to the 1880s, the term "cruiser" was not recognized as a single group of ships, being composed of frigates, corvettes, and sloops. By the 1890s, however, the new class had taken on a well-defined identity of its own. Capable of long-range action independently of battle fleets, cruisers were able to engage in commerce raiding or to protect national interests in far-flung places. By the turn of the century, cruisers had become the single largest class of warship in service; some navies never commissioned a more powerful, or modern, vessel.

Square sail on foremast

▲ SEIKI

Commissioned 1876	**Origin** Japan
Displacement 900 tons	
Length 200ft (61m)	
Top speed 9.5 knots	

Barque-rigged (with square sails on the fore- and main masts and fore and aft on the mizzen) and wooden-hulled, the screw-sloop *Seiki* was the first ship built at the Yokosuka Navy Yard, to a French design.

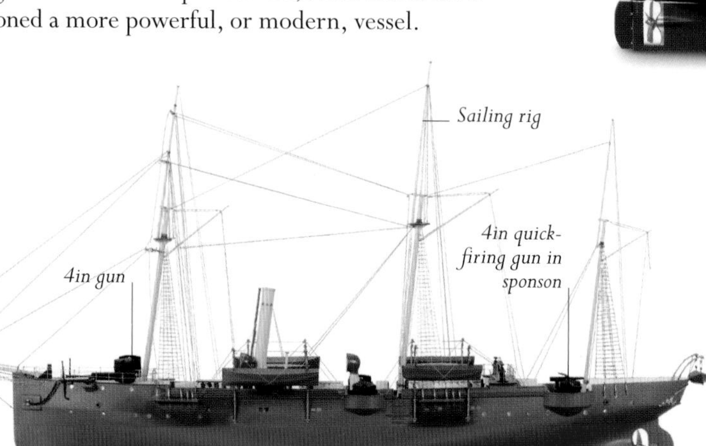

▲ HMS RATTLER

Commissioned 1887	**Origin** UK
Displacement 810 tons	
Length 165ft (50.3m)	
Top speed 13 knots	

A "composite gunboat," with wooden hull-planking on iron frames, the *Rattler* was one of a group of about 30 essentially similar general-purpose, small warships built between 1875 and 1890 for colonial service in Africa and Asia.

▲ TAKAO

Commissioned 1889	**Origin** Japan
Displacement 1,750 tons	
Length 231ft (70.4m)	
Top speed 15 knots	

The first steel-hulled warship built in Japan, the *Takao* was devoid of all protection save for its armament. Built to a French design (by Émile Bertin), and under French supervision, it showed considerable Gallic influence.

▼ HMS GIBRALTAR

Commissioned 1894	**Origin** UK
Displacement 7,700 tons	
Length 387ft (118.1m)	
Top speed 18 knots	

One of a class of nine first-class protected cruisers—with armored decks and no side-armor, but with coal loaded in the hull to give protection—the *Gibraltar* was built for service in the tropics, and its steel hull was clad in wood and copper.

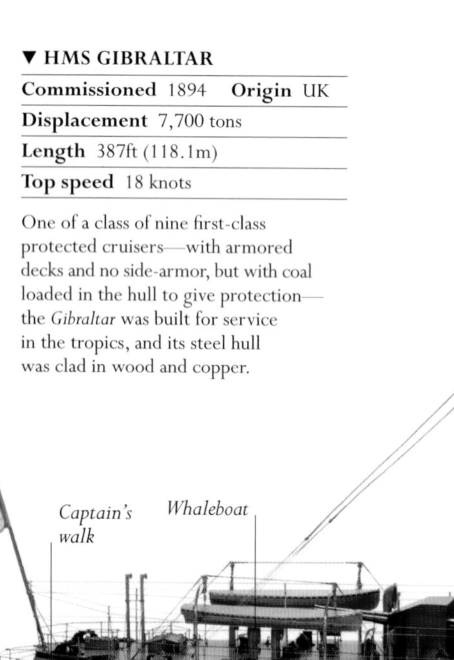

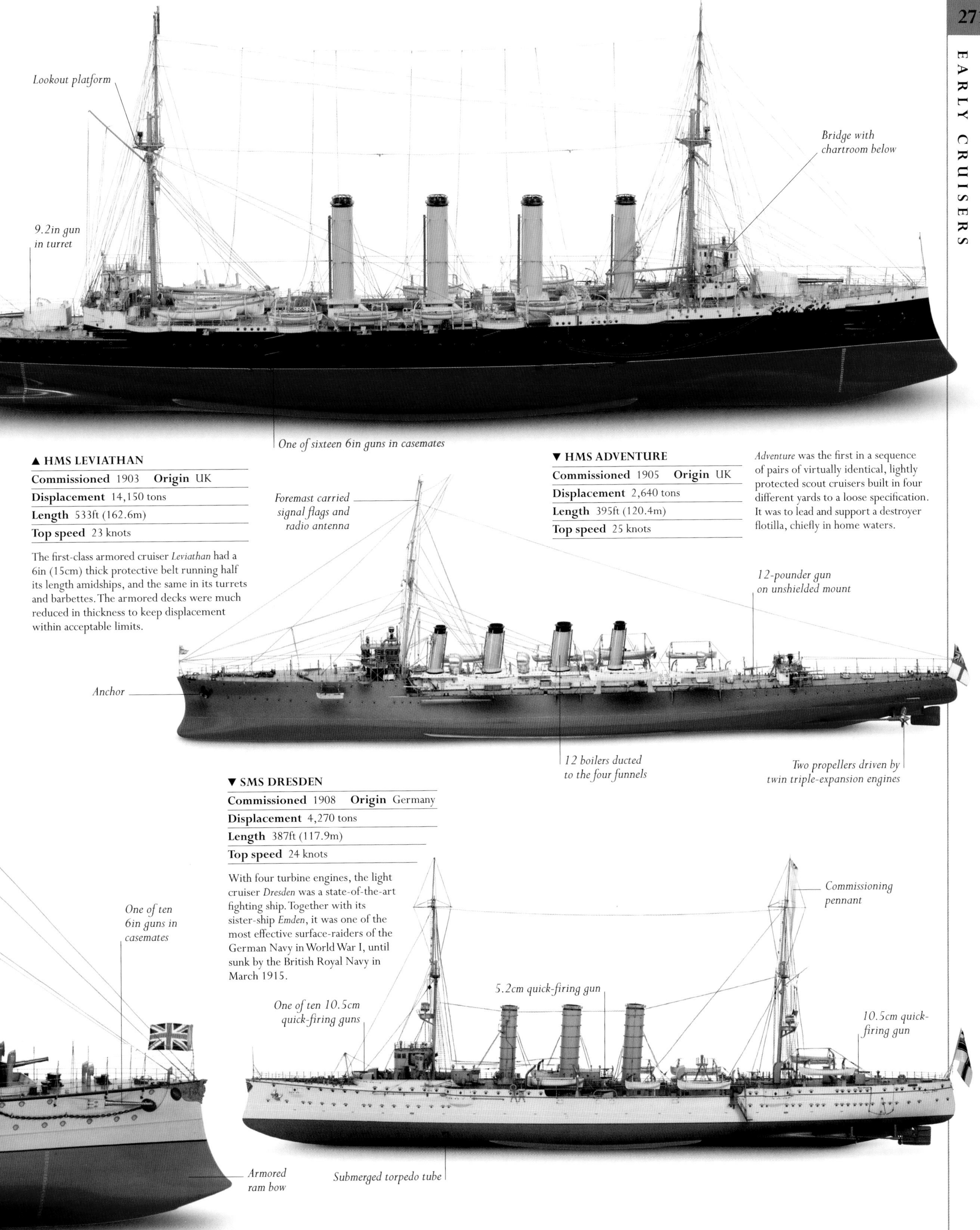

▲ HMS LEVIATHAN

Commissioned 1903 **Origin** UK

Displacement 14,150 tons

Length 533ft (162.6m)

Top speed 23 knots

The first-class armored cruiser *Leviathan* had a 6in (15cm) thick protective belt running half its length amidships, and the same in its turrets and barbettes. The armored decks were much reduced in thickness to keep displacement within acceptable limits.

▼ HMS ADVENTURE

Commissioned 1905 **Origin** UK

Displacement 2,640 tons

Length 395ft (120.4m)

Top speed 25 knots

Adventure was the first in a sequence of pairs of virtually identical, lightly protected scout cruisers built in four different yards to a loose specification. It was to lead and support a destroyer flotilla, chiefly in home waters.

▼ SMS DRESDEN

Commissioned 1908 **Origin** Germany

Displacement 4,270 tons

Length 387ft (117.9m)

Top speed 24 knots

With four turbine engines, the light cruiser *Dresden* was a state-of-the-art fighting ship. Together with its sister-ship *Emden*, it was one of the most effective surface-raiders of the German Navy in World War I, until sunk by the British Royal Navy in March 1915.

TORPEDO BOATS, DESTROYERS, AND SUBMARINES

The perfection of the locomotive torpedo by English engineer Robert Whitehead at Fiume (modern-day Rijeka) in the 1860s changed the face of naval warfare forever. Craft were soon developed specifically to deploy the new weapon, leading to the production of torpedo-boat "destroyers" to combat the threat. Destroyers quickly established themselves as a valuable component of the fleet, taking over the torpedo boats' offensive role when necessary. The torpedo also proved vital to a third class of vessel, the submarine, providing submariners with a viable weapon for use when submerged against surface ships.

▲ LIGHTNING

Commissioned 1876 **Origin** UK
Displacement 33 tons
Length 87½ft (26.7m)
Top speed 18.5 knots

The first torpedo boat built for the British Royal Navy—at the urging of constructor John Thornycroft—was used as an experimental craft. It embodied a variety of innovative features including a divided rudder ahead of the propeller.

Torpedo in drop collars

▲ TB 64

Commissioned 1880 **Origin** UK
Displacement 13 tons
Length 63ft (19.2m)
Top speed 16.5 knots

Second-class torpedo boats, such as the TB 64, were intended to be carried aboard battleships or large cruisers, but were also employed for harbor defense. Drop collars later gave way to tubes for launching their weapons.

4.7in quick-firing gun

▲ ALMIRANTE SIMPSON

Commissioned 1896 **Origin** Chile
Displacement 800 tons
Length 240ft (73.2m)
Top speed 21.5 knots

Strictly speaking, *Almirante Simpson* was a torpedo gunboat, very similar in design, although not in looks, to the British Royal Navy's *Alarm*-class of 1894. This is not surprising given that it was also built by Laird in Birkenhead, England.

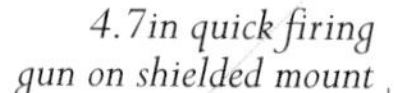

4in quick-firing gun

▲ HMS JACKAL

Commissioned 1911 **Origin** UK
Displacement 990 tons
Length 246ft (75m)
Top speed 27 knots

Jackal was an *Acheron*-class destroyer ordered under the British Royal Navy's 1910–11 Program. It was designed for sturdiness and good seakeeping over speed.

▼ HMS STURGEON

Commissioned 1896 **Origin** UK
Displacement 340 tons
Length 190ft (57.9m)
Top speed 27 knots

Sturgeon was one of the "27-knotters," prototype torpedo-boat destroyers built by 14 different builders to a basic specification but no fixed pattern. It was constructed by Vickers at its Barrow-in-Furness yard, and discarded in 1912.

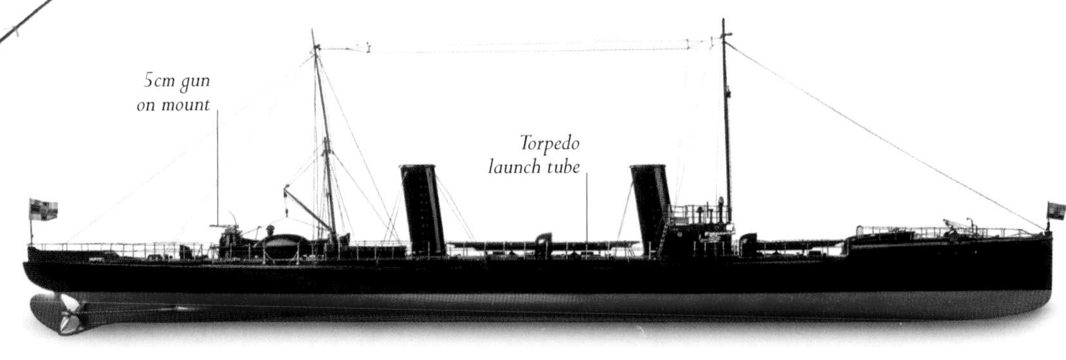

▲ SMS S101

Commissioned 1901 **Origin** Germany
Displacement 388 tons
Length 207ft (63m)
Top speed 26.5 knots

Although officially classed as destroyers, these Schichau-built vessels were, in effect, enlarged torpedo boats, their gun armament being extremely light. Those still in use in September 1914 were reclassified as such, and some were rearmed with 8.8cm guns.

▼ HMS HOLLAND NO. 1

Commissioned 1901 **Origin** UK
Displacement 113 tons (122 tons submerged)
Length 64ft (19.5m)
Top speed 7.5 knots

Britain's Royal Navy came late to submarines, the first such boats—built to an American design by Vickers at Barrow-in-Furness—being delivered 13 years after France commissioned its first, the *Gymnôte*, and four years behind the US Navy.

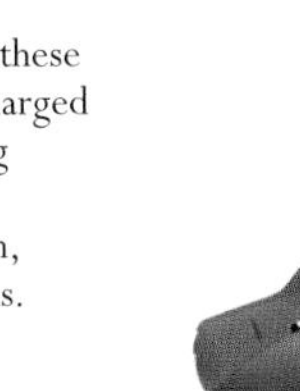

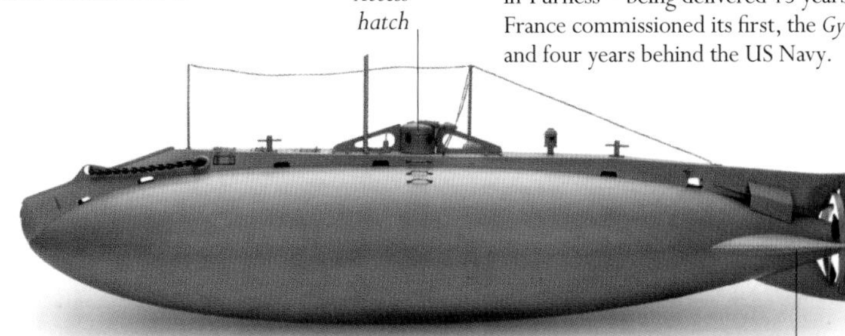

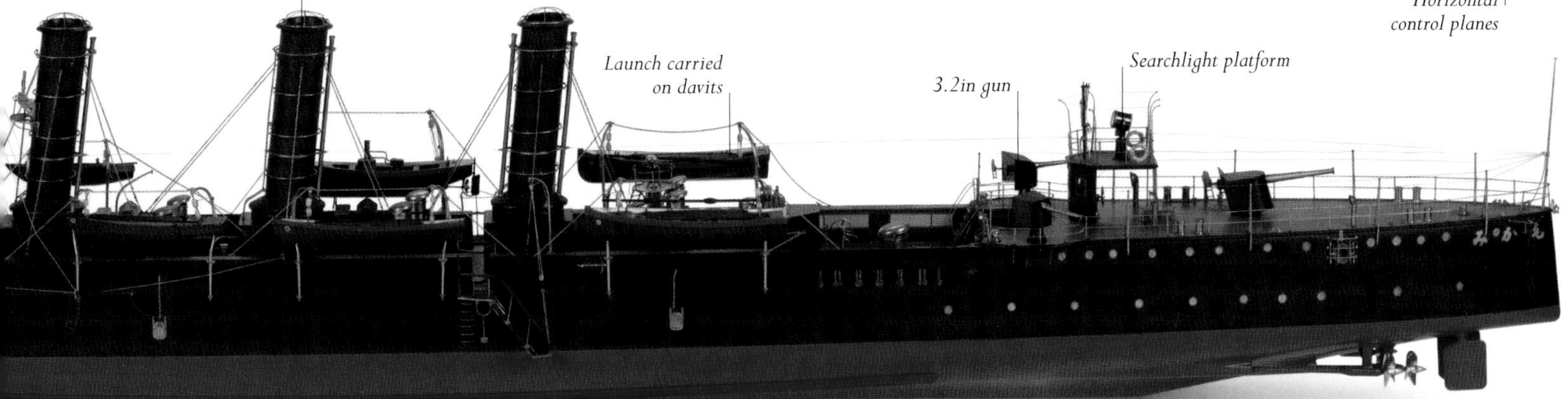

▲ MOGAMI

Commissioned 1908 **Origin** Japan
Displacement 1,350 tons
Length 316ft (96.3m)
Top speed 23 knots

Officially classified as a "despatch vessel," and in fact a miniature protected cruiser, *Mogami* was the first turbine-engined Japanese warship. Its original function was rendered obsolete even before completion by the introduction of wireless telegraphy.

▼ HMS MASTIFF

Commissioned 1914 **Origin** UK
Displacement 1,100 tons
Length 274ft (83.6m)
Top speed 35 knots

By 1914, destroyers had increased considerably in both size and speed. Several of the *M*-class ships were built experimentally, and *Mastiff* was said to be the fastest warship afloat following her sea trials.

1914–1945

THE WORLD WARS

104

INTRODUCTION

The two world wars, from 1914 to 1918, and from 1939 to 1945, were the most destructive conflicts in human history. In terms of technology, the period was marked by the spectacular development of aviation and of motorized warfare, especially tanks.

The pace of development was by no means even. Infantry firepower increased over time, from the introduction of light machine-guns and mortars, to sub-machine-guns, automatic rifles, and, late in World War II, assault rifles. But there is no comparison between this scale of change and the absolute transformation of aerial warfare. Armies entered World War I with a few hundred flimsy, unarmed reconnaissance aircraft. By 1945, however, fleets of thousands of multi-engined bombers were able to devastate enemy cities, while ground forces could barely operate if their opponents controlled the skies. Dominance in naval battles shifted from large battleships to aircraft carriers, while submarines established themselves, unexpectedly, as potentially war-winning commerce raiders.

The tank, a useful—if clumsy—adjunct to World War I infantry operations, was vital to the fast-moving motorized warfare of World War II, when coordinated by radio with ground-attack aircraft serving as aerial artillery. The motor truck eventually made horse-drawn transport obsolete, although, as late as 1941, Germany still used hundreds of thousands of horses for its invasion of the Soviet Union.

The pressure of war generated a search for "wonder weapons," as scientists were enlisted to help the military effort. Poison gas proved indecisive in World War I, and chemical weapons were not used between 1939 and 1945. The jet aircraft, V-1 flying bomb, and V-2 ballistic missile were all introduced by Germany late in World War II, without affecting the outcome of the conflict; however, the atom bomb, developed by the United States between 1942 and 1945 at vast cost, truly heralded a new era in warfare.

KEY DATES

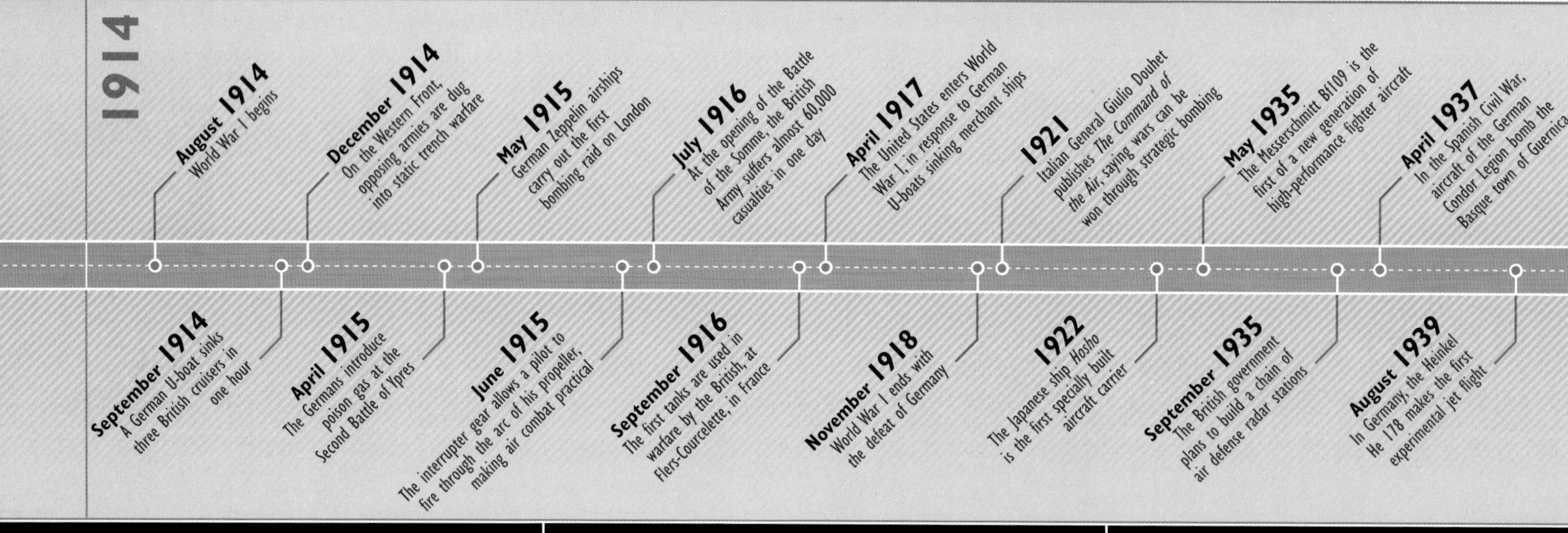

THE BATTLE OF VERDUN—1916

THE BATTLE OF ARRAS—1917

US GROUND FORCES—c.1943

September 1939
World War II begins in Europe

April 1940
The Germans drop parachute troops during their invasion of Norway

May–June 1940
The German army defeats the British and French using "Blitzkrieg" tactics

June 1940
The Battle of Britain begins—the first battle fought exclusively in the air

September 1940
German aircraft bomb London, opening the Blitz, which went on until May 1941

June 1941
Germany and its allies invade the Soviet Union, in Operation Barbarossa

December 1941
A strike by Japanese naval aircraft devastates the US fleet at Pearl Harbor, in the Pacific

June 1942
The Battle of Midway is fought between American and Japanese aircraft carriers in the Pacific

February 1943
After months, Soviet troops win a decisive victory at Stalingrad

July 1943
Allied bombers destroy the German city of Hamburg, killing 40,000 people

July–August 1943
The largest tank battle of World War II is fought at Kursk, on the Eastern Front, between the Soviet Union and Germany

June 1944
The D-day landings in Normandy are the world's largest amphibious operation

June 1944
German V-1 flying bombs strike London, England

September 1944
Germany attacks Allied cities with V-2 ballistic missiles

April–May 1945
Soviet troops occupy the German capital, Berlin, ending World War II in Europe

August 1945
The United States drops atom bombs on the Japanese cities of Hiroshima and Nagasaki

1945

THE BATTLE OF LEYTE GULF—1944

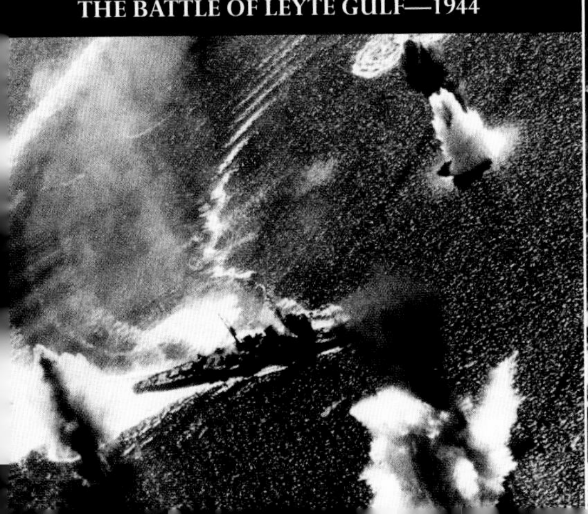

THE BOMBING OF DRESDEN—1945

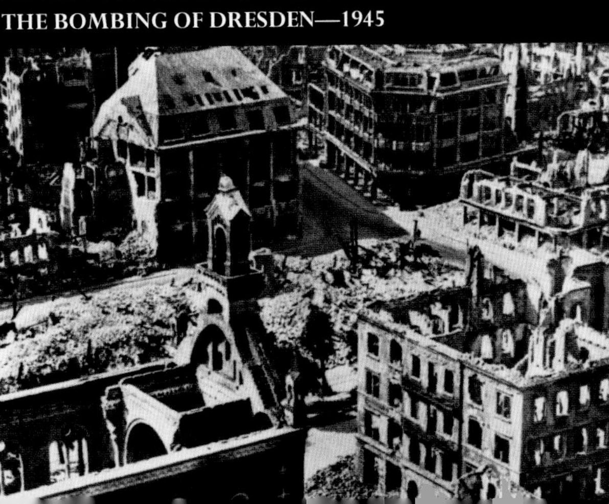

DIVE-BOMBER—c.1945

KEY **BATTLE**

BATTLE OF VERDUN
1916

In February 1916, the Germans attacked the French trenches at Verdun, firing over a million shells in their preliminary bombardment. A battle of attrition followed, in which more than 500,000 men died, with little gain to either side.

▲ French soldiers advance across no-man's-land, in a 1928 film recreating the infantry assault at Verdun.

▼ PASSCHENDAELE
Australian soldiers advance across duckboards during the Battle of Passchendaele, on the Western Front, in 1917. Artillery shells and wet weather combined to create nightmarish fighting conditions, with movement hampered by thick mud and deep, water-filled craters.

KEY DEVELOPMENT

TRENCH WARFARE

World War I (1914–18) was industrialized conflict on a massive scale, with factories supplying weapons and munitions for armies totaling millions. Trench warfare, born out of this new, large-scale firepower, favored the defenders, especially if they were protected behind barbed wire.

By 1915, a double line of trenches stretched across France and Belgium, with troops facing one another across no-man's-land. This new kind of field fortification was a response to increasing artillery and infantry firepower, as was the adoption of steel helmets by all armies. Trenches developed into elaborate defense systems: the Germans in particular constructed complexes of concrete bunkers and concealed machine-gun nests that extended for miles behind the front line (see pp.286–87).

ATTACK AND DEFENSE

Offensives in the initial stages of trench warfare involved a sustained preliminary artillery bombardment—designed to destroy enemy defenses by sheer quantity of high-explosive shells—followed by a frontal infantry assault. Often, however, the defenders survived the bombardment, and slaughtered the attackers as they tried to cross no-man's-land, using machine-guns and rapid-fire rifles. Even when enemy front-line trenches were captured, assaults floundered as the attackers pushed farther forward over ground that had been churned up by shells. The advancing troops could no longer communicate with their own lines by field telephone, with the result that the defenders were often able to move reserves to a danger spot quicker than the attackers could reinforce their offensive. Cavalry units, the only forces capable of rapid movement, were highly vulnerable to infantry and artillery fire, and hampered by barbed wire and shell craters.

BREAKING THE DEADLOCK

Commanders began to seek technological solutions to address or overcome the stalemate of trench warfare. The Germans introduced poison gas, which was first pumped from cylinders and later delivered by artillery shells. Used by both sides,

◂ CANADIAN TROOPS GO "OVER THE TOP" The moment of climbing out of the frontline trench to advance on the enemy—known as going "over the top"—was dreaded by every infantryman. Junior officers traditionally led the way into no-man's-land, themselves unarmed or carrying only a pistol.

gas claimed many thousands of lives and contributed to the general misery of trench life, but it had no decisive effect.

The British placed great faith in tanks. These slow-moving armored vehicles advanced in front of the infantry in many offensives from 1916 onward. However, their effectiveness was limited by their tendency to break down and, in spite of their heavy armor, their vulnerability to artillery fire.

In the end, trench warfare was transformed by a gradual evolution of artillery and infantry tactics, integrating new technology in effective ways. Aerial observation from aircraft and tethered balloons, linked to the ground by radio, improved the targeting of big guns. Flash-spotting and sound-ranging techniques allowed gunners to pinpoint and destroy enemy batteries, based on the sight and sound of their gunfire. The tight coordination of artillery and infantry was crucial to the "rolling barrage"—a curtain of supporting shellfire advancing only 165ft (50m) ahead of the soldiers. Light machine-guns, grenades, portable mortars, and flame-throwers improved the armament of attacking troops, while German elite Stormtroopers used shock assault tactics to punch holes in enemy defenses. In 1918, Germany's assault on Allied trenches—and its eventual failure—signaled the end of trench warfare in World War I.

KEY EVENTS

1914–18

- **November 1914** After an initial phase of mobile warfare, the armies on the Western Front settle into entrenched positions.
- **April 1915** The Germans make the first effective use of poison gas, releasing chlorine from cylinders against unprotected French colonial and Canadian troops at the Second Battle of Ypres.
- **July 1916** On the first day of the Somme offensive, British troops suffer more than 57,000 casualties, including 19,000 killed.
- **June 1917** At Messines, 19 mines explode simultaneously in tunnels dug under German lines, killing 10,000 and allowing a British advance.
- **November 1917** Massed British tanks help infantry achieve a breakthrough at Cambrai, although the opportunity is not exploited.
- **March 1918** German forces, spearheaded by Stormtroopers, achieve a major breakthrough in the Michael offensive. Mobility returns to the war, which ends in the defeat of Germany, in November.

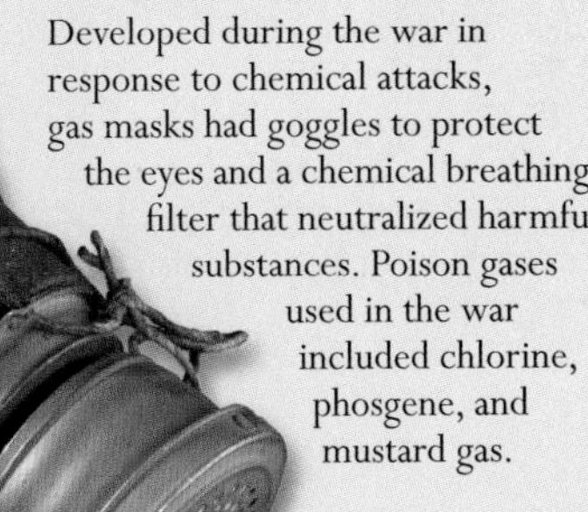

◂ A GERMAN GAS MASK Developed during the war in response to chemical attacks, gas masks had goggles to protect the eyes and a chemical breathing filter that neutralized harmful substances. Poison gases used in the war included chlorine, phosgene, and mustard gas.

> "[The regiment's] assault **failed of success** because **dead men** can advance no farther"
>
> **GENERAL BEAUVOIR DE LYLE**, ON THE NEWFOUNDLAND REGIMENT, JULY 1, 1916

UNIFORMS AND EQUIPMENT

Until the latter years of the 19th century, a soldier went into battle wearing the same colorful outfit he wore on the parade ground, but this changed with the advent of revised infantry tactics. The need for concealment led to the adoption of khaki, field-gray, and similar neutral tones. Protective body armor, which was abandoned when plate and mail proved vulnerable to bullets, was not to return until the development of flak jackets in World War II.

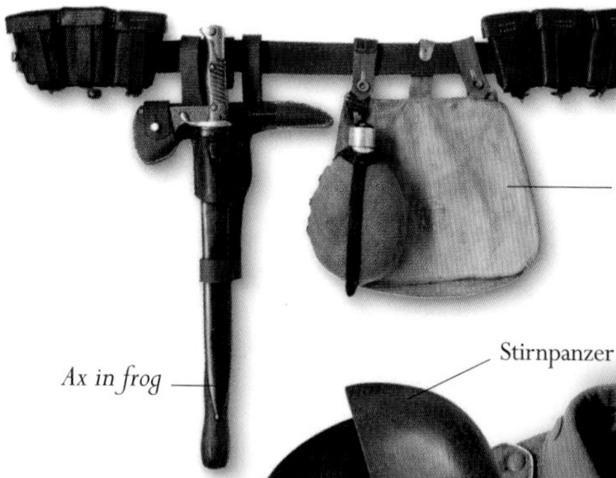

Water bottle in holder

Ax in frog

◀ STORM TROOPER EQUIPMENT

Date 1916

Origin Germany

Material Leather, cotton, brass

German storm troopers were issued with a belt kit that included bags for grenades to supplement ammunition pouches, frogs to hold an ax and the favored short bayonet-cum-trench knife, and a water bottle.

▶ BRITISH UNIFORM

Date 1902

Origin UK

Material Wool

British troops in India took up khaki uniforms as early as the 1850s. They were formally adopted in 1897, and the darker shade shown here came into use in 1902. Also shown is the belt of the 1908-pattern webbing system, with ammunition pouches and a bayonet "frog"—a strap for suspending an item from the belt.

Service dress tunic

Stirnpanzer

Nickel/silicon steel

▶ GERMAN STORM TROOPER UNIFORM

Date 1916

Origin Germany

Material Wool, leather

When the first "Stormtroop" (*Sturmabteilung*) detachments went into action in 1916, they adopted a combat dress with leather reinforcing patches on the elbows and knees, along with lighter boots. Based on the medieval sallet, the original *Stahlhelm* helmet had ventilators above each temple, from which a much heavier brow plate could be hung. This plate, the *Stirnpanzer*, weighed 8¾lb (4kg) and was worn only when absolutely necessary.

Reinforcing leather patch

Distinctive reinforcing band

▲ ITALIAN UNIFORM

Date 1915

Origin Italy

Material Wool, steel

Italy switched to a gray-green uniform, similar to the German *feldgrau*, in 1915. The army also adopted a steel helmet similar to the French "Adrian," with its reinforcing band running back across the crown.

▼ FRENCH UNIFORM

Date Up to 1915

Origin France

Material Wool, leather, brass

The French army was one of the last to give up its brightly colored field uniform—red breeches and a long-tailed blue coat—in favor of drab colors. Conversely, it was the first to adopt a steel helmet in place of the cloth *képi*.

Heavy leather belt-and-braces and ammunition pouches

Uniform made from "horizon blue" cloth

Triple-edged Lebel bayonet, nicknamed "Rosalie"

Red woolen breeches

French army boots

▼ RUSSIAN UNIFORM

Date 1914

Origin Russia

Material Wool, leather, sheepskin

Russia adopted light brown for its field uniform in 1907. Cossack units continued to wear the traditional sheepskin *Papakha* hat, while artillerymen were issued a short sword instead of a bayonet.

Sheepskin Papakha *hat*

▼ AMERICAN UNIFORM

Date 1917

Origin US

Material Wool

The US Army introduced olive uniforms in 1902, although some troops had worn the color in the Spanish-American War of 1898. The hat was a hangover from earlier times, but when US forces appeared in Europe in 1917, they had copies of the British steel helmet.

▶ AMERICAN EQUIPMENT

Date 1917

Origin US

Material Cotton, brass

American soldiers were issued webbing comprising a belt and braces, which held ammunition pouches and a water-bottle holder, plus a bayonet frog.

Ammunition pouch

Water-bottle holder

HEAVY MACHINE-GUNS

The most significant and deadly weapons used on the battlefield in World War I, "heavy" machine-guns accounted for more casualties than any other weapons except for artillery. They were capable of maintaining sustained fire for hours on end as long as simple precautions were observed, such as changing barrels regularly. Sited to cover vulnerable features, these guns usually operated in batteries, firing through fixed, interlocking arcs. When combined with barbed wire, they made it almost impossible for infantry to advance without taking enormous losses. Only with the development of effective armored fighting vehicles (AFVs) was their omnipotence overcome.

▶ DWM MG08

Date	1908
Origin	Germany
Weight	58½lb (26.5kg)
Barrel	28¼in (71.9cm)
Caliber	7.92mm Mauser

Soon after the German army acquired its first Maxims in 1895, Deutsche Waffen und Munitionsfabriken (DWM) began modifying the design, and the final version was adopted as the *schweres Maschinengewehr 08*. It had a heavy sledge-style mount, known as the *Schlitten*.

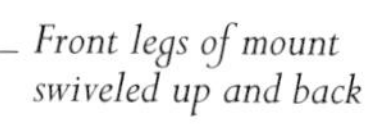

Front legs of mount swiveled up and back

Cooling water in jacket reached boiling point after 600 rounds of rapid fire

Rear sight

Firing grip

Muzzle booster

▲ VICKERS-MAXIM "NEW LIGHT" MODEL 1906

Date	1906
Origin	UK
Weight	43¼lb (19.6kg)
Barrel	28½in (72.3cm)
Caliber	7.7mm

The first departure from Maxim's original design, the "New Light" saw the original brass fittings exchanged for much lighter steel, but continued to employ the downward-breaking locking toggle that made the receiver large. The Russians adopted it as the M1910.

▶ RUSSIAN MAXIM M1910

Date	1910–42
Origin	Russia
Weight	52½lb (23.8kg)
Barrel	28½in (72.1cm)
Caliber	7.62mm

The Imperial Russian arsenal at Tula began manufacturing the Vickers "New Light" model in 1910; it stayed in production until 1942. They were mounted on Sokolov wheeled carriages, which incorporated a turntable, while some, such as this one, were fitted with shields.

Metal, rather than fabric, ammunition belts used

Extended firing grips

Elevation screw

▶ VICKERS "LIGHT PATTERN" MODEL 1908

Date	1908
Origin	UK
Weight	40lb (18.1kg)
Barrel	28½in (72.3cm)
Caliber	7.7mm

Designed to resolve shortcomings in the Vickers-Maxim "New Light" model, the locking toggle was modified in this gun: it now broke upward, reducing the size of the receiver. The "disappearing" tripod mount allowed the gun to be fired from the cover of a parapet.

▶ SCHWARZLOSE M07/12

Date	1912
Origin	Austria-Hungary
Weight	43¾lb (19.9kg)
Barrel	20¾in (52.6cm)
Caliber	8mm Mannlicher

The Schwarzlose was the only heavy machine-gun to use an unlocked "blowback" system, better suited to pistol-caliber ammunition, relying on a very heavy breechblock and return spring to slow the rate of fire. Massively over-engineered, it proved almost indestructible in normal use.

▶ HOTCHKISS MODÈLE 1914

Date	1914
Origin	France
Weight	52lb (23.58kg)
Barrel	30½in (77.5cm)
Caliber	8mm Lebel

The Modèle 1914 was a slight improvement on earlier designs, but was still prone to overheating. It had a problematic feed system that used 24-round metallic strips, rather than fabric belts. However, it was still reliable when used correctly, and saw service until the early 1940s.

▼ FIAT-REVELLI MODEL 1914

Date	1914
Origin	Italy
Weight	37½lb (17kg)
Barrel	25¾in (65.4cm)
Caliber	6.5mm Mannlicher-Carcano

This model employed a delayed "blowback" system to fire underpowered rounds, fed from a 50-round stack magazine and oiled on their way to the chamber. The oiled rounds picked up dust and dirt, causing the gun to jam regularly.

▲ BROWNING M1917

Date	1917
Origin	US
Weight	33lb (14.97kg)
Barrel	24in (61cm)
Caliber	.3in

John Browning produced a poor design of machine-gun for Colt, the gas-operated M1895 "Potato Digger" (see p.245), but later reverted to recoil actuation and improved on Maxim's method of locking barrel and breech together to create the M1917. It saw service in the latter months of World War I, but soon lost its water jacket to become the air-cooled M1919. It remained in use in that form until the 1960s.

LIGHT MACHINE-GUNS AND MACHINE-PISTOLS

Although rapid-fire weapons ruled the battlefields of World War I, they were far too cumbersome to be carried into attack. The first step was to abandon ammunition belts, water-cooling, and the impossibly heavy static mount for magazines, and adopt lighter barrels and the sort of "furniture" found on rifles. These innovations led to the light machine-gun (LMG), which was handy enough, just about, for a man to fire from the hip on the move. The next stage in the development of automatic weapons was a complete departure. The machine-pistol was an entirely new form of a much lighter weapon, firing pistol-caliber ammunition in bursts.

▲ **LEWIS GUN M1914**

Date 1913
Origin US
Weight 26lb (11.8kg)
Barrel 26in (66cm)
Caliber .303in

The air-cooled Lewis Gun was the first LMG used on the Western Front. Taken up by the Belgians, then by the British, it remained in service on the ground, in the air (when it was usually stripped of its barrel shroud), and even at sea until World War II.

▲ **MG13**

Date 1914
Origin Germany
Weight 24lb (10.9kg)
Barrel 28¼in (71.7cm)
Caliber 7.92mm Mauser

The MG13 was developed from a weapon Louis Schmeisser designed and Dreyse produced from 1909. That gun was water-cooled, but the MG13 swapped the water jacket for a perforated shroud, and gained a tubular butt stock and a pistol grip-and-trigger group.

▲ **MAXIM MG08/15**

Date 1915
Origin Germany
Weight 30¾lb (14kg)
Barrel 28½in (71.9cm)
Caliber 7.92mm Mauser

To turn it into an LMG, the MG08's receiver was abbreviated and it got a slimmer water jacket, a bipod, a butt, and a pistol grip and trigger. Ammunition belts were contained in drums.

▲ **BROWNING AUTOMATIC RIFLE (BAR) M1918**

Date 1918
Origin US
Weight 16lb (7.28kg)
Barrel 24in (61cm)
Caliber .30-06 Springfield

John Browning responded to pleas to provide infantrymen with a weapon they could fire in bursts from the hip while advancing. The gas-operated BAR was too heavy and cumbersome ever to be a success in that role, but it survived as the US Army's stock LMG until the 1950s.

▼ BERGMANN LMG15NA

Date	1916
Origin	Germany
Weight	28½lb (12.9kg)
Barrel	28½in (72.6cm)
Caliber	7.92mm Mauser

Bergmann's LMG was adopted in 1910, but it was not until the appearance of a modified version in 1916 that it found favour. Its ammunition was contained in a metal link belt, fed from a drum-like container.

▼ DMW LMG08/15 (LUFTGEKÜHLT MASCHINENGEWEHR)

Date	1915
Origin	Germany
Weight	26½lb (12kg)
Barrel	28¼in (71.9cm)
Caliber	7.92mm Mauser

Though it was also used by infantrymen, fitted with a buttstock and pistol grip, the LMG08/15 was developed as a fixed gun for use in aircraft. In this form, it had a synchronizer cable linked to an interrupter gear, which allowed it to fire through the propeller's arc.

▲ MG08/18

Date	1918
Origin	Germany
Weight	28¾lb (13kg)
Barrel	28¼in (71.9cm)
Caliber	7.92mm Mauser

The MG08/15 was never entirely suitable for use as an assault weapon. Just before the war ended, this revised air-cooled version with a slimmed-down perforated barrel shroud was introduced. It was almost 8¾lb (4kg) lighter than the MG08/15, but came too late to see widespread use.

▲ PARABELLUM LMG14/17

Date	1917
Origin	Germany
Weight	21½lb (9.8kg)
Barrel	27¾in (70.5cm)
Caliber	7.92mm Mauser

Arguably the best of the German Maxims, the Parabellum LMG was produced in response to a specification for a weapon for flexible mounting in aircraft and airships. Its barrel shroud was later slimmed down, and it was issued to selected infantry units in this form toward the end of the war.

▲ BERGMANN MP18/1

Date	1918
Origin	Germany
Weight	9¼lb (4.2kg)
Barrel	7¾in (19.6cm)
Caliber	9mm Parabellum

The strong, sturdy MP18/1 was the first effective machine-pistol. It was chambered for the Parabellum round Luger had developed for the P08 pistol, although that resulted in feed problems until a simpler box magazine was designed.

WORLD WAR I DEFENSES

BAYERNWALD TRENCH

For much of World War I, a line of trenches ran for 435 miles (700km) from the Belgian coast to the Franco-Swiss border west of Basel. Bayernwald was a German trench near Ypres, in Flanders.

Following the "Race to the Sea" after the Battle of the Aisne, in September 1914, the opposing armies dug in to face each other. At first, the trenches they excavated were little more than ditches, but as the deadlock persisted trenches evolved into permanent fortifications incorporating bunkers and protected by belts of barbed wire. The "no-man's-land" between the opposing lines was sometimes as little as 28 yards (25m) wide, but was typically 10 times that.

The height of the trench walls was generally well over that of the soldiers, with sides "riveted" with lumber, wattle, corrugated iron, and sandbags, and their bottoms lined with planks. Strongpoints were constructed using poured concrete or prefabricated blocks brought in at night. The nature of the trenches varied with the terrain, but in low-lying areas like Flanders they were always at risk of flooding, and daily life was a constant struggle against the mud. Since the Germans took up their positions first, they often had the advantage of choosing higher ground that was drier and less exposed to enemy fire.

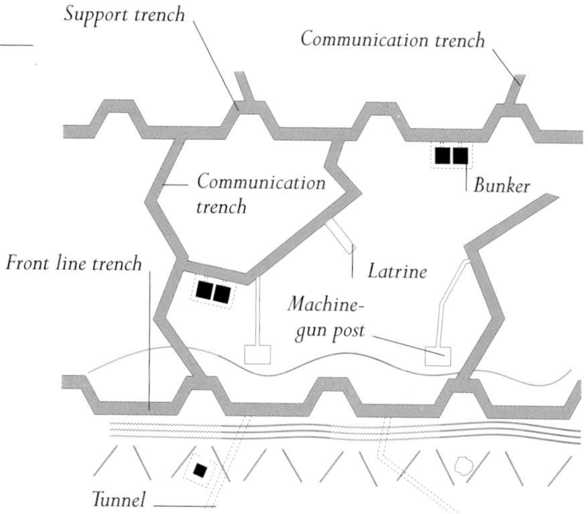

SIMPLIFIED GERMAN TRENCH SYSTEM
Reserve troops and supplies were moved from the support trench to the front via communication trenches, along which telephone lines also ran.

TRENCH STRUCTURE

► FIRESTEP
A simple wooden framework supported a step on which a man could stand to fire over the parapet. This was a risky business, so many soldiers equipped their rifles with a form of periscope.

◄ TRENCH LINE
Trenches followed a meandering, zigzag path. This gave some protection to the occupants against shrapnel and blasts from artillery rounds and grenades. It also prevented an enemy who had managed to break in from firing along the trench.

▲ SHALLOW TRENCH
Built in a raised location overlooking the enemy, the Bayernwald trench could be shallower than usual yet still protect troops from direct fire.

▲ CROSS-TIMBER
Trenches were bridged with timber beams; they supported roof sections, telephone lines, or hoses to pump out water.

BUNKERS AND TUNNELS

▶ **SHELTER**
There were 10 two-room bunkers on this site. They were not strong enough to withstand a direct hit from artillery, but did protect their occupants from shrapnel and small-arms fire.

▲ **CONSTRUCTION**
The bunkers were built from pre-cast concrete blocks, carried in from a nearby narrow-gauge railway. Four bunkers and a protected mortar emplacement survive.

▲ **CONFINED SPACES**
Headroom within the bunkers was no more than 4ft (1.2m). In part, this was to ensure that troops sheltering inside would never get too comfortable.

▲ **TUNNEL ENTRANCE**
When conditions allowed, both sides tried to tunnel under the opposing lines, usually in order to explode mines.

▲ **ACCESS SHAFT**
Vertical shafts gave access to the tunnels. Fierce fighting broke out when opposing tunnelers broke into each other's workings.

FIELD GUNS, SIEGE GUNS, AND HOWITZERS

The artillery pieces in use by 1914 were capable of inflicting casualties on an industrial scale. They ranged from mountain guns that could be broken down quickly and carried by mules, and light guns such as the 18-pounder quick-firer—which were used on the battlefield rather than fired from a dug-in position—to howitzers such as the British Army's 9.2in Mark I. The latter arrived in France early in 1915 and became the most effective counter-battery weapon of the war, capable of hurling a 290lb (130kg) high-explosive shell to a distance of more than 5½ miles (9km). Guns mounted on railway tracks that could reach a target more than 25 miles (40km) away were used for long-range bombardment.

▼ 2.75IN MOUNTAIN GUN

Date	1911
Origin	UK
Weight	1,290lb (585kg)
Length	6ft (1.84m)
Caliber	2.75in
Range	3.41 miles (5.5km)

This was an improved version of the tried-and-tested 10-pounder mountain gun. For transportation, the barrel broke down into two sections and the rest of the gun into a further three. It could be carried by six mules, or towed.

Barrel could be depressed to -15° and elevated to +22°

Recoil recuperator

◀ 6IN (30CWT) HOWITZER

Date	1896
Origin	UK
Weight	3.86 tons (3.5 tonnes)
Length	7ft (2.13m)
Caliber	6in
Range	4.28 miles (6.9km)

The 6in howitzer could be fired as a siege gun on a static siege platform or on a field carriage. It was employed by the British Army during the Second Boer War and in the early months of World War I.

Recuperator wrapped with rope

Goniometric sight for indirect fire

Gun captain to traverse the weapon

Single-pole trail

Recoil recuperator

▲ 18-POUNDER QF MARK II

Date	1904
Origin	UK
Weight	1.41 tons (1.28 tonnes)
Length	7¾ft (2.34m)
Caliber	3.3in
Range	3.72 miles (6km)

The standard British field gun for almost four decades, the 18-pounder was first introduced in 1904. It fired a wide variety of projectiles, including high explosive, shrapnel, gas, and armor-piercing rounds. Its six-man crew could fire 20 rounds per minute for short periods.

▶ 9.2IN SIEGE HOWITZER MK I

Date	1914
Origin	UK
Weight	13.2 tons (12 tonnes)
Length	11ft (3.4m)
Caliber	9.2in
Range	5.71 miles (9.2km)

This was the Allies' most effective counter-battery weapon, destroying enemy artillery from concealed positions well behind the fighting front. More than 650 were employed on the Western Front by the British and US armies.

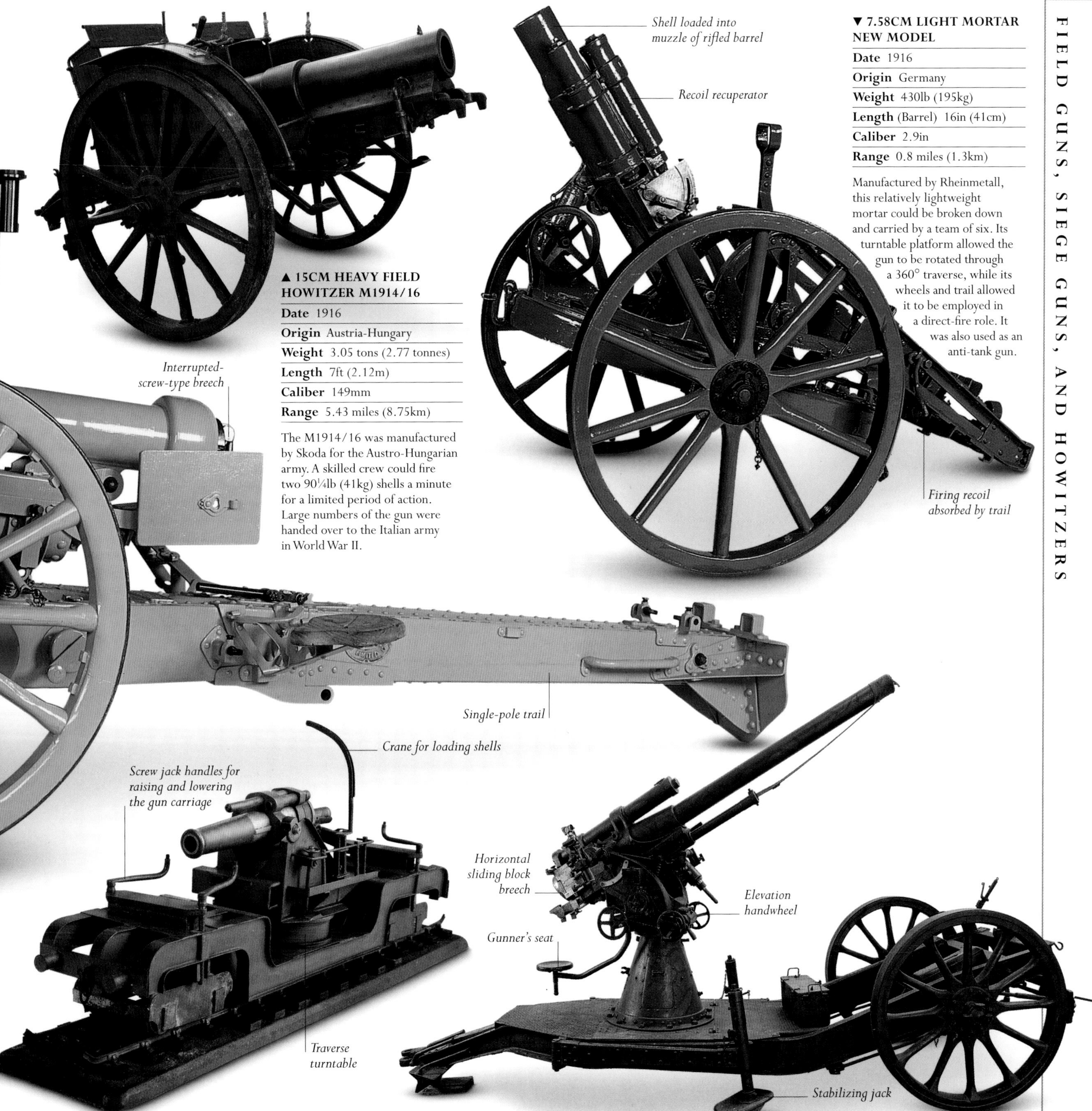

▼ 7.58CM LIGHT MORTAR NEW MODEL

Date	1916
Origin	Germany
Weight	430lb (195kg)
Length	(Barrel) 16in (41cm)
Caliber	2.9in
Range	0.8 miles (1.3km)

Manufactured by Rheinmetall, this relatively lightweight mortar could be broken down and carried by a team of six. Its turntable platform allowed the gun to be rotated through a 360° traverse, while its wheels and trail allowed it to be employed in a direct-fire role. It was also used as an anti-tank gun.

▲ 15CM HEAVY FIELD HOWITZER M1914/16

Date	1916
Origin	Austria-Hungary
Weight	3.05 tons (2.77 tonnes)
Length	7ft (2.12m)
Caliber	149mm
Range	5.43 miles (8.75km)

The M1914/16 was manufactured by Skoda for the Austro-Hungarian army. A skilled crew could fire two 90¼lb (41kg) shells a minute for a limited period of action. Large numbers of the gun were handed over to the Italian army in World War II.

▲ 12IN HOWITZER MARK I ON RAILWAY MOUNTING

Date	1916
Origin	UK
Weight	64.81 tons (58.81 tonnes)
Length	12ft (3.7m)
Caliber	12in
Range	6.31 miles (10.17km)

Manufactured by the Elswick Ordnance Company for the British Army, 12in railway howitzers were operated in pairs by British Royal Garrison Artillery. The short-barrelled Mark I was soon superseded by the longer-barrelled Mark III, which had 40 per cent greater range, and the Mark V, which had much-improved traverse.

▲ 7.7CM SOCKEL-FLAK

Date	1916
Origin	Germany
Weight	2.27 tons (2.06 tonnes)
Length	8¾ft (2.7m)
Caliber	77mm

The 7.7cm Sockel-flak was responsible for bringing down many of the 1,600 Allied aircraft that fell victim to anti-aircraft guns in World War I. It fired a 15lb (6.8kg) shell, which a skilled crew of six could fire at a rate of more than 20 rounds per minute. The effective ceiling of this gun was 15,584ft (4,750m).

TRENCH-FIGHTING WEAPONS

Throughout World War I, assaults on enemy positions almost inevitably ended in hand-to-hand combat in the confined spaces of trenches and dugouts. Pistols came into their own in such circumstances, but were issued mainly to officers. Individual soldiers armed themselves with the rifle-and-bayonet as well as expedient weapons such as knives and axes, which were chosen for their ability to disable or kill at a single stroke. The design of early grenades, although not entirely satisfactory, soon improved dramatically.

▶ LUGER P08

Date 1908–42
Origin Germany
Weight 31oz (880g)
Barrel 4in (10cm)
Caliber 9mm Parabellum

Georg Luger's Pistole '08—the P08 or "Parabellum"—was the German officer's handgun of choice during World War I. Its 9mm Parabellum round (9×19mm) was more powerful than others of similar dimensions, and became a world standard.

▼ STICK GRENADE

Date 1915
Origin Germany
Weight 21oz (595g)
Length 14¼in (36.5cm)

The *Stielhandgranate* first saw service with German troops, and became one of the Stormtroopers' iconic weapons. The handle gave the thrower a significant range advantage over one armed with grenades such as the Mills bomb.

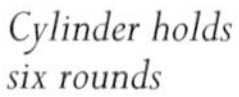

▶ COLT NEW SERVICE

Date 1909–41
Origin US
Weight 2½lb (1.15kg)
Barrel 5½in (14.4cm)
Caliber .45 Colt

American officers were issued with Colt "automatics" but some felt that they were likely to jam. Most preferred the last revolver produced for the US Army—the .45-caliber Colt New Service.

▼ SMLE MKIII RIFLE WITH WIRE-CUTTING ATTACHMENT

Date 1907
Origin UK
Weight 8lb (3.7kg)
Barrel 25in (64cm)
Caliber .303in

The battlefields of World War I were festooned with barbed-wire entanglements, and many methods for dealing with this were tested. One involved fitting sprung cutting jaws to the muzzle of an SMLE rifle, but this proved ineffective.

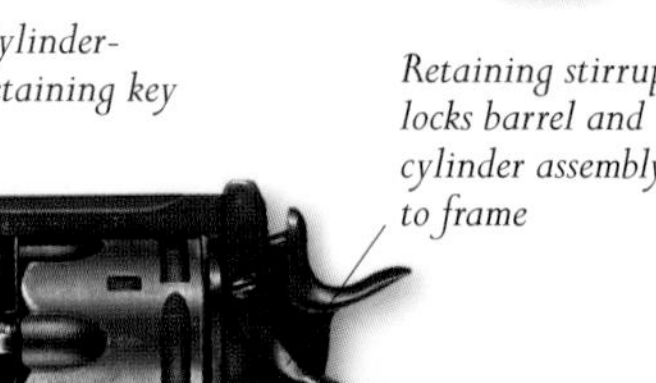
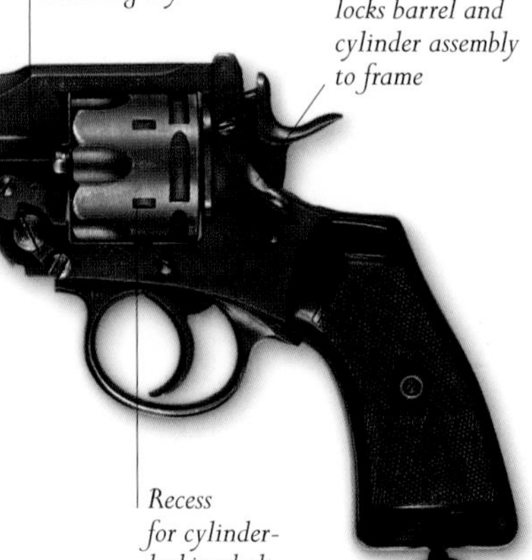

▶ WEBLEY & SCOTT MK VI

Date 1915
Origin UK
Weight 2¼lb (1.05kg)
Barrel 6in (15.2cm)
Caliber .455 Eley

Birmingham arms manufacturer Webley & Scott began supplying pistols to the British Army in 1887. The Mk VI was the last of them, and was prized for its rugged reliability.

▶ TRENCH AX

Date 1916
Origin UK

Issued to British troops as a general-purpose tool, the trench ax was widely employed as a weapon in close-quarter fighting during raids and assaults on enemy positions.

▲ WINCHESTER TRENCH GUN

Date	1897
Origin	US
Weight	8lb (3.6kg)
Barrel	20in (51cm)
Caliber	12-bore

The Winchester Repeating Arms Company commissioned gun-designer John Moses Browning to develop a pump-action shotgun, and he produced the M1897. Its six-round magazine made it extremely useful to the combat infantryman.

▼ NAILED COSH

Date	1916
Origin	UK

The simplest trench-fighting weapons were clubs and truncheons, often—as in this example—with nails or spikes added to increase their lethality, and usually with a retaining loop.

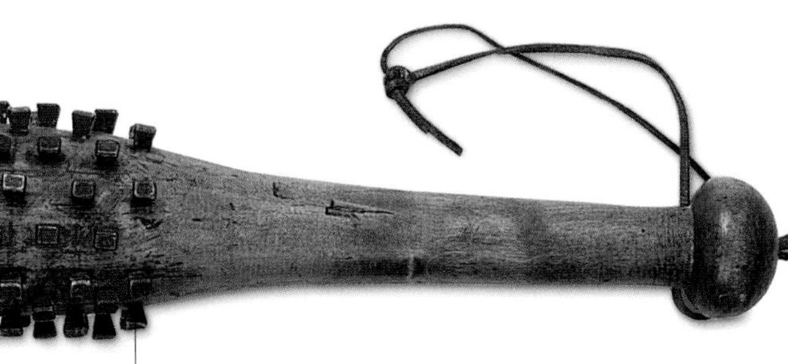

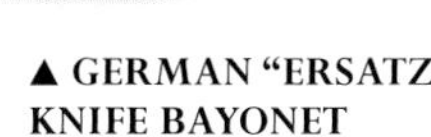

▲ GERMAN "ERSATZ" KNIFE BAYONET

Date	1917
Origin	Germany
Weight	7¾oz (220g)
Length	10¼in (26.1cm)

This short, double-edged bayonet, developed privately to fit the Mauser GeW'98 rifle, doubled as a combat knife, and many German soldiers bought one for themselves.

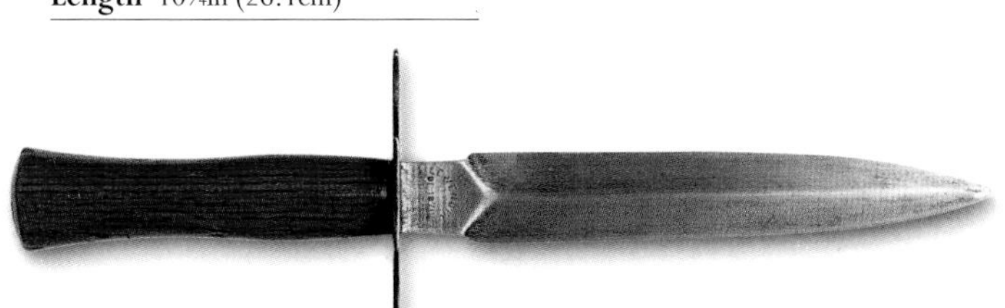

▲ BRITISH SPIKED CLUB

Date	c.1916
Origin	UK

This club, hand-whittled from hardwood, incorporates both horseshoe nails and a stabbing spike in its enlarged head. It also has serrations to improve the grip, and a wrist strap for security.

▲ FRENCH TRENCH KNIFE

Date	1916
Origin	France

This was a simple stabbing and slashing weapon with a double-edged blade, a steel cross-guard, and an unadorned wooden grip, perhaps made at Laguiole in the Aveyron *département* of south-central France.

▶ NO. 36 MILLS BOMB

Date	1915
Origin	UK
Weight	27oz (765g)
Length	3¾in (95.2mm)

Grenades became more effective when reliable time-fuses became available. The British Mills Bomb, with its "pineapple" casing filled with a TNT-based explosive called Baratol, was the first of its type, and was widely copied.

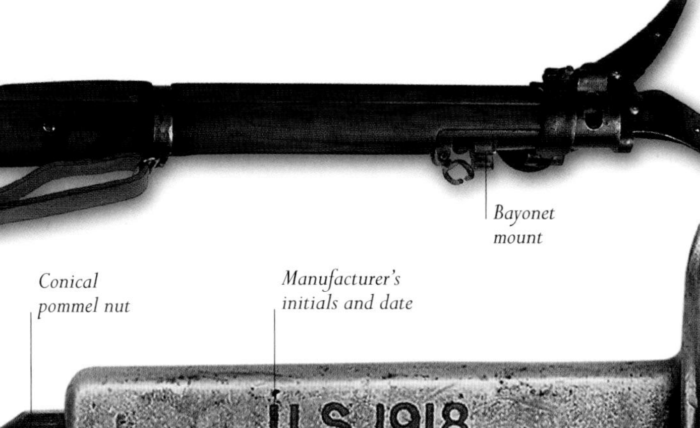

◀ AMERICAN KNUCKLE-DUSTER TRENCH KNIFE

Date	1918–45
Origin	US
Weight	17½oz (500g)
Length	22in (56cm)

This combination weapon's conical pommel nut was designed to puncture the human skull. The spiked knuckle-duster made a punch potentially lethal, while the blade was used to slash or stab.

THE BATTLE OF ARRAS

Caught in the stalemate of trench warfare, armies on the Western Front in World War I sought a fresh approach. In the Battle of Arras in April 1917, British and Commonwealth forces had initial success in infantry assaults on German lines, but fell short of the longed-for breakthrough.

British commanders at Arras were determined to avoid the disasters of the Somme offensive the previous year, when troops had plodded in lines toward machine-gun fire. Artillery and infantry planned to mount a skillful combined assault on the German positions, including the well-held Vimy Ridge. Before the operation, tunnels leading to the front were excavated to shelter the assembling troops. The longest of these tunnels was over a mile in length. Short trenches or "saps" stretched into the no-man's-land between the trench lines to provide advanced jumping-off points for the assault. Artillery observers, meanwhile, plotted the positions of German heavy guns, using sophisticated sound-ranging techniques and spotting their muzzle flashes when they fired. This enabled British gunners to deliver accurate counter-battery fire, suppressing the German artillery when the attack began. Infantry and artillery officers also worked on coordinating a "creeping barrage"—a moving screen of exploding shells in front of advancing Allied troops.

The offensive was preceded by a week-long bombardment of the German lines by more than 900 guns. This sacrificed any hope of surprise, but special fuses allowed shells to effectively break up the barbed wire in front of the German trenches—an essential preparation for the infantry advance. The attack was launched at 5:30am on Easter Monday, April 9, with Canadian troops assigned to the sector in front of Vimy Ridge.

Soldiers moved forward, keeping some 50 yards (46m) behind the creeping artillery barrage. Other guns subdued the German batteries and fired poison gas shells into their defenses. Massed British machine-guns meanwhile fired over advancing troops and onto German trenches, while dozens of tanks lumbered forward in support of the infantry.

The first wave of attackers reached the German frontline trenches in most places, at which point a fierce close-quarters struggle ensued with grenades and bayonets. A second wave of troops then passed through the first to continue the advance. British troops overcame German machine-gun nests using flexible small-unit tactics: one half of a platoon gave covering fire as their comrades dashed forward to attack. By the end of the first day's fighting, Vimy Ridge was in Canadian hands and other British troops had advanced about 3 miles (5km).

RETURN TO STALEMATE

On April 11 British General Edmund Allenby claimed that his army was "pursuing a defeated enemy." Cavalry were sent forward in expectation of a breakthrough into open country, but this proved vastly overoptimistic. The artillery had performed impressively, but had also churned up the ground over which the advance had to proceed. While engineers prepared a path on which the British heavy guns could move forward, the Germans reinforced their defenses. By April 14, the advance had ground to a halt in the face of fresh German troops and uncut barbed wire. As was so often the case in World War I, doomed attempts to revive the offensive then went on for far too long, producing heavy casualties for little or no further gain.

PREPARING FOR ACTION
British infantry at Arras dig a reserve trench before moving up to the frontline. Trenches were always dug in a zigzag pattern to limit exposure to fire down their length.

TANKS AND ARMORED VEHICLES

With the deadly combination of artillery, machine-guns, and barbed wire dominating the battlefield, the "poor bloody infantry" could not function effectively without some form of adequate protection in attack. The support offered by motor vehicles was limited due to their unreliability and difficulty in maneuvering under all but ideal conditions. This led to the development of a form of armored tractor that could run on continuous tracks rather than wheels, and had sufficient armor to be impervious to bullets and shrapnel. "Tanks," as they came to be called, were first deployed during the Battle of the Somme, in 1916, but it was not until the following year, at Cambrai, that they were first used with any real degree of success.

◀ TANK CREW HELMET

Date	1916
Origin	UK
Material	Steel, leather

Bullets striking the tank caused metal splinters to fly. British tankers were thus issued with these leather-covered steel helmets.

▶ ROLLS-ROYCE ARMORED CAR

Date 1915	**Origin** UK
Weight	3.9 tons (3.56 tonnes)
Length	16ft (4.93m)
Top speed	45mph (72kph)
Engine	80hp (59.7kW)

The Rolls-Royce armored car, built using the chassis of the "Silver Ghost" touring car, first saw service with the British armed forces in Belgium in December 1914. The design was later modified for use in the desert.

▼ "LITTLE WILLIE"

Date 1915	**Origin** UK
Weight	20.2 tons (18.3 tonnes)
Length	21½ft (6.53m)
Top speed	2mph (3kph)
Engine	105hp (78.3kW)

"Little Willie" was a prototype armored fighting vehicle that was built to prove the viability of the concept to British military chiefs.

LITTLE WILLIE
~1915~

6mm mild steel bodywork

Track tensioner

Hotchkiss machine-gun

Continuous "caterpillar" track driven from the front

6-pounder gun

Command cupola

102

2324

◀ MARK IV TANK

Date 1917	**Origin** UK
Weight	31.4 tons (28.4 tonnes)
Length	26¼ft (8.02m)
Top speed	4mph (6kph)
Engine	105hp (78.3kW)

The improved Mark IV tank was built in large numbers. Crew safety was ensured by moving the gasoline tank to the outside of the vehicle, a measure that also improved ventilation and comfort.

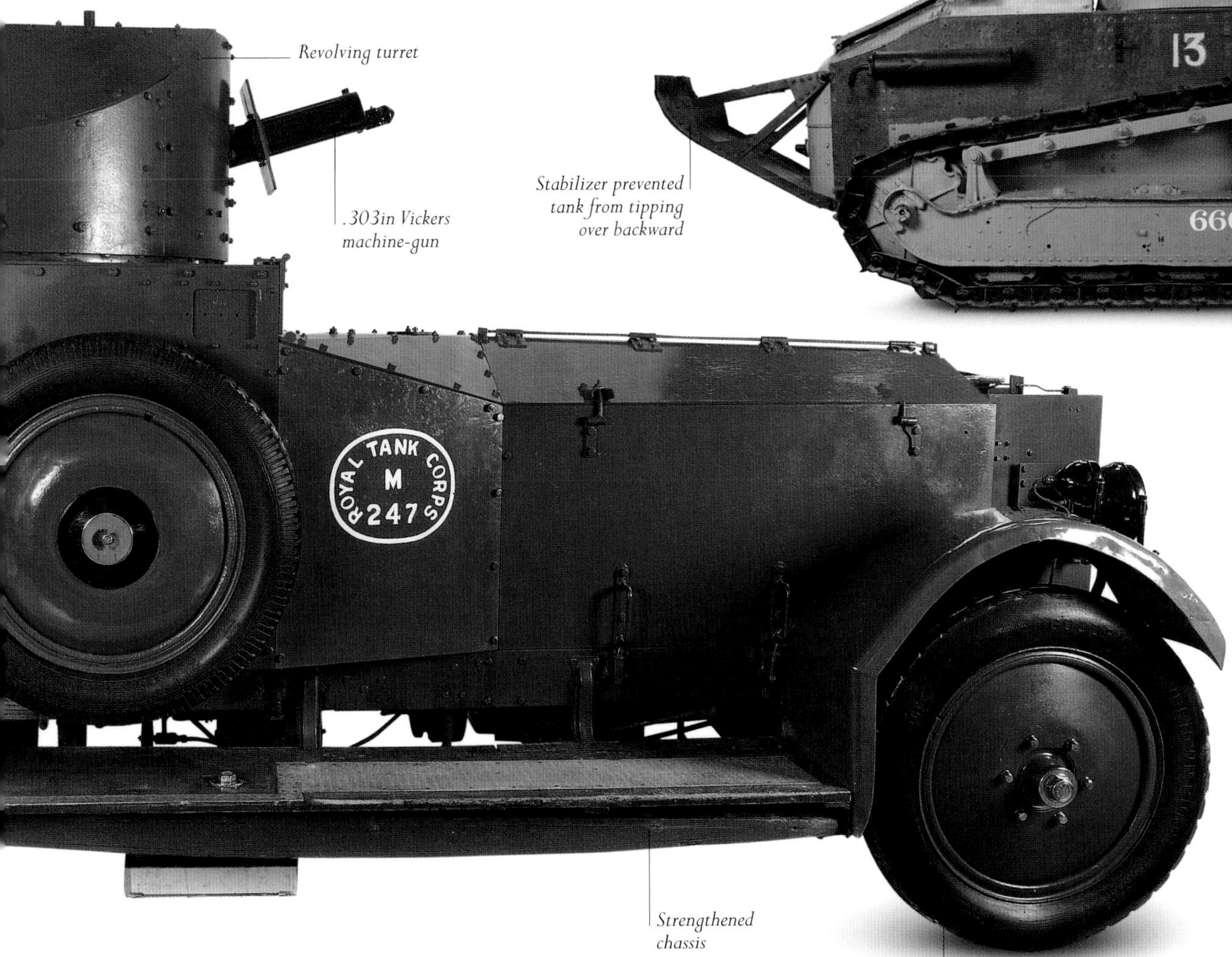
Revolving turret
.303in Vickers machine-gun
ROYAL TANK CORPS
M
247
Strengthened chassis
Solid tires

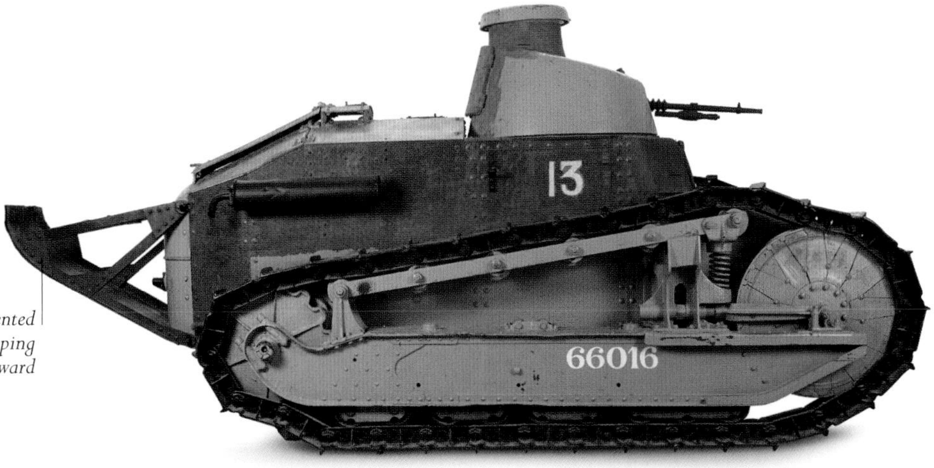
Stabilizer prevented tank from tipping over backward
13
66016

▲ RENAULT FT-17

Date 1917 **Origin** France
Weight 7.7 tons (7 tonnes)
Length 16½ft (5.02m)
Top speed 5mph (8kph)
Engine 35hp (26.1kW)

Also adopted by the US Army, the Renault FT-17 became the most widely used tank after World War I, and more than 3,500 were built.

▼ A7V STURMPANZERWAGEN

Date 1918 **Origin** Germany
Weight 33 tons (29.8 tonnes)
Length 24ft (7.34m)
Top speed 8mph (13kph)
Engine Two 100hp (74.6kW)

The A7V tank, based on an American tracked tractor, came into service only in the last year of World War I, and just 30 were built. It had two Daimler-Benz gasoline engines.

▼ MEDIUM MARK A WHIPPET

Date 1917 **Origin** UK
Weight 15.6 tons (14.2 tonnes)
Length 33ft (10.1m)
Top speed 7mph (12kph)
Engine Two 45hp (33.6kW)

Developed as a scouting tank by cavalry units, the Whippet's tracks were each driven by a separate, 45hp (33.6kW), 6-cylinder gasoline engine. The vehicle was turned by varying one engine's speed relative to the other. The fixed turret had three or four machine-guns.

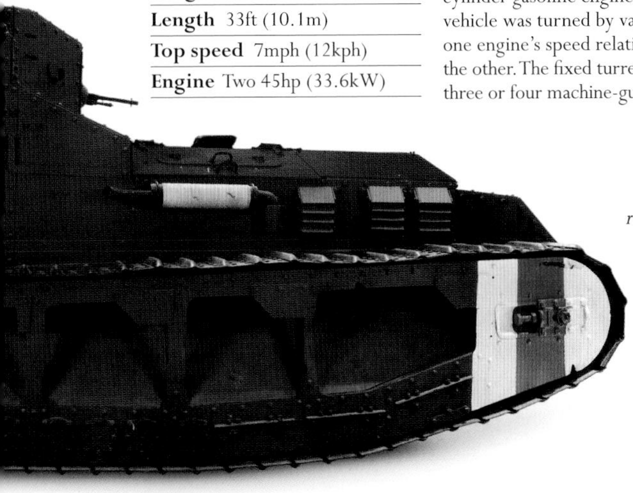

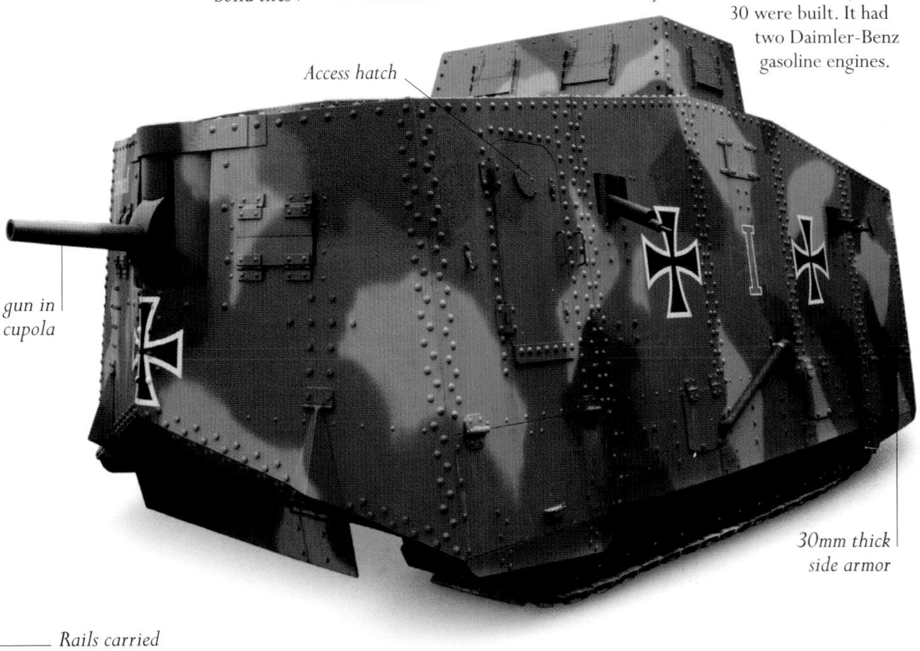
Access hatch
5.7cm gun in rotating cupola
30mm thick side armor

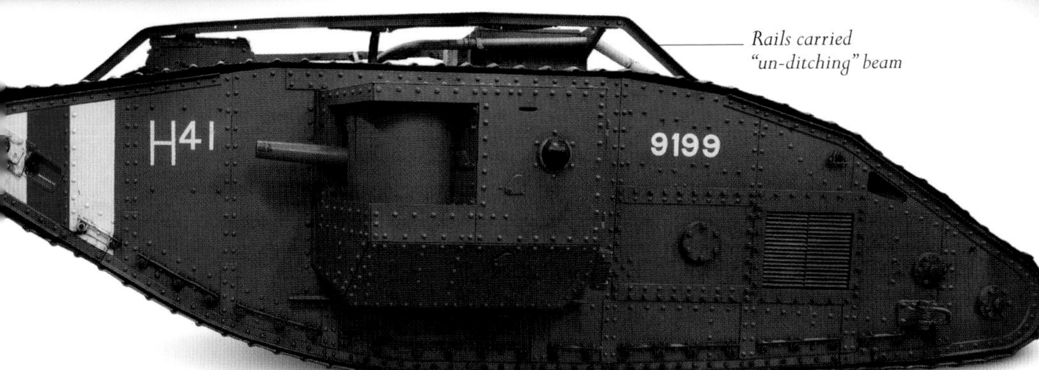

Rails carried "un-ditching" beam
H41
9199

◀ MARK V TANK

Date 1918 **Origin** UK
Weight 32.5 tons (29.5 tonnes)
Length 26½ft (8.05m)
Top speed 5mph (8kph)
Engine 150hp (111.8kW)

The Mark V tank saw the introduction of epicyclic gearing, enabling the tank to be steered by one man instead of the four previously required. When chained to the tracks, its "un-ditching" beam was carried under the tank to free it when stuck in mud.

WORLD WAR I TANK

MARK V TANK

Tanks were first used by the British on the Somme in September 1916. Early models were unreliable, but showed strong fighting potential. Over 400 Mark Vs had entered service before the war's end.

The Mark V, introduced in 1918, was the last of the lozenge-shaped British heavy tanks to fight on the Western Front. As with all of its predecessors, the Mark V's thick armor reduced both its speed and mobility. The tank was employed to lead infantry across no-man's-land, smashing a path through barbed wire and trenches.

Although resistant to machine-guns, heavy tanks were vulnerable to artillery fire, and when operated over muddy ground pitted with shell holes, they could also get stuck or break down. At the Battle of Cambrai in 1917, around 324 British heavy tanks carried out a mass attack on firm ground and demonstrated what the vehicle could achieve if properly used. Lighter, quicker tanks, such as the British Whippet and the French Renault FT-17—which introduced the rotating gun turret—proved their worth in the relatively open combat of the war's later stages.

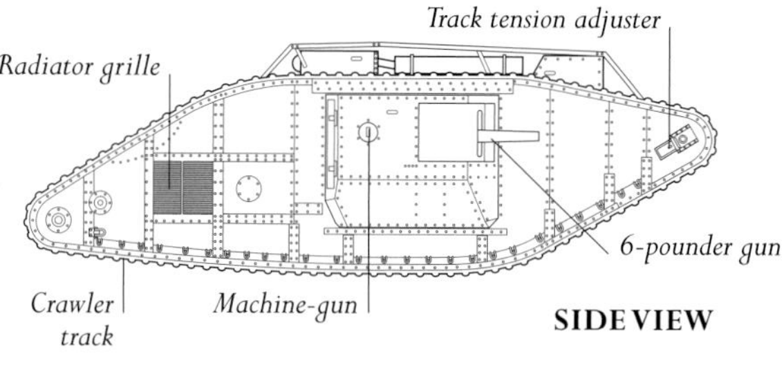

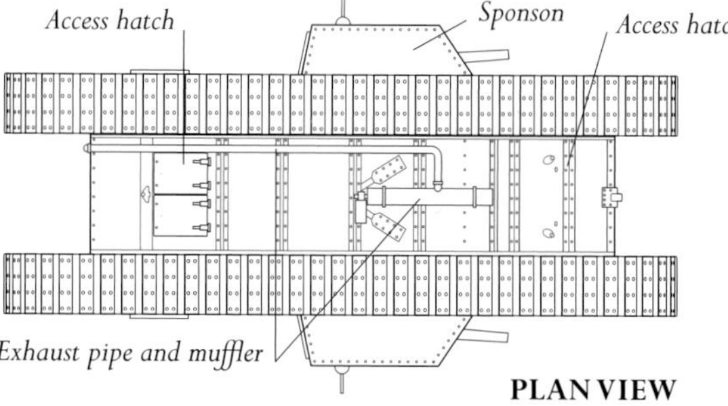

▲ **MARK V TANK**
The tank was 26½ft (8.05m) long and weighed 32.5 tons (29.5 tonnes). Its 150hp (112kW) Ricardo engine gave it a top speed of 4½mph (7.4 kph).

TANK EXTERIOR

▲ **CRAWLER TRACK**
The tank moved on two tracks—loops of riveted metal links that ran around rollers.

▲ **FRONT VIEW**
Enemy troops trained their fire on the vision ports, so tank crews began to wear face masks.

▶ **"MALE" TANK**
Versions with two 6-pounder guns and four Hotchkiss machine-guns were known as "male" tanks; "female" tanks were equipped only with machine-guns.

▼ **ADJUSTER NUT**
To give the correct traction, the tension in the tracks was altered by turning adjuster nuts.

▲ **6-POUNDER GUN**
Two crew manned each of the quick-firing 6-pounders, which were located on either side of the tank in armored projections called sponsons. Each sponson also mounted a machine-gun.

▲ **ARMOR**
The Mark V was clad in riveted steel plates, up to ½in (14mm) thick, which could withstand German armor-piercing bullets. The engine radiator grille is visible on the left.

INSIDE THE TANK

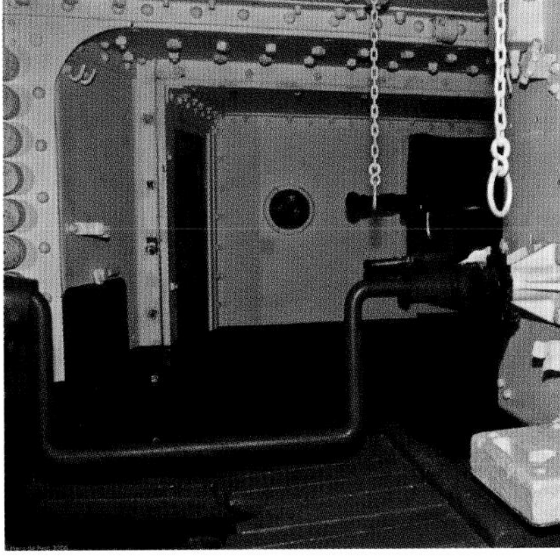

▲ **STARTER CRANK**
The water-cooled engine was started by four members of the crew turning a large crank handle.

► **DRIVER'S SEAT**
The driver sat to the commander's right. He had to bring the tank to a halt to turn it, which made it an easy target.

▼ **INTERIOR CONDITIONS**
The crew—commander, driver, and six gunners—worked in hot, cramped, noisy, fume-filled conditions. Bullets hitting the exterior sent steel splinters flying inside the tank, so the men wore protective clothing.

▲ **UNCOVERED ENGINE**
The engine was exposed so that it could be kept lubricated while running.

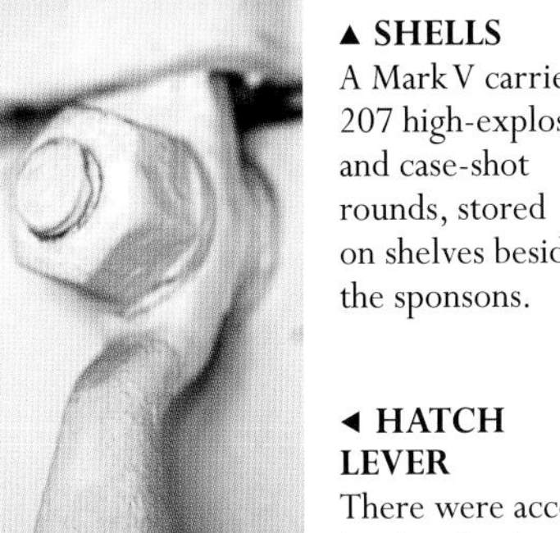

▲ **SHELLS**
A Mark V carried 207 high-explosive and case-shot rounds, stored on shelves beside the sponsons.

◄ **HATCH LEVER**
There were access hatches for the crew on the roof, on the sponsons, and at the rear of the tank.

COMMUNICATIONS EQUIPMENT OF WORLD WAR I

As battlefields and armies grew in size, the need for effective long-distance communication became more urgent. Paper messages were carried by human couriers, as well as carrier pigeons and dogs, with varying degrees of reliability. Traditional signaling systems such as semaphore, flares, and heliographs were joined on the battlefield by new forms of telegraphy, based on electricity. Cable telegraphy, which depended on long wires connecting fragile telegraph machines, and wireless telegraphy, which demanded cumbersome hardware, were vulnerable to interception by the enemy. Notably, the entry of America into the conflict in 1917 was precipitated by the interception of a German telegram.

Flags were made from serge or silk; silk flags were quicker to manipulate

◄ SEMAPHORE FLAGS

Date 1914–1918
Origin UK
Type Signaling

The semaphore flag signaling system was developed for use as a way of communicating between ships in the 19th century, and remained in use until rendered obsolete by the introduction of lightweight radios. A practiced signaler could signal a dozen or more words per minute.

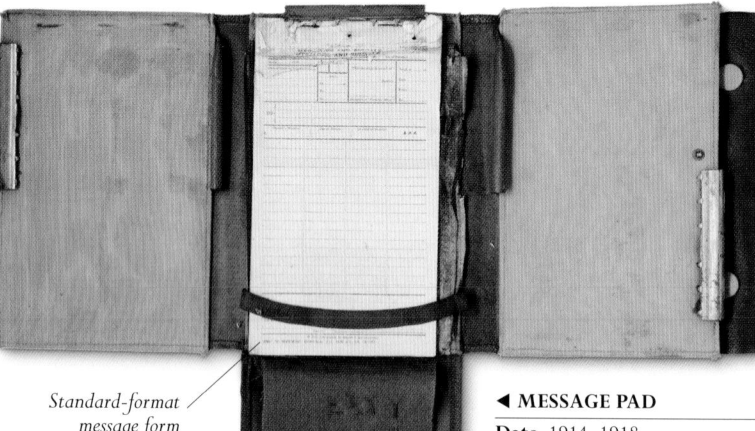

Standard-format message form

◄ MESSAGE PAD

Date 1914–1918
Origin UK
Type Message dispatch

Officers in the front line were supplied with message pads bound in leather and canvas covers. Carbon paper was used to produce a duplicate copy, which the sender retained.

Leather collar with secure pocket

◄ DOG COLLAR

Date 1914–1918
Origin UK
Type Message dispatch

Under some circumstances, usually in areas where it was deemed too dangerous to send a man, trained dogs were used to carry messages, secreted either in harnesses or simple collars.

Plane mirror

◄ HELIOGRAPH MARK V

Date 1916
Origin UK
Type Signaling

The first practical heliograph—a mirror used for flashing sunlight—was developed in India in the 1860s. Lightweight, needing no power source, and difficult to intercept, they were extremely useful and remained in service until the 1970s.

▼ WHEATSTONE TELEGRAPH

Date 1914–1918
Origin UK
Type Telegraphy

Based on technology developed by British scientist Charles Wheatstone in the 1830s, the Wheatstone telegraph used a punch-tape system to transmit up to 100 words per minute.

Reader for punched paper tape

▶ PIGEON MESSAGE CAPSULE

Date 1914–1918

Origin UK

Type Message dispatch

During the war, thousands of messenger pigeons were used by the British and German armies. Messages written on rice paper and folded to fit into containers such as this were attached to the birds' legs.

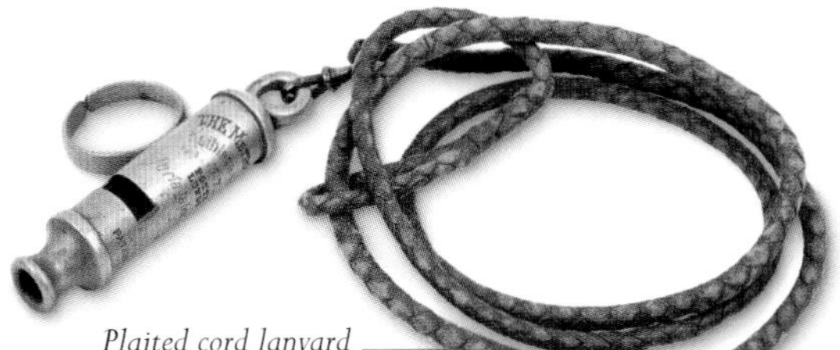

Leg clip

Message capsule

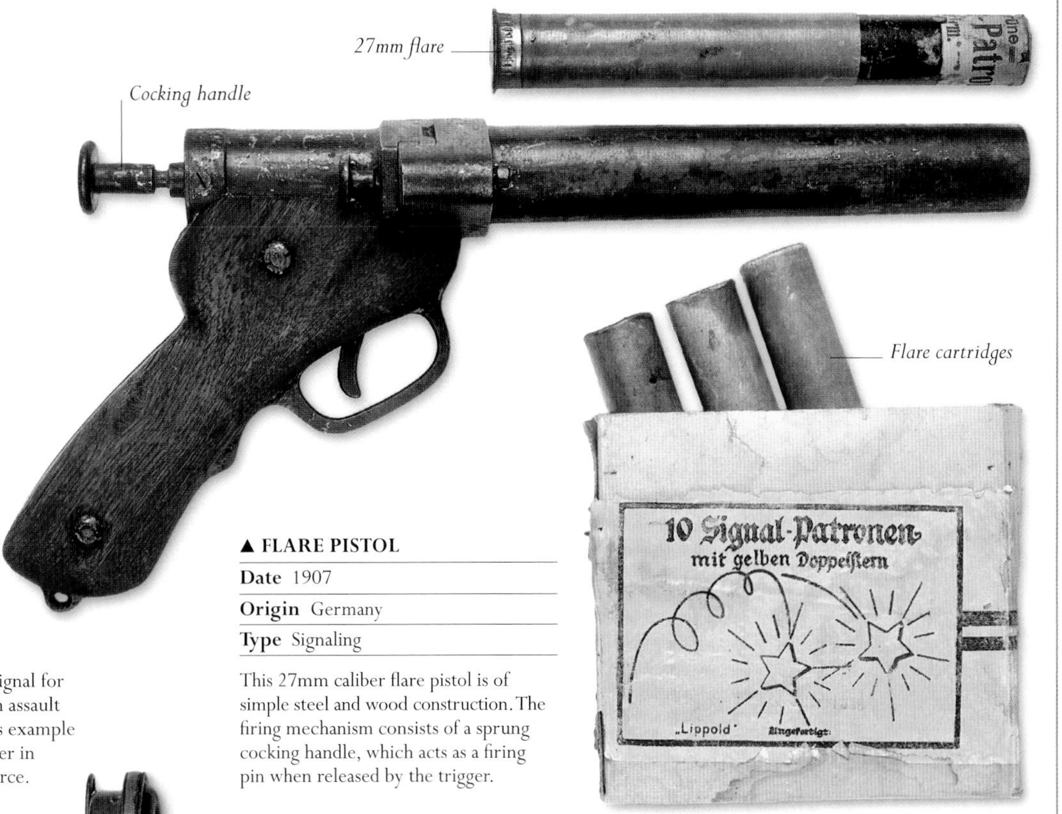

27mm flare

Cocking handle

Flare cartridges

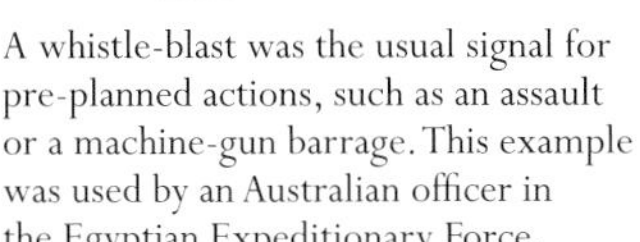

Plaited cord lanyard

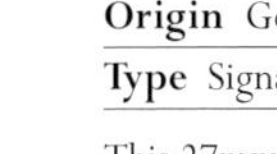

▲ SIGNALING WHISTLE

Date 1914

Origin UK

Type Signaling

A whistle-blast was the usual signal for pre-planned actions, such as an assault or a machine-gun barrage. This example was used by an Australian officer in the Egyptian Expeditionary Force.

▲ FLARE PISTOL

Date 1907

Origin Germany

Type Signaling

This 27mm caliber flare pistol is of simple steel and wood construction. The firing mechanism consists of a sprung cocking handle, which acts as a firing pin when released by the trigger.

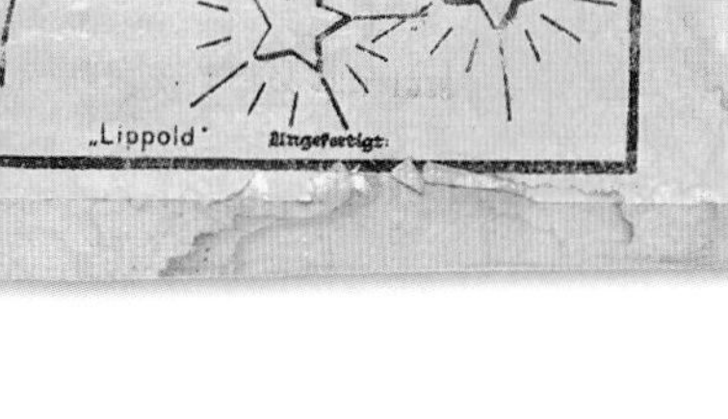

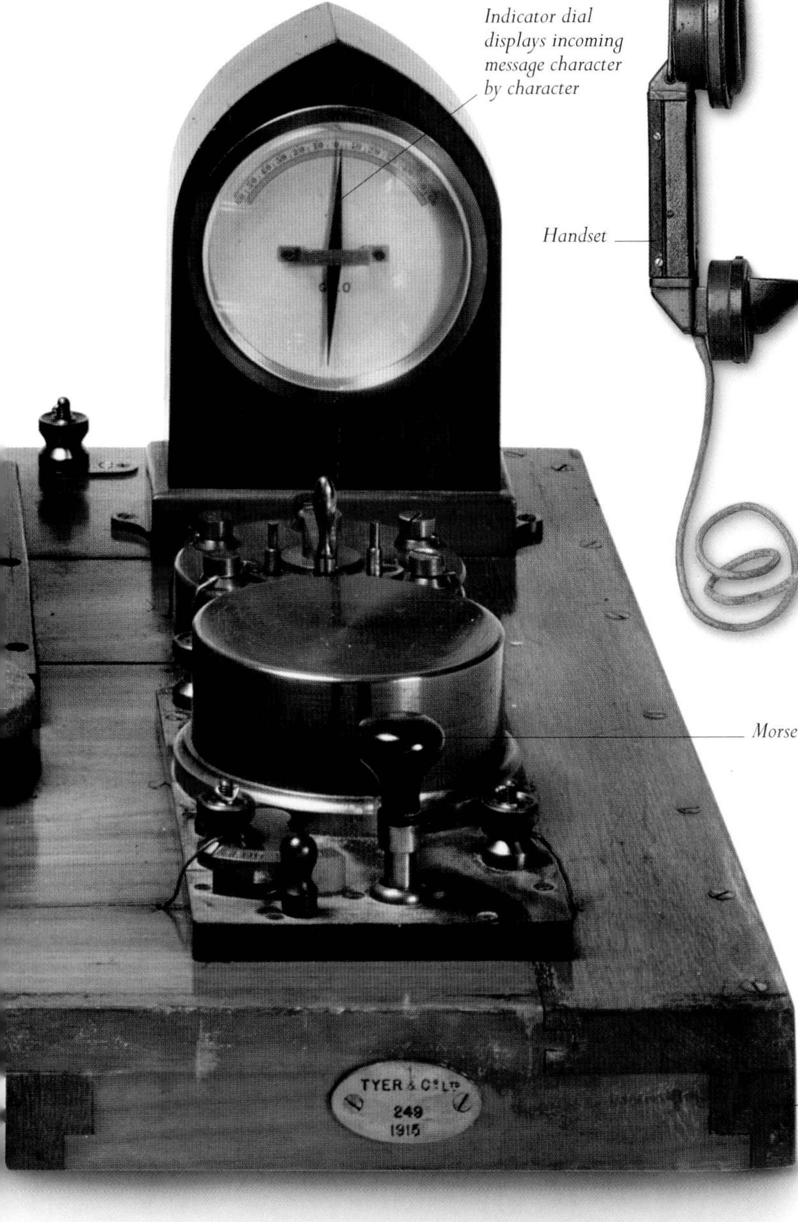

Indicator dial displays incoming message character by character

Handset

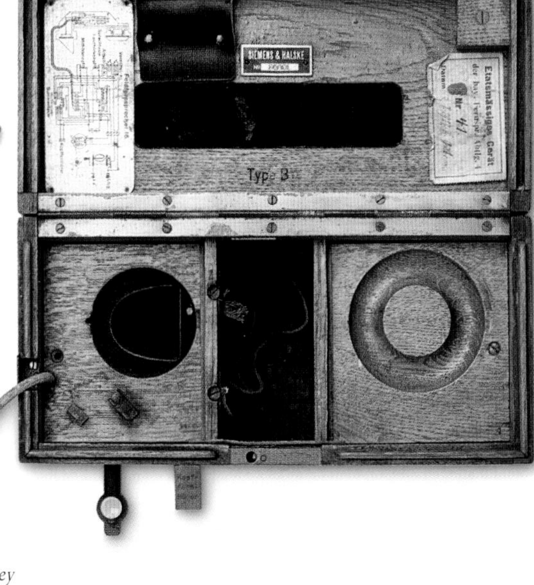

◀ FIELD TELEPHONE

Date 1914–1918

Origin Germany

Type Telephony

Field telephones were used extensively throughout World War I, mostly to allow front-line units to communicate with headquarters to the rear. However, they relied on cables that were extremely fragile and had to be repaired frequently.

Morse key

Wooden baseboard

Cutaway for the nose

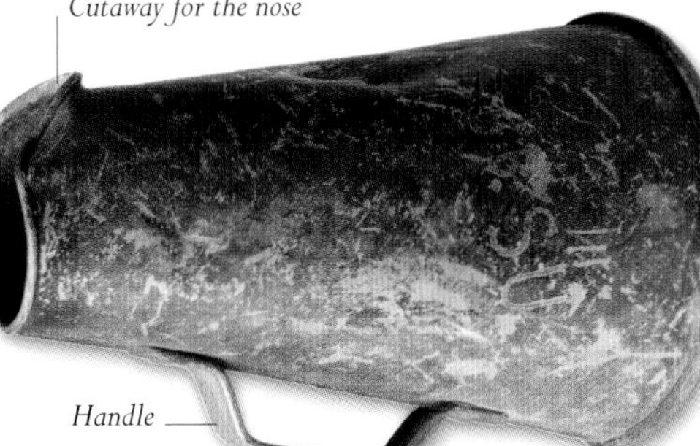

Handle

◀ MEGAPHONE

Date 1915

Origin UK

Type Signaling

This loudhailer megaphone was recovered from the area known as Shrapnel Gulley at Anzac Cove on the Gallipoli Peninsula, together with other artifacts used by 2nd Field Company, Royal Australian Engineers, between April 25 and December 20, 1915.

KEY **EVENTS**

1914–45

■ **1915** The invention of the interrupter gear allows a pilot to fire a machine-gun through his propeller arc, leading to the development of the first fighter planes.

■ **1935** The UK begins work on an air defense system, based on a chain of coastal radar stations, to give early warning of aerial threats.

■ **1937** German aircraft intervening in the Spanish Civil War destroy the Basque town of Guernica by aerial bombing.

■ **1938** The Boeing B-17 Flying Fortress (see pp.314–17) heavy bomber is introduced. This all-metal monoplane can carry a 6,000lb (2,700kg) bomb load.

■ **1944** The German Messerschmitt Me 262 Schwalbe ("Swallow") is the first jet-engined fighter to enter service.

■ **1945** American B-29 bombers drop atomic bombs on the Japanese cities of Hiroshima (see pp.378–79) and Nagasaki; Japan then surrenders.

KEY DEVELOPMENT

THE GROWTH OF AIR POWER

The most influential innovation in warfare between 1914 and 1945 was the development of air power. Combat aircraft became not only a vital adjunct to army and navy operations, but also an instrument for direct attack upon the enemy's homeland and infrastructure.

Although there had been a few minor uses of aircraft in war before 1914, it was World War I that saw the first true age of military aviation. The main combatants entered the war with about 500 flimsy flying machines between them. By 1918, the UK alone had 22,000 aircraft in service.

The prime functions of aircraft were that of reconnaissance and artillery spotting—giving army gunners feedback on where their shells had landed. Experimental raids were also mounted on targets behind enemy lines, with small bombs dropped by hand. Fighter aircraft were later sent up to shoot down bombers and reconnaissance planes, and, by 1916, fighters from opposing sides were engaged in aerial combat over the Western front. Air aces, the most successful fighter pilots, were celebrated as "knights of the air."

STRATEGIC BOMBING

Military chiefs soon realized that aircraft could also be used for strategic bombing—direct air attacks on enemy cities. Germany led the world in lighter-than-air flight, and their massive Zeppelin and Schütte-Lanz rigid airships launched night raids on London and other cities from 1915. Airships proved too slow-moving and vulnerable once the UK deployed night fighters in defense, and were replaced by heavier-than-air bomber aircraft. From

▶ **THE BOMBING OF DRESDEN**
In February 1945, some 1,300 Allied bombers attacked the German city of Dresden, causing a firestorm that killed around 25,000 people. The incident became a focus for criticism of strategic bombing.

"Fighting in the air is **not sport**, it is **scientific murder**"

US PILOT EDDIE RICKENBACKER, *FIGHTING THE FLYING CIRCUS*, 1919

1917, German Gothas heavy bombers attacked London and Paris, and, by the war's end, the UK and France were mounting their own bombing raids against German cities. After the war, some air commanders argued—wrongly—that future wars would be won by strategic bombing alone.

NEW AIRCRAFT

World War I airmen fought mostly in wood-and-canvas biplanes. During the 1930s, air forces were transformed by streamlined monoplanes—many of all-metal construction—with more powerful engines and improved performance. These new aircraft, including the Messerschmitt Bf 109 fighter and the dive-bombing Junkers Ju 87 Stuka, were first used by German forces in the Spanish Civil War (1936–39).

In the early years of World War II, from 1939 to 1941, Germany achieved a series of victories through coordinated air–ground warfare. This was based on radio contact between tanks and aircraft, operating as "aerial artillery." They also pioneered the use of airborne troops, landed by parachute or glider. However, the UK's radar-based air defense system enabled the Royal Air Force to prevent the *Luftwaffe* gaining command of the air in the Battle of Britain, in the summer of 1940. A sustained night bombing campaign against British cities, from September 1940 to May 1941, caused devastation, but failed to break the UK's will to fight.

As World War II progressed, the US and the UK achieved air superiority over Germany and Japan, chiefly through their ability to manufacture aircraft in huge quantity. The US built about 300,000 military aircraft during World War II, used to support operations in ground attack, tactical bombing, transport, and airborne troop landing roles, along with independent strategic bombing offensives. A day-and-night campaign by Allied bombers eventually reduced German cities to rubble, although still not to decisive effect.

Innovations such as the first jet aircraft or the first military helicopters were of marginal effect, but the arrival of the atomic bomb in 1945 heralded a new era in warfare.

▼ BOMBER CREW KIT
In World War II, American B-17 bomber crews flew at high altitude in unpressurized aircraft. They were issued with oxygen masks to aid breathing and heated flying suits to protect against cold.

KEY **FIGURE**

BARON VON RICHTHOFEN

1892–1918

Germany's most famous World War I air ace, Manfred von Richthofen served as cavalry officer before becoming a fighter pilot. Credited with downing 80 enemy aircraft—more than any other pilot in the war—the "Red Baron" was himself shot down and killed in April 1918.

▲ Von Richthofen led a squadron that was nicknamed the "Flying Circus" due to its planes' bright colors; the baron himself flew a red Fokker Dr.I triplane.

◄ AMERICAN BOMBERS
A medium-range Mitchell B-25 bomber flies a bombing raid in France during World War II. Air superiority proved essential to the success of armies in combat.

RECONNAISSANCE AND FIGHTER AIRCRAFT

Initially, military aircraft were employed to observe the battlefield, but there was soon an imperative to control the airspace over it. The first aerial "dogfights" involved pistols and rifles, and were inconclusive. Machine-guns, which could be fired in bursts while the pilot corrected his aim, were the answer. However, it was not until a method was developed of allowing such weapons to follow the pilot's natural sightline, and fire through the propeller's arc, that the fighter aircraft really came into its own. The first such attempts saw propeller blades fitted with strips of steel to deflect bullets, but soon thereafter "interrupter" mechanisms were developed, which shut off the gun while the blade passed through the line of fire.

Upper wings with short ailerons

Skid prevented aircraft nosing-over on landing

▲ AVRO 504K

Date 1917 **Origin** UK
Wingspan 36ft (10.97m)
Length 29½ft (8.97m)
Top speed 90mph (145kph)
Engine 110hp (82kW) Le Rhône 9Ja single-bank 9-cylinder rotary

Early versions of the Avro 504 served as reconnaissance and combat aircraft, but the two-seater 504K came into its own as a trainer. Over 10,000 were built over a period of almost 20 years.

.303in (7.7mm) Lewis MG

Tail skid

.31in (7.92mm) LMG 08/15 or LMG 14 fires between propeller blades

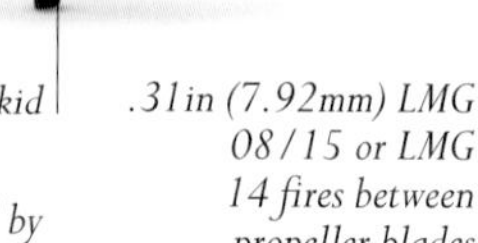

► S.E.5A

Date 1917 **Origin** UK
Wingspan 26½ft (8.11m)
Length 21ft (6.38m)
Top speed 140mph (225kph)
Engine 200hp (149.13kW) Hispano-Suiza 8b or Wolseley W4a "Viper" in-line V-8

The S.E.5a was an upgraded version of what was already an extremely powerful aircraft. It was superior to the contemporary Fokker D.VII in terms of stability and speed, and had much better high-altitude performance.

"Fat" cantilevered wing section gave improved lift

Radial engine had "horseshoe" semi-cowl

Wing braced by cables anchored on a central mast

Box section fuselage

Tail plane has no fixed fin

◄ FOKKER EII

Date 1915 **Origin** Germany
Wingspan 26¼ft (8m)
Length 24ft (7.3m)
Top speed 93mph (150kph)
Engine 100hp (74.5kW) Oberursel U.19 single-bank 9-cylinder rotary

Dutchman Anton Fokker's monoplane was an improved copy of the Morane-Saulnier. Its short-lived success was due solely to it being the first aircraft fitted with synchronizing interrupter gear for its gun.

Two .31in (7.92mm) LMG 08/15 machine-guns

6-cylinder in-line engine protrudes from faired-in nose

Two .31in (7.92mm) LMG 08/15s

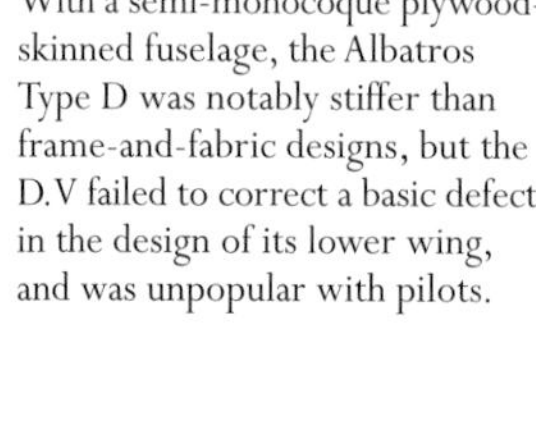

▼ ALBATROS D.V

Date 1917 **Origin** Germany
Wingspan 29½ft (9m)
Length 24ft (7.33m)
Top speed 110mph (175kph)
Engine 200hp (149.13kW) Daimler-Benz D.III in-line 6-cylinder

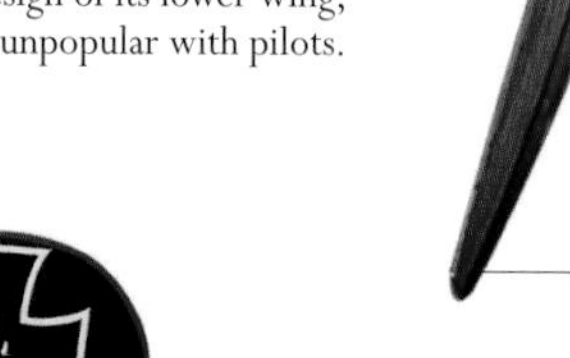

With a semi-monocoque plywood-skinned fuselage, the Albatros Type D was notably stiffer than frame-and-fabric designs, but the D.V failed to correct a basic defect in the design of its lower wing, and was unpopular with pilots.

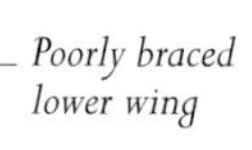

Poorly braced lower wing

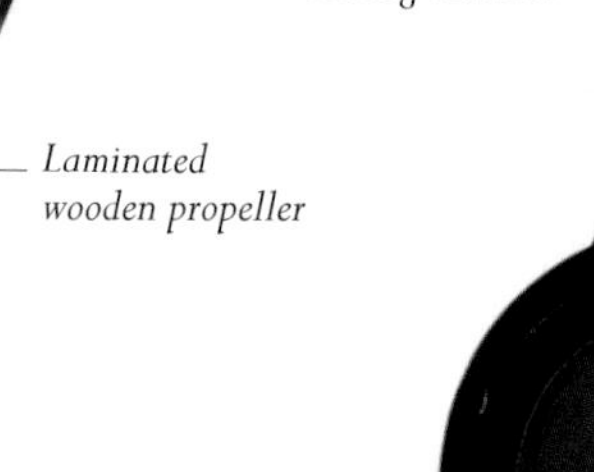

Automobile-type cooling radiator

Laminated wooden propeller

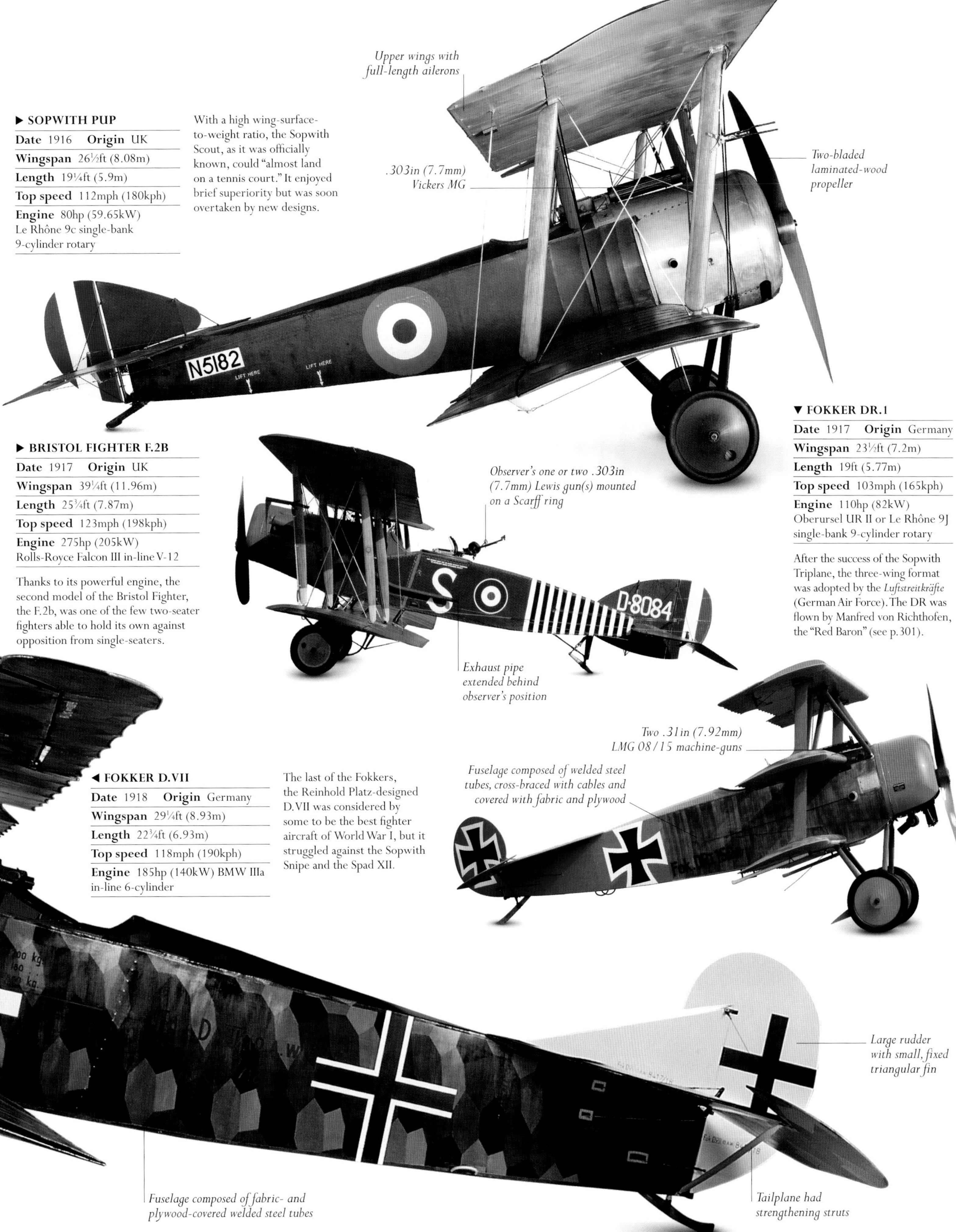

▶ SOPWITH PUP

Date 1916 **Origin** UK
Wingspan 26½ft (8.08m)
Length 19¼ft (5.9m)
Top speed 112mph (180kph)
Engine 80hp (59.65kW) Le Rhône 9c single-bank 9-cylinder rotary

With a high wing-surface-to-weight ratio, the Sopwith Scout, as it was officially known, could "almost land on a tennis court." It enjoyed brief superiority but was soon overtaken by new designs.

▶ BRISTOL FIGHTER F.2B

Date 1917 **Origin** UK
Wingspan 39¼ft (11.96m)
Length 25¾ft (7.87m)
Top speed 123mph (198kph)
Engine 275hp (205kW) Rolls-Royce Falcon III in-line V-12

Thanks to its powerful engine, the second model of the Bristol Fighter, the F.2b, was one of the few two-seater fighters able to hold its own against opposition from single-seaters.

▼ FOKKER DR.1

Date 1917 **Origin** Germany
Wingspan 23½ft (7.2m)
Length 19ft (5.77m)
Top speed 103mph (165kph)
Engine 110hp (82kW) Oberursel UR II or Le Rhône 9J single-bank 9-cylinder rotary

After the success of the Sopwith Triplane, the three-wing format was adopted by the *Luftstreitkräfte* (German Air Force). The DR was flown by Manfred von Richthofen, the "Red Baron" (see p.301).

◀ FOKKER D.VII

Date 1918 **Origin** Germany
Wingspan 29¼ft (8.93m)
Length 22¾ft (6.93m)
Top speed 118mph (190kph)
Engine 185hp (140kW) BMW IIIa in-line 6-cylinder

The last of the Fokkers, the Reinhold Platz-designed D.VII was considered by some to be the best fighter aircraft of World War I, but it struggled against the Sopwith Snipe and the Spad XII.

BOMBER AIRCRAFT

Aircraft were first used to bomb ground targets during the Italian campaign to wrest Libya from the Ottoman Empire in 1911, but, as World War I progressed, it became imperative to produce machines designed specifically for the task. Progress was slow, however, and even by the war's end aerial bombardment was still a haphazard affair: only what was later known as "area bombing" of built-up areas was at all effective. Large aircraft were required to carry payloads over long distances, and, vulnerable to attack by fighters, they soon began to operate under cover of darkness.

Enclosed flight deck, with large cabin behind

Space for crew of eight

▲ SIKORSKY "ILYA MOUROMETZ"

Date 1915	**Origin** Russia
Wingspan 113ft (34.5m)	
Length 57½ft (17.5m)	
Top speed 68mph (110kph)	
Engine Four 148hp (108.8kW) Sunbeam Crusader in-line V-8s	

The great Russian designer Igor Sikorsky was responsible for the first four-engined aircraft; he built it as a commercial transport, but with war looming it was soon adapted as the basis for a heavy bomber. No two were identical.

Observer had two Lewis guns, one pointing forward, the other up and to the rear

Engine behind pilot

▲ RAF F.E.2

Date 1915	**Origin** UK
Wingspan 47¾ft (14.5m)	
Length 32¼ft (9.8m)	
Top speed 90mph (145kph)	
Engine 160hp (107.6kW) Beardmore 6-cylinder	

Originally intended as a fighter, the "pusher" F.E.2 was technically obsolete even before its prototype flew, but it proved to be a success as a light bomber. Over 2,000 were built.

Engine located behind pi...

▶ VOISIN 8

Date 1916	**Origin** France
Wingspan 61¾ft (18.2m)	
Length 36¼ft (11.02m)	
Top speed 82mph (132kph)	
Engine 220hp (161.8kW) Peugeot BAa in-line 8-cylinder	

The French *Service Aéronautique Militaire*'s first specially built night bomber, the Voisin 8, was never more than mediocre, but many of its shortcomings could be traced to its Peugeot engine. Replacing it with a 300hp (220.6kW) Renault V-12 made a considerable difference.

Forward gun position; a 37mm cannon can be substituted for the machine-gun

Wings staggered in a semi-sesquiplane layout

Observer had one or two Lewis guns

Tail skid

Lower wing roots cut away to improve observer's view of the ground

▶ RAF R.E.8

Date 1916	**Origin** UK
Wingspan 42½ft (12.98m)	
Length 27¾ft (8.5m)	
Top speed 103mph (165kph)	
Engine 140hp (102.9kW) RAF 4a in-line V-12	

The "Harry Tate" (rhyming slang for R.E.8; Tate was a music-hall artist) proved to be little more maneuverable than the aircraft it replaced (the B.E.2), but it was better armed and carried a greater payload. It remained in service until the end of the war.

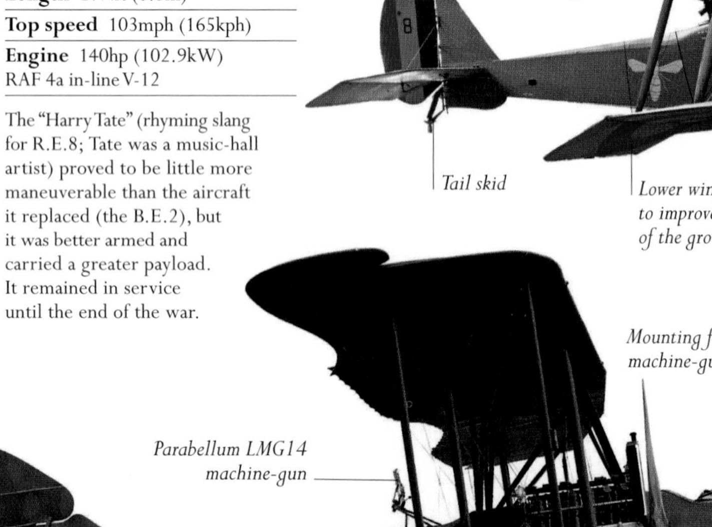

Mounting for machine-gun

Parabellum LMG14 machine-gun

Under-wing racks could carry a 880lb (400kg) bomb load

◀ AEG G.IV

Date 1916	**Origin** Germany
Wingspan 60¼ft (18.4m)	
Length 31¾ft (9.7m)	
Top speed 103mph (165kph)	
Engine Two 260hp (191.2kW) Daimler-Benz D.Iva in-line 6-cylinders	

While the limited range of the G.IV meant that it was used mainly as a tactical bomber attacking battlefield targets, it was also used on the Italian front to bomb cities, including Padua, Venice, and Verona.

Ailerons extending beyond wing-top

Bracing strut

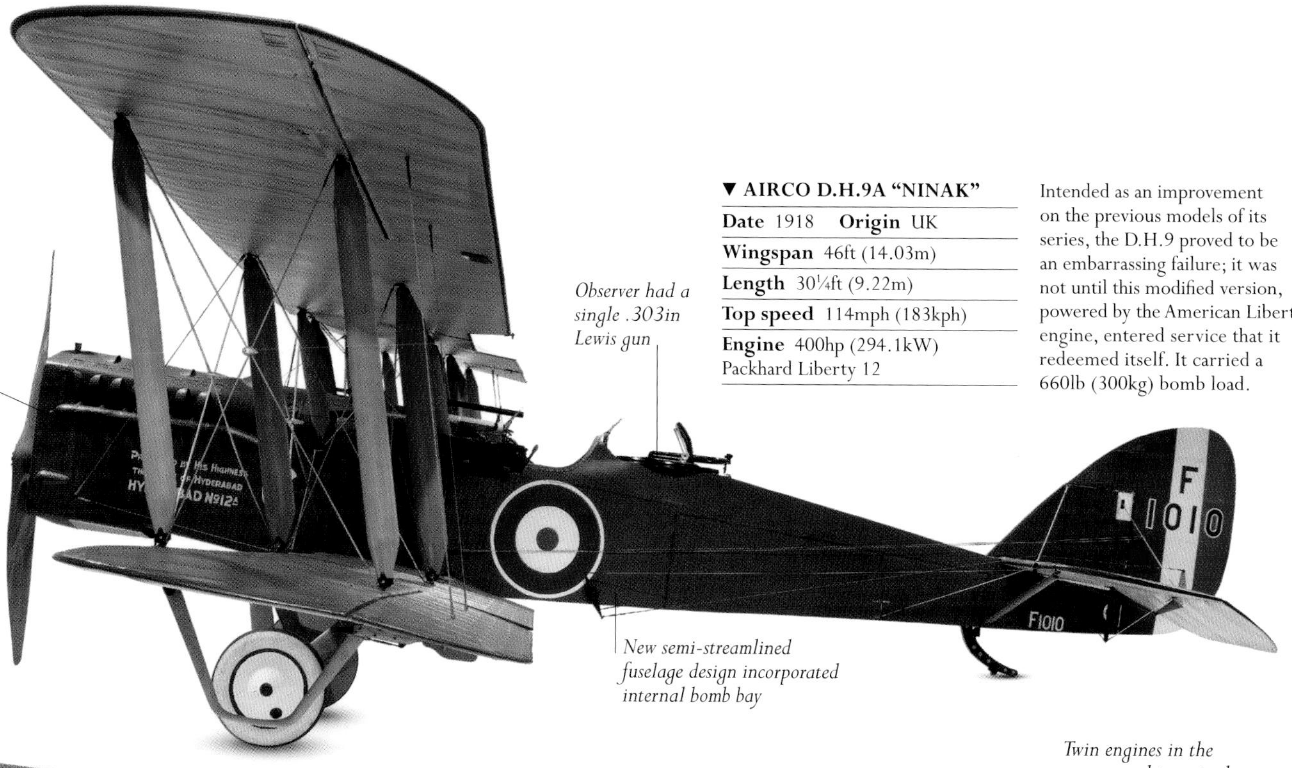

▼ AIRCO D.H.9A "NINAK"

Date 1918 **Origin** UK
Wingspan 46ft (14.03m)
Length 30¼ft (9.22m)
Top speed 114mph (183kph)
Engine 400hp (294.1kW) Packhard Liberty 12

Intended as an improvement on the previous models of its series, the D.H.9 proved to be an embarrassing failure; it was not until this modified version, powered by the American Liberty engine, entered service that it redeemed itself. It carried a 660lb (300kg) bomb load.

▼ VICKERS VIMY

Date 1918 **Origin** UK
Wingspan 68ft (20.75m)
Length 43½ft (13.28m)
Top speed 100mph (160kph)
Engine Two 360hp (264.7kW) Rolls-Royce Eagle VIII in-line V-12s

The Vimy missed combat service during World War I by a matter of weeks, but it went on to be the British Royal Air Force's lead bomber until 1925. By that time it had achieved everlasting fame as the first aircraft to cross the Atlantic.

▲ ZEPPELIN STAAKEN

Date 1917 **Origin** Germany
Wingspan 138½ft (42.2m)
Length 72½ft (22.1m)
Top speed 84mph (135kph)
Engine 4 x 220hp (161.8kW) Daimler-Benz Bz.IVs in wing nacelles; 2 x 160hp (117.6kW) D.IIIs in nose

The most remarkable aircraft built for the *Luftstreitkräfte* (the German Air Force), the giant R-series Zeppelins had four, five, or six engines, and could deliver a ton or more of bombs to targets (such as those in London, England), with precision.

FIGHTER AND FIGHTER-BOMBER AIRCRAFT 1939–42

Although much faster and more maneuverable than their predecessors, the fighter aircraft of 1918 were little changed from those of 1914. During the 1930s, all-metal monoplane fighters came into their own (a rare exception being the Hawker Hurricane, which had a fabric covering), with vastly more powerful engines, the ability to mount additional machine-guns, and heavier "cannon." By 1939, the most capable aircraft were reaching speeds in excess of 348mph (560kph), and could climb to 34,000ft (10,360m). Experts believed that such enhanced performance would put an end to the dogfights that were the essence of aerial combat during World War I, but they were soon proved wrong.

Equal-length wings

▲ GLOSTER GLADIATOR

Date 1937 **Origin** UK
Wingspan 32¼ft (9.83m)
Length 27½in (8.36m)
Top speed 255mph (415kph)
Engine 830hp (610.4kW) Bristol Mercury IX air-cooled single-bank 9-cylinder radial

Although technically outdated, the Gladiator saw front-line service with the RAF in France, Norway, and (most famously) Malta. It was also deployed by numerous other countries, including China, Finland, Norway, and Greece.

Cockpit bulged to improve pilot's field of view

Metal constant-pitch propeller

Wing could accommodate cannon and machine-guns

▶ SUPERMARINE SPITFIRE

Date 1939 **Origin** UK
Wingspan 36¼ft (11.23m)
Length 30ft (9.12m)
Top speed 378mph (605kph)
Engine 1,470hp (1,081.1kW) Rolls-Royce Merlin 45 in-line V-12

The Spitfire's superb handling characteristics ensured its immediate success. Its continuous development—it was to be built in 13 main variants—kept it in service until well after the end of the war.

▼ MESSERSCHMITT BF 110

Date 1940 **Origin** Germany
Wingspan 53⅓ft (16.3m)
Length 40½ft (12.3m)
Top speed 350mph (560kph)
Engine Two 1,100hp (809kW) Daimler-Benz DB 601A in-line V-12s (inverted)

Designed originally as a long-range bomber escort, the early Bf 110 displayed serious shortcomings in that role. Later, -F and -G variants were significantly more successful, particularly as radar-equipped night-fighters.

Tailplane had twin fins and rudders

Radar antenna

Underwing load for bombs or extra fuel tanks

Light alloy propeller

MG17 machine-guns mounted in wings

▲ MESSERSCHMITT BF 109

Date 1941 **Origin** Germany
Wingspan 32⅓ft (9.85m)
Length 28⅓ft (8.65m)
Top speed 355mph (570kph)
Engine 1,300hp (956.1kW) Daimler-Benz DB 601E in-line V-12 (inverted)

The Bf 109 beat stiff competition to become the *Luftwaffe*'s first modern fighter aircraft. In all, some 35,000 were built in nine versions and many variants, with engines from Junkers or Daimler-Benz.

▶ FOCKE-WULF FW 190 WÜRGER

Date 1941 **Origin** Germany
Wingspan 34½ft (10.5m)
Length 29ft (8.84m)
Top speed 410mph (655kph)
Engine 1,540hp (1,132.6kW) BMW 801C2 air-cooled 2-bank 14-cylinder radial

The most advanced fighter aircraft when it entered service, the Fw 190 remained unbeatable until confronted by the Spitfire Mk IX. An active development program saw improved versions produced until 1945. The Fw 190 was the first important fighter of World War II to have a radial engine.

◄ DEWOITINE D.520

Date 1940 **Origin** France
Wingspan 33½ft (10.2m)
Length 28¼ft (8.6m)
Top speed 330mph (535kph)
Engine 935hp (687.6kW) Hispano-Suiza 12Y 45 in-line V-12

Without doubt the most capable fighter aircraft produced in France, the D.520 was a match for the Bf 109Es it fought in 1940, but only 400 had been produced before France capitulated. It had a service ceiling of 34,500ft (10,500m) and a range of 950 miles (1,530km).

Cockpit had limited field of view
Three-bladed constant-pitch propeller
Capacity for a 1,500lb (680kg) bomb load

▲ CURTISS P-40 WARHAWK

Date 1941 **Origin** US
Wingspan 37⅓ft (11.38m)
Length 33⅓ft (10.15m)
Top speed 340mph (550kph)
Engine 1,200hp (882.5kW) Allison V-1710-81 in-line V-12

While respected for its agility, the Warhawk, even in its later variants, could not compete with the Messerschmitt Bf 109 or the Focke-Wulf Fw 190, which could attain higher altitudes. Nonetheless, it was the mainstay of the UK's Desert Air Force in North Africa, and saw action in China and the Southwest Pacific.

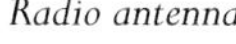
Radio antenna
Early-pattern camouflage paintwork
Squadron markings

◄ HAWKER HURRICANE

Date 1940 **Origin** UK
Wingspan 40ft (12.2m)
Length 32¼ft (9.85m)
Top speed 340mph (550kph)
Engine 1,185hp (871.5kW) Rolls-Royce Merlin XX V-12 in-line

The Hurricane was something of an anomaly: a modern interceptor with a fuselage covered with fabric rather than sheet aluminum. It was much easier to produce and to repair than its all-metal Spitfire counterpart.

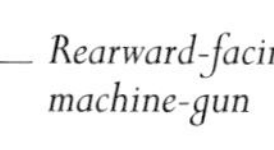
Cockpit accommodated both pilot and gunner
Rearward-facing machine-gun
Plywood monocoque rear fuselage

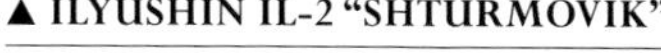

▲ ILYUSHIN IL-2 "SHTURMOVIK"

Date 1942 **Origin** Soviet Union
Wingspan 47¾ft (14.6m)
Length 38ft (11.6m)
Top speed 255mph (410kph)
Engine 1,700hp (1,250.3kW) Mikulin AM-38F in-line V-12

Built around a 1,540lb (700kg) armored shell that contained the crew, engine, and fuel tank, the Il-2, the "flying tank," was designed purely as a ground-attack aircraft. Over 42,000 were constructed.

"Bubble" cockpit canopy gave good all-round vision

Hardpoints for bombs

▲ NAKAJIMA KI-43 HAYABUSA "OSCAR"

Date 1942 **Origin** Japan
Wingspan 35½ft (10.84m)
Length 29⅓ft (8.92m)
Top speed 330mph (530kph)
Engine 1,150hp (845.8kW) Nakajima Ha-115 2-bank 14-cylinder radial

The Japanese Army's equivalent to the IJN's Mitsubishi A6M, the *Hayabusa* (Peregrine Falcon) weighed just 2.5 tons (2.3 tonnes). Due to its light weight it was highly maneuverable and had an impressive rate of climb. The *Hayabusa* was well regarded by its pilots, even though it was slow by contemporary standards and poorly armed.

FIGHTER AND FIGHTER-BOMBER AIRCRAFT 1943–45

Some combatant nations—notably the Japanese—initially favored lightweight, lightly armored fighter aircraft, on the grounds that maneuverability was all-important; others preferred better protection and more powerful weaponry, and it was the latter that were to prove more effective. Such fighter aircraft were also more easily adapted to the ground-attack role, and this became increasingly important on both European fronts, and in the Pacific Theater. After the brief appearance of rocket-powered aircraft, jet propulsion technology took its first faltering steps in aircraft of this type toward the war's end, and within ten years piston-engined fighters had all but disappeared.

Four 30mm cannon mounted in the nose

Retractable nose wheel

Small ailerons

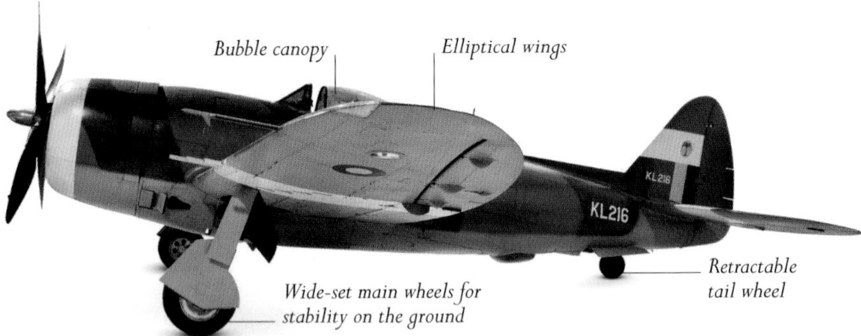

Bubble canopy

Elliptical wings

Wide-set main wheels for stability on the ground

Retractable tail wheel

▲ REPUBLIC P-47 THUNDERBOLT

Date 1942 **Origin** US

Wingspan 40¾ft (12.42m)

Length 36ft (11m)

Top speed 435mph (700kph)

Engine 2,535hp (1,890.3kW) Pratt & Whitney R-2800-59W Double Wasp radial

Nicknamed the "Jug" due to its bulky shape, the Thunderbolt was admired for its high-altitude performance—no German aircraft could out-dive it—and its ability to take punishment. It proved extremely effective as a ground-attack fighter-bomber.

Each wing could carry one 500lb (226.8kg) bomb or four 3in rockets

▲ HAWKER TEMPEST MK II

Date 1944 **Origin** UK

Wingspan 41ft (12.5m)

Length 33½ft (10.26m)

Top speed 432mph (695kph)

Engine 2,590hp (1,931.3kW) Bristol Centaurus V radial

The last and best of the British piston-engined fighter aircraft, the Tempest was a fast and maneuverable interceptor—capable of taking on the jet-powered Messerschmitts and Arados when deployed intelligently—while also excelling in the ground-attack role.

Rolls-Royce Merlin engine

Four-bladed Hamilton propeller

Each wing could carry four machine-guns and 1,700 rounds of 0.5in ammunition

▲ NORTH AMERICAN P-51 MUSTANG

Date 1943 **Origin** US

Wingspan 37ft (11.3m)

Length 32¼ft (9.83m)

Top speed 438mph (705kph)

Engine 1,590hp (1,185.6kW) Packard Merlin V-1650-7 V-12

Produced in response to a request from the UK, the Mustang was an underachiever until it was fitted with a Rolls-Royce Merlin engine. It went on to become a mainstay of the US Army Air Forces, both as an escort and as a fighter-bomber. Its rear fuselage and tail were completely redesigned during the aircraft's production.

Large fin and rudder improved stability and maneuverability

Retractable tail wheel

Plywood-covered rear fuselage

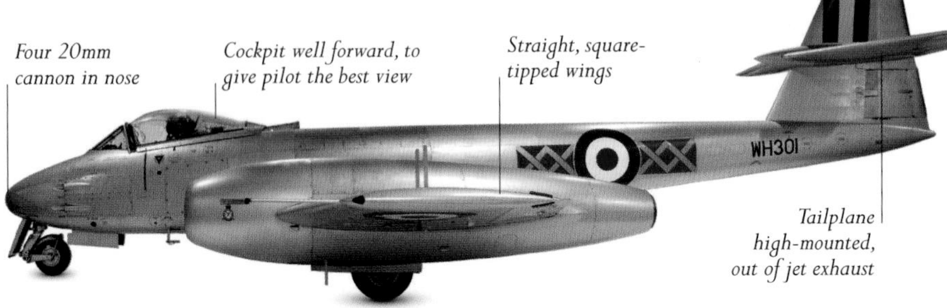

Four 20mm cannon in nose

Cockpit well forward, to give pilot the best view

Straight, square-tipped wings

Tailplane high-mounted, out of jet exhaust

◄ GLOSTER METEOR

Date 1944 **Origin** UK

Wingspan 37¼ft (11.3m)

Length 44½ft (13.6m)

Top speed 600mph (965kph)

Engine Twin 3,500lb (1,590kg) Rolls-Royce Derwent turbojets

The Allies' first operational jet aircraft, the Meteor was the product of a long development program. It saw active service in World War II and in Korea; its last variant was withdrawn as late as 1965.

Tailplane mounted high, out of jet exhaust

◀ MESSERSCHMITT ME 262 SCHWALBE

Date 1944 **Origin** Germany
Wingspan 41½ft (12.6m)
Length 34¾ft (10.6m)
Top speed 540mph (870kph)
Engine Twin 1,985lb (900kg) Junkers Jumo 004B-1 turbojets

The first turbojet-powered combat fighter, the Me 262 quickly proved effective against the US Air Force's daylight bombing campaign, but it was produced too late to affect the outcome of the war.

Large wings needed for heavy aircraft (16 tons)

Four 20mm cannon in belly nacelle

▲ NORTHROP P-61 BLACK WIDOW

Date 1944 **Origin** US
Wingspan 66ft (21.1m)
Length 49½ft (15.1m)
Top speed 365mph (590kph)
Engine Twin 2,250hp (1,677.8kW) Pratt & Whitney R-2800-65W Double Wasp radials

The P-61 was the first US aircraft designed as a night-fighter, and was the first aircraft specifically designed to carry radar for this purpose. It was capable of "loitering" in the skies for up to eight hours at a time.

One 30mm cannon in each wing-root

Swept-back wing form

Landing skid; wheels were dropped on takeoff

◀ MESSERSCHMITT ME 163 KOMET

Date 1944 **Origin** Germany
Wingspan 30½ft (9.33m)
Length 18¾ft (5.7m)
Top speed 600mph (960kph)
Engine 3,750lb (1,700kg) Walter HWK 109-509A-2 liquid-fuel rocket

The only rocket-powered aircraft to see active service, the Me 163 relied on its ability to overtake high-altitude bombers and to make one diving pass before its engine cut out.

Two machine-guns mounted above the engine to fire through the propeller's arc

20mm cannon fired through propeller boss

Pilot sat in armored tub

Two 30mm cannon housed in wing roots

Air intake

"Spats" improved aerodynamic performance with wheels retracted

▲ YAKOVLEV YAK-3

Date 1944 **Origin** Soviet Union
Wingspan 30¼ft (9.2m)
Length 28ft (8.5m)
Top speed 410mph (655kph)
Engine 1,300hp (969.4kW) Klimov VK-105PF-2 V-12

Offering high performance and yet easy to maintain, the Yak-3 was a favorite with ground-crew and pilots alike. Many pilots who flew the Mustang, the Spitfire, and the Yak-3 regarded the Yak as the superior aircraft.

Two 0.5in machine-guns mounted above engine

13mm-thick armored plate behind pilot's seat

Air intake

Stressed aluminum fuselage

▶ KAWASAKI KI-100

Date 1945 **Origin** Japan
Wingspan 39¼ft (12m)
Length 29ft (8.8m)
Top speed 360mph (580kph)
Engine 1,500hp (1,118.5kW) Mitsubishi Ha 112-II radial

Influenced by the German Focke-Wulf Fw 190, the Ki-100 was one of the best fighter aircraft the Japanese air force deployed during World War II—highly maneuverable and with a high altitude capacity. However, it came too late to make any difference to the outcome of the war.

BOMBER AIRCRAFT 1939–42

During World War II, two different types of bomber aircraft emerged: those designed to fly long-range "strategic" missions against infrastructure targets, or drop bombs onto industrial cities in the hope of causing significant disruption to manufacturing; and "tactical" bombers, which were employed on and around the battlefield. Both had vital roles to play, but it was the "heavies," the four-engined aircraft capable of carrying many tons of bombs, which came to define the type. Aircraft such as these did not begin to enter service until war was already under way, operating alongside the twin-engined types, which had dominated production during the 1930s.

▲ HEINKEL HE 111

Date 1941 **Origin** Germany

Wingspan 74ft (22.6m)

Length 54ft (16.4m)

Top speed 275mph (440kph)

Engine Two 1,300hp (1,969.4kW) Junkers Jumo 211F-1 in-line V-12s (inverted)

The most numerous of the medium bombers with which the *Luftwaffe* entered the war, the He 111 was built in a bewildering array of variants, the most outlandish of which was the twin-fuselage, five-engined He 111Z.

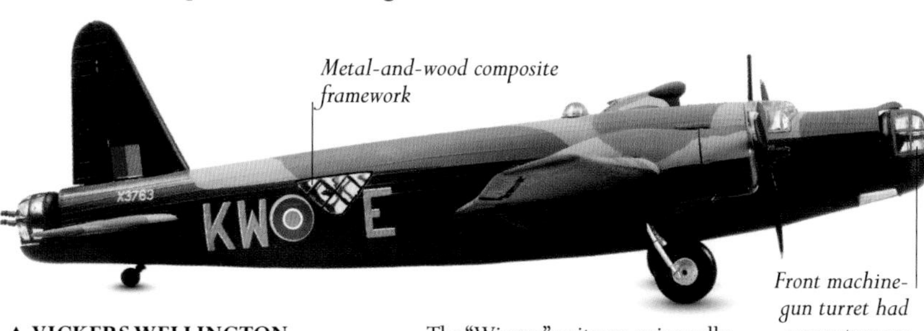

▲ VICKERS WELLINGTON

Date 1941 **Origin** UK

Wingspan 86¼ft (26.26m)

Length 61ft (18.54m)

Top speed 255mph (410kph)

Engine Two 1,500hp (1,118.5kW) Bristol Hercules XI two-bank 14-cylinder radials

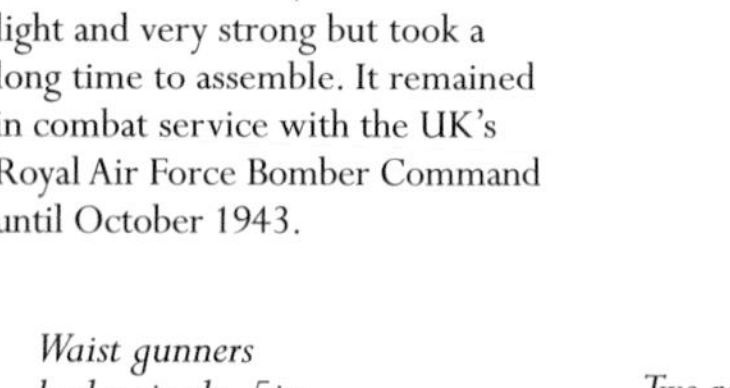

The "Wimpy," as it was universally known, had a fabric-covered metal-and-wood airframe, which was light and very strong but took a long time to assemble. It remained in combat service with the UK's Royal Air Force Bomber Command until October 1943.

▲ DORNIER DO.17

Date 1938 **Origin** Germany

Wingspan 59ft (18m)

Length 52ft (15.79m)

Top speed 255mph (410kph)

Engine Twin 1,000hp (745.7kW) BMW Bramo 323P "Fafnir" single-bank 9-cylinder radials

The Do.17—the "Flying Pencil"—was relatively unimportant when compared to other German bombers of the early war years, especially the He 111. Thanks to its agility, however, it was a favorite with its crew.

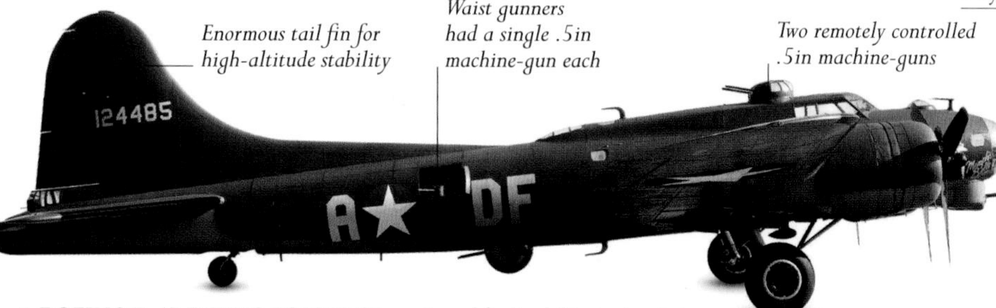

▲ BOEING B-17 FLYING FORTRESS

Date 1943 **Origin** US

Wingspan 103¾ft (31.62m)

Length 74⅓ft (22.66m)

Top speed 285mph (460kph)

Engine Four 1,200hp (894.8kW) Wright R-1820-97 Cyclone single-bank 9-cylinder radials

Famed for its ability to absorb damage, the Flying Fortress's (see pp.314–17) weakness was its limited bomb load—just half that of the Lancaster. Bristling with guns, Fortresses flew in "combat box" formation for mutual defense against fighters during daylight raids.

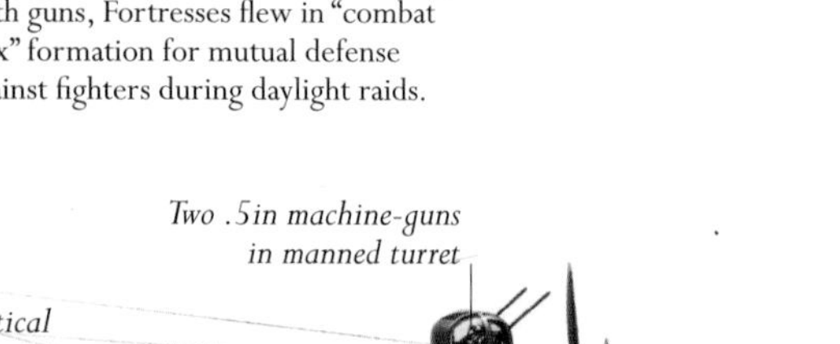

▲ B-25 MITCHELL

Date 1943 **Origin** US

Wingspan 67½ft (20.6m)

Length 54ft (16.45m)

Top speed 272mph (438kph)

Engine Two 1,700hp (1,267.6kW) Wright R-2600-92 Cyclone two-bank 14-cylinder radials

With war imminent, the US Army Air Corps ordered the B-25 Mitchell medium bomber "off the drawing board," without waiting for a prototype. Eventually, almost 10,000 were built in six main variants, including the B-25H/J gunships, which had up to 18 machine-guns and a 75mm cannon.

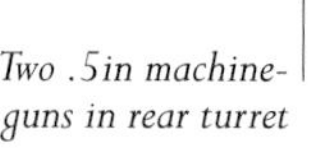

"Mid-upper" turret had two machine-guns

Spacious fuselage

Engines mounted centrally in "thick" wings that incorporated fuel tanks

◀ **SHORT STIRLING MK I**

Date 1940 **Origin** UK

Wingspan 99ft (30.2m)

Length 87¼ft (26.6m)

Top speed 255mph (410kph)

Engine Four 1,030hp (768.1kW) Bristol Hercules II two-bank 14-cylinder radials

The Short Stirling was the first of the British Royal Air Force's "heavies" to reach operational service. It was used in bombing raids over Germany, but was soon superceded by the Handley-Page Halifax and the Avro Lancaster.

Enlarged cockpit canopy gave better visibility for pilot and rear gunner

Bristol Hercules radial engines

Bomb-aimer's position

Bomb-aimer's position in "beetle-eye" glazed nose, with single machine-gun

Navigator's and wireless operator's positions below cockpit

Tail had turret containing four machine-guns

▲ **HANDLEY-PAGE HALIFAX MK III**

Date 1942 **Origin** UK

Wingspan 104¼ft (31.75m)

Length 71½ft (21.82m)

Top speed 282mph (455kph)

Engine Four 1,615hp (1,204.3kW) Bristol Hercules XVI two-bank 14-cylinder radials

The Halifax never achieved the legendary status of the Lancaster, even though it was more versatile and preceded it into service. It carried out maritime patrols and all kinds of special operations.

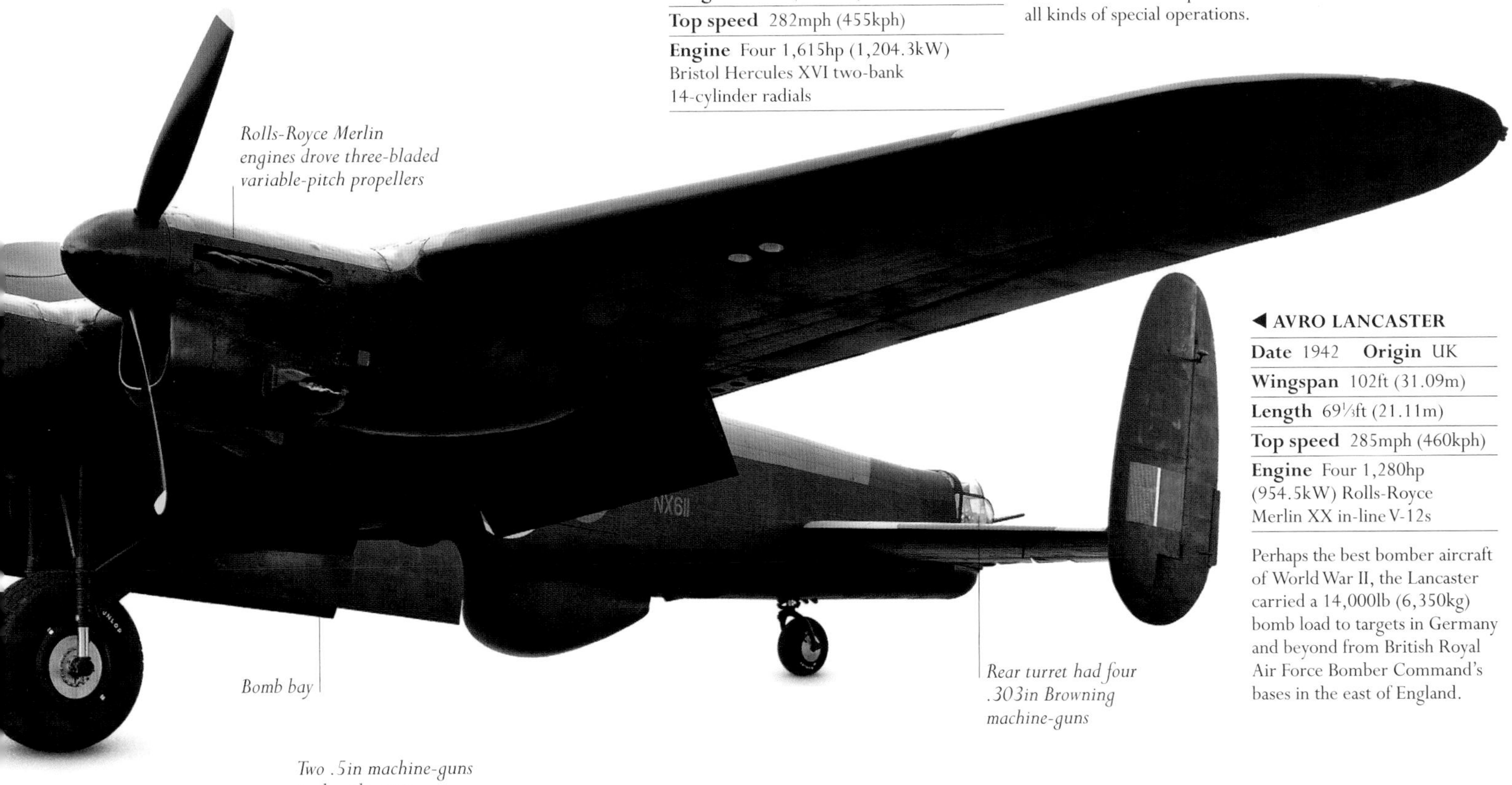

Rolls-Royce Merlin engines drove three-bladed variable-pitch propellers

Bomb bay

Rear turret had four .303in Browning machine-guns

◀ **AVRO LANCASTER**

Date 1942 **Origin** UK

Wingspan 102ft (31.09m)

Length 69⅓ft (21.11m)

Top speed 285mph (460kph)

Engine Four 1,280hp (954.5kW) Rolls-Royce Merlin XX in-line V-12s

Perhaps the best bomber aircraft of World War II, the Lancaster carried a 14,000lb (6,350kg) bomb load to targets in Germany and beyond from British Royal Air Force Bomber Command's bases in the east of England.

Two .5in machine-guns in dorsal turret

Forward gun turret

◀ **CONSOLIDATED B-24 LIBERATOR**

Date 1943 **Origin** US

Wingspan 110ft (33.5m)

Length 67⅔ft (20.6m)

Top speed 290mph (470kph)

Engine Four 1,200hp (894.8kW) Pratt & Whitney R-1830-65 Twin Wasp two-bank 14-cylinder radials

Lighter, faster, and with a greater carrying capacity than the B-17, the Liberator was to be the most prolific Allied bomber of World War II. However, it was harder to fly than the Flying Fortress, and was never as popular with crews.

BOMBER AIRCRAFT 1943–45

Strategic bombers evolved during the course of World War II, their capacities enhanced by the development of more powerful engines, and their capabilities improved by the introduction of radar-based guidance systems and the first effective predictive bombsights. By 1944, the best of these could deliver heavy bomb loads with great accuracy onto targets thousands of miles from their home bases, but they were still sustaining major losses—the British Royal Air Force (RAF) Bomber Command alone lost over 12,000 aircraft during the course of the war.

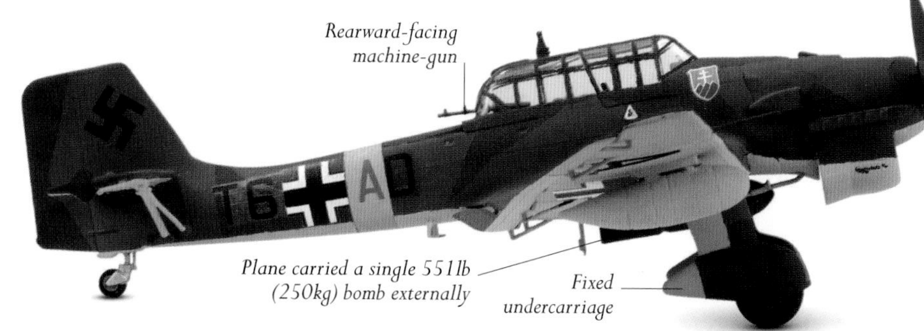

Rearward-facing machine-gun

Plane carried a single 551lb (250kg) bomb externally

Fixed undercarriage

▲ JUNKERS JU 87D STUKA

Date 1941	**Origin** Germany
Wingspan 45½ft (13.8m)	
Length 36ft (11m)	
Top speed 240mph (390kph)	
Engine 1,400hp (1,044kW) Junkers Jumo 211J V-12	

Perhaps the most recognizable of all German aircraft of the period, the Ju 87 *Sturzkampfflugzeug* first saw combat in Spain, in 1937. It was still operational—armed with twin 3.7cm cannon—in the last days of World War II, by which time around 6,500 had been built in six main variants.

Tall tail fin and rudder gave stability

Bomber versions could carry a 4,000lb (1,800kg) bomb load

▲ DE HAVILLAND MOSQUITO B.16

Date 1942	**Origin** UK
Wingspan 54ft (16.5m)	
Length 41½ft (12.6m)	
Top speed 415mph (670kph)	
Engine Two 1,710hp (1,275kW) Rolls-Royce Merlin 76 V-12s	

The Mosquito was an anomaly: a modern aircraft built largely from wood. Its first flight was in November 1940. It was to become one of the most successful aircraft the British RAF operated during World War II, serving in bomber, day- and night-fighter, and reconnaissance roles.

Two .5in machine-guns in remote-controlled turret

Rear turret housed two manned .5in machine-guns

Plane carried a 4,000lb (1,800kg) bomb load

◄ MARTIN B-26 MARAUDER

Date 1942	**Origin** US
Wingspan 71ft (21.65m)	
Length 58¼ft (17.8m)	
Top speed 290mph (460kph)	
Engine Two 1,900hp (1,417kW) Pratt & Whitney R-2800-43 Double Wasp radials	

The Marauder was designed and operated as a medium bomber. It saw service in the Pacific Theater, Europe, and the Mediterranean. Despite being difficult to fly and having stability problems early on, due to a poorly designed fin, it ended the war with the lowest loss rate of any US Army Air Force aircraft.

Two .5in machine-guns

▼ HEINKEL HE 177 GRIEF

Date 1942	**Origin** Germany
Wingspan 103ft (31.45m)	
Length 72¼ft (22m)	
Top speed 350mph (565kph)	
Engine Two 2,600hp (1,939kW) Daimler-Benz DB 610 W-24s	

The *Grief* (Griffin) was the only specially built long-range heavy bomber operated by the *Luftwaffe* during World War II. An inspired design that was flawed in execution, many of its shortcomings could be traced to its over-complicated engine and to the requirement that it function as a precision dive bomber.

Remote-controlled ventral gondola housed a single cannon and a single machine-gun

Crew of two

2,000lb (910kg) of bombs carried internally

Cockpit accommodated pilot and navigator side-by-side

Three-bladed variable-pitch propeller

◀ **DOUGLAS A-20 HAVOC**

Date 1942	**Origin** US
Wingspan 61⅓ft (18.7m)	
Length 48ft (14.6m)	
Top speed 340mph (549kph)	
Engine Two 1,700hp (1,267.7kW) Wright R2600-A Twin Cyclone radials	

The Havoc—"Boston" to the British RAF, which also operated it—was intended as a light/attack bomber, but also saw service as a night-fighter. A total of almost 7,500 were built by Douglas and Boeing between late 1939 and September 1944.

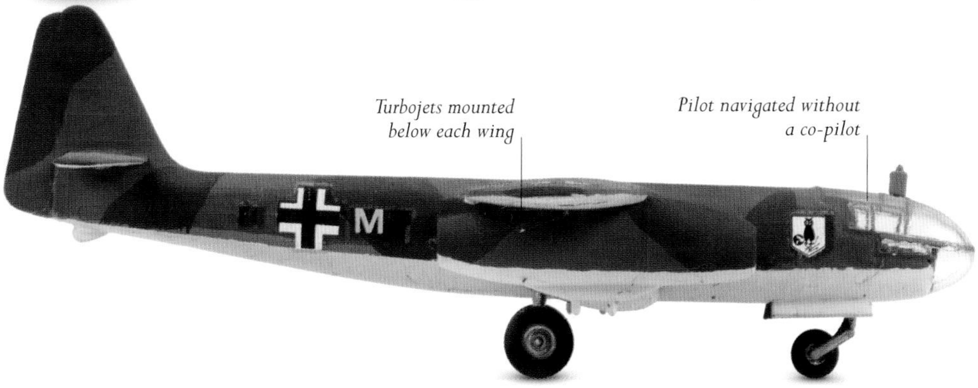

Turbojets mounted below each wing

Pilot navigated without a co-pilot

▲ **ARADO AR 234B-2**

Date 1944	**Origin** Germany
Wingspan 46¼ft (14.1m)	
Length 41½ft (12.63m)	
Top speed 460mph (740kph)	
Engine Two 1,985lb (900kg) Junkers Jumo 004B-1 turbojets	

The second turbojet to enter service with the *Luftwaffe*, the Ar 234B-2 first flew in June 1943. Within a year it had proved to be a capable reconnaissance aircraft, and while this became its main role, it also flew a number of bombing missions, most notably an attempt to destroy the last remaining Rhine Bridge at Remagen.

Pilot very exposed in torpedo-like airframe

Warhead contained 2,650lb (1,200kg) of Amatol high explosive

▲ **YOKOSUKA MXY7 OHKA**

Date 1944	**Origin** Japan
Wingspan 16¾ft (5.12m)	
Length 19¾ft (6.06m)	
Top speed 575mph (927kph)	
Engine Three 587lb (266kg) Type 4 rocket motors	

The *Ohka* was a manned flying bomb powered by three solid-fuel rocket motors. It was intended to be used against warships, and was carried to its target below a mother-aircraft—usually a Mitsubishi G4M "Betty." Around 850 of the *Ohka* were produced, but only seven of them sank or damaged US ships. Several more successful *kamikaze* (see p.342) attacks were carried out by conventional aircraft.

▼ **BOEING B-29A SUPERFORTRESS**

Date 1944	**Origin** US
Wingspan 141¼ft (43.1m)	
Length 99ft (30.2m)	
Top speed 357mph (575kph)	
Engine Four 2,200hp (1,640kW) Wright R-3350-23 Duplex Cyclone radials	

The largest and most capable of the Allies' strategic bombers, with pressurized fuselage and remotely controlled guns, the B-29A first flew in September 1942, and was operational against targets in Japan (from a base in China) from June 1944. Its most famous missions were those that saw nuclear bombs dropped on the Japanese cities of Hiroshima (see pp.378–79) and Nagasaki.

Remote-controlled ventral turret housed two .5in machine-guns

Pressurized fuselage

WORLD WAR II LONG-RANGE HEAVY BOMBER

BOEING B-17 FLYING FORTRESS

Conceived in the 1930s, the B-17 epitomized a new type of bomber aircraft, able to carry heavy loads over long distances. Supplied to Great Britain by the US under the Lend-Lease Act, it became one of the mainstays of the Allied bombing offensive in Europe.

The B-17C was the first version to go to war, in July 1941, but only with the arrival of the B-17E two months later did the aircraft begin to make its mark. Its reputation was assured when the definitive B-17G was introduced in October 1943.

For short-range missions, a B-17G could carry a 8,000lb (3,600kg) bomb load, but that was reduced to 6,000lb (2,700kg) when the aircraft was fueled for 2,000 miles (3,200km). The top speed was 287mph (462kph), although in mass formation the planes did not exceed 180mph (290kph).

Flying by day made B-17s vulnerable, in spite of their heavy armament, but losses fell after long-range fighters were developed to escort them. In all, 12,671 B-17s were built, and around 37 percent of these were lost.

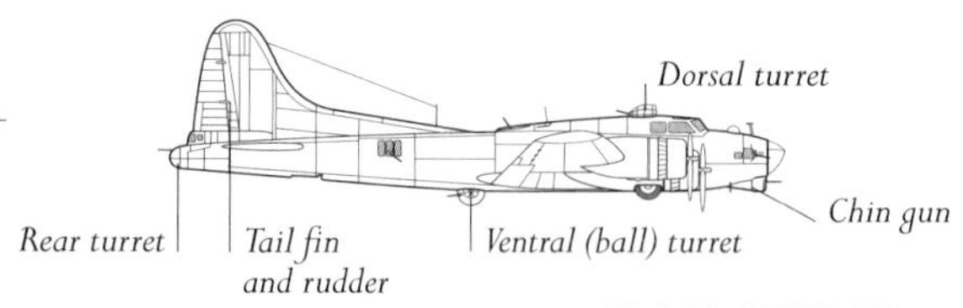

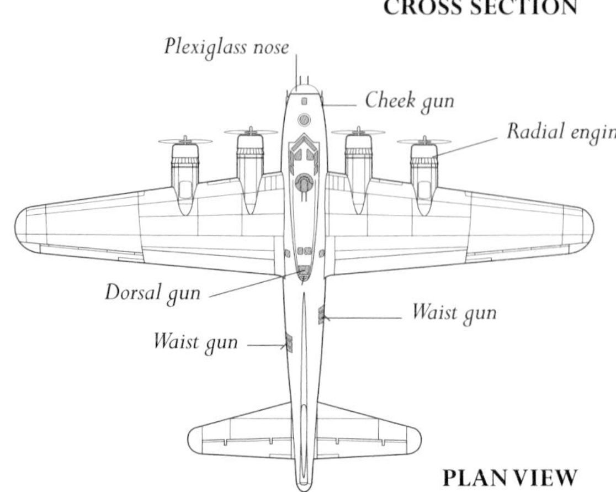

BOMBER PROFILE
The B-17 had a wingspan of 103¾ft (31.62m) and measured 74⅓ft (22.66m) from nose to tail. The huge tail fin gave the aircraft a distinctive profile.

THE STRUCTURE

▲ **ROBUST UNDERCARRIAGE**
To support a loaded weight of almost 25.5 tonnes (25 tons), the undercarriage struts had to be robust, with massive hydraulic shock-absorbers.

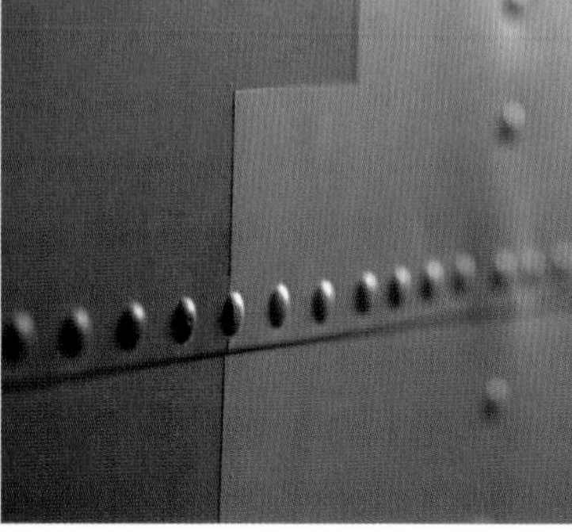

▲ **ALUMINUM SKIN**
The wings and fuselage were clad with light-gauge aluminum, riveted to the frames underneath.

▲ **WING ROOT**
Construction was not sophisticated; no effort was made to improve the airflow by counter-sinking the fastenings.

► **RADIAL ENGINE**
The B-17's four 1,200hp Wright radial engines were equipped with turbo-superchargers to improve high-altitude performance.

THE GUNS

▲ **AT THE NOSE**
The bombardier had a clear view of the target through the plexiglass nose. He also operated the twin .5in Browning M2 machine-guns in the chin turret below, by remote control.

◄ **DORSAL TURRET**
The forward dorsal guns were mounted above the cockpit in a hydraulically powered turret with 360° traverse and 90° elevation; they were operated by the flight engineer.

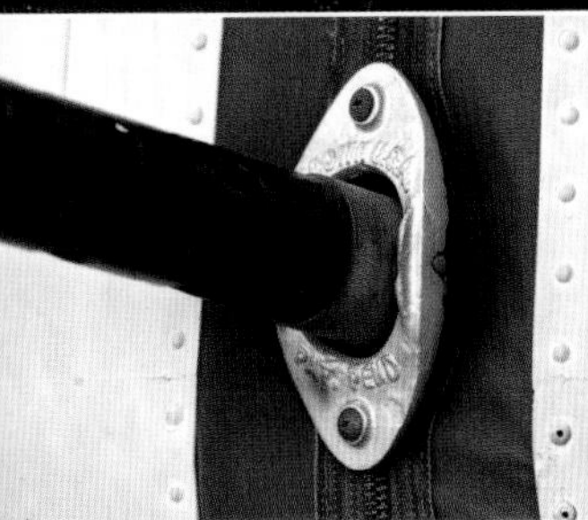

▲ **CHIN GUN**
A chin turret was added on the B-17G after research showed that the plane was vulnerable to head-on attacks.

▲ **CHEEK GUN**
Single flexibly mounted M2 machine-guns were mounted just aft of the bombardier's position; they were operated by the navigator.

▲ **BALL TURRET**
The F and G variants featured a ventral (ball) turret that was suspended on a gimbal from a tube attached to the fuselage ceiling.

▲ **WAIST GUN**
Along the fuselage in staggered positions, port (aft) and starboard (forward), were single, flexibly mounted M2s, each with its own gunner.

◄ **A MIGHTY FORTRESS**
With a ten-man crew, the B-17 was cramped, but its crews set great store by its ability to get them home even when badly damaged.

INSIDE THE B-17

Much of the B-17's slim fuselage was taken up by the bomb bay. The pilot and co-pilot in the cockpit, and the flight engineer behind them, were relatively comfortable, as were the radio operator, bombardier, and navigator, though the latter two had to squirm into their positions in the nose via a narrow opening. The tail and ball-turret gunners, however, had to be contortionists to reach their places. They and the waist gunners wore electrically heated suits.

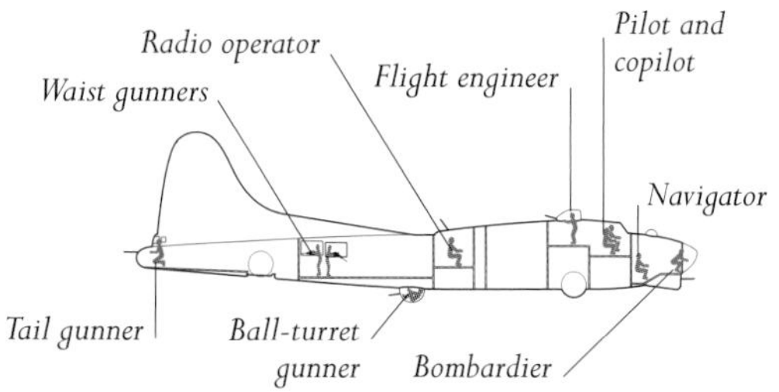

CROSS SECTION

▲ FLIGHT DECK
Both the pilot, who sat on the left, and the copilot had a control yoke, with the throttle controls for each individual engine located between the two of them.

▶ FORWARD VIEW
Looking toward the radio operator's position from the starboard waist gun, the fuselage ribs are clearly visible. The black column supports the ball turret below the fuselage.

▼ PITCH CONTROLS
The propellers' pitch and the throttle settings had to be adjusted to regulate the aircraft's airspeed, and this required the attention of both men.

THE OXYGEN SUPPLY

▲ OXYGEN REGULATOR
Each crewman was supplied with oxygen from a central source. He used a portable bottle (*below*) if he needed to move around the aircraft.

▲ CENTRAL SUPPLY
There were 18 large oxygen cylinders in the lower fuselage. Oxygen was vital at the B-17's operating height of over 25,000ft (7,600m).

▲ CONTROL CABLES
Cables running from the flight deck through the fuselage to the control surfaces activated the rudder, ailerons, and elevators.

THE GUNS AND BOMBS

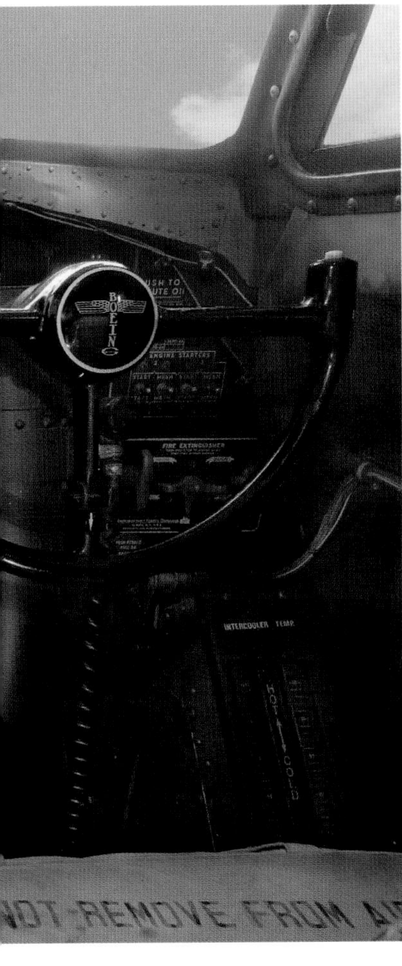

◀ **TOP GUNS**
There were three dorsal machine-guns. In addition to the pair in the powered turret above the cockpit, the radio operator had a single .5in M2 gun in a flexible mount above his own position.

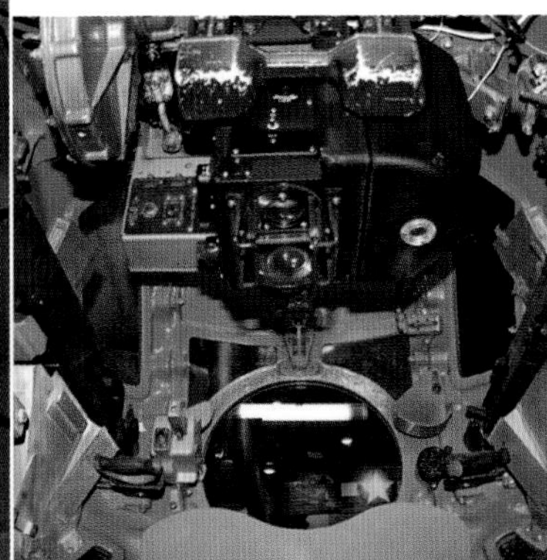

▲ **BALL TURRET**
The gunner for the ball turret climbed into position after takeoff. Lack of space forced him to sit with his knees against his chest. In an emergency, he donned a parachute only after clambering back into the fuselage.

▼ **TAIL TURRET**
Like the ball-turret gunner, the tail gunner had very limited space. He had to operate his paired M2 machine-guns from a kneeling position.

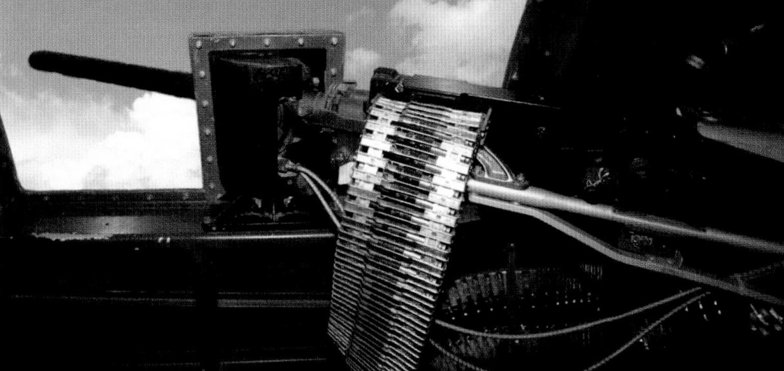

◀ **WAIST GUN**
The two single machine-gun positions in the waist were open to the elements until the E model was introduced. There was no recovery system for spent cartridge cases, which littered the floor.

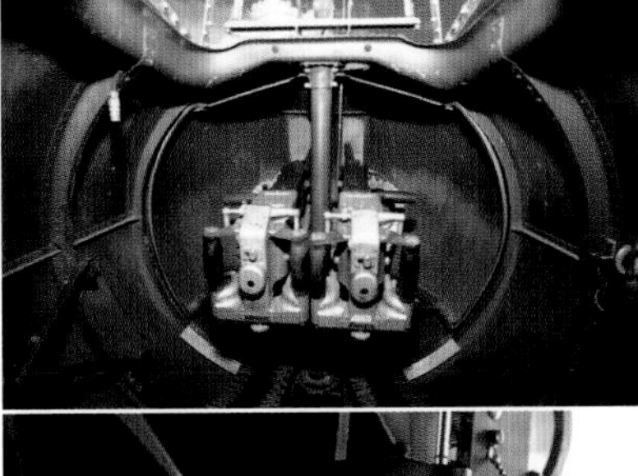

▲ **GUN SIGHT**
The waist guns had compensating sights that could be programmed with the aircraft's speed and altitude to give the "lead" required to hit a moving target.

▲ **NORDEN BOMB SIGHT**
One of the most sophisticated pieces of equipment in the entire aircraft, the bomb sight was a predictive computer that allowed the bombardier to compensate for such factors as the aircraft's altitude and forward speed, and the type of bombs carried.

▲ **BOMB BAY**
From his position, the bombardier could see into the bomb bay, below and aft of the flight deck.

▼ **BOMB LOAD**
A typical load included high explosive bombs and mixed incendiary devices.

BOMBS AND MISSILES OF WORLD WAR II

Initially, aerial bombs were simple iron cylinders filled with explosives and fused to detonate on impact; sometimes they had rudimentary fins, but were still only suitable for hitting areas rather than specific targets. Aerodynamic casings and more effective fins made flight paths more predictable, but even the best bombs were far from accurate. As soon as appropriate technologies became available, bombs were fitted with guidance systems, some of them built-in, others requiring a controlling hand in the launch aircraft. By 1944, following much experimentation with rocketry, the first generation of "surface-to-surface" missiles appeared (i.e. launched from the ground to strike ground targets), and promised to change the very nature of the war in the air.

Wingspan was 21ft (6.4m)

▲ BLOHM & VOSS BV246 HAGELKORN

Date 1943
Origin Germany
Charge 960lb (435kg)
Length 11½ft (3.5m)

The *Hagelkorn* ("Hailstone") glide-bomb was an unpowered air-to-surface missile, its gliding ability allowing it to be dropped at a distance from the target rather than above it. Its development program was curtailed in favor of the V-1 flying bomb.

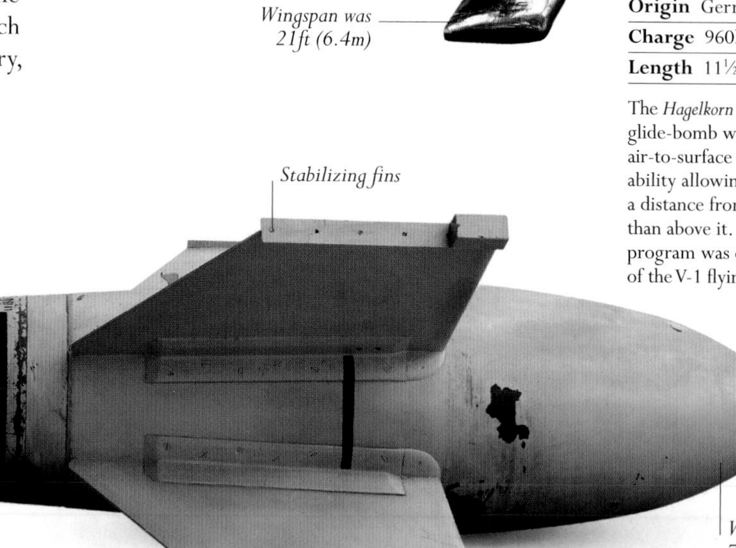

▲ RUHRSTAHL/KRAMER X-1 "FRITZ X"

Date 1943
Origin Germany
Charge 705lb (320kg)
Length 11ft (3.3m)

The most successful guided bomb of the war, the "Fritz X" was steered to its target by an operator aboard the launching aircraft. It was a marked success, with the *Luftwaffe*'s specialist unit, *Kampfgeschwader* 100, sinking the British ship HMS *Warspite* at Salerno.

▼ FIESLER FI103 (V1)

Date 1944
Origin Germany
Charge 1,830lb (830kg)
Length 27⅓ft (8.32m)

The first long-range surface-to-surface missile, the FI103 was launched from a ramp by a steam catapult, and was powered by a simple pulse-jet motor. It was deployed from June 13, 1944 against targets in the UK and later against Antwerp.

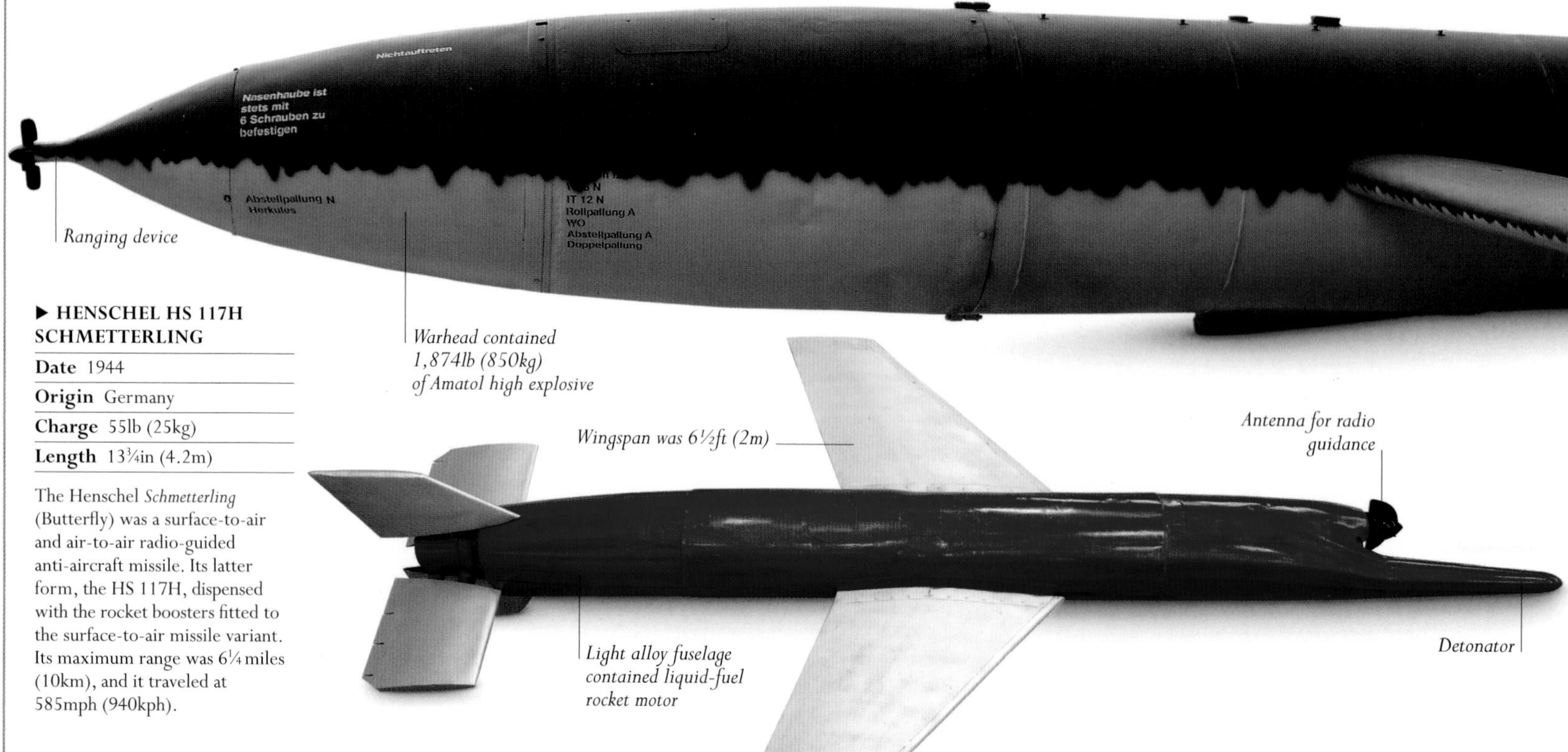

▶ HENSCHEL HS 117H SCHMETTERLING

Date 1944
Origin Germany
Charge 55lb (25kg)
Length 13¾in (4.2m)

The Henschel *Schmetterling* (Butterfly) was a surface-to-air and air-to-air radio-guided anti-aircraft missile. Its latter form, the HS 117H, dispensed with the rocket boosters fitted to the surface-to-air missile variant. Its maximum range was 6¼ miles (10km), and it traveled at 585mph (940kph).

▲ RUHRSTAHL X-4 AAM

Date	1944
Origin	Germany
Charge	44lb (20kg)
Length	6½ft (2m)

The X-4 air-to-air (i.e. aircraft-to-aircraft) missile was developed as a "stand-off" weapon, to be delivered from outside the range of the target aircraft's guns. Powered by a liquid-fuel rocket, it had a range of up to 2½ miles (4km), and flew at over 683½mph (1,100kph). It was guided by a wire connecting it to its mother-aircraft.

▶ A4 (V2)

Date	1944
Origin	Germany
Charge	2,150lb (975kg)
Length	46ft (14.05m)

The A4 was the world's first ballistic missile, with a maximum range of 205 miles (330km), which allowed it to hit London from launch sites in the Netherlands. Horizontal and vertical gyroscopes guided the rocket.

Warhead contained 2,205lb (1,000kg) of Amatol high explosive

Rocket motor

Stabilizing fins

▼ ATOMIC BOMB MK I "LITTLE BOY"

Date	1945
Origin	US
Charge	15,000 tons TNT equivalent
Length	12¼ft (3m)

"Little Boy" was the codename given to the first nuclear device used in war. The US Army Air Forces dropped it over Hiroshima (see pp.378–79), in Japan, from the B-29 Superfortress "Enola Gay" bomber aircraft on August 6, 1945, to devastating effect.

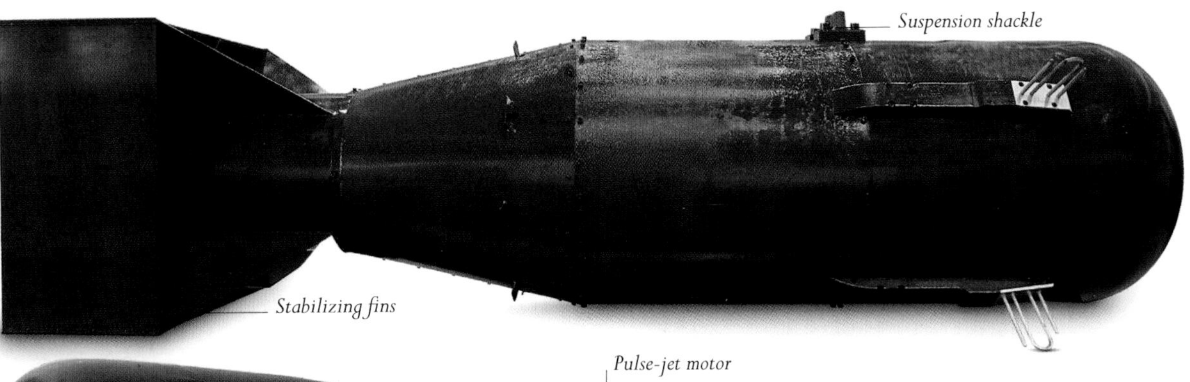

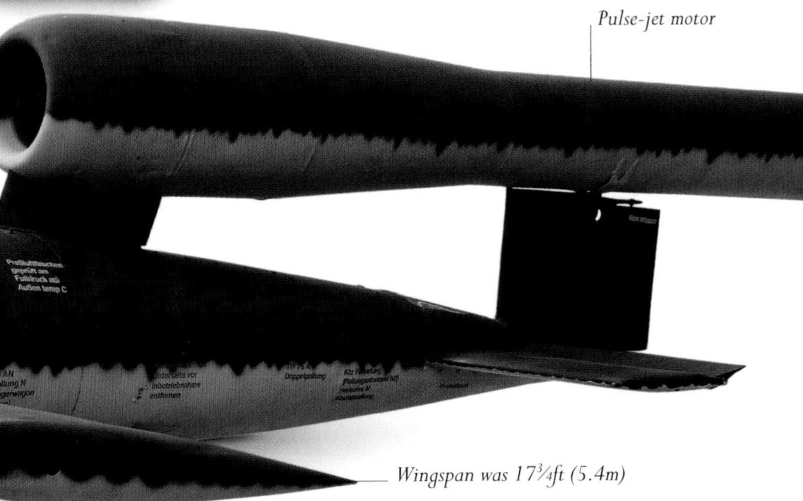

▶ ATOMIC BOMB MK II "FAT MAN"

Date	1945
Origin	US
Charge	21,000 tons TNT equivalent
Length	10¾ft (3.3m)

"Fat Man" was the second nuclear device dropped by the US Army Air Forces on Japan, this time on the city of Nagasaki, on August 9, 1945. It was a completely different design from that of "Little Boy," using plutonium in place of uranium.

TRANSPORT, RECONNAISSANCE, AND LIAISON AIRCRAFT

The first military transport aircraft were commercial airplanes developed during the interwar period, but specially built designs better suited to military operations soon began to appear. Specialist reconnaissance aircraft were developed, too: some, especially those designed to undertake maritime operations, doubled up in the attack role, while others dispensed with armament completely in the interest of being able to fly higher and faster than any armed interceptor the enemy could send against them—a principle that has held into the modern era. Light aircraft were also pressed into military service to operate both in and away from the combat zone.

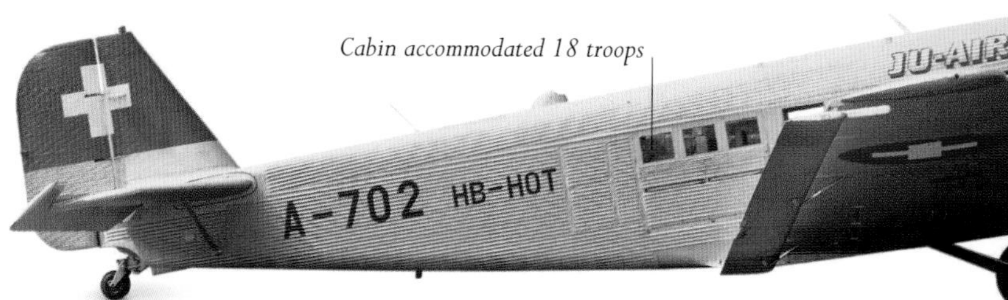

Cabin accommodated 18 troops

▲ **JUNKERS JU. 52/3M**

Launched 1932 **Origin** Germany

Wingspan 95¾ft (29.25m)

Length 62ft (18.9m)

Top speed 165mph (265kph)

Engine Three 715hp (533kW) BMW 132 radials

With its three motors, rectangular fuselage and corrugated Duralumin skin, the Ju. 52 was instantly recognizable. Originally produced as a 17-seater airliner, it was taken up for military service in 1935. In combat zones, losses were invariably high; 280 were lost in May 1940 during the invasion of the Netherlands.

High-mounted wing gave a good field of view

▲ **CONSOLIDATED PBY CATALINA**

Launched 1936 **Origin** US

Wingspan 104ft (31.7m)

Length 64ft (19.5m)

Top speed 196mph (315kph)

Engine Two 1,200hp (895kW) Pratt & Whitney R-1830-92 Twin Wasp radials

Designed as a "patrol bomber," the Catalina is the most successful flying boat ever produced; many are still in use, chiefly to fight wildfires, 75 years after it was introduced.

Loop antenna for finding direction

▲ **FOCKE-WULF FW. 200 CONDOR**

Launched 1937 **Origin** Germany

Wingspan 107¾ft (32.85m)

Length 77ft (23.45m)

Top speed 225mph (360kph)

Engine Four 1,200hp (895kW) BMW 323R radials

The Condor was built for Lufthansa as a long-range airliner, but was adapted for military service in mid-1939. It was not robust enough to be a success as a military transport craft, but was better suited to maritime reconnaissance and for attacking shipping. A total of 276 were built, most of which were lost during the war.

Flaps extended the full length of the wings

Cockpit had space for pilot and observer

Large rudder for maneuverability

Entire aircraft weighed just 2,800lb (1,270kg)

▲ **FIESELER FI.156 STORCH**

Launched 1937 **Origin** Germany

Wingspan 46¾ft (14.3m)

Length 32½ft (9.9m)

Top speed 110mph (175kph)

Engine 240hp (177kW) Argus As 10V8

The *Storch* (Stork) was designed as an army liaison aircraft. Unusually for a land-based aircraft, it had wings that could be folded back along its fuselage. Its approach speed was so low that in a headwind it appeared to land almost vertically.

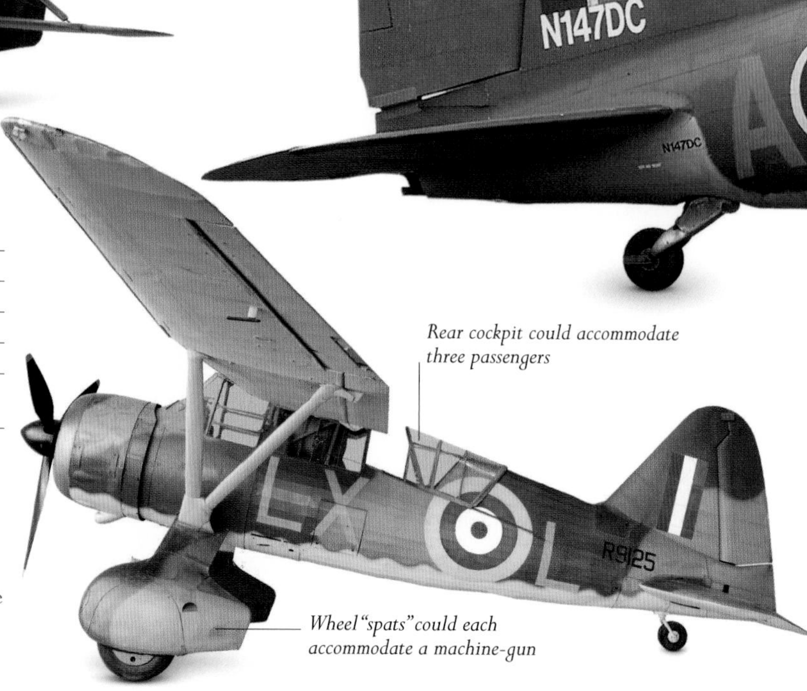

Rear cockpit could accommodate three passengers

Wheel "spats" could each accommodate a machine-gun

▶ **WESTLAND LYSANDER**

Launched 1938 **Origin** UK

Wingspan 50ft (15.25m)

Length 30½ft (9.3m)

Top speed 211mph (340kph)

Engine 870hp (649kW) Bristol Mercury XX radial

The Lysander was used for World War II army operations, perhaps most famously by the British Royal Air Force's 138 (Special Duties) and 161 Squadrons, which employed it to insert and recover agents in enemy-occupied territory. A total of 1,786 were built, all of which were withdrawn from service at the war's end.

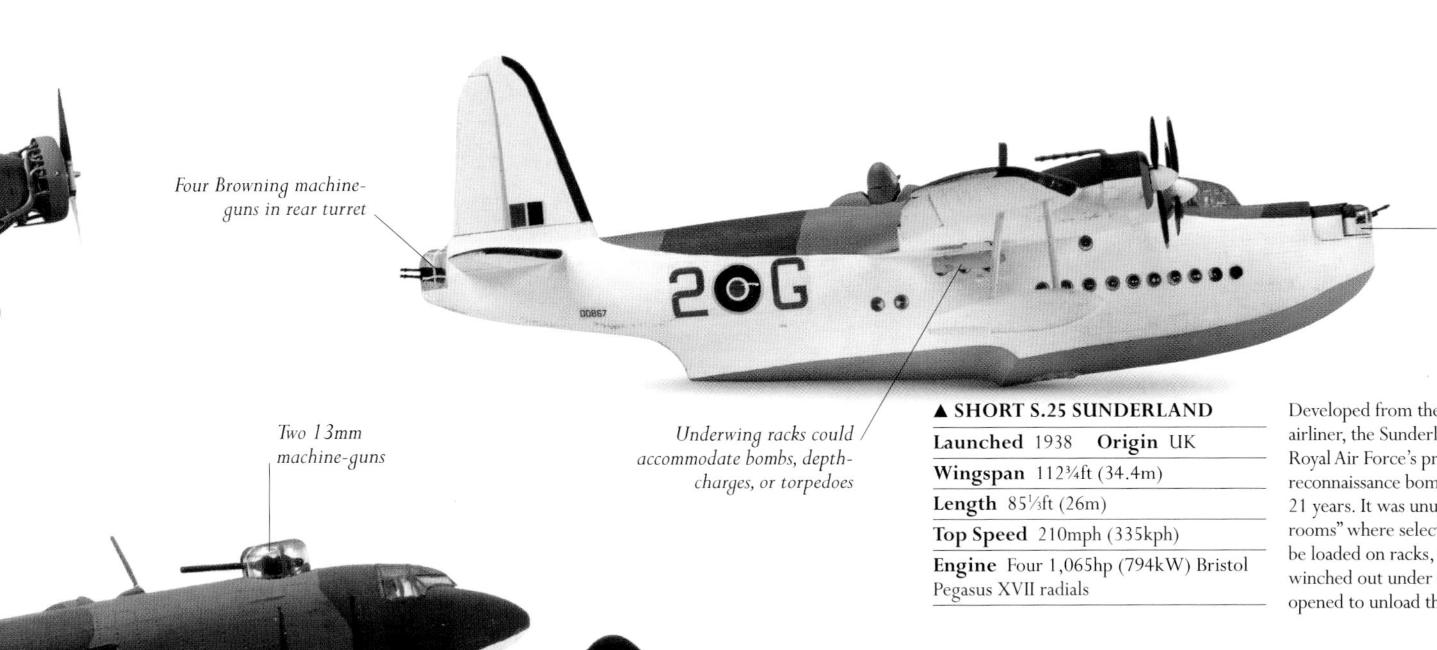

▲ SHORT S.25 SUNDERLAND

Launched 1938 **Origin** UK
Wingspan 112¾ft (34.4m)
Length 85⅓ft (26m)
Top Speed 210mph (335kph)
Engine Four 1,065hp (794kW) Bristol Pegasus XVII radials

Developed from the successful Empire airliner, the Sunderland was the British Royal Air Force's principal patrol/reconnaissance bomber flying boat for 21 years. It was unusual in having "bomb rooms" where selected ordnance could be loaded on racks, which were then winched out under the wings and opened to unload the bombs.

Two 13mm machine-guns

Remote-controlled 20mm cannon

Wings and fuselage of fabric-on-wood construction

Glider pilots were also combat soldiers

▲ AIRSPEED HORSA GLIDER

Launched 1941 **Origin** UK
Wingspan 88ft (26.8m)
Length 67ft (20.4m)
Top speed 100mph (160kph)
Engine None

The *Luftwaffe* used gliders during the invasion of Belgium and France in 1940, and the British soon followed. The Horsa was larger than the German DFS 30, and could carry 25 troops. Some 4,000 were built, over 1,200 of which were expended in Operation Market Garden (see pp.372–73).

▼ DOUGLAS C-47 SKYTRAIN

Launched 1936 **Origin** US
Wingspan 95¼ft (29m)
Length 64¾ft (19.7m)
Top speed 230mph (370kph)
Engine Two 1,100hp (820kW) Wright R-1820 Cyclone radials

Introduced as a commercial airliner by American Airlines, the DC-3 soon entered military service as the C-47. Over 10,000 were built for this purpose by 1945; some 400 were still in use at the end of the 20th century. A C-47 originally cost just under US $80,000 to build.

Crew of two

Three-bladed propeller driven by radial engine

Cabin could accommodate 32 paratroopers

Four 18ft (5.5m) rotor blades

Tail rotor counteracted turning movement of main rotor

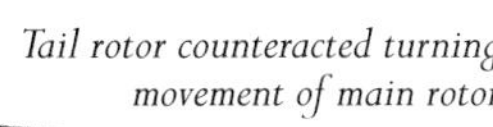

▶ SIKORSKY R-4 HOVERFLY

Launched 1943 **Origin** US
Rotor diameter 37¾ft (11.5m)
Length 33½ft (10.2m)
Top speed 75mph (120kph)
Engine 200hp (149kW) Warner R-550 radial

Developed from the experimental VS-300 for liaison and rescue work, the Hoverfly was the US Army Air Forces and the British Royal Air Force's first operational rotary-wing aircraft. A total of 131 were built up to 1944, when the type was superseded by the R-5.

COMMUNICATIONS AND CODE-BREAKING EQUIPMENT OF WORLD WAR II

Between World War I and World War II great strides were made in both wired and wireless communications technology, the latter reaching a point at which it was possible to build reliable transmitter/receiver sets (transceivers) that would fit into a small suitcase. By 1939, mechanical calculators were commonplace in the business world, and the technology they employed was increasingly used to mechanize the encoding of messages, making them very difficult to decipher if intercepted. During World War II, these two apparently disparate disciplines joined forces to create the first electromechanical (and later electronic) computers, which were developed specifically as aids to code-breaking.

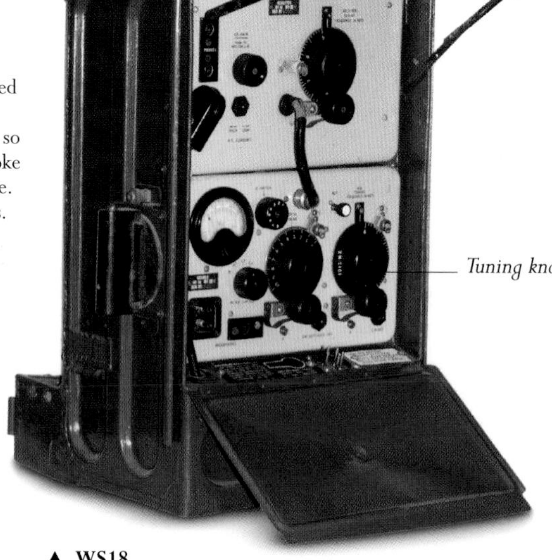

▲ WS18

Date 1939

Origin UK

Type Radio transceiver

Described as being "for short range telephony in forward areas," the Wireless Set 18 had an effective transmission range of 5 miles (8km). It was issued in 1939, and was the first "man-pack" radio transceiver put into series production for the British Army.

▼ ENIGMA

Date 1926–1950s

Origin Germany

Type Encoding/decoding device

The operator turned Enigma's rotors to a random setting and typed the message to be encoded using the keys below—each keystroke advancing the rotors so that repeating the same keystroke gave a different result each time. Decoding reversed this process.

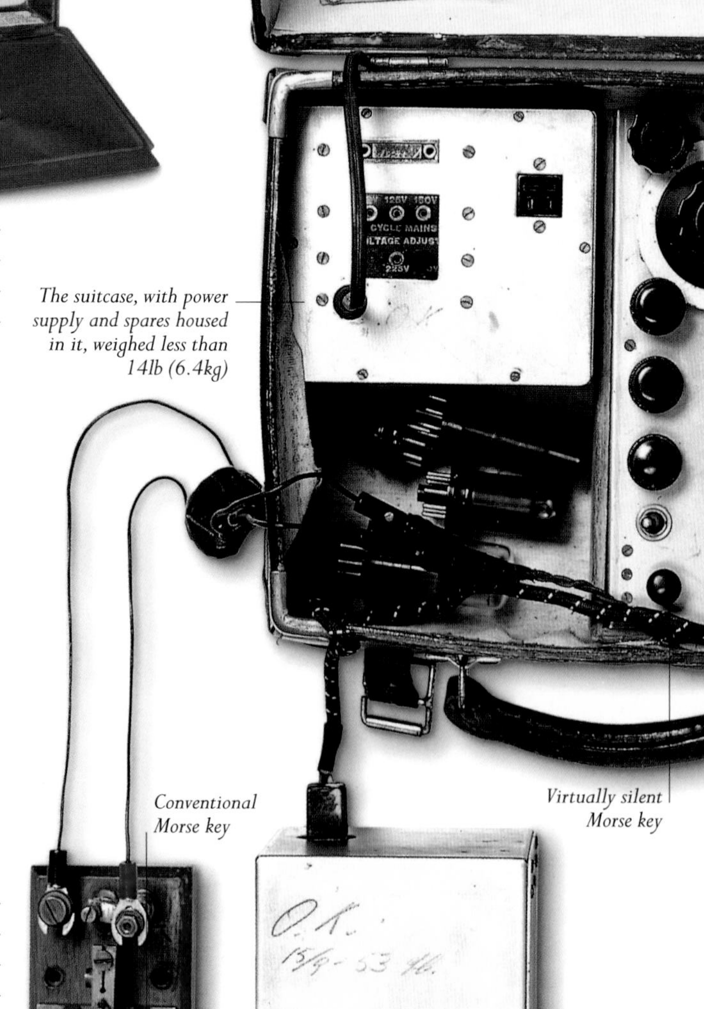

▶ PARASET SUITCASE RADIO TRANSCEIVER

Date 1940

Origin UK

Type Radio transceiver

The first miniature radio transceiver for clandestine use, the Whaddon Mk VII Paraset was the absolute minimum needed to set up two-way communication over distances of up to 500 miles (800km). It included a built-in Morse key that was almost silent in operation.

▶ TYPE EE-8-B US ARMY FIELD TELEPHONE

Date 1944

Origin US

Type Field telephone set

For security reasons, battlefield communication during the war, especially between rear-echelon command posts and front-line units, was still carried out by means of land lines rather than by radio wherever possible. This was to avoid the need for time-consuming encoding and decoding.

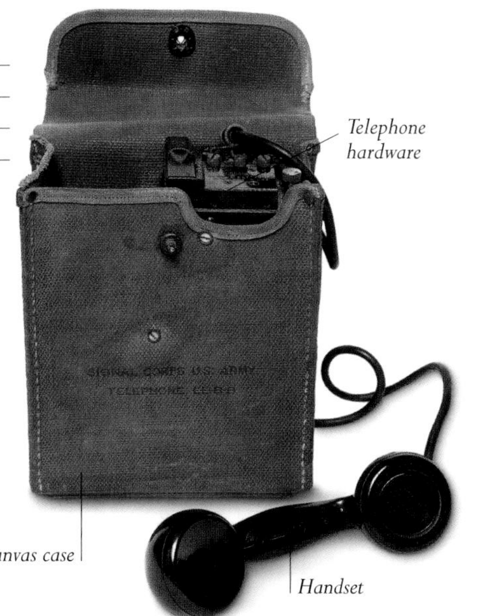

Telephone hardware

Canvas case

Handset

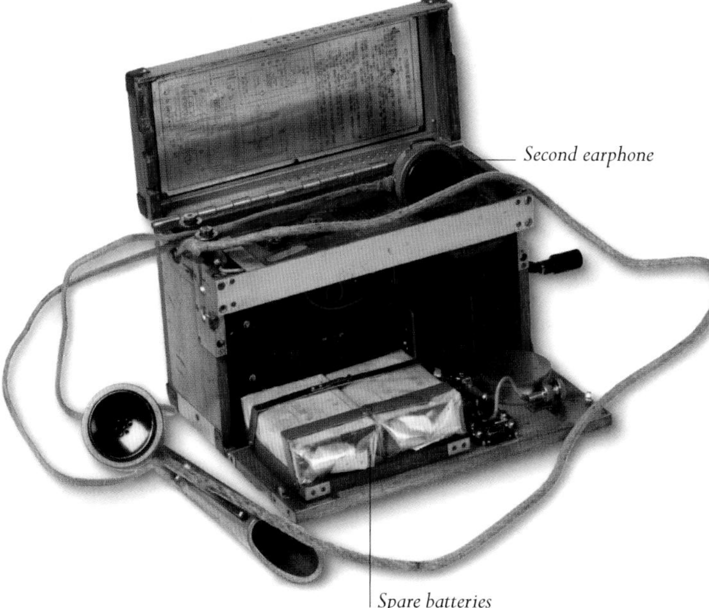

Second earphone

Spare batteries

▲ FIELD TELEPHONE MODEL 92

Date 1932

Origin Japan

Type Field telephone set

Developed in peacetime by the Oki Electric Co, this field telephone was manufactured to a very high standard. The wooden case housed a generator, the headset, batteries, and spares. The Japanese employed the "ground return" system, which was both less secure and less reliable than using twin cables.

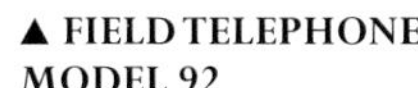

▶ KRYHA

Date 1920s–1940s

Origin Germany

Type Encoding/decoding device

Simpler in character than Enigma, Kryha was considerably less secure—a 1,135 characters-long test message was successfully broken by an American team within three hours. This purely mechanical device, however, had the advantage of being much smaller and lighter.

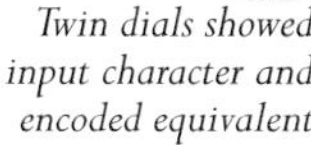

Twin dials showed input character and encoded equivalent

▼ TYPE A MK III SUITCASE RADIO TRANSCEIVER

Date 1944

Origin UK

Type Radio transceiver

This was the most widely used of the British "spy radios," and technically the best of them. It had a transmission range of over 500 miles (800km). Packed into a suitcase just 4in (10cm) deep, along with spares and accessories, it weighed only 8¾lb (4kg) in total.

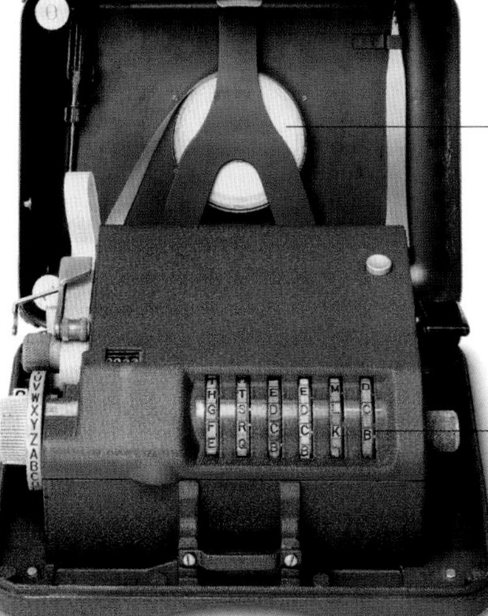

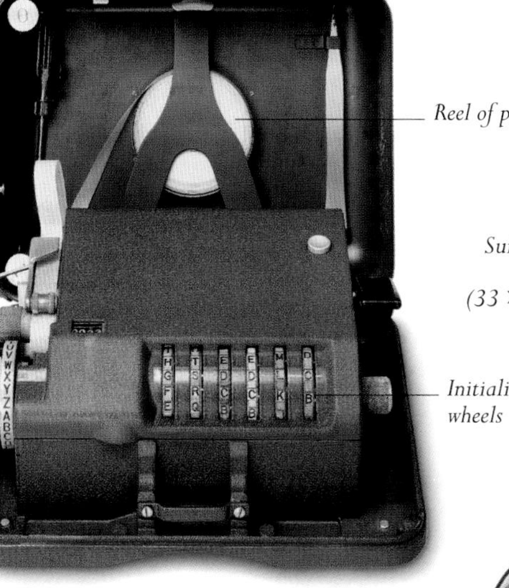

Spare valve

Reel of paper tape

Initializing wheels

Crystal assembly

▲ M209B

Date 1940–1955

Origin US

Type Encoding/decoding device

A purely mechanical encryption device, the M209 employed six alphabetic wheels to set up the initial key. The message was then entered one character at a time via the wheel on the left. The result was printed on paper tape, and the rotor settings advanced. Reversing the procedure permitted decoding. M209's output was decoded by German code-breakers by early 1943.

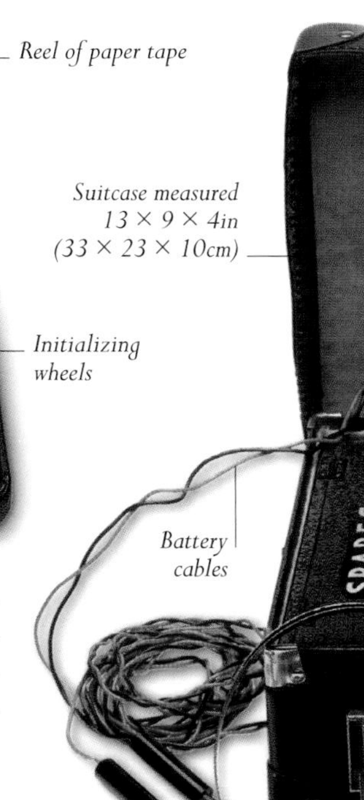

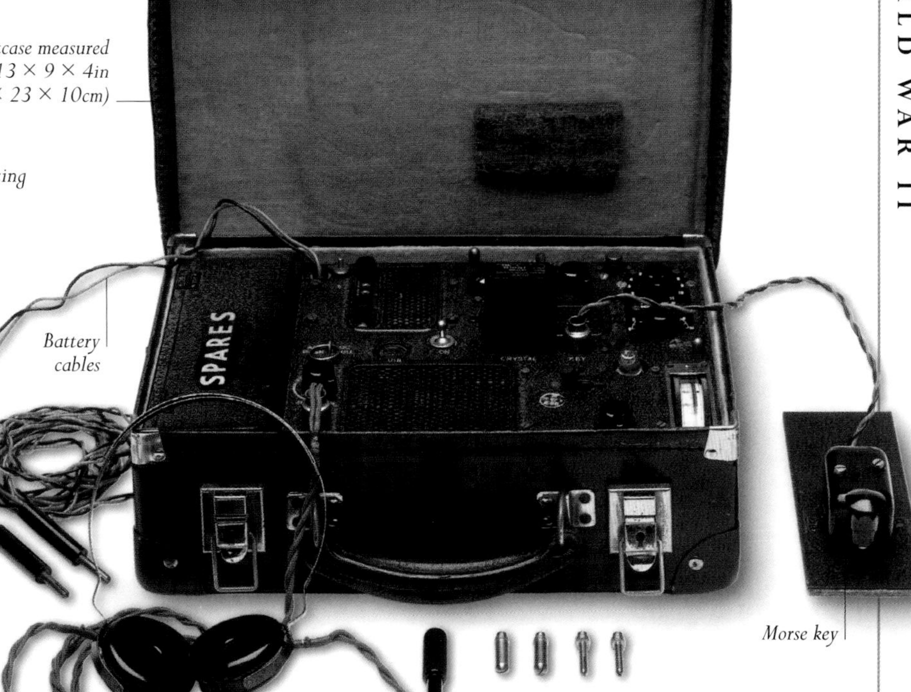

Suitcase measured 13 × 9 × 4in (33 × 23 × 10cm)

Battery cables

Morse key

WORLD WAR ERA MEDALS

The World Wars saw countless acts of individual gallantry amid the mass actions of huge armies. Medals continued to be awarded for acts of exceptional bravery, and the sheer numbers of combatants meant that more were issued than ever before. Some medals that had been introduced previously took on a new significance during this period—notably Germany's "Blue Max" and the USA's Purple Heart.

◀ **WORLD WAR I VICTORY MEDAL**

Date 1919

Origin US

The Victory Medal, as it was first known, was issued to US forces who had served in World War I and actions in Russia (1919–20).

Bronze Maltese cross with swords between the arms

▶ **CROIX DE GUERRE**

Date 1915

Origin France

This medal was issued to individuals for bravery or other military virtues displayed on the battlefield during World War I, World War II, and in other campaigns not fought on French soil. The example pictured is a World War II medal.

▲ **OTTOMAN WAR MEDAL**

Date 1915

Origin Turkey

Conflict World War I

Better known as the Gallipoli Star, this decoration was awarded for the duration of World War I to Turkish soldiers and their allies for gallantry in battle.

Golden eagles between the arms of the cross

▶ **POUR LE MÉRITE (BLUE MAX)**

Date 1740–1918

Origin Germany

This order was both a civillian and military honour until 1810, when it was restricted to serving military personnel. One of the first airmen to receive the award was World War I flying ace Max Immelmann; his fame led to the order becoming known as the Blue Max.

▲ **MILITARY CROSS**

Date 1914

Origin UK

Instituted in 1914 as a gallantry award for British army officers of a lower precedence than the Victoria Cross (see p.258) and the Distinguished Service Order, from 1993 onward, the Military Cross has been open to all ranks for gallantry in land operations.

▶ **IRON CROSS**

Date 1914

Origin Germany

The Iron Cross was issued to all ranks, but only those who had already received a 2nd Class award could receive the 1st Class version. In World War I, around 4 million 2nd Class and 145,000 1st Class medals were awarded. The medal shown is a 1939 design with a central swastika.

▲ **MEMORIAL PLAQUE**

Date 1919

Origin UK

Conflict World War I

Awarded to the next-of-kin of those who lost their lives as a result of active service in World War I, this bronze plaque, 4¾in (120mm) in diameter, bears the name of the dead serviceman.

▶ **ORDER OF THE PATRIOTIC WAR**

Date 1942

Origin Soviet Union

Conflict World War II

This silver-and-enamel medal was awarded to Soviet military personnel who fought on the Eastern Front, and to partisan fighters for personal bravery. The Order of the 1st Class was issued 344,000 times, while 1,028,000 2nd Class awards were made.

▶ DISTINGUISHED FLYING CROSS

Date 1918

Origin UK

Introduced for officers of the British Royal Air Force, the Distinguished Flying Cross (DFC) was awarded for acts of valor. World War I saw approximately 1,100 DFCs issued, while 20,354 were awarded during World War II. The DFC was opened to all ranks in 1993.

Propeller design on vertical arms

T-35 tank depicted on front

▲ MEDAL FOR COURAGE

Date 1938

Origin Soviet Union

First introduced to recognize displays of courage in battle by military personnel in the defense of the Soviet Union, this medal continued to be awarded by Russia after the break-up of the USSR. Its recipients receive a monthly pension and travel free on Russian public transportation.

▼ PURPLE HEART

Date 1782

Origin US

The original Purple Heart was instituted by George Washington in 1782 as the Badge of Military Merit, and was issued to only three Revolutionary War soldiers. The award was not proposed again until 1932. Approximately 1.9 million Purple Hearts have been issued since that date.

Hammer and sickle emblem of the Soviet Union

Golden background rays denote a 1st Class award

Black, yellow, and blue stripes represent night flying, enemy searchlights, and the sky

▲ AIR CREW EUROPE STAR

Date 1945

Origin UK

Conflict World War II

The rarest World War II campaign star, this medal was awarded for operations over Europe from UK bases from September 3, 1939 to June 5, 1944. The recipient had to hold the 1939–45 Star and have flown in operations for two months between these dates.

Ribbon colors said to represent blood, snow, and death

◀ EASTERN FRONT MEDAL

Date 1942

Origin Germany

Conflict World War II

Commonly known as the "Ostmedaille," this award marked service on the Eastern Front between November 15, 1941 and April 15, 1942. In reference to the hardship endured during that winter, campaign, it was nicknamed the "Gefrierfleischorden" (Frozen Meat Medal).

Eagle and swastika motif

KEY EVENTS

1914–45

■ **1914** In the second month of World War I, a single German U-boat in the North Sea sinks three British cruisers in one hour.

■ **1916** Forty-four battleships—28 British and 16 German—are present at the Battle of Jutland, but only a few are sunk in what is an indecisive encounter.

■ **1941** The British battleship HMS *Prince of Wales* and the battle cruiser HMS *Repulse*, sailing off Malaya without air cover, are sunk by land-based Japanese bombers and torpedo aircraft.

■ **1944** The US Navy deploys more than 200 ships against the Japanese at the battle of Leyte Gulf (see pp.348–49), off the Philippines, one of the largest naval battles in history.

■ **1945** The German Type XXI U-boat enters frontline service. It is the first submarine able to submerge for long periods, rather than diving occasionally, and can travel at speed underwater.

KEY DEVELOPMENT

BATTLES AT SEA IN THE WORLD WARS

Command of the seas was a vital element in both world wars. The impact of submarines and aircraft created logistical complications, as well as new dangers, for surface fleets, which were themselves increasingly devoted to the support of amphibious landings.

Given the fleets of heavily gunned battleships built in the years leading up to the war, the naval battles of World War I did not follow expectations: there was no climactic, pitched battle between the German High Seas Fleet and the British Grand Fleet. On the only occasion when the two met, at Jutland in the summer of 1916, the Germans fled on discovering the full extent of the British fleet deployed against them, and escaped due to a bungled pursuit. In fact, British superiority in numbers was simply too great to be challenged, even though German warships proved to have better range-finding equipment, better protection against shells, and better night-fighting skills.

German surface warships had been expected to pose a serious threat to British merchant shipping, but it was the German U-boats that turned out to be the biggest threat. Having disposed of the majority of Germany's warships early in the conflict, Britain's Royal Navy were frighteningly vulnerable to mines and submarines, leading to caution in all fleet operations. The belated introduction of convoys accompanied by Royal Navy warships, from the summer of 1917, reduced losses, but U-boats remained a constant danger.

▼ **AN AMPHIBIOUS TRUCK**
The American DUKW (or "Duck") was one of the ingenious vehicles developed for amphibious operations in World War II. It could carry 25 soldiers ashore and up a beach.

POST-WORLD WAR I

Proof of the effectiveness of submarines, and growing evidence for the importance of naval air power, failed to discourage navies from building bigger and better battleships after 1918. In the 1920s, the Royal Navy thought it had found the answer to the U-boat menace with the ASDIC sonar system, which pinpointed vessels underwater—not considering that they could attack by night on the surface, where their low profile made them virtually undetectable.

World War II brought epic naval conflicts in the Atlantic, Pacific, and Mediterranean, with the British, German, Italian, American, and Japanese navies engaged in fierce combat. This time the major shock for navies was the vulnerability of even the most powerful warships to air attack. Within range of hostile aircraft, surface ships were dangerously exposed without air cover. German magnetic mines caused havoc

"The only thing that ever **truly frightened me** during the war was the **U-boat peril**"

BRITISH PRIME MINISTER WINSTON CHURCHILL

at the start of the war, until the technique of degaussing ship's hulls (reducing their magnetism) was introduced.

Meanwhile, U-boats, coordinated by radio and with improved range, were even more destructive to merchant shipping than they had been in World War I. A combination of tactical and technological innovations were employed to meet this threat: these included improved radar on convoy escort ships, and high-frequency radio direction-finding equipment ("huff-duff").

When gun battles between large surface warships did occur, victory usually went to the side with superior radar and night-fighting equipment, as in the fighting between Japanese and American fleets around Guadalcanal in 1942, or between the British and Italians in the Mediterranean. Eventual naval superiority allowed the Allies to mount numerous amphibious landings: the largest of these, at Normandy in June 1944, was supported by more than 1,200 warships.

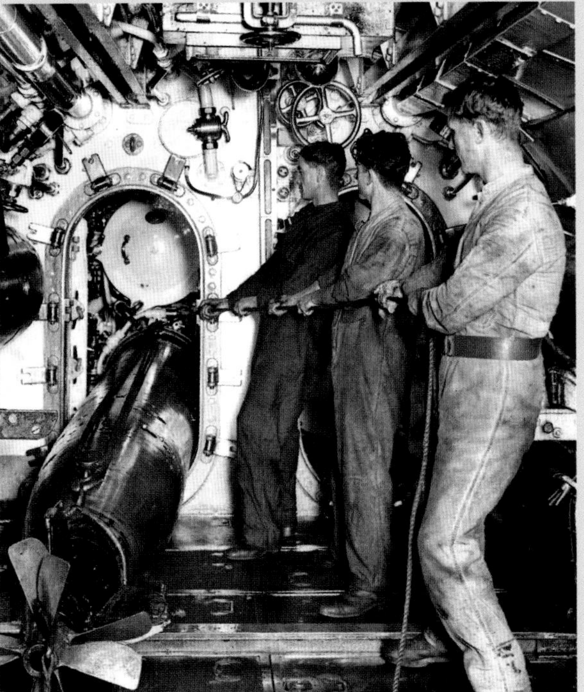

◄ **LOADING A TORPEDO**
The cramped conditions on World War II submarines made loading torpedoes in the torpedo tubes extremely difficult. On German U-boats—as with British submarines—the torpedo room also served as living accommodation.

◄ **PEARL HARBOR**
The USS *Nevada* was among the 18 American ships sunk or damaged in Japan's surprise attack on the US Pacific fleet on December 7, 1941, at Pearl Harbor. The Japanese force consisted of 353 fighter, bomber, and torpedo aircraft launched from six aircraft carriers, supported by midget submarines.

KEY **FIGURE**

ADMIRAL ISOROKU YAMAMOTO

1884–1943

Having fought as an ensign at the Battle of Tsushima in 1904, Yamamoto rose to be commander-in-chief of the Japanese Combined Fleet by 1939. An advocate of naval air power, he planned the attack on Pearl Harbor that started the Pacific War in 1941.

▲ Yamamoto died when his transport aircraft was ambushed and shot down by US fighters.

CAPITAL SHIPS

Although the term "capital ship" was not actually defined until the 1920s, by the outbreak of World War I it was already being applied to the most powerful craft in the fleet: battleships and battlecruisers, which sacrificed armor for speed as a means of protecting themselves. Battleships seemed to dominate the field of naval warfare during World War I, but in fact the expected large-scale battle between the German and British fleets did not materialize. After the war, they bore the brunt of internationally mandated cuts, but their heyday was already past in any case. In the early stages of World War II they proved themselves sickeningly vulnerable to air attack, and the pride-of-place they once enjoyed passed to the aircraft carrier.

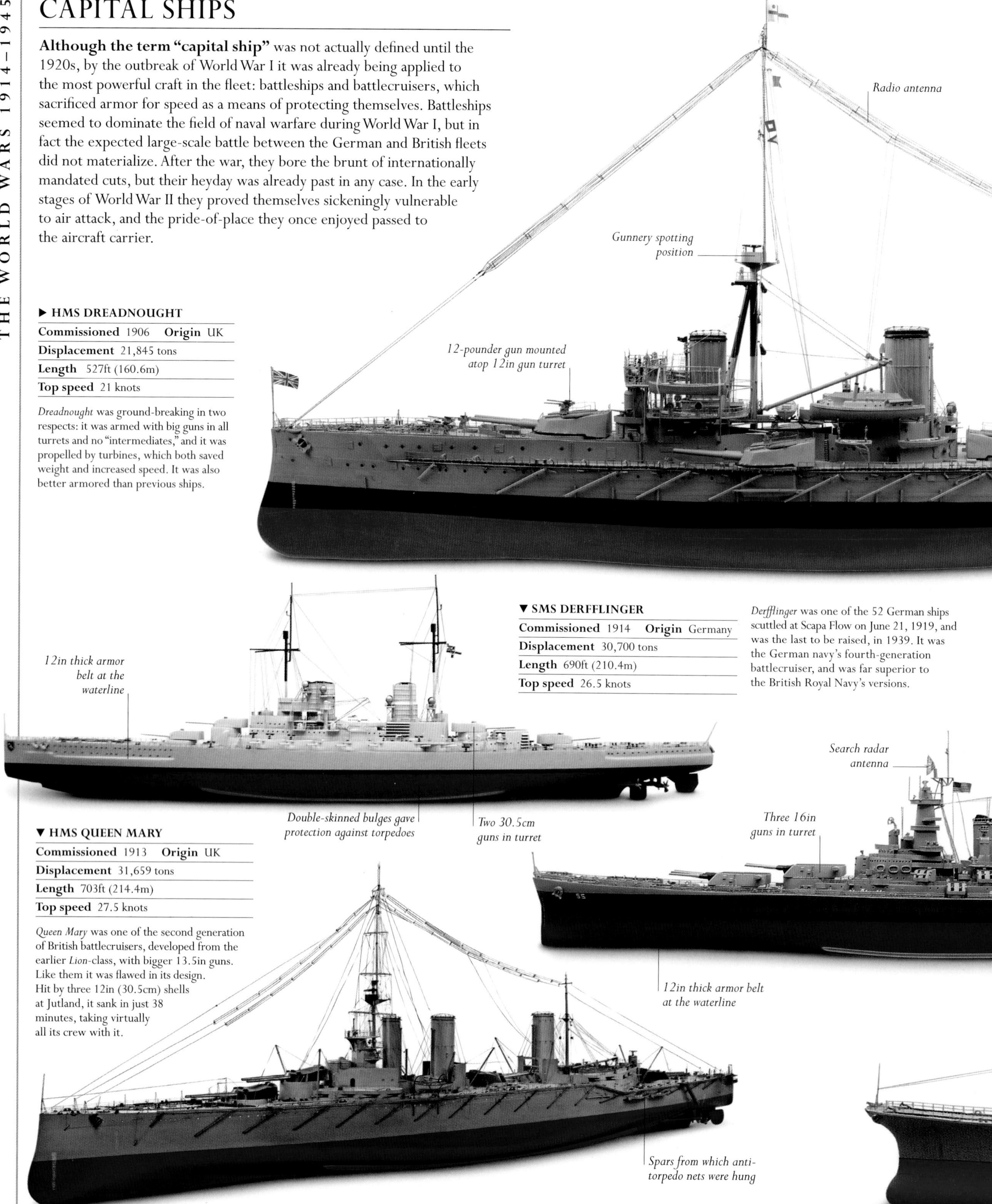

▶ HMS DREADNOUGHT

Commissioned 1906 **Origin** UK
Displacement 21,845 tons
Length 527ft (160.6m)
Top speed 21 knots

Dreadnought was ground-breaking in two respects: it was armed with big guns in all turrets and no "intermediates," and it was propelled by turbines, which both saved weight and increased speed. It was also better armored than previous ships.

▼ SMS DERFFLINGER

Commissioned 1914 **Origin** Germany
Displacement 30,700 tons
Length 690ft (210.4m)
Top speed 26.5 knots

Derfflinger was one of the 52 German ships scuttled at Scapa Flow on June 21, 1919, and was the last to be raised, in 1939. It was the German navy's fourth-generation battlecruiser, and was far superior to the British Royal Navy's versions.

▼ HMS QUEEN MARY

Commissioned 1913 **Origin** UK
Displacement 31,659 tons
Length 703ft (214.4m)
Top speed 27.5 knots

Queen Mary was one of the second generation of British battlecruisers, developed from the earlier *Lion*-class, with bigger 13.5in guns. Like them it was flawed in its design. Hit by three 12in (30.5cm) shells at Jutland, it sank in just 38 minutes, taking virtually all its crew with it.

Armored conning tower

Three 16in guns in turret

Supermarine Walrus seaplane

14in thick armor belt at the waterline

◀ **HMS RODNEY**

Commissioned 1927	**Origin** UK
Displacement 45,200 tons	
Length 710ft (216.4m)	
Top speed 23 knots	

Built to the limits imposed by the Washington Naval Treaty, *Rodney* and its sister-ship *Nelson* were characterized by the unconventional layout of their main armament—their 16in guns were all located forward, in three triple turrets.

Turret with two 38cm guns

Gunnery control radar

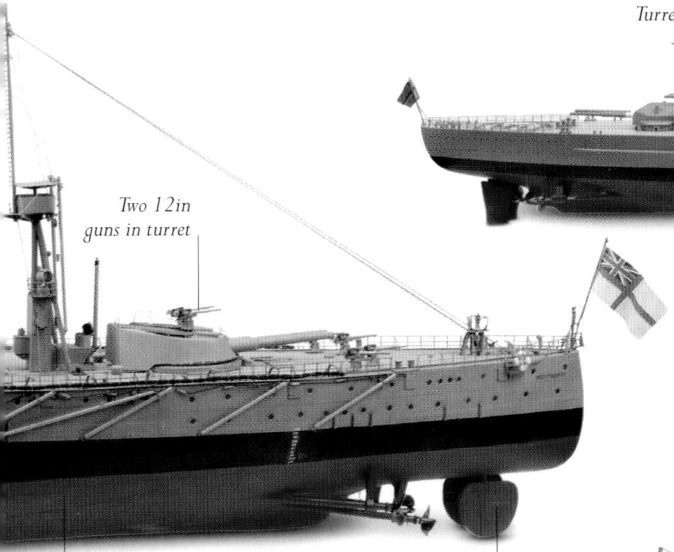

Two 12in guns in turret

11in thick armor belt at the waterline

Twin rudders

▲ **BISMARCK**

Commissioned 1940	**Origin** Germany
Displacement 50,900 tons	
Length 814ft (248m)	
Top speed 29 knots	

The pride of the Kriegsmarine, *Bismarck* and its sister-ship *Tirpitz* achieved iconic status. Both ships acted as a deterrent that drained British naval resources, although *Bismarck*'s effective action was limited to the destruction of HMS *Hood*. It was sunk in 1941 after being holed by British torpedo bombers.

90mm anti-aircraft gun

▼ **VITTORIO VENETO**

Commissioned 1940	**Origin** Italy
Displacement 45,030 tons	
Length 780ft (237.8m)	
Top speed 30 knots	

One of just three fast battleships built for the Regia Marina between the world wars, *Vittorio Veneto* spent over five years in construction, during which time its specification was altered significantly. It carried its main guns in triple turrets, two forward and one aft.

Three 152mm guns in turret

Turret with three 381mm guns

Catapult with spotter aircraft

Catapult for launching spotter aircraft

◀ **USS NORTH CAROLINA**

Commissioned 1941	**Origin** US
Displacement 44,380 tons	
Length 729ft (222.1m)	
Top speed 28 knots	

North Carolina and its sister-ship *Washington* marked a departure in US battleship design when they were built. They were bigger and much faster than those laid down at the end of World War I, and were equipped with much more powerful armament. *North Carolina*, "The Showboat," is preserved at Wilmington in its home state.

▼ **YAMATO**

Commissioned 1941	**Origin** Japan
Displacement 69,990 tons	
Length 863ft (263m)	
Top speed 27 knots	

Yamato and its sister-ship *Musashi* were the biggest battleships ever constructed, and mounted the most powerful armament. However, both succumbed to air attack. Another of the same class, *Shinano*, was completed as an aircraft carrier, but was sunk before being completed by a US submarine, the *Archerfish*.

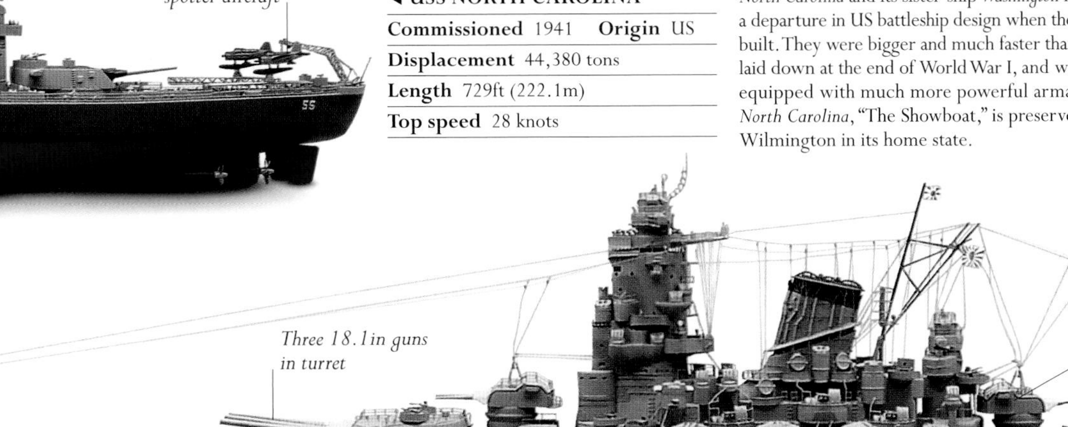

SUPER-DREADNOUGHT BATTLESHIP

USS TEXAS

The *Texas* was the product of the naval arms race that preceded World War I. A "super-dreadnought", it earned five battlestars during a long service career that spanned more than 30 years.

With a main armament of ten 14in guns, the *Texas* entered service in 1914 as the world's most powerful warship. In some respects it was behind the times, especially in using coal-fired reciprocating engines rather than oil-fired steam turbines. An extensive modernization in 1927 installed oil-fired boilers, improved the ship's armor, and upgraded its fire-control systems. Later changes included the addition of many anti-aircraft guns and fire-control and air-defense radars.

By World War II, the *Texas* was too slow to keep up with more modern capital ships in combat, but its guns still packed a powerful punch. The *Texas* escorted convoys in the Atlantic before the USA entered the war. Later, the ship was prominent in a shore bombardment role, providing fire support for landings in North Africa, Normandy (see pp. 340–41), Iwo Jima, and Okinawa. The *Texas* suffered only one combat fatality, when its conning tower was hit by a shell from a German shore battery in 1944.

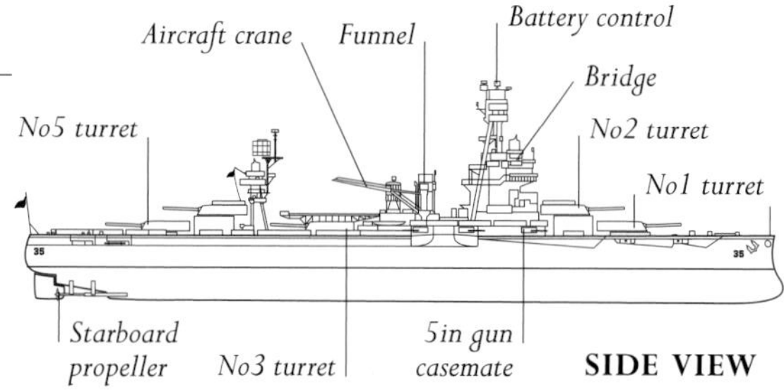

SIDE VIEW

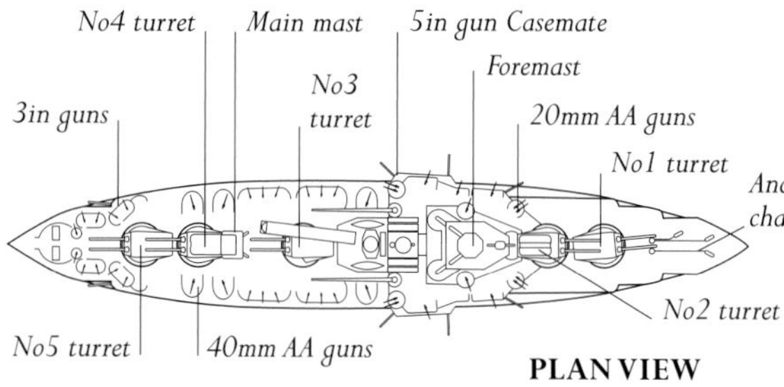

PLAN VIEW

USS *TEXAS*
A New York class battleship, the *Texas* was built at a cost of around $6 million. It was 574ft (175m) long, displaced 27,000 tons, and had a top speed of 21 knots.

AROUND THE DECK

▲ REAR VIEW OF FOREMAST
Below the battery control are other areas that need a high, clear line of sight such as the bridge and lookout platforms.

▶ SHIP'S BELL
Used to mark the time of day and regulate duty watches, this large brass bell on the deck was engraved with the ship's name.

▲ ANCHOR CAPSTANS
In front of the 14in bow guns, two large electric capstans rotated to raise or lower the anchors. At the stern there are other capstans, which were used for towing.

▲ BATTERY CONTROL
Observers in the battery control relayed readings for range, speed, and bearing to the plotting room below deck, which, in turn, sent instructions to the gunners.

▶ SOLE SURVIVOR
Decommissioned in 1946, the USS *Texas* is now a museum ship at San Jacinto, Texas. It is the last surviving battleship of the dreadnought era.

▸ **FORWARD GUN TURRETS**
The 14in guns could fire 1,500lb (680kg) shells at targets over 13 miles (20km) away, at a rate of one round every 45 seconds.

▴ **ANTI-AIRCRAFT GUNS**
During the late 1920s, the *Texas* received sixteen 5-inch and eight 3-inch anti-aircraft guns.

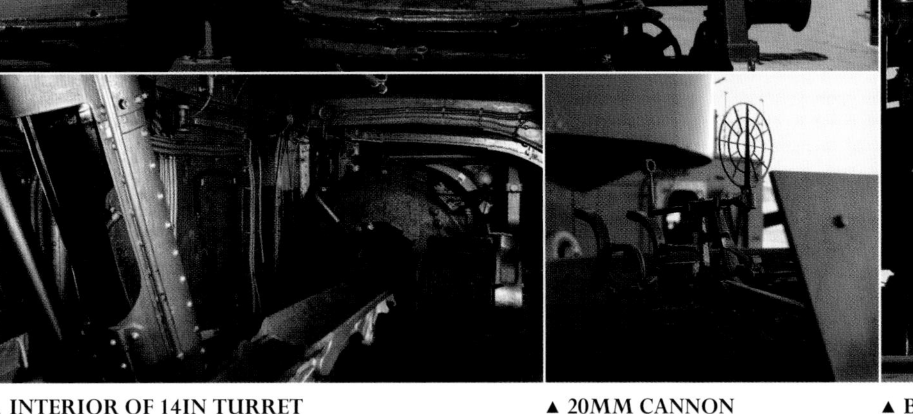

▴ **INTERIOR OF 14IN TURRET**
Shells raised from the magazine were rolled onto the loading tray. The shell and charge bags were rammed into the breech and the breech door closed, ready for firing.

▴ **20MM CANNON**
As a last-ditch defense against aircraft, the *Texas* carried forty-four 20mm Oerlikon cannon.

▴ **BOFORS 40MM GUN**
The ship's 40 Bofors anti-aircraft guns, a World War II addition, were remotely controlled.

▴ **PARAVANE**
The two paravanes were towed from the bow to snag the lines of submerged mines.

▴ **LINE CUTTER**
Each paravane had a blade to cut mines loose so that they floated to the surface.

BELOW DECKS

Home to a complement of about 1,800 men and officers by 1945, the *Texas* was like a small town, with a post office, dentist, and barber's shops—but no liquor store, because alcohol consumption was banned on all US Navy ships. There were few frills on board: most men ate where they slept, and toilet and bathing facilities were quite primitive. It was, however, a well-organized world in which each man knew his place, and in which basic needs of health and nutrition were properly addressed.

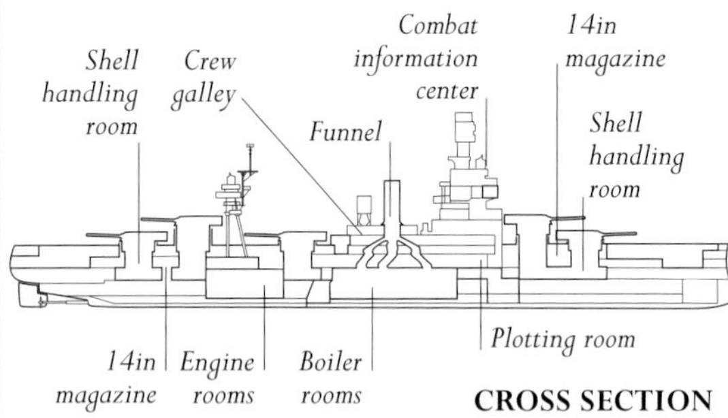

CROSS SECTION

COMMAND AND CONTROL

▲ **COMBAT ROOM**
Staff in the Combat Information Center assessed data from the radar (a World War II addition) and other sources. They also coordinated the weapons systems.

▲ **PILOT HOUSE**
The pilot house, located on the bridge, contained the main steering position. It was equipped with wheel, compass, rudder-angle indicator and engine room telegraph.

◄ **CHART ROOM**
Adjacent to the pilot house, the chart room was where the navigating officer worked. The devices on the wall above the chart table are depth and speed indicators.

SHELLS AND POWDER

▲ **14IN SHELL HOIST**
Shells and charges stored in magazines well below the waterline were brought up to the handling rooms and readied for use.

▲ **POWDER SCUTTLES**
Propellent powder, stored far from the shells, was sent to the handling rooms via flash-proof scuttles to prevent accidental ignition.

BOILERS AND RUDDER

◄ **BURNER NOZZLE DETAIL**
The burners forced fuel oil through atomizers, creating a spray of mist that was burned to heat the water. The red bar was used to adjust the volume and fineness of the spray.

▲ **EMERGENCY STEERING POSITION**
Normally the twin rudders were turned by electric motors, but if the power failed, the ship could be steered manually by teams of 16 men, using four large wheels.

► **OIL-FIRED BOILER**
After the Texas's refit in 1927, steam to drive the two vertical, triple-expanding engines was produced by six oil-fired boilers. Each boiler had eight burners; three have been removed here to reveal the interior.

▲ ENLISTED MEN'S GALLEY
The galley, on the main deck, could be opened up on three sides to provide ventilation. Food was sent down to the cafeteria on the deck below.

◀ BAKERY
The bakery was positioned near the galley on the port side of the main deck, so that the ovens could be cooled by fresh air.

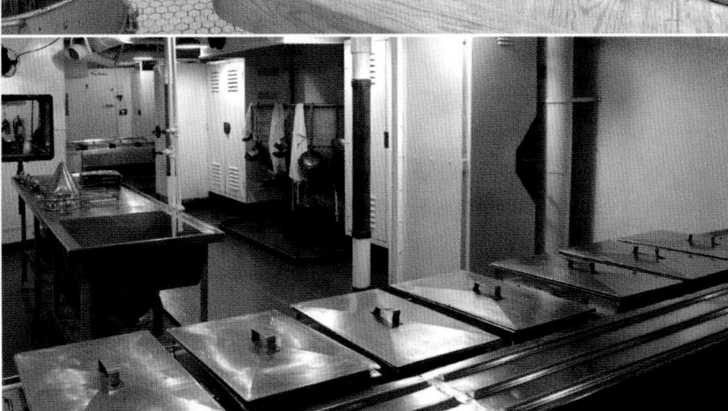

◀ CAFETERIA
Food arriving from the galley above via dumbwaiter was put into heated serving containers. Most enlisted men ate off foldaway tables in their berthing areas.

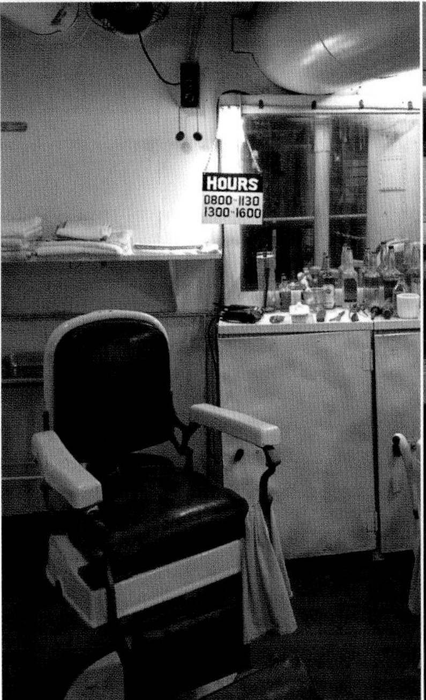

▲ BARBER'S SHOP
This barber's shop looked after the enlisted men—officers had their own barber's shop farther forward.

▲ MARINE BERTHS
Like enlisted sailors, the marines on the ship slept in bunks stacked three or four high. Most berthing areas were on the second deck.

▲ POST OFFICE
Letters from family, friends, and loved ones reached the sailors through the ship's post office, providing an important boost to crew morale.

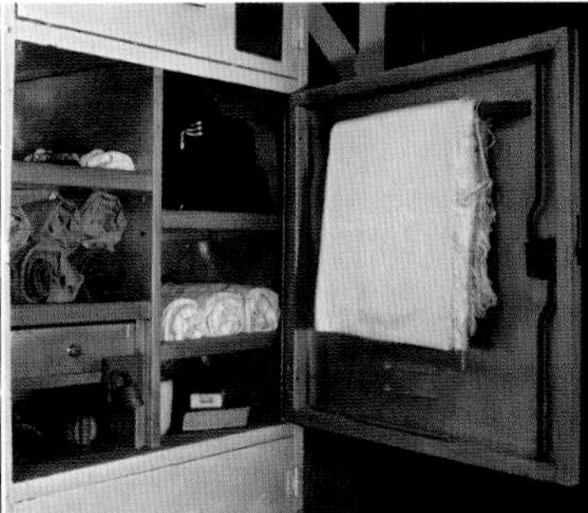

▲ CREW LOCKER
Privacy and space were limited, but each person had a locker for personal possessions.

CRUISERS

Traditionally, "cruisers" were warships big enough to be able to undertake protracted voyages and operate for long periods. By the early years of the 20th century, they were subdivided into three classes: "scout," "protected," and "armored," with additional subcategories—but within a decade, new builds conformed to a single pattern. Later, they would be described as "light" if armed with 6in guns, and "heavy" if they mounted anything larger. Later still, an anti-aircraft cruiser emerged, with high-angle guns to protect against bombers.

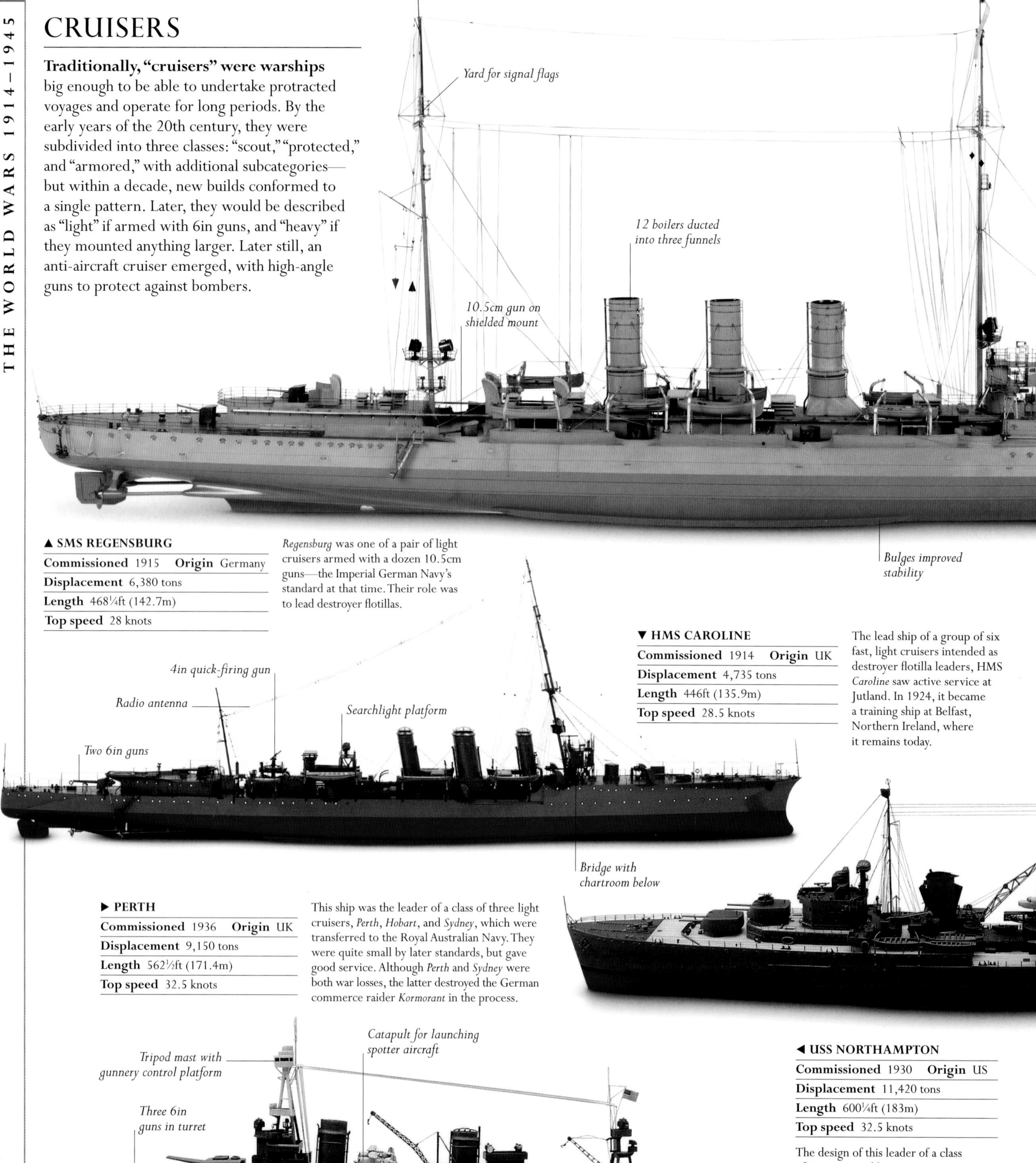

▲ SMS REGENSBURG

Commissioned 1915 **Origin** Germany
Displacement 6,380 tons
Length 468¼ft (142.7m)
Top speed 28 knots

Regensburg was one of a pair of light cruisers armed with a dozen 10.5cm guns—the Imperial German Navy's standard at that time. Their role was to lead destroyer flotillas.

▼ HMS CAROLINE

Commissioned 1914 **Origin** UK
Displacement 4,735 tons
Length 446ft (135.9m)
Top speed 28.5 knots

The lead ship of a group of six fast, light cruisers intended as destroyer flotilla leaders, HMS *Caroline* saw active service at Jutland. In 1924, it became a training ship at Belfast, Northern Ireland, where it remains today.

► PERTH

Commissioned 1936 **Origin** UK
Displacement 9,150 tons
Length 562½ft (171.4m)
Top speed 32.5 knots

This ship was the leader of a class of three light cruisers, *Perth*, *Hobart*, and *Sydney*, which were transferred to the Royal Australian Navy. They were quite small by later standards, but gave good service. Although *Perth* and *Sydney* were both war losses, the latter destroyed the German commerce raider *Kormorant* in the process.

◄ USS NORTHAMPTON

Commissioned 1930 **Origin** US
Displacement 11,420 tons
Length 600¼ft (183m)
Top speed 32.5 knots

The design of this leader of a class of six armoured heavy cruisers was compromised by the constraints of the Washington Naval Treaty of 1922. It was ultimately sunk by torpedoes during the short but hectic Battle of Tassafaronga on the night of November 30, 1942.

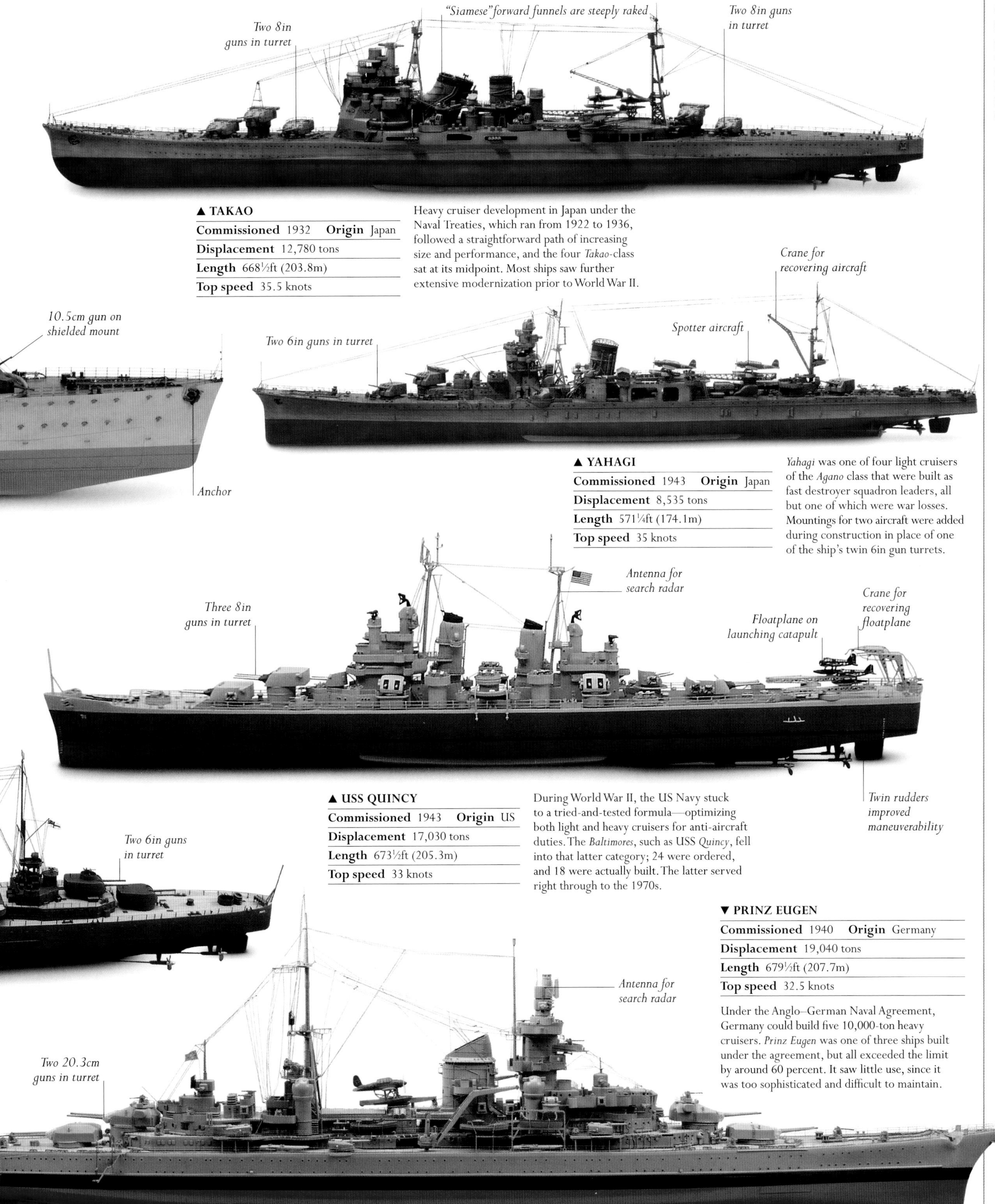

▲ TAKAO

Commissioned 1932	**Origin** Japan
Displacement 12,780 tons	
Length 668½ft (203.8m)	
Top speed 35.5 knots	

Heavy cruiser development in Japan under the Naval Treaties, which ran from 1922 to 1936, followed a straightforward path of increasing size and performance, and the four *Takao*-class sat at its midpoint. Most ships saw further extensive modernization prior to World War II.

▲ YAHAGI

Commissioned 1943	**Origin** Japan
Displacement 8,535 tons	
Length 571¼ft (174.1m)	
Top speed 35 knots	

Yahagi was one of four light cruisers of the *Agano* class that were built as fast destroyer squadron leaders, all but one of which were war losses. Mountings for two aircraft were added during construction in place of one of the ship's twin 6in gun turrets.

▲ USS QUINCY

Commissioned 1943	**Origin** US
Displacement 17,030 tons	
Length 673½ft (205.3m)	
Top speed 33 knots	

During World War II, the US Navy stuck to a tried-and-tested formula—optimizing both light and heavy cruisers for anti-aircraft duties. The *Baltimores*, such as USS *Quincy*, fell into that latter category; 24 were ordered, and 18 were actually built. The latter served right through to the 1970s.

▼ PRINZ EUGEN

Commissioned 1940	**Origin** Germany
Displacement 19,040 tons	
Length 679½ft (207.7m)	
Top speed 32.5 knots	

Under the Anglo–German Naval Agreement, Germany could build five 10,000-ton heavy cruisers. *Prinz Eugen* was one of three ships built under the agreement, but all exceeded the limit by around 60 percent. It saw little use, since it was too sophisticated and difficult to maintain.

DESTROYERS AND ESCORTS

By the outbreak of World War I, destroyers had grown in size, and now displaced 1,000 tons or more. They were still built for speed—well over 30 knots was normal—and mounted 4-inch guns or larger, as well as torpedoes. Their primary function during conflict was to defend the battle fleet against attack from similar ships or torpedo-boats, although they were also used to hunt submarines. The battle fleet became an obsolete concept by 1939, but destroyers survived. Enlarged still further, up-gunned, and armed with an array of depth-charges, they were employed—along with a new generation of smaller escorts—to guard convoys of merchant ships against attack from submarines and aircraft.

▲ HMS SNAPDRAGON

Commissioned 1915	**Origin** UK
Displacement 1,250 tons	
Length 268ft (81.7m)	
Top speed 16 knots	

Flower-class sloops, such as the *Snapdragon*, were fleet minesweepers, but were widely used for towing, reprovisioning, and crew transfers. They were built in large numbers by nonspecialized yards.

▶ SMS G37 (1914)

Commissioned 1915
Origin Germany
Displacement 1,050 tons
Length 260ft (79.5m)
Top speed 34.5 knots

Krupp-Germaniawerft's *G37*-class followed an experimental design. They had a shorter forecastle in an attempt to improve their rough-weather performance. *G37* was mined in November 1917, in the North Sea.

Bridge with chartroom below

8.8cm gun on pedestal mount

Torpedo tube

Smaller forecastle for stability in bad weather

▼ HMS AVON VALE

Commissioned 1941	**Origin** UK
Displacement 1,625 tons	
Length 280ft (85.3m)	
Top speed 27 knots	

Avon Vale was the first of the second group of *Hunt*-class destroyer-escorts built in the early years of World War II. This multirole ship was designed to protect merchant convoys from attack from both submarines and aircraft.

Four 2-pounder "pom-pom" anti-aircraft guns

Twin propellers driven by steam turbines

▼ HMS ACANTHUS

Commissioned 1940	**Origin** UK
Displacement 1,245 tons	
Length 205ft (62.5m)	
Top speed 16.5 knots	

Corvettes such as HMS *Acanthus* were the smallest specially built warships used for convoy escort duties during World War II. Their design was based on that of commercial whale-catchers, and they were powered by piston engines, rather than turbines.

Depth Charges

Light anti-aircraft gun

4in gun

K01

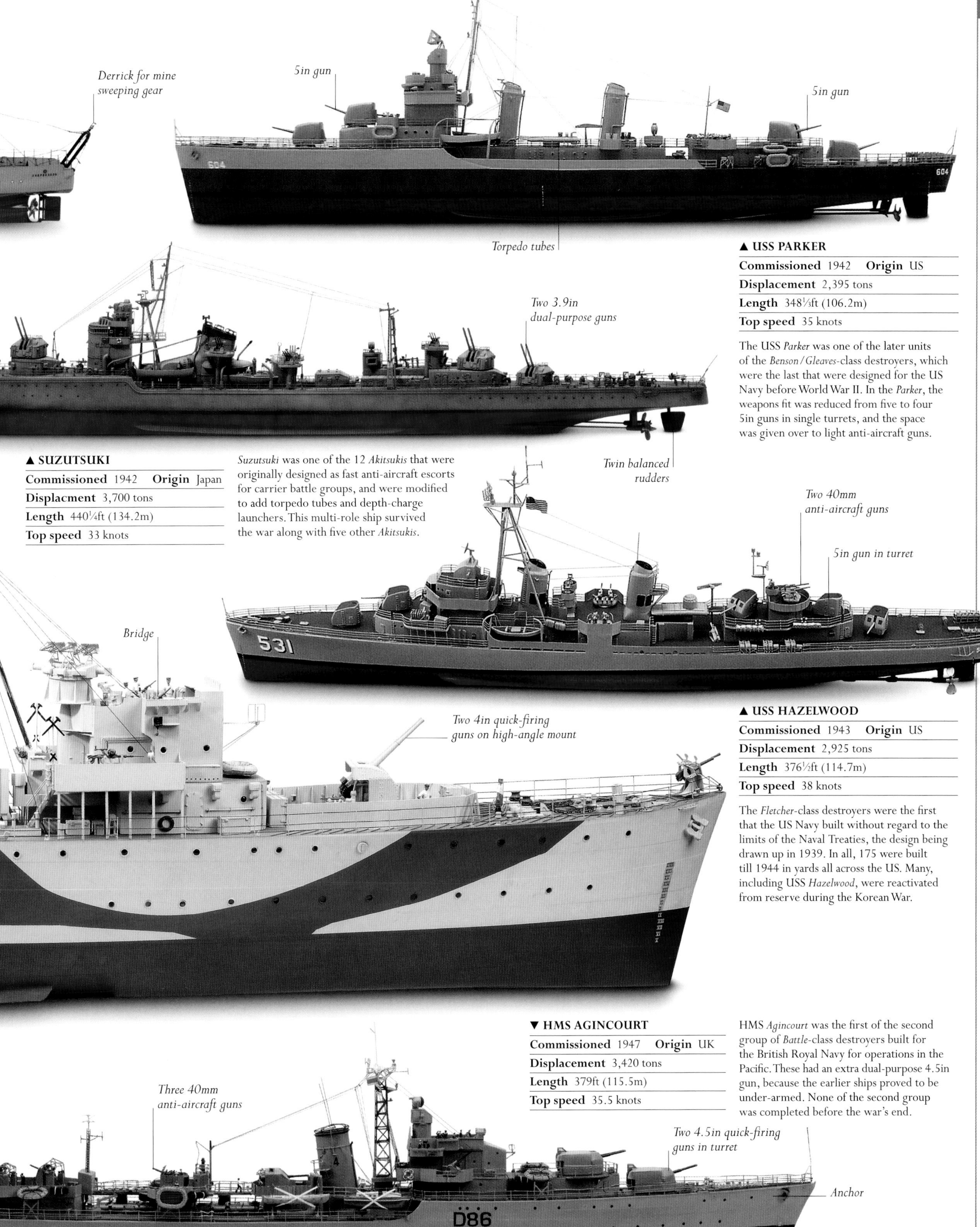

▲ USS PARKER

Commissioned 1942	**Origin** US
Displacement 2,395 tons	
Length 348⅓ft (106.2m)	
Top speed 35 knots	

The USS *Parker* was one of the later units of the *Benson/Gleaves*-class destroyers, which were the last that were designed for the US Navy before World War II. In the *Parker*, the weapons fit was reduced from five to four 5in guns in single turrets, and the space was given over to light anti-aircraft guns.

▲ SUZUTSUKI

Commissioned 1942	**Origin** Japan
Displacment 3,700 tons	
Length 440¼ft (134.2m)	
Top speed 33 knots	

Suzutsuki was one of the 12 *Akitsukis* that were originally designed as fast anti-aircraft escorts for carrier battle groups, and were modified to add torpedo tubes and depth-charge launchers. This multi-role ship survived the war along with five other *Akitsukis*.

▲ USS HAZELWOOD

Commissioned 1943	**Origin** US
Displacement 2,925 tons	
Length 376½ft (114.7m)	
Top speed 38 knots	

The *Fletcher*-class destroyers were the first that the US Navy built without regard to the limits of the Naval Treaties, the design being drawn up in 1939. In all, 175 were built till 1944 in yards all across the US. Many, including USS *Hazelwood*, were reactivated from reserve during the Korean War.

▼ HMS AGINCOURT

Commissioned 1947	**Origin** UK
Displacement 3,420 tons	
Length 379ft (115.5m)	
Top speed 35.5 knots	

HMS *Agincourt* was the first of the second group of *Battle*-class destroyers built for the British Royal Navy for operations in the Pacific. These had an extra dual-purpose 4.5in gun, because the earlier ships proved to be under-armed. None of the second group was completed before the war's end.

SUBMARINES

Submarines came into their own during World War I, and Germany, in particular, used them to excellent effect, especially against enemy merchant ships carrying vital supplies to Europe. During World War II, when Germany's surface fleet was severely limited by Hitler's prejudice against it, it was the "U-boats" that provided the Kriegsmarine with the bulk of its victories: it is a widely held view that they came close to bringing Britain to its knees. As a consequence, both Britain's Royal Navy and the US Navy were forced to make considerable investments in measures to combat the "submarine menace," which took some time to take effect. The Battle of the Atlantic could be fully declared won only after these measures had yielded results.

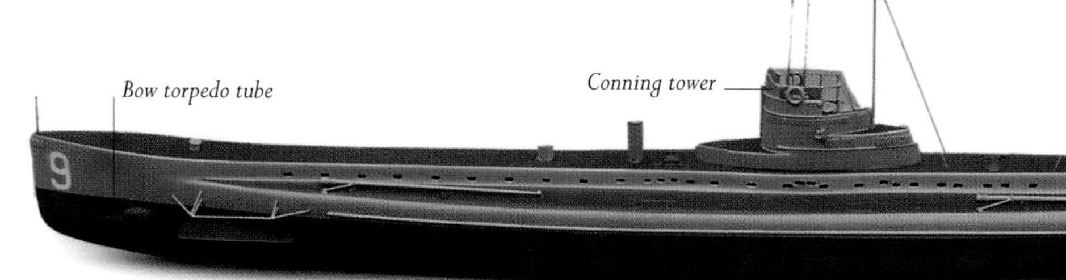

▲ U-9

Commissioned 1910	**Origin** Germany
Displacement 495 tons (610 tons submerged)	
Length 188¼ft (57.4m)	
Top speed 14.2 knots (8 knots submerged)	

The *U-9* was leader of a class of four Type U-9 coastal submarines constructed at the Danzig Navy Yard in the Baltic. Like all German submarines built prior to 1912, they had both electric motors and petrol engines. Though these were experimental boats, they also saw combat, and all but *U-9* were war losses.

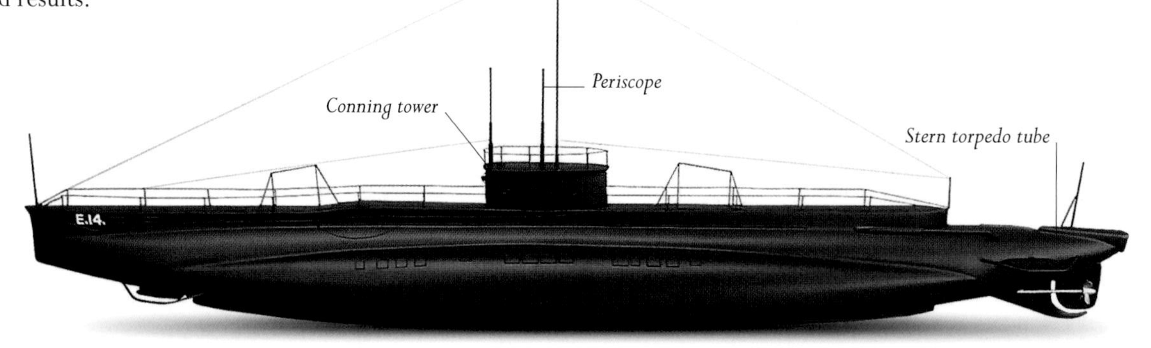

▶ RN E-CLASS

Commissioned 1913–17	**Origin** UK
Displacement 670 tons (810 tons submerged)	
Length 181ft (55.2m)	
Top speed 15 knots (9 knots submerged)	

Built in two groups, the British Royal Navy's *E*-class submarines were ocean-going boats with a range of 3,000 nautical miles (5,556km). At the outbreak of the war, 16 were in service or nearing completion, and 40 more were hastily constructed in no less than eight different yards. Six were constructed as minelayers; each of these were fitted with three torpedo tubes and carried 20 mines.

▲ U-25

Commissioned 1936	**Origin** Germany
Displacement 860 tons (985 tons submerged)	
Length 237½ft (72.4m)	
Top speed 18.5 knots (8.3 knots submerged)	

One of a pair of Type IA double-hulled ocean-going boats, the *U-25* was built by Deschimag for the Kriegsmarine in the mid-1930s, after a protracted and secretive design process. It sunk north of Terschelling, in August 1940, after hitting a mine that it had laid itself.

▲ RN T-CLASS (1937–44)

Commissioned 1938–45	**Origin** UK
Displacement 1,320 tons (1,575 tons submerged)	
Length 275ft (83.8m)	
Top speed 15.5 knots (9 knots submerged)	

T-class boats were built for Britain's Royal Navy in three large groups from 1937 to 1944, undergoing considerable improvement in the process. Later builds remained in service until the 1960s. Maximum dive depth was 300ft (91m), which increased to 350ft (106m) in the last group.

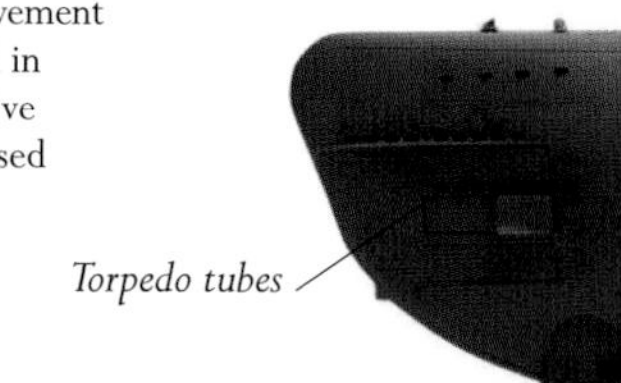

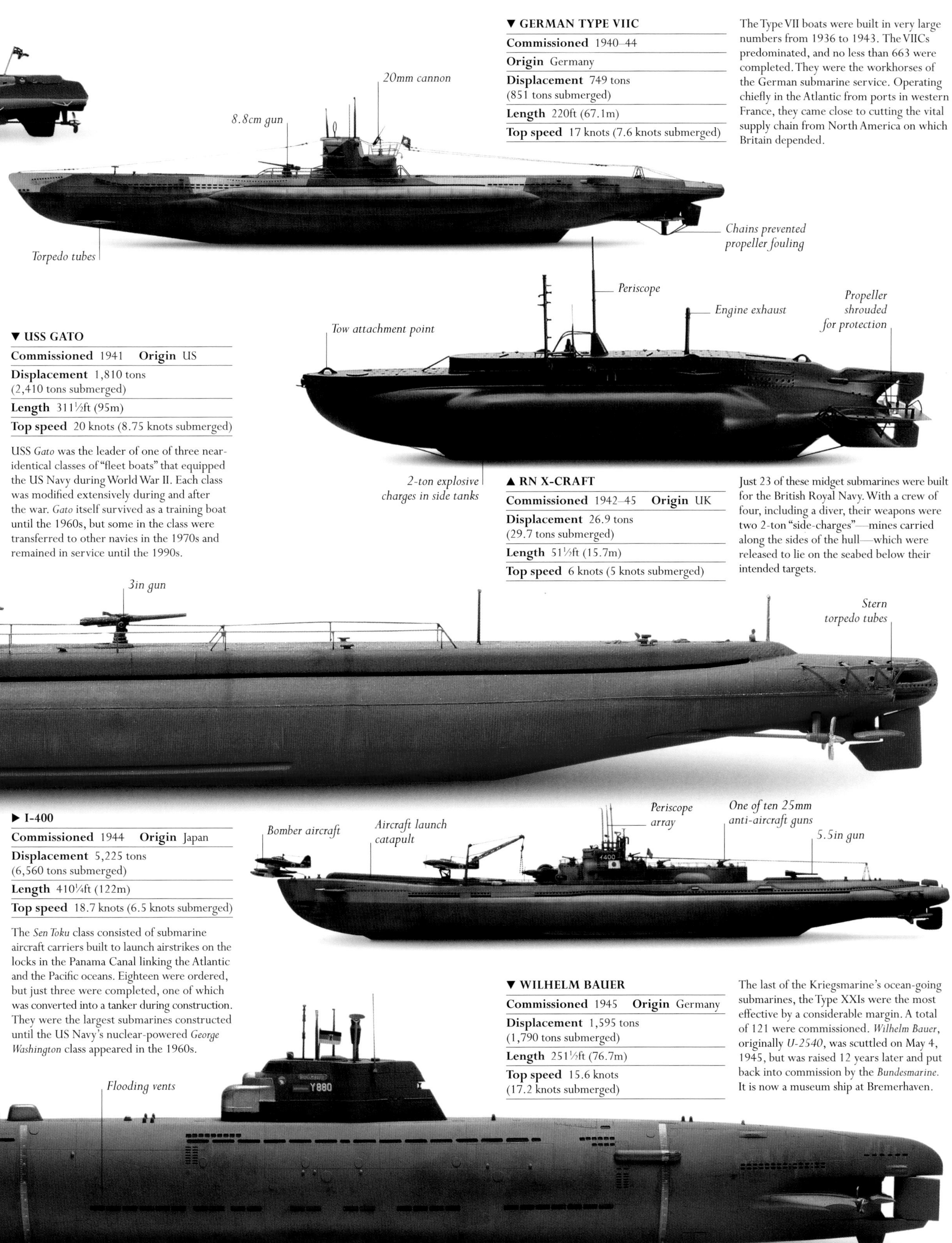

▼ GERMAN TYPE VIIC

Commissioned 1940–44	
Origin Germany	
Displacement 749 tons (851 tons submerged)	
Length 220ft (67.1m)	
Top speed 17 knots (7.6 knots submerged)	

The Type VII boats were built in very large numbers from 1936 to 1943. The VIICs predominated, and no less than 663 were completed. They were the workhorses of the German submarine service. Operating chiefly in the Atlantic from ports in western France, they came close to cutting the vital supply chain from North America on which Britain depended.

▼ USS GATO

Commissioned 1941	**Origin** US
Displacement 1,810 tons (2,410 tons submerged)	
Length 311½ft (95m)	
Top speed 20 knots (8.75 knots submerged)	

USS *Gato* was the leader of one of three near-identical classes of "fleet boats" that equipped the US Navy during World War II. Each class was modified extensively during and after the war. *Gato* itself survived as a training boat until the 1960s, but some in the class were transferred to other navies in the 1970s and remained in service until the 1990s.

▲ RN X-CRAFT

Commissioned 1942–45	**Origin** UK
Displacement 26.9 tons (29.7 tons submerged)	
Length 51½ft (15.7m)	
Top speed 6 knots (5 knots submerged)	

Just 23 of these midget submarines were built for the British Royal Navy. With a crew of four, including a diver, their weapons were two 2-ton "side-charges"—mines carried along the sides of the hull—which were released to lie on the seabed below their intended targets.

▶ I-400

Commissioned 1944	**Origin** Japan
Displacement 5,225 tons (6,560 tons submerged)	
Length 410¼ft (122m)	
Top speed 18.7 knots (6.5 knots submerged)	

The *Sen Toku* class consisted of submarine aircraft carriers built to launch airstrikes on the locks in the Panama Canal linking the Atlantic and the Pacific oceans. Eighteen were ordered, but just three were completed, one of which was converted into a tanker during construction. They were the largest submarines constructed until the US Navy's nuclear-powered *George Washington* class appeared in the 1960s.

▼ WILHELM BAUER

Commissioned 1945	**Origin** Germany
Displacement 1,595 tons (1,790 tons submerged)	
Length 251½ft (76.7m)	
Top speed 15.6 knots (17.2 knots submerged)	

The last of the Kriegsmarine's ocean-going submarines, the Type XXIs were the most effective by a considerable margin. A total of 121 were commissioned. *Wilhelm Bauer*, originally *U-2540*, was scuttled on May 4, 1945, but was raised 12 years later and put back into commission by the *Bundesmarine*. It is now a museum ship at Bremerhaven.

THE NORMANDY LANDINGS

The Allied landings on Normandy beaches on D-day, June 6, 1944, comprised the largest amphibious operation ever. With around 160,000 soldiers put ashore in a single day despite heavy resistance, the invasion was a masterpiece of planning and organization on a vast scale.

The outcome of the Normandy landings depended upon experience accumulated by the Allies since the beginning of World War II—on Sicily and the Italian mainland, in the Dieppe Raid of 1942, and by US Marines in the Pacific. The most important lesson learned had been never to underestimate the difficulty of such an enterprise.

Successful landings required command of the air and sea, and the Allies achieved this on D-day. With most of the German Luftwaffe assigned to the Eastern front, or to homeland defense, Allied aerial dominance over the beaches was assured. Meanwhile, Allied navies deployed more than 1,200 warships for the invasion which, in combination with mines and air patrols, deterred attacks by German surface ships and submarines.

A second necessity for the landings was tactical surprise. The enemy knew an invasion was being prepared, but not where or when it would come, and deception operations made them expect an attack on the more obvious Pas-de-Calais. Poor weather in early June delayed this invasion by a day, but also put the defenders off their guard, since they believed landings would not be attempted in such conditions.

The five target beaches were codenamed Utah, Omaha, Gold, Juno, and Sword. Utah and Omaha were assigned to American troops, Gold and Sword to the British, and Juno to the Canadians. The invasion fleet set off from ports across the south of England on the night of June 5–6, assembling south of the Isle of Wight. Minesweepers led the way across the English Channel, clearing a passage for other warships and troop transports, while airborne troops landed by parachute and glider to seize objectives behind the beaches. At dawn Allied warships, including six battleships, opened fire on the German Atlantic Wall coastal defenses. This was the first warning the German defenders had of the impending invasion.

THE FINAL APPROACH

Allied soldiers transferred into more than 4,000 landing craft for the final approach. The craft were a mixture of flat-bottomed plywood Landing Craft, Vehicle, Personnels (LCVPs), Landing Craft Assaults (LCAs), and others, with ramps in the bow that lowered for the men to exit. Other specialized landing craft transported tanks or provided supporting fire.

Conditions were difficult. Tanks with floats designed to "swim" sank in the rough waters. Seasickness was rife, and on leaving the boats troops had to wade through deep water straight into enemy fire. Some soldiers who exited their crafts too far from shore drowned, dragged under by the weight of their equipment.

Despite losses of around 10,000 casualties, the landings succeeded, giving the Allies a foothold in occupied Europe. Only at Omaha beach were soldiers nearly driven back into the sea; many US tanks and engineers were lost before reaching shore, and defenses were strong after inaccurate Allied bombing. Even there, with the help of well-directed naval gunfire, American troops established a secure beachhead by nightfall, and floating Mulberry harbors were towed into position to enable the troops ashore to receive supplies.

GOING ASHORE
An aerial photograph taken over the Normandy coast on D-day shows American vehicles advancing off the beach as landing craft continue to unload troops at the shoreline.

KEY **TACTIC**

KAMIKAZE
1944–45

In October 1944, Japan began to adopt suicide tactics, deliberately crashing their aircraft into American ships with the aim of crippling or sinking them. The kamikaze ("divine wind") units were initially made up of only elite flyers, but, by 1945, suicide attack had become a task for thousands of poorly trained novice pilots. An estimated 322 Allied ships were hit by kamikaze planes, and at least 34 of them sank.

▲ A Japanese Zero fighter seen just before it crashed into the USS *Missouri*, in 1945. The battleship suffered only superficial damage.

► **THE DIVE-BOMBER**
One of a new generation of high-performance American carrier aircraft introduced during World War II, the Curtiss SB2C Helldiver could bomb accurately enough to hit ships, unlike most conventional bombers.

KEY DEVELOPMENT

AIR AND SEA BATTLES

The growth of air power between 1914 and 1945 transformed naval warfare. Capable of deciding the outcome of battles with the long-range strike power of their aircraft, carriers took over from battleships as the most potent warships in a fleet.

▲ **THE FAIREY SWORDFISH**
The UK entered World War II with the outdated Fairey Swordfish biplane as its torpedo bomber. The slow-flying "Stringbag" was surprisingly effective, notably in an attack on the Italian fleet at Taranto in 1940.

Navies were at the forefront of the early development of military aviation. Naval commanders could see the advantages of aerial reconnaissance and were quick to experiment with both airplanes and airships when war broke out in 1914.

At first, seaplane tenders carried float aircraft, which were winched over the side to take off from the sea and—hopefully—recovered from the sea after returning from their mission. In 1916, the British Royal Navy began replacing seaplanes with wheeled landplanes. These might take off from a platform mounted on a warship's revolving gun turret or from a raft towed behind a destroyer. To land, these light, canvas-and-wood aircraft simply ditched into the sea, and were then hoisted aboard the ship.

In 1917, the British cruiser HMS *Furious* was fitted with a long flight deck, on which landing trials were carried out with a Sopwith Pup biplane. A converted ocean liner, HMS *Argus*, came closer to achieving a successful aircraft carrier design, recognizing the need to avoid

the turbulence created by a traditional ship's superstructure. The *Argus* was just entering service as World War I ended.

BETWEEN THE WARS

During the inter-war years there was impressive progress in the development of aircraft carriers in France, Japan, and the US, among others, despite the determination of some naval commanders to concentrate on battleships. The first specially built carriers appeared in the 1920s. British naval aviation was held back after the decision to give control of all military aircraft to their Royal Air Force. By 1939, when this unsatisfactory arrangement ended, the British Royal Navy had good-quality carriers, but its aircraft were obsolete. This allowed the US and Japan to take the lead in naval aviation.

▲ A CROWDED FLIGHT DECK
Taking off and landing aircraft on the deck of a carrier was a complex and accident-prone procedure under combat conditions. Here, Douglas SBD Dauntless dive-bombers form a line on the deck of USS *Yorktown*.

The US Navy followed the conversion of its USS *Lexington* and USS *Saratoga* battlecruisers, built 1920–27, with the specially built Yorktown class of carriers, introduced from 1937 onward. Japan was especially successful in developing a carrier fleet, placing great importance on pilot training and the design of naval aircraft. It soon became apparent that dive-bombers and torpedo bombers were the best aircraft types for attacking enemy ships.

WAR IN THE PACIFIC

The early years of World War II repeatedly demonstrated that even the most heavily gunned warships were vulnerable to air attack. This was especially true in the Pacific War. The surprise attack mounted by a Japanese carrier task force on the US naval base at Pearl Harbor, Hawaii, in December 1941, was an unforgettable illustration of the devastating potential of naval air power, and forced American naval commanders to recognize that carriers were their capital ships. As a result, battleships, cruisers, and destroyers were given the role of protecting them.

The vast industrial capacity of the US helped to turn the tide. Carriers and naval aircraft were produced in astonishing quantity, enabling them to overwhelm and even eliminate the Japanese carrier fleet over the course of 1944. By 1945, the Allies had 40 carriers in their fleet off Okinawa, and the Americans had established themselves as undisputed world leaders in naval aviation.

> "The war would end with the **aircraft carriers** the fleet's **main striking force**"
>
> **BRITISH FLEET AIR ARM PILOT CHARLES LAMB**, *WAR IN A STRINGBAG*, 1977

KEY **EVENTS**

1914–45

- **1914** Britain's Royal Naval Air Service attacks airship sheds at Cuxhaven, Germany, in the first sea-launched attack on a land target.
- **1922** The Japanese navy commissions *Hosho*, the first specially built aircraft carrier. Britain's HMS *Hermes*, which was laid down in 1918, is completed shortly after.
- **1941** Japanese carrier-borne aircraft attack the US naval base at Pearl Harbor, Hawaii, sinking or damaging 18 American ships.
- **1942** The Battle of Midway—a long-range duel between American and Japanese aircraft carriers—is fought in the mid-Pacific. The opposing fleets do not engage with their guns.
- **1943** The US Navy establishes a Fast Carrier Task Force to spearhead its Pacific campaign. The Task Force comprises a core of aircraft carriers escorted by big-gun warships.
- **1945** Japan's *Yamato*, the largest and most heavily armed battleship ever built, is sunk by American naval aircraft.

AIRCRAFT CARRIERS

The earliest aircraft-carrying ships actually functioned as floating seaplane bases. Although experimentation had taken place earlier, it was not until after World War I that true aircraft carriers, capable of launching aircraft and recovering them, entered service. By 1939, significant advances had been made, and the British Royal Navy had a dozen such carriers in operation or under construction. The Imperial Japanese Navy had a similar number, and the US Navy had eight. It was the US Navy that subsequently embraced the type most wholeheartedly, constructing huge numbers of "fleet" carriers, and lighter, less-capable "escort" carriers during the course of World War II. Many such escort carriers were also constructed in the US for the British Royal Navy.

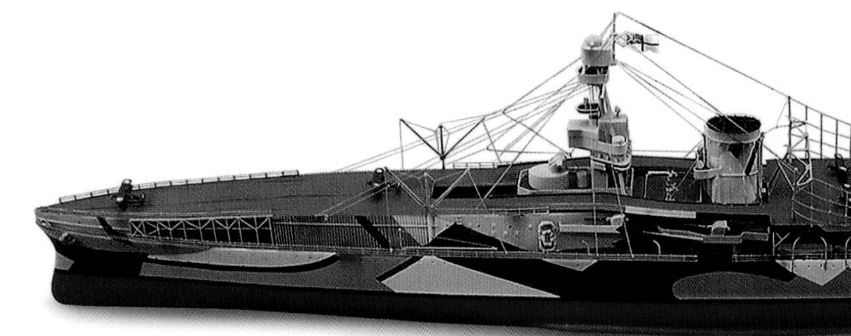

▲ **HMS FURIOUS**

Commissioned 1917 **Origin** UK
Displacement 22,890 tons
Length 786½ft (239.7m)
Top speed 30 knots

Ordered as a light battlecruiser, *Furious* was completed as a makeshift aircraft carrier with a short flying-off deck forward. It was later completely reconstructed from the main deck upwards, and equipped to operate 36 aircraft. It served with distinction, almost unscathed, until September 1944.

▲ **USS SARATOGA**

Commissioned 1927 **Origin** US
Displacement 43,055 tons
Length 888ft (270.7m)
Top speed 33 knots

Ordered as part of a group of six battlecruisers at the end of World War I, *Saratoga* and sister-ship *Lexington* were selected for completion as carriers. It became the US Navy's first effective carrier, and survived World War II, winning seven battle stars.

▲ **AKAGI**

Commissioned 1927 **Origin** Japan
Displacement 42,750 tons
Length 855½ft (260.7m)
Top speed 31 knots

Akagi was completed as a carrier with a three-level flight deck, which allowed aircraft to take off from hangar-deck levels and land on the (truncated) upper deck. The boiler flues were on the starboard side, and an island was not fitted until *Akagi* was comprehensively rebuilt along more orthodox lines between 1935–38.

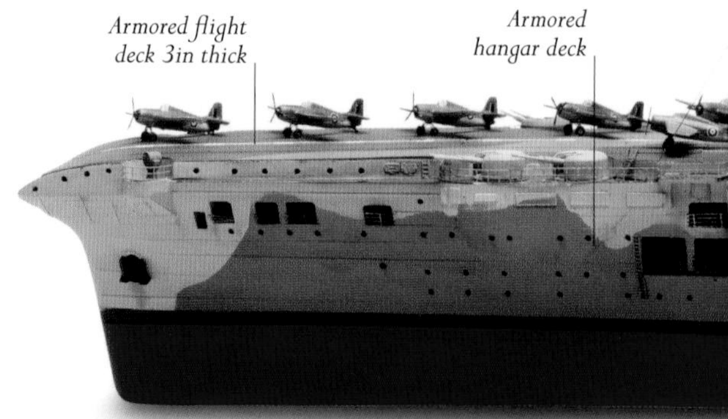

▼ **HMS ARK ROYAL**

Commissioned 1938 **Origin** UK
Displacement 27,720 tons
Length 800ft (243.8m)
Top speed 31 knots

The British Royal Navy's first large purpose-built aircraft carrier, *Ark Royal* introduced many design elements—including steam catapults—that were used in later types. Although well protected, it succumbed to a torpedo in the Mediterranean in 1941, having ferried much-needed aircraft to Malta.

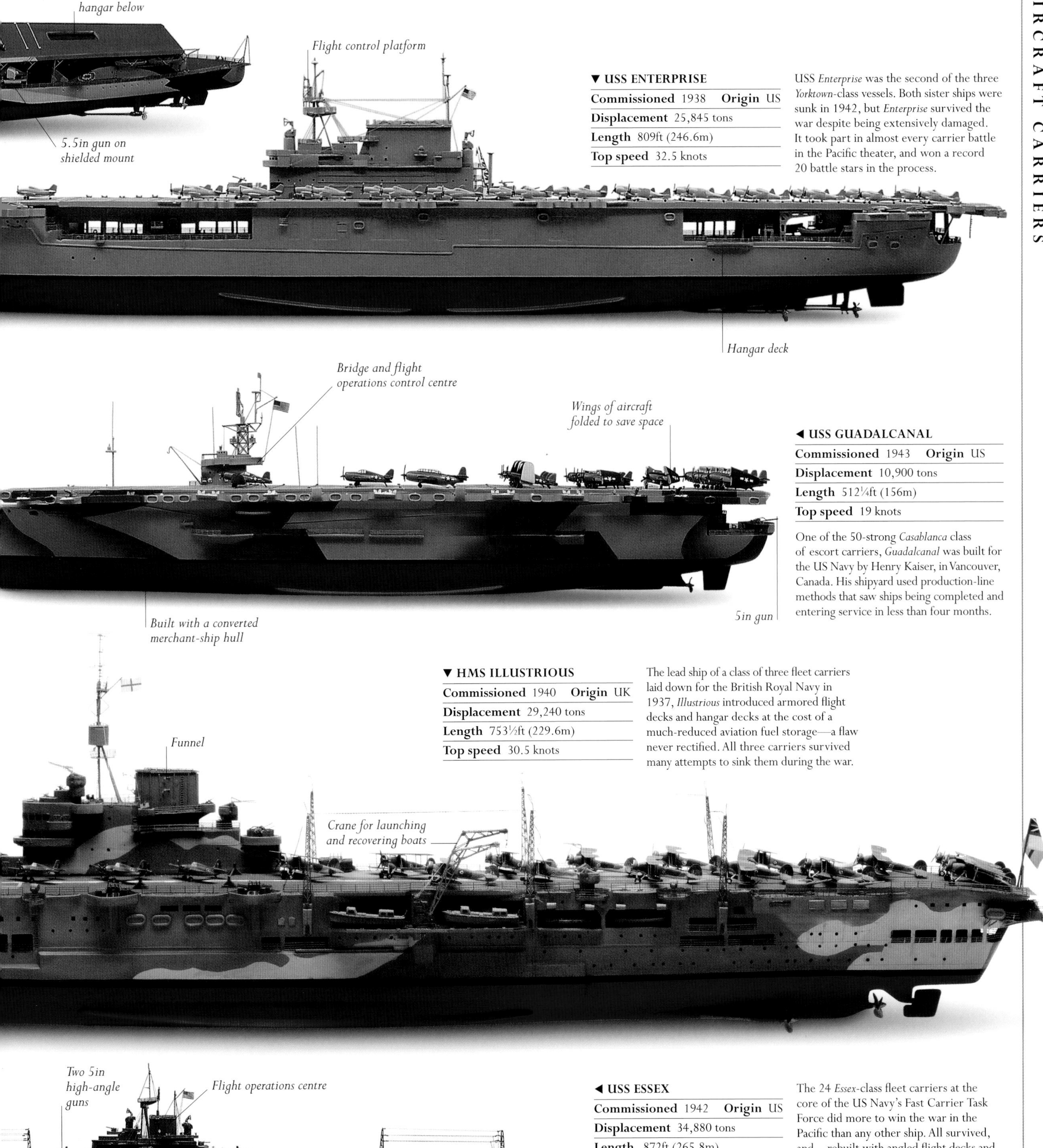

▼ USS ENTERPRISE

Commissioned 1938 **Origin** US

Displacement 25,845 tons

Length 809ft (246.6m)

Top speed 32.5 knots

USS *Enterprise* was the second of the three *Yorktown*-class vessels. Both sister ships were sunk in 1942, but *Enterprise* survived the war despite being extensively damaged. It took part in almost every carrier battle in the Pacific theater, and won a record 20 battle stars in the process.

◀ USS GUADALCANAL

Commissioned 1943 **Origin** US

Displacement 10,900 tons

Length 512¼ft (156m)

Top speed 19 knots

One of the 50-strong *Casablanca* class of escort carriers, *Guadalcanal* was built for the US Navy by Henry Kaiser, in Vancouver, Canada. His shipyard used production-line methods that saw ships being completed and entering service in less than four months.

▼ HMS ILLUSTRIOUS

Commissioned 1940 **Origin** UK

Displacement 29,240 tons

Length 753½ft (229.6m)

Top speed 30.5 knots

The lead ship of a class of three fleet carriers laid down for the British Royal Navy in 1937, *Illustrious* introduced armored flight decks and hangar decks at the cost of a much-reduced aviation fuel storage—a flaw never rectified. All three carriers survived many attempts to sink them during the war.

◀ USS ESSEX

Commissioned 1942 **Origin** US

Displacement 34,880 tons

Length 872ft (265.8m)

Top speed 32.7 knots

The 24 *Essex*-class fleet carriers at the core of the US Navy's Fast Carrier Task Force did more to win the war in the Pacific than any other ship. All survived, and—rebuilt with angled flight decks and other improvements—went on to form the basis of the post-war carrier fleet.

CARRIER AND MARITIME STRIKE AIRCRAFT

Initially, the planes borne on aircraft carriers were no different to those that operated from terrestrial fields, but, by the mid-1920s, deliveries of aircraft modified for shipboard performance had begun. From that point on, the designs of carrier- and land-based aircraft began to diverge, although the latter were still useable on ships. As well as fighters, whose primary role was to defend the mother ship and other ships in the fleet, long-range reconnaissance aircraft and specialist attack aircraft armed with torpedoes or bombs were also commissioned. The latter were dominated by dive bombers during this period.

Pilot's, wireless operator's, and gunner's positions all open to the elements

Wings could be folded back for storage

Torpedo carried below fuselage

▲ FAIREY SWORDFISH

Date 1936	**Origin** UK
Wingspan 45½ft (13.87m)	
Length 35¾ft (10.87m)	
Top speed 140mph (225kph)	
Engine 690hp (514.5kW) Bristol Pegasus IIIM.3 radial	

Though considered obsolete even before the start of World War II, the "Stringbag" (so called because of wide variety of equipment it was cleared to carry) scored some notable successes, sinking an Italian battleship and damaging two more at Taranto in November 1940. Six months later a Swordfish disabled the German battleship *Bismarck*, allowing her to be sunk.

▲ GRUMMAN F4F WILDCAT

Date 1940	**Origin** US
Wingspan 38ft (11.6m)	
Length 28¾ft (8.8m)	
Top speed 320mph (515kph)	
Engine 1,200hp (895kW) Pratt & Whitney R-1830-86 Twin Wasp radial	

When it came to developing a monoplane fighter, Grumman adapted the F3F biplane to create the F4F Wildcat, adding an improved tail and mid-mounted wing, and specifying a more powerful engine. Although capable, it was never a match for the Japanese Zero.

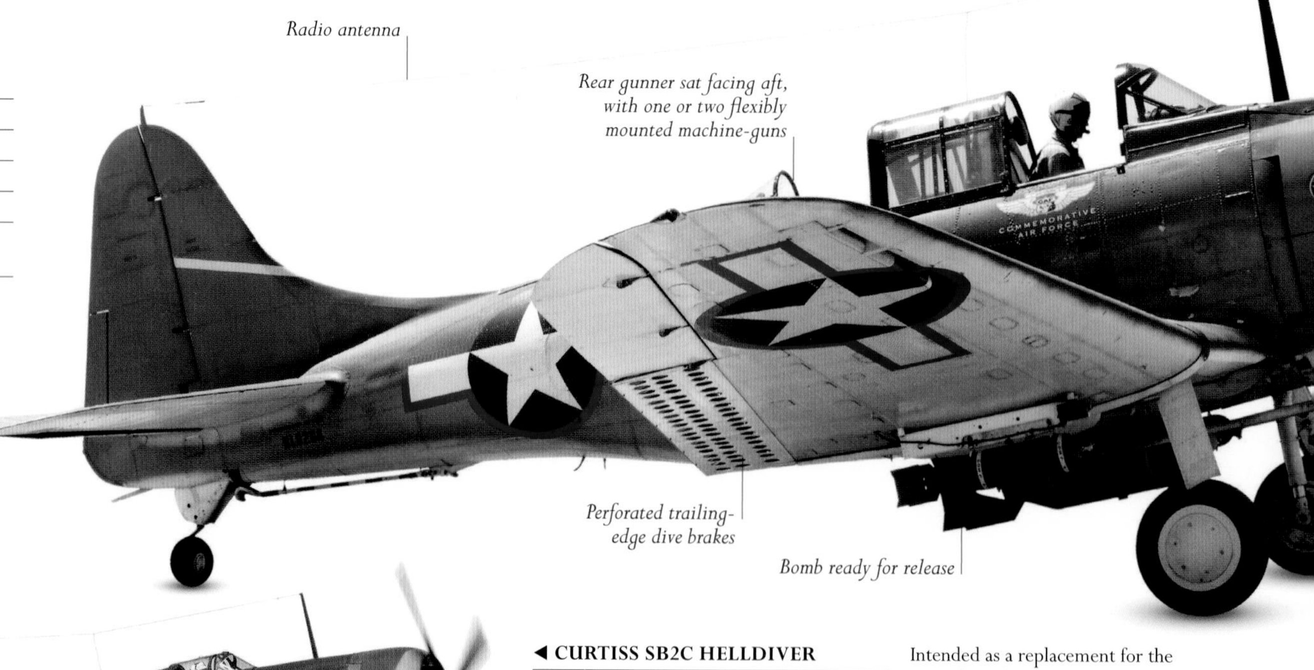

▶ DOUGLAS SBD DAUNTLESS

Date 1942	**Origin** US
Wingspan 41½ft (12.66m)	
Length 33ft (10.09m)	
Top speed 255mph (410kph)	
Engine 1,200hp (895kW) Wright R-1820-60 Cyclone radial	

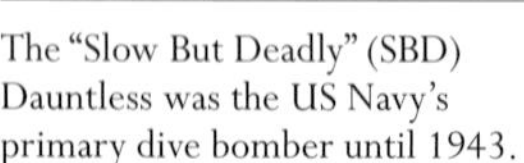

The "Slow But Deadly" (SBD) Dauntless was the US Navy's primary dive bomber until 1943. Rugged and dependable, it sank more Japanese ships than any other American aircraft, and later evolved into the A-1 Skyraider employed in Korea and Vietnam.

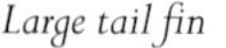

◀ CURTISS SB2C HELLDIVER

Date 1943	**Origin** US
Wingspan 49¾ft (15.17m)	
Length 38¾ft (11.81m)	
Top speed 295mph (475kph)	
Engine 1,900hp (1,416.8kW) Wright R-2600-20 Twin Cyclone radial	

Intended as a replacement for the Dauntless, the Helldiver suffered from a vast number of design flaws that had to be corrected before it could enter service. It had poor handling characteristics, but it ended the war with an admirable combat record.

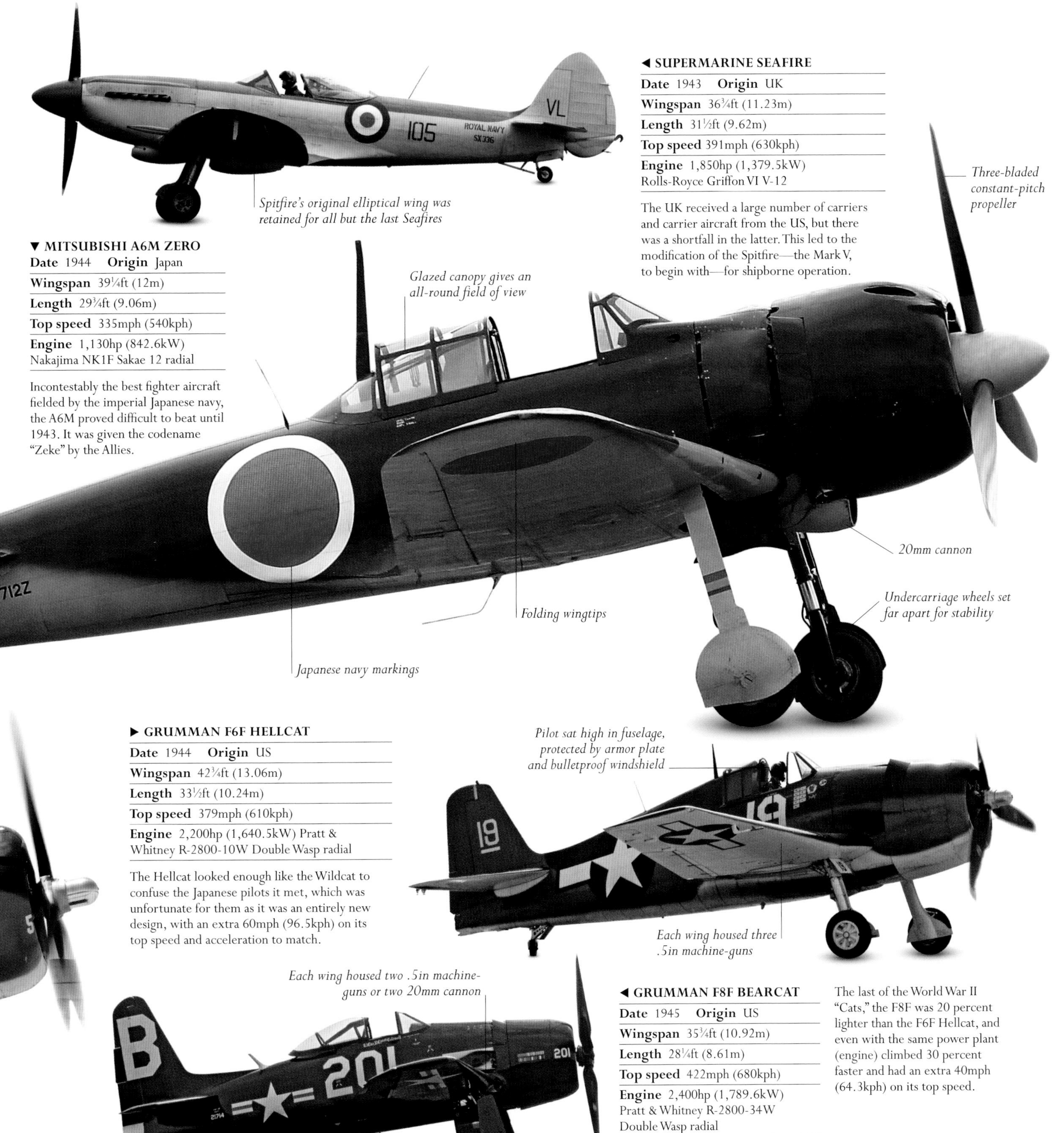

◀ SUPERMARINE SEAFIRE

Date 1943 **Origin** UK

Wingspan 36¾ft (11.23m)

Length 31½ft (9.62m)

Top speed 391mph (630kph)

Engine 1,850hp (1,379.5kW) Rolls-Royce Griffon VI V-12

The UK received a large number of carriers and carrier aircraft from the US, but there was a shortfall in the latter. This led to the modification of the Spitfire—the Mark V, to begin with—for shipborne operation.

▼ MITSUBISHI A6M ZERO

Date 1944 **Origin** Japan

Wingspan 39¼ft (12m)

Length 29¾ft (9.06m)

Top speed 335mph (540kph)

Engine 1,130hp (842.6kW) Nakajima NK1F Sakae 12 radial

Incontestably the best fighter aircraft fielded by the imperial Japanese navy, the A6M proved difficult to beat until 1943. It was given the codename "Zeke" by the Allies.

▶ GRUMMAN F6F HELLCAT

Date 1944 **Origin** US

Wingspan 42¾ft (13.06m)

Length 33½ft (10.24m)

Top speed 379mph (610kph)

Engine 2,200hp (1,640.5kW) Pratt & Whitney R-2800-10W Double Wasp radial

The Hellcat looked enough like the Wildcat to confuse the Japanese pilots it met, which was unfortunate for them as it was an entirely new design, with an extra 60mph (96.5kph) on its top speed and acceleration to match.

◀ GRUMMAN F8F BEARCAT

Date 1945 **Origin** US

Wingspan 35¾ft (10.92m)

Length 28¼ft (8.61m)

Top speed 422mph (680kph)

Engine 2,400hp (1,789.6kW) Pratt & Whitney R-2800-34W Double Wasp radial

The last of the World War II "Cats," the F8F was 20 percent lighter than the F6F Hellcat, and even with the same power plant (engine) climbed 30 percent faster and had an extra 40mph (64.3kph) on its top speed.

▶ VOUGHT F4U CORSAIR

Date 1942 **Origin** US

Wingspan 41ft (12.5m)

Length 33ft (10.1m)

Top speed 416mph (670kph)

Engine 2,000hp (1,491.3kW) Pratt & Whitney R-2800-8 radial

The Corsair was undoubtedly the most capable carrier-based fighter aircraft of World War II, and also gave very good service as a fighter-bomber. A total of 12,571 were produced between 1942 and 1953.

UNDER AIR ATTACK
A Japanese cruiser takes evasive action at the Battle of Leyte Gulf. The vulnerability of large warships to air strikes was a shock to all navies in World War II, requiring changes in tactics and making carriers the most important ships.

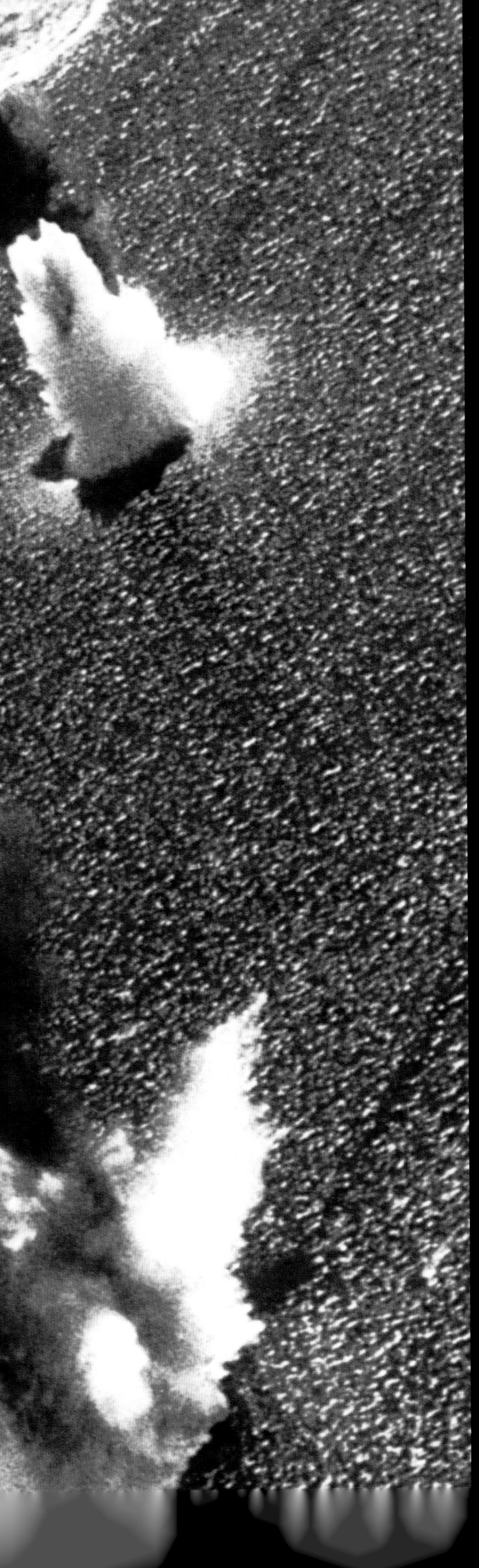

AIR–SEA COMBAT

THE BATTLE OF LEYTE GULF

The warfare between the Japanese Imperial Navy and the US Navy in the Pacific during World War II was remarkable for the significant role of aircraft and the epic scale of the combat. The Battle of Leyte Gulf in October 1944 was one of the largest sea battles ever fought.

By autumn 1944 Japanese naval aviation was a battered remnant of the force that had shocked the United States with its attack on Pearl Harbor almost three years earlier. Japan still possessed an impressive array of battleships and cruisers, but without adequate air cover, a sortie by these heavily gunned warships had become almost suicidal. Nonetheless, when the United States began amphibious landings on Leyte Island in the Japanese-occupied Philippines on October 20, the Imperial Navy sent every available vessel to attack the landing force. The Japanese divided their striking forces in two, one sailing south of Leyte Island and the other to the north. Land-based aircraft on the Philippines would supply air cover, while Japan's few remaining carriers were used as a decoy. Without their aircraft they headed away from the action, in the hope that the carriers of Admiral William F. Halsey, Jr.'s Third Fleet would follow.

The Japanese southern force, including two battleships and four cruisers, was ambushed by Admiral Thomas Kinkaid's Seventh Fleet while attempting the passage of the Surigao Strait on the night of October 24–25. American destroyers and PT boats first made torpedo runs, scoring a series of hits that sank the battleship *Fuso* with all hands. The Japanese then encountered the American main force of six battleships and eight cruisers, some equipped with advanced radar fire control that allowed them to hit Japanese warships at a range of over 20,000 yards (18,280m) in the dark. The second Japanese battleship, *Yamashiro*, was among the ships sunk by armor-piercing shells. Only a handful of crew survived.

Meanwhile, the approach of the other Japanese naval force through the Sibuyan Sea on October 24 had triggered a fierce air–sea battle. Halsey's carrier aircraft swarmed to attack the battleship *Musashi*, one of the largest, most powerfully gunned warships ever built. Hit by 19 bombs and 17 torpedoes in five successive air strikes, the massive ship sank with the loss of over 1,000 lives. Attacks by Japanese land-based aircraft inflicted some damage on US naval forces, but little in relation to their own losses of pilots and machines.

In the hope of at least dying to some effect, a group of Japanese pilots volunteered to carry out suicide attacks, crashing their aircraft into enemy ships. The first American ship sunk by kamikaze pilots was the escort carrier USS *St. Lo* on October 25.

THE END OF AN ERA

The battle almost ended badly for the Americans. After the sinking of the *Musashi*, Halsey accepted the bait of the decoy Japanese carriers and pursued them to destruction. In the absence of the main American carrier force, Japanese heavy cruisers slipped through the San Bernadino Strait and surprised escort carriers and destroyers supporting the troop landings. The US Navy was briefly at the mercy of Japanese naval guns, but bold torpedo runs by the destroyers and attacks by aircraft from the escort carriers drove the Japanese off. Having lost three battleships, eight cruisers and four carriers, the Imperial Navy had fought its last major battle.

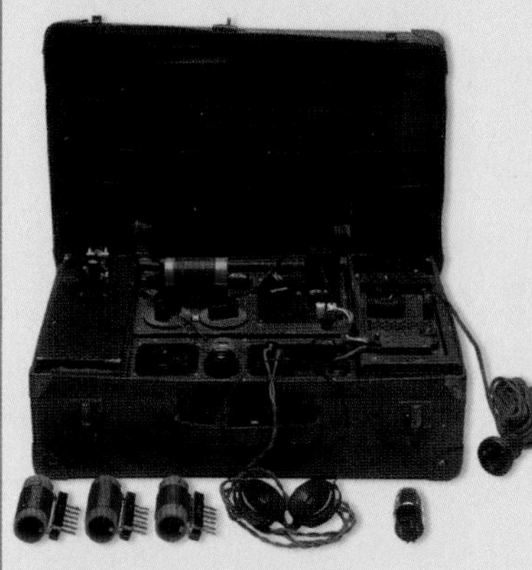

▲ A SUITCASE RADIO
The British Mk III Suitcase Transceiver was designed for use by agents of Britain's Special Operations Executive (SOE) and resistance groups. All its components were miniaturized, although it still required valves, as transistors had not yet been invented.

KEY DEVELOPMENT

TANKS AND INFANTRY IN WORLD WAR II

Land-based conflict in World War II extended across the globe, from the North African desert to the jungles of New Guinea and the streets of Berlin. Tanks and trucks made warfare more mobile, but did not eradicate the need for grueling infantry combat.

Between the two World Wars, a number of army officers, including J. F. C. Fuller in the UK, Heinz Guderian in Germany, and Mikhail Tukhachevsky in the Soviet Union, explored the use of tanks as the key strike force. Developments in tank design—improving speed, reliability, and armament—lent this vision credibility.

BLITZKREIG

Nazi Germany gave fullest rein to armored war, and defeated Allied ground forces in France in May–June 1940. Using their *Blitzkreig* ("lightning war") tactics, German tanks and motorized infantry, supported by aircraft as "aerial artillery," broke through Allied lines in the Ardennes. Mobile radios solved the communication problems of World War I, allowing generals to keep in touch with advancing forces, and facilitating combined ground and air maneuvers. As the war progressed, countermeasures were introduced, including mines, anti-tank guns, and infantry anti-tank weapons. The development of self-propelled guns provided artillery support for mobile forces, and also gave extra firepower to destroy advancing tanks.

Most infantry entered the war with the same bolt-action rifles issued in World War I, although the US Army had adopted the semi-automatic M1 Garand in 1936. By the end of the war, German

► TANK WARFARE
Following variable battlefield performance in World War I, the tank became a crucial part of land forces in World War II, both for Allied and Axis armies.

KEY **FIGURE**

GENERAL PATTON
1885–1945

George S Patton first commanded tanks during World War I. During World War II, he became America's most aggressive practitioner of armored warfare, from North Africa and Sicily, to the spectacular dash across France in the summer of 1944. He excelled in defeating a desperate, final counteroffensive by the Germans in the Ardennes, in the winter of 1944–45.

▲ Patton was a controversial commander, often feared as well as respected.

troops had the Sturmgewehr, the first assault rifle. Heavy, general-purpose, and light machine-guns were ubiquitous, as were submachine-guns, including the British Sten and the American Thompson ("Tommy") gun. Cavalry were mostly absent, although some armies still used horse-drawn supply trains—Germany assembled over 600,000 horses for its 1941 invasion of the Soviet Union.

TACTICS AND FORCES

Airborne troops emerged as a new elite branch of infantry, delivered to battle by parachute or glider. The Allies also conducted amphibious operations on a massive scale—particularly the US Marines in their "island-hopping" campaign against the Japanese in the Pacific. Resistance groups mounted guerrilla warfare in occupied territory, and irregular forces fought behind enemy lines.

However, land warfare in World War II was not only about mobility; infantry fought at close quarters for long periods at Stalingrad in the Soviet Union in 1942–43, and on Iwo Jima in the Pacific in 1945. Often, defensive positions were attacked by artillery barrage and infantry assault, supported with armored vehicles—similar tactics, albeit with improved technology, to those used in World War I.

> "The real secret is speed—**speed of attack** through **speed of communication**"
>
> **GENERAL ERHARD MILCH**, DISCUSSING *BLITZKRIEG*, 1939

◄ **US MARINES ON GUADALCANAL**
World War II soldiers had to fight in a wide variety of environments. The Pacific island of Guadalcanal, the scene of intense combat between American and Japanese troops in 1942, was difficult jungle terrain.

KEY **EVENTS**

1919–45

- **1919** British Army officer J. F. C. Fuller presents a plan for offensives based on penetration in depth by a strike force of massed tanks, supported by aircraft and motorized infantry battalions.
- **1928** American engineer J. Walter Christie completes his design for a high-speed tank with a revolutionary suspension system.
- **1936** The US Army adopts the semi-automatic M1 Garand rifle, with an eight-round "en-bloc" clip (with cartridges and clip inserted in a fixed magazine)—a significant advance on existing bolt-action rifles.
- **May–June 1940** German *Blitzkrieg* tactics combine tanks, aircraft, and motorized infantry to break deep into enemy territory.
- **May 1941** An invading force of German paratroopers land on Crete.
- **July 1943** Massed German tanks are defeated at the Battle of Kursk by Soviet defenses, including minefields and anti-tank guns.
- **1945** American troops make extensive use of flamethrowers on Iwo Jima and Okinawa.

ALLIED ARMORED FIGHTING VEHICLES

Although Allied tanks seldom reached the standard of their German counterparts in terms of technical excellence, they were far better equipped to meet the demands of mass production. This was especially the case with the Soviet T-34/85 and the US M4 Sherman tanks, which were manufactured in the tens of thousands and played a pivotal role in defeating the Germans on both the Eastern and Western fronts. France produced some good tank designs in the 1930s, but failed to use them effectively when Germany invaded France in 1940. British tanks often proved inadequate for combat conditions, although the gunned-up Sherman Firefly proved to be a potent battle-winning weapon.

▲ SOMUA S35

Date 1936 **Origin** France
Weight 21.5 tons (19.5 tonnes)
Length 18ft (5.38m)
Top speed 25mph (40kph)
Engine SOMUA 8-cylinder 190hp (142kW) gasoline engine

An effective 1930s design that utilized a powerful main gun and a cleverly sloped armor, the three-man SOMUA equipped France's cavalry divisions, complementing the infantry's Char B1-bis. One drawback, however, was that the commander was also required to act as the gunner inside the very cramped turret.

▼ CHAR B1-BIS HEAVY TANK

Date 1936 **Origin** France
Weight 30.8 tons (28 tonnes)
Length 20¾ft (6.37m)
Top speed 17mph (28kph)
Engine Renault 6-cylinder 307hp (229kW) gasoline engine

The French army's B1-bis was a formidable tank in its day, even if it was slow and not very reliable. Heavily armored, it had the unusual distinction of being equipped with two main armaments—a howitzer for firing high explosives against enemy fortifications, and a turret-mounted anti-tank gun.

▶ M4A1 MEDIUM TANK (SHERMAN)

Date 1941 **Origin** US
Weight 35.6 tons (32.3 tonnes)
Length 19ft (5.84m)
Top speed 30mph (48kph)
Engine Continental R975 400hp (298kW) gasoline radial engine

The M4 tank was the most important tank fielded by the Western Allies, equipping the armored divisions of the US and UK. Although easy to produce and maintain, it was inadequately armored and its gun could not take on the Panther and Tiger tanks of the German armed forces.

▼ CRUISER MK VIII (A27M) CROMWELL TANK

Date 1943 **Origin** UK
Weight 30.7 tons (27.9 tonnes)
Length 20¾ft (6.35m)
Top speed 40mph (64kph)
Engine Rolls Royce V12 603hp (450kW) gasoline engine

One of the more successful British tanks designs of World War II, the five-man Cromwell combined reasonable armored protection with an effective main gun. It was widely used in a reconnaissance role because of its impressive top speed, reliability, and ease of handling.

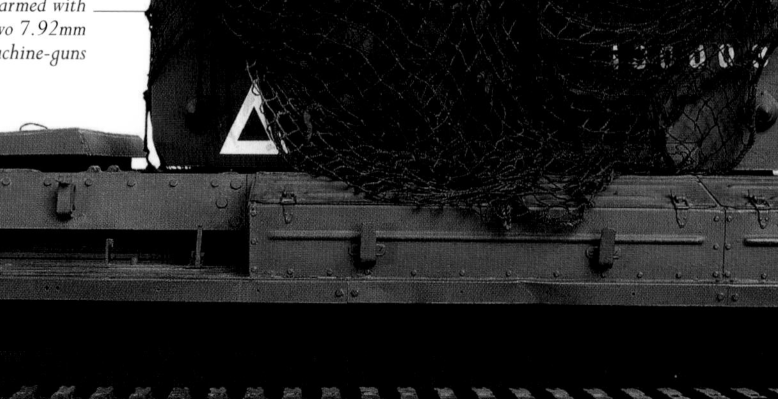

75mm M6 gun

Commander's cupola

▲ T17E1 STAGHOUND LIGHT ARMORED CAR

Date 1943 **Origin** US
Weight 15.3 tons (13.9 tonnes)
Length 18ft (5.49m)
Top speed 55mph (89kph)
Engine Two GMC 270 6-cylinder 97hp (72kW) gasoline engines

Although designed and built in the US, the Staghound was used almost exclusively by British and Commonwealth forces. Reliable and popular with its crew, a number of variants were developed, which included a close-support version armed with a 75mm howitzer, and an anti-aircraft version with two .5in Browning machine-guns. It was operated by a crew of five.

▲ M24 CHAFEE LIGHT TANK

Date 1944 **Origin** US
Weight 20.2 tons (18.4 tonnes)
Length 16¼ft (4.99m)
Top speed 35mph (56kph)
Engine Two Cadillac M44T24 110hp (82kW) engines

The US Army's requirement for a light tank with a more powerful armament than the standard 37mm gun led to the introduction of the M24 with a 75mm gun. Reliable and swift, it was a popular armored fighting vehicle, operating with a crew of five. However, it only arrived at the front line in Europe during the closing stages of World War II.

◀ T-34/85 MEDIUM TANK

Date 1944 **Origin** Soviet Union
Weight 35.3 tons (32 tonnes)
Length 22ft (6.68m)
Top speed 31mph (50kph)
Engine 12-cylinder 496hp (370kW) diesel engine

The T-34/85 represented a superb combination of firepower, armor protection, and mobility. When the Germans first encountered the T-34/85 in 1941, armed with the smaller 76.2mm gun, they realized they were facing a tank far superior to anything they could field. Even after the development of a new range of German tanks, it remained a formidable armored fighting vehicle.

75mm main gun

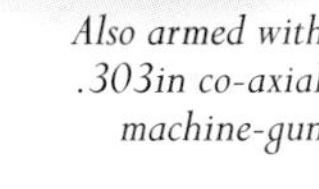

▲ M4 MEDIUM TANK (SHERMAN FIREFLY)

Date 1944 **Origin** US/UK
Weight 36.4 tons (33 tonnes)
Length 19¼ft (5.89m)
Top speed 25mph (40kph)
Engine Chrysler 425hp (317kW) multibank engine

The lack of a powerful main gun hampered the standard M4 tank, but this was rectified by the introduction of a British 17-pounder main armament in the Firefly. This high-velocity gun was capable of taking on German heavy tanks, although the tank's light armor remained inadequate for operations in Northwest Europe in 1944–45.

Front idler

AXIS ARMORED FIGHTING VEHICLES

As the nation that developed the concept of *Blitzkrieg*, it was hardly surprising that Germany should develop some of the most advanced and effective armored fighting vehicles (AFVs) of World War II. The Panther and Tiger tanks struck fear in their Allied opponents, but, unlike the Allies, German tank manufacturers could not utilize the methods of mass production, as their vehicles were slow and expensive to build. Germany's Axis partners, Italy and Japan, produced some effective designs in the 1930s, but were unable to develop them further as the war progressed.

▲ PANZERKAMPFWAGEN II LIGHT TANK, AUSF F

Date 1935 **Origin** Germany
Weight 11 tons (10 tonnes)
Length 15¼ft (4.64m)
Top speed 34mph (55kph)
Engine Maybach 6-cylinder 140hp (104kW) gasoline engine

The Panzer II, manned by a crew of three, was originally created to function as a training tank. However, the shortage of more powerful models brought it into the front line, where it was used in huge numbers for the invasions of Poland and France.

▲ TYPE 95 HA-GO LIGHT TANK

Date 1936 **Origin** Japan
Weight 8.1 tons (7.4 tonnes)
Length 14¼ft (4.38m)
Top speed 28mph (45kph)
Engine Mitsubishi NVD 6120 6-cylinder 120hp (89kW) diesel engine

Entering service in the 1930s, this three-man tank was typical of its time. While it proved successful during the war in China, it was outclassed by US armor and anti-tank guns during World War II.

► CARRO VELOCE L3-33 FLAMETHROWER

Date 1936 **Origin** Italy
Weight 3.5 tons (3.2 tonnes)
Length 10½ft (3.17m)
Top speed 26mph (42kph)
Engine SPA CV3 43hp (32kW) gasoline engine

Developed from the British Carden-Lloyd tankette, this modified version of the L3-35 replaced its twin machine-guns with a flamethrower nozzle. The flame fuel was carried in a 132-gallon (500-liter) trailer towed by the vehicle.

Muzzle brake

88mm KwK 43 main gun

Mantlet

Armed with 75mm KwK 40 main gun as well as two or three 7.92mm machine-guns

▲ PANZERKAMPFWAGEN IV MEDIUM TANK

Date 1936 **Origin** Germany
Weight 27.5 tons (25 tonnes)
Length 19¼ft (5.89m)
Top speed 24mph (38kph)
Engine Maybach HL 120TRM 12-cylinder 300hp (224kW) gasoline engine

Intended to adopt the role of an infantry support vehicle, the Panzer IV developed into a potent main battle tank as a result of a series of upgrades that improved protection and firepower. With a crew of five, the Panzer IV was the only German tank to remain in service throughout the war.

◀ PANZERKAMPFWAGEN III MEDIUM TANK, AUSF M

Date 1939 **Origin** Germany
Weight 25.9 tons (23.5 tonnes)
Length 21ft (6.41m)
Top speed 25mph (40kph)
Engine Maybach HL 120TRM 12-cylinder 300hp (224kW) gasoline engine

The Panzer III entered service in 1939 as the German army's main battle tank, but by the end of 1941 its inferiority to the Soviet T-34 had become evident and it was adapted to act as a chassis for other armored vehicles. This mark was manned by five crew.

◀ PANZERKAMPFWAGEN V PANTHER MEDIUM TANK, AUSF G

Date 1943 **Origin** Germany
Weight 49.4 tons (44.8 tonnes)
Length 22½ft (6.88m)
Top speed 29mph (46kph)
Engine Maybach HL230 P30 12-cylinder 700hp (522kW) gasoline engine

Although designated as a medium tank, the five-man Panther was an exceptionally powerful armored fighting vehicle, and, once initial teething problems were rectified, it became one of the most effective tanks of World War II.

▲ PANZERKAMPFWAGEN VI TIGER I HEAVY TANK, AUSF E

Date 1942 **Origin** Germany
Weight 61.7 tons (56 tonnes)
Length 20¼ft (6.20m)
Top speed 24mph (38kph)
Engine Maybach HL230 P45 12-cylinder 700hp (522kW) gasoline engine

Adopting a design philosophy that emphasized protection and firepower, the Tiger was a fearsome weapon, but it lacked maneuverability. It was also costly to manufacture.

◀ PANZERKAMPFWAGEN VI TIGER II HEAVY TANK, AUSF B

Date 1944 **Origin** Germany
Weight 76.9 tons (69.8 tonnes)
Length 23¾ft (7.26m)
Top speed 24mph (38kph)
Engine Maybach HL230 P30 12-cylinder 700hp (522kW) gasoline engine

The Tiger II (or King Tiger), which was operated by five crew members, was arguably the most powerful tank fielded by any side in World War II. However, its immense weight caused a series of reliability problems, which hampered its battlefield performance.

WORLD WAR II ARMORED VEHICLE

T-34 TANK

Although crudely finished, noisy, and cramped, the Soviet Union's T-34 was perhaps the most successful tank of World War II, taking on and eventually beating the formidable German panzers.

Designated the T-34/76, the tank first saw action in 1941. It mounted a 76.2mm main gun and two 7.62mm DT machine-guns, one in the turret and one in the hull. The coaxial machine-gun in the turret fired tracer rounds to guide the main gun. The T-34 had a four-man crew, with the tank commander doubling as the main gunner.

Thanks to its simple design, the T-34 was easy to mass-produce—nearly 40,000 were built before the war's end—and to repair. Relatively light in weight, it could achieve an impressive 32mph (51kph) and coped well with mud, snow, and broken ground. Its sloped armor, 4in (100mm) thick, gave good protection, while the high-velocity gun penetrated enemy armor effectively.

In 1944, with the T-34 outclassed by more advanced German tanks, the T-34/85 model entered service. Its upgraded 85mm gun gave greater firepower, and the more spacious turret, which had room for three crew, allowed the roles of commander and gunner to be separated.

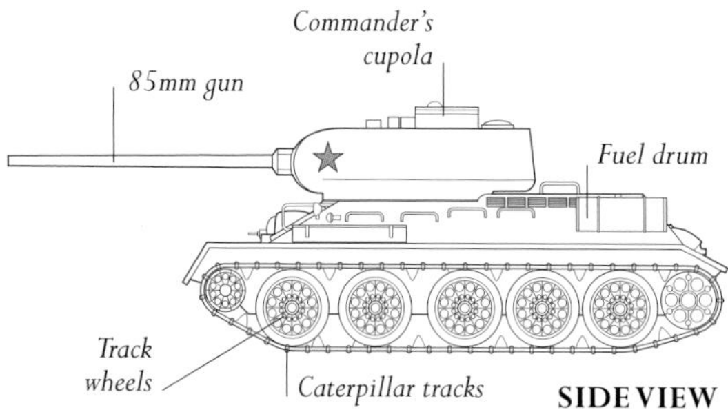

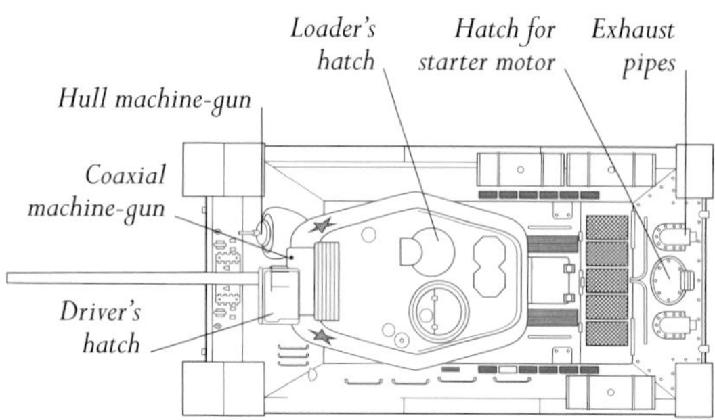

SOVIET T-34/85
The five-man T-34/85 had a longer main gun than its predecessor. Its flatter turret gave it a lower profile and made it a more difficult target.

TANK EXTERIOR

▲ HULL MACHINE-GUN
The machine-gun muzzle was able to pivot on its mounting. The hole above the muzzle is a gun sight.

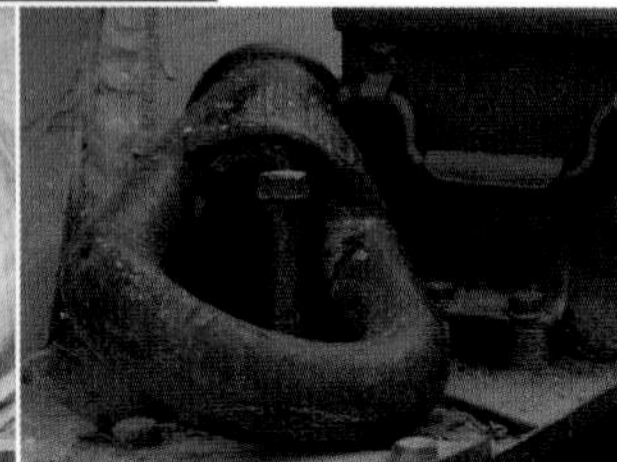

▲ TOWING ROPE EYE
A wire hawser (large rope) ran along the side of the tank. It could be used to haul damaged vehicles from the battlefield.

▲ FUEL DRUMS
The drums of spare diesel fuel were a fire hazard in battle, so they were usually emptied before combat.

▼ DRIVER'S HATCH
The entrance hatch for the driver was usually left open to give him a better view of the way ahead.

◀ SPARE TRACK ON TURRET
Spare links for repairing the T-34's wide tracks were carried on the outside of the tank.

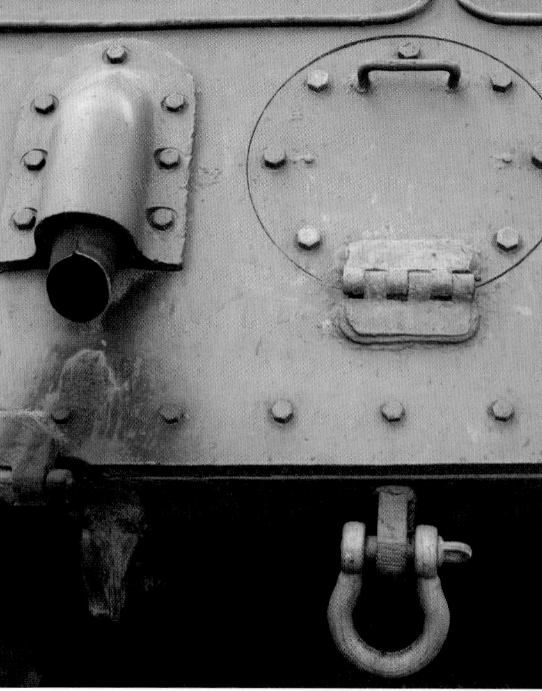

▲ EXHAUST PIPES AND STARTER MOTOR HATCH
The exhausts tended to billow clouds of smoke when the engine started up. The noisy engine could be heard from 500 yards (450m) away.

◄ **TROOP CARRIER**
Several soldiers could ride into battle on the rear platform of the T-34 and on the sides of its hull, providing instant infantry support.

TANK INTERIOR

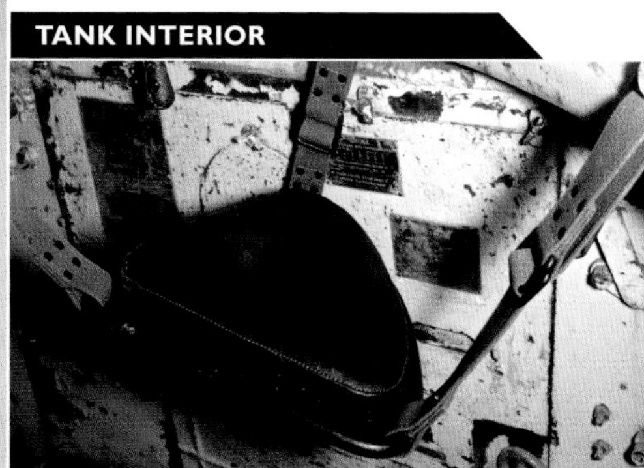

▲ **LOADER'S SEAT**
While dodging the main gun's recoil, the loader fetched shells from bins under the turret floor.

▲ **TURRET TRAVERSE WHEEL**
The gunner turned a wheel to traverse (rotate) the turret, and was responsible for firing the static coaxial machine-gun, in the turret to the right of the main gun.

▲ **RUNNING GEAR**
The suspension was based on an American design that had been rejected by the US Army.

▲ **AMMUNITION DRUMS**
Tracer rounds (often fired as range finders) for the coaxial machine-gun lay ready to hand.

◄ **DRIVER'S SEAT**
Sitting beside the hull machine-gunner, the driver could see only straight ahead. He steered mainly to instructions from the commander.

ANTI-TANK WEAPONS

The advent of the tank forced arms designers to come up with weapons powerful enough to counter this threat. For the infantry, who bore the brunt of the armored assault, armor-piercing rifles came as a solution. Weapons such as the Panzerbüsche were also successful, but improvements in tank armor during World War II rendered them obsolete. Lightweight, short-range weapons firing shaped-charge projectiles became more useful. The most effective anti-tank weapon, however, was a high-velocity artillery piece.

◀ PAK 36 ANTI-TANK GUN

Date 1934
Origin Germany
Weight 723lb (328kg)
Length 5½ft (1.66m)
Caliber 37mm
Armor penetration 1½in (38mm) at 400 yards (365m)

Designed for warfare in the 1930s, the light PAK 36 was obsolete by 1940. It was nicknamed the "doorknocker" for the way its shells bounced off the armor of Allied tanks.

▼ BOYS MK1 ANTI-TANK RIFLE

Date 1937
Origin UK
Weight 36lb (16.33kg)
Barrel 35¾in (91cm)
Caliber .55in
Armor penetration ¾in (21mm) at 330 yards (302m)

The Boys anti-tank rifle fired a heavy tungsten-steel round, and had a correspondingly violent recoil. However, it was only able to pierce light armor, and was replaced by the PIAT.

▶ FLAK 36 AA/AT GUN

Date 1936
Origin Germany
Weight 8.1 tons (7.4 tonnes)
Length 19ft (5.79m)
Caliber 88mm
Armor penetration 6¼in (159mm) at 1,094 yards (1,000m)

Designed as an anti-aircraft (AA) gun, the famed "88," as it was known, was found to be highly effective as an anti-tank gun. It could be put in position very quickly—within three minutes—although its bulk and height made it difficult to conceal. It was able to fire up to 20 rounds per minute.

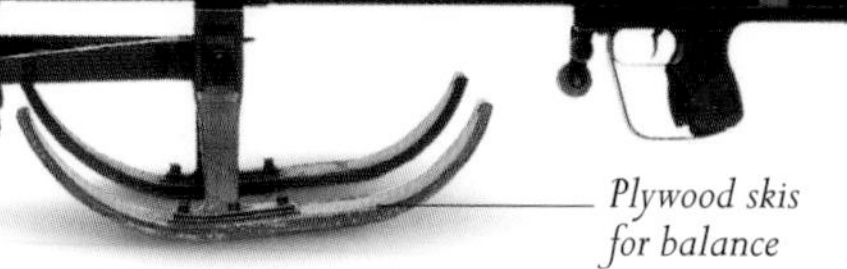

▲ LAHTI L39 ANTI-TANK RIFLE

Date 1939
Origin Finland
Weight 109lb (49.5kg)
Barrel 4¼ft (1.3m)
Caliber 20 × 138Bmm
Armor penetration 1¼in (30mm) at 109 yards (100m)

The L39's enormous size and weight gave it the nickname "Elephant Gun." It was used to good effect during the Winter War of 1939–40.

▼ PANZERBÜSCHE 39 ANTI-TANK RIFLE

Date 1940
Origin Germany
Weight 27¾lb (12.6kg)
Barrel 3½ft (1.08m)
Caliber 7.92 × 94mm
Armor penetration 1in (25mm) at 328 yards (300m)

The Panzerbüsche 39 relied on its very high muzzle velocity and tungsten-cored bullet to penetrate enemy armor. It was, however, expensive to manufacture, and was only produced in small numbers.

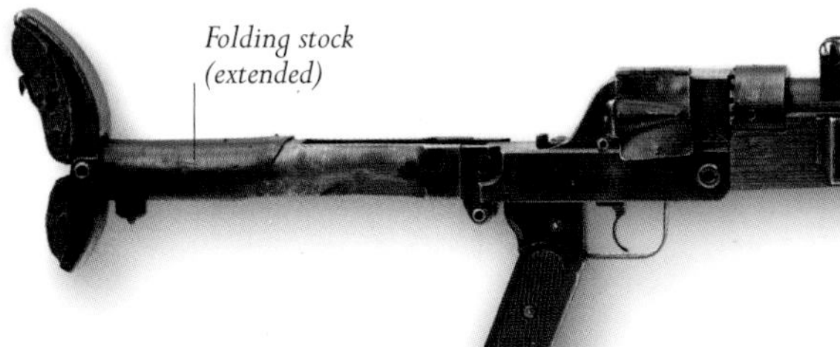

▲ M1A1 "BAZOOKA"

Date 1942

Origin US

Weight 13¼lb (6kg)

Length 4½ft (1.37m)

Caliber 60mm

Armor penetration 4¾in (120mm) at 150 yards (138m)

The Bazooka was essentially a tube that launched a solid fuel rocket with a shaped-charge warhead. It was operated by two men—one who fired and one who loaded.

▼ PIAT

Date 1942

Origin UK

Weight 32lb (14.5kg)

Length 39in (99cm)

Armor penetration 3in (75mm) at 120 yards (110m)

The PIAT (Projector, Infantry, Anti-Tank), like the Sten, was a wartime expedient design that put function before form. It was actually a spigot mortar that fired a bomb with a shaped-charge warhead.

▼ M1942 FIELD/ ANTI-TANK GUN

Date 1942

Origin Soviet Union

Weight 2 tons (1.73 tonnes)

Length 13¾ft (4.18m)

Armor penetration 3¼in (98mm) at 545 yards (500m)

Although designed as a divisional field gun, the M1942 could also destroy armor with high-explosive and armor-piercing rounds.

◄ SD. KFZ. 173 JAGDPANTHER

Date 1944

Origin Germany

Weight 50.7 tons (46 tonnes)

Length 32½ft (9.9m)

Top speed 28½mph (46kph)

Armor penetration 7½in (193mm) at 1,094yards (1,000m)

Arguably the finest armored fighting vehicle of the war, the Jagdpanther tank destroyer combined mobility, armor protection, and a devastating high-velocity main gun.

TRUCKS, HALF-TRACKS, AND LIGHT VEHICLES

While tanks and other armored fighting vehicles have been regarded as the most effective vehicles of World War II, it was the trucks, cars, half-tracks, and other light vehicles that provided the vital logistical backup to the vast armies of the Allies and the Axis powers. For the first time in history, troops in auxiliary services began to outnumber front-line troops. Such support was vital. Not only was there a vast range of vehicles, but a specific model could also come in a bewildering range of variants, each designed to suit a particular role in differing conditions.

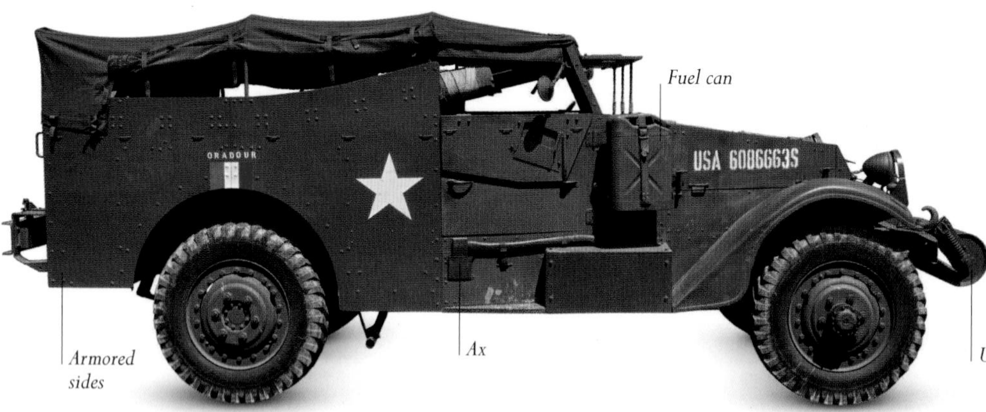

Fuel can

Armored sides

Ax

Unditching roller

▲ M3A1 SCOUT CAR

Date 1940 **Origin** US

Weight 4.4 tons (4.03 tonnes)

Length 18¼ft (5.6m)

Top speed 55mph (89kph)

Engine Hercules JXD 6-cylinder 110hp (82kW) gasoline engine

Developed as a light armored car to support American mechanized formations, the M3A1 suffered from poor off-road mobility, although its best design features were incorporated into the half-tracks that succeeded it.

▲ SDKFZ 251-8 AUSF C HALF-TRACK

Date 1940 **Origin** Germany

Weight 8.6 tons (7.8 tonnes)

Length 19ft (5.8m)

Top speed 33mph (52.5kph)

Engine Maybach HL 42 6-cylinder 100hp (74.6kW) gasoline engine

Although originally intended as an APC (Armored Personnel Carrier), the SDKFZ 251 half-track proved so useful that at least 22 separate variants were developed, including this 251-8 battlefield ambulance. Other variants included anti-tank, rocket launcher, and anti-aircraft versions.

Helmet and canteen on spare wheel, mounted on sidecar

Cylinder head

Side pannier

► R75 MOTORCYCLE COMBINATION

Date 1941 **Origin** Germany

Weight 882lb (400kg)

Length 7¼ft (2.4m)

Top speed 59mph (95kph)

Engine Four-stroke 2-cylinder flat-twin 25hp (19kW) gasoline engine

Manufactured by BMW, the R75 was powered by a 750cc engine and utilized a drivetrain that powered the rear wheels of both the bike and the sidecar. Many were armed with a 7.92mm MG34 machine-gun.

Windshield (folded forward)

Wheel with four-wheel-drive transmission

► WILLYS JEEP

Date 1941 **Origin** US

Weight 1.14 tons (1.04 tonnes)

Length 11ft (3.33m)

Top speed 55mph (89kph)

Engine Willys 4-cylinder 60hp (45kW) gasoline engine

Technically known as a truck, but more commonly called a jeep, this iconic World War II vehicle was rugged, reliable, and eminently versatile. It had space for four crew.

Angled armor plate

▶ DODGE T214-WC56 COMMAND RECONNAISSANCE LIGHT TRUCK

Date 1942 **Origin** US
Weight 2.7 tons (2.45 tonnes)
Length 14ft (4.24m)
Top speed 54mph (87kph)
Engine Dodge T214 6-cylinder 92hp (69kW) gasoline engine

One of a series of light trucks, the command reconnaissance (WC56) was often used by senior officers. It was fitted with map boards and internal lighting, as well as a canvas top and side-screens.

Engine hood
Radio aerial
Spare wheel
Fuel can

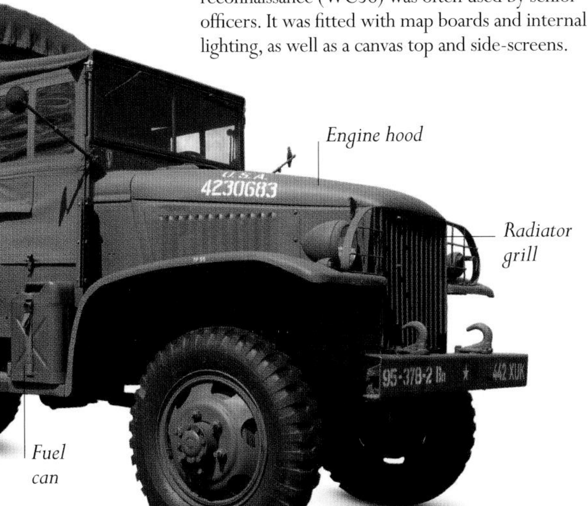

▲ GMC 2½-TON 6X6 TRUCK

Date 1939 **Origin** US
Weight 5.05 tons (4.58 tonnes)
Length 21¼ft (6.5m)
Top speed 45mph (72kph)
Engine 6-cylinder 90hp (67.3kW) gasoline engine

Nicknamed the "Jimmy," the GMC-produced truck was one of the workhorses of American logistics in Europe from 1944 to 1945. Reliable, with a good cargo load, the six-wheel-drive vehicle could cope with all but the roughest conditions.

Rear machine-gun
Haversacks slung on external rail
Forward machine-gun
Fuel can
Caterpillar tracks

▲ M5 HALF-TRACK

Date 1942 **Origin** US
Weight 10.2 tons (9.3 tonnes)
Length 20¾ft (6.33m)
Top speed 42mph (68kph)
Engine International Harvester RED-450-B 6-cylinder 141hp (105kW) gasoline engine

Designed to provide mobility and protection for infantry advancing into battle, this M5 was broadly similar to its more famous M3 cousin. More than 40,000 half-tracks of various specifications were used by the US during World War II.

▼ SCHWIMMWAGEN

Date 1942 **Origin** Germany
Weight 2,006lb (910kg)
Length 12½ft (3.83m)
Top speed 50mph (80kph); 6mph (10kph) on water
Engine 4-cylinder air-cooled 25hp (18.4kW) gasoline engine

Based on the Volkswagen, the *Schwimmwagen* (swimming car) was a fully amphibious four-wheel-drive vehicle, which could tackle snow, mud, and water obstacles encountered on campaign.

UNIFORMS AND EQUIPMENT

During World War II, military uniforms went through a transitional phase as old gave way to new. Traditional uniforms—such as those worn by the Japanese infantryman—distinguished the soldier from both the enemy and civilians, and provided him with a sense of solidarity with his fellow troops. The new functional uniforms, however, typically worn by specialists such as fliers and armored troops, were designed with practical considerations in mind. This approach to uniform would become increasingly common in the post-war era.

◀ FELDMÜTZE

Date 1934

Origin Germany

Material Wool

Nicknamed the *Schiffchen* (little ship) by the ordinary soldier, the *Feldmütze* (side cap) was issued to Panzer (tank) troops, and included the famous death's head insignia of Prussia's Black Hussars.

▲ PANZER JACKET

Date 1930s

Origin Germany

Material Wool

Panzer crews were issued with black, hip-length, double-breasted jackets. The color helped conceal oil and grease stains.

Cuff title of SS-Leibstandarte Adolf Hitler division, Hitler's personal bodyguard

Leather peak

Rank insignia

▲ IMPERIAL JAPANESE ARMY UNIFORM

Date 1930

Origin Japan

Material Cotton (wool in winter)

This infantryman's uniform was worn during the early stages of World War II. It consisted of a peaked cap and the single-breasted M90 tunic, which had a stand-and-fall collar.

▶ BRODIE HELMET

Date 1939

Origin UK

Material Steel

Designed by the British inventor John Brodie, this was the standard steel helmet worn by British troops during both world wars. Based on the shape of a medieval kettle hat, the helmet gave protection from shrapnel and shell splinters.

Helmet pressed from single steel sheet

▶ BATTLEDRESS JACKET

Date 1942

Origin UK

Material Wool

Battledress was a new uniform adopted by the British Army from 1939 onward. It included trousers and a short jacket (or blouse). This simpler P40 battledress jacket utilized less fabric and was introduced in 1942.

Formation insignia

P40 "austerity version" without pleated pockets and front fly

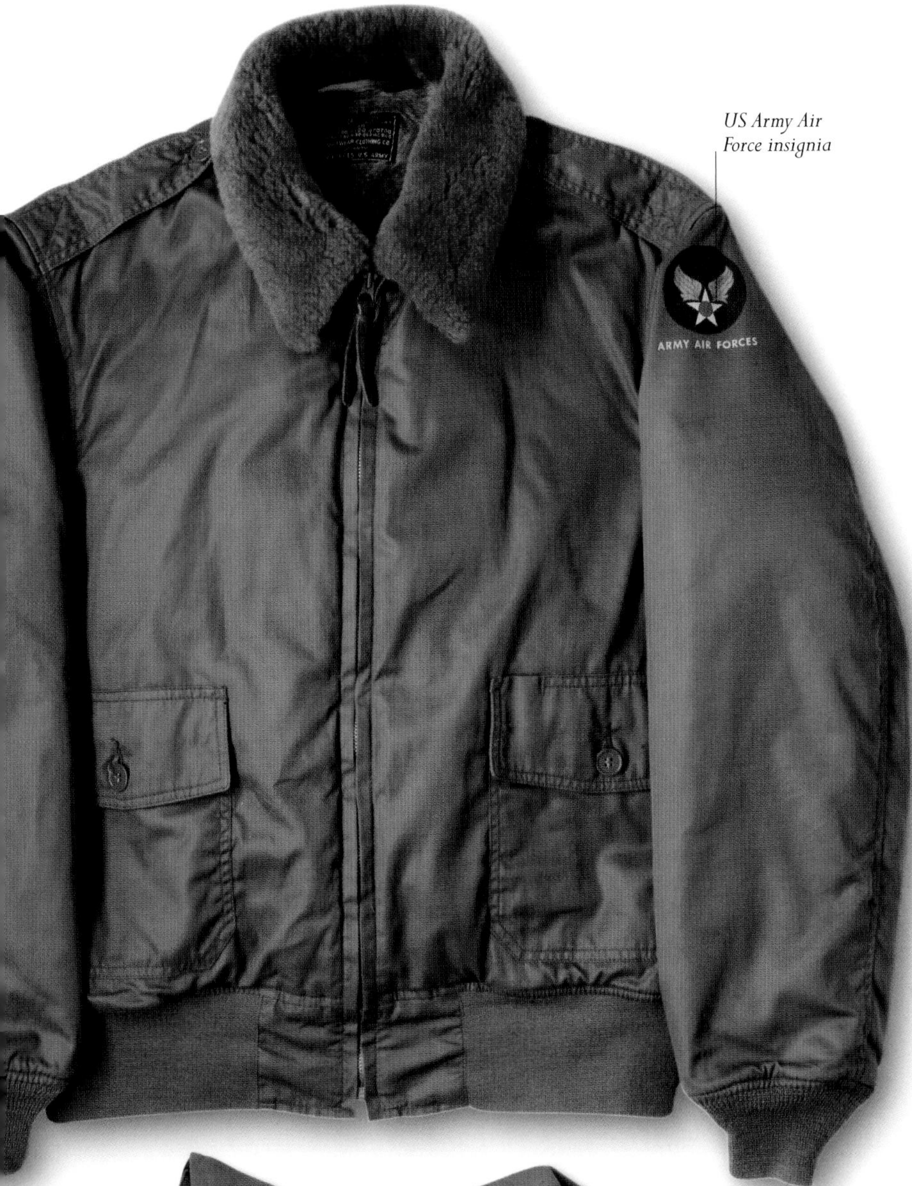
US Army Air Force insignia
ARMY AIR FORCES

Apron to protect lower abdomen
Webbing with red quick-release tab

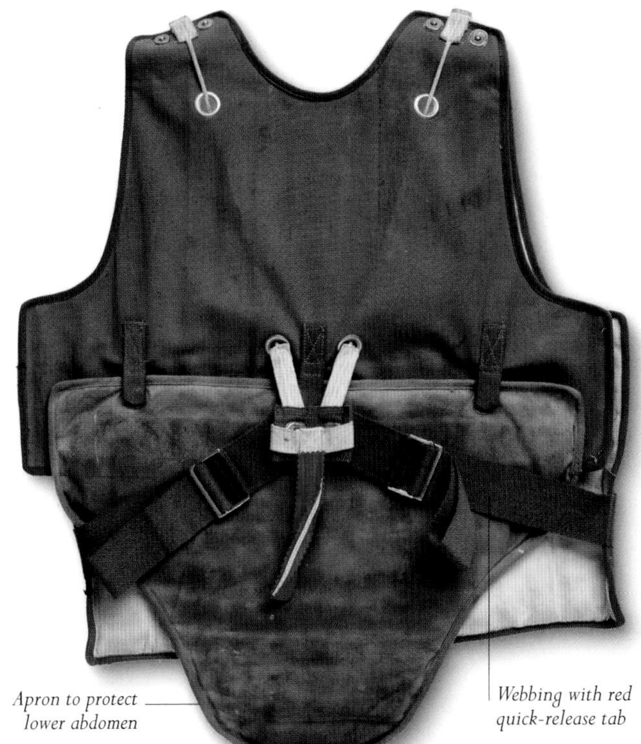

▲ FLAK JACKET

Date 1942

Origin US

Material Nylon, steel

Designed to protect US bomber crews from low-velocity fragments, these early examples of flak jackets consisted of steel plates sewn into a multi-layered nylon jerkin.

◄ B10 FLYING JACKET

Date 1943

Origin US

Material Cotton (with alpaca lining)

Issued to US air crews, the B10 featured a fur collar and zip opening. It also had knitted wrists and waistband to help its wearer retain body warmth.

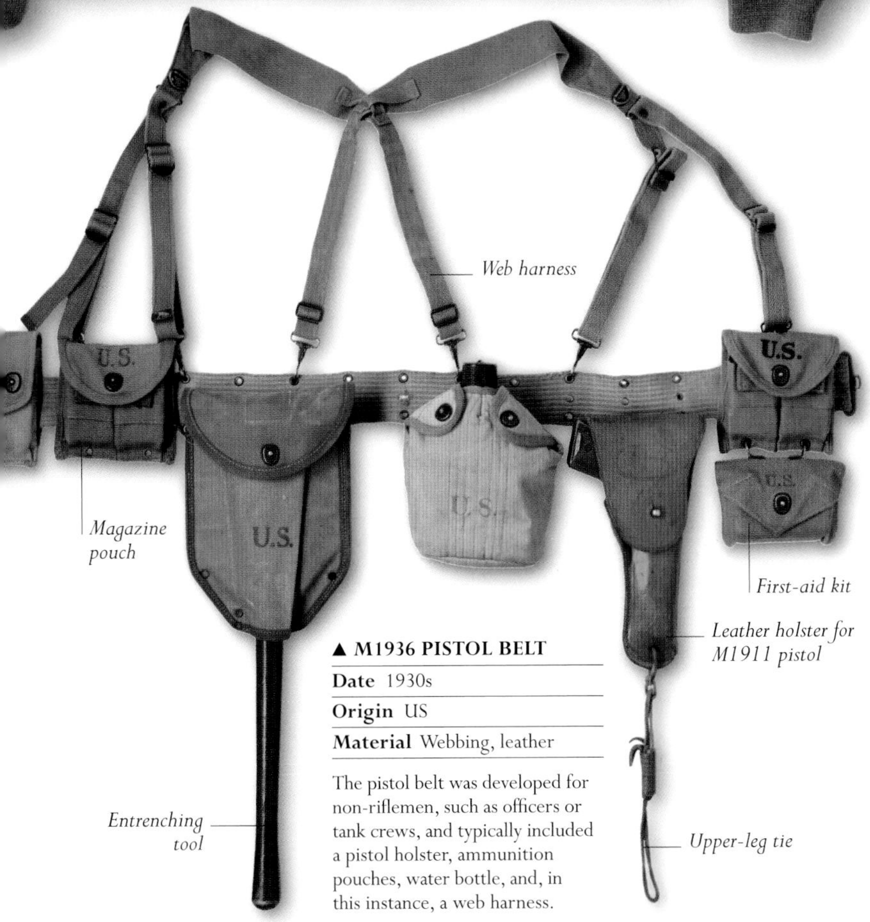
Web harness
Magazine pouch
First-aid kit
Leather holster for M1911 pistol
Entrenching tool
Upper-leg tie
U.S.

▲ M1936 PISTOL BELT

Date 1930s

Origin US

Material Webbing, leather

The pistol belt was developed for non-riflemen, such as officers or tank crews, and typically included a pistol holster, ammunition pouches, water bottle, and, in this instance, a web harness.

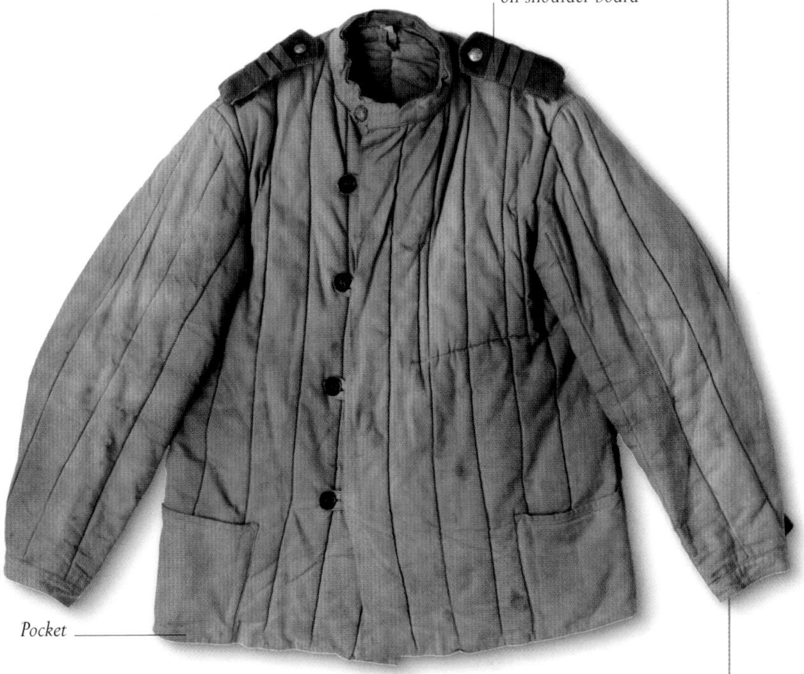
Sergeant's rank insignia on shoulder board
Pocket

▲ TELOGREIKA

Date 1930s

Origin Soviet Union

Material Cotton, cotton wool

The *telogreika* (body warmer) was a quilted jacket issued to Soviet troops during the winter months. The fabric of the jacket was stuffed with cotton wool, which helped keep out the worst of the cold.

SELF-LOADING RIFLES

The old bolt-action rifles developed during the final years of the 19th century were still in service at the outbreak of World War II, and despite their age remained highly effective. But the war proved to be a transitional stage for the rifle. The first major breakthrough took place with the introduction of the self-loading rifle, which allowed repeated shots to be fired by simply pulling the trigger. The key development, however, came with the German Sturmgewehr 44, the first assault rifle and forerunner of the AK47, its revolutionary medium-powered 7.92 × 33mm cartridge allowing soldiers to deliver effective automatic fire for the first time.

▲ **MAUSER INFANTERIEGEWEHR 98**

Date 1898
Origin Germany
Weight 9lb (4.15kg)
Barrel 29in (74cm)
Caliber 7.92mm

The Gewehr 98 was issued to the German army during both world wars. Although somewhat cumbersome when used in confined spaces, the rifle was rugged, reliable, and accurate.

Fixed-focus eyepiece

▶ **MOSIN-NAGANT M1891/30PU**

Date 1930
Origin Soviet Union
Weight 8¾lb (4kg)
Barrel 29in (73cm)
Caliber 7.62mm

The M1891/30 was the standard rifle of the Red Army during World War II. Selected models of the rifle were fitted with a 3.5-power PU telescopic sight, to be used by snipers.

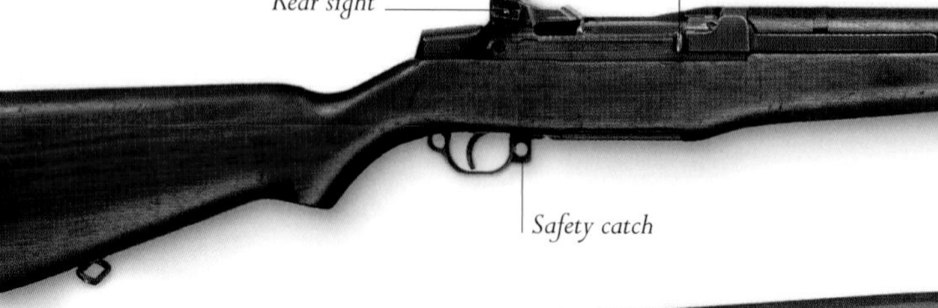

▲ **M1 GARAND RIFLE**

Date 1932
Origin US
Weight 9½lb (4.31kg)
Barrel 24in (61cm)
Caliber .30-06

Designed by John Garand, the M1 rifle was the first general issue self-loading rifle to be accepted for military service. By the end of World War II, over five million of them had been manufactured.

Ten-round detachable box magazine

▲ **LEE ENFIELD RIFLE NO. 4**

Date 1939
Origin UK
Weight 9lb (4.1kg)
Barrel 25in (64cm)
Caliber .303in

A successor to the SMLE rifle of World War I fame, the Lee Enfield rifle No. 4 had a heavier barrel and a relocated rear sight, and was designed for mass production.

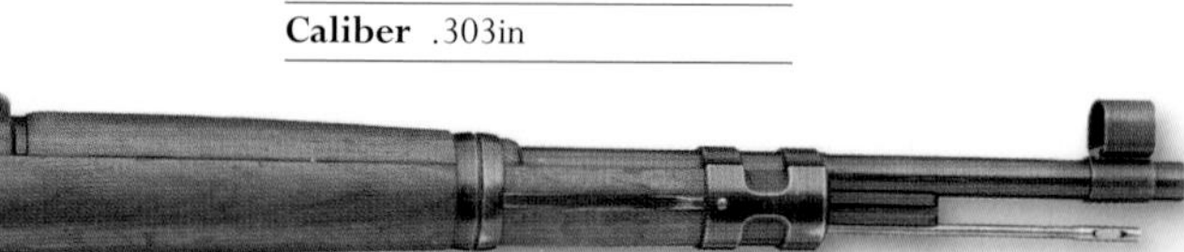

▲ **MAUSER KAR98K**

Date 1935
Origin Germany
Weight 8½lb (3.9kg)
Barrel 23½in (60cm)
Caliber 7.92mm × 57

The "Karabiner" 98K was a modified version of the Gewehr 98, and became the standard German rifle of World War II. More than 14 million were manufactured between 1935 and 1945. During that time, the design was further simplified to speed up production.

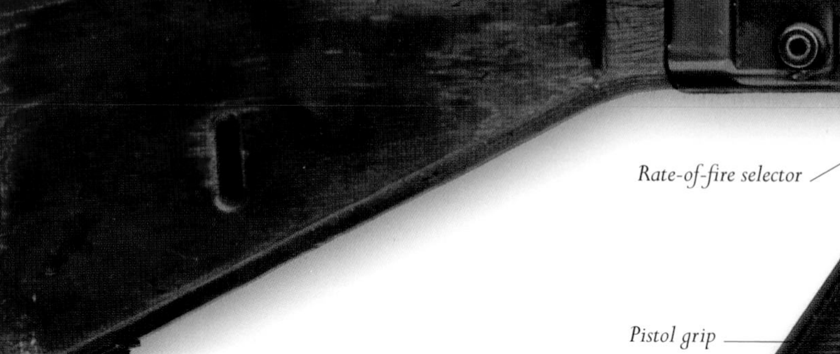

▲ **TOKAREV SVT40**

Date 1940
Origin Soviet Union
Weight 8½lb (3.9kg)
Barrel 24in (61cm)
Caliber 7.62mm × 54R

During the 1930s, the Soviet designers worked on the development of a self-loading rifle, and this led to the introduction of the SVT40—usually issued to NCOs or trained marksmen.

▲ **M1 CARBINE**

Date 1941
Origin US
Weight 5¼lb (2.4kg)
Barrel 18in (46cm)
Caliber .30in Carbine

The M1 carbine was a popular lightweight weapon. It used an intermediate cartridge, the power of which was between that of a rifle and pistol. It was also produced with a folding butt for paratroopers.

▲ **GEWEHR 43**

Date 1943
Origin Germany
Weight 9½lb (4.35kg)
Barrel 22in (56cm)
Caliber 7.92mm × 57

The German army's request for a self-loading rifle to increase infantry firepower led to the introduction of the successful Gewehr 43. A number of them were fitted with telescopic sights and used as sniper rifles.

▲ **STURMGEWEHR 44**

Date 1943
Origin Germany
Weight 11¼lb (5.1kg)
Barrel 16½in (41.8cm)
Caliber 7.92mm × 33 Kurz

One of the most influential firearms of the 20th century, the StG 44 was manufactured using pressed-steel that was easier to produce. Its medium-powered cartridge enabled properly controlled automatic fire.

▼ **MOSIN-NAGANT CARBINE M1944**

Date 1944
Origin Soviet Union
Weight 8½lb (3.9kg)
Barrel 20¼in (51.7cm)
Caliber 7.62mm × 54R

In 1910, the Mosin-Nagant rifle was modified to produce a carbine by shortening its barrel. In 1938, it was revamped, and in 1944, it attained its final form with the addition of a folding bayonet.

PERSONAL WEAPONS

While the rifle was the prime weapon of the infantryman, other troops, such as officers, NCOs, tank crews, and airmen, required something more maneuverable for their personal protection. The solution to their requirement was provided by submachine-guns, pistols, and revolvers—all of which used the light but low-powered pistol round. In practice, revolvers and pistols were rarely used in combat, but the submachine-gun, which was light and had a high rate of automatic fire, proved to be a key weapon of World War II. It was particularly useful in close-combat conditions, such as house-clearing and jungle fighting.

▶ COLT M1911A1

Date 1924
Origin US
Weight 2½lb (1.1kg)
Barrel 5in (12.7cm)
Caliber .45in ACP

Adopted in response to demands for a handgun with guaranteed stopping power, the Browning-designed M1911A1 replaced the M1911 of World War I. It was used by the US armed forces during World War II and after.

Recoil spring housing
Butt houses seven-round removable magazine

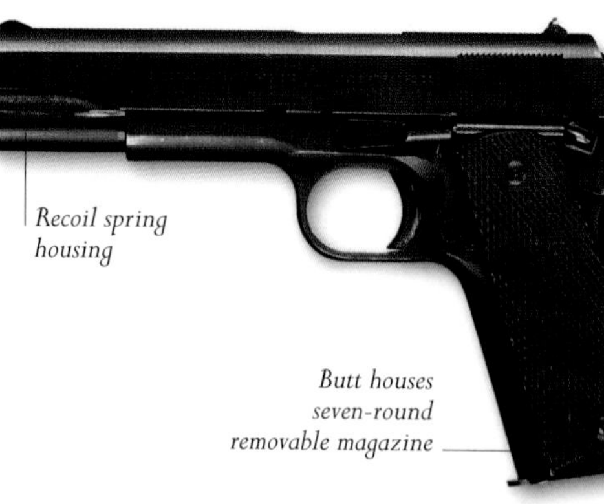

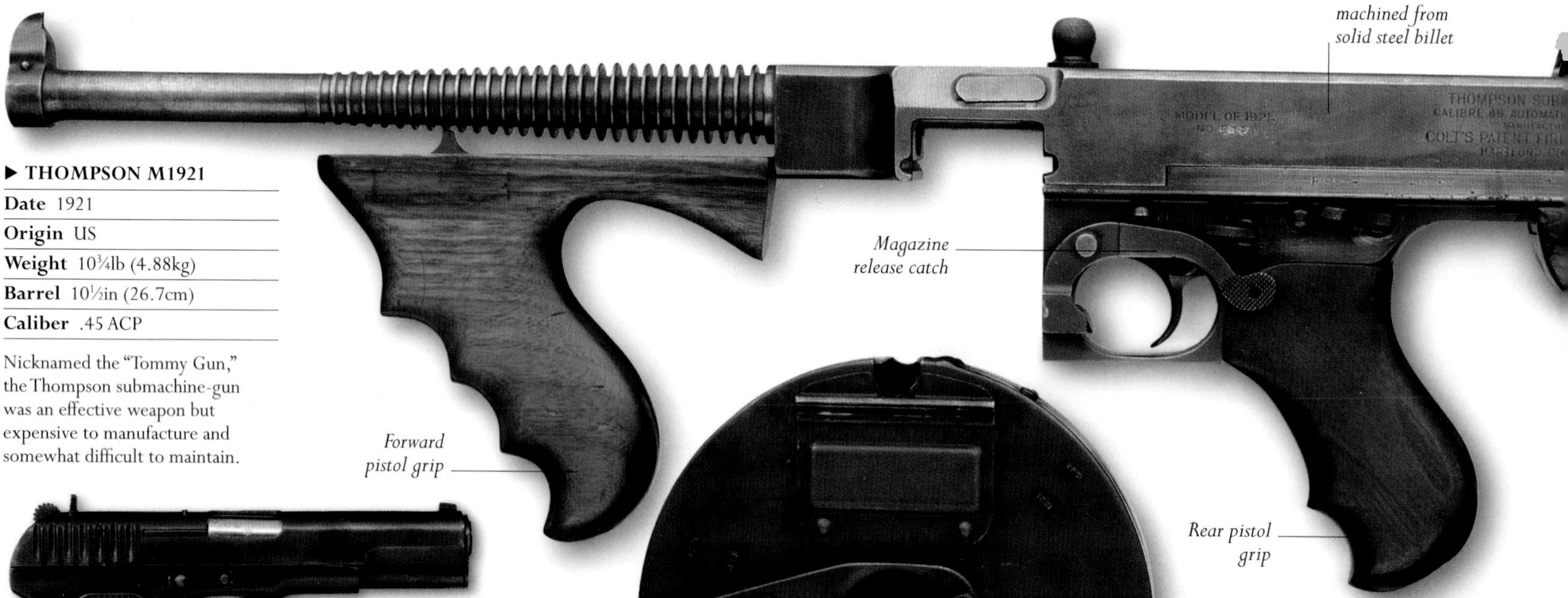
Receiver machined from solid steel billet
Magazine release catch
Forward pistol grip
Rear pistol grip

▶ THOMPSON M1921

Date 1921
Origin US
Weight 10¾lb (4.88kg)
Barrel 10½in (26.7cm)
Caliber .45 ACP

Nicknamed the "Tommy Gun," the Thompson submachine-gun was an effective weapon but expensive to manufacture and somewhat difficult to maintain.

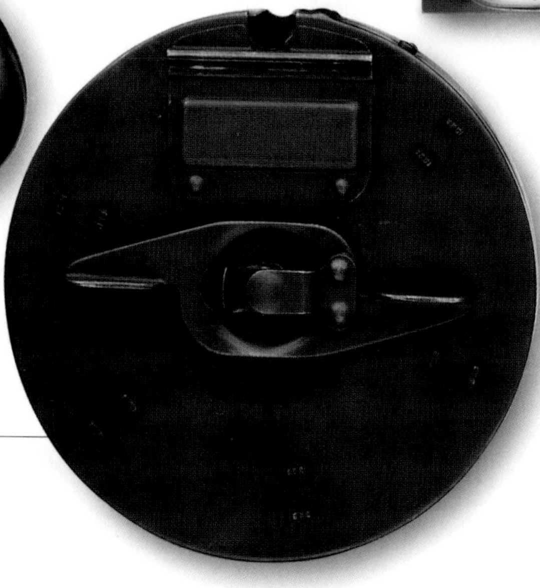
Winder for clockwork mechanism

50-ROUND
DRUM MAGAZINE

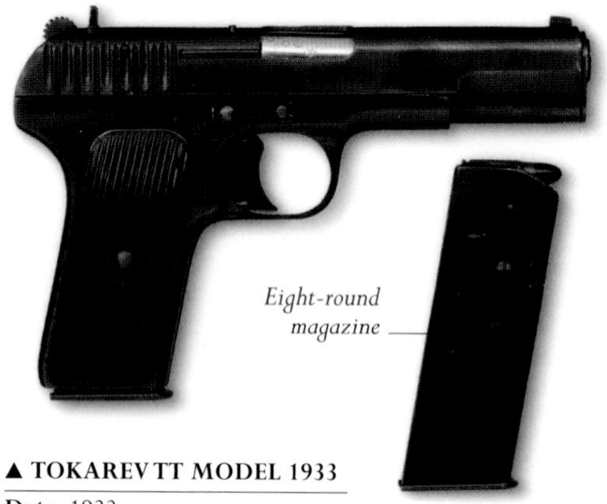
Eight-round magazine

▲ TOKAREV TT MODEL 1933

Date 1933
Origin Soviet Union
Weight 29½oz (830g)
Barrel 4½in (11.6cm)
Caliber 7.62mm

The Tokarev TT33 was the first self-loading pistol to be issued to the Red Army. It lacked a safety catch, but could be put on half-cock.

▼ ASTRA M901

Date 1927
Origin Spain
Weight 4¾lb (2.1kg)
Barrel 6½in (16cm)
Caliber 7.63mm Mauser

This self-loading pistol was part of the Astra 900 series, a copy of the Schnellfeuer ("Rapidfire") version of the Mauser C/96. It had an automatic-fire capability, but was difficult to control in that mode.

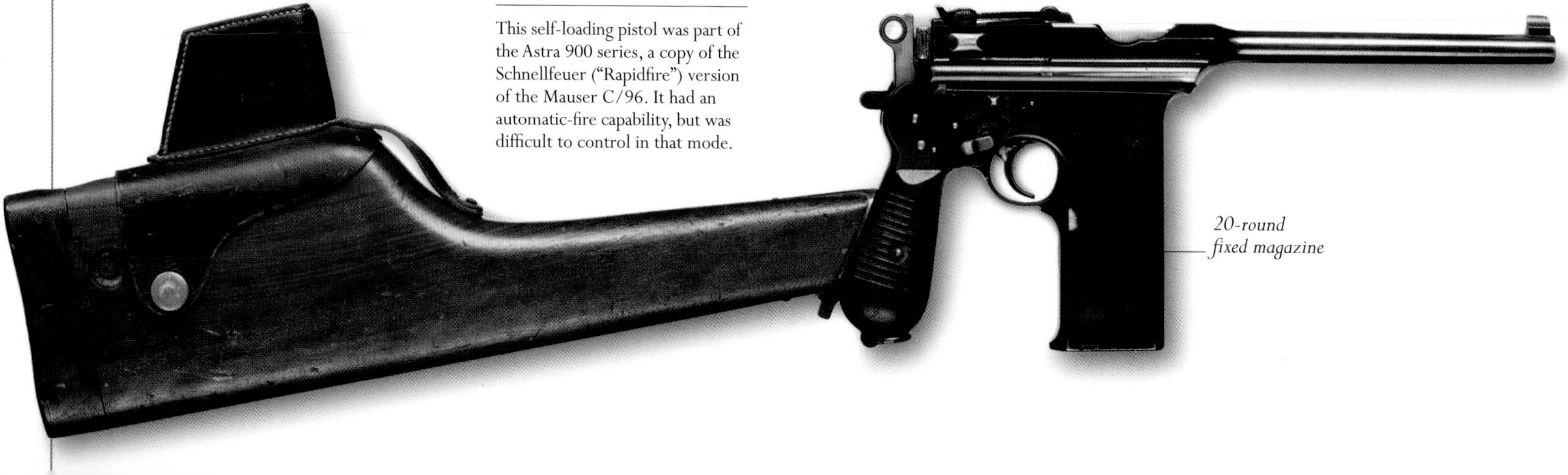
20-round fixed magazine

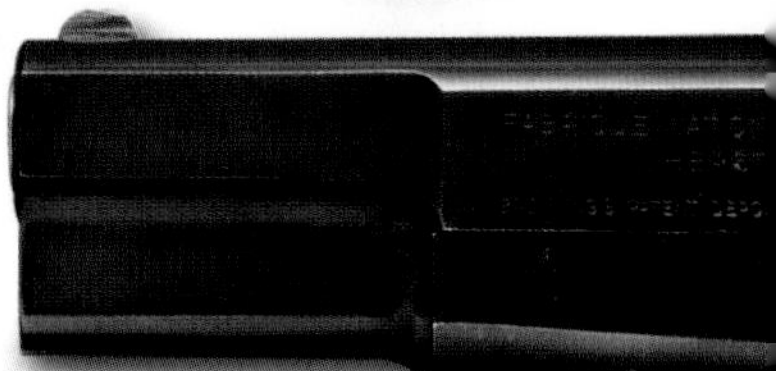

▶ BROWNING GP35

Date 1935
Origin Belgium
Weight 35oz (990g)
Barrel 4¾in (11.8cm)
Caliber 9mm Parabellum

A Browning-designed pistol, the GP35 was used by both Allies and Germans during World War II. It proved to be both rugged and reliable and continues in use today.

▶ PPSH-41

Date 1939
Origin Soviet Union
Weight 7¾lb (3.5kg)
Barrel 10½in (27cm)
Caliber 7.62mm

Over five million examples of this sturdy and dependable weapon had been manufactured for the Red Army by the end of World War II.

Cocking-handle cover acts as safety catch

Rear sight adjustable for windage and elevation

Flash suppressor

Retractable skeleton butt

Carrying sling

30-round detachable box magazine

▲ M3A1

Date 1940s
Origin US
Weight 8lb (3.66kg)
Barrel 8in (20.3cm)
Caliber .45in ACP

The M3 "Grease Gun," and the improved M3A1 version, was cheap to produce and simple to strip, clean, and maintain. It fired the same heavy pistol round used in the Colt M1911A1.

Wooden butt stock, removable in some models

▶ MP40

Date 1940
Origin Germany
Weight 9lb (4.03kg)
Barrel 10in (24.8cm)
Caliber 9mm Parabellum

The MP40 had a revolutionary design that used simple steel pressings, die-cast parts, and plastics. It was an improved version of its predecessor the MP38, and was much cheaper to produce because it had fewer machined parts.

Skeleton butt stock (folded)

32-round magazine

Rear sight

Fixed steel butt stock

▲ STEN MARK II

Date 1941
Origin UK
Weight 8¼lb (3.7kg)
Barrel 7¾in (19.7cm)
Caliber 9mm

Cheap and easy to manufacture, the Sten was a stop-gap weapon that was to prove itself an effective submachine-gun. The gun was fitted with a 32-round magazine.

Butt houses 13-round removable magazine

▲ BERETTA MODELLO 1938/42

Date 1942
Origin Italy
Weight 7¼lb (3.27kg)
Barrel 8½in (21.3cm)
Caliber 9mm

One of the finest weapons of its type to see service during World War II, the M38/42 was well-made, reliable, and, for a submachine-gun, surprisingly accurate.

High-quality wooden stock

Double trigger for automatic and single-shot fire

Extended 40-round magazine

WATER- AND AIR-COOLED MACHINE-GUNS

The air-cooled machine-guns of World War II marked a shift away from the water-cooled models of World War I, although a notable exception was the tried-and-tested Vickers. Another trend was the twin development of the light machine-gun, with examples such as the Bren and the Breda, and the heavy machine-gun, exemplified by the Degtyarev DShK1938 and the Browning M2 HB. The key technological development came from Germany, however, with the introduction of the MG34. The first general-purpose machine-gun, it combined the sustained-fire role of the heavy or medium machine-gun with the portability of the light machine-gun.

▶ **VICKERS MK I**

Date	1912
Origin	UK
Weight	40lb (18.1kg)
Barrel	28½in (72.1cm)
Caliber	.303in

Employed in both world wars, the water-cooled Vickers was an extremely reliable medium machine-gun, and, when firing the Mk 8Z bullet, was capable of a range of up to 2.54 miles (4.1km).

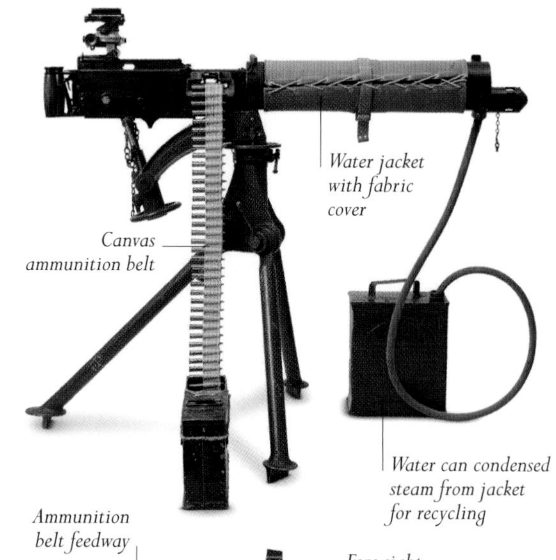

▶ **BROWNING M1919**

Date	1919
Origin	US
Weight	31lb (14.06kg)
Barrel	24in (61cm)
Caliber	.3in

The M1919 was an air-cooled version of the earlier M1917, and it proved to be a first-rate medium machine-gun, supporting US infantrymen throughout World War II.

▼ **BREDA MODELLO 30**

Date	1930
Origin	Italy
Weight	22¾lb (10.32kg)
Barrel	20½in (52cm)
Caliber	6.5 × 54mm

The standard light machine-gun of the Italian army, the Breda Modello 30 utilized a novel 20-round-strip feed system, but proved chronically unreliable and too delicate for battlefield conditions.

▼ **FM MODEL 1924/29**

Date	1930s
Origin	France
Weight	19½lb (8.93kg)
Barrel	20in (50cm)
Caliber	7.5 × 57mm

With a firing mechanism based on that of the Browning BAR, the FM M1924/29 suffered from cartridge problems, which were resolved by the time it became the French army's standard light machine-gun in World War II.

▲ BROWNING M2 HB

Date 1933

Origin US

Weight 84lb (38.1kg)

Barrel 3¾ft (1.14m)

Caliber .5in

The highly effective "fifty cal" M2 HB (heavy barrel) has been used as key armament in aircraft, on armored vehicles, and by ground troops. It remains in service even today.

▼ MG34

Date 1935

Origin Germany

Weight 25¼lb (11.5kg)

Barrel 24¾in (62.7cm)

Caliber 7.92 × 57mm

The MG34 was a revolutionary design—light, yet robust enough to deliver sustained fire at 900 rounds per minute. However, it was difficult and expensive to manufacture and was subsequently replaced by the MG42.

▼ BREN GUN

Date 1938

Origin UK

Weight 22¼lb (10.15kg)

Barrel 25in (63.5cm)

Caliber .303in

Originally developed in Brno, Czechoslovakia, and modified at Enfield in London (hence its name), the dependable Bren was the British Army's light machine-gun during World War II, and remained in service until the 1980s.

▼ DEGTYAREV DSHK1938

Date 1938

Origin Soviet Union

Weight 73½lb (33.3kg)

Barrel 3½ft (1m)

Caliber 12.7 × 108mm

Employed as the Red Army's heavy machine-gun, the DShK1938 was similar to the .5in Browning M2. It enjoyed a similar range of uses and longevity—some are still in service.

◄ MG42

Date 1942

Origin Germany

Weight 25¼lb (11.5kg)

Barrel 21in (53.3cm)

Caliber 7.92 × 57mm

A successor to the MG34, the MG42 had an extraordinarily high rate of fire—over 1,200 rounds per minute—and, when used with a tripod, was capable of sustained long-range fire.

ARTILLERY

The story of artillery in World War II was one of evolution from the firepower of the previous world war. Field pieces gradually became more mobile, ranges increased, and radio communications improved tactical flexibility. One new development, however, was the widespread introduction of rocket artillery, such as the German Nebelwerfer, which were able to cover large areas with a carpet of high explosive. Artillery continued to play a key role in both attack and defence, and this was the reason that the Soviet armed forces described it as the "Red God of War."

◀ 40MM BOFORS ANTI-AIRCRAFT GUN

Date	1934
Origin	Sweden
Weight	2.6 tons (2.4 tonnes)
Length	7¼ft (2.25m)
Caliber	40mm
Range	4½ miles (7.2km)

Considered to be one of the finest anti-aircraft guns of the war, combining accuracy, range, and a decent-sized projectile, the Bofors was exported throughout the world, and used by both Axis and Allied armies.

Automatic ammunition feed

Road wheels

Stabilizing outrigger

Muzzle brake

▼ 50MM LIGHT MORTAR 36

Date	1936
Origin	Germany
Weight	31lb (14kg)
Caliber	50mm
Range	568½ yards (520m)

Despite its designation as a light mortar, with the tube and baseplate combined the M36 was a somewhat heavy mortar, and its complex and costly design led to it being phased out of service from 1941.

Carrying handle

Baseplate

Long 40-caliber barrel

▶ 155MM M1A1 GUN

Date	1941
Origin	US
Weight	15.3 tons (13.9 tonnes)
Length	24ft (7.36m)
Caliber	155mm
Range	14½ miles (23.22km)

The M1A1 was the mainstay of US long-range artillery during World War II, capable of firing a 95lb (43kg) high-explosive shell. Other ammunition included smoke, chemical, illuminating, and even anti-tank rounds.

Muzzle of short howitzer barrel

Steel wheels and pneumatic tires of M8 carriage

▲ 75MM M1A1 PACK HOWITZER

Date	1940
Origin	US
Weight	1,440lb (653kg)
Length	12ft (3.68m)
Caliber	75mm
Range	5½ miles (8.79km)

Developed for use on rough terrain, where it could be broken down into separate pieces to be carried by pack animals, the lightweight M1A1 howitzer was also successfully assigned to US airborne forces.

▼ 122MM M1938 HOWITZER

Date	1939
Origin	Soviet Union
Weight	3.4 tons (3.1 tonnes)
Length	19¼ft (5.9m)
Caliber	122mm
Range	7½ miles (11.8km)

Also known as the M30, this field howitzer was a mainstay of the Red Army's artillery division. Maintained by a crew of eight, it was capable of a rate of fire of six rounds per minute.

▼ 25-POUNDER GUN-HOWITZER (MK II)

Date	1940
Origin	UK
Weight	2 tons (1.8 tonnes)
Length	15ft (4.6m)
Caliber	88mm
Range	7¾ miles (12.25km)

An effective compromise between the gun and the howitzer, the 25-pounder came into its own in the North African Campaign, where it was pressed into service as an ad hoc anti-tank gun.

◀ 150MM NEBELWERFER 41

Date	1941
Origin	Germany
Weight	1,195lb (542kg)
Caliber	150mm
Range	4¼ miles (6.9km)

Initially developed to fire poisonous gas and smoke (for battlefield concealment), the six-barreled Nebelwerfer could also fire high-explosive rounds to devastating effect against target areas.

▲ 4.2IN MORTAR

Date	1942
Origin	UK
Weight	805lb (365kg)
Caliber	4.2in
Range	2½ miles (3.75km)

The 4.2in mortar was the British Army's heavy mortar, and was manned at divisional level by crews from the Royal Artillery. It was capable of firing up to 20 rounds of 20lb (9.1kg) high-explosive ammunition in a minute.

LANDING BEHIND ENEMY LINES
Allied forces land by parachute and glider near Arnhem in the German-occupied Netherlands during Operation Market Garden. The attempt to seize and hold the bridge over the Rhine at Arnhem was ambitious and, ultimately, a costly failure.

AIRBORNE ASSAULT

OPERATION MARKET GARDEN

Launched in September 1944, Operation Market Garden was the largest airborne assault to date, aimed at seizing tactical objectives in the Netherlands. It might have shortened the war; but its successes and eventual failure showed both the strengths and weaknesses of airborne forces.

In August 1944, British and American airborne troops were placed under unified command as the First Allied Airborne Army. General Bernard Montgomery of the British Army planned to use this force to open a path through the German-occupied Netherlands and into northern Germany. Airborne troops, both parachute and glider infantry, were to seize and hold a series of bridges and canals to allow the British 30th Corps, advancing from the Allied front line, to move toward the German border.

The scale of the airborne operation was unprecedented. Taking off from England on September 17, the first wave involved over 20,000 troops packed into more than 1,500 transport aircraft and 500 gliders. Allied air supremacy allowed this aerial armada to fly to its target areas in daylight, dropping parachutists and their equipment with varied accuracy. The gliders, towed by "tug" aircraft, also mostly landed safely. But once on the ground, the airborne forces were in a risky position. Although some heavy equipment was landed with them, they were unsupported infantry deep inside hostile territory. Once the enemy recovered from the surprise of the initial assault, the lightly armed troops would have to resist counterattacks until the arrival of the British corps' tanks and artillery.

US 101st Airborne Division landed near Eindhoven, closest to the Allied front line. They quickly took four of the five bridges assigned to them and were joined by the advancing British armored forces on September 18. US 82nd Airborne were assigned responsibility for seizing crossings of the Maas and Waal Rivers. Engaged in heavy fighting, they succeeded in repelling German counterattacks but failed to take the vital bridge at Nijmegen; meanwhile a second round of airdrops and glider landings that should have brought reinforcements was delayed by poor weather. The British corps successfully made contact with 82nd Airborne on September 19, but the bridge was not taken until the next day, after a high-casualty river crossing by troops in rowing boats.

BEST-LAID PLANS

These delays placed Britain's First Airborne Division, attempting to take the final bridge over the Rhine at Arnhem, in a desperate situation. The paratroops had landed too far from their target; with radio and navigation problems, they lost coherence in the advance toward Arnhem, and only one battalion reached the bridge. German counter-attacks, meanwhile, were ferocious. The presence of two SS panzer divisions in the area had been reported by intelligence sources before the operation, but the information had been ignored: now, infantry divisions with only light artillery support found themselves fighting for their lives against German tanks.

The arrival of the Polish Parachute Brigade to reinforce the British was delayed until September 21, and even then they were dropped in the wrong place. After heroic resistance, the battalion at the bridge surrendered, on the same day. On September 25, efforts turned to evacuating surviving soldiers across the Rhine. In total 2,398 were saved, but 1,485 had been killed and 6,414 taken prisoner. The operation had failed.

AIRBORNE FORCES UNIFORM AND KIT

World War II witnessed an expansion in the use of parachute-equipped troops. The strength of airborne formations was their strategic mobility, but once the paratrooper landed he became a heavily burdened infantryman, lacking both tactical mobility and firepower. Miniaturized motorcycles and simple folding bicycles were used to improve his capability but had limited success. Light mortars and shoulder-launched anti-tank weapons, used by conventional infantry, provided the paratrooper with portable "artillery."

◀ M2 PARATROOPER HELMET

Date	1942
Origin	US
Material	Steel

The airborne helmet had a D-ring chinstrap holder and a spray-paint camouflage, applied by its owner. The "Gingerbread Man" was the emblem of the 509th Airborne Battalion.

▶ M1942 JUMP JACKET

Date	1942
Origin	US
Material	Cotton poplin

The olive green jacket was spray-painted at unit level. The uniform was sprayed while on the body, the soldier covering his head with a cardboard box. This left the collar untouched by paint.

▼ JUMP BOOTS

Date	1942
Origin	US
Material	Leather, rubber, canvas

The coveted status symbol of the US airborne forces, jump boots were designed for parachuting safety, with reinforced toecaps, internal ankle supports, and a beveled heel to prevent the heel from snagging on the uneven aircraft floor.

▼ M1A1 CARBINE

Date	1942
Origin	US
Weight	5¼lb (2.36kg)
Barrel	18in (45.7cm)
Caliber	.3in

The M1 Carbine had already proved to be popular with soldiers who needed a lightweight weapon. For airborne forces, this special M1A1 variant was produced, complete with a folding stock for use during parachute drops.

◀ M36 MUSETTE BAG

Date 1936

Origin US

Material Canvas

This versatile mini-haversack held ammunition, rations, and personal effects. The rope was included in case the soldier needed to free himself from a tree or building on landing.

Attachment straps

Rope 33ft (10m) in length

Standard issue raincoat folded under flap

◀ TYPE T5 PARACHUTE

Date c.1940

Origin US

Material Silk (later rayon)

The T5 was the standard parachute used by the US Army throughout World War II. Static lines attached to the plane automatically deployed the parachute as the paratrooper jumped from the aircraft.

Pull-out panel covering main parachute

Leg straps of cotton webbing

▶ MK3 FIGHTING KNIFE

Date 1943

Origin US

Weight 8½oz (240g)

Length 11½in (29.5cm)

Based partly on the British Fairburn-Sykes commando knife, the Mk3 was intended for hand-to-hand combat. Paratroopers strapped the knife on to their lower leg for ease of access.

Leather washers form grip

Recurved quillons

Diamond-section blade

▼ FG42 AUTOMATIC RIFLE

Date 1943

Origin Germany

Weight 10lb (4.53kg)

Barrel 19¾in (50.2cm)

Caliber 7.9mm

The FG42 was a fully automatic weapon designed to provide long-range firepower to paratroopers on the ground. It pioneered a "straight-line" butt-to-muzzle layout and employed a gas-operated firing mechanism.

Folding sight

Metal butt stock

Bipod legs

Slanting pistol grip

▶ AIRBORNE GRAVITY KNIFE

Date 1937

Origin Germany

Weight 12½oz (350g)

Length 10in (25.3cm)

Issued to German paratroopers, this knife could be opened with one hand. When the operating lever was opened, the blade fell forward due to gravity. It was intended primarily to help the soldier free himself from a tangled parachute harness.

Spike

▶ BSA FOLDING BICYCLE

Date 1943

Origin UK

Weight (Frame) 4½lb (2kg)

The armed forces had used folding bicycles extensively during World War I, but this lightweight model was designed especially for commandos and airborne forces, to provide them some much-needed mobility.

RESISTANCE WEAPONS AND EQUIPMENT

Formed in July 1940, the British Special Operations Executive (SOE) was given the task of conducting irregular warfare throughout German-occupied Europe, providing support to local resistance movements. SOE placed a premium on lightweight, covert communications equipment, so that when its agents were operating behind enemy lines they could maintain contact with Britain. There was also a requirement for stealth weapons that could silently eliminate sentries or assassinate selected individuals. SOE was subsequently joined in its espionage operations by the American Office for Strategic Services (OSS), which placed a similar emphasis on specialized weapons.

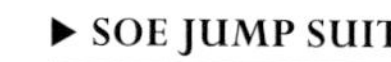

▶ SOE JUMP SUIT

Date 1941

Origin UK

Material Weatherproofed cotton

Designed for use by covert-action personnel parachuting into occupied territory, the camouflage suit protected the clothing underneath from damage. It also had numerous pockets to hold vital equipment.

Inner pockets to hold kit securely

Full-length zipper to allow quick removal of jump suit

RADIO ANTENNA

Headset

Microphone

Cable

◀ SOE S-PHONE TRANSCEIVER

Date c.1942

Origin UK

Type Ultra-high frequency duplex radio telephone

A miniaturized transmitter and receiver, the S-Phone weighed just 15lb (7kg), and enabled an agent to speak to the pilot of an aircraft 30 miles (48km) away at a height of up to 10,000ft (3,050m).

DUPLEX TRANSCEIVER

Radio concealed in leather suitcase

▶ SOE TYPE 3 (MK II) SUITCASE RADIO

Date c.1942

Origin UK

Type Portable transmitter/receiver station

Designed for agents working in enemy territory, the radio could transmit and receive messages to ranges of up to 500 miles (800km). It contained a modular receiver, transmitter, power supply unit, and miniature Morse key.

▲ V44 SURVIVAL KNIFE

Date 1934
Origin US
Weight 2½lb (1.1kg)
Length 13½in (34.5cm)

Originally ordered by the US Army Air Corps as a survival aid for downed aircrew, this fearsome-looking weapon became popular with US troops fighting in the Pacific Theater of Operations—the area of operations of US forces during the Pacific War.

▲ "MIDDLE EAST" PATTERN KNUCKLE-DUSTER KNIFE

Date c.1943
Origin UK
Weight 15¾oz (450g)
Length 11¾in (30cm)

Cast from a single piece of brass, this knife had four protruding studs on the hilt for punching. The steel blade had a single cutting edge that swept upward to a point, making this knife suitable for stabbing upward.

▲ "BIG JOE" CROSSBOW AND BOLT

Date c.1943
Origin US
Weight 8¾lb (4kg)
Length 26in (66cm)

This OSS crossbow was powered by rubber loops that were tensioned by a windlass handle before firing. The front frame and shoulder stock could be folded for ease of transport.

▲ WELROD SILENCED PISTOL

Date c.1943
Origin UK
Weight 2½lb (1.2kg)
Barrel 12in (30.5cm)
Caliber 9mm

Developed at SOE's Station IX, the Welrod was an exceptionally quiet assassination weapon, especially when firing subsonic ammunition. The sights were marked with fluorescent paint for low-light conditions.

◄ FP-45 LIBERATOR PISTOL

Date 1942
Origin US
Weight 15¾oz (450g)
Barrel 4in (10cm)
Caliber .45in

Designed by OSS as a simple and very cheap gun, the Liberator was intended to be paradropped to resistance groups. It had ten rounds of ammunition and was delivered with illustrated strip instructions for use.

◄ STEN MK6

Date 1944
Origin UK
Weight 10lb (4.5kg)
Barrel 7¾in (19.7cm)
Caliber 9mm

The silenced version of the Mk5, the Mk6 featured improvements such as a wooden butt stock and pistol grip. It was produced on request from SOE for guerrilla operations in Europe.

HIROSHIMA IN RUINS
The city was targeted partly because there were no hills to deflect the force of the explosion. Only earthquake-proof structures of reinforced concrete were left standing; the rest were destroyed in the blast or went up in flames.

NUCLEAR WARFARE

THE BOMBING OF HIROSHIMA

When US aircraft dropped atom bombs on the Japanese cities of Hiroshima and Nagasaki in August 1945 in a bid to end World War II, it opened a new perilous chapter in the history of warfare. For the first time, weapons had been created that were so destructive that their use had to be avoided at all costs.

The first test of a nuclear device took place at Alamogordo in the New Mexican desert on July 16, 1945. The explosion was equivalent to nearly 20,000 tons of TNT and generated temperatures three times hotter than the core of the Sun. The detonation was the culmination of the top-secret Manhattan Project, which had been initiated in December 1941 and headed by General Leslie Groves.

The objective of the project was to produce an atom bomb and deliver it on an enemy target, and to this end Groves had not only directed teams of scientists and engineers, but also set up a special flying group to drop the bomb. Group 509 of the US Army Air Force, commanded by Colonel Paul Tibbets, was equipped with the Boeing B-29 Superfortress, America's latest bomber aircraft, which had the range to strike Japanese cities from US-held Pacific island bases.

In late July and early August, components for a uranium-based atomic bomb, codenamed "Little Boy," and several plutonium-based bombs, codenamed "Fat Man," were delivered to the island of Tinian in the Marianas, where Colonel Tibbets' B-29s were based. The intention was to drop the bombs on selected Japanese cities as soon as the components had been assembled and when weather conditions permitted.

On July 26, after the Potsdam conference attended by America, Britain, and the Soviet Union, the US and its allies called on Japan to surrender or face "prompt and utter destruction." When this call was rejected by Japan two days later, preparations for the world's first nuclear strike went ahead.

Hiroshima had been chosen as the first target because it was arguably of military significance, with a barracks and port, and was also largely undamaged, unlike most Japanese cities already devastated by conventional bombing. A large and flat urban area with a population of 300,000, Hiroshima would demonstrate the maximum effect of the bomb.

Colonel Tibbets chose to lead the operation in person. He piloted the B-29 designated to carry the "Little Boy" bomb and had his mother's maiden name, *Enola Gay*, written on the aircraft's side.

The *Enola Gay* was escorted by two other B-29s and arrived over Hiroshima at 8:15am on August 6 after an uneventful flight from Tinian. The aircraft released the bomb from an altitude of 30,000 feet, and it detonated in the air a minute later over the center of the city.

TOTAL DESTRUCTION

The destruction surpassed all expectations: almost every building was destroyed over an area of 7.5 miles (12 square km) and estimates of the death toll range from 80,000 to 140,000. Of this number, those not killed immediately by the effect of the heat flash and blast died of radiation sickness over the following months.

Three days later the "Fat Man" plutonium bomb was dropped on another city, Nagasaki. It killed an estimated 35,000 to 80,000 people —a lower figure because hills had restricted the bomb's effectiveness. Japan surrendered on August 15, heralding the end of World War II. No nuclear device has been used in warfare since.

1945–PRESENT

THE NUCLEAR AGE

INTRODUCTION

After World War II, developments in military technology were driven by the Cold War confrontation between the two "superpowers"—the United States and the Soviet Union. At the same time, guerrilla warfare and terrorism have proved enduringly resistant to the world's most advanced military arsenals.

From the late 1940s, a nuclear arms race between the US-led NATO alliance and the Soviet Union created weaponry of awesome destructive power. With long-range bombers replaced by missiles as nuclear delivery systems, by the 1960s the world had entered the era of MAD—Mutually Assured Destruction. Peace between the superpowers was maintained by the certainty of unbearable losses in the event of a nuclear war. At the same time, each side sought to surpass the other in every area of conventional military technology, from the performance of aircraft and submarines, to guidance systems and military satellites. Although World War III never materialized, much of the non-nuclear technology was tried out in the 1960s and 1970s, in wars between Israel and its Arab neighbors, and by the US in Vietnam. However, it was the 1991 Gulf War—the first major post-Cold War conflict—that revealed the true scale of technological progress, showcasing such wonders as smart bombs, stealth aircraft, and cruise missiles.

The post-WWII era has also seen the rise of guerrilla warfare and terrorism. Although they generally lack access to advanced weaponry, guerrillas have benefited from modern infantry weaponry and explosives, while the arms industry has fueled low-level conflicts across the globe with a ready supply of automatic weapons and ammunition. Despite the fact that technological progress made the need for a mass citizen army outdated by the end of the 20th century, when major powers fought guerrilla forces, they found there was no alternative to putting troops on the ground and sustaining the losses this entailed.

KEY DATES

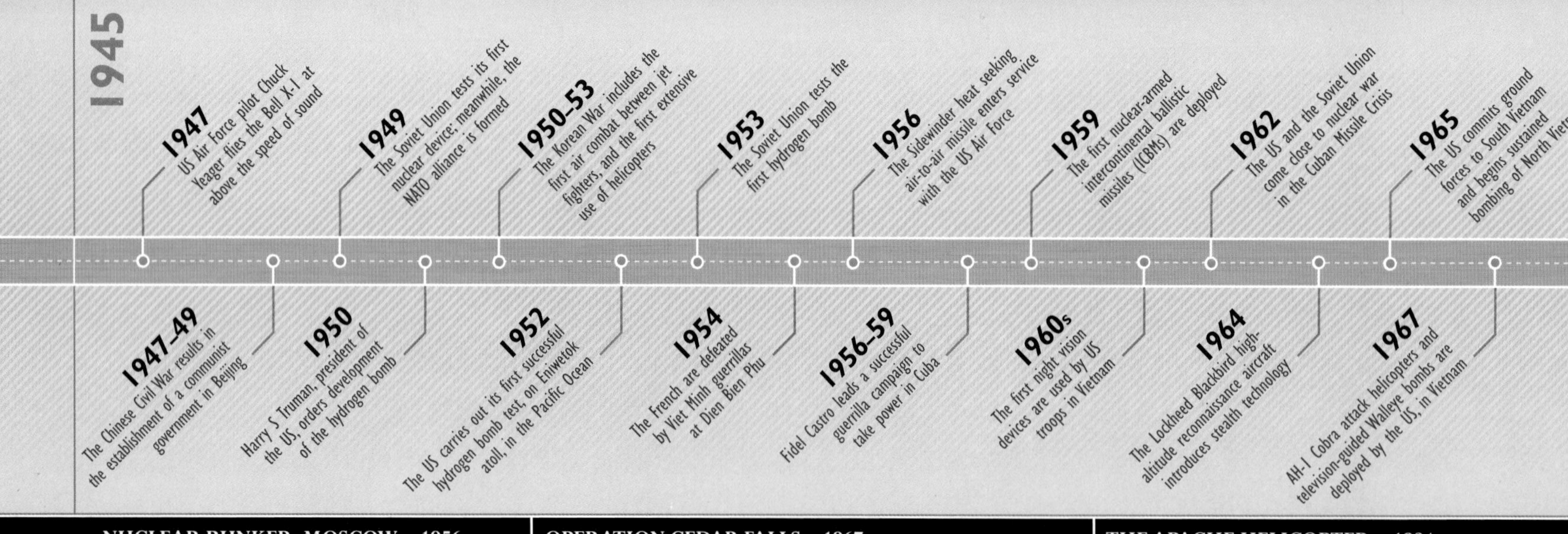

NUCLEAR BUNKER, MOSCOW—1956

OPERATION CEDAR FALLS—1967

THE APACHE HELICOPTER—1984

THE TWIN TOWERS—2001

BAGHDAD—2003

COMBAT IN AFGHANISTAN—2010

KEY **STRUCTURE**

NUCLEAR SHELTER

Away from the cataclysmic center of a nuclear explosion, people sheltering in deep underground bunkers would have a chance of survival. But the ensuing radioactive fallout would force survivors to remain underground for extended periods, requiring supplies of uncontaminated food, water, and recyclable air.

▲ This nuclear bunker was built in Moscow in 1956, anticipating the fear of an all-out nuclear conflict.

KEY **EVENTS**

1945–1955

■ **August 6, 1945** A US B-29 aircraft drops an atomic bomb on Hiroshima, marking a new era of nuclear warfare.

■ **May 22, 1947** President Harry S. Truman commits the US to providing military assistance to any nation threatened by Communist aggression. This becomes known as the Truman Doctrine.

■ **April 4, 1949** The North Atlantic Treaty Organization (NATO) is formed, to provide a military bulwark against the Soviet Union.

■ **November 1, 1952** The US carries out the first successful test of a hydrogen bomb, on the Eniwetok atoll in the Pacific. The Soviet Union follows suit in 1953.

■ **May 14, 1955** The Warsaw Pact is agreed, a mutual defense treaty between the Soviet Union and the Communist states of eastern Europe.

KEY DEVELOPMENT

THE COLD WAR ERA

The end of World War II witnessed the emergence of the Soviet Union and the US as global superpowers, and their ideological hostility was to define international politics for the remainder of the 20th century.

The enmity between these two superpowers was made especially dangerous by the advent of nuclear weapons. The US, the first of the two nations to develop an atomic bomb, used its nuclear supremacy to devastating effect against the Japanese cities of Hiroshima (see pp. 378–79) and Nagasaki in 1945; it lost its lead in 1949, however, when the Soviet Union developed its own atomic bomb. This marked the beginning of an arms race, as the two superpowers developed ever-more powerful weapons and more complex and accurate delivery systems. Scientists invented the hydrogen bomb in the mid-1950s: the blast from the first hydrogen explosion was measured at 10.4 megatons, 450 times more powerful than the bomb dropped on Nagasaki.

Nuclear weapons were initially carried in bomber aircraft, but their vulnerability to air-defense systems soon became apparent. The solution was to supplement the use of bombers with ballistic missiles, which were difficult to intercept. They could be fired from concealed concrete silos and had the range to hit population

▸ A US NUCLEAR TEST, NEVADA
US troops watch the mushroom cloud of an atomic explosion while on a field exercise in Nevada, in November 1951. They are just 6 miles (9.5km) from the explosion.

"Mankind must put an **end to war** or war will put an end to **mankind**"

US PRESIDENT JOHN F. KENNEDY, SEPTEMBER 25, 1961

centers deep within the territory of any potential enemy. Further refinements included the use of multiple warheads on a single missile, and submarines that were able to fire nuclear weapons while hidden underwater.

The US, exploiting its technical superiority over the Soviet Union, made repeated attempts to construct missile-launched anti-ballistic-missile systems, of which the space-based "Star Wars" defense was the most ambitious. None, however, were successful. Meanwhile, some soldiers were equipped with NBC (Nuclear, Biological, Chemical) suits to help those who survived an initial blast to operate in a radiation-contaminated atmosphere. In an attempt to ensure the continuity of government in the event of nuclear onslaught, extensive underground bunkers were constructed to shelter officials at the onset of war.

NUCLEAR DEADLOCK

In terms of civilian casualties, however, it was clear that hundreds of millions of people on both sides would be killed if a full nuclear exchange took place, and that life for those who did survive might well be unendurable. Thus, US military policy during the 1960s was driven by the doctrine of Mutually Assured Destruction (MAD), the acronym reflecting the conviction that a nuclear war was effectively unwinnable.

This was the Cold War, when the antagonism between West and East was, paradoxically, moderated by the power of nuclear weapons, each side fearing the consequences of an all-out "hot war" (although during the Cuban missile crisis of 1962, East-West tensions almost let to nuclear war, after US spy aircraft discovered Soviet missile bases in Cuba.) This fear did not, however, prevent the leaders of the US and the Soviet Union from aggressively pursuing their interests elsewhere. In what became termed "limited warfare," the armies of the Communist East and capitalist West engaged in military operations to establish dominance over each other. They refrained from direct confrontation, and instead supported other states or groups in secondary conflicts.

In many cases, local disputes became proxy wars between the superpowers. In Vietnam (see pp. 398–99), the people's attempt to overthrow colonial rule was transformed into full-scale war by the provision of Soviet (and Chinese) military aid to the Vietnamese Communists, countered by US aid to France, and finally full US military involvement. In the Middle East, the US aligned itself with Israel, while the Soviet Union supported Israel's Arab opponents. In conflicts in Africa, and Central and South America, military assistance given to one side was countered by similar support from the rival superpower. The Cold War may not have resulted in nuclear war, but the tactic of avoiding direct conflict between the superpowers had the side-effect of exporting warfare all around the globe.

▲ **AN UNDERWATER LAUNCH**
A Trident ballistic missile is fired from a submarine far out in the ocean. The Trident missile has a range of 4,400 miles (7,100km) and can carry eight independently targeted nuclear warheads.

▼ **AN NBC SUIT**
The Nuclear, Biological, Chemical (NBC) suit provided basic protection against radiological and other hazards. It could be worn for several days before needing to be replaced.

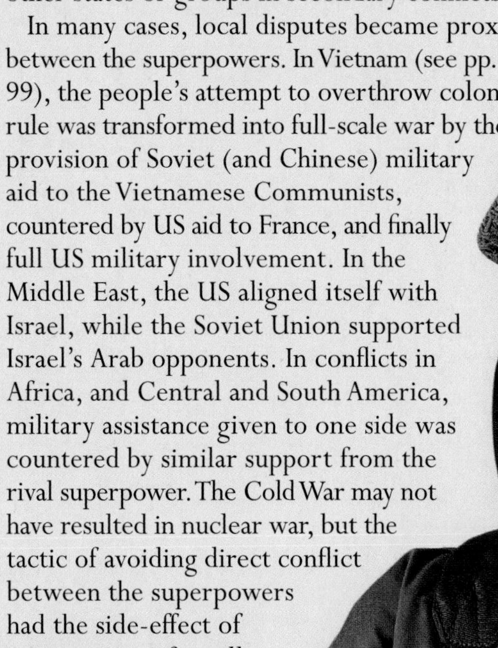

NUCLEAR BOMBERS AND INTERCEPTORS

For twenty years after the attacks on Hiroshima (see pp. 378–79) and Nagasaki in 1945, the long-range strategic bomber—which had to be fast and capable of carrying a heavy payload—remained a vital element in every nuclear power's arsenal. A new type of fighter aircraft was produced to counter this threat—the exceptionally fast "interceptor," whose role was to shoot down bombers before they could do any significant damage. By the mid-1960s, however, the development of Intercontinental Ballistic Missiles (ICBMs), such as the submarine-launched Polaris missile, rendered the strategic bomber obsolete; the role of the interceptor was reduced accordingly.

Tail armed with two 20mm cannon

Twin-jet mounting

Landing gear

▲ BOEING B-47 STRATOJET

Date 1950 **Origin** US
Wingspan 116¼ft (35.4m)
Length 106¾ft (32.6m)
Top speed 606mph (980kph)
Engine Six 7,185lb (3,266kg) General Electric J47-GE-25 turbojets

One of the first jet bombers to serve with the US Strategic Air Command, the B47 featured a swept-back wing and a substantial internal bomb load.

▼ TUPOLEV TU-95 "BEAR"

Date 1955 **Origin** Soviet Union
Wingspan 164½ft (50.1m)
Length 151½ft (46.2m)
Top speed 562mph (905kph)
Engine Four 15,000 Kuznetsov NK-12M turboprops

Although equipped with turboprop engines, the Tu-95 demonstrated high performance characteristics that included an exceptional range (with bomb load) of 9,300 miles (15,000km) without refueling.

Swept-back wings (35° angle)

Turboprop engine

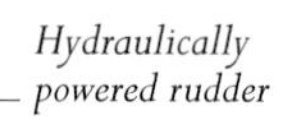

▼ BOEING B-52 STRATOFORTRESS

Date 1955 **Origin** US
Wingspan 185ft (56.4m)
Length 161ft (50.2m)
Top speed 650mph (1,046kph)
Engine Eight 13,750lb (6,237kg) Pratt & Whitney J57-43WB turbojets

The long-serving B-52 was designed to drop nuclear bombs on the Soviet Union (which it never did), but subsequently evolved into a launch platform for cruise missiles and a conventional bomber of awesome power.

Hydraulically powered rudder

Aircraft carried four nuclear free-fall or 20 AGM-69 SRAM missiles, or up to 60,000lb (27,200kg) of conventional bombs

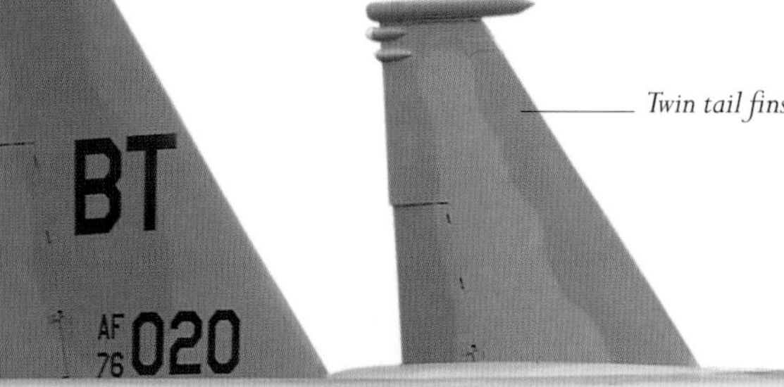

▼ AVRO 698 VULCAN B2

Date 1956 **Origin** UK
Wingspan 111¼ft (33.9m)
Length 100ft (30.5m)
Top speed 640mph (1,029kph)
Engine Four 22,000lb (9,992kg) Bristol Siddeley Olympus turbojets

During the late 1950s, the British nuclear deterrent was spearheaded Vulcan B2. It had a distinctive delta wing that helped ensure good load-carrying capabilities and a high subsonic speed.

◀ ENGLISH ELECTRIC LIGHTNING F.1A

Date 1960 **Origin** UK
Wingspan 34¼ft (10.6m)
Length 50ft (15.2m)
Top speed 1,386mph (2,230kph) or Mach 2.1
Engine Two 16,000lb (71.17kN) Rolls Royce Avon 301R turbojets

The Lightning was the first British aircraft to exceed Mach 2 (twice the speed of sound) in level flight. This, combined with its excellent rate of climb, made it Britain's main air-defense fighter.

▼ DASSAULT MIRAGE III C

Date 1961 **Origin** France
Wingspan 27ft (8.2m)
Length 50¾ft (15.5m)
Top speed 1,460mph (2,350kph)
Engine 13,225lb (6,000kg) SNECMA Atar 9B afterburning turbojet

The delta-winged Mirage III series has been exported to 21 countries, including Israel, which used the aircraft with great success during the Six-Day War of 1967.

▲ CONVAIR B-58 HUSTLER

Date 1961 **Origin** US
Wingspan 56¾ft (17.3m)
Length 96¾ft (29.5m)
Top speed 1,319mph (2,122kph) or Mach 2
Engine Four 15,020lb (6,815kg) General Electric J79-GE-5A/B/C afterburning turbojets

This highly ambitious supersonic nuclear bomber utilized many of the latest advances in aviation technology. Although difficult to fly, it was capable of a high maximum speed.

▼ MCDONNELL DOUGLAS F-15C EAGLE

Date 1976 **Origin** US
Wingspan 42¾ft (13m)
Length 63¾ft (19.4m)
Top speed 1,650mph (2,660kph)
Engine Two 17,450lb (77.62kN) Pratt & Whitney F100-100 augmented turbofans

Built as a response to the MiG-25, the F-15C Eagle emerged as one of the world's foremost fighter and strike aircraft, utilizing advanced avionics with immense power and performance.

Bubble cockpit canopy

Hughes APG-63 radar scanner in nose

Aircraft armed with a single 20mm cannon, four AIM-7F/M Sparrow, and four AIM 9L/M Sidewinder air-to-air missiles

▲ MIKOYAN-GUREVICH MIG-25 "FOXBAT"

Date 1970 **Origin** Soviet Union
Wingspan 46ft (14m)
Length 64¾ft (19.8m)
Top Speed 1,868mph (3,000kph) or Mach 3.2
Engine Two 24,651lb (11,200kg) Tumansky R-15B-300 turbojets

Built for speed and high altitudes, the MiG-25 caused consternation in the West. Capable of exceeding Mach 3 (three times the speed of sound), it remains the world's fastest combat aircraft.

NUCLEAR ATTACK SUBMARINE

USS NAUTILUS

When the *Nautilus* entered service in 1954, it was the world's first nuclear-powered submarine. Its advent in the early part of the Cold War (see pp.384–85) marked a revolutionary step in naval warfare.

Three reactors enabled the *Nautilus* to travel for long periods without having to surface or refuel, unlike conventional submarines. In 1955, the ship set a new record for a submerged voyage, covering 1,381 miles (2,222km) in 90 hours. Three years later it became the first submarine to travel under the ice cap to the North Pole.

On the *Nautilus*'s upper deck was the attack center—the heart of the ship's role as a warship. Forward of that were captain's and officers' quarters. The lower deck housed the control room, from where the ship was steered when underwater, and the crew's mess and galley. The engines and reactors were near the stern.

The *Nautilus* was not especially fast underwater and carried only conventional torpedoes. Apart from the reactors, its major innovations were dispensing with a deck gun, providing a bunk for each crew member, and (on its 1958 sub-Arctic trip) an inertial navigation system. By 1959, the *Nautilus* was being superseded by submarines that, through improved hull design and the use of new materials, could travel faster and reach greater depths than before. Nuclear submarines would soon dominate naval warfare, either as torpedo-carrying attack submarines or as nuclear missile carriers. Retired in 1980, the *Nautilus* is now a museum.

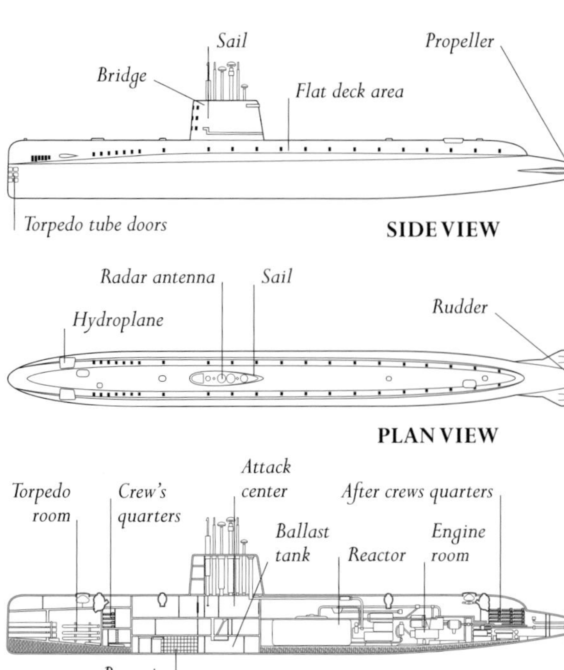

USS *NAUTILUS*
Displacing 3,533 tons (4,092 tons submerged), the *Nautilus* was 323½ft (98.6m) long and carried a crew of 116. It had a top speed of 23 knots and could dive to a maximum depth of 700ft (213m).

OPERATING SYSTEMS

▲ CONTROL ROOM
Two planesmen operated the hydroplanes to adjust the ship's angle and depth. To their right, the helmsman operated the rudder.

▲ ALARMS
Alerts were sounded before the craft began to dive or if there was danger of a collision.

▲ WATER LEVELS
Dials indicated the amount of water contained in the ship's ballast tanks.

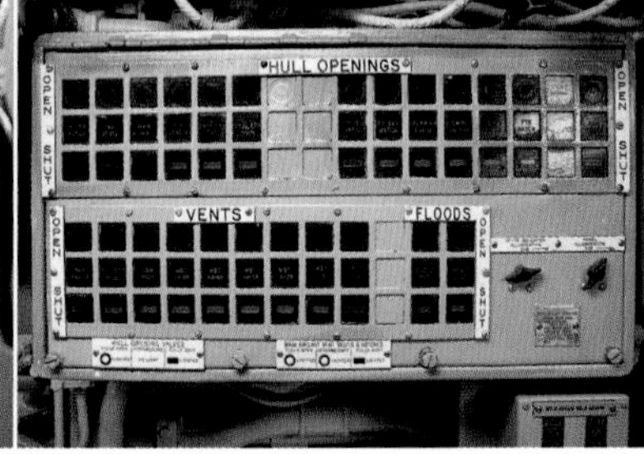

▲ DISPLAY PANEL
Prior to diving, this panel was checked to determine the status of the craft's numerous hatches and vents.

▲ ELECTRONIC COUNTERMEASURES
These devices detected signals from other vessels and helped foil attempts to track the ship from its own transmissions.

▲ SONAR ROOM
Sonar equipment and displays were used to locate ships and other submarines, follow target objects, and avoid underwater collisions.

▶ SUBMARINE SAIL
When travelling on the surface, the *Nautilus* was steered from the bridge, located at the top of the submarine's "sail" (conning tower).

LIFE ON BOARD

▲ **WARDROOM**
The captain and officers dined and relaxed in the wardroom. For the first time on a submarine there was an attempt at decoration, with pipes and ducts covered by panels.

▲ **GALLEY**
The crew's meals were made in a stainless-steel galley. There were also ice cream and drink machines.

▲ **CREW'S QUARTERS**
Each crew member had his own bed—an improvement on previous submarines, which used a shift system for bunks.

BATTLE STATIONS

► **TORPEDO**
The only armaments on the *Nautilus* were torpedoes. Some were kept in the tubes, ready for firing. Others were stored on racks in the torpedo bay.

▲ **TORPEDO BAY**
In the bow were 24 Mk 14 torpedoes, and the launching mechanisms. The door of one of the six torpedo tubes can be seen on the left.

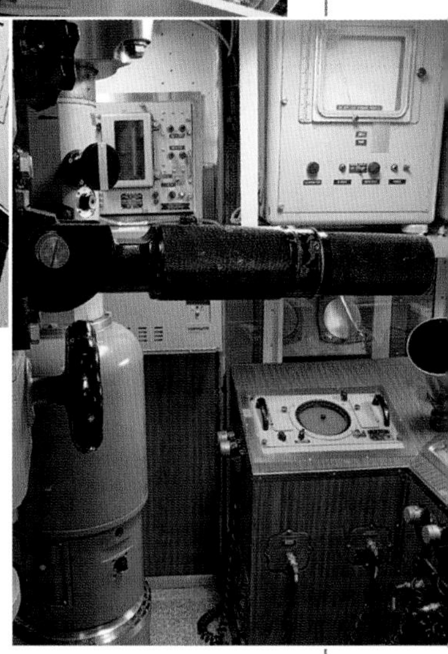

► **ATTACK CENTER**
Combat instructions were given from this area, which housed two periscopes, torpedo-firing controls, and navigational equipment.

KEY DEVELOPMENT

GUERRILLAS AND TERRORISTS

Guerrilla warfare has existed for centuries, but it was the Chinese Communist leader Mao Zedong who, during the Chinese civil war, gave it its modern form. Mao gathered support within rural communities, and built a grass-roots force that he used to wage a campaign of armed harrassment against the Chinese government. Mao later expanded his guerrilla forces to conduct conventional military operations.

Guerrilla war, inspired by leaders such as Mao and, later, Cuban revolutionary Fidel Castro, gained enormous influence in the postwar period, when nationalists in Asia and Africa were fighting for independence from European colonial rule—notably the Algerian nationalists against the French in Algiers. However, the emergence of the Cold War (see pp.384–85) complicated matters, because it tended to polarize all such conflicts into a broader struggle of East versus West.

CONFLICT IN VIETNAM

This polarization was epitomized by events during the war in Vietnam, which saw the development of a new model of guerilla warfare. Adopting Mao's strategy as an initial template, a Vietnamese Nationalist–Communist coalition rose up against the French administration in 1945. Using classic guerrilla hit-and-run tactics, their lightly armed, highly mobile forces wore down the French army, and then, in 1954, defeated it in a pitched battle at Dien Bien Phu. The subsequent peace settlement was followed by elections, which the US sabotaged for fear that North Vietnamese Communist leader Ho Chi Minh would win. This, in turn, was the trigger for hostilities between the Communist north and the US-backed south.

At first, it seemed inevitable that the better-equipped US would crush the insurgency with superior weapons and air power. The Vietnamese Communists received extensive military assistance from China and the Soviet Union; although this consisted mainly of World War II-era rifles and machine-guns to begin with, the Vietnamese were also tenacious and focused on their objectives, while the Americans lacked a coherent counterinsurgency strategy. Years of bitter guerrilla warfare failed to secure victory for the US; disillusioned and exhausted, it withdrew its forces in 1972—a prelude to a North Vietnamese takeover of the country.

With the demise of colonial empires by the mid-1970s, guerrilla conflicts became more diverse. The US sponsored its own insurgent

KEY **FIGURE**

MAO ZEDONG

1893–1976

The son of a farmer, Mao went to university in Beijing, where he studied the works of Marx, and co-founded the Chinese Communist Party (CCP) in 1921. In contrast to the conventional Communist reliance on urban workers, Mao mobilized the rural peasants, who became the bedrock of his military revolution.

▲ After defeating the Nationalists in 1949, Mao dominated Chinese political life until his death in 1976.

◀ **GUERRILLA WEAPONS**
Iraqi insurgents often use RPGs (an abbreviation of the Russian for "manually operated anti-tank grenade launcher"), and improvised explosive devices (IEDs), which are cheap but effective against occupying forces' vehicles. Other tactics include sniping, mortar strikes, and suicide bombings.

◀ **AMERICAN AIRBORNE ASSETS**
Troops from the US First Cavalry Division leap from a UH-1 Iroquois helicopter (a "slick" Huey), in Vietnam. Although the Americans exploited their aerial advantage with skill, they were unable to prevail.

KEY **EVENTS**

1945–PRESENT

- **October 1, 1949** The People's Republic of China is founded, after more than two decades of warfare, under Mao Zedong's leadership.
- **May 7, 1954** French forces besieged in Dien Bien Phu, in Vietnam, surrender to the communist Vietminh. The French had hoped that they could defeat the Vietminh in a conventional military operation, but found themselves totally overwhelmed.
- **March 8, 1965** US Marines land near Da Nang, as part of an American effort to combat communist insurgency.
- **October 13, 1977** A Lufthansa airliner is hijacked by guerrillas in support of the German Red Army Faction. German special forces subsequently storm the aircraft in Mogadishu, Somalia, and release the 86 passengers unharmed.
- **December 24, 1979** The Soviet occupation of Afghanistan begins, prompting the US to supply Afghan Mujahideen resistance fighters covertly with money and arms.
- **December 29, 1992** A hotel in Aden, used by US troops on their way to Somalia, is bombed. It is al-Qaeda's first attack.
- **September 11, 2001** Al-Qaeda (see p.408) launches terror attacks on America.

"Politics is **war without bloodshed**, while **war is politics with bloodshed**"

MAO ZEDONG, *ON PROTRACTED WAR*, MAY 1938

campaigns—the Contras, against the left-wing Nicaraguan government, and the Mujahideen, against the Soviet Union's Red Army in Afghanistan. Toward the end of the 20th century, low-intensity, guerrilla-style warfare had also become endemic in parts of Africa—notably in the failed states of the the Congo basin and the Horn of Africa—as warring bands fought for local supremacy. Guerrilla wars were predominantly rural in origin and character, while terrorism was mainly an urban phenomenon. Typical terrorist tactics such as assassination, extortion, kidnapping, and bombings were used by guerrilla groups—but from the 1960s onward, terrorism began to develop a character of its own.

If guerrilla insurgencies were violent attempts to gain control of a state, terrorism was an extreme form of protest, often an attempt to publicize a cause, or destabilize a society. Terrorism took many forms, reflecting the differing backgrounds and grievances of its participants. It included middle-class angst against the capitalist state, given violent form by the German Red Army Faction, the spate of plane hijackings in support of the Palestinian cause in the 1970s, and assassinations in Spain by the Basque separatist movement, ETA. However, for the West, the most worrying trend was the emergence of radical Islamist terrorists in the 1990s. Characterized by resentment toward the US and its allies, their attacks on the World Trade Center and the Pentagon in the US, in 2001, ushered in a new era in which the threat of large-scale terrorist attacks on civilian populations is never far from the public consciousness.

▼ **HECKLER & KOCH MP5**
Used by anti-terrorist forces, this submachine-gun is accurate, reliable, and has a relatively low recoil, enabling controlled automatic fire.

ASSAULT RIFLES

After World War II, there was a demand for infantrymen to be equipped with fully automatic rifles, but the full-powered rifle cartridge was too powerful for accurate automatic fire. The solution lay in the intermediate cartridge that had been pioneered in the German StG44, a development followed by the widespread reduction in caliber sizes that led to the NATO 5.56 × 45mm cartridge replacing the heavier 7.62 × 51mm equivalent. The resulting weapon—the assault rifle—was further adapted to incorporate other new ideas, among them the "bullpup" design in which the trigger group was fitted forward of the magazine, making the rifle more compact.

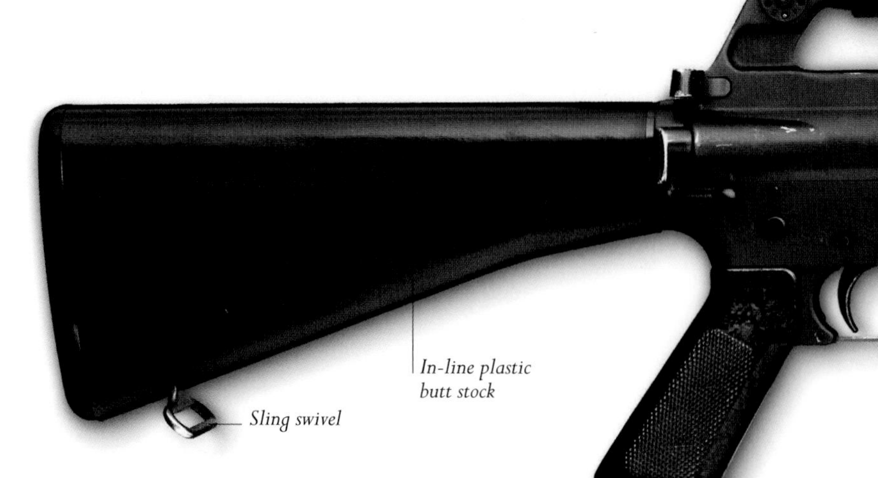

▲ M16A1 ASSAULT RIFLE

Date 1967
Origin US
Weight 8lb (3.64kg)
Barrel 20in (50.8cm)
Caliber 5.56 × 45mm

Introduced in the Vietnam War, the M16 series has developed into one of the world's key small arms. This example is fitted with an M203 grenade launcher.

Muzzle brake · *Rear sight* · *Fire selector*

▲ FN FAL PROTOTYPE

Date 1950
Origin Belgium
Weight 9¼lb (4.2kg)
Barrel 23½in (60cm)
Caliber .280

The FAL was originally developed with the German 7.92 × 33mm intermediate cartridge, although it went on to become a major export success (the basis for the British SLR) when rechambered for the 7.62 × 51mm NATO round.

Rear sight · *30-round detachable magazine*

▲ AK47 TYPE 56S

Date 1957
Origin China
Weight 11¼lb (5.13kg)
Barrel 16¼in (41.4cm)
Caliber 7.62 × 39mm

The most famous assault rifle in the world, the AK47 has undergone a number of changes over the years and has been widely copied. This Type 56S civilian variant was made in China.

Stamped steel body · *30-round detachable box magazine*

Shrouded rear sight · *Butt stock* · *30-round detachable box magazine*

▲ STONER 63

Date 1963
Origin US
Weight 7¾lb (3.52kg)
Barrel 20in (50.8cm)
Caliber 5.56 × 45mm

Designed as a modular firearm, the Stoner 63 can be assembled to produce different variants that include a carbine, assault rifle (shown here), and several machine-gun configurations.

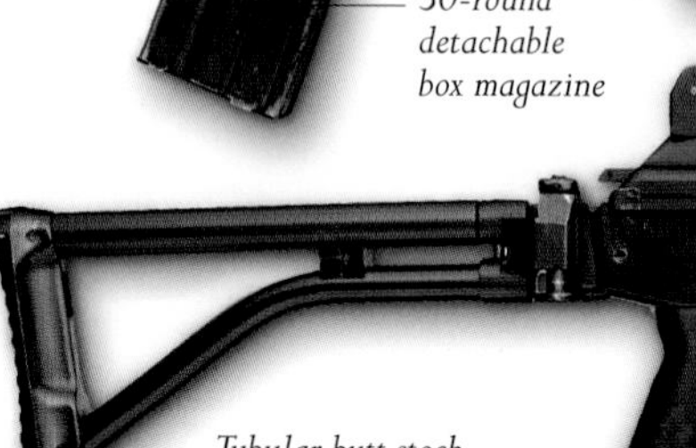

Cocking handle · *Tubular butt stock folds to the right* · *35-round detachable magazine*

▶ GALIL

Date 1972
Origin Israel
Weight 8¾lb (3.95kg)
Barrel 18in (46cm)
Caliber 5.56 × 45mm

The Galil is based on the Finnish Valmet M62, itself derived from the AK47. The Galil comes in a number of variants that include a standard assault rifle, light machine-gun, and sharpshooter rifle.

▲ AK74

Date 1978
Origin Soviet Union
Weight 7¼lb (3.3kg)
Barrel 16¼in (41.5cm)
Caliber 5.45 × 39mm

Based closely on the AKM, the AK74 is an improved version rechambered for the high-velocity intermediate 5.45 × 39mm cartridge. The example shown here has been equipped with a GP25 grenade launcher.

▼ L85A1 (SA80)

Date 1985
Origin UK
Weight 11lb (4.98kg)
Barrel 20½in (51.8cm)
Caliber 5.56 × 45mm

Although dogged by early development problems, the "bullpup"-configured SA80 is now firmly established as the infantry rifle of the British Army, featuring the use of high-impact plastics and optical sights as standard.

▲ STEYR AUG

Date 1978
Origin Austria
Weight 9lb (4.1kg)
Barrel 20in (50.8cm)
Caliber 5.56 × 45mm

Dating back to the 1970s, the futuristic and highly successful AUG was among the first assault rifles to utilize an integral optical sight, plastic components, and a "bullpup" configuration.

◀ FAMAS F1

Date 1978
Origin France
Weight 8lb (3.61kg)
Barrel 19¼in (48.8cm)
Caliber 5.56 × 45mm

A "bullpup" design, the FAMAS F1 is a very compact weapon, and has been used by the French armed forces since the late 1970s. Like many assault rifles, it makes full use of plastics and metal stampings.

▲ HECKLER & KOCH G41

Date 1981
Origin Germany
Weight 9lb (4.1kg)
Barrel 18in (45cm)
Caliber 5.56 × 45mm

A progression from H&K's 7.62mm G3 rifle, the G41 was rechambered to take the 5.56 × 45mm NATO round, and could be fitted with other NATO standard features including a universal sight mount and magazine. It had limited military use.

INFANTRY FIREPOWER

Although the modern assault rifle is a highly capable weapon, it lacks sufficient firepower to support infantry fighting on their own, and for this reason portable weapons with greater firepower were developed. The light machine-gun (LMG) is one of the oldest support weapons, capable of providing sustained automatic fire. At the next level is the grenade launcher, followed by the mortar, which provides infantry with miniaturized artillery. Portable anti-tank devices have also proved highly successful—ranging from the light RPG-7V to the just-portable MILAN, which fires missiles that the operator guides by wire to avoid defensive countermeasures.

▼ RPG-7V

Date 1961
Origin Soviet Union
Weight 13¾lb (6.3kg)
Barrel 37½in (95cm)
Caliber 40mm
Range 546¾ yards (500m)
Grenade type AT, AP, HE, thermobarbic

The shoulder-launched RPG-7 fires a projectile with a two-stage launcher/sustainer propellant. As well as optical sights, the weapon has backup iron sights and a passive infrared sight.

▲ PKM

Date 1969
Origin Soviet Union
Weight 16½lb (7.5kg)
Barrel 25¼in (64.5cm)
Caliber 7.62mm × 54R

A general-purpose machine-gun (GPMG), the PKM is gas-operated, belt-fed, and air-cooled. It is an improved variant of the Mikhail Kalashnikov-designed PK. The butt plate is hinged and contains a cleaning kit.

▶ MILAN ANTI-TANK MISSILE

Date 1972
Origin France, West Germany
Weight (Loaded) 75lb (34kg)
Length 4ft (1.2m)
Caliber 125mm
Armor penetration 25½in (650mm)

The MILAN is an anti-tank weapon that enables an operator to guide the missile to its target via signals sent along long, thin wires attached to the missile. Although many MILANs are vehicle-mounted, they can be deployed by a two-man infantry crew.

◀ FN MINIMI

Date 1975
Origin Belgium
Weight 15lb (6.83kg)
Barrel 18¼in (46.5cm)
Caliber 5.56 × 45mm

An outstanding gas-operated, air-cooled light machine-gun, the Minimi has been adopted by the British Army and the US Army, among others, where it has been designated the M249 Squad Automatic Weapon (SAW).

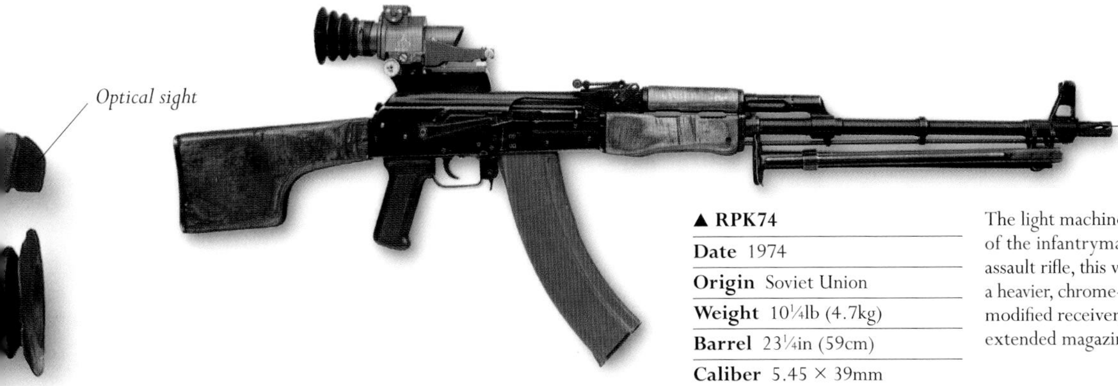

Optical sight
Muzzle brake

▲ RPK74

Date	1974
Origin	Soviet Union
Weight	10¼lb (4.7kg)
Barrel	23¼in (59cm)
Caliber	5.45 × 39mm

The light machine-gun version of the infantryman's AK74 assault rifle, this weapon features a heavier, chrome-plated barrel, a modified receiver, a bipod, and an extended magazine.

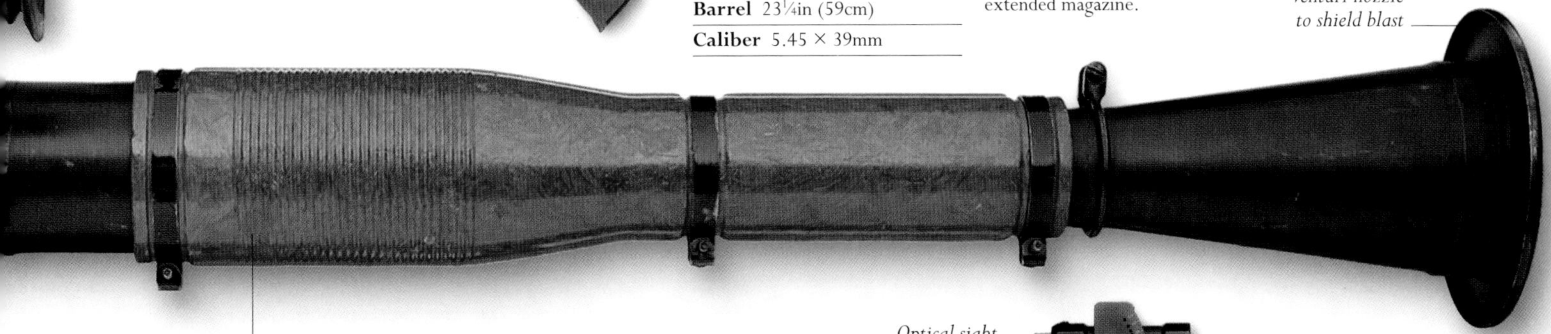

Venturi nozzle
to shield blast
Wooden heat shield to
protect operator's shoulder

▼ NEGEV

Date	1988
Origin	Israel
Weight	15¾lb (7.2kg)
Barrel	18in (46cm)
Calibre	5.56mm

Israel Military Industries' Negev is one of a breed of lightweight automatic weapons that has blurred the distinction between LMG and GPMG. Chambered for the SS109 NATO bullet in 5.56mm caliber, it can deliver automatic fire at 700 or 900 rounds per minute (rpm).

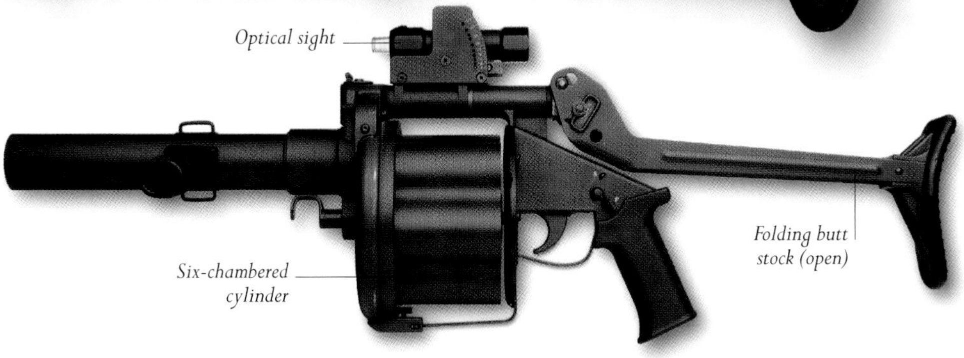

Optical sight
Six-chambered
cylinder
Folding butt
stock (open)

Fore sight
Barrel
Bipod folded under
gas cylinder

▲ MILKOR MGL

Date	1983
Origin	South Africa
Weight	11¾lb (5.3kg)
Barrel	11¾in (30cm)
Caliber	40mm
Range	382¾ yards (350m)
Grenade type	HE, HEAT, anti-personnel, pyrotechnic

The Milkor is a semiautomatic multiple grenade launcher (MGL) that fires its projectiles from a six-chambered revolver-style magazine. The Milkor has been exported to more than 30 countries, including the US.

British SUSAS
optical sight
Hinged folding
butt stock
Trigger guard
Safety catch

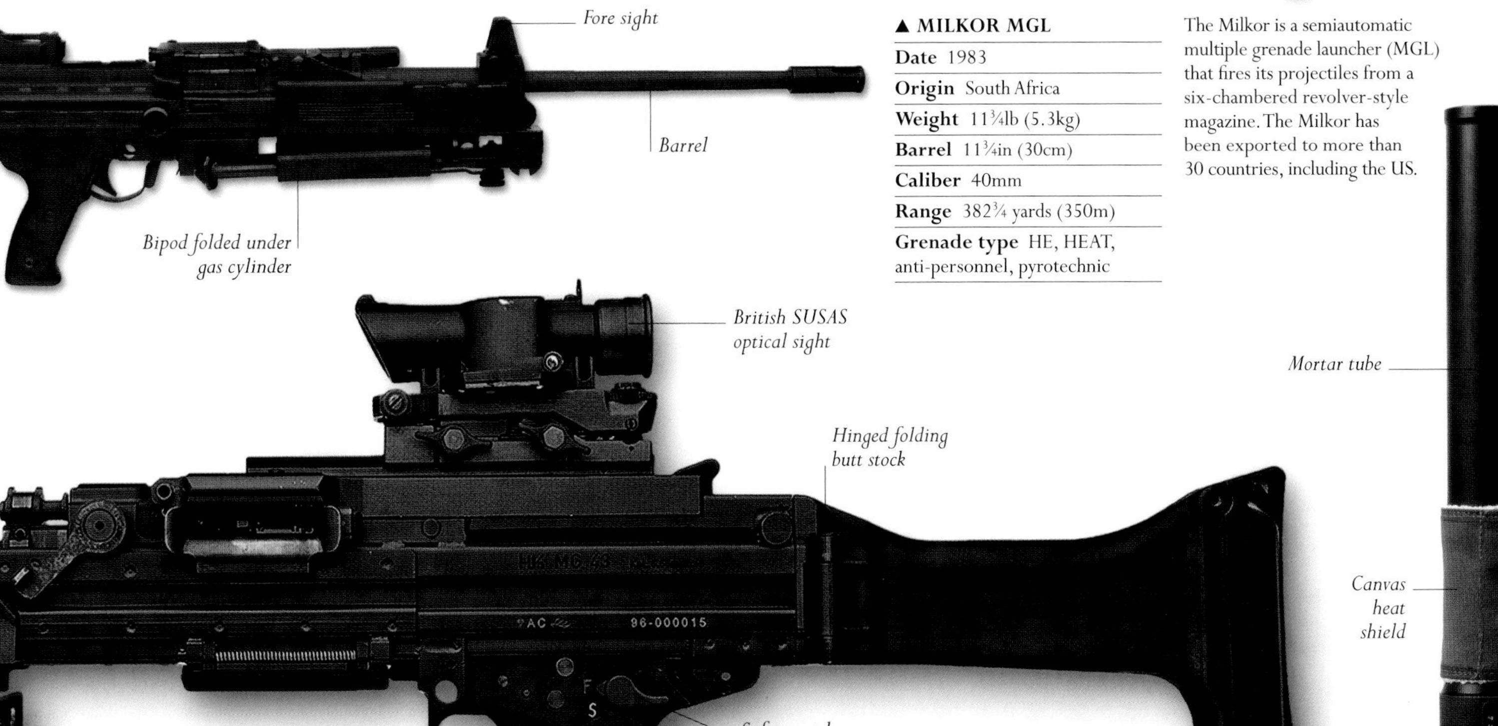

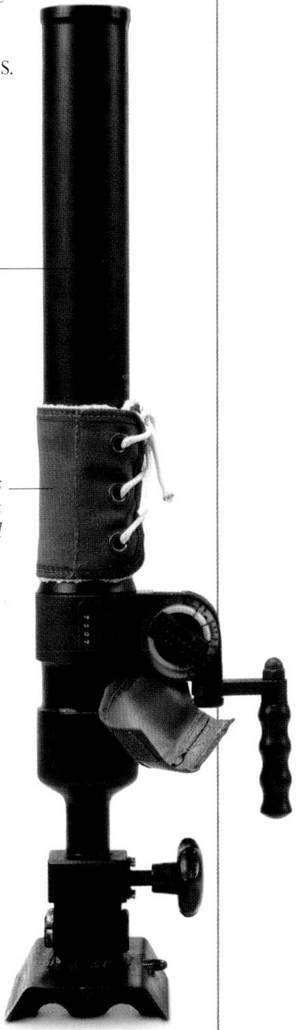

Mortar tube
Canvas
heat
shield

▲ HECKLER & KOCH MG43

Date	2001
Origin	Germany
Weight	18¾lb (8.55kg)
Barrel	18¾in (48cm)
Caliber	5.56 × 45mm

A rival to the FN Minimi, the MG43 is a belt-fed light machine-gun that features a folding butt stock and a quick-change barrel. In a slightly modified form, it has been designated the MG4 by the German army.

▶ SOLTAM COMMANDO MORTAR

Date	2006
Origin	Israel
Weight	13¾lb (6.2kg)
Length	21in (53.3cm)
Caliber	60mm
Range	874¾ yards (800m)

This lightweight mortar can be carried and fired by a single person. Its high rate of fire—up to 16 rounds per minute—makes it a valuable asset for infantry.

US MARINE UNIFORM AND KIT

When the US Marines were first deployed in Vietnam in 1965, they were ill-equipped for an environment in which terrible heat exhausted the infantrymen and incessant rain ruined their kit and uniforms. And so, lightweight, camouflage uniforms were issued in 1966–67, replacing the heavy olive-green "Utility" uniform. The hazards of patrols and sweeps in Vietnam—where ambushes and booby-trap devices inflicted a heavy toll of casualties—meant that personal protection was of high priority, hence the wearing of flak jackets and the eventual adoption of reinforced jungle boots.

▶ M1 HELMET

Date 1960s
Origin US
Material Manganese-steel

The M1 was a slightly modified version of the famous World War II helmet. It featured a pressure clip, which was introduced to reduce the risk of choking.

▶ COAT TROPICAL WR CLASS II

Date 1960s
Origin US
Material Cotton, poplin

The tight weave on this shirt made it wind-resistant and almost waterproof. The fabric was found to offer a good mix of breathability and defense against biting insects.

▼ JUNGLE BOOTS

Date 1960s
Origin US
Material Leather, canvas, nylon, rubber

These tropical combat (or jungle) boots were among the most common type issued to Marines. Their hard rubber soles were directly molded on since stitching tended to rot in the hot climate. From 1967, Panama sole boots were issued, with an embedded steel plate to protect against punji-stick booby-traps.

▲ M61 WEBBING

Date 1960s
Origin US
Material Nylon

The straps of the M61 webbing looped over the Marine infantryman's shoulders to help take the weight of the equipment hung around his waistbelt.

▶ **1941 PACK**

Date 1941
Origin US
Material Nylon, cotton

This small pack was used to hold rations and personal effects, while the rolled sheet of camouflage canvas formed half of a "pup" tent when joined to a second sheet.

Mitchell-pattern camouflage issued only to Marine Corps

M1943 folding entrenching shovel

MAP OF SAIGON BASE AREA

PARACHUTE FLARE

ANGLE HEAD FLASHLIGHT

◀ **M1955 ARMORED VEST**

Date 1960s
Origin US
Material Fiberglass, plastic, nylon

The Doron-armored (fiberglass and plastic) vest—heavy and unsuitable for tropical conditions—would have little chance of stopping a bullet, but it was an effective defense against shrapnel.

▼ **M14 RIFLE**

Date 1959
Origin US
Weight 9¾lb (4.4kg)
Barrel 22in (55.8cm)
Caliber 7.62mm

Designed to use the then-standard NATO round, the US M14 replaced the old M1 rifle. The M14 possessed a fully automatic fire capability and was equipped with a larger magazine. By the late 1960s, it was replaced by the M16.

Rear sight

Flash hider

20-round detachable magazine

Safety pin ring

◀ **M67 GRENADES**

Date 1960s
Origin US
Weight 1lb (0.45kg)
Length 3½in (89mm)

The M67 "baseball" grenade had a notched-wire interior designed to fragment into many small pieces on the detonation of its high-explosive charge.

▼ **M79 GRENADE LAUNCHER**

Date 1961
Origin US
Weight 6lb (2.75kg)
Barrel 12in (30.5cm)
Caliber 40mm
Range 985ft (300m)

With a maximum range of 985ft (300m), the M79 grenade launcher bridged the gap between the hand grenade and the mortar. As well as firing high explosive, the M79 could fire antipersonnel, smoke, and illuminating rounds. Two were issued to each rifle squad.

Fold-down leaf sight, graduated to 1,150ft (350m)

Rubber pad absorbs recoil

▼ **M60 MACHINEGUN**

Date 1963
Origin US
Weight 23lb (10.51kg)
Barrel 23½in (59.9cm)
Caliber 7.62mm

The M60 was the US example of the general-purpose machinegun—inheriting some design features from the German MG42. It was widely used by the US Marine Corps in Vietnam and is still in service today.

Carrying handle

Feed cover

Heat shield

Fore sight

Pistol grip

Bipod (folded)

SOLDIERS ON PATROL
US troops continue a "Search and Destroy" patrol in Vietnam, while an armored vehicle secures the helicopter landing area. The strategy was to airlift in troops to destroy the enemy and their supplies, then airlift troops out again, instead of taking and holding enemy territory.

OPERATION CEDAR FALLS

American ground troops were committed to a war against communist guerrillas in South Vietnam in 1965. US commander General William Westmoreland adopted an aggressive strategy, directing forces in large-scale "search and destroy" operations in guerrilla-controlled areas. Operation Cedar Falls in January 1967 exemplified the successes and failures of this approach.

Operation Cedar Falls was directed against the Iron Triangle, a guerrilla stronghold 25 miles (40km) from the South Vietnamese capital Saigon. Over many years the guerrillas had fortified the area with a complex system of tunnels protected by booby-traps and concealed firing positions. The Americans planned to encircle and destroy the guerrillas in a "hammer and anvil" operation. Troops along the southwest side of the Triangle would be the "anvil," blocking the guerrillas' escape as they were hit by the "hammer"—forces attacking from the north and east. The plan relied on helicopters to lift infantry swiftly into their combat positions, thereby bypassing difficult forested terrain and avoiding possible ambushes to convoys on roads. Helicopter gunships were not yet available, but the infantry received supporting firepower from tactical bombers, fixed-wing gunships, and artillery firebases.

The operation began on January 8 with the placing of the "anvil" forces, including elements of the South Vietnamese Army. One of the first objectives was to secure the village of Ben Suc, considered a hotbed of guerrilla activity. A flight of 60 helicopters zoomed in at treetop level and landed an entire American infantry battalion at positions around the village, which was then occupied with only light casualties. Other airmobile formations and mechanized infantry executed the "hammer" element of the operation over the following days. Traveling in M113 armored personnel carriers, the mechanized infantry were protected against the anti-personnel mines and sniping that took such a toll on soldiers on foot patrol. Newly introduced Rome plows, designed for heavy land-clearance, carved swathes through the jungle, while specially trained and equipped soldiers were sent in to search the dark maze of tunnels. These "tunnel rats" found caches of weapons and munitions, uniforms, food dumps, and an abundance of documents valuable to US intelligence.

DESTRUCTION OF RESOURCES

The Americans and South Vietnamese allies went on to render the Iron Triangle unusable for guerrilla forces. Tunnels were filled with acetylene gas and blown up, while much of the area was sprayed from the air with Agent Orange herbicide, poisoning forest and agricultural land. The peasant population was evacuated at gunpoint to refugee camps and Ben Suc was totally destroyed, the buildings burned, then flattened by bulldozers. But the objective of locating and destroying communist soldiers largely failed. The lightly equipped guerrillas were expert at concealment and slipped through the US cordon. The combination of the Americans' firepower and mobility allowed them to clear populated regions of guerrillas—but at the cost of devastating the peasant society that sustained them and laying waste to land US troops were deployed to defend. What American forces could not do was bring enemy formations to decisive combat and destroy them.

HELICOPTERS

The helicopter has been a major force in transforming warfare on the modern battlefield. Transport helicopters—such as the CH-47 Chinook and the UH-60 Black Hawk—are able to deliver heavy stores to forward troops, and having no need for a runway they can do this in almost any type of terrain. More important still has been the introduction of the attack helicopter, or "helicopter gunship," which provides close air support to ground troops and targets enemy armor. The Russian MI-24 Hind is a rare hybrid—a gunship that doubles up as a troop carrier.

▼ **BELL UH-1 IROQUOIS**

Date 1959	**Origin** US
Rotor span	48ft (14.63m)
Length	57ft (17.4m)
Top speed	135mph (217kph)
Engine	1,100hp (820kW) Lycoming T53-L-11 turboshaft

The UH-1 "Huey"—which first saw service during the Vietnam War—was a workhorse of the US Army, operating in many roles, including gunship, troop transport, search and rescue, liaison, and casualty evacuation.

Fenestron shrouded tail rotor

Tail boom

Wide sliding side door

Underfloor skids

Hydraulic power units and tanks (cover open)

Cabin window (jettisonable)

Utility hatch

Fuel tank

Cargo hook

▶ **BOEING VERTOL CH-47 CHINOOK**

Date 1962	**Origin** US
Rotor span	60ft (18.3m) each
Length	99ft (30.2m)
Top speed	196mph (315kph)
Engine	Two 3,750hp (2,796kW) Lycoming T55-GA-712 turboshafts

The twin-rotor CH-47 has been one of the longest-serving and most effective of cargo-carrying helicopters. Large loads can be slung underneath the helicopter, and a wide loading ramp is situated at the rear.

Engine exhaust duct

Two-crew tandem cockpit

TOW missiles (four on each stub wing)

Two 7.62mm miniguns

▲ **BELL AH-1 COBRA**

Date 1967	**Origin** US
Rotor span	44ft (13.6m)
Length	52.3ft (16.1m)
Top speed	196mph (315kph)
Engine	1,800hp (1,300kW) Lycoming T53-L-703 turboshaft

The first dedicated gunship—with a fighter-style two-man cockpit—the AH-1 Cobra proved highly effective in Vietnam, providing close fire support to slower and more vulnerable helicopters such as the UH-1.

▼ **MESSERSCHMITT-BÖLKOW-BLOHM BO-105**

Date 1971	**Origin** West Germany
Rotor span	32¼ft (9.84m)
Length	39ft (11.86m)
Top speed	167mph (270kph)
Engine	Two 420hp (313kW) Allison 250-C20B turboshafts

The BO-105 was the first helicopter to offer the safety provided by twin engines. Its low weight and agile performance were combined with a potent punch provided by six HOT (High subsonic Optical remote-guided fired from Tube) anti-tank missiles.

Tail boom with German Air Force insignia

◀ SA GAZELLE

Date 1971 **Origin** France
Rotor span 34½ft (10.5m)
Length 39ft (11.97m)
Top speed 193mph (310kph)
Engine 590hp (440kW) Turbomeca Astazou IIIA turboshaft

A lightweight utility helicopter produced for the French army, the Gazelle was also produced in the UK. Variants were armed with TOW (Tube-launched, Optically tracked, Wire-guided) anti-tank missiles, 20mm cannon, and Mistral air-to-air missiles.

▲ MIL MI-24 HIND

Date 1973 **Origin** Soviet Union
Rotor span 56½ft (17.3m)
Length 57¼ft (17.5m)
Top speed 215mph (346kph)
Engine Two 2,200hp (1,641kW) Isotov TV3-117 turboshafts

The Hind is a very large gunship and troop transporter. Its armament includes a rotary-barrel heavy machine-gun under the nose, as well as under-wing pylons for a variety of missile types.

▶ SIKORSKY UH-60 BLACK HAWK

Date 1979 **Origin** US
Rotor span 53¾ft (16.36m)
Length 64¾ft (19.76m)
Top speed 222mph (357kph)
Engine Two 1,890hp (1,410kW) GET700-GE-701C turboshafts

The UH-60 is a twin-engined utility helicopter able to ferry up to 14 soldiers, carry cargo, and evacuate up to six stretcher cases at a time. It can also be configured as a gunship.

◀ APACHE AH MK1

Date 2004 **Origin** UK
Rotor span 48ft (14.6m)
Length 58¼ft (17.7m)
Top speed 227mph (365kph)
Engine Two 2,100hp (1,566kW) Rolls-Royce RTM322 turboshafts

The Apache AH Mk1 (or AugustaWestland Apache) is the UK version of the Boeing AH-64D Apache Longbow helicopter. It has been successfully deployed by the British Armed Forces in Afghanistan (see pp.436–37).

ATTACK/RECONNAISSANCE HELICOPTER

AH-64 APACHE

The anti-armor AH-64 is used by a number of the world's armed forces. It employs many of the offensive and defensive technologies that dominate the modern battlefield.

Initially developed by Hughes Helicopters and now produced by Boeing, the twin-engined AH-64 Apache was introduced in 1984. It performed well in the Gulf War of 1991 and subsequently during the invasions of Afghanistan in 2001 and Iraq in 2003. Shown here is the AH1—a version of Boeing's AH-64D Apache Longbow built under licence by AugustaWestland for the British Army.

The Apache's weaponry includes a chain gun, rockets, and its primary armament of Hellfire missiles. Using target-acquisition and fire-control systems, the crew can merely select targets and fire; the missiles will then lock on to the targets and do the rest. This "fire-and-forget" capacity allows the Apache to take evasive action as soon as it has launched its own weapons.

To make this slow-flying helicopter less vulnerable in battle, the Apache is equipped with a variety of defensive systems. These include the suppression of infrared radiation (to avoid detection by hostile heat-seeking missiles), and sensors that give advance warning of incoming threats.

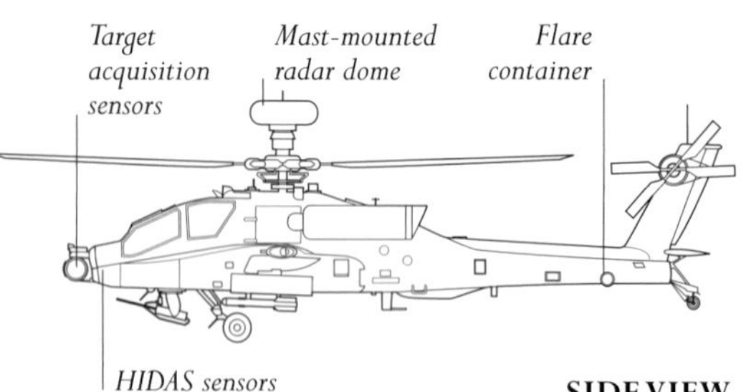

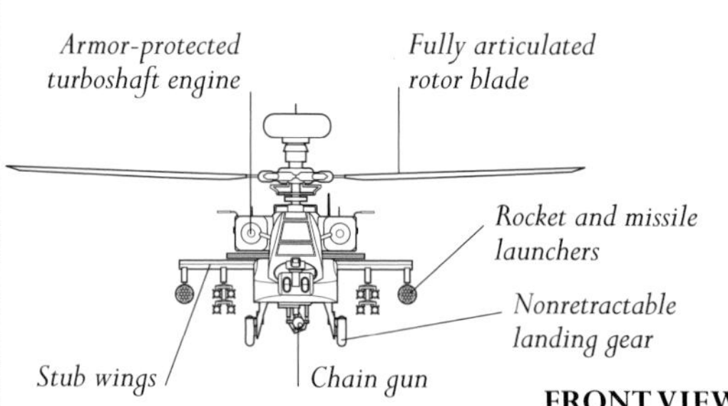

AH-64D APACHE LONGBOW
The helicopter's fuselage is 51ft (15.5m) in length and the main rotor diameter measures 48ft (14.6m). With a range of 334 miles (537km), the Apache has a cruising speed of around 162mph (260kph).

WEAPONS SYSTEMS

▲ 30MM CHAIN GUN
The Hughes M230 chain gun can fire 625 rounds per minute, fed from a 1,200-round magazine by an electrically driven chain mechanism.

▲ MISSILE
Up to 16 Hellfire guided missiles can be carried (a training round is shown above). These anti-armor weapons have a range of 5 miles (8km).

▲ ROCKET POD
Mounted under the wings, the two rocket pods are for use against infantry and light armor. Each one can launch 19 unguided 70mm rockets.

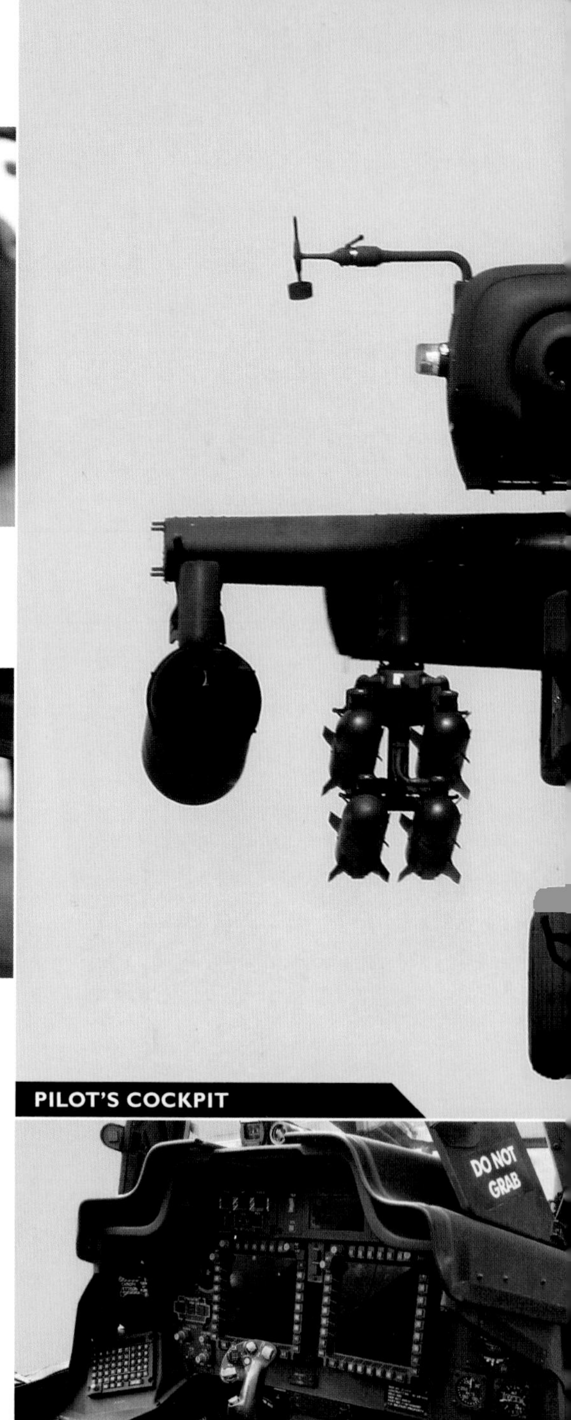

PILOT'S COCKPIT

▲ INSTRUMENT PANELS
The pilot sits above and behind the co-pilot/gunner. All the helicopter's systems are displayed in both cockpits and managed using the buttons around the screens.

◂ **RADAR "HAT"**
The hatlike structure above the main rotor is the Longbow radar. It gives the crew a 360-degree electronic picture of the battlefield, regardless of conditions, and locates enemy targets.

HELICOPTER EXTERIOR

◂ **HIDAS SENSORS**
The Helicopter Integrated Defensive Aids System (HIDAS) automatically detects and responds to enemy missiles.

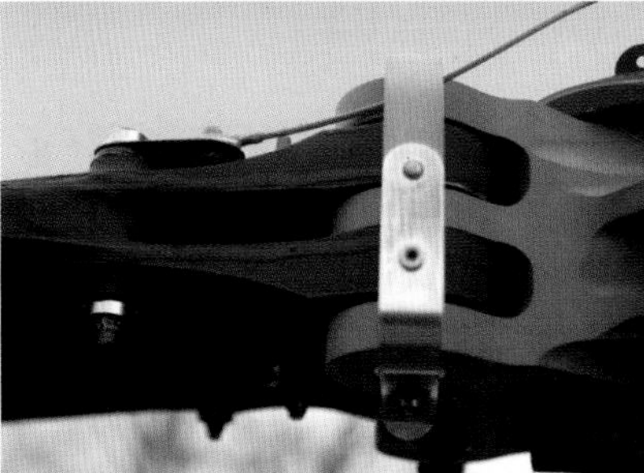

◂ **MAIN ROTOR ASSEMBLY**
The rotor blades are attached to the hub by laminated steel straps. The blades can easily be folded or removed for transportation by air or ship.

▴ **WIRE CUTTER**
Blades on the airframe can cut through power cables and telephone wires that could bring the craft down.

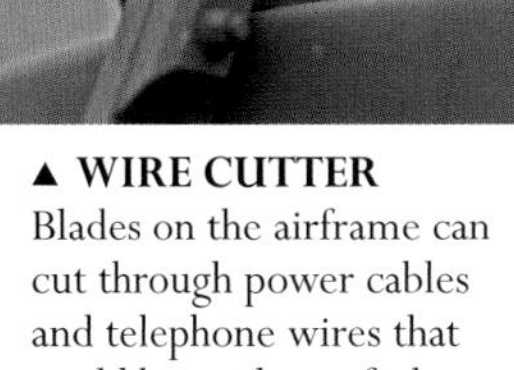

▴ **FLARE CONTAINER**
Decoy flares housed near the tail are fired by the helicopter's automatic defense system to confuse hostile missiles.

▴ **CANOPY JETTISON**
The armored cockpit canopy can be jettisoned in an emergency.

◂ **PILOT'S MONOCLE**
The monocle provides thermal (infrared) imaging and flight information in all conditions.

▴ **SAFETY BELT**
An array of safety features gives the crew a good chance of surviving crash landings.

◂ **CONTROL STICK**
Both pilot and gunner have flight and weapons controls. They can take over from each other if necessary.

SPECIAL FORCES WEAPONS

Special Forces units are sometimes required to deploy specialized weapons. Rock-solid reliability is a precondition for any such selection; a high-level of firepower makes small arms such as the Franchi shotgun and the Glock pistol popular choices. At other times stealth weapons are needed. But the most interesting recent development has been the introduction of the Personal Defense Weapon (PDW), such as the FN P90. This dispenses with the old Parabellum submachine-gun cartridge in favor of a smaller but more powerful round that can penetrate body armor.

Recoil spring housing

▲ FN BROWNING HP35

Date	1935
Origin	Belgium
Weight	2¼lb (1kg)
Barrel	4¾in (11.8cm)
Caliber	9 × 19mm

John Moses Browning's last design, this high-capacity weapon set the standard for modern self-loading pistols, and has been used by British, German, and Canadian forces.

Fore sight

Cocking handle

Attachment lugs for barrel-mounted accessories such as a suppressor

► HECKLER & KOCH MP5

Date	1966
Origin	Germany
Weight	6¾lb (3.1kg)
Barrel	8¾in (22.5cm)
Caliber	9 × 19mm

The most important and widely used submachine-gun of the modern period, combining accuracy and reliability, the MP5 has three rates of fire: single-shot, three-round burst, and automatic.

Weapon can be fitted with a 15- or 30-round magazine

Magazine release catch

Suppressor

▲ INGRAM M10

Date	1970
Origin	US
Weight	7½lb (3.4kg)
Barrel	4½in (11.4cm)
Caliber	0.45in

With a cyclical rate of fire of well over 1,000 rounds per minute, the Ingram M10 can empty its magazine in just over a second. The suppressor is essential to retain control over firing.

Retractable butt stock

Combined pistol grip and magazine holding 32 rounds

Optical sight

Muzzle

Cocking handle

Folding butt stock

▲ FRANCHI SPAS 12

Date	1978
Origin	Italy
Weight	9¾lb (4.4kg)
Barrel	21½in (54.5cm)
Caliber	12-bore

Developed as a close-combat weapon for both police and military, the Special Purpose Automatic Shotgun (SPAS) is gas-operated (with an optional pump mode) and holds eight rounds in an under-barrel tubular magazine.

▲ RUGER MODEL 10/22

Date	1980s
Origin	US
Weight	6¼lb (2.8kg)
Barrel	18½in (47cm)
Caliber	0.22in

When fitted with an integral suppressor, the 10/22 fires a lightweight bullet that is useful in relatively close-range situations, where a full-power cartridge could cause collateral damage.

▶ GLOCK 17

Date	1982
Origin	Austria
Weight	1¼lb (0.6kg)
Barrel	4¼in (11.4cm)
Caliber	9 × 19mm

Famous for its all-plastic frame, the Glock is a leading modern-generation automatic pistol, fitted with a 17-round magazine housed in the pistol grip.

▲ STEYR SPP

Date	1993
Origin	Austria
Weight	2¾lb (1.3kg)
Barrel	5in (13cm)
Caliber	9 × 19mm

A cut-down version of Steyr's TMP submachine-gun, the SPP—or Special Purpose Pistol—fires on semiautomatic only, and can take either a 15- or 30-round magazine housed in the pistol grip.

▼ FN P90

Date	1990
Origin	Belgium
Weight	6lb (2.68kg)
Barrel	10¼in (26.3cm)
Caliber	5.7 × 28mm

A ground-breaking PDW, the FN P90's nonmechanical body components are all moulded from plastic, and its unique horizontal ammunition feed allows the magazine to be incorporated within the receiver.

▲ HECKLER & KOCH MP7

Date	2001
Origin	Germany
Weight	4¼lb (1.9kg)
Barrel	7in (18cm)
Caliber	4.6 × 30mm

Similar in concept to the FN P90, the MP7 is a PDW that fires one of the new-generation reduced caliber, high-velocity rounds, in this case the 4.6 × 30mm cartridge. The fully ambidextrous design accommodates both left- and right-handed operators.

MEDALS OF THE MODERN ERA

The fragmentation of the colonial empires and the rise of new nations led to different forms of conflict, often without defined battles, but for which the combatants needed to be recognized. Some military operations, such as in Korea and Kosovo, involved forces acting on behalf of international organizations, rather than countries, which therefore issued medals. While the nature of war was changing, traditional acts of valor continued to provide the grounds for the award of many long-standing medals.

◀ **LIAOHSI MEDAL**

Date 1950

Origin China

Conflict Korean War

The distinctive bronze Liaohsi Medal for the Struggle to Resist the United States of America and Support Korea was issued to Chinese "volunteers" in the Korean War (1950–53). The enamelled front bears a map showing the Korean Peninsula and China.

▲ **ETHIOPIAN CONGO MEDAL**

Date 1964

Origin Ethiopia

Conflict Congo Crisis

This medal was awarded to Ethiopians who served under the UN banner during the Congo Crisis of 1960–64. About 3,000 troops from the Imperial Bodyguard and part of an air squadron carried out peacekeeping duties.

▶ **UN KOREA MEDAL**

Date 1950

Origin UK/United Nations

Conflict Korean War

Different versions of the UN Korea Medal were awarded to forces from each participating nation, although all shared the same ribbon. The British medal (shown) was issued to British and Commonwealth forces who had served at least one full day in Korea.

▲ **GENERAL SERVICE MEDAL**

Date 1962

Origin UK

This award was made for minor operations and campaigns—those short of full-scale war. It was open to all the UK armed services. Thirteen clasps were awarded and 130,000 medals with the Northern Ireland clasp (shown) were issued (1969–2007).

◀ **ORDER OF THE RED STAR**

Date 1930

Origin Soviet Union

The Red Star was awarded for achievements in the defense of the Soviet Union (both in war and peace) in the fields of state security, military science, weapons development, and courage and valor in battle. More than 4 million people received the order of the Red Star, with the last award made in 1991.

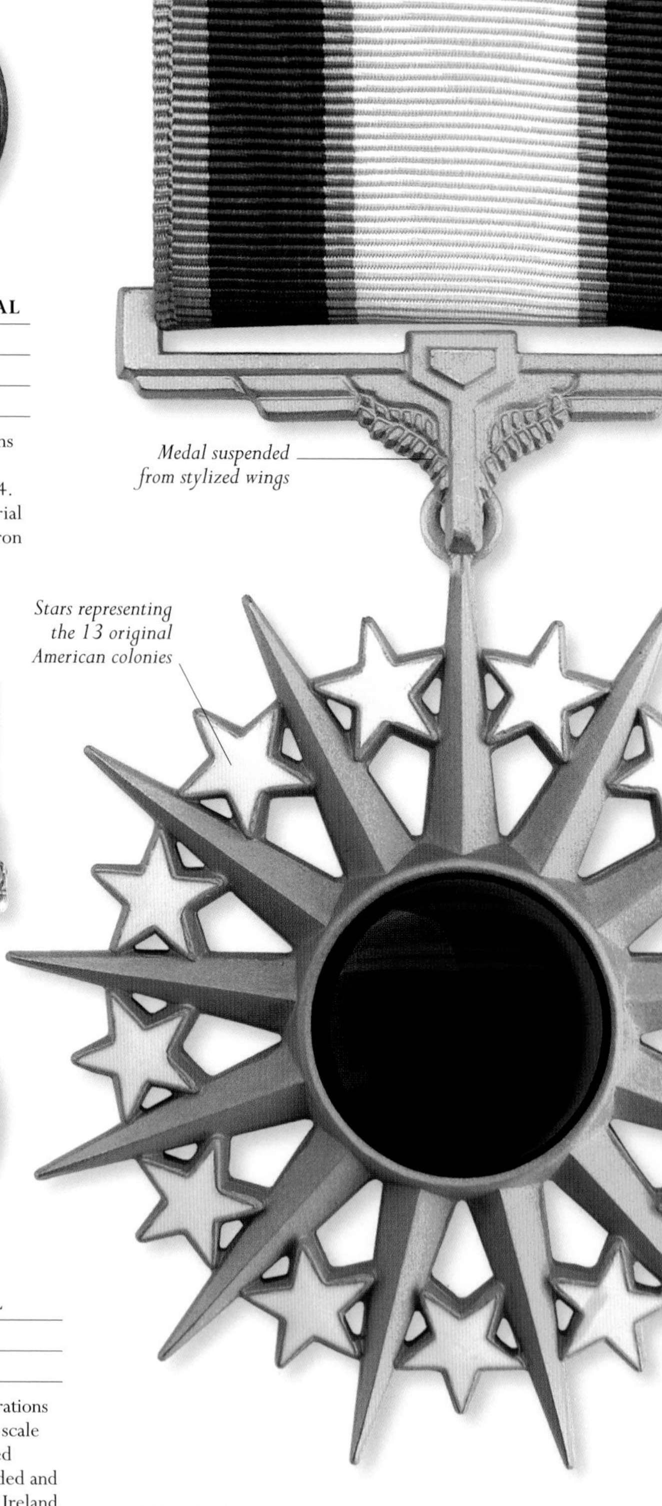

▲ **AIR FORCE DISTINGUISHED SERVICE MEDAL**

Date 1960

Origin US

This medal has a sunburst motif with a central blue stone representing the sky. Generally issued to high-ranking officers, it is awarded for "exceptionally meritorious service in a duty of unique and great responsibility," in a combat or non-combat role.

Head of Queen Elizabeth II

▲ **VIETNAM SERVICE MEDAL**

Date 1965

Origin US

Conflict Vietnam War

Depicting an oriental dragon and a bamboo grove on the front, the Vietnam Service Medal was awarded to military personnel who took part in combat or support operations in Vietnam, Thailand, Laos, or Cambodia between July 4, 1965 and March 28, 1973.

▲ **VIETNAM MEDAL**

Date 1968

Origin Australia/New Zealand

Conflict Vietnam War

The first operational service medal to be designed and produced in Australia, this was awarded to members of the Australian and New Zealand armed forces who served in Vietnam between May 1964 and January 1973. The reverse shows a figure of a man standing between two spheres.

▼ **KOSOVO NATO SERVICE MEDAL**

Date 1999

Origin NATO

Conflict Kosovo War

This bronze medal bearing the NATO star emblem set in a wreath of olive leaves was first instituted to reward personnel who took part in operations during the Kosovo War (1998–99) in the former Yugoslavia, for 30 days continuous service inside the country.

▲ **SOUTH ATLANTIC MEDAL**

Date 1982

Origin UK

Conflict Falklands War

The South Atlantic Medal was issued to all UK military personnel involved in the liberation of South Georgia and the Falkland Islands after Argentina's invasion in 1982. The coat of arms of the Falklands appears on the reverse. A rosette on the medal ribbon denotes service in the battle zone.

Lamassu, a winged bull with a man's head

"For Valor" inscribed on scroll

◀ **IRAQ MEDAL**

Date 2004

Origin UK

Conflict Iraq War

This award was given to all military and civilian participants in British actions in Iraq from 2003 to 2011, known as Operation Telic. Those who saw combat from March 19, 2003 were awarded a silver ribbon rosette. The reverse of the medal (shown) depicts a lamassu (a figure from Assyrian mythology).

Cross motif formed by four-bladed propeller

◀ **DISTINGUISHED SERVICE CROSS**

Date 1918

Origin US

The second highest military decoration after the Medal of Honor, this medal is awarded to US forces for extreme gallantry and risk of life in actual combat. Just over 1,000 were issued in the Vietnam War—400 of which were awarded posthumously.

▶ **DISTINGUISHED FLYING CROSS**

Date 1927

Origin US

This bronze medal for air crew is given for "heroism or extraordinary achievement while participating in an aerial flight," and has been awarded in all the major US conflicts since its institution, most recently in Iraq and Afghanistan (see pp.436–37).

KEY DEVELOPMENT

THE CONTEMPORARY ERA

The most significant developments in recent military technology have been driven not by increased firepower, but by the integration of electronics and computers into weapons systems; many modern conflicts bear witness to the advantage these technologies can provide.

The first steps toward precision-guided ("smart") weapons date back to the final stages of World War II, but it was not until the late 20th century that these devices truly transformed the military environment. The combination of vast leaps in computer power with the miniaturization of electronics over recent decades has led to the development of projectiles with their own guidance systems, enabling exceptional accuracy over long ranges. This process has extended from the radar and heat-seeking guidance systems that are now commonplace in missiles, to some artillery shells, ground-launched rockets, and even man-portable projectile weapons.

Modern military aircraft are fitted with a huge array of electronics to improve missile accuracy and acquire targets alongside devices that help counter anti-aircraft weapons. Remote-control guidance has been extended to the weapons themselves: the "drone," or Unmanned Aerial Vehicle (UAV), is one such example. This remote-controlled aircraft can fly over hostile territory to provide detailed photographic reconnaissance, or even to conduct strike missions, without the risk of a pilot being killed or captured.

SOUND AND VISION

Battlefield communications have improved vastly over recent years. The "fog of war"—which prevented a general from knowing what was going on in battle—is mostly a thing of the past, with individual radios allowing officers and troops to communicate directly. Global Positioning Satellites (GPS) enable a commander back at base to maintain close control over patrols or armored vehicles, with constant, real-time updates on their position and battlefield capability. For the troops on the frontline, laser range-finders improve the accuracy of weapons, and nightfall no

KEY **ATTACK**

AL-QAEDA ATTACKS AMERICA

SEPTEMBER 11, 2001

The assault by al-Qaeda on the US homeland in 2001 exposed the inherent vulnerability of an open society to attack. The terrorists, armed only with knives, were able to hijack four civilian airliners, crashing two of them into the World Trade Center, and one into the Pentagon.

▲ The second aircraft crashes into the World Trade Center; 2,977 civilians died in the attacks that day.

▼ AFGHANISTAN
A US Army CH-47 Chinook helicopter provides aerial security in Khost Province, Afghanistan, in early 2012.

◀ **BAGHDAD, MARCH 2003**
This apocalyptic image shows Baghdad burning during the opening stages of the coalition assault. US electronic countermeasures suppressed Iraqi air-defenses, leaving the city fatally vulnerable to attack.

longer brings military operations to a halt. Night-vision equipment was initially based on heavy, infra-red scopes, but improvements, including the arrival of light-intensifying starlight scopes, have made the 24-hour battlefield a reality.

The 1991 Gulf War proved the value of these, when a US-led force using the latest battlefield technology succeeded in ejecting the army of Iraqi dictator Saddam Hussein from Kuwait with little difficulty. The importance of the US and coalition forces' advanced weapons was confirmed a few years later in the success of the well-coordinated 2003 invasion of Iraq, against a much less well-equipped Iraqi army. This mastery has given the armed forces of advanced nations—especially the US—a significant advantage over the less well-equipped conventional armies of other nations.

However, terrorists armed with the simplest weapons have still been able to wreak havoc in Western societies, for example in the attacks on the US in 2001. In Iraq, insurgent groups emerged from the ruins to wage a sustained war against occupying forces, and in Afghanistan, the materially superior US and its allies have been unable to defeat Taliban fighters. The latter use classic guerrilla tactics—striking at weak points before melting back into the civilian population, or using civilians as human shields during firefights. For all their advanced technology, the armies of the West have yet to overcome simply-armed, determined insurgents, some of whom would rather face death than be defeated.

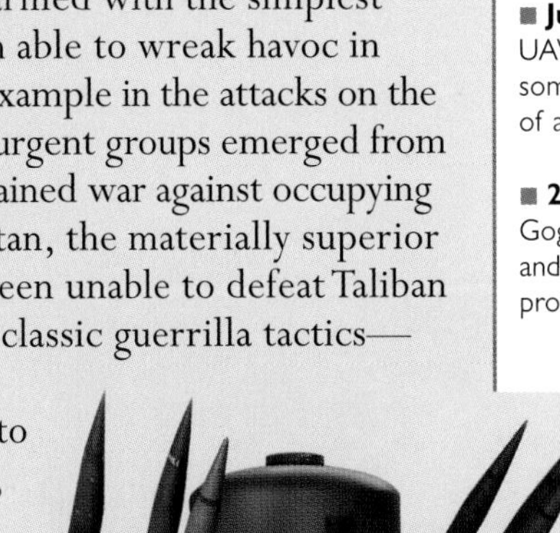

◀ **RAPIER SURFACE-TO-AIR MISSILE LAUNCHER**
The Rapier is noted for its accuracy and fast reaction time; it is used for ground-to-air defense by nine countries, including Switzerland, Turkey, and Iran. A mobile, tracked version is also in service.

KEY **EVENTS**

20TH–21ST CENTURY

- **September 1943** An air-launched radio-controlled German bomb ("Fritz-X") hits the Italian battleship *Roma*. This is the first use of a guided weapon in combat.
- **April–May 1972** US aircraft destroy the Thanh Hoa bridge in North Vietnam with laser-guided bombs; the bridge had survived 800 previous US sorties using conventional bombs.
- **1960s** The first night-vision devices are used, by US troops in the Vietnam conflict.
- **1991** Operation Desert Storm sees the first mass use of precision-guided munitions against military targets in Iraq, including laser-guided bombs (LGBs).
- **July 1995** The US Predator UAV enters service, and is seen by some military theorists as the future of air warfare in the 21st century.
- **2000s** Panoramic Night Vision Goggles (PNVGs) are developed and assigned to selected US aircrews, providing 95-degree vision.

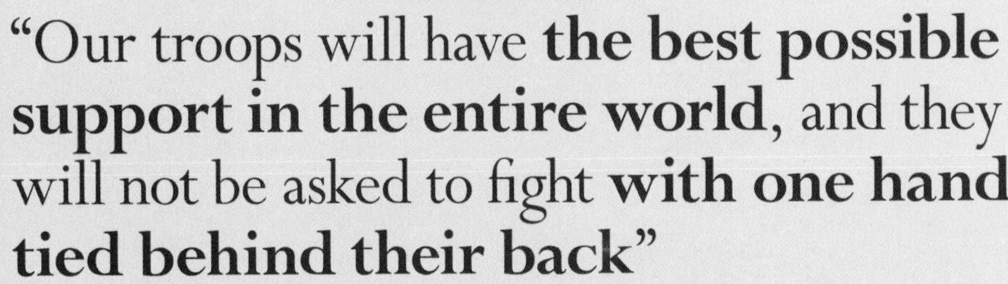

"Our troops will have **the best possible support in the entire world**, and they will not be asked to fight **with one hand tied behind their back**"

US PRESIDENT GEORGE H.W. BUSH, 1991

FIGHTER AND STRIKE AIRCRAFT

Fighter aircraft have been transformed since the first subsonic jets fought each other in the Korean War (1950–53). Today, they have the capacity to travel at over twice the speed of sound, and are also capable of carrying an enormous weight of missiles, rockets, and bombs—well in excess of the bomb loads carried by World War II heavy bombers such as the B17 (see pp. 314–17). The most recent advances, however, have been made in the field of aviation electronics. The latest fly-by-wire (i.e. computerized) control systems allow a maneuverability that would be impossible using conventional mechanical or human means, while weapons can be guided toward their target with pinpoint accuracy.

Armed with six .5in machine-guns, plus up to 5,300lb (2,400kg) of bombs / rockets

Bubble canopy

Fuel drop tank

▲ NORTH AMERICAN F-86 SABRE

Date 1949 **Origin** US

Wingspan 39¼ft (11.93m)

Length 38¾ft (11.84m)

Top speed 692mph (1,114kph)

Engine 5,910lb (26.3kN) General Electric J73-GE-3D

The first swept-wing fighter in the US Air Force, the F-86 was also a highly successful fighter that was able to take on the MiG-15. Including all variants, over 9,000 F-86s were built—more than any other Western jet fighter.

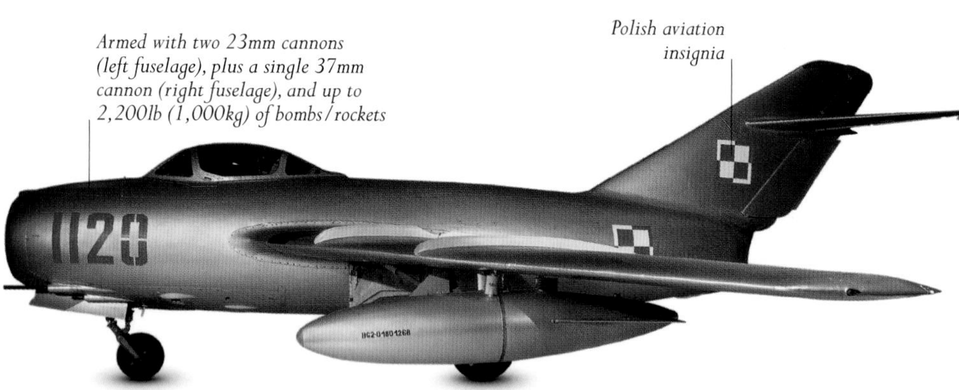

Armed with two 23mm cannons (left fuselage), plus a single 37mm cannon (right fuselage), and up to 2,200lb (1,000kg) of bombs / rockets

Polish aviation insignia

▲ MIKOYAN-GUREVICH MIG-15

Date 1949 **Origin** Soviet Union

Wingspan 33ft (10.08m)

Length 33ft (10m)

Top speed 684mph (1,100kph)

Engine 5,950lb (26.5kN) Klimov VK-1 turbojet

The Soviet Union broke new ground with this advanced fighter that saw the first ever jet combat with the US F-86 over Korea. The MiG-15 was also manufactured in China, Czechoslovakia, and Poland.

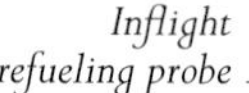

Inflight refueling probe

Variable exhaust nozzle

Armed with 20mm M61 Gatling Cannon, plus guided missiles and up to 17,000lb (7,700kg) ordnance

Ventral fin (port)

▲ GENERAL DYNAMICS F-16C FIGHTING FALCON

Date 1978 **Origin** US

Wingspan 32¾ft (9.96m)

Length 49½ft (15.06m)

Top speed 1,500mph (2,410kph)

Engine 17,155lb (76.3kN) F110-GE-100 turbofan

The multirole F-16 was built in response to the US Air Force's demand for a lightweight fighter. One of the first aircraft to use fly-by-wire controls, it was fast and extremely maneuverable.

▼ BAE HARRIER II GR9A

Date 1989 **Origin** UK

Wingspan 30⅓ft (9.25m)

Length 46⅓ft (14.12m)

Top speed 662mph (1,065kph)

Engine 21,750lb (96.7kN) Rolls-Royce Pegasus Mk 105 vectored turbofan

The most advanced of all the Harriers, a series that began in 1969, the GR9A is a Vertical / Short Takeoff and Landing (V / STOL) jet aircraft. This model is primarily used as a light strike aircraft.

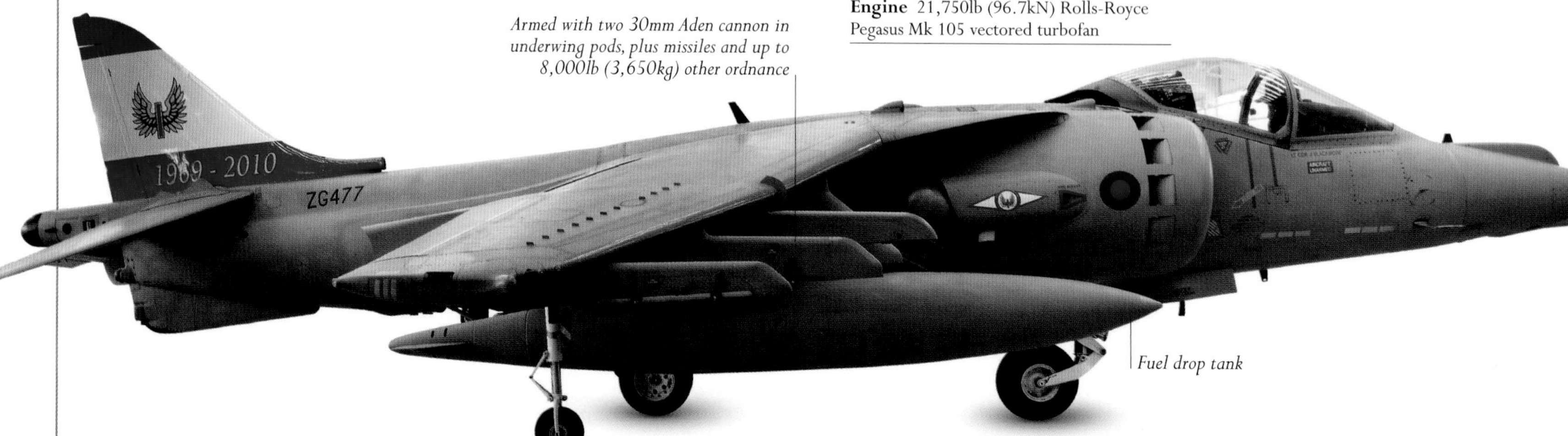

Armed with two 30mm Aden cannon in underwing pods, plus missiles and up to 8,000lb (3,650kg) other ordnance

Fuel drop tank

▲ SUKHOI SU-27 "FLANKER"

Date 1984 **Origin** Soviet Union
Wingspan 48¼ft (14.7m)
Length 72ft (21.9m)
Top speed 1,550mph (2,494kph)
Engine Two 16,910lb (75.22kN) Saturn/Lyulka AL-31F turbofans

Developed in response to the American F-15, the Su-27 is a large twin-engined multirole aircraft employing advanced avionics. In order to minimize weight, large sections of the Su-27 have been built from titanium.

◀ DASSAULT MIRAGE 2000D

Date 1995 **Origin** France
Wingspan 30ft (9.13m)
Length 47¾ft (14.55m)
Top speed 1,453mph (2,338kph)
Engine 14,500lb (64.3kN) SNECMA M53-p2 turbofan

The 2000D is the conventional strike aircraft counterpart of the nuclear-armed 2000N. The single-engined 2000D employs advanced avionics and has seen active service over the former Yugoslavia, Afghanistan, and Libya.

▲ EUROFIGHTER TYPHOON

Date 2003
Origin Germany/UK/Italy/Spain
Wingspan 36ft (10.95m)
Length 52½ft (15.96m)
Top speed 1,550mph (2,500kph)
Engine Two 13,000lb (60kN) Eurojet EJ 200 turbofans

The Typhoon is a twin-engined multirole fighter that has an extra pair of forward canard ("duck") wings. The advanced fly-by-wire artificial stability makes the aircraft exceptionally easy to maneuver.

▼ LOCKHEED MARTIN F-35A LIGHTNING II

Date 2006 **Origin** US
Wingspan 35ft (10.7m)
Length 51½ft (15.67m)
Top speed 1,200mph (1,930kph)
Engine 28,000lb (125 kN) Pratt & Whitney F135 turbofan

The advanced-stealth-technology-equipped F-35 comes in three different models: the F-35A (conventional take-off and landing); the F-35B (short take-off and vertical landing), and the F-35C (carrier-based aircraft).

STEALTH GROUND-ATTACK AIRCRAFT

LOCKHEED F-117 NIGHTHAWK

The first operational aircraft designed around stealth technology, the F-117 used faceting—sharply angled surfaces—to reduce its radar signature, enabling it to strike undetected at heavily defended targets.

The F-117 was a direct descendant of Have Blue, an experimental stealth aircraft that Lockheed began developing in 1975. The USAF received its first F-117s in 1982, but the plane's existence remained a secret until 1988. Despite its F (fighter) designation, the Nighthawk was a ground-attack aircraft. It typically carried a pair of 2,000lb (910kg) laser-guided bombs in its internal weapons bay, but had no air-to-air capability. During the Gulf War of 1991, F-117s carried out more than 40 percent of all strategic air strikes. The aircraft was retired in 2008.

Stealth technology gave the F-117 a radar signature equivalent to that of a small bird. Its angled surfaces scattered incoming radar waves instead of reflecting them back at their source, and a coating of matt-black radar-absorbent material (RAM) further reduced the signature. To avoid detection the aircraft could not use radar itself, so navigation was by GPS and an inertial guidance system. Efforts to conceal the Nighthawk from heat-seeking missiles included dispensing with afterburners on the engines and cooling the exhaust by channeling it through long ducts lined with heat-absorbent material.

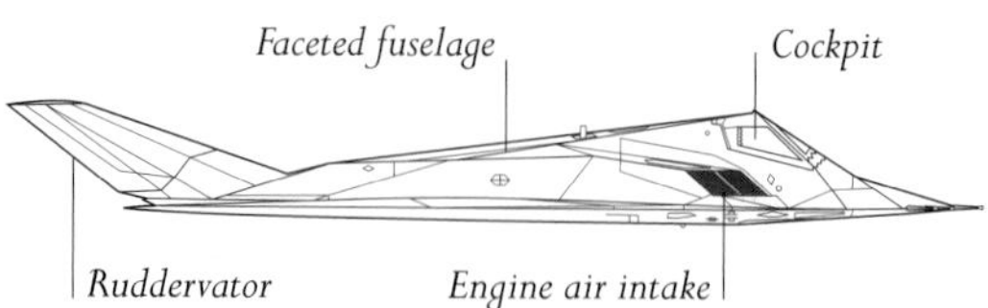

SIDE VIEW

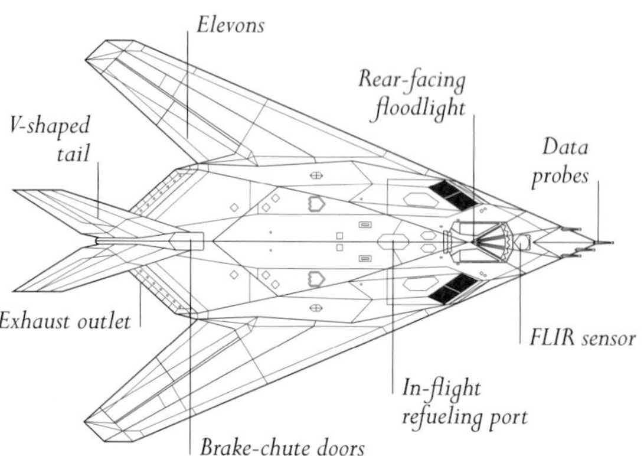

PLAN VIEW

▲ **LOCKHEED F-117 NIGHTHAWK**
Nearly 66ft (20.1m) long and with a wingspan of 43⅓ft (13.2m), the F-117 was powered by two General Electric F404 non-afterburning turbofans.

DATA SENSORS

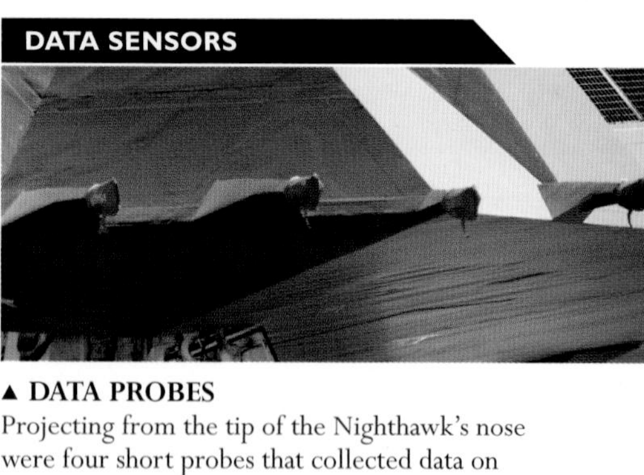

▲ **DATA PROBES**
Projecting from the tip of the Nighthawk's nose were four short probes that collected data on the aircraft's airspeed and angle of attack.

▲ **INFRARED SENSOR**
The Forward-Looking Infrared Sensor (FLIR) was used to locate targets. There was also a downward-looking sensor (DLIR) by the front undercarriage.

► **IN FLIGHT**
Stealth affected flying abilities: the F-117 was limited to subsonic speeds, and its shape made it unstable. Known as the "Wobblin' Goblin," it could be flown only with a computer-controlled fly-by-wire system.

FUSELAGE AND WINGS

▲ **ANGULAR WINDOWS**
The windows had a thin gold coating to absorb radar energy into the airframe. Dogtooth patterns along window and canopy edges, and on other openings and panels, helped disrupt radar reflections.

◀ **PARACHUTE**
The wings possessed elevons but no flaps, so the landing speed was quite high. A brake-chute was used to reduce the length of the landing run.

◀ **FORWARD VIEW FROM TAIL**
At night, a rear-facing floodlight on top of the canopy illuminated the in-flight refueling port (the central panel just below the light). Brake-chute doors were located at the base of the ruddervators.

▲ **FRONT WHEEL**
The F-117 "borrowed" parts from other existing planes: the front undercarriage, for example, was taken from the Lockheed A-10 Thunderbolt.

▲ **V-SHAPED TAIL**
Sometimes referred to as "ruddervators," the two forks of the tail combined the functions of rudders and elevators.

▲ **INTAKE GRILLES**
Fine-mesh grilles over the engine air intakes prevented radar from reflecting off the compressor blades.

INSIDE THE COCKPIT

▲ **HEAD-UP DISPLAY**
Located on top of the instrument decking, the head-up display (HUD) projected key information onto the pilot's forward view through the windscreen.

▲ **INSTRUMENT DECKING**
The F-117's cockpit included a central screen for infrared imagery, twin multi-function color displays for flight and weapons data, and a digital moving-map system.

ELECTRONIC WARFARE AND RECONNAISSANCE AIRCRAFT

Aerial reconnaissance plays a vital role in intelligence gathering, whether at a tactical level via the MiG-21 and OV-1 Mohawk, or at a strategic level via the U-2 or SR-71. These "eyes in the sky" reached a new level of sophistication with the introduction of Airborne Early Warning (AEW) aircraft, which can build up an electronic picture of enemy movements from enormous distances. These in turn have evolved into Airborne Warning and Control System (AWACS) aircraft, which provide all-weather command, communications, and surveillance.

▲ LOCKHEED P-3C ORION

Date 1962 **Origin** US
Wingspan 99¼ft (30.4m)
Length 116¾ft (35.6m)
Top speed 466mph (750kph)
Engine Four 4,600hp (3,700kW) Allison T56-A-14 turboprops

Developed from the Electra commercial airliner, the Orion acts as a maritime surveillance and anti-submarine aircraft. Its Magnetic Anomaly Detector (MAD) boom is used to track the presence of submerged submarines.

▶ LOCKHEED U-2

Date 1957 **Origin** US
Wingspan 103ft (31.4m)
Length 63ft (19.2m)
Top speed 500mph (805kph)
Engine 19,000lb (8,618kg) General Electric F118-101 turbofan

A strategic reconnaissance aircraft, the U-2—capable of cruising at heights of 70,000ft (21,000m)—was used by the Central Intelligence Agency (CIA) as a spy plane. It earned infamy when one was shot down in Soviet airspace in 1960.

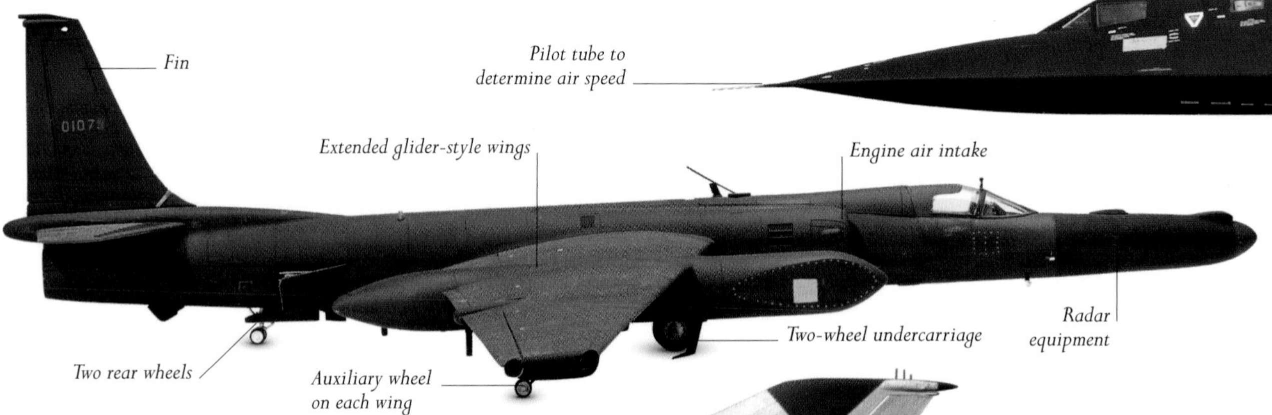

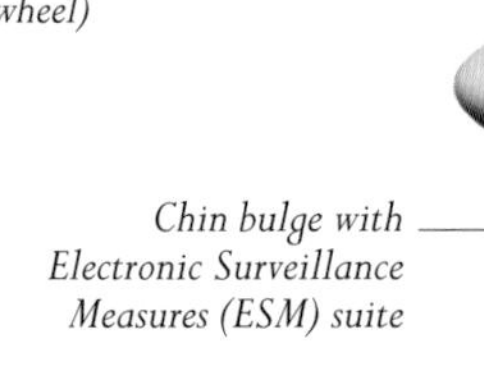

▲ MIKOYAN-GUREVICH MIG-21R

Date 1959 **Origin** Soviet Union
Wingspan 23½ft (7.15m)
Length 51¾ft (15.76m)
Top speed 1,385mph (2,230kph)
Engine 14,550lb (6,600kg) Tumansky R-13-300 turbojet

One of the most prolific aircraft in the Soviet armory, the MiG-21R was a tactical reconnaissance variant in which guns were replaced by optical and infrared cameras, either mounted within the airframe or in external wing pods.

◀ GRUMMAN OV-1 MOHAWK

Date 1959 **Origin** US
Wingspan 48ft (14.63m)
Length 41ft (12.5m)
Top speed 450mph (724kph)
Engine Two 1,400hp (1,044kW) Lycoming T53-L-701 turboprops

Designed for battlefield surveillance, the Mohawk was fitted with optical cameras and a Side-Looking Airborne Radar (SLAR) that provided a detailed picture of enemy movements on the ground.

▶ GRUMMAN E-2C HAWKEYE

Date 1964 **Origin** US

Wingspan 80½ft (24.56m)

Length 57½ft (17.54m)

Top speed 374mph (602kph)

Engine Two 4,910hp (3,663kW) Allison T56-A-425 turboprops

The first true Airborne Early Warning (AEW) aircraft, the Hawkeye's distinctive rotating radome was able to discover and track enemy aircraft, and then direct friendly aircraft to intercept them.

Flexible outer skin designed for high speed

Adjustable engine air intake cones

U.S. AIR FORCE

17959

959

▲ LOCKHEED SR-71 BLACKBIRD

Date 1966 **Origin** US

Wingspan 55½ft (16.94m)

Length 107½ft (32.74m)

Top speed 2,275mph (3,661kph)

Engine Two 32,500lb (14,742kg) Pratt & Whitney J58-1 turbo ramjets

A strategic reconnaissance aircraft that saw extensive operational service during the Vietnam War, the SR-71 is not only the world's fastest aircraft, it has also set the sustained altitude record of 98,192ft (29,929m).

▼ BOEING E-3A SENTRY (AWACS)

Date 1977 **Origin** US

Wingspan 145¼ft (44.4m)

Length 153ft (46.6m)

Top speed 530mph (853kph)

Engine Four 21,000lb (9,540kg) Pratt & Whitney TF33-PW-100 turbofans

The US Air Force's Airborne Warning and Control System (AWACS) is a converted Boeing 707 airliner. The rotating dish antenna can detect aircraft within a radius of 245 miles (395km). Onboard computers assess the threat and control friendly aircraft in defense.

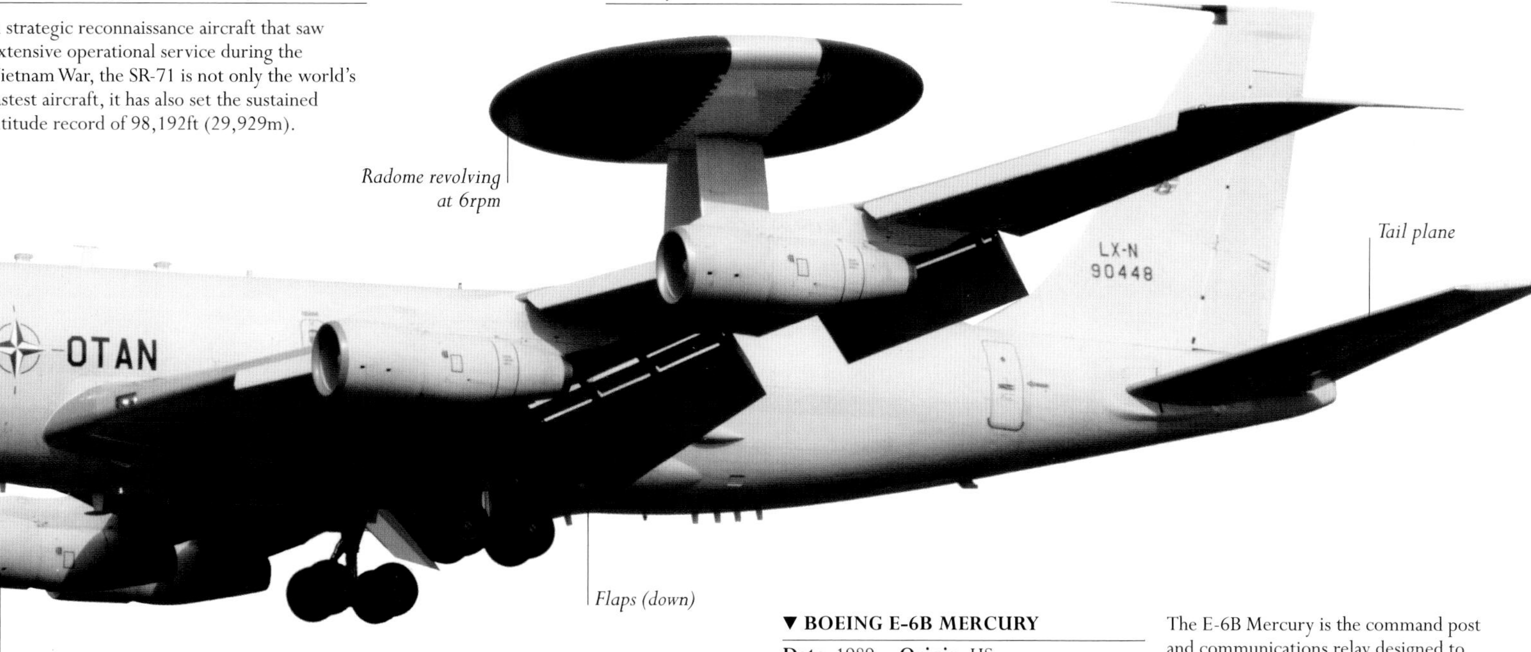

▼ BOEING E-6B MERCURY

Date 1989 **Origin** US

Wingspan 148¼ft (45.2m)

Length 150¼ft (45.8m)

Top speed 600mph (970kph)

Engine Four 34,000lb (150kN) CMFI CFM56-2A-2 turbofans

The E-6B Mercury is the command post and communications relay designed to maintain control of America's nuclear forces if ground-based control became impossible during a nuclear war.

Dorsal blister containing satellite communications

NAVY

POST-WAR TANKS

After 1945, a new class of armored fighting tank or vehicle evolved: the Main Battle Tank (MBT), which was more heavily armored, had a more powerful engine, and was armed with a more potent gun than its World War II predecessors. Although light and medium tanks were still manufactured, it was the MBT that dominated tank production and tactics. The major design development in this period was the introduction of new armor types. Conventional steel armor had become vulnerable to high-explosive anti-tank (HEAT) projectiles, and, to solve this problem, composite armors were introduced, of which the composite Chobham type, used on the Challenger and Abrams tanks, was the best known.

Snorkel for deep-water fording

Plastic side skirts

▲ T72

Date 1971 **Origin** Soviet Union
Weight 45.7 tons (41.5 tonnes)
Length 22¾ft (6.95m)
Top speed 37mph (60kph)
Engine 12-cylinder 780hp (582kW) diesel engine

The three-man T72 was an effective, if not particularly advanced, tank that dispensed with the usual fourth crew member in favor of an automatic loader. It was widely exported to countries around the world.

◀ AMX-13

Date 1952 **Origin** France
Weight 15.9 tons (14.5 tonnes)
Length 16ft (4.88m)
Top speed 37mph (60kph)
Engine Model 8Gxb 8-cylinder 250hp (190kW) gasoline engine

Developed as an air-portable light tank to support airborne forces, the AMX-13 featured an unusual two-part turret and an automatic loading system with two six-round magazines. It was manned by three crew.

▶ T62

Date 1961 **Origin** Soviet Union
Weight 44 tons (40 tonnes)
Length 21¼ft (6.63m)
Top speed 31mph (50kph)
Engine V-55 12-cylinder 581hp (433kW) diesel engine

A development from the T55, the T62 was equipped with infrared night-vision equipment. It was operated by a crew of four men: the commander, driver, gunner, and loader. It was the first modern tank to be armed with a smoothbore main gun.

▼ STRIDSVAGN 103

Date 1966 **Origin** Sweden
Weight 42.9 tons (39 tonnes)
Length 29½ft (9m)
Top speed 31mph (50kph)
Engine Rolls-Royce 490hp (223kW) diesel/Caterpillar gas turbine engine

Often known as the S-Tank, this radical turret-less tank was armed with a fixed gun that was traversed by engaging the left or right tracks, and elevated by adjusting the hull suspension. It was operated by three crew.

▶ CHALLENGER 1 MBT

Date 1983 **Origin** UK
Weight 68.3 tons (62 tonnes)
Length 37¾ft (11.5m)
Top speed 35mph (56kph)
Engine Rolls-Royce 12-cylinder 1,200hp (895kW) diesel engine

Manned by four crew, the Challenger 1 was one of the first armored vehicles to use Chobham ceramic composite armor. It was a considerable improvement over the underpowered Chieftain tank, and has now been superseded by the Challenger 2.

◀ M1A1 ABRAMS MBT

Date 1986 **Origin** US
Weight 67.5 tons (61.3 tonnes)
Length 26ft (7.93m)
Top speed 42mph (67kph)
Engine Honeywell 1,500hp (1,120kW) multi-fuel turbine engine

The four-man M1A1 has become the US Army's MBT, seeing service in the 1991 Gulf War and the 2003 invasion of Iraq. Its main armament has been uprated from the M1's 105mm gun, and it features a gas-turbine engine.

◀ LEOPARD C2

Date 2000 **Origin** West Germany
Weight 46.2 tons (42 tonnes)
Length 27¼ft (8.29m)
Top speed 40mph (65kph)
Engine MB 838 10-cylinder 819hp (610kW) multi-fuel engine

Developed in West Germany during the 1960s, the Leopard 1 proved to be a highly effective MBT. Several models were created for export, such as the improved C2 version that was adopted by the Canadian Army, among others.

◀ T90 MBT

Date 1993 **Origin** Russia
Weight 52.3 tons (47.5 tonnes)
Length 31½ft (9.63m)
Top speed 40mph (65kph)
Engine V-84 12-cylinder 840hp (618kW) diesel engine

An evolutionary design based on the T72, the three-man T90 is the Russian army's MBT. It includes a new main gun, an increased array of electronic devices, and greatly improved armor protection.

INFANTRY UNIFORMS AND EQUIPMENT

The latter part of the 20th century saw the widespread introduction of body armor as part of the basic infantry kit in the armies of all developed countries. New synthetic materials, such as Kevlar and Spectra, were used to make vests that could protect against small-arms fire; plates made from ceramic or composite materials could be fitted into special pockets in the vests to protect vulnerable areas of the body against high-velocity rounds. Cutting-edge technology also shaped the development of uniforms, which incorporated flame-retardant and even anti-malarial elements.

▲ ADVANCED BOMB SUIT

Date 1990s

Origin UK

Material Nomex, Kevlar, foam, armored plates

Bomb suits are constructed from many layers of armored material, since they are meant to protect against both explosive fragments and a bomb's blast wave. To minimize body heat, they are also fitted with their own cooling system.

▶ MK 6 HELMET

Date 1986

Origin UK

Material Ballistic nylon

This helmet was developed for the British Army to improve protection and to be worn in a variety of environments, including inside armored vehicles.

▶ DESERT CAMOUFLAGE UNIFORM

Date 1990

Origin UK

Material Cotton, nylon

Designed for the conditions encountered in Iraq and Afghanistan, this two-color Disruptive Pattern Material (DPM) desert uniform combines effective camouflage with a material adapted for use in high temperatures.

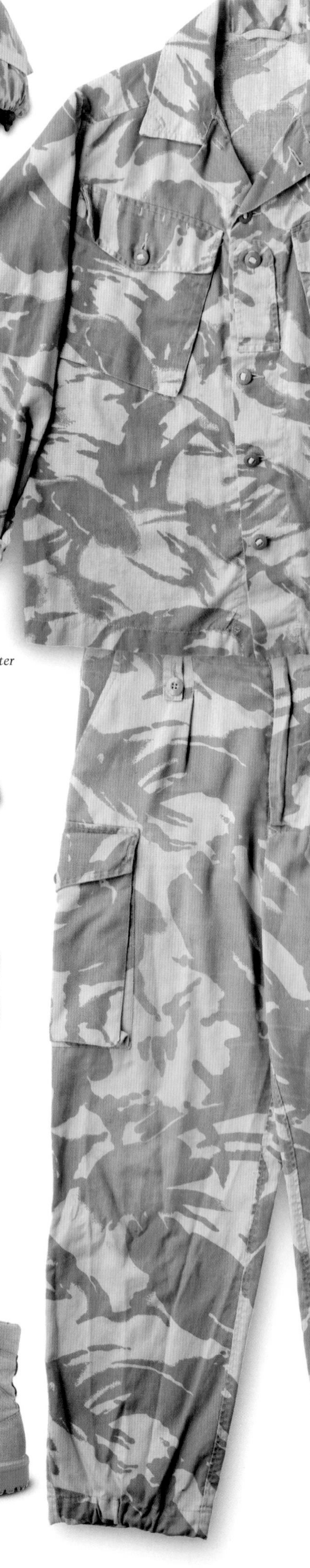

▼ 6B5 BODY ARMOR

Date 1986

Origin Soviet Union

Material Nylon, Kevlar, titanium/ceramic plates

Used extensively during the conflict in Chechnya in the 1990s, 6B5 body armor was made of Kevlar sheets, with inserts of either ceramic or titanium to provide extra ballistic protection.

▼ DESERT BOOTS

Date 1990s

Origin UK

Material Suede, Cordura, rubber

Lightweight patrol boots were designed for use in warm weather. They have been used extensively by British troops operating in Iraq and Afghanistan.

Two-color camouflage

Nozzle connected to drinking-water supply system

▲ OSPREY BODY ARMOR

Date 2006

Origin UK

Material Kevlar, ceramic plates

Developed as a modular system, Osprey Body Armor enables protective elements for the upper arms, neck, and throat to be added to the main vest, which protects the torso.

Cloth cover in Universal Camouflage Pattern (UCP)

◀ US ARMY ADVANCED COMBAT HELMET

Date 2003

Origin US

Material Ballistic fiber

The US Army's successor to the PASGT helmet, the Advanced Combat Helmet (ACH) shares similarities with the US Marines Lightweight Helmet (LWH). Like the LWH, the ACH is lighter and smaller than its predecessor and makes use of the latest ballistic-material technology.

Mounting bracket for night-vision aids

◀ US MARINE CORPS LIGHTWEIGHT HELMET

Date 2004

Origin US

Material Ballistic armor

Developed for the US Marines, the Lightweight Helmet (LWH) has a complex suspension and chinstrap configuration, which offers greater comfort and less weight than its predecessor, the PASGT.

Two-tone desert Disruptive Pattern Material (DPM)

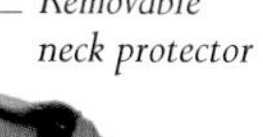

Removable neck protector

Groin protector

► INTERCEPTOR BODY ARMOR

Date 2007

Origin US

Material Kevlar, ballistic panels

Developed to improve protection for US ground troops, the modular Interceptor Body Armor (IBA) is capable of stopping most bullets, although wearing a complete set does burden the soldier with an extra 33lb (15kg).

Formation insignia: 101st Airborne

Mandarin collar, worn up with body armor

Flame-resistant material in UCP

▲ ARMY COMBAT UNIFORM

Date 2002

Origin US

Material Cotton/nylon mix

The Army Combat Uniform (ACU) makes extensive use of Velcro fastenings. The cloth material is both flame-resistant and impregnated with the insecticide permethrin.

SNIPER RIFLES

Military sniper rifles traditionally derived from two sources: first, the improved military rifle, fitted with a telescopic sight and firing match-grade ammunition; and secondly, the hunting rifle, which although highly accurate was often insufficiently robust for field conditions. During the late 1960s, small-arms designers finally began to produce rifles specifically designed for sniping. The M40 and the SS69 led the way, and were followed by a succession of superbly accurate firearms, such as the L96A1. Recent developments include the introduction of the 50-caliber heavy sniper rifle, and the .300 Winchester and .338 Lapua Magnum rounds, which are increasingly replacing the standard 7.62mm NATO cartridge.

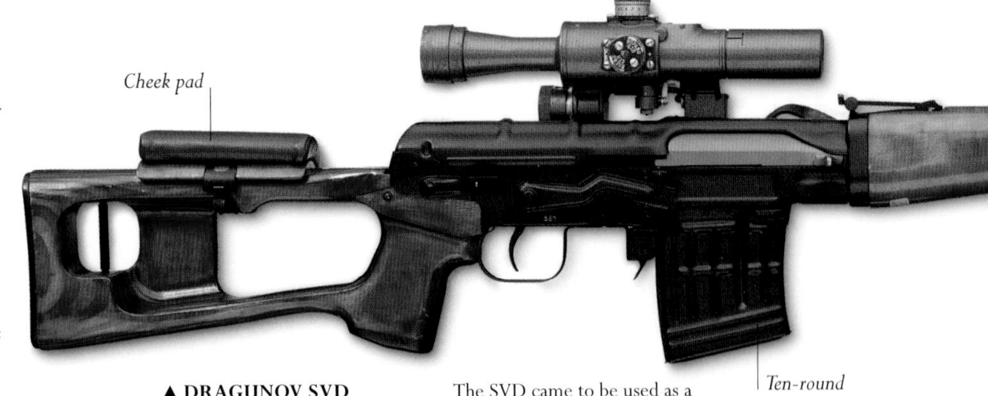

▲ **DRAGUNOV SVD**

Date	1963
Origin	Soviet Union
Weight	9½lb (4.3kg)
Barrel	24in (61cm)
Caliber	7.62 × 54R

The SVD came to be used as a sharpshooter platoon-support weapon by Warsaw Pact armies in the 1960s. Its four-power PSO-1 telescopic sight has limited infrared capability.

▲ **M40 SNIPER RIFLE**

Date	1966
Origin	US
Weight	6¾lb (3.1kg)
Barrel	24in (61cm)
Caliber	7.62 × 51mm

A military version of the Remington 700 sporting rifle, the M40 was first used by the US Marine Corps in Vietnam. Subsequent models were equipped with a fiberglass stock and a Unertl ten-power scope.

Elevation adjustment

Bolt handle

Five-round removable box magazine

Ten-power telescopic sight

▼ **STEYR SSG69**

Date	1969
Origin	Austria
Weight	8½lb (3.9kg)
Barrel	25½in (65cm)
Caliber	7.62 × 51mm

Developed for the Austrian army, the SSG also proved popular with police organizations. The SSG69 was unusual in its use of a five-round rotating spool magazine housed within the rifle body.

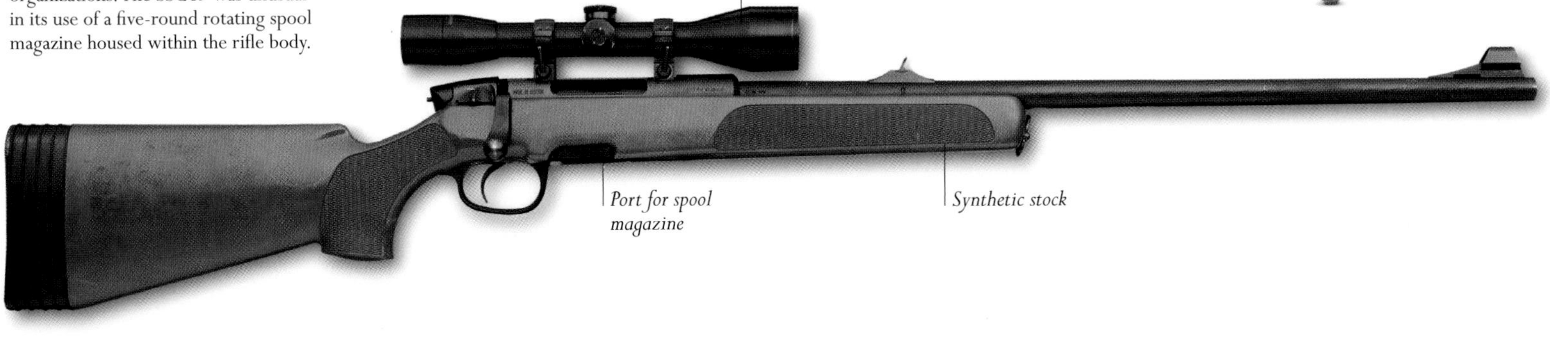

Six-power Kahles ZF69 telescopic sight

Port for spool magazine

Synthetic stock

▶ WALTHER WA2000

Date	1978
Origin	Germany
Weight	15¼lb (6.95kg)
Barrel	25½in (65cm)
Caliber	.300 Win Mag/7.62mm

Developed primarily for police use, the WA2000 employed a "bullpup" configuration and a semiautomatic action fed by a six-round magazine. High manufacturing costs ended its production in 1988.

◀ L96A1

Date	1984
Origin	UK
Weight	14¼lb (6.5kg)
Barrel	25¾in (65.5cm)
Caliber	7.62 × 51mm

The British Army's L96A1 sniper rifle was the first to be developed specifically for sniping, and it became the forerunner of a whole series of sniper rifles produced in a variety of calibers.

▶ HECKLER & KOCH PSG-1

Date	1985
Origin	Germany
Weight	17¾lb (8.1kg)
Barrel	25½in (65cm)
Caliber	7.62 × 51mm

Intended as a sniper rifle for the German police, the Heckler & Koch PSG-1 employed a semiautomatic action and was fitted with a heavy free-floating barrel, an adjustable butt stock, and a six-power telescopic sight.

▲ BARRETT MODEL 90

Date	1995
Origin	US
Weight	23½lb (10.7kg)
Barrel	29in (73.7cm)
Caliber	.50 BMG

Ronnie Barrett pioneered the anti-materiel (AM) rifle in the early 1980s. This model, noteworthy for its compact "bullpup" design, is an effective sniping weapon for ranges in excess of 5,900ft (1,800m).

▼ HECATE II SNIPER RIFLE

Date	1993
Origin	France
Weight	30½lb (13.8kg)
Barrel	27½in (70cm)
Caliber	.50 BMG

As with other Western heavy sniper rifles, the Hecate II fires the .50 BMG (12.7 × 99mm NATO) round, and is based around PGM's metallic skeleton system, complete with a high-efficiency muzzle brake.

▼ C14 TIMBERWOLF SNIPER RIFLE

Date	2005
Origin	Canada
Weight	15lb (6.8kg)
Barrel	26in (66cm)
Caliber	.338in Lapua Magnum

Following recent trends in antipersonnel sniper-rifle design, the Timberwolf has been chambered for the powerful .338in Lapua Magnum round, which extends a rifle's effective range to over 3,940ft (1,200m).

MODERN FRIGATES AND DESTROYERS

While the aircraft carrier and the nuclear-powered submarine are the capital ships of today's major naval forces, smaller escort vessels remain as necessary as ever. The distinction between destroyers and frigates has become more indefinite during the post-war era, with the (larger) destroyer and the (smaller) frigate dispensing with some of their guns in favor of an array of guided missiles as their main armament. Escort vessels have usually been classified into anti-aircraft or anti-submarine vessels, but most are capable of performing a variety of tasks.

Funnel
Twin 5-inch guns

▲ USS HERBERT J THOMAS

Commissioned 1945 **Origin** US
Displacement 3,460 tons
Length 390ft (119m)
Top speed 36.8 knots

One of 98 *Gearing*-class anti-aircraft destroyers, the *Herbert J Thomas* was designed for long-range patrols in the Pacific, and was armed with six 5-inch guns in three turrets. It took part in both the Korean and Vietnam Wars.

▶ HMS DIAMOND

Commissioned 1952 **Origin** UK
Displacement 3,580 tons
Length 390ft (119m)
Top speed 30 knots

As a *Daring*-class destroyer, *Diamond* was the last such vessel in the British Royal Navy to be fitted with guns as its main armament before the widespread introduction of guided missiles.

Turret with two 4.5in guns
D35

▶ HMS LANCASTER

Commissioned 1992 **Origin** UK
Displacement 4,200 tons
Length 436ft (133m)
Top speed 32 knots

A Type-23 frigate, *Lancaster* is a versatile multi-role vessel, armed with Sea Wolf anti-aircraft missiles, Harpoon anti-ship missiles, and Stingray anti-submarine torpedoes.

▲ HMNZCS CANTERBURY

Commissioned 1971 **Origin** UK
Displacement 2,960 tons
Length 372ft (113.4m)
Top speed 28 knots

The *Canterbury* was a broad-beam *Leander*-class frigate commissioned into the Royal New Zealand Navy. The ship saw service in a number of peacekeeping operations in the Pacific and Persian Gulf.

▼ HMS SHEFFIELD

Commissioned 1975 **Origin** UK
Displacement 4,350 tons
Length 410ft (125m)
Top speed 30 knots

A Type-42 Guided Missile Destroyer, *Sheffield* took part in the Falklands campaign of 1982. While on patrol off the Falkland Islands, *Sheffield* was sunk by an Exocet missile fired by an Argentinian naval aircraft.

Type 10006 radar
Type 992Q radar
Anti-aircraft radar
Hangar
4.5in gun turret
Sea Dart surface-to-air missile
D80

Missile launcher

◀ **USS PHARRIS**

Commissioned 1974	**Origin** US
Displacement 4,070 tons	
Length 438ft (133.5m)	
Top speed 27 knots	

The *Pharris* was launched as a *Knox*-class destroyer, and was later reclassified as a frigate. It was intended for anti-submarine warfare duties, being armed with Anti-Submarine Rocket (ASROC) and Harpoon missiles.

Missile launcher

Radar and electronics mast

▲ **USS OLIVER HAZARD PERRY**

Commissioned 1977	**Origin** US
Displacement 3,485 tons	
Length 436ft (133m)	
Top speed 28 knots	

The lead ship in its frigate class, the *Oliver Hazard Perry* was designed as a general-purpose escort vessel, protecting merchant convoys or acting as part of a carrier battle group.

Sea Wolf missile system

4.5in Mark 8 gun

Hull painted with anti-fouling paint to increase speed

◀ **USS ARLEIGH BURKE**

Commissioned 1991	**Origin** US
Displacement 8,375 tons	
Length 505ft (154m)	
Top speed 30 knots	

The first destroyer to be fitted with the advanced AEGIS missile system, the *Arleigh Burke* also incorporates the latest stealth technology. It is the lead-ship of its class of guided-missile destroyers.

Vertical-launch missile deck

▶ **HMCS VANCOUVER**

Commissioned 1993
Origin Canada
Displacement 4,750 tons
Length 440ft (134m)
Top speed 30 knots

The second *Halifax*-class series vessel of the Canadian Navy, the *Vancouver* is a modern multirole frigate, able to deal with surface and aerial threats while possessing a full anti-submarine capability.

AMERICAN AIRCRAFT CARRIER

USS GEORGE WASHINGTON

Aircraft carriers are the ultimate symbol of naval power. The *George Washington* is one of 10 Nimitz-class supercarriers in the US Navy—the largest military vessels ever to take to the seas.

Commissioned in 1992, the *George Washington* can accommodate 85 aircraft, including fighter, strike, and transport planes, airborne early warning (AEW) aircraft, and helicopters. It is also a floating home for around 6,000 service men and women. Although designed primarily to offer an offensive strike capability, the ship is equipped with its own defenses, such as anti-aircraft and anti-missile weapon systems, and rapid-fire 20mm guns.

On the starboard side and overlooking the deck is the island superstructure—the ship's command-and-control center, which houses the bridge and primary flight-control area. From here, officers keep a careful watch on the massive flight deck, which covers 4.5 acres (1.8 hectares)—about the size of two-and-a-half football fields.

During flying operations, the deck is a hive of activity, with aircraft taking off and landing, and being maneuvered, refueled, and armed. Aircraft are launched by four catapults, two at the forward end of the angled deck and two in the bows. The landing deck is angled to the port side to allow other activities to take place as aircraft return to the ship. When touching down, a pilot must ensure that the plane's tailhook catches one of four high-tensile steel arrestor wires that run across the flight deck. These decelerate the aircraft rapidly and bring it to a halt within two seconds.

When not in use, most aircraft are stored beneath the flight deck in the vast hangar, which stretches for much of the ship's length. On the decks below are living quarters for the ship's personnel.

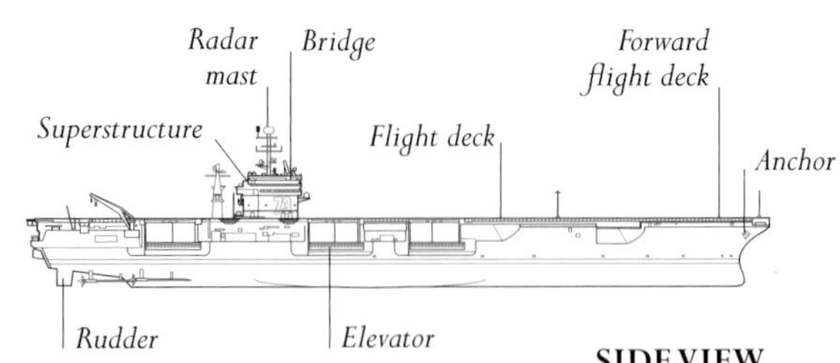

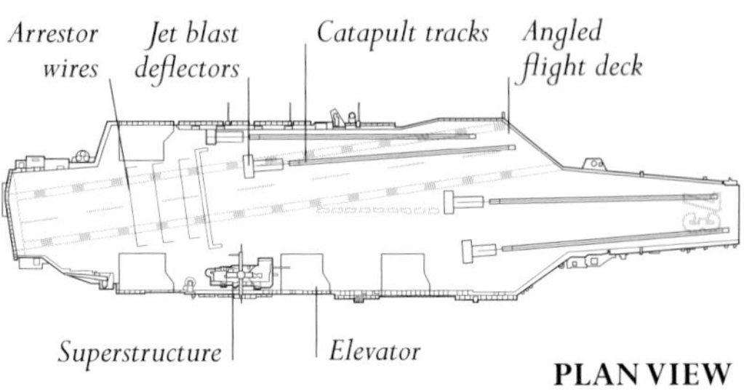

▲ **USS *GEORGE WASHINGTON***
The sixth Nimitz-class carrier, the *George Washington* is 1,092ft (333m) long and displaces about 103,000 tons. It is powered by two nuclear reactors.

▼ **PREPARING FOR TAKE-OFF**
Deck crew secure a Northrop Grumman E-2C Hawkeye AEW aircraft to a catapult shuttle.

TAKE-OFF AND LANDING

▲ **CATAPULT CONTROL POD**
This observation pod, which retracts below the flight deck, enables the crew controlling catapult launches to see what is happening while remaining safe from moving aircraft and their exhausts.

▲ **CATAPULT SHUTTLE**
For a catapult launch, a shuttle is attached to a plane's undercarriage and propelled along a track by a steam-powered piston.

▲ **SHUTTLE TRACK**
The catapult shuttle runs along a track set into the surface of the ship's flight deck.

▲ **JET-BLAST DEFLECTOR**
The yellow deflector shield behind this McDonnell Douglas F/A-18 Hornet prevents the plane's exhaust from causing damage or injury during takeoff. The deflector shield is cooled by sea water.

▲ **GRUMMAN F-14 TOMCAT LANDING**
A pilot increases the throttle at touch-down, so that if the aircraft fails to catch the arrestor wires it still has enough speed to take off again and attempt another landing—a practice called "touch and go."

AROUND THE DECK

▲ **AIRCRAFT WEAPONRY**
Most of the *George Washington*'s formidable firepower is reserved for its aircraft. The range of airborne weapons include bombs, rockets, guided missiles, and torpedoes.

▲ **ELEVATOR**
Four hydraulic lifts, one to port and three to starboard, move aircraft between the hangar and the flight deck. They also take containers of stores or spare parts to and from the hangars.

▶ **HELICOPTER MAINTENANCE**
An aircraft carrier's helicopters perform many roles, including anti-submarine work, rescue missions, and the transportation of personnel.

▲ **ISLAND SUPERSTRUCTURE**
Much of the electronics, including radar and satellite communications equipment, is based on the island, which has the ship's number painted on its sides.

▼ **FLOATING AIRSTRIP**
Carriers such as the *George Washington* provide the strategic benefit of a mobile strike platform that can operate from anywhere in international waters.

INSIDE AND DOWN BELOW

The control rooms are based in the island superstructure up above and elsewhere below deck. In addition to the aircraft hangar, the lower-deck areas include the catapult and arrestor gear machinery, 44 magazines, and the power plant and engine room. Facilities for the thousands of crew and air wing include messes, medical facilities, and a gym.

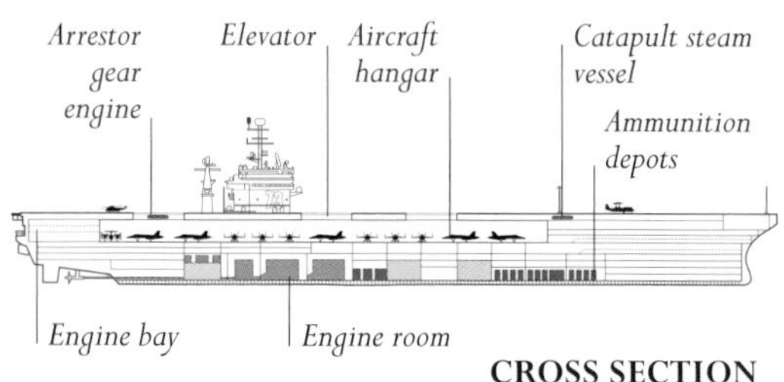

CROSS SECTION

LAUNCH AND CATCH

▲ ARRESTING GEAR PISTON
Huge hydraulic pistons below the *George Washington*'s flight deck provide the power to rein in the arrestor wires as they are caught by planes landing at speeds of up to 150mph (240kph).

▲ INSTRUMENT PANEL
Gauges show the steam pressure in the catapult mechanisms. The ship can launch four planes per minute.

CONTROL ROOMS

▲ PRIMARY FLIGHT CONTROL
Overlooking the deck, the air boss in charge of the ship's aircraft coordinates all takeoffs and landings. The windows are angled to reduce glare.

▲ BRIDGE
The bridge gives panoramic views of the sky and ocean. From here, the captain or watch officer oversees navigation and steering.

▲ REACTOR CONTROLS
The reactors are controlled remotely from this room. The ship can run for a year on a fuel pellet the size of a soft drink can. It has enough fuel to run nonstop for 18 years.

AIRCRAFT HANGAR

◄ NO. 3 PUMP ROOM
JP5 aviation fuel is pumped up to the flight deck. To reduce the risk of fire, JP5 has a lower ignition temperature than commercial fuel.

LIFE BELOW DECKS

▲ OPERATIONS ROOM
Staff monitor takeoffs, landings, and activities on the flight deck via television screens, and use radar to direct airborne planes. In the event of an attack, the defense systems are also operated from here.

◄ PROPELLER SHAFT
An engineer checks a shaft that drives one of the four propellers. Powered by the ship's twin nuclear reactors, a quartet of five-bladed propellers give *George Washington* a top speed in excess of 30 knots.

▼ BAKERY
Along with the galley, the bakery helps provide around 18,000 meals each day. The large ovens are visible in the background.

◄ HANGAR
Aircraft are serviced in the hangar. Each of the staff involved have a specific jacket color that denotes their role: for example, a general maintenance petty officer wears a green one, while brown denotes a plane captain—responsible for the upkeep of a specific aircraft.

► ANCHOR CHAINS
The *George Washington* has a pair of 30-tonne, stockless anchors. The anchor chains run through the bows, where they are stored when not in use. Each chain link weighs approximately 360lb (160kg).

▼ ENGINE BAY
The maintenance, testing, and storage of engines takes place in this bay. An F-14 Tomcat engine can be seen here, with the engine of an F/A-18 Hornet visible in the background.

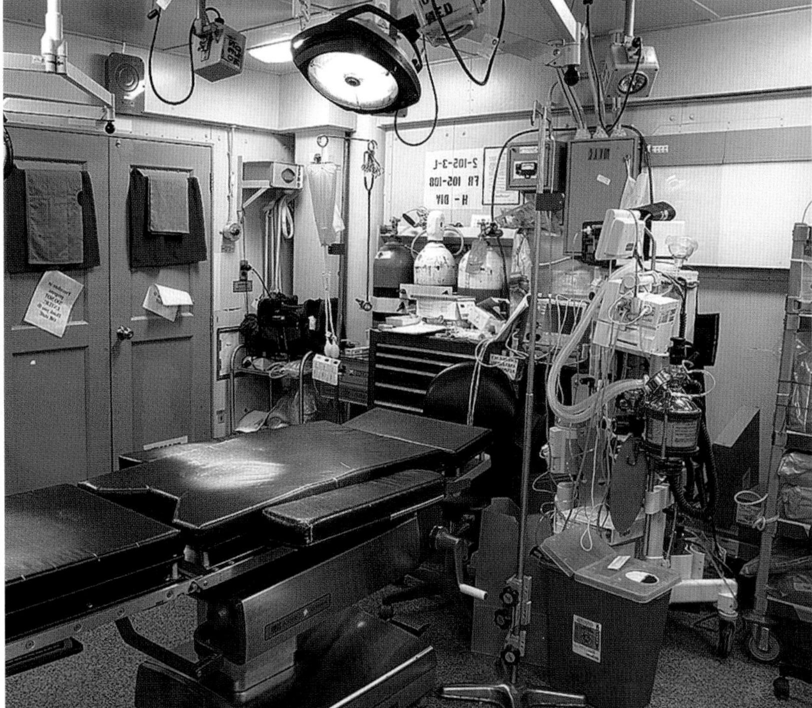

▲ OPERATING ROOM
The ship's medical department must be ready for almost any kind of illness, accident, or battle casualty. In an average year, the medical team sees over 10,000 patients, processes around 3,000 X-rays, and performs more than 100 surgical operations.

▲ BRIEFING ROOM
Flight instructions are given in the briefing room. Each seat is assigned to a specific pilot.

▲ DRINKING FOUNTAIN
Distilling plants daily produce 330,000 gallons (1.5 million liters) of freshwater from seawater.

KEY **OPERATION**

OPERATION NEPTUNE SPEAR
MAY 2, 2011

The killing of the al-Qaeda (see p.408) leader Osama bin Laden by US SEAL Special Forces, on May 2, 2011, was achieved through a combination of intelligence and technology. Bin Laden's Pakistani hideout was observed by satellites, and then by the covert Sentinel stealth UAV. The US SEALs were transported by stealth UH-60 Black Hawk helicopters and carried the latest equipment, including suppressed carbines, night-vision goggles, and body armor.

▲ Osama bin Laden was the founder of al-Qaeda, the jihadist group responsible for the terrorist attacks on the US, on September 11, 2001 (see p.408).

KEY DEVELOPMENT

THE HIGH-TECH BATTLEFIELD

The pursuit of technology to improve battlefield performance continues at an ever-increasing pace. In a race currently led by the US, all the major military nations are incorporating the latest scientific and technological advances into their weapon systems.

The development of the unmanned aerial vehicle (UAV) has brought about a profound change to the way battles are fought. Toward the end of the 20th century, the UAV had already established itself as a valuable reconnaissance tool; in particular, the RQ-4 Global Hawk and the Predator and Reaper drones have revolutionized the process of gathering strategic and tactical intelligence. Post-2000, the UAV has also assumed the role of hunter-killer. The MQ-9 Reaper, for example, can be armed with up to 14 Hellfire air-to-ground missiles or two Paveway II laser-guided bombs. It has seen extensive use in Afghanistan, where it is controlled via a real-time satellite link from an air force base in Nevada, some 6,000 miles (9,600km) away. A further advantage of the UAV is its airborne endurance: the Israeli Eitan, for example, can stay airborne for up to 70 hours.

UNMANNED VEHICLES ON LAND

As part as the American-led move toward the "automated battlefield," unmanned vehicles are also used on land. This began with remote-controlled bomb-disposal machines, but in recent years, larger, more complex vehicles have been produced, including the remote-controlled Black Knight tank, which is based on the M2 Bradley infantry combat vehicle. An intriguing development has been the Israeli remote-controlled robotic snake. Used for surveillance in confined, hostile environments, it is equipped with a camera and microphone.

Progress made in applying stealth technology to standard front-line aircraft (such as the US F-35) has now been extended to warships and armored vehicles. Developments in Adaptive Camouflage allow such high-profile ground objects as a main battle tank to be hidden from infra-red sensors. And, heading into the realms of science fiction, research has also been conducted into a material called Metaflex, which may be able to hide soldiers behind a kind of "invisibility cloak."

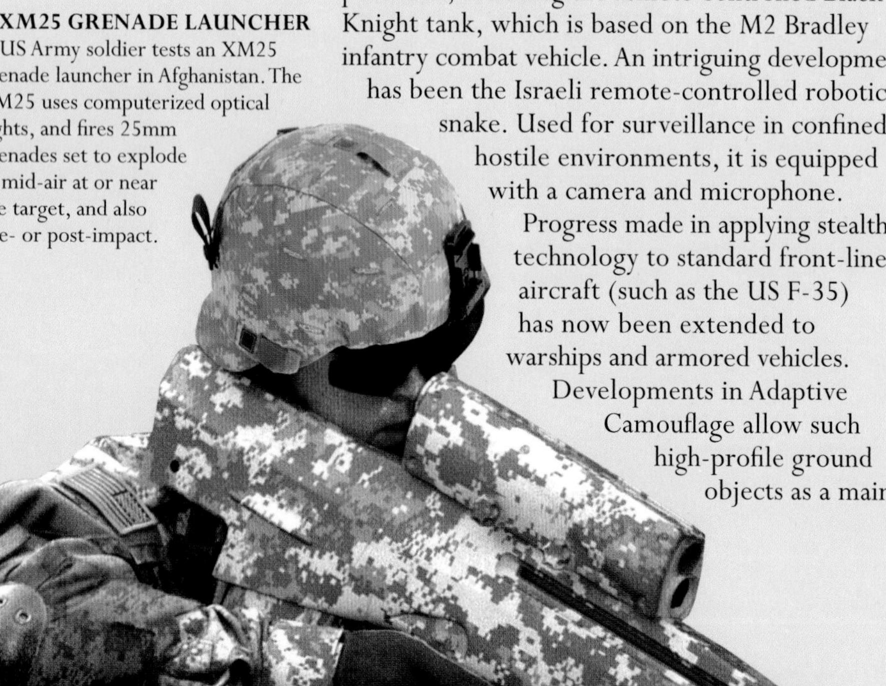

▼ XM25 GRENADE LAUNCHER
A US Army soldier tests an XM25 grenade launcher in Afghanistan. The XM25 uses computerized optical sights, and fires 25mm grenades set to explode in mid-air at or near the target, and also pre- or post-impact.

"Our **moral authority** is as **important** [as] our **troop strength** and our **high-tech weapons**"

ROBERT REICH, FORMER US SECRETARY OF LABOR, JULY 2004

Laser weapons have evolved into two distinct categories. Laser rifles, such as the American TR3 and PHASR, cause temporary blindness, and are intended to discourage rather than kill. A second line of development consists of very powerful lasers, such as the experimental Laser Avenger, which is designed to shoot down incoming missiles.

For the soldier on the battlefield, the conflict in Afghanistan has been a testing ground for a whole range of new weapons. The XM-26 LSS under-barrel shotgun—which attaches to an M4 or M16-type assault rifle—enables door-breaching and close-range firepower, and can fire non-lethal projectiles such as tear gas. Another innovation is the H&K XM25 Counter-defilade Target Engagement (CDTE). This 25mm semi-automatic grenade launcher uses a "smart" laser range finder to ensure precise detonation of the grenade to a range of up to 1,090 yards (1,000m). The grenade measures the distance it travels by counting its own rotations.

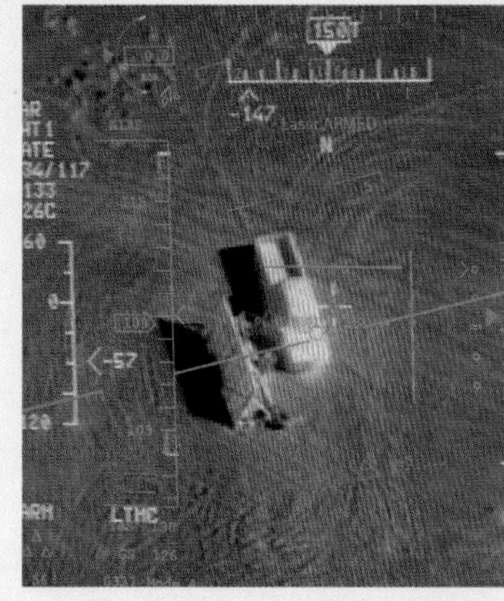

▲ **AN MQ-9 REAPER IMAGE**
A display screen in a ground control station at a US Air Force base shows the view captured by a MQ-9 Reaper camera during a training mission.

KEY **EVENTS**

1970–PRESENT

- **1972** The Wheelbarrow bomb-disposal robot is developed for the British Army for use in Northern Ireland.
- **1982** The Lockheed F-117, the first aircraft to feature stealth technology, is adopted by the US Air Force (see pp.412–13).
- **1994** The Predator UAV makes its first flight. It is designed for reconnaissance only.
- **2001** The Reaper UAV is developed. It is larger and more versatile than the Predator.
- **2006** The F-35 Lightning II—a jet fighter with advanced stealth technology—goes into production.
- **2007** Reaper UAVs begin combat missions over Afghanistan.
- **2009** Combat field trials of the IAWS take place in Iraq and Afghanistan.
- **2010** Metaflex "invisible" material is developed.

◀ **A TALON 3B ROBOT**
A claymore land mine is removed from a sand dune by a Talon 3B robot during a training exercise in Bahrain. Designed to search and destroy Improvised Explosive Devices (IEDs), the robot is operated remotely by technicians using monitors and video equipment attached to the unit.

GUIDED-MISSILE DESTROYER

USS DONALD COOK

The US Navy's guided-missile destroyer *Donald Cook* saw action in the Iraq War. Deployed in Operation Iraqi Freedom in March 2003, it was among the first ships to launch strikes against Iraqi targets.

The *Donald Cook* and her fellow Arleigh Burke-class destroyers are among the most advanced surface warships in service today. Launched in 1997 and the 25th ship in the class, the *Donald Cook* belongs to Flight II, which embodies significant advances in armaments and electronics on earlier versions. The ship is packed with diverse weaponry, giving her what the US Navy calls "multi-mission offensive and defensive capabilities." The heart of the destroyer's offensive capabilities are the two Mk41 Vertical Launch Systems (VLS). These can fire anti-aircraft missiles, anti-submarine missiles, missiles for destroying other surface ships, and cruise missiles for strike operations against land targets. The ship also has a launch pad from which an attack helicopter can operate.

The destroyer's design is intended to maximize its chances of surviving. The Arleigh Burke class were among the first ships to incorporate "stealth" technology, with buried funnels and angled shapes that reduce their radar profile, as well as features to suppress infrared emissions. They were also the first all-steel American warships. Using steel rather than aluminum for the destroyer's superstructure reduces damage in the event of a missile hit. The *Donald Cook* has a crew of 30 officers and over 300 enlisted personnel.

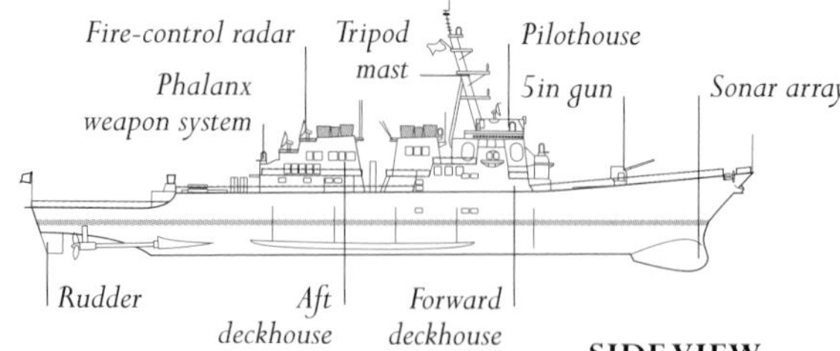

SIDE VIEW

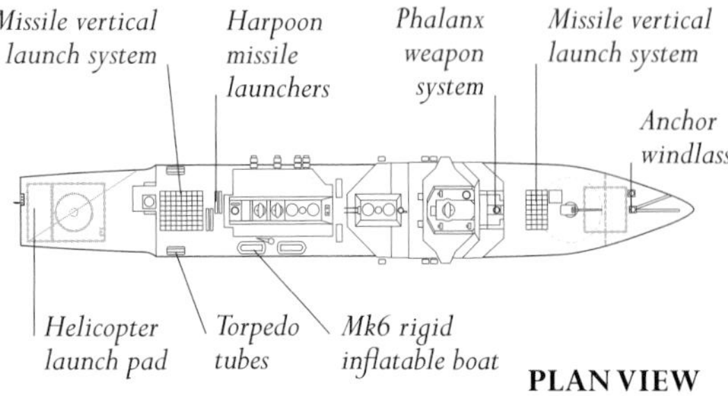

PLAN VIEW

USS *DONALD COOK*
Despite being classed as a destroyer, *Donald Cook* is over 500ft (150m) long and displaces 8,400 tons, making her similar in size to many World War II cruisers.

DECK FEATURES

▲ **ANCHOR CHAIN**
The two anchors are carefully positioned so that they do not strike the large sonar bulge on the ship's hull as they are lowered and raised.

▲ **HELICOPTER LANDING-LIGHTS**
Green lights indicate a good approach, amber signal caution, and red mean that an incoming helicopter is too low. Flashing reds tell the pilot to abort the landing.

▲ **HELICOPTER LANDING PAD**
The ship can embark and refuel a Sikorsky SH-60 Seahawk helicopter for search and attack missions or for transporting personnel and cargo.

▲ **CHAFF AND DECOY LAUNCHER**
The Super Rapid Bloom Offboard Chaff system launches chaff and infrared decoys to confuse enemy missiles and fire-control systems.

▼ **DECK PROFILE**
Compact weaponry, some of it concealed, gives the deck a rather bare look. Later ships in the class have a covered hangar forward of the landing-pad.

THE WEAPONS SYSTEMS

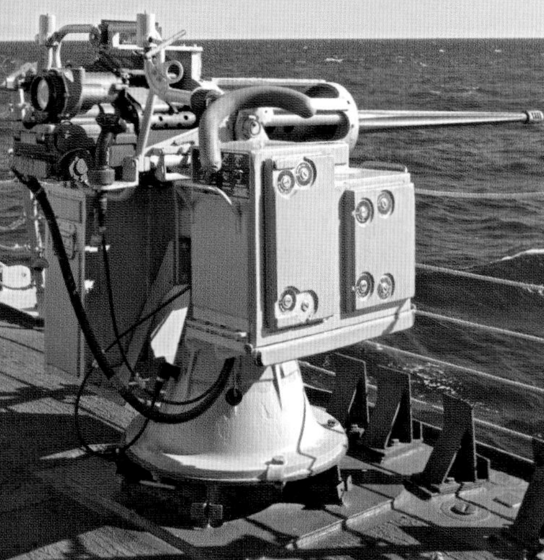

▲ **25MM CHAIN GUN**
Fed ammunition by an electrically operated chain mechanism, two Mk38 guns provide defense against patrol boats or floating mines.

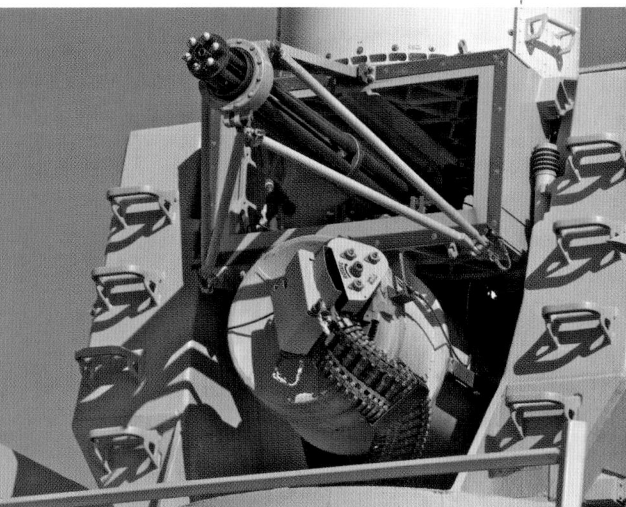

▲ **20MM ROTARY CANNON**
The two Phalanx Close-In Weapons Systems use automated radar-controlled cannon to identify, track, and destroy incoming missiles.

▲ **TORPEDO TUBES**
There are two sets of Mk32 triple torpedo tubes. The torpedoes are fired using compressed air from a flask at the rear of the tubes.

◀ **5IN GUN**
The Mk45 gun is designed for use against surface ships or aircraft, or for shore bombardment.

INSIDE AND BELOW DECK

Battle operations are coordinated by the Combat Information Center (CIC). This is dominated by the computer-based AEGIS combat system, which can simultaneously engage in air, surface, and subsurface warfare. Steel bulkheads are located throughout the ship in case a hit is suffered, and vital equipment is also protected by Kevlar shields. An air filtration system helps guard against nuclear, biological, and chemical attack.

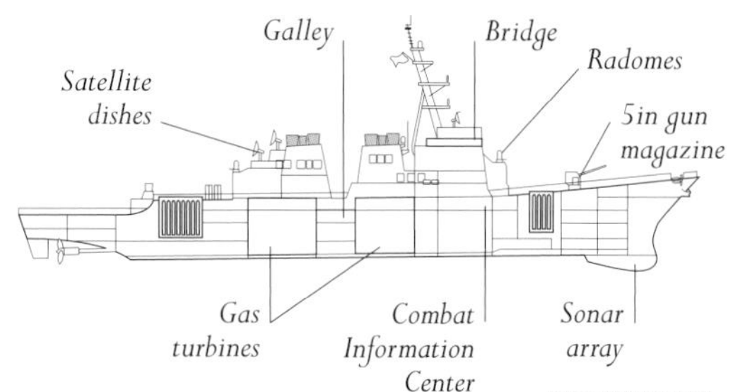

SIDE VIEW

CONTROL AND COMBAT

▲ **SHIP'S BRIDGE**
The helmsman steers from the helm station in the center of the bridge. There is also an automated digital steering system that allows a course to be entered and automatically maintained.

POWER PLANT

▲ **GAS TURBINE**
The four LM2500 gas turbines, derived from the engines used on jets such as the Boeing 747, give a top speed of over 30 knots.

▲ **MAIN PASSAGEWAY**
Double-plated bulkheads and interior airlock doors provide protection and allow vital areas—such as the turbine control room at the end of the passageway—to be isolated in the event of an attack.

▲ **MAIN ENGINE ROOM**
Two purification systems, one in each of the two main engine rooms, remove solid contaminants and water from the fuel supply.

▲ **HATCH**
Airtight hatches separate the ship into zones to protect against contamination by biological or chemical agents.

▲ **TACTICAL COORDINATOR**
A group of specialists staff the CIC, each of whom has a specific role. For example, the Tactical Information Coordinator seen here handles tactical data coming in from allied ships.

AMMUNITION SYSTEM

◄ **AMMUNITION LOADING SYSTEM**
In combat situations, a small team in the 5in gun magazine operates a computerized loading system. The system ensures that there is an uninterrupted supply of ammunition to the Mk45 gun on the deck above.

▲ **5IN GUN MAGAZINE**
Situated beneath the Mk45 gun mounting, the *Donald Cook*'s 5in shell magazine stores 680 rounds of ammunition. The yellow markings on the shells indicate that they are high-explosive rounds.

▲ **PROPELLANT STORE**
The propellant powder used to fire shells from the Mk45 gun is also stored in the magazine. The gun discharges up to 20 rounds per minute.

◄ **BATTLE ROOM**
Based in the CIC, the AEGIS combat system controls and coordinates the ship's weapons and its electronic countermeasures devices.

◄ **CIC SCREEN**
AEGIS integrates and displays data from radar, sonar, and satellite systems. The AN/SPY 1-D phased array radar can track hundreds of different targets simultaneously.

LIFE ON BOARD

▲ **SHIP'S GALLEY**
The spacious and well-equipped kitchens on board the *Donald Cook* allow the ship's galley staff to prepare three hot meals a day, with a choice of dishes, for the crew of more than 330 officers and enlisted men and women.

◄ **MESS TABLES**
Enlisted crew members eat in an informal self-service canteen next to the ship's galley.

◄ **FIREFIGHTING GEAR**
Fire stations with hoses, protective overalls, and breathing apparatus are located around the decks.

POST-WAR SUBMARINES

Nuclear-powered submarines and their armament of submarine-launched ballistic missiles (SLBMs) are arguably the most potent weapon system ever developed. Hidden beneath the waves, they are able to launch their deadly missiles without warning and are virtually immune from retaliatory action by the enemy. Their high level of concealment also provides them with an invaluable second-strike capability. More conventional attack submarines, powered either by nuclear reactors or diesel-electric motors, operate against surface vessels or hunt down other submarines.

▲ USS NAUTILUS (SSN-571)

Commissioned 1954 **Origin** US

Displacement 3,535 tons (4,090 tons submerged)

Length 324ft (98.8m)

Top speed 22 knots (25 knots submerged)

A ground-breaking vessel, the *Nautilus* was the world's first operational nuclear-powered submarine and, in 1958, the first to complete an underwater transit of the North Pole.

▼ USS MARYLAND (SSBN-738)

Commissioned 1992 **Origin** US

Displacement 16,000 tons (18,700 tons submerged)

Length 561ft (171m)

Top speed 20 knots (25 knots submerged)

An *Ohio*-class ballistic missile submarine, *Maryland* is at the forefront of America's nuclear deterrent. Its 24 Trident missiles are capable of delivering up to 12 warheads per missile to a range of 7,021 miles (11,300km).

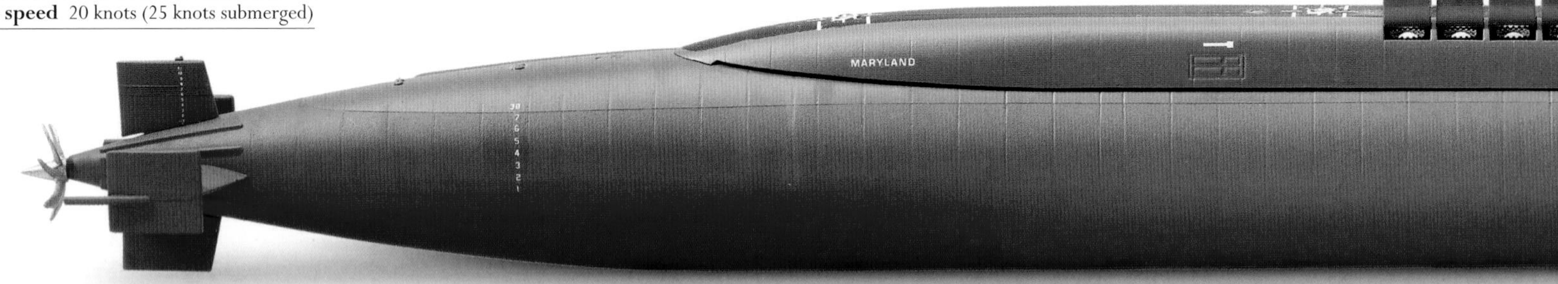

▶ NOVOSIBIRSK (B-401)

Commissioned 1984

Origin Soviet Union

Displacement 2,325 tons (3,075 tons submerged)

Length 220ft (67m)

Top speed 15 knots (24 knots submerged)

A diesel-electric attack submarine of the *Kilo* class, *Novosibirsk* was armed with minelaying equipment and conventional torpedoes, as well as anti-ship and anti-aircraft missiles.

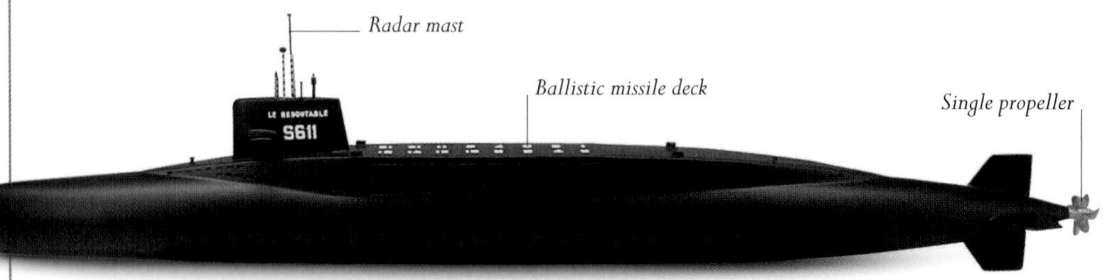

◀ LE REDOUTABLE (S611)

Commissioned 1971 **Origin** France

Displacement 8,045 tons (8,940 tons submerged)

Length 420ft (128m)

Top speed 18 knots (25 knots submerged)

Le Redoutable was the lead vessel in its class and France's first ballistic missile submarine. Its original M1 missiles had a range of 1,243 miles (2,000km) while carrying a 450 kilotonne warhead.

▲ AKULA CLASS

Commissioned 1981

Origin Soviet Union

Displacement 18,500 tons (25,000 tons submerged)

Length 574ft (175m)

Top speed 22 knots (27 knots submerged)

Codenamed Typhoon by NATO, the Russian *Akula* ("shark") class of submarines were the largest undersea vessels ever built. They were designed to fire SLBMs while hidden under the Arctic ice.

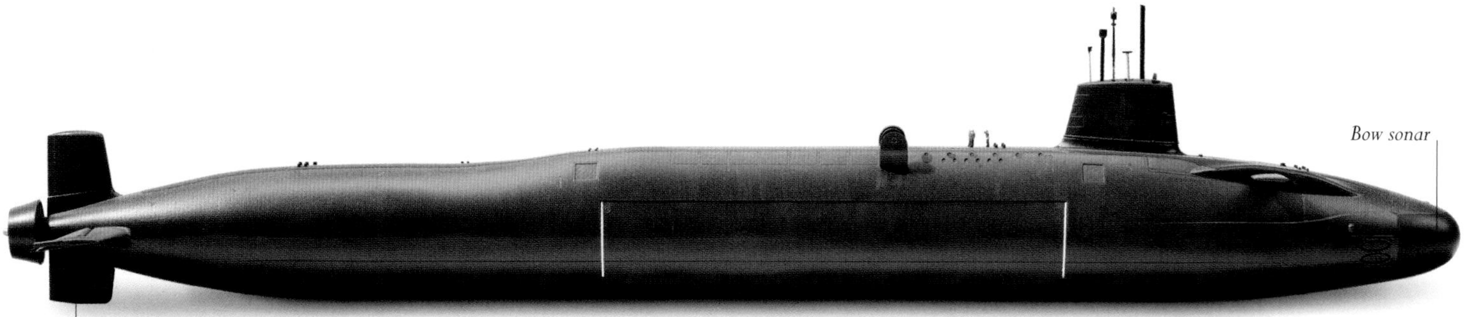
Bow sonar
Lower fin segment

▲ HMS VANGUARD (S28)

Commissioned 1993 **Origin** UK

Displacement 15,160 tons (16,190 tons submerged)

Length 492ft (150m)

Top speed 25 knots submerged

The lead vessel of its class, the nuclear-powered *Vanguard* is armed with 16 Trident SLBMs, each containing up to 12 warheads. It also has four tubes for Spearfish guided torpedoes.

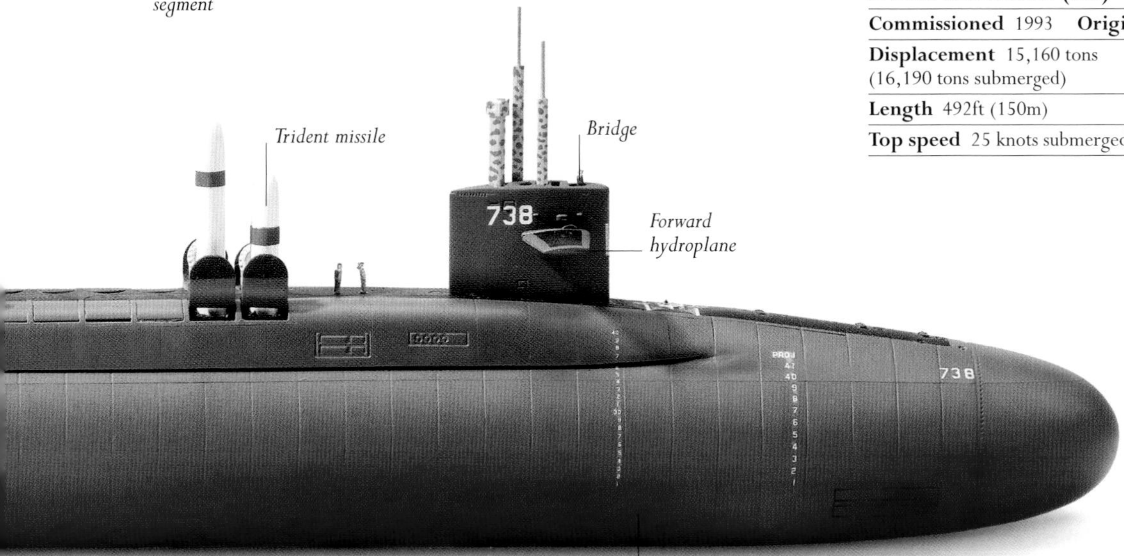
Trident missile
Bridge
Forward hydroplane
Pressurized hull

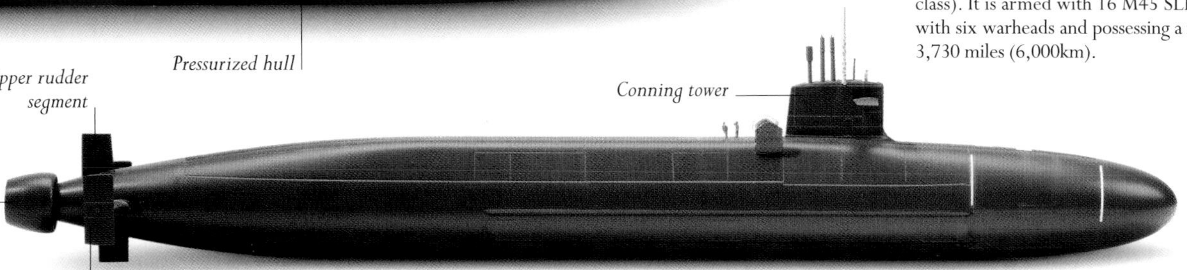
Upper rudder segment
Shrouded pumpjet propulsor
Conning tower
Hydroplane

▼ LE TRIOMPHANT (S616)

Commissioned 1997 **Origin** France

Displacement 12,640 tons (14,335 tons submerged)

Length 453ft (138m)

Top speed 20 knots (25 knots submerged)

Le Triomphant is the lead vessel of its class (a replacement for the French navy's *Redoutable* class). It is armed with 16 M45 SLBMs, each with six warheads and possessing a range of 3,730 miles (6,000km).

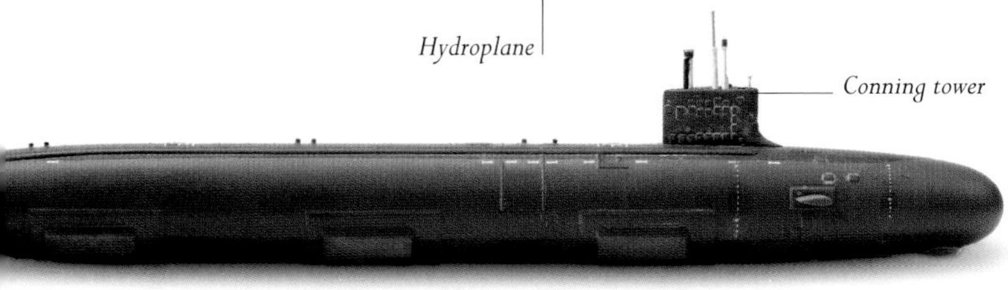
Conning tower

◀ USS VIRGINIA (SSN-74)

Commissioned 2004 **Origin** US

Displacement 6,455 tons (7,101 tons submerged)

Length 377ft (115m)

Top speed 25 knots (32 knots submerged)

The *Virginia*—lead vessel in its class—is a nuclear-powered attack submarine, armed with Mark 48 guided torpedoes and Tomahawk cruise missiles. It features a pressure chamber that can release SEAL divers while submerged.

▶ HMS ASTUTE (S119)

Commissioned 2010 **Origin** UK

Displacement 7,130 tons (7,535 tons submerged)

Length 318ft (97m)

Top speed 20 knots (30 knots submerged)

A nuclear-powered attack submarine, *Astute* is the lead vessel of its class. Along with conventional torpedoes, the vessel is armed with Spearfish guided torpedoes and Tomahawk cruise missiles.

Propeller within sound-minimizing shroud
Forward hydroplane
Torpedo port

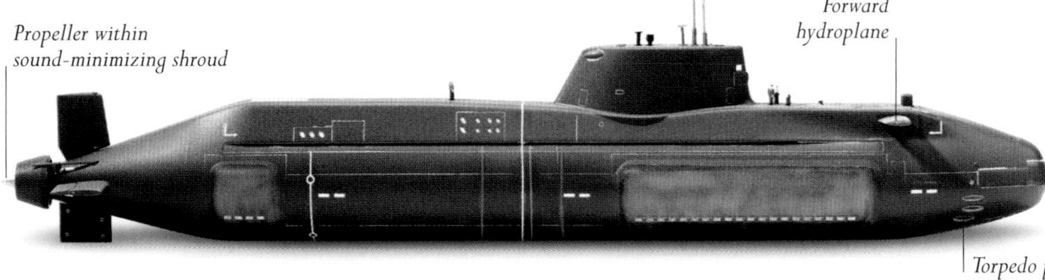

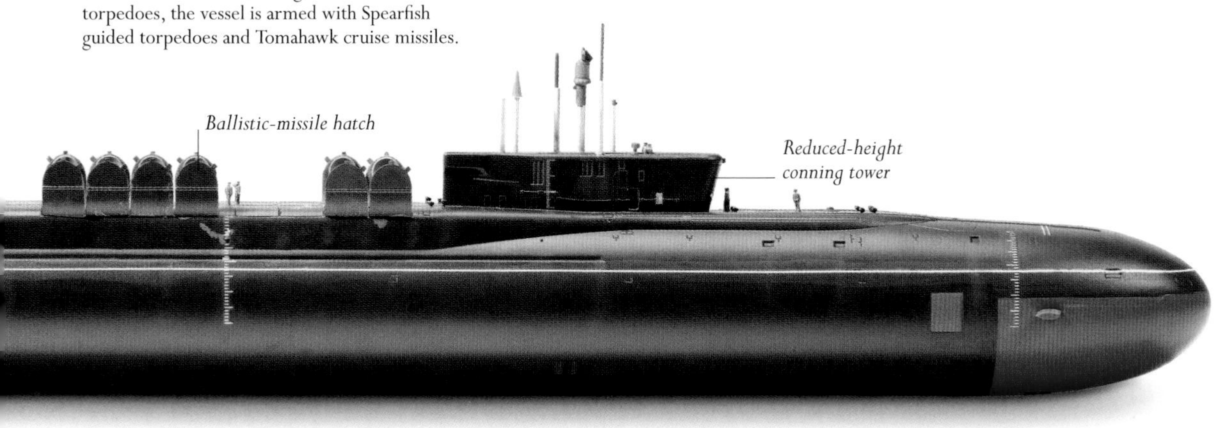
Ballistic-missile hatch
Reduced-height conning tower

◀ YURI DOLGORUKI

Commissioned 2012 **Origin** Russia

Displacement 14,490 tons (23,620 tons submerged)

Length 558ft (170m)

Top speed 15 knots (29 knots submerged)

One of the latest *Borey*-class nuclear-powered submarines, the *Yuri Dolgoruki* is armed with 16 RSM-56 Bulava SLBMs, each missile containing six warheads with a range of up to 6,214 miles (10,000km).

COUNTERINSURGENCY

COMBAT IN AFGHANISTAN

The soldiers of the International Security Assistance Force (ISAF) operating against Taliban insurgency in Afghanistan had access to the most advanced military technology available in the early 21st century. But as Operation Moshtarak showed in February 2010, this still left infantrymen vulnerable.

Operation Moshtarak was a large-scale offensive into a Taliban-controlled area of Helmand Province in southern Afghanistan. Some 15,000 American, British, Canadian, and Afghan army troops were sent in to wrest control of the area in order to disrupt poppy cultivation and drug-trafficking networks, and install government rule. The insurgents were hiding among the local population and occupying the towns of Marjah and Showal.

Equipped with the latest night-vision optics, the ISAF was able to launch the operation under cover of darkness. Small special forces units that had infiltrated the target area—British SAS and US Navy SEALs—called in strikes by Predator unmanned aerial vehicles (UAVs) and Apache attack helicopters against Taliban positions. About two hours before dawn, Super Stallion and Chinook helicopters, escorted by helicopter gunships, airlifted troops to landing sites near the target towns. The soldiers advanced with caution across ground scattered with improvised explosive devices (IEDs), the cause of two-thirds of ISAF casualties in Afghanistan. Using portable aluminum bridges, they were able to cross the numerous irrigation ditches without traversing existing bridges that would inevitably be mined. While the airlifted troops approached the Taliban-held towns, other US forces began advancing from their bases overland into Taliban territory. M1 Assault Breacher Vehicles led the way along the heavily mined and booby-trapped roads; occasionally line charges (rockets towing cables of plastic explosive) were fired ahead to blow up any concealed devices.

The opening day of the operation was impressively efficient and successful, with pockets of Taliban resistance overcome. US Marines established themselves inside Marjah and British troops entered Showal. Most Taliban forces had probably left by this stage, but sufficient insurgents remained in the towns to pose a serious threat. The typical Taliban armory of AK assault rifles, RPG-7 rocket-propelled grenade launchers, PK machine-guns, and bolt-action sniper rifles was a match for ISAF infantry weapons in an environment that offered plentiful concealment.

WAR AMONG THE PEOPLE

Clearing the town house by house was a demanding task. The obvious tactic for the Americans and British, eager to keep their own casualties low, was to identify the buildings occupied by Taliban elements and call in air strikes or use surface-to-surface missiles to destroy them. Modern guidance systems ensured that specific targets could be hit with a high degree of accuracy most of the time, but there was still a grave risk of politically undesirable civilian casualties. Indeed, on the second day of the operation, two missiles fired by an American High Mobility Artillery Rocket System (HIMARS)—a truck-mounted multiple rocket launcher— killed 12 Afghans in Marjah, including children.

Although the main towns were officially under Afghan government control within 12 days of the start of the operation, draining low-level combat continued, with sniper fire and IEDs imposing a steady toll on ISAF and Afghan soldiers. In time, the outcome would prove inconclusive.